D1565984

CHRISTIANITY
IN CHINA

From the Eighteenth Century
to the Present

CHRISTIANITY
IN CHINA

*From the Eighteenth Century
to the Present*

EDITED BY DANIEL H. BAYS

STANFORD UNIVERSITY PRESS

Stanford, California

Published with the assistance of the University of Kansas
Scholarly Revolving Fund

Stanford University Press

Stanford, California

©1996 by the Board of Trustees of the Leland Stanford
Junior University

Printed in the United States of America

CIP data are at the end of the book

This volume is dedicated
to the life and work of
John King Fairbank

96061

Preface

This volume constitutes the largest but by no means the only product of the History of Christianity in China Project, which covered the years 1985–92 and was funded by the Henry Luce Foundation, Inc. The project itself was inspired by John K. Fairbank, who had long believed that the large historical story of the modern Christian missionary movement in China, documented by voluminous missions records, was an understudied one.[1] Although clearly Fairbank had in mind studying not just missions, but their interactions with Chinese society and the diverse manifestations of Chinese Christianity, throughout the 1970s and early 1980s there were few scholars from the field of China studies who followed up his suggestion, and it proved impossible for him to promote this topic of study by mobilization of a funded committee to encourage and oversee research, as he originally wished to do. Missions were of scant interest to most historians of China who received their training in the 1960s and 1970s, and "Chinese Christianity" seemed like an oxymoron to some.

There were understandable reasons for this. In the 1960s and 1970s, it seemed to many, including me, that the historical verdict on the significance of Christianity in modern Chinese history was that for the most part it had been a false start, a failed endeavor. Despite its record of some contribution to intellectual change and social modernization, it was apparent that Christianity, like other religions, but especially so because of its ineradicable foreign connections, was doomed slowly to die out in China. Nationalism and the secular state, embodied in the Chinese Communist movement, had swept it away, and the number of visible Christians in China was fast dwindling—and all of them were elderly, it appeared. Besides its disappearance as a factor in contemporary China, it seemed moreover that the study of Christianity in Chinese history could tell us only limited things about the large forces affecting Chinese society in recent centuries, because it was so strongly tied to the foreign sector. Study of Christianity meant study of foreign missions and missionaries, it was assumed, and that was not the mainstream of Chinese history, the pursuit of which required a "China-centered" approach.[2]

The premises justifying this relative lack of interest were undercut after 1980 by two factors. One was the resurgence of solid academic research and discussion of missions history, shorn of the religious or cultural triumphalism that had characterized much earlier missions history and hagiography, and had made it of only marginal use to most area specialists interested in the indigenous societies to which missions were sent. A corollary of this resurgence was a deep interest in the history of Christianity in non-Western societies, stressing the growth and spread of Christianity as a world religion, not as a reflection of Western culture — much less an appendage of Western political forces. The "world Christianity" approach is one that can bridge and make relevant to each other the respective endeavors of missiologists knowledgeable about non-Western societies and of China specialists and other area studies scholars. The fact is that Christianity is now more non-Western than Western in its worldwide makeup, and the transcultural interactions and social changes that have brought that about in recent history should have compelling interest for scholars of the non-Western world.[3] For example, a recent set of studies of the worldwide process of conversion to Christianity finds it most profitable to "explore Christianity as a world religion rather than as a uniquely Eurocentric one."[4]

The other factor that neutralized the premise that the study of Christianity in Chinese history was neither as interesting nor as important as many other topics in Chinese studies was the dramatic revival of religious activity, including Christianity, in China after 1980. This was by far the more important of the two factors in piquing the interest of China scholars, because studies of the growth of Christianity in other non-Western societies did not necessarily seem particularly relevant to a China in which overt religious expression, either institutional or personal, was essentially nonexistent from the early 1960s to 1979. Despite the interesting phenomenon of rampant popular religious expression in Taiwan, accelerating along with economic growth and modernization, it seemed that the secularizing pressures on all religions in China had nearly eliminated popular religiosity there. However, historians of early modern Chinese history did find very stimulating the pathbreaking studies of the surprisingly lively role of popular religion in pre-1900 China provided by Susan Naquin, Daniel Over-myer, and other scholars after 1976.[5] Then, after 1980, the loosened strictures on religious expression in China released a flood of manifestations of revival of religion, especially popular religion, which was nothing short of spectacular, and of intense interest to many China scholars. Religion — temples, churches, monasteries and nunneries, sects and popular cults of all kinds — surged back into public visibility in the 1980s.[6]

One of the most intriguing aspects of this religious revival has been the rapid growth of Christianity, especially Protestant Christianity, in the past fifteen years. It seems clear that there are now at least twenty to thirty million Chinese Christians, possibly more, at any rate a number perhaps ten times the number of believers in 1949. Moreover, there are considerably more Protestants than Catholics now, an interesting reversal of their proportions a half-century ago. This phenomenon is obviously not part of some foreign cultural or political presence, or simply a carry-over from the days of foreign missions, which have been gone from China for over forty years. Rather, I believe, it shows how thoroughly Christianity has become Chinese, and part of the Chinese social scene.[7] At the same time it reveals some of the other aspects of Chinese society today, such as the dynamics of private associations (Christians are practically the only state-recognized religious groupings that are congregational in nature); the role of associational or congregational religion should probably be taken into account in the discussions of the likelihood of there developing a "public sphere" or "civil society" in China.[8] And of course, varying expressions of Christianity, as well as of other religions, reveal something of the search for meaning in a secular society, and continuing popular religious consciousness, in contemporary China.

Thus, when John Fairbank suggested to me in 1984 that I propose a study project on missions and Chinese Christianity, the intrinsic interest in such an endeavor, on my own part and presumably that of other China scholars, was much higher than it would have been a decade earlier. My own judgment was that the largest contribution could be made by simply focusing on the history of Chinese Christianity, not excluding missions, but only highlighting them when they were a central part of a story centered on Chinese Christians. Moreover, because, with some exceptions, earlier studies on the subject had tended to use Western-language mission records and neglect the application of Chinese-language sources, I decided that use of Chinese materials should be given a high priority in such a project. The Henry Luce Foundation, Inc., generously funded the project, and an illustrious advisory council was assembled to establish guidelines and distribute postdoctoral awards for what came to be called the History of Christianity in China Project, administered at the University of Kansas, 1985–92.

The presumption that both established and upcoming scholars would be attracted not only to postdoctoral fellowship monies but also to pursuing the historical origins and development of the continuing lively presence of Christianity in China was borne out by the high quality of the proposals we received. In fact, we discovered that a number of historians of China were already working, peripherally if not centrally, to reinvestigate and revise our picture of the place of Christianity in Chinese social, political, and intellectual history. In the process, as they viewed Christianity as a more natural (if sometimes disruptive) part of the Chinese scene, they came upon insights into the dynamics of Qing and twentieth-century history visible through analysis of this "Christian factor," as it were. We were able to fund some of these research projects that were already underway, several of them by non-U.S. scholars, as well as to help new ones to gain momentum (for a full list of all the grants made over the four years of awards, 1986–89, see Appendix A). The result has been the creation of a large number of significant studies, some of them appearing as chapters in this volume, some appearing as monographs or articles elsewhere, others still underway as monographic studies.[9] In general, these studies have aimed at the elucidation of basic forces of modern Chinese history, while at the same time, by using materials relating to Christianity, they often shed light on the growth and indigenization of the Chinese church and the role of missions. On the whole, use of Chinese materials and a focus on Chinese participants have been the hallmark of these studies.

All but one of the chapters in this volume were written as part of the History of Christianity in China Project. They were originally presented in two symposia, held in Lawrence, Kansas, in 1989 and 1990. Thirty-four papers were written for the project and presented at one of those two symposia. Included were seven from the PRC, and one each from Taiwan, Korea, Canada, and Hong Kong. Because the original funding for the proposals was made on the basis of individual scholarly quality and promise, not how they related to one another, there was not an automatic complementarity among the finished essays presented at the symposia. Still, several groupings were obvious each year, and both symposia were characterized by good presentations and lively and insightful discussions, not only by the assigned critics (including "outside" commentators), but the whole group attending. The full rosters and presentation titles of the two symposia are included in Appendix B. After the second symposium, in 1990, the task of fashioning out of almost three dozen papers a manageable volume appeared quite daunting; indeed, it was daunting. Of the present volume's twenty chapters, eighteen are directly derived from the presentations made at one of the symposia. My own is a different essay; and Professor Kwok's essay was specially commissioned later.

Twenty chapters are a large chunk to digest, even for the dedicated scholar-reader. Accordingly, I have divided them into four broad sectors, Parts I through IV, and before each part I have provided a short introduction that highlights what are in my opinion the significant themes brought out in the chapters in that part. As an overview, several important aspects of modern Chinese history and the place of Christianity in it are illuminated by these chapters. In Part I, the dynamics of Qing local society, from the role of "religious" factors to other aspects of ritual or community life, and even a case study of an individual missionary's influence on imperial court society, are shown in rich texture. Parts II and III show clear links between Christianity and ethnicity, and between Christianity and Chinese women's identity and roles. These chapters give, I believe, an unprecedentedly detailed picture of how questions of ethnicity and gender, as well as (in the ethnic studies) local configurations of political power, can be approached through materials relating to missions and church-related institutions. Several of the chapters in Parts II and III also make excellent use of interviews.

The six chapters of Part IV constitute a partial profile, over the span of a century and a half, of the immensely complex process of making the foreign imported religion a domestic product. This was a long and arduous task, still underway today, much of it accomplished under the coercive pressures of mass nationalism, Japanese occupation, or Communist intolerance and repression. These chapters provide a concrete sense of this process of changeover from a foreign mission identity to a Chinese Christian identity. They also provide several striking case studies of the inherent tensions and conflicts within the Christian community as some Chinese Christians, who, themselves propelled by the same forces and emotions as non-Christian Chinese, strove for autonomy and independence in a missions-dominated Christian arena.

These chapters do not, of course, tell the whole story of Christianity in China in the past more than two centuries. And they do not always tell us with certainty how the parts of that story are best interpreted by scholars with command of Chinese sources as well as familiarity with relevant missions sources and other Western materials. Some large gaps remain in the volume, as indeed they existed in the coverage of topics funded by the History of Christianity in China Project. There are no studies here on the important topic of Catholicism after the early 1900s; nor do any directly address the interesting issue of the connection between Christianity and the formation of an upwardly mobile Chinese urban business community from the late nineteenth century on. And the whole question of linkage between Christianity and modernization is not treated directly in this volume, although several chapters provide access into the problem. Thus many topics, large and small, remain to be investigated in this area. The scholars involved in the History of Christianity in China Project, and in this volume, hope that the significance of the subjects we have addressed, and the multinational nature of the venture, will make the volume a benchmark — a baseline against which to measure further work, and also a source of insight into issues of comparative history, studies of Chinese religions, and some basic patterns of social change in China's recent history. Christianity in China at the turn of the twenty-first century may be in the latter stages of a process of inculturation that will make it as much a part of the Chinese scene as Buddhism became over a thousand years ago. We hope that we have illuminated some aspects of that process.

D.H.B.

Acknowledgments

The research and study project out of which this volume has emerged began in 1984. Late in that year, while I was in Taiwan on a Fulbright research grant, I received from John Fairbank a letter that was also a bequest: his encouragement to pursue on a more systematic and programmatic basis what I was researching at the time, modern Chinese Christianity. It is only fitting that the volume be dedicated to his memory; he treated me like one of his own academic offspring, though I never attended Harvard, and his fingerprints are, figuratively, on most if not all the pages of this work.

My sincere appreciation goes to the Henry Luce Foundation, Inc., and especially to Terrill E. Lautz, then program officer and now vice president of the foundation, for funding what must have seemed at the time to be a rather uncertain venture. They were steady in encouragement, and were willing to add extra funding for fellowships after the initial two rounds of postdoctoral awards showed the large number of well-qualified applicants with excellent proposals. The continuing interest and support of Terry was very meaningful to me as the project meandered through the swampland of preparing the volume for submission to a publisher, and I am gratified that its appearance vindicates those years of support.

My hearty thanks to the members of the Advisory Council of the History of Christianity in China Project: besides John Fairbank, they included K. C. Liu, of the University of California, Davis; Richard P. Madsen, University of California, San Diego; Lucian W. Pye, MIT; and Grant Wacker, then of the University of North Carolina, Chapel Hill, now of Duke University Divinity School. Each contributed sage advice on myriad subjects, and in particular helped to forge a solid roster of grantees for the project fellowship awards in our enjoyable annual meetings in New York. I must single out K. C. Liu for special thanks for his constant encouragement, as faithful friend and as a source of many fertile ideas. Thanks also to all the participants in the two symposia, presenters as well as commentators (they are all listed in Appendix B), including the student assistants in 1989 and 1990, respectively, Charles Keller and Xiao Tian.

Besides the Henry Luce Foundation, Inc., my own research, reflected in my chapter in this volume and in related efforts, was supported at various times by the General Research Fund of the University of Kansas, the U.S. Office of Education for a Fulbright-Hays grant to Taiwan in 1984–85, and the Committee on Scholarly Communication with China for four months' research in China in 1986. At that time, I was well treated by my host institution, Nanjing University, and by its affiliate, the Jinling Theological Seminary, where Professor Xu Rulei received me graciously; special research assistance, and treasured personal friendship, were provided by Professor Li Shiyu, now of the Tianjin Academy of Social Sciences. The Pew Charitable Trusts have funded another project that I am directing, time from which I have taken in 1993 and 1994 to do most of the last work of editing and assembling the volume. The final editing work before publication was done while I was a research fellow at the Joyce and Elizabeth Hall Center for the Humanities at the University of Kansas in fall 1994; I am grateful for the helpful staff there, and for the peaceful office in which to pull it all together and write the connecting parts.

Sandee Kennedy did much of the typing and word processing at various stages; I am grateful for her professionalism, high standards of accuracy, and cheerfulness. A special word of thanks goes to Pam LeRow, Lynn Porter, Paula Courtney, and Tonya Elmore of the College Word-Processing Center of the University of Kansas, for amiably greeting me each time I came by with another ungainly pile, and efficiently whipping into final shape the many pieces of what was at times a very unwieldy manuscript. Wang Dong provided invaluable help with the Character List, and Charles Keller proofread efficiently. I appreciated Lynn Stewart's and Laura Bloch's careful and responsive management of the production process, and Richard Gunde's wonderfully meticulous copyediting.

Finally, Janny, thanks for understanding how important this was to me, and helping in so many ways.

D.H.B.

Contents

A photo section follows p. 173.

Contributors

DANIEL H. BAYS received his Ph.D. from the University of Michigan in Ann Arbor, and is professor of history at the University of Kansas, Lawrence.

TIMOTHY BROOK, who teaches in the Department of History, the University of Toronto, is a social historian of the Ming dynasty who is currently researching Chinese wartime collaboration with Japan.

NICOLE CONSTABLE received her Ph.D. from the University of California, Berkeley, and is assistant professor of anthropology at the University of Pittsburgh.

NORMA DIAMOND, who received her Ph.D. at Cornell University, is a professor of anthropology and an associate of the Center for Chinese Studies at the University of Michigan in Ann Arbor.

ROBERT E. ENTENMANN received his Ph.D. in history and East Asian languages at Harvard University; he teaches East Asian history at St. Olaf College in Northfield, Minnesota.

GAO WANGZHI, formerly director and professor of Christian studies, the Institute of World Religions, Chinese Academy of Social Sciences, lately has been a post-doctoral research associate of the University of California, Berkeley.

EMILY HONIG received her Ph.D. from Stanford University, and is currently professor of women's studies and history at the University of California, Santa Cruz.

DONALD P. KELLY is a doctoral candidate in the Department of Sociology, the University of California, San Diego.

KWOK PUI-LAN received her Th.D. from the Divinity School, Harvard

University, and is now associate professor of theology at the Episcopal Divinity School, Cambridge, Massachusetts.

CHARLES A. LITZINGER received his Ph.D. at the University of California, Davis, and teaches East Asian history at California State University, Bakersfield.

JUDITH LIU received her Ph.D. at the University of California, San Diego, and now teaches in the Department of Anthropology and Sociology, the University of San Diego.

JESSIE G. LUTZ received her Ph.D. in Chinese history from Cornell University, and is professor of history, emeritus, at Rutgers University.

R. RAY LUTZ is professor of European history, emeritus, at Kean College of New Jersey.

HEIDI A. ROSS received her Ph.D. in comparative education from the University of Michigan at Ann Arbor, and is associate professor of education and Asian studies at Colgate University.

MURRAY A. RUBINSTEIN received his Ph.D. from New York University, and is professor of history at Baruch College at the City University of New York.

JOHN R. SHEPHERD received his Ph.D. from Stanford University, and is assistant professor of anthropology at the University of Virginia.

ALAN RICHARD SWEETEN received his Ph.D. in history from the University of California, Davis. He is an independent researcher and businessman presently completing a study of Christianity in Jiangxi Province in the nineteenth century.

ROGER R. THOMPSON received his Ph.D. from Yale University, and was assistant professor of history at the University of Maryland at College Park.

TSOU MINGTEH, formerly instructor in the Department of Social Sciences, Shanghai Jiaotong University, is a Ph.D. candidate in history, Michigan State University.

PETER CHEN-MAIN WANG received his Ph.D. in history at the University of Arizona; he has taught at Tamkang University and Chung-hsing University, Taiwan, and is now teaching in the Department of History, National Chung-cheng University, Chia-yi, Taiwan.

ERNEST P. YOUNG, who received his Ph.D. from Harvard University, is professor of history and associate of the Center for Chinese Studies at the University of Michigan in Ann Arbor.

Abbreviations

A/G	Assemblies of God
ADNantes	Archives Diplomatiques de Nantes
AMAE	Archives du Ministère des Affaires Étrangères
AME	Archives des Missions Étrangères
Annales CM	*Annales de la Congrégation de la Mission*
BMG	Basler Missionsgesellschaft, Archiv
CCC	Church of Christ in China
CCJ	Church of Christ in Japan
CCP	Chinese Communist Party
CIM	China Inland Mission
CMYB	*China Mission Year Book*
CPPCC	Chinese People's Political Consultative Conference
CR	*Chinese Recorder*
CWM	Council for World Mission, Archives
ELCA	Evangelical Lutheran Church in America, Archives
FO	Foreign Office, United Kingdom
GMD	Guomindang
GX	Guangxu
HK	Hong Kong
ISRR	Institute of Social and Religious Research
JSZ	*Jindaishi ziliao*
JWJAD	*Jiaowu jiaoan dang*
MECS	Methodist Episcopal Church, South
MEP	Société des Missions Étrangères de Paris
Methodists	Archives of the United Methodist Church (USA)
MHCC	Mission Among the Higher Classes of China
MMS	Methodist Missionary Society
MSCC	Missionary Society of the Church of Canada Archives
NCC	National Christian Council

NCCU	North China Christian Union
NCDN	*North-China Daily News*
NDA	Nanjing District Association (of CCC)
OMFA	Overseas Missionary Fellowship Archives, Selly Oak College
PRC	People's Republic of China
QL	Qianlong
SMJ	Archives du Secrétariat des Missions Jésuites
TZ	Tongzhi
UCA	United Church of Canada Archives
WS	*Wenshe yuekan*
YMCA	Young Men's Christian Association
YWCA	Young Women's Christian Association
ZLD2	Zhongguo dier lishi dang'anguan
ZZD	Zhang Zhidong, *Zhang Wenxiang-gong quanji*

CHRISTIANITY
IN CHINA

*From the Eighteenth Century
to the Present*

PART I

Christianity and the Dynamics of Qing Society

Christianity and the Dynamics of Qing Society

DANIEL H. BAYS

In the concrete cases provided, the detail in which they are described, and the variety of sources employed, several of the chapters in this section enable us to test and modify two major interpretive schemes put forward in recent years to explain the links between Christianity and Chinese society, those of Jacques Gernet and Paul Cohen.

Gernet's persuasively argued hypothesis, dealing with the seventeenth century, was that the Chinese were basically unable to absorb and understand the essential concepts of Christianity, because of their cultural, including linguistic, predispositions.[1] The only chapter in this part dealing with the pre-1800 period, that by Robert E. Entenmann, tends to contradict this hypothesis, in that it describes Chinese Catholic communities whose Chinese priests and leaders had no insurmountable barriers to adopting and internalizing Christianity—although the different cultural flavor of belief and behavior, compared with that of the European missionaries, is also apparent. The pre-1800 period was also addressed at the History of Christianity in China Project symposia in papers by Gail King, Lin Jinshui, David Mungello, and Joanna Waley-Cohen (see Appendix B). Mungello's work, in book form, also argues against Gernet's interpretation through a Hangzhou case study, as does Erik Zürcher's 1990 essay on early Fujian Christianity.[2] The second chapter in this section, by Alan Sweeten, also gives us an impression of Catholic Christianity being strongly, not superficially, rooted in Jiangxi society in the late nineteenth century. The whole issue of the Christian presence outside the court between the early eighteenth century and the 1840s appears to be much more complex than previously thought, with Catholic communities growing and prospering in at least some parts of the empire, despite imperial proscription.

One of the discussion themes of the 1989–90 symposia, conceptualized and well articulated by K. C. Liu, was a two-track model of attraction to Christianity, or conversion. One was popular, the other intellectual or rational; or as Liu put it, one related to popular religious millenarianism, and the other to the stress on moral orthodoxy, both already strongly present on the Chinese scene.[3] This may be a concept useful for the whole period from the late-Ming decades through the twentieth century. The ability of Christianity occasionally to win local officials' approval or at least benign tolerance, despite its popular sectarian aspects and ready confusion with the White Lotus tradition, indeed despite its outright illegality, was perhaps due to its partial similarity to other expressions of moral orthodoxy.[4] Probably even more important was the other strand of access to Chinese society, through popular religiosity. Entenmann's chapter gives us some impressions of local Catholic life and worship in the context of popular culture, including the White Lotus tradition. This social sector, that of syncretic popular religion or "superstition," is an obvious one in which to find linkages between Christianity and Chinese society, despite the disapproval in which much of this contact would have been held by the European missionary priests.[5]

The entire structure of the Christian presence in China was changed, of course, by several factors in the nineteenth century, most importantly the creation through the treaty system of a whole new structure of interaction between foreign missionaries and Chinese society, which also had direct impact on the status and role in society of Chinese Christians. Concrete ideas for understanding the ensuing frequent local disputes and violence deriving from these relationships, which characterized the whole last part of the nineteenth century and (as Ernest P. Young's chapter shows) the early twentieth century, were provided more than thirty years ago by Paul Cohen.[6] In a nutshell, Cohen showed clearly how the presence and activities of Christian missionaries, in addition to stirring up old phobias about heterodoxy, also directly challenged the status and roles of the gentry, or the Confucian local elite. They, in turn, naturally mobilized what resources they could muster, including instigation of mass violence, to counter the missionaries. This remains a useful interpretation, but several of our chapters go well beyond it and in effect modify it.

It seems to me that the new (post-1842) political context of the unequal treaty system was the single most important factor in creating the many cases of urban violence involving missionaries and Chinese Christians. But in the countryside, the local elite were not ubiquitous, and the documented cases involving missionary/Christian–local conflict, as

Sweeten's chapter shows, often did not even involve the local elite, or involved them in ways that did not include defense of their status and power. Here I see some continuity between Entenmann's Sichuan Catholic communities of the previous century and Sweeten's late nineteenth century Jiangxi Catholics in their being, in many cases, an integrated part of the local community. One of the chief contributions of Sweeten's work is its recounting, in remarkable detail, the variety of issues and disputes that could result in a legal record or report of some kind. He shows that the Christian identity of many of the parties to "Christian cases" (*jiaoan*) was incidental. Indeed, if not for the national political situation that often involved the Zongli yamen in haggling with foreign diplomatic representatives and the passing of documents back and forth between Beijing and local levels, much of the documentation in the *JWJAD* collection never would have had reason to go beyond the district or prefectural level. The *JWJAD* documents, used by four of the writers in this section (Sweeten, Litzinger, Thompson, and Young), give us a good deal of information on county and prefectural legal procedures, including interrogations and testimony of parties involved. This collection should probably be used more by historians of Chinese law than it has been in the past.

Despite Entenmann's and Sweeten's stress on Christian groups often being integrated parts of the local community, nevertheless there remains the undeniable fact that there were frequently disruptive results when a portion of a village or local community became Christians. This often had little or nothing to do with the prerogatives and status of the local elite, but as Charles Litzinger shows, it was frequently tied up with the thorny problem of temple fair and theatrical subscriptions — Christians claimed exemption from them — and more broadly with the whole concept of the cultural and social unity of the village as represented by the local temple and activities centered on it. There is much in this short chapter, but Litzinger makes his main point clear: the village temple association, and its central symbolic role for the community, could easily become an important arena of conflict between Christians and non-Christians, due to the synonymity of cultural and social integration at the village level. Insofar as Chinese Catholics, by refusing (under treaty rights) to pay temple exactions, challenged the cultural premises of what the temple represented, they seemed to undermine the integrity of the whole community.

Roger R. Thompson's chapter follows directly on Litzinger's, and reinforces the latter's main theme. Its beginning, with the joint agreement of missionaries and Chinese officials in 1901 that the basic problem of the past several decades of tension, culminating in the Boxer violence, derived from opera subscription disputes and resentment, is revealing. Thompson's three case studies from Shanxi add more evidence to Litzinger's. And by bringing in early twentieth century events as well, Thompson successfully ties the idea of the unitary, integrated sacred/secular village world, and what Christian conversion did to it, to the broader linear process of the desacralization of rural China. In his treatment, nineteenth-century Christianity, related as it was to (foreign) political power, was a portent of the twentieth-century phenomenon of the Chinese state, in its successive versions, desacralizing the unitary village for the extractive purposes of state-building.

Lest it be assumed that disputes over opera subscriptions were only a nineteenth-century phenomenon, or that they simply resulted from Chinese Christians cynically taking advantage of the unequal treaty system at the time, let me quote from a recent (1994) letter to the editor of *Tianfeng*, the Chinese Protestant monthly published in Shanghai. It is from a local Chinese Christian in Inner Mongolia.

There is a superstitious custom in our village which has come down through the ages: on the 15th day of the first lunar month and the 8th day of the fourth month, incense and paper are burned in the temple and idols are worshipped. Sometimes there is a performance of local opera and everyone in the village is asked to contribute their share of the expense. We Christians, concerned to keep our faith pure and maintain the true way, refused to give any money, and so relations between believers and non-believers went sour, causing conflicts and disagreements. This gave us a bad image in the non-believers' eyes. They called us selfish and tight-fisted.[7]

Today, these Christian villagers are more likely to want to use funds saved from "superstitious" opera and worship to invest in economic development projects; the desacralization of the old unitary village is still underway.

Ernest P. Young's chapter gives us the fascinating story of the tragic and mysterious death of magistrate Jiang in Nanchang in 1906, which set off an apparently nineteenth century–style fit of popular violence and diplomatic complications. But some things had changed by the early twentieth century. A modern student class, motivated by the modern force of nationalism, played an important role in the events. Young also shows clearly the beginnings of a more moderated stance of foreign governmental intervention, in this case the French government, in local disputes relating to Christianity, and he profitably uses a "ladder of arenas" concept to elucidate factors either intensifying or reducing pressures tending to confrontation and violence. The field will look forward to Young's continuing broader work on the French religious protectorate.

Tsou Mingteh's chapter on Gilbert Reid, describing the evolution of his early missionary career and his role in the post-1894 reform movement in Beijing, comes from a longer study of Reid's entire career until his death in 1927. It reminds us that in considering the role of missionaries and Christianity in interaction with Chinese society, we should not overlook the few missionaries who managed to have an apparently remarkable degree of access to figures around the court in the mid-1890s. Besides Reid, Timothy Richard is of course a well-known figure in this regard. Here, it was not Christianity as either popular religion or reinforcer of moral orthodoxy that was operative, but Christianity as associated with reformist trends to benefit society as a whole. Tsou highlights Reid's own role, or his claims of playing a certain role, by using hitherto ignored Chinese writings of Reid, and other previously unused Reid materials from various repositories. Whether Reid actually had the hundreds of interviews and visits with Beijing officials and literati that he claimed in the reports and promotional literature of the MHCC is an intriguing question. He is not given such a prominent place in previous accounts of this period.[8] But if Tsou is correct in crediting Reid with a bigger role than we previously knew, this may also indicate a greater degree of openness and flexibility than we had earlier surmised on the part of the Chinese elite, and even some officials, in the crisis atmosphere immediately after the disaster of the Sino-Japanese War.

CHAPTER I

Catholics and Society in Eighteenth-Century Sichuan

ROBERT E. ENTENMANN

In 1724 the Qing government outlawed Catholicism and consigned it to the category of "perverse sects and sinister doctrines," which already included the White Lotus sect of folk Buddhism. Both religions were suspected of fostering superstition, immorality, political subversion, and social conflict. Catholicism was suspect only in part because of its connection with foreigners. The authorities generally regarded it primarily as another type of heterodox folk religion, such as the White Lotus, even when they were aware of its foreign origins.

Over the course of the eighteenth century, persecution and apostasy reduced the number of Catholics in China by about a third, from about 300,000 to 200,000. In Sichuan, however, Catholicism fared better than elsewhere in China. The frontier environment of Sichuan, populated mostly by recent settlers from Central and South China and their descendants, proved hospitable for illegal and "heterodox" sects.

Indeed, the Catholic church in eighteenth-century China accorded in many ways with Ernst Troeltsch's definition of a sect.[1] Although some were born into Catholic families, many Catholics freely elected membership in the church, generally as a result of a conversion experience. Suspicious and wary of the secular world, they often did not recognize the demands of secular society. According to Troeltsch, sects generally fall into two types of relationship to the world: militant oppositionist and passive. In eighteenth-century Sichuan the White Lotus was sometimes the former, the Catholics without exception the latter.

Chinese Catholics, almost always a small minority in their communities, nevertheless maintained social and economic relations with their non-Catholic neighbors. There was a certain amount of intermarriage, and virtually every Catholic had close non-Catholic relatives. There were also many former Catholics, particularly after persecutions. Many eventually rejoined the church, but some joined the persecutors.

The local persecutions of 1746 and 1755 in the district of Jiangjin provide particularly rich sources of information on the complex relationships between Catholics and non-Catholics and between Catholics and the authorities.

The city of Jiangjin lies on the south bank of the Yangzi River in southeastern Sichuan, about 80 kilometers upstream from Chongqing. During the Qing dynasty it was the seat of a district within Chongqing Prefecture. The larger part of the district was on the south bank, stretching down to the border of Guizhou. Although dwarfed by the prefectural city of Chongqing, the district seat of Jiangjin was an important commercial center. It ranked as a "greater city" in G. William Skinner's central-place hierarchy.[2] It was also an important river crossing point, as the very name of the city, literally "river crossing," indicates.

Along with the rest of the Sichuan basin, Jiangjin was devastated by the depredations of the mid-seventeenth century: the rebellion of Zhang Xianzhong, the Manchu invasion and Ming resistance, the rebellion of the Three Feudatories, and the famine and disease that attended these military campaigns. The population of the province fell from perhaps four million to a quarter or half that; the demographic loss was heaviest in major cities and towns such as Jiangjin on major transport routes.[3]

No Ming population data for the district appear to be available. The official and very unreliable figures for 1669 are 9,833 households and 39,271 *dingkou*, the latter a tax unit theoretically related to the number of adult males. By 1766 the figures rose to 68,411 households and 281,847 *dingkou*.[4] Sichuan proper, excluding tribal areas, increased in population from roughly two million in 1680 to perhaps fifteen million 80 years later.[5]

This demographic growth resulted primarily from immigration from South and Central China, particularly from Hubei, Guangdong, Fujian, and Jiangxi. For the first half of the eighteenth century Sichuan was a frontier province that attracted a heterogeneous mixture of settlers seeking land and livelihood, and the region continued to receive immigrants long after it had regained its demographic losses.

These settlers had left behind their native places, their clan and temple organizations, and often even their immediate families to move to Sichuan, where government control was often weak and social order elusive. Settlers and natives alike relied on institutions that offered mutual support, protection, and fellowship to make their lives more secure. Religious affiliation often provided them with a sense of community, companionship, mutual support, and spiritual solace. It provided an alternative society and an explanation of the world that to many made more sense than that provided by orthodox Confucianism. Popular religions based in congregations gave adherents a sense of membership in a community of the elect and an important substitute for broken kinship and village ties. They also promised better fortune in this life and salvation in the next. Although the White Lotus sect was the most important of the popular religions of eighteenth-century Sichuan, the Roman Catholic church also fulfilled these functions.

The Origins of Catholicism in Jiangjin

Catholicism has a long history in southeast Sichuan. Jesuit missionaries established a church in Chongqing as early as 1642, but few of the Catholics in late Ming Sichuan survived the rebellions and warfare of the Ming-Qing transition.[6] In 1660 the French Jesuit Claude Motel came to Chongqing at the invitation of a Christian official, Xu Zuanzeng, to minister to Christian immigrants from other provinces. Motel stayed only two years but baptized 170 converts.[7] The Catholic population of the Chongqing area grew gradually, through immigration as well as conversion.

Missionary activity was renewed in Chongqing in 1702 with the arrival of two Lazarist missionaries, Johannes Mullener and Luigi Appiani. Their activities reached the surrounding countryside and, according to Mullener, there were Catholics in Jiangjin as early as 1713.[8] Missionary jurisdiction for the area was later transferred to the Société des Missions Étrangères de Paris.

The most eminent of the Catholic families in Jiangjin was the Luo family. The Luos, possibly Hakkas, had originated in Guangdong but had settled in Nankang district in Jiangxi, probably in the 1690s. In 1695 the family converted to Catholicism. Shortly thereafter, perhaps in 1700 or 1701, the brothers Luo Liangwei and Luo Liangyi migrated to Sichuan with their families. Liangyi died shortly after arriving in the province. His brother, following a Buddhist rather than a Catholic custom, cremated the corpse and buried the ashes in a jar.

According to the Luo family genealogy, Luo Liangwei encountered the French missionary Jean Basset preaching in a market town one day. Luo recited scripture to Basset to demonstrate that he was a Catholic. The missionary was delighted to learn that there were Christians in the area and accepted Luo's invitation to visit his house. All in Luo's household accepted the Catholic faith during Basset's visit.[9]

According to the Luo family genealogy, the Luo family came to Sichuan with several other Catholic families, named Wu, Wang, Ma, Qiu, and Song. Evidently they first settled in Luoranggou, a major Catholic settlement in south-central Sichuan, then in about 1723 they moved to Jiangjin. Luo Liangwei bought land in the village of Zhaojiazhuang, where he established a hamlet named Shengchongping, a community too small to locate on any available map but apparently to the north of the Yangzi; it is located thirty li or about fifteen kilometers from Youxi, a market town on the north bank of the Yangzi. He also purchased land near Longmentan, a market town on the south bank of the Yangzi not far downstream from Youxi.

The family grew large and prosperous. The descendants of the two brothers eventually formed six branches of the lineage. Some remained fervent Catholics; others left the faith. Other families intermarried with the Luos, often converting to Catholicism in the process. In the 1740s one member of the family, known by his Latin Christian name of Matthaeus, went to the French seminary in Siam, but died before being ordained. At least one woman in the family, Anna, joined the order of Catholic women known as the Christian Virgins.[10]

In 1734 the French missionary Joachim Enjobert de Martiliat spent four months with the family, who built him a thatched hut. During his stay he heard 220 confessions and baptized twelve adults.[11]

Shengchongping acquired a resident priest in 1736 when Johannes Mullener, now bishop and vicar apostolic of Sichuan, assigned Joannes-Baptista Gu Yaowen responsibility for eastern Sichuan. Gu, a native of Beijing who had studied at the College of the Holy Family in Naples, established a residence in the hamlet. Martiliat found Gu to be well versed in moral and scholastic theology, but deficient in Latin, which he could understand well but speak only with difficulty.[12] Over one hundred Catholics in Shengchongping contributed money and labor to build a brick church and parsonage for Gu.[13]

The enthusiasm of local Catholics for Gu was not always shared by his European colleagues, and many of the far-flung Catholics under Gu's jurisdiction thought he neglected them. The Italian Dominican missionary Luigi Maggi complained that Gu tolerated superstitious practices — or practices Maggi considered superstitious, says Martiliat. Young Catholics fifteen years of age had not yet had their first communion; many Catholics were ignorant about their faith and did not even know how to genuflect. This complaint suggests that they showed their devotion by kowtowing instead. Moreover, Maggi complained, Gu played chess with members of his flock. Martiliat noted that Gu rarely traveled from Shengchongping.

The Christians at Changshou complained that he had abandoned them; he saw them rarely and went by like lightning. He spent at most one day with each family and neglected to visit many.[14] He apparently considered himself the parish priest of Shengchongping and had a loyal following there.

The Persecution of 1746

Three contemporaneous accounts of the persecution of 1746 exist, two by firsthand observers and one by a Chinese priest who visited the Catholic communities of Jiangjin four years later. Martiliat, after 1744 bishop and vicar apostolic of Yunnan and superior of Huguang and Sichuan, narrowly escaped capture and recounted his experiences in a letter written soon after the event.[15] In August 1746 Gu Yaowen sent an account in Chinese to Martiliat, who forwarded it to Paris along with a Latin translation.[16] Finally, Andreas Ly, left as the senior priest in Sichuan after the departure of European missionaries in 1746, left an account based on his investigation in 1750 of the persecution.[17]

The persecution was province-wide. It initially targeted not the Catholics but the White Lotus, "a species of fanatics," according to Martiliat, "who await I don't know what kind of liberator, and against whom the magistrates carry out an investigation every year, in which Christians have been involved many times." A little before Easter in 1746 a White Lotus leader was arrested in Xindu, a district not far from Chengdu. It was rumored that he and 400 of his followers had planned to set fire to Chengdu and put its inhabitants to the sword.

A few days later a *baojia* chief noticed a picture of the Virgin Mary on the wall of the mission's house in Chengdu. He reported it to his superiors, perhaps thinking that the picture represented Wusheng laomu, the Eternal and Venerable Mother worshipped by the White Lotus sect. The local authorities stationed guards at the house, questioning all who came and went, and asking in particular about a man named Ma, reputed to be the leader of the Christians. Ma Qingshan was the Chinese name of Martiliat, who with the other French missionary in Chengdu, Hyacinthe de Verthamon, went into hiding. Rumors spread that the imprisoned White Lotus leader had implicated the Christians in his confession.

Martiliat and Verthamon escaped from the city. Martiliat was severely ill, feverish and coughing blood. His condition obliged him to ride on horseback, making him dangerously conspicuous. The two missionaries slowly made their way to Shengchongping, probably choosing that refuge because it was an isolated but important Christian community and Gu's residence, and because of Martiliat's friendship with the Luo family. Their arrival in Shengchongping was noticed by the neighboring non-Catholics. Although Martiliat and Verthamon stayed inside all day, they would stroll outside and converse in the evening hours, unaware that they were being observed.

The Catholic community was well known in the area, and the local Catholics did not behave with the circumspection one would expect of an underground church. Because the hamlet was the home of one of the few priests in eastern Sichuan, Catholics from as far away as Chongqing and the neighboring districts of Yongchuan, Tongliang, He Zhou, and Fu Zhou came to the hamlet seeking Gu to receive sacraments and to participate in worship. On holy days the crowd numbered as many as 400. "The faithful prayed in loud voices and sang publicly with all their lungs," Andreas Ly reported, not only on feast days but also daily for matins and evening prayers. "Many did not know how to pray without shouting." Worship was accompanied by music from flutes, tambourines, and gongs.[18]

The immediate cause of the local persecution in Jiangjin was a festival celebrating the summer solstice and the 24 June feast day of St. John the Baptist, Gu Yaowen's patron saint. The celebration also commemorated the third anniversary of the death of Gu's grandmother, when according to Chinese custom Gu stopped wearing mourning garments. In addition, the assembly celebrated the betrothal of an infant girl to an infant boy in the Luo family. The custom of child betrothal, although condemned by the church, was still common among the Chinese Catholics, and in this case seems to have been condoned by Gu. The festival thus combined features of Catholicism and Chinese popular culture.

The Catholics of Shengchongping celebrated with three days of banquets, to which their non-Catholic neighbors were invited. The local *baojia* chief Liu Mianshi and others of high rank were present and joined Gu at the head table, where however they were seated at inferior places. As the guests grew intoxicated, Liu Mianshi began to insult and abuse the priest. Gu angrily dared Liu to denounce him to the authorities.

This incident was symptomatic of underlying hostilities between the wealthy Luo family and its neighbors. Some of the local non-Catholics were hostile to the Luos because of lawsuits they had lost regarding landownership.[19] Two neighbors, including Liu Mianshi, reported to the authorities that the Luo family fasted—a practice associated with the White Lotus— and were members of the White Lotus sect.[20]

On 14 July Peng Weiming, magistrate of Jiangjin, having learned of the presence in Shengchongping of two European missionaries, sent over 50 soldiers to the hamlet with orders to arrest them. Martiliat and Verthamon were alerted and fled to the woods, where they stayed hidden in a dark, stuffy hut for eighteen days. Verthamon and a servant then made their way to Youxi, and thence to Chongqing; Martiliat, too sick to travel, remained hidden for several days more. Finally he reached the river, where he hired a boat to take him to Chongqing.

On 15 July armed soldiers bearing torches and lanterns arrived before dawn at the house of the Luo family. The neighing of horses and barking of dogs awakened the family, but before they could escape the men were seized and the women confined to their rooms. The soldiers searched every room with lanterns, tore up floorboards, looked under beds, and opened storerooms and closets. They found crucifixes, images, and religious books in Chinese, but did not discover Gu Yaowen's European books, hidden above a water buffalo's stall.

Four men were arrested at the house and taken to the magistrate in the district capital. They were Gu Yaowen; Thaddaeus Li Kuishan, a tailor originally from Fujian; Andreas Luo Youxiang, the head of the Luo family; and Luo's nephew Ignatius Luo Junzuo, son of Andreas Luo Youxiang's late elder brother. Two days later the four were interrogated by the magistrate.

Gu, conspicuous because of his Beijing accent and said to be the leader of the Catholics, was interrogated first. He was particularly suspect because Sichuan had virtually no settlers from North China. Gu explained his presence in Shengchongping by falsely claiming to be related to the Luo family and said that he had been hired to teach the family's children. He also claimed to conduct business in the local market towns of Shimen and Youxi. He said that the Luo family numbered 30 to 40, all Catholics. When asked about other Catholics in the district, Gu was remarkably forthcoming, naming Catholics not only in Youxi but also in the nearby district of Changshou. The magistrate questioned Gu about the religious practices of the Catholics, asking whether there was a chapel in Shengchongping, and whether men and women met together to chant scripture (*nian jing*).

"Usually they pray separately," Gu replied, "but on some occasions they pray together. This is allowed, since they are all relatives."

"How many holy days do you have in each month?"

"We have several saints' days, and once a week there is a sabbath. The Muslims call it *zhuma* [Arabic: *Juma*, Friday], the Catholics call it *zhuri* [Lord's day]."

"Who is this copper figure of a man hanging from a cross?"

"That is a memento from antiquity we honor."

"What is his name?"

"Yesu [Jesus]."

"Where does the name Yesu come from?"

"It comes from Europe, by way of Macao."

"Are Ye and Su two saints of your religion whom you honor under the name of Yesu?"

Gu, apparently dumbfounded, declined to answer. The magistrate, convinced that Gu was not a White Lotus teacher, told him that he could preach his religion as far as the neighboring districts of Chongqing and He Zhou.

Andreas Luo Youxiang was interrogated next. He was asked what province he had come from, when he had arrived in Sichuan and when he had acquired his land, who were in his family and who were related to him by marriage, and whether the women in his family were married to Catholics or non-Catholics. He was asked when he had become a Christian, whether he had converted others to his religion, whether he had a chapel on his property, and why he had a gathering of Catholics in his home against the express prohibition of such meetings. The magistrate also questioned him about two heterodox sect leaders also named Luo, an uncommon surname. He also asked about the two other sect leaders, presumably referring to Martiliat and Verthamon. Finally, he asked, who was Jesus and who had given him that name?

Magistrate Peng then interrogated Thaddaeus Li Kuishan about his province of origin and occupation. He also asked Li to explain how Mary could be both virgin and mother of God. Finally Ignatius Luo Junzuo was questioned about the objects found in his home and was asked whether he was related to the sect leaders named Luo.

All four declared that they followed no perverse religion, that is to say the White Lotus sect, nor did they fast, a term that referred to the vegetarianism practiced by White Lotus. They declared that they were Catholics and had received their religion from their parents. The magistrate, satisfied that they were indeed relatively harmless Catholics rather than White Lotus sectarians, released them, saying, "go, practice your religion, read your books, but do not assemble in your house."[21]

Martiliat, who soon learned from Gu Yaowen what had transpired, was disturbed by Gu's evasive replies to questions about Jesus, whom Gu did not acknowledge as Christ the Redeemer during the interrogation. Moreover, Gu's claims to be related to the Luo family were false. Martiliat wrote to Gu, charging that such dishonesty, especially in the presence of other Christians, set a bad example.[22]

Gu replied indignantly that his answers about Catholicism were not those of an apostate. The magistrate had asked the questions in passing and was primarily concerned about possible affiliations with the White Lotus. The Luos had claimed that Gu was a relative, and Gu had no choice but to corroborate their testimony. In any case Gu was following the examples of Abraham, who had once falsely claimed that his wife was his sister, and Martiliat himself, who had dissembled about his native place in 1740 while under arrest.[23] Martiliat did not reply.[24]

Despite the magistrate's clemency, Gu Yaowen, fearful of further persecution, left Shengchongping in the autumn to visit Catholics in neighboring districts, a pastoral responsibility he had neglected in the past. Early in 1747 he returned to his native city of Beijing, where he spent the remainder of his life. Thaddaeus Li Kuishan also left Jiangjin, abandoning his wife and children.

This was not the end of the ordeal of the Luo family. On 12 February 1747, during the absence from Jiangjin of the district magistrate, the local jail warden summoned Andreas Luo for interrogation, evidently hoping to secure a bribe.

"I know that you have become rich from European money. Is that why you're a Christian?"

"When I was a boy my parents taught me, and with my entire family I practice my religion."

"How many children and grandchildren do you have? Who of your granddaughters have married, and to whom?"

"One of my granddaughters was given in marriage to the native Sichuanese Luo family now living in Chongqing; another to the Zhang family, originally of Zhejiang, that has settled in Changshou."[25]

"Are those families Christian?"

"Yes."

"Why did you marry your granddaughters to families so far away from you, and all Christians, unless it is prohibited by your religion to marry anyone but a Christian?"

"Not at all, considering that another of my granddaughters has been married to a non-Catholic named Liu, not far from me."

"How many disciples have you taught?"

"I have not taught any."

"Why do you have a chapel in your house?"

"I am only a farmer, and I have no chapel. I have a school, where in past years children have been taught by the teachers Gu [Yaowen] and He [Paulus He Baolu, a layman]."

Luo was asked about other Catholics in Jiangjin, but did not reveal their names. He was beaten ten strokes as a result. The warden then interrogated Ou [Wu] Tchao-ming, a Catholic from Youxi, about other Catholics in the area. Ou named all of them, and was praised as sincere and candid. Luo, on the other hand, was scolded and beaten again. He then identified four of his tenants at Longmentan as Catholics. The warden interrogated sixteen others. Three admitted to being converts. The others all claimed to have been raised as Catholics by their parents — being raised as a Catholic was considered a lesser offense than converting to Catholicism, since one's Catholicism was presumably then based upon filial piety rather than volition. The warden fined Andreas Luo 72 taels for teaching Catholicism to others. All were forced to sign statements of apostasy, declaring that they had through error and ignorance been introduced to the perverse Christian religion by their parents and others, and that they would not return to it in the future.

Two months later Magistrate Peng returned to Jiangjin from a visit to Chengdu. He accepted the statements of apostasy. In the fifth month of 1747, after rebels claiming to be Christians had been captured elsewhere in the province, he again summoned the Catholics and told them that he would punish them severely and exile them if he ever found a Christian book or image among them, "even as small as the palm of the hand."[26]

The magistrate reported his investigation to the prefect of Chongqing, forwarding as well the statements of apostasy. The prefect in turn reported the matter to the provincial capital. The confiscated books and images were sent to Chengdu, where they were burned. The prefect granted clemency to the Catholics provided that they not return to the religion.[27]

The persecution of 1746 was aimed at heterodoxy, not specifically Christianity. Its immediate cause in Jiangjin was economic rivalry and social tension between the Luo family and its non-Catholic neighbors. The family's adherence to an illegal religion and its association with foreign missionaries rendered it vulnerable to persecution.

The Persecution of 1755

The Catholics continued to practice their religion, secretly but without further harassment, until another local persecution in 1755. Those who had publicly abjured their faith during the persecution had incurred excommunication, although they had not considered themselves bound by such formal statements. As the church historian Adrien Launay notes, "to the pagans this formula was synonymous with a pledge of apostasy; for Christians with few scruples it was a means of extracting themselves from the affair without punishment and without entangling their conscience, for, they say, our religion is not perverse and cannot be referred to by that expression."[28] Local officials, hoping to be spared further trouble, were often willing to tolerate the quiet practice of Catholicism as long as it did not come to their notice. They generally recognized that Catholicism, unlike the White Lotus sect, was not potentially seditious.

At the beginning of 1749 Andreas Ly made a pastoral visit to Jiangjin. His major task was to reconcile to the church those who had given statements of apostasy to the authorities. He received apostates back into the church with a ceremony, believing that public sins such as apostasy required public penance.[29] During his stay in the market town of Longmentan, which was home to about 100 Catholics, Ly lifted the excommunication of ten people and absolved them from the sin of apostasy. He sadly noted, however, that the lack of a catechist or lay leader made many grossly ignorant of their faith.[30]

From Longmentan Ly crossed the Yangzi and went by foot in the dark of night to Shengchongping, where he stayed at the house of Andreas Luo. He absolved Luo and four others from apostasy, and lifted their excommunication.[31]

In the years that followed, the authorities of Jiangjin took no notice of the Catholics. On one occasion in 1753 the new district magistrate, Zhang Zhihe, ordered the chief Daoist priest (*primarius Taosseorum*) of Jiangjin to investigate perverse sects such as the White Lotus and the Dasheng sect. He interrogated Thaddaeus Siu of Youxi, apparently a suspected sect member. On learning that Siu was a Catholic, the Daoist priest observed that Catholicism was an upright and ancient religion, unlike the perverse sects.[32]

Although Andreas Luo was forced to sell some of his land to pay his fine and bribes to local officials, he remained prosperous. Besides his land in Shengchongping he owned land in Longmentan. His tenants in Longmentan included two Catholic families related to each other by marriage, the Wang and the Qiu. After Baptista Wang died, some of his sons left the church. One, a reputed thief named Joseph, a nephew of Andreas Luo and son-in-law of a man named Nicholaus Qiu, moved into his father-in-law's house. Luo, fearing that his tenant's notoriety would cause him difficulty, canceled their lease and rented the land instead to another Catholic, Lucius Ma Yongyao. Joseph Wang and Nicholaus Qiu brought a complaint against Luo before the local gentry (*primariis regionis*), who compelled him to pay the plaintiffs seven or eight taels in compensation.[33] Although Luo agreed to the settlement, Wang and Qiu found it inadequate. Nicholaus Qiu then destroyed some of his own household utensils to incriminate Luo and denounced him to the local jail warden, as follows:

I, Khieou [Qiu] Tso-tchy, compelled to fast and destroy idols, hereby denounce the perverse religion. For over ten years I have been a tenant of Andreas Luo, and with great effort have brought his land, which had been wilderness, into cultivation and tended it carefully. I have never caused him any trouble. The landlord, Andreas Luo, has many times forced me to obey perverse fasts, which have been prohibited by the highest authorities. This was prohibited by the former magistrate Peng [Weiming]. Yet Andreas Luo was not moved to obey the prohibition.

On the 21st of the seventh month of the Qianlong reign [28 August 1755], Andreas Luo and his disciple Lucius Ma Yongyao and Ma's sons, along with Luo's nephew Petrus, came to my house to force me and all the members of my family, of both sexes, to fast. I could never agree to this because of the strict official prohibition of all fasting. They became violent and not only did they destroy my altar to the gods, my ancestral tablets, and my incense burner, they also destroyed my domestic utensils and injured me on my right arm, as you can see, and expelled me from the land.

I denounced this violence to the local gentry [*primariis istius regionis*], Houang Meou-sin and others, seeking justice, but this only incited their malice and anger toward me. Such casual violation of the laws, compelling people to fast, destroying statues, and expelling innocent tenants from the land, leaves me no recourse but to denounce them to the authorities. QL 20/7/23 [30 August 1755].

This accusation did not have the desired result. Qiu therefore sent an accusation directly to the district magistrate, Wang Zhengyi:

I, Khieou Tso-tchy, fearful of violating the law, offer this accusation. On the 21st [*sic*] of this month I denounced Andreas Luo to the jail warden for enticing me into perverse religion. The jail warden accepted my accusation and promised to investigate its accuracy, but did not keep his promise.

My father was once enticed into this religion by the said Andreas Luo. When an official edict condemned fasters, my father was penitent, obeyed the law, and mended his ways. His dying command to me was never to profess that religion prohibited by law. But Andreas Luo, in violation of the law, forced me to return to that disgusting religion [*vomitus*] on the 14th of the eighth month [September 19]. He, his disciple Lucius Ma, Luo's nephew Petrus, and three others brought me an image I am unfamiliar with [a crucifix], a rosary, and a calendar, and forced me to fast. I accepted these objects but was not willing to fast. I ask your mercy for my transgressions, oh magistrate, and beg you to investigate.

The magistrate agreed to examine the matter.

Soon thereafter Joseph Wang made a much more serious accusation against Andreas Luo, his uncle. Luo, he charged, kept in his house not only a military banner and weapons but also five or six virgins, soon to be the queens of rebels. Although there were no weapons at the house, there were in fact a few members of the Institute of Christian Virgins. The magistrate, fearful of potential rebellion, immediately raided a house belonging to

Andreas Luo in Longmentan. There he found a small catechism, a book of prayers, and a crucifix belonging to Thomas Song Fong-tsiang, a barber and immigrant from Fujian.

The magistrate also ordered two officers to search Andreas Luo's house in Shengchongping for virgins and military weapons. The Christian Virgins, alerted just before the magistrate's arrival, fled into the woods, while two or three married women and widows stayed at the house. The officials found no weapons or virgins but uncovered a number of religious books and images. The magistrate reported his investigation to the prefect of Chongqing as follows:

I, Wang, magistrate of Jiangjin, inform the prefect of my investigation into perverse religions. On QL 20/8/29 [4 October 1755] a certain common man [*plebeius*] of an important village of my district, named Wang, reported to me that his late father Joannes-Baptista, who had once spread the Christian religion, had abandoned it after it was investigated. But Wang's uncle Andreas Luo still observed the religion in violation of the law, with his disciple Lucius Ma and others. Wang, fearing lest he be implicated with his uncle, begged me to investigate. The same day members of the local gentry, Tchang Kho-sin, Sou Kien-jin, and Houang Meou-sin, made similar statements to me. These accounts led me to interrogate Joseph Wang in private.

This Andreas Luo, who had once renounced Christianity [during the persecution of 1746], was persuaded by Thomas Song, a native of Fujian, to begin praying and fasting with his disciples Lucius Ma and Nicholaus Khieou [Qiu] Tso-tchy. Moreover, Wang's elder brother was also made to embrace the religion. So I sent the centurion Ouang Suen-yeou and the deputy Tchang Tchy-y to search several houses.

They found nothing in the houses of Lucius Ma, Khieou Tso-tchy, or Thomas Song, but in the house of Andreas Luo they seized four prayer books, one in which was inscribed "written by Joseph Tshien, Yongzheng 12 [1734]." Another was inscribed "copied by Thomas Song, Qianlong 18 [1753]." There was also a catechism for confirmation, a book of rules for meeting on feast days, a book of funeral ritual, and a four-volume work on the rudiments of Christianity. These books were hard to understand at first, but after repeated readings I learned that they concerned avoiding misfortune and doing penance for sins. We also found four calendars indicating fast days, two little square images, and a cross of wood on which a copper figure was attached.

All was brought to the district office. I took testimony from Tchang Kho-sin, Sou Kien-jin, and Houang Meou-sin, and learned that in fact Andreas Luo prays, fasts, and makes idols in his house. Joseph Wang testified that Andreas Luo is a Christian, and for that reason he denounced him, but he is not a member of any other religion.

I summoned Andreas Luo, who testified as follows: "I am a native of Jiangxi, and have land in the main village of the district [Longmentan]. I learned Christianity from my ancestors. In QL 13 [1748], when the sect leader Lieou Khy's plot against the emperor was uncovered, I burned my prayer books, and with my entire family ate meat, never fasting again. At the beginning of the eighth month of this year, the barber Thomas Song persuaded me, with books and images, to return to prayer and fasting. Khieou Tso-tchy and Carolus Wang Tso-yuen [presumably Joseph Wang's elder brother] also wanted to join the faith."

I then summoned Lucius Ma, Khieou Tso-tchy, and Carolus Wang Tso-yuen, who all admitted knowledge of the books and images Thomas Song had given to Andreas Luo, and all admitted that they had once fasted, and later ate meat.

I then interrogated Thomas Song who said that he was a native of Fujian, and that in the sixth month of this year he had traveled from his native province to Sichuan. Passing by boat through Hankou, he encountered an old man who said that one could be freed from whatever punishment one was liable to if one does penance and prays. That man gave Thomas Song books and images as well as a calendar noting the days to fast, and said that he was a Christian. At the beginning of the eighth month Song gave the images and books to Andreas Luo but did not propagate the religion to others.

I interrogated him further. Why are the names Joseph Tshien and Thomas Song in the book? Where are they from? [Thomas] Song Fong-tsiang replied that Thomas was his school name, but he didn't know who Joseph Tshien was, or why his name was in the book.

The magistrate completed the investigation, sent the confiscated books and images to the provincial authorities, and referred the matter to the prefect of Chongqing. Eventually those interrogated, including the original plaintiffs, Nicholaus Qiu and Joseph Wang, were all imprisoned for a few months.

The Catholic communities of Shengchongping and Longmentan survived the ordeal, and the Catholics of Jiangjin remained undisturbed for the rest of the eighteenth century, although their religion remained illegal until 1844. The Luos continued to be the most important Catholic family in the area. One branch moved to the nearby district of Yongchuan. Of the 52 Chinese priests from Sichuan ordained between 1825 and 1856, five were members of the Luo family.[34]

Of the other eighteenth-century Catholic families in Jiangjin, only the Wu family remained by the early twentieth century. The Wangs had disappeared, or more likely had abandoned Catholicism and no longer appeared in church records. The Ma family had migrated to nearby Baxian, the Qius to Fu Zhou, and the Songs to Tongliang.[35] All other Catholics in the district were descended from later converts, mostly after the legalization of Christianity.

Conclusion

The sources available on the Catholics of Jiangjin, particularly on the persecutions of 1746 and 1755, make it possible to make some generalizations about them and their relations with the larger society in which they lived.

They, like their non-Catholic neighbors, were not a community with deep roots in the area. The relatively well-established Luo family, for example, had in 1746 been in Jiangjin for little over twenty years and had lived in Sichuan for less than half a century. Other Catholics mentioned in the sources were immigrants from Fujian and elsewhere. Like most inhabitants of mid-eighteenth-century Sichuan, the Catholics of Jiangjin were immigrants or their immediate descendants.

The Catholics did not all belong to one social stratum. The writings of the missionaries often described the poverty of the Chinese Catholics, but it does not seem that as a group they were poorer than others. The evidence in fact supports the observations several decades later by Abbé Huc. He noted that although in most of China Catholics had been recruited primarily from the most indigent classes, the greatest number in Sichuan were to be found in the middle ranks of society.[36] Indeed, some prospered. Chinese Catholicism was not always the religion of the dispossessed.

Indeed, the Luos of Shengchongping became targets of resentment because of their landed wealth. They seem to have been supported by the local gentry, who in 1755 initially rejected the accusation of Nicholaus Qiu, a poor tenant, and cooperated with the persecution only when the matter reached the district magistrate. Yet because of their illegal religion, the Luos could never be secure from the threat of persecution. Their enemies exploited this vulnerability. The persecution of 1746 was caused in part over resentments stemming from a land dispute; the 1755 persecution resulted from a dispute between a landlord and tenant. Ironically, the initiator of the persecution of 1755 was himself a Catholic and was ultimately punished for that reason.

Catholicism was persecuted because it was considered heterodox. Its apparent similarity to the most subversive of the sects, the White Lotus, made it appear dangerous. As Daniel Bays has shown, Christianity paralleled the indigenous Chinese sectarian tradition in many ways. Both that tradition and Christianity practiced congregational worship with liturgy, singing, reading of scripture, and preaching. The description of the festival in June 1746 clearly shows the influence of Chinese popular religion on Chinese Catholic practice as well. Even Catholic and White Lotus theologies had many similarities: both believed that humanity had become alienated from its creator, but salvation was possible through repentance and reliance on an intermediary. Both religions awaited the coming of a messiah.[37]

The authorities sometimes suspected a connection between the White Lotus and Christianity. The accusations and interrogations of Catholics during the persecutions in Jiangjin demonstrate this suspicion. The Catholics were accused of fasting and chanting scripture in mixed meetings of men and women, both practices associated with the White Lotus. Although the Catholics were not vegetarians, they fasted on certain days, referring to this practice as *zhai*, the same word used by White Lotus sectarians in reference to their vegetarianism.[38]

The authorities sought, in their interrogations, to discover the network of Catholic believers and teachers, questioning Catholics about their family background and relationships. They assumed, not unreasonably, that Catholicism spread through networks of lay teachers and relatives, as did White Lotus teachings. They had little knowledge of the religion they were investigating, as Peng Weiming's questions about Jesus indicate. Once the authorities determined that the Catholics were law-abiding, apart from their religion, they treated them with leniency.

By the mid-eighteenth century Catholicism had become a popular religion with roots in Chinese society. The foreign provenance of the religion did not seem particularly important to its adherents, their neighbors, or even the authorities. Indeed, the persecution of 1755 involved no foreigners at all. Chinese Catholics usually lived in peace with their non-Christian neighbors. When conflict arose between them, the Catholics' membership in an illegal religion gave their adversaries an advantage in the dispute. Yet such strife was generally caused not by religious differences but merely reflected the ordinary economic and social conflicts of eighteenth-century China.

CHAPTER 2

Catholic Converts in Jiangxi Province: Conflict and Accommodation, 1860–1900

ALAN RICHARD SWEETEN

Most studies of Christianity in China, preoccupied with the diplomatic ramifications of various incidents or with the cultural gap as revealed in certain conflicts, have not looked closely at Christianity at the local or community level. It was after all at this level—be it in a city or town neighborhood or in a village or rural district—where the actual contact between missionaries, Christians, and non-Christians occurred. In these tightly knit communities people often spent their entire lives living and working close together while constrained mainly by Confucian standards of behavior and the need for social harmony. When individuals, whether as members of a family, a lineage, or a community, converted to Christianity their relationship with others may have changed, but they and non-Christians still had to deal with everyday matters of personal and oftentimes mutual concern: conflict or accommodation resulted.[1]

The focus of this study is on how Catholicism functioned among the common people of Jiangxi at the local level. Some of the questions to be addressed are: What was the conversion process for Catholics and what did it mean to become Catholic? Did Chinese tend to convert as individuals or en masse as families and lineages? Who were the Chinese Catholics and what was their socioeconomic background? Were Catholics, as Paul A. Cohen has written, "confined almost entirely to poor peasants and towns-people, criminal elements and other unsavory types" and were those that adopted Catholic beliefs and social practices "to a great extent, a community apart, isolated and often estranged from their fellow Chinese"?[2]

In broader terms, why was there friction between converts and non-converts? Is the pattern of conflict that Cohen has analyzed for urban settings applicable to rural conflict? Did the gentry instigate and take the lead in the rural incidents that involved Catholics as they had in major urban cases? These are just some of the questions that must be asked in order to broaden and clarify our understanding of Christianity for both urban and rural China. On the basis of information available for Jiangxi Province over a four-decade period we may begin to answer these important questions.

Catholicism in Jiangxi

Catholic missionaries first began work in Jiangxi in 1595.[3] Although they faced enormous difficulties, such as the political turmoil and warfare of dynastic change and Qing imperial proscription of Christianity from 1724 to 1844, still missionaries persevered and made gradual progress. Little is known, however, about the day-to-day work of the missionaries or about the people who converted during this early period.[4] Although there were probably 200,000 or more Chinese Catholics in the eighteenth and early nineteenth century, precise data on the number of converts and where they lived are lacking.

After 1844, with their presence in China guaranteed by Sino-foreign treaties, missionaries intensified proselytization. Jiangxi became a separate vicariate apostolic in 1846 under the control of a titular bishop from the Congregation of the Mission (Lazarist); the number of converts began to grow quickly. One estimate for the 1840s has 4,500 Catholics scattered about the province. Another rough count for the early 1900s found approximately 36,000 Catholics in Jiangxi.[5]

Conversion to Catholicism and Some Individual Catholics

These may seem like small numbers when compared to the province's mid-nineteenth-century population of approximately twenty million people, but to missionaries and native priests these converts were just the beginning of future success. Catholic clergy used every manner of means to win new adherents to the faith. Through sermons, medical work, aid to the poor; through establishment of schools, orphanages, opium refuges; and through intervention in lawsuits and other ways, potential converts were attracted.

In Jiangxi the subsequent course of religious instruction by the Lazarists was similar to that for the various other Catholic orders working in China.[6] The vicar apostolic for Guizhou, Louis Faurie, described in 1864 the process and the ceremony by which one became an "adorer."

When a pagan has been told what he is to understand by the true religion and . . . declares his belief in one God and his desire to become a Christian, he is . . . taught the sign of the cross. As soon as he can do this without being prompted two candles are lighted on the altar and he is placed on his knees. He holds in his hands a paper on which is printed all that he has to repeat. An old Christian kneels near him, so as to be able to direct him how to answer. The ceremony commences by making the sign of the cross: then five prostrations while reciting the following words:

First prostration. "I believe in God. I abjure all my past errors."

Second prostration. "I hope that God in His infinite goodness, will forgive all my sins."

Third prostration. "I love and adore God, all beautiful, almighty, more than anything else in this world."

Fourth prostration. "I detest with all my heart the sins of my past life and I firmly resolve never to commit them again."

Fifth prostration. "I pray the Blessed Virgin Mary, my mother, to obtain for me from God, by her powerful intercession, the grace of final perseverance."

After this the Apostles' Creed is recited, also Our Father, Hail Mary, and the Ten Commandments. Then is added this declaration:

"The commandments of God that I have just recited are contained in these two: To love God above all things and one's neighbor as oneself. These ten command-ments have been dictated by God that all nations might observe them. Those who keep them faithfully will be recompensed with eternal glory in heaven. Those who disobey them will be condemned by Him to the eternal torments of hell."[7]

The applicant "then concluded with five thanksgivings — for the cre-ation, nourishment, and preservation of his life, for redemption, for pardon for sins, for having been brought to a knowledge of the true religion, and for all other blessings." The ceremony thus ended and the applicant was enrolled as an adorer. The priest expected the adorer to attend mass and to follow Catholic precepts. Significantly, the adorer now considered himself to be a Catholic.[8]

If over a period of about one year the adorer mastered the rudiments of Catholic doctrine and if the adorer disavowed native beliefs and idols and discontinued ancestor worship then enrollment as a catechumen came next. The Catholic church decreed that before admittance to baptism one not only had to study devoutly but also had to observe church doctrine. In other words, the catechumen was on probation: probation often lasted another year. When the catechumen demonstrated thorough knowledge of "his catechism, the chief mysteries of the Faith, the more important Cath-olic symbols, the Lord's prayer, the Ten Commandments, the precepts of the church, and the effect of baptism," and when the catechumen demon-strated through action that there was no involvement with opium, concubines, or other behavior the church considered immoral, the catechumen could then be baptized.[9]

After baptism a few converts became catechists with certain important responsibilities. Whatever the catechists' motivation, training, and progression as Catholics they became in fact local lay leaders. There may have been one or more for each community.[10] Between the infrequent visits of the priest, catechists instructed those who had not yet been baptized and undertook the general religious care of the Catholic community. In addition, catechists often added to the flock by making the first all-important overture to interest potential converts in Catholicism. It is remarkable that catechists could undertake such responsibilities without the extended training received by priests.

Missionary accounts from different times and places in China confirm the importance of the catechists.[11] Likewise, within primary Chinese sources for cases involving missionaries and converts (*jiaoan*) in Jiangxi, one regularly encounters adult male converts identified as *jiaotou*. This appears to be the Chinese equivalent of catechist, but I believe the term is best translated as "lay leader." *Jiaotou* is the term such leaders themselves used. Converts knew them by this title, and *jiaotou* freely disclosed their position to local officials.

Most importantly, *jiaotou* were the vital link in conversion. According to one commoner in Jiangxi, "on 1 April 1874 I took [*jiaotou*] Zou Yaya as my teacher and studied Catholicism."[12] In the same locality this teacher-student or master-disciple relationship was attributed to several other men by new converts: it can be inferred that they were *jiaotou*, as well.[13] *Jiaotou* also possessed the power to reject converts if they acted wrongly. "On 27 February 1873 I became a Catholic," stated one man. "Later, because I was not friendly with [other] converts the *jiaotou* expelled me."[14]

In such accounts we begin to see conversion in more personal terms. For some individuals conversion to Catholicism was such a noteworthy event that the exact date could be marked. For others, the significance was in terms of family history. The Xiaos, proprietors of a bean curd shop in Potou (a market place in Lüling County), proudly stated that their family had been Catholic for ten generations.[15] A man from the same county stated that "[my family] has been Catholic for three generations."[16] Regardless of when the commitment to Catholicism was made, it was memorable.

Given the male domination of traditional China, it is not surprising that the conversion of adult men had considerable impact on other family members. One man, Wu Aiyao, expressed it this way: "when I was young I followed my father in converting to Catholicism."[17] Another man revealed an even stronger paternal influence: "since my father converted so did the entire family."[18] In a rural area of Xinchang County during February 1868 one Yan Bingyi and his whole family converted at the same time.[19] Within another family a father did not oppose the conversion of an adult son because the former saw it as an act of self-improvement. The son's wife and concubine converted with him.[20] And, in one instance at least, an adult man led his widowed mother to Catholicism.[21] Although there is no evidence of women exercising a parallel influence, still there were devout Catholic women, some of whom resolutely kept the faith as widows.[22]

The question remains whether it was typical in Jiangxi for entire families to convert together. With so many variables involved in family life, the preliminary answer seems to be no, although a conclusive answer must await the compilation of more data. Regarding the conversion of entire lineages or villages, I reach the same conclusion. To be sure, there are reports of the conversion of entire — probably single-lineage — villages in neighboring Guangdong; yet the conversion of entire villages does not seem to have occurred in Jiangxi.[23] Within the *jiaoan* documents for the period 1860–1911, there is only one brief mention of a rural village in southern Jiangxi that was entirely Christian, and it had been so for a long time.[24] Unfortunately, the documents do not disclose any details on this village.

Where lineages are clearly visible in Jiangxi, Catholics are always in the minority. According to information from one lineage in Longquan County, altogether there were more than 180 adult men (*dingkou*) among whom there were only six convert families.[25] Except for one village in southern Jiangxi, no evidence of conversion by entire lineages or large groups of people has been seen for Jiangxi. Furthermore, if the hypothesis regarding lineage division along socioeconomic axes is correct, it cannot be said that Jiangxi converts came from just the disadvantaged half.[26]

The Socioeconomic Background of Converts

In Jiangxi converts came from all walks of life and continued to live and to work in the community. At one end of the social spectrum virtual outcasts, namely "mean people" (*jianmin*), became Catholics and at the other end a few lower-degree holders (*jiansheng* and *shengyuan*) converted.[27] Not one convert with higher-degree status was visible in any Jiangxi *jiaoan*.[28] Among converts were both property-owning and tenant farmers as well as agricultural laborers, barbers and tanners ("mean professions"), shopkeepers, and the unemployed and the very poor.[29] All of these people remained part of the community in which they lived and did not form separate enclaves.[30]

Most converts who became involved with the law were not trouble-makers or habitual criminals. Certainly the vast majority of converts were commoners, but so were most Chinese. This cannot serve as an indictment. Because of the social and occupational diversity of converts found in Jiangxi it is difficult to conclude that they were from "among the populace least likely to support the established order."[31] On the contrary, there are signs that converts supported the Qing. A Nankang County local militia director, for example, was Catholic and fought against Vegetarian Sect bandits (*zhaifei*) who threatened the area during the 1850s.[32] And in 1874 a French missionary set an example for local converts by voluntarily furnishing information that led to the arrest of men planning an uprising in Wuning County.[33]

Yet, at times, Catholicism did attract men susceptible to illegal behavior. Rather than recounting the various crimes of assault, robbery, and extortion perpetrated against the well-to-do of Yihuang County by a group of Catholic converts, a social profile will be drawn. Of the ten men arrested, one indicated he was a laborer; the rest stated they were without profession and unemployed. Not one had heavy family obligations or restraints; only one man was married and most indicated that one or both parents were deceased. Of the ten men, nine had converted during a two-month period shortly before the illegal activities began, and one man had been "expelled" from the ranks of the converts by a *jiaotou* (but remained part of the band). Finally, in converting to Catholicism several of the men established a teacher-student relationship with different people, one of whom was identified as a *jiaotou*.[34] This teacher-student bond, it should be noted, was organizationally important among some sectarian groups.[35]

I would venture that the above profile is more revealing of a pattern of local discontent than a pattern of conversion. To be sure, Catholicism may have been one tie that drew these men together, but their socioeconomic plight seems more significant. After all, one man was rejected as a Catholic yet stayed with the group as they targeted the wealthy; religion appears incidental to how and why the men acted out their dissatisfaction. Therefore, the case is atypical of convert-commoner conflict and cannot serve as proof that Catholics were more disloyal than any other segment of the population.

No matter how Catholics are described, local authorities tended to watch them closely and the Zongli yamen endeavored continuously to regulate the activities of both missionaries and converts. Although Paul Cohen has explained the Chinese and Western positions on major urban *jiaoan* for the 1860s, and other works fill in most of the gap for the remainder of the nineteenth century, the full story of *jiaoan* within a diplomatic context has yet to be written.[36] Similarly, we await a comprehensive analysis of *jiaoan* within a domestic setting and with stress on local socioeconomic issues.[37] For Jiangxi we may observe a certain type of conflict between converts and non-Catholics that resulted in litigation. These small and mostly rural cases help us understand the often personal nature of some of the conflict and allow us to see from another perspective Catholicism in the community setting.

A Priest's Claim of Religious Persecution

During 1872 the magistrate of Chongren County ordered Wang Po and other local gentry to reinstitute *baojia* registration in Qiuxi, a market town where numerous converts lived. Converts, however, refused household registration cards and moreover rejected requests for contributions to the next local operatic performance. Subsequently, at the operatic performance Wang Po spotted a convert and scolded him for freeloading. The convert along with a *jiaotou* later avenged the insult by assaulting Wang. Community concord soon evaporated and county authorities had to intervene to reestablish order.

To Father Antoine Anot, the Qiuxi trouble smacked of persecution. He reported that after January 1873 converts had been repeatedly beaten, robbed, and subjected to extortion: altogether there were more than 30 incidents.[38] The Chongren acting magistrate retrieved from the county files 34 complaints made by converts. However, no trial had been possible in 26 instances because plaintiffs and witnesses could not be found or because insufficient information precluded further investigation.[39] From the eight cases tried several examples will serve to highlight the actual nature of the Chongren conflict.

A local quarrel. Wang Faxing, a convert, quarreled with an intoxicated man who had been publicly discussing Catholicism (evidently in uncomplimentary terms). Wang took the man to the local church where he was forced to apologize. Later a relative of the man, who was active in the local *baojia* bureau, sought out Wang to discuss the matter. Outside Wang's carpentry shop the two men argued and a crowd gathered. At that time someone slipped into the shop and stole some tools. Wang thought the whole incident had been staged and filed suit. The acting magistrate disagreed, but still ordered reimbursement for Wang's loss.[40]

An unpaid loan. Mrs. Hu née Huang formally complained that because her husband was Catholic he had been wanted for arrest by one Zou Jiaxiang and others. After her husband fled, without leaving a clue as to his whereabouts, Zou and others extorted money from her. The acting magistrate ascertained that the Hus had borrowed money from Zou. While Hu was gone on business, Zou came to collect. Mrs. Hu delayed and Zou made threats until she repaid the money. Because Mrs. Hu felt both threatened and insulted she accused Zou of extortion. The acting magistrate ruled the complaint unwarranted and took no further action.[41]

Harassment of a Catholic beggar. Mrs. Huang née Liao, a convert, filed a complaint stating that the directors of the local *baojia* bureau had tried to arrest her husband because he was Catholic. He fled to avoid arrest, leaving his family behind. A young son then died of starvation and exposure to freezing temperatures. The acting magistrate discovered that Huang had indeed left his family because he feared repercussions of the converts' attack on Wang Po, but that Mrs. Huang had not complained immediately. Moreover, in court she could not identify the defendants. The acting magistrate determined that the Huangs were beggars and that after the father left, a son had indeed died. The acting magistrate made no mention of whether or not the *baojia* directors had actually attempted to arrest Huang. Instead, the acting magistrate ruled that the *baojia* directors were not responsible for the death of Huang's son; the case thus ended.[42]

These three brief cases, and others too, reveal the multicausal nature of convert-commoner conflict and litigation. Catholicism was one element, yet the facts do not support Father Anot's claim of religious persecution. The situation was more complex than that, as the incisive commentary of Li Xucheng, a local gentryman, reveals.

This is the home area of commoners and converts. Is there ordinarily contact [between them] or not? [Of course,] debts are owed, rents are due, and there are I.O.U.'s. These are the endless affairs [of any community. From the rift caused by converts who would not register for the *baojia* or contribute money for the opera, relations between] commoners and converts were not friendly. Here and there, payments of rents and debts were sought. [There were] arguments and quarrels and [some] desired to have people arrested and prosecuted by officials in order to recover [money] or because of various things that were taken in lieu of the debts.

Subsequently, the real situation was obliterated and complaints were made of extortion, assault, and robbery. There were many inaccuracies, and it was feared [by some] that a judicial settlement would come from these lies. Therefore, many hid and would not be questioned [in court]. Now both sides recognize that there were misunderstandings. The commoners and converts are once again amicable.[43]

In 1875 Father Anot again reported the persecution of converts, this time over 100 separate instances in Anren County.[44] Local officials investigated altogether 63 complaints, most pivoting on a claim of robbery or extortion. The Anren magistrate concluded that in 52 of these cases no such incident had occurred. Except for one case settled by the magistrate, all the others were dismissed.[45] In 37 of the complaints not one plaintiff could be located (one man was deceased), nor could anyone with a similar name within seven to ten miles of Dengjia market town, the site of the supposed persecution.[46] Therefore, the magistrate held no trials.

Acting Governor Liu Bingzhang commented that "in all litigation between commoners and converts, if the converts' facts are lacking [they then] hide and will not come [to court] in order to get the missionary to intervene and argue [the case on their behalf]."[47] With his claim refuted by the official investigation, Father Anot requested that the case be closed because the converts were either elsewhere or too sick to come to court.[48]

The tension between the common people and converts of Chongren and Anren counties was real enough; after all, two churches were destroyed. Although convert-commoner animus took the form of complaints and accusations, the intent was not necessarily to go to court, as evidenced by the many converts who failed to show up in court. Furthermore, the complaints (even if false) centered on concrete problems involving material things. That this was the main theme has two implications: converts had intimate ties with the community at large, and Catholicism itself was not a consuming issue. Hence when examples of conflict involving converts are taken from the community setting the religious elements are too easily given prominence. We should keep in mind, as Li Xucheng pointed out, that many problems between converts and their neighbors were not of a special kind.

Secular Problems Involving Catholics

Throughout the nineteenth century in Jiangxi we find situations comparable to those described above for Chongren and Anren counties. For example, on 27 February 1899 the French minister complained to the Zongli yamen about Chinese mistreatment of one of their missionaries in Chongren County. The Zongli yamen ordered provincial officials to investigate the complaint at hand and the overall situation.[49] This led in turn to an official inquiry into the *jiaoan* of several counties. The magistrates of Shangrao and Lüqi counties reviewed their respective files and reported case summaries of litigation that involved converts.[50] Significantly, these cases had all been settled locally: the magistrates had not previously reported these cases to their superiors nor had missionaries previously complained about the cases to the French authorities. All of these cases point clearly to local, secular problems as the main source of conflict.

A soured business relationship. In early 1894 Gui Bogao moved from Linchuan County to Tashui in the countryside of Shangrao County. There he became partners with Xu Yunjin in making and selling grasscloth. Gui lived and worked at Xu's home and continued to do so after Xu ended the partnership two months later. Gui, who was a convert to Catholicism, continued the business alone while living at Xu's home. He paid room and board to Xu. When Gui took a short trip sometime in late 1897 or early 1898, Xu confiscated his grasscloth and bedding as security for Gui's unpaid rent.

Gui took the matter to court. The magistrate questioned both sides and then ruled that Gui should pay the rent owed to Xu and that Xu should return Gui's property to him. On 23 February 1899 the magistrate closed the file on this case.[51]

A widow and her false complaint. Mrs. Xu née Xia, a widow and mother of Xu Yunjin (from the case above), complained to the magistrate that her son was without a proper profession and had sold land belonging to her without her permission. To redeem the property and clear the title she had had to pay the buyer $200. Secondly, she complained that her nephew, Xu Yunzhang, who was Catholic, had purchased land from her in 1889. He had not paid her all the money due and now refused to make further payments. The widow claimed that because of her advanced age she now needed the money for the purchase of a coffin and other items.

According to Xu Yunzhang, however, his cousin, Xu Yunjin, actually owed him money but in order to avoid repayment he instigated his mother to file a false legal complaint. On 15 March 1899 the Shangrao magistrate stated there was no evidence to support the widow's complaint against her nephew. The magistrate granted leniency to the widow because of her age and ordered Xu Yunjin punished for his misdeeds.[52]

An illegal purchase of grain. In 1899 Yan Huaxing, a commoner and Catholic, went to Shangrao City. There he made arrangements with two gentrymen for the purchase of a small amount of grain held in storage. As Yan and a helper carried the grain in shoulder-pole baskets out of the city via the south gate, Fang Defu, another gentryman, stopped them and confiscated the grain. Yan filed a complaint with the magistrate.

The magistrate investigated and determined that Yan Huaxing and his family were well-off. In attempting to purchase grain held in reserve Yan had broken the law. This was not unusual, according to the magistrate, because commoners frequently worried about grain shortages before the new harvests were in. "The little people compare trifling amounts constantly and the circumstances [of this case] originated in this. Since not much grain was purchased [we] should forego further deliberations." The magistrate closed the case by ordering Fang Defu to compensate Yan for the confiscated grain.[53]

A dispute over farm land and irrigation. The convert and commoner Wang Fuheng complained to the magistrate that a neighbor had ignored an earlier judicial decision by excavating a new irrigation embankment that when filled with water would endanger Wang's own property. Wang also disputed the location of another neighbor's lime store and adjacent cesspool. The latter neighbor counter-charged that Wang had in the construction of a new home disturbed a grave mound, thus necessitating a new burial site.

The documents on this dispute are not detailed, but it appears that the various parties involved did not want to pursue the matter and refused summonses to appear in court. Nonetheless, the Shangrao magistrate, based on the information gathered, ruled that Wang's fields had actually benefited from the new irrigation embankment. Wang, however, was responsible for having disturbed a grave site and should pay his neighbor $6 in compensation for the reburial expenses. Since no one petitioned to continue the litigation, the magistrate noted the case as closed on 20 June 1899.[54]

A village school property dispute. Fu Jingxing, a *juren*, and others formally complained to the Lüqi magistrate in June–July 1884 that 30 years earlier they had on behalf of the village school purchased a dilapidated building and land from Lin Xiaozou and his wife, née Fu. The building served as the school's office. In 1889 several side rooms of the repaired building were rented out to one Lin Chunfa, who was Lin Xiaozou's brother's grandson. Lin Chunfa made regular rent payments to the school. When his father, Lin Xi'en, his mother, née Chen, and his brother, Lin Ruijin (a convert), moved in with him two years later they refused to pay rent. They claimed that this section of the building had not been sold to the school. On the contrary, Lin née Chen protested to the magistrate that Fu Jingxing had usurped their property and was now simply trying to use the school's possession of the property as a way to swindle them.

The magistrate looked into the complaints of both sides in order to piece together the property's ownership history. He discovered that during the Taiping Rebellion, at the time of Lin Xiaozou's sale, Lin Xi'en and his family had fled to Fujian. Before they returned to Lüqi County Lin Xiaozou died. Meanwhile the village school took possession of the purchased building and the one next door. When Lin Xi'en and his family returned they moved back into their old house. They refused to pay rent to the school and wanted the school to vacate Lin Xiaozou's property. Upon Lin Xi'en's death, Lin née Chen found stored in a wooden chest an old deed that she supposed was proof that the building sold to the school was in fact the common property of the Lin lineage; thus her lawsuit.

The Lüqi magistrate determined that the deed of sale held by the school was valid since it had been signed by Lin née Fu and Lin Xi'en. Lin née Chen and her son, Ruijin, realized their wrongdoing and pleaded for leniency. The magistrate documented their plea for the records and ended the trial.[55]

Marital problems between a husband, wife, and concubine. Throughout China it was common practice for churches to care for orphans and waifs. A church in Lüqi County reared a girl with the surname of Zhang. She converted to Catholicism and when she was grown the church assisted in her marriage to one Deng Tuanpeng, a nonconvert. She and Deng had no children and because of this Deng lineage elders worried. Not only was Deng Tuanpeng without offspring but so too were all of his brothers. The lineage wanted blood heirs, and consequently ordered Deng Tuanpeng to take another wife. If the two then produced a male, the lineage hoped that this "one son could take the place of two for the ancestral hall."

At that time, one Lu Sanyuan was married to a woman with the surname of Rao. Lu, however, was too poor to support a wife and sold her to Deng Tuanpeng. The woman became Deng's concubine in order to bear him sons. In the beginning Deng née Zhang, the legal wife, and Deng née Rao were on peaceful terms. Later the two women had frequent arguments about trifling domestic matters. Deng Tuanpeng often had to intervene in these disputes. In doing so Deng née Zhang thought her husband took the concubine's side, which made the wife more quarrelsome than ever. After the wife began to hear about neighborhood gossip regarding the household's problems she pressed her husband to get rid of the other woman. When he refused, Deng née Zhang left him, returning to the church where she grew up.

During May–June 1897 Deng née Zhang filed a formal complaint with local officials that her husband had mistreated her and had favored the concubine. The Lüqi magistrate ordered runners to summon those involved. Once in court Deng née Zhang stated that she now regretted having listened to gossip. She feared that her complaint might cause her husband "to suffer a loss" (*shoukui*). For her husband's sake she begged the magistrate for mercy. A spokesman for the Deng lineage also appeared in court and stated that Deng Tuanpeng was willing to divorce Deng née Rao. Tacitly, and under the circumstances, the lineage agreed. Deng Tuanpeng later deposed that "Deng née Rao had been divorced and [she] can remarry. Deng née Zhang had returned and [they] were living together; all is well." He requested that the magistrate forgo further deliberations. The magistrate agreed to close the files because this was simply a case of suspicions and not one of adultery or favoritism.[56]

Hard feelings over a church loan. In mid-1897 there was a small disturbance at a Catholic church in Songshi, a market town about twenty miles northwest of the Lüqi county seat. Yang Xing, the church manager, formally requested the magistrate to arrest Liu Wanzu and other non-Catholics he held responsible. The magistrate responded by ordering an investigation and by ordering runners to summon those involved to court for questioning.

From the depositions taken in court, the magistrate learned that Liu Wanzu had earlier mortgaged agricultural land he owned to the church. He had repaid all the loan except for $4. When Liu decided to move from the Songshi area, he went to the church to settle the debt and to retrieve his deed to the land. Although the documents on this case do not provide the details, someone — probably Yang Xing — stipulated that to clear the mortgage Liu not only had to make the final payment but also had to express thanks to the church for making the loan. This angered Liu and he refused. Later, according to Yang Xing, Liu and other men returned to the church looking for trouble and spoke vilely of destroying the church building. A worker at the church took exception to these threats and argued with the men. Since Liu and the men could not make the worker back down, they beat and injured him. They did not harm anyone else or damage the church.

With the investigation and inquiry concluded, the Lüqi magistrate found Liu completely to blame. The magistrate ordered Liu to pay the church the $4 that he still owed on the mortgage and to reimburse the church worker for his medical expenses. This settlement apparently satisfied everyone and the case ended.[57]

Although all the above cases involved Catholics, as we have seen the conflict did not center on religion. Rather it had a mundane tone to it and suggests that religious affiliation was not a barrier blocking contact and day-to-day dealings. The same appears true of contact between, at least, some converts to Catholicism and Protestantism, as illustrated in the case below.

An Overdue Loan Leads to Murder

On 14 March 1898 Fan Youqi reported to the Fengcheng magistrate that his nephew, Fan Zhewu, had been murdered by Li Jingzheng and Cai Mingliu.[58] The subsequent investigations reveal how a seemingly trivial matter could suddenly explode into a major criminal case. Although the victim and the two defendants were all converts to Christianity, religion had nothing to do with the case itself. Instead, the facts of the case center on the purely personal matter of a loan and the failure to repay it.

According to the deposition of Li Jingzheng, he was a native of Fengcheng County and lived in a village near an area called Jiaokeng. He was 66 years of age and had no close family members alive at the time. In addition, he was a *jiansheng* degree holder and a convert to Protestantism. During January–February 1898 Li loaned 50 copper cash to Fan Zhewu, a man with whom he was well acquainted and who wanted the money to purchase salt. Fan was a 36-year-old commoner and either a farmer or a laborer. He had converted to Catholicism and lived in a neighboring village. Li and Fan had had no previous conflict or hard feelings toward one another.

Fan and Li agreed on a deadline for repayment of the loan. The deadline passed, however, and on 10 March Li encountered Fan on a local roadway and took the opportunity to demand repayment. When he did so, Li stated, "Fan Zhewu cursed me and said I should not block his path and demand repayment. Subsequently, we cursed each other and quarreled. I would not submit [to him]. We quarreled [more but] I feared that he was a violent [man] so I departed for home. [My] heart was filled with hatred so [I] conceived the idea of getting help to beat [Fan and thus] vent my anger."

Later that same day Cai Mingliu, who was also a convert to Protestantism and Li's friend, came to visit at Li's home. Li told him of the confrontation with Fan. At Li's request Cai agreed to help Li beat up Fan Zhewu. The two men then went out in search of Fan. Sometime during the afternoon they found him. At that time Fan was returning home and happened to be carrying with him a sharp tree-pruning knife. Li once again cursed Fan for repudiating the loan. Fan then swung the knife at them, according to Li. Cai Mingliu reacted quickly, grabbing Fan in order to take away the knife. In doing so Cai accidentally wounded Fan on the forehead. Fan continued to be aggressive and fought more with Cai. Li did not intervene but stood to the side cursing Fan. Fan got the worse of it; he suffered another knife wound to the forehead and fell to the ground. The wounds were unexpectedly serious and a short time later Fan died. Li Jingzheng and Cai Mingliu both fled the scene.

Deng Renjiu witnessed the fight and informed the deceased's uncle, Fan Youqi. Since the local *dibao* position was at the time vacant, no other report of the murder had been made when Fan Youqi contacted the Fengcheng magistrate.[59] Magistrate Tang Dingxuan sent runners to arrest the accused and to summon witnesses. According to procedure, the magistrate also ordered an autopsy. The coroner examined Fan Zhewu's body and determined that he had died from a knife wound to the head.

Magistrate Tang's successor, Wen Jukui, continued the investigation. On 4 November 1898 Wen obtained the revocation of Li Jingzheng's purchased *jiansheng* degree and ordered runners to arrest him. Cai Mingliu remained at large and officials never succeeded in arresting him. The only witness to the murder, Deng Renjiu, did not appear in court because he had left the county on business. In judging the case Magistrate Wen depended on evidence he gathered, but mainly on Fan Youqi's testimony and Li Jingzheng's deposition.

Wen Jukui's replacement as magistrate and the Nanchang prefect each repeated the investigation and trial. Likewise, the acting judicial commissioner of Jiangxi investigated and personally questioned Li Jingzheng. None of these officials found any discrepancies in the original trial report or in the description of the case as presented above. The officials ruled that although Li did not act in the assault and homicide still he was the original conspirator. According to Qing legal statutes, officials sentenced Li to 100 blows of the heavy bamboo and permanent banishment to a distance of 3,000 li.[60]

It is significant that the three principal men involved in this case were converts and relevant to note that local Catholics and Protestants were in contact with and did business with one another. Still, religion was not at issue, contrary to what officials had suggested earlier in reports about Catholic-Protestant feuding in Fengcheng County.[61] This case boiled down to conflict between two men over a small, unpaid loan. The amount of the loan did not financially make or break Li Jingzheng, but Fan Zhewu's repudiation of the loan and aggressive attitude could and did affect Li's temper and sense of face. This had become a matter of principle. Given the age, physical, and occupational differences between Li and Fan, it is not surprising that Li involved a third party for assistance. Cai Mingliu wanted to help a friend and fellow convert, not to commit murder. Yet the affair ended in Fan's death because emotions such as anger and psychological elements like face overruled rational behavior.

Conclusion

In Jiangxi the Congregation of the Mission was responsible for Catholics in the entire province's numerous cities and countless villages. The Lazarist missionaries and priests were few in number and their actual presence in the scattered Catholic congregations was restricted to periodic visits.[62] Consequently, the priests had to rely heavily on *jiaotou* — the local lay leaders. These lay leaders played a crucial role in sustaining and preserving the Catholic congregations. Lay leaders conducted religious services and in general tended to the religious needs of the converts. Most significantly, lay leaders frequently initiated contact with non-Catholics, who converted mostly as individuals and occasionally as families. Lay leaders were the catalyst for conversions and their importance cannot be overstressed.

Missionaries and lay leaders found converts to Catholicism among Chinese of all walks of life, including the lower gentry. Converts, however, were predominantly common people and this should be expected in a society where the latter were the overwhelming majority. Otherwise, converts defy categorization; we find among them lower-degree holders and beggars; yeoman farmers, agricultural laborers, handicraft workers, and carpenters; people of the "mean professions" and people without profession; men and women, old and young; married, widowed, and single. The socioeconomic background of converts cannot be predicted or prejudged. I can find no justification for the labeling of converts as the dregs, miscreants, outcasts, and disloyal members of Chinese society.

In the *jiaoan* documents Chinese officials sometimes pointed out that converts were still to be considered Chinese.[63] One unavoidable interpretation of this fact is that conversion to Catholicism or Protestantism did not remove converts from the Chinese context, be it a legal or social one. The findings presented above indicate that many Chinese Catholics remained in close contact with non-Catholic kith and kin. Cases for Chongren, Shangrao, and Lüqi counties illustrate that converts had all types of business dealings with members of the local non-Catholic community. Since religious affiliation did not preclude business contact should we presume that it precluded social or personal relations? Of course not, for as we observed in one case above, Catholics who managed an orphanage in Lüqi County demonstrated their ties to the world around them by permitting the marriage of a woman they raised to a local non-Catholic. Other cases in other ways support the conclusion that converts neither segregated themselves from nonconverts nor lived in separate enclaves.

Regular contact between converts and nonconverts did lead to personal disagreements and to local socioeconomic disputes. With converts as both plaintiffs and defendants these problems led on occasion to litigation. From the cases under study, we may conclude that some, if not all, of the conflict must be viewed as having many causes, of which religion was only one. Missionaries were naturally sensitive to the religious aspect of the conflict or tried to emphasize it to their and their converts' advantage. The nonreligious aspects cannot be ignored, however. Many of the disputes in which Catholics were involved actually pivoted on specific and concrete issues like unpaid debts, land ownership, marital problems, and claims (both true and false) of extortion, robbery, even wrongful death. Whether in the countryside or in the towns and cities of Jiangxi, some of these problems occurred before missionary intervention and sometimes were precipitated by the converts themselves and not by nonconverts or by local gentry.

As we look into the day-to-day workings of a society in which the gentry played an active role it is not surprising to find their presence or involvement in various cases. Yet the involvement of the gentry does not guarantee that ideological or doctrinal issues were paramount.[64] In the countryside of Jiangxi, we cannot single out the gentry as instigators of *jiaoan*, much less find in these cases an anti-Christian movement masterminded and led by the gentry. Instead, we find gentry like Li Xucheng of Chongren County who observed, without voicing a single worry about Catholicism as a heterodoxy or as a sociopolitical threat, that regular contact between converts and nonconverts had led to problems typical of any community and that these practical, even mundane, problems were at the center of the *jiaoan*.

CHAPTER 3

Rural Religion and Village Organization in North China: The Catholic Challenge in the Late Nineteenth Century

CHARLES A. LITZINGER

In the last 40 years of the nineteenth century, thousands of villagers in North China struggled over the penetration into their midst of a foreign religious sect: Roman Catholicism. This struggle may seem to many as yet another in that long series of more or less acrimonious confrontations between rival religious systems contorting the face of human history. But for the historian this richly documented conflict also offers a rare possibility of gaining an understanding of rural religion and village organization in late traditional China. Because the struggle involved foreign missionaries and believers in a foreign sect that was protected by foreign diplomatic representatives in Beijing, documentation of hundreds of cases of conflict has been preserved in the archives of the Zongli yamen (after 1901 reorganized as the Waiwu bu, Ministry of Foreign Affairs), the office responsible for foreign relations in the Qing government of the late nineteenth and early twentieth centuries.[1]

Prasenjit Duara in *Culture, Power, and the State* has demonstrated that religious institutions provided the most significant element in the "cultural matrix" producing legitimacy in rural North China. Without doubt one of the most important of these religious institutions was the village temple. In multilineage villages the temple organization probably functioned as the chief agency of power and control.[2] In these villages the temple association provided organizational forms, elsewhere provided by lineage associations, and supplied the structures of social integration for villagers who although belonging to different lineages shared residence and social relationships in the same village.

The material presented in this chapter seems important not only for the rare view it gives of nineteenth-century temples as functioning social institutions. It also tends to alter the view that Chinese villages were not on the whole "well-organized, energetic communities" and that peasants "did not play a prominent role in any work that called for organizing ability."[3]

This chapter will throw light on the structure and activities of rural religion in several villages in Zhili (Hebei) Province in the second half of the nineteenth century. These are revealed as the backdrop against which the struggle for the division of temple land and property took place when Catholicism penetrated to the village level.

The Village Temple, Public Property, and the Public Good

A Chinese missionary had made converts in Saili Village, Baixiang County in southwestern Zhili in the first year of the Tongzhi reign (1862), and at first no difficulty arose. A dispute, however, soon developed over the possession and use of temples and temple lands in the village. There were two temples in the village. One was dedicated to Guanyin; the other, apparently also of Buddhist origins, was called Xipo Si. The incense land (*xianghuo di*) of the temples amounted to over ten mu (1 mu = approx. ⅙ acre). Trouble began when the missionary wished to occupy at least part of this property and set up a Catholic church. Others in the village objected on the grounds that these assets were the public property of the whole village (*hecun gonggong zhi shi*).[4]

Nonetheless, the Catholics set up a church in the temple of Guanyin and proceeded to hold services. A lawsuit was brought in 1865 when, as was the custom each year from the first to the fifth day of the fourth lunar month during the Xuanwu Mountain temple fair, the entire village (*hecun gong-gong*) as a public endeavor wished to set up a tent at the Guanyin temple to serve tea. The Xuanwu Mountain temple was apparently nearby and the tea was probably provided for those traveling through Saili on their way to and from the fair. The Catholics refused to allow this.[5]

The magistrate asked the Catholics to vacate the temple temporarily during the fair with the understanding that they could return thereafter. At the time both sides agreed to this solution but subsequently there was ceaseless legal wrangling. In the spring of 1868 the magistrate, apparently unable to bring about a successful settlement, requested that the case be transferred to the *zhou* level. Here it was ruled that the villagers should select some other land that they could exchange for the Catholics' share in the two temples and on which the Catholics could build a new church. Because no land was specifically designated, however, the Catholics continued to hold school and to conduct religious services in the Guanyin temple.

Unrest continued in the village, and the Catholic missionary reported in the fall of 1869 that, though a major fire had been prevented, someone had attempted to burn the main gate of the temple where Catholic services were being held. The magistrate arrested those responsible, issued a proclamation forbidding such acts of vandalism and exhorting both sides to mutual harmony. After the incident he sent reliable yamen runners to keep the church under surveillance. Although the proclamation held that regardless of whether they belonged to the church, the villagers were all children of the reigning dynasty (*guojia chizi*), it does not seem that this opinion counted for much in the village. The Zongli yamen worried that settlements of this kind might incite others to use the foreign religion as a pretext for robbing the people of their property and urged special vigilance in such cases in the future.[6]

Another case concerned with disputes over the ownership and use of temples and of temple property occurred in Pingshan and Lingshou counties in Zhengding Prefecture in western Zhili. As the Catholics increased in number in a village, they asked for their share of the community property of the local temples. Not surprisingly, the non-Christian villagers were reluctant to see the arrangements regarding these centers of village life altered. In these two areas in Zhengding Prefecture tensions were generated which led to serious outbreaks of violence in 1864. The case was in adjudication for nearly five years and was not settled until 1869.

The temple in Shuinian Village, Pingshan County, boasted an ancient gold-leafed Buddha in the main hall. Behind it were four smaller images in wood, bronze, and plaster. In the rear hall of the temple was an image of Bodhisattva Guanyin.[7]

The terminology used by the villagers in describing this temple leaves no doubt that, although it was obviously originally a Buddhist institution, its membership included the entire village community. The temple is described as the public temple of the village community (*cunzhong gonggong dasi*) or more simply as the village temple (*cunmiao*). The lands owned by the temple are said to be the public property of the village temple (*cunmiao gongchan*) and to comprise a total of 105 mu. Of this total, 35 mu had been contributed by a member of the local elite, a *gongsheng* named Liu Xide. Trees were grown on the temple lands to provide wood and revenue for the upkeep of the temple. Of the over two hundred households in the village, eighteen had been converted to the Catholic faith by 1863. After conversion the Catholics demanded that the common property be divided. After much dispute a settlement was arrived at in which the Catholics received 35 mu, and 70 mu were retained by the villagers as public property. The trees continued to be reserved for public use of the villagers (*cunmin gongyong*).[8]

Jishan Temple was located in Zhangfuan Village in Fuan Pai, Lingshou County. This temple was maintained jointly by the six villages in the *pai*.[9] First built in the Tang period, it faced south and was located to the west of the village. The temple lands comprised over 170 mu. To the front of the temple was the hall of the King of Heaven (*Tianwang dian*) in which were four statues of that deity, two on the east side and two on the west. In the Sangharama hall (*Jialan dian*), was an image of Shuai Jiang holding a hammer in his hand. In the meditation hall (*chan dian*) were two bronze Buddhas. The monk Guanglun resided at this temple and was charged with its care. He had entered the monastic state at Chengfu Monastery in Goutai Pai, Lingshou County. In 1863, with gentry (*shenshi*) of Fuan Pai acting as guarantors, Guanglun was examined and licensed by the county magistrate to reside at and take care of Jishan Temple.[10]

As early as the first year of the Tongzhi reign (1862), not only this temple but also others in the area had been troubled by vandals whom the local leaders identified as Catholics. The Catholics were also accused of appropriating commonly owned property in the area and of taking stones from temple walls for use in building their church. These activities were carried out on the assumption that this property, although attached to formally religious organizations, was in fact the common property of all residents.[11]

With regard to Jishan Temple itself, the Catholics were said to have tried unsuccessfully to convert the monk in charge to Catholicism. The monk refused and the Catholics then asked for a division of the commonly owned lands attached to the monastery. According to the Catholics' opponents, when with the villagers' support the monk refused, the monastery was vandalized and the sacred images in the meditation hall were destroyed.[12]

Outraged by the renewed vandalism, a large crowd gathered on the night of TZ 3-2-19 (26 March 1864)[13] and went to "reason" with the Catholics. Warned of the possibility of trouble, most of the Catholics fled beforehand. Still several were placed under arrest and a great deal of property belonging to Catholics appears to have been stolen.

The settlement of the case and the restoration of harmony in the villages took over five years. What is important to note here is that the monastery was obviously well organized, with lower-gentry leadership, and responded forcefully to the Catholic assault. The assumptions of the Catholics in demanding a share of the commonly owned property are perhaps the best proof of the existence of a corporate entity of an ostensively religious character but to which all in the community belonged not by voluntary association but simply by the fact of residency.

Finally, a case in Shahe County in southwestern Zhili in the late 1860s illustrates most clearly the coincidence of village and temple communities, and the radical change brought by the conversion to Catholicism of some villagers. In Beizhang Village in that county there were several temples that were supported by land and trees commonly owned (*hecun gongchan*) by all members of the village. After some of the villagers joined the Catholic church in the spring of TZ 6 (1867), they refused to allow commonly owned trees to be cut down and sold to finance the repair of the walls of a Buddhist temple west of the village. This precipitated a quarrel in the village in which at least two people were wounded.[14]

A legal dispute resulted in which the final decision held that the temples, their trees, and their lands were indeed the common property of the whole village. The Catholics in the village had like everyone else held shares. But now that they had become Catholics and started a new way of life (*shengmian*), they formed a category distinct from the ordinary commoner households. Further, theirs was an unorthodox path (*yitu*) and mutual harmony with them was no longer possible. It was ordered, therefore, that the common property be distributed fairly according to the number of households in each group. Since the temples themselves could not be divided, the Catholics received a cash settlement for their shares and were to make no further claims.[15]

Village Social Integration and Community Custom

Several disputes occurred in Baixiang County in southwestern Zhili as a result of the Catholic attempt to extricate converts from activities dictated by local custom and which were, at least in the formal sense, religious. In the summer of the first year of the Tongzhi reign (1862) in Xiaoli Village prayers were offered for rain, and Catholics were ordered by the village leaders to participate. They alleged that when they refused, they had been beaten, and so brought a suit before the *zhou* magistrate. The Catholic missionary argued that prayers for rain were an affair undertaken voluntarily by the rural people (*nongmin ziwei zhi shi*) and that Catholics should not be forced to participate.[16]

One of the converts who was principally involved in the case said that on the day the dispute occurred, a local gentry bully (*jingun*) and the *xiang* headman (*xiangzhang*) had come leading the community in procession carrying a statue of Guan Di, praying for rain.[17] They attempted to force the Catholics to worship the deity, but having been warned often by the missionaries that such ceremonies were contrary to church regulations, the Catholics refused. Taking advantage of their numbers, the villagers barricaded the homes of the Catholics for three days, subjecting them to verbal harassment. Finally some of the villagers forced their way into the Catholic chapel carrying the image of Guan Di and ordered the Catholics to kowtow to it. Some of the Catholics were beaten up and money and property were stolen from the chapel. The Catholics also alleged that a monk who was apparently accompanying the procession struck and broke the image of Guan Di, hoping to blame the Catholics for the sacrilege and thus bring the even greater wrath of the community down upon them. The Catholics brought a suit at the county yamen to no avail and then went to the *zhou* magistrate with like results.[18]

The "gentry bully" to whom the Catholics referred was a 31-year-old *shengyuan* of the village who made his living as a teacher. His version of happenings in the village leading to the confrontation was quite different from that of the Catholics. According to him, a French Catholic bishop had come to the village in the first month of the current year. At least two families in the village were converted, and a chapel was set up on the east side of the village. All went well until TZ 1-6-28 (24 July 1862), when the scholar and others in the village, concerned about the dryness of the weather, according to the custom of the area (*zhaoyi xiangyue*) requested that all in the village community (*tong cunzhong*) participate in a procession of the image of Guan Di to various temples in the area to burn incense and pray for rain. The Catholics in the village were not willing to participate, but at that time there was no discussion with them about their refusal.[19]

According to this account, on 7-1 (27 July), after it had rained in the area, the scholar and the others again organized a procession for the image of Guan Di to visit the various temples to give thanks. This time when the villagers were passing by the Catholic chapel, they encountered some Catholics. The villagers got into an argument with the Catholics saying that although they had entered the church, they all still had crops in the fields. They had not participated in the procession praying for rain, but they had still obviously benefited from the prayers of the village community. The Catholics disagreed and a fight broke out in which the father of the leader of the Catholics in the village was wounded, and the mother of the scholar in a fit of anger stole four sets of sacred books from the Catholic chapel. The long court suit, hinted at above, then ensued and was finally settled only by referral to provincial authorities.[20]

The assumptions behind the reasoning used by the villagers made it clear that cultural and social integration in the village community were nearly synonymous; the world of social interaction mirrored the world of meaning almost perfectly. The prayers for rain were a matter of custom handed down from antiquity (*xisu xiangyan*). The necessity of participation was based on residence in the village. A Buddhist monk in the village was taking part in the processions although apparently not as a religious leader. The villagers participated as a community (*cunzhong*). Further it seemed reasonable to the villagers that all who profited from the rain should give thanks for its gracious provision.[21]

The Catholics, on the other hand, were clearly attempting a fundamental change in local institutions. The system of social interaction which presupposed a cultural consensus in the village was now being challenged. The Catholics did not any longer wish to recognize the community character of certain village undertakings and wished to redefine them as practices in which one was free to participate or not at will (*ziwei zhi shi*). Since cultural and social integration in the village were so closely intertwined, the behavior of the Catholics inevitably violated both.

A similar dispute, also in Baixiang County in the 1860s, concerned the refusal of Catholics to participate in a harvest thanksgiving festival. In the second year of the Tongzhi reign (1863), after the introduction of Catholicism in Neibu Village, there had been a series of disputes between the 39 Catholic families and their fellow villagers. Catholics were accused before the county magistrate of refusing to pay taxes and to make the payments in lieu of corvée. The Catholics testified that what they had refused to pay was an assessment for a local temple folk opera performance. They complained to the bishop that the magistrate supported the false charges of the villagers, although he was well aware of the real situation, and punished the Catholics. In the aftermath of the suit several Catholic families, apparently under coercion, went to the county yamen and publicly renounced their newly acquired faith.[22]

At the center of this controversy was a convert named Liu Ziqiang. According to the 80-year-old widow Liu Zhangshi, who had become a Catholic, Liu Ziqiang was her adopted grandson. Mrs. Liu's own son had a daughter but no son, so she had bought him a concubine. The concubine, however, bore no children at all. The elder Mrs. Liu then arranged for the adoption of Liu Ziqiang, the second son of a *shengyuan* who was head of the Liu lineage, to provide her son with a male heir. Her son had sometime later died and soon thereafter the concubine fell from the path of virtue, "carrying on like a beast" (*xingtong qinshou*) with one of Mrs. Liu's hired hands. The two even went so far as to plot to have Liu Ziqiang returned to his ancestral home and to have a son who had issued from their liaison replace him as heir. The widow then ordered Liu Ziqiang to fire the hired hand and from that time on the latter held a grudge against Liu.[23]

The year before the trouble between the Catholics and their opponents, at a time when the village was holding an opera at the local temple, the hired hand conspired with others in the village to force Liu to contribute money. When Liu refused, they tied him up, took him to the county magistrate, and charged him with refusing to make the payments in lieu of corvée. The magistrate punished Liu and held him in jail for four months. Emboldened by their success the hired man and his friends then convinced Mrs. Liu's daughter-in-law to charge her adopted son in court of unfilial conduct. The magistrate this time ordered that Liu Ziqiang's adoption be rescinded and that he be returned to his ancestral home. At this juncture Liu, according to his adopted grandmother, took the case to the provincial authorities.[24]

Although the documents preserved in the Zongli yamen archives do not indicate the final resolution of the case, what interests us most here is the dispute arising out of Liu Ziqiang's refusal to make a contribution for the temple folk opera. Neibu Village held a festival each year in thanksgiving for the harvest; to support the festival activities, proceeds from the sale of the produce of community-owned land, which amounted to something over two mu, were used. This land was cultivated each year by the villager who was serving his turn as head of the harvest thanksgiving association (*xieqiu hui*). After the harvest it was this person's responsibility to organize the festival, which included a thanksgiving procession and a folk opera.[25]

It happened that in the first year of the Tongzhi period (1862) it was the turn of Liu Ziqiang to act as association head. He was not then a Catholic and served his term. However, the following year, after becoming a Catholic, according to the villagers he refused to return the common land he had cultivated in his capacity as leader. The village community (*cunzhong*) then brought a suit against him before the county magistrate.[26]

The Catholics argued that Liu had, in fact, resigned from the association because he had become a Catholic and that he wished to return the fields he had cultivated for the association along with feed for the ox and seed which had apparently also been provided. It was rather that the village leaders, whom the Catholics claimed belonged to the Momo sect, would not allow him to resign because they wanted to use this alleged refusal as a pretext to destroy the church in the village. The leaders had brought the suit, and the magistrate had supported and upheld them in court. It was then that sixteen or seventeen of the thirty-nine Catholic families in the village were said to have left the church.[27]

As mentioned above, the archives do not contain the documents which show the final judgment in the case. In correspondence with the provincial authorities who settled the case, the Zongli yamen described the bishop pleading the Catholic cause with French officials in the capital as an experienced pettifogger (*xi ji'nian songgun shoubi*).[28]

Regardless of the legal outcome, it is clear that both sides acknowledged that the refusal of Liu Ziqiang and other Catholics to take part in an autumn thanksgiving festival was one of the roots of the trouble in the village. As in other areas of North China where Catholics made similar refusals, the Neibu villagers, seeing the fee as required of all members of the village community, charged their Catholic neighbors with failure to make a payment in lieu of corvée.

Again, as in the Xiaoli Village case, it is obvious that Neibu Village functioned as a social whole. Supporting this social integration we can infer a cultural world whose meanings included all in the village. When the weather is dry, all must pray to Guan Di. When the rain comes, all profit from it and all should give thanks. The Catholic attempt to make these activities voluntary would seem perverse in such a cultural context. An aggressive refusal to observe such customs might be expected to provoke a violent response.[29]

A third Zhili case involving disruption of village social integration clarifies the tension created by the Catholic attempt to withdraw from the financing of local sacrifices, festivals, and folk operas. The Chinese officials involved in this case believed that matters were made worse by the intransigence of the French missionaries. First reports were received at the Zongli yamen late in 1874, indicating Catholic claims that at Xiban Village, Ding Zhou, in west central Zhili a man named Zhu Luoheng, a leader of the White Lotus sect in the area, was out to destroy Catholicism in the village.[30] Investigations by Chinese officials including Li Hongzhang found that difficulties in the village had begun because of a claim that a Catholic, Zhang Liang, had advocated refusing to pay taxes. Hearings were held but officials could find no proof of the charge.[31]

Later one of the village leaders reported that a Catholic named He Junbao was forcing others in the village to join the Catholic religion, was refusing to make the payments in lieu of corvée, and had gotten into a fight with a man named An Gouer. However, in court An was found guilty of starting the fight and had been punished.[32]

Early in 1875 the Zongli yamen received a new report in the case, disclosing deeper roots for the conflict than previously indicated. Late in 1873 a religious festival and folk opera (*saihui yanxi*) had been held in the village and the local leaders, including Zhu Luoheng, "not handling matters according to the treaties," had assessed the Catholics. Again, early the following year during the Lantern Festival the Catholics were assessed to obtain funds to purchase oil. An Zhenji, the Catholic teacher in the village, refused to pay and mutual suspicions had been aroused. This was the situation that had led to the fight between He Junbao and An Gouer and to several other disputes in the village. After a personal investigation in the village, the magistrate issued a proclamation stating that Catholics were exempt from levies for local sacrifices and other religious activities.[33] The settlement, whose eventual outcome is not evident in the documents, was now further delayed by new demands by the Catholic bishop and other missionaries.

In summing up the case for the Zongli yamen, the officials forwarding the report wrote that rural people still frequently did not recognize becoming a Catholic as a good act nor did they know that the proscription against Catholicism had been rescinded. They looked upon the assessment for sacrifices to the local spirits, religious festivals, and folk operas as "matters of public duty in the area" (*xiangjian gongshi*); and they, of course, wished to collect them from everyone. Unruly elements in the community sometimes took advantage of this situation so that the people could not live in harmony with their Catholic neighbors and lawsuits never ceased.[34]

In this case it seems clear that the social integration of the village had been shattered because of the Catholic withdrawal from those social activities in the life of the village community that were considered matters of public duty for all. Here as elsewhere it appears that the assessments for such activities, some of which were in a formal sense religious, were confused with public obligations such as taxes and the payments in lieu of corvée. In fact, the first official investigation in the case heard accusations of tax refusal and only later was it discovered that the underlying causes of the disquiet and fighting in the village were the assessment for the folk opera in connection with a temple festival and the buying of oil for the Lantern Festival.

The Temple Community Equals the Village Community

From the disputes over temples and their activities and property described above, we have a picture of the temple as an institution to which the entire village community belonged by virtue of residence in the village and which functioned as the center of village social life. Earlier writers such as Hsiao Kung-chuan, construing temples narrowly as religious institutions rather than as community-wide social institutions, came to the conclusion that no "village communities," if this term implied communal property, existed in China "throughout historical times." If our analysis is correct, this view was certainly in error.[35]

In the minds of the villagers the temple land was clearly community land and could not be disposed of without community consent.[36] Temples regardless of their religious provenance are called "village temple" as though any consciousness of their sectarian religious origins had been lost. The monk-caretaker of a Buddhist temple is licensed only after having been guaranteed by the gentry of the entire community served by the temple. A Buddhist monk is resident at a temple whose name implies that its origins were Daoist.[37]

The repair of the temple and its activities were financed by the whole community, often through a "tax" on land.[38] These local levies were sometimes collected by the same people responsible for the collection of regular taxes: the *difang*, the *dibao*, the *xiangdi*, the *xiangzhang*.[39] To meet a special levy imposed on the village by the county magistrate for the repair of the walls of the county seat, the village was expected to borrow against the temple property, which was considered the property of the village community.[40] Temple obligations and village obligations were not distinct in the minds of the villagers.[41]

Temple activities were community activities. The most common of these was the holding of folk operas for the entertainment of the temple deity and the community. These operas were called "public operas" (*gongxi*).[42] Prayers for a fruitful year, for rain, or in thanksgiving for a plentiful harvest reflected concerns shared by the entire rural community and envisaged benefits from which all alike would profit.[43] The buying and selling that accompanied temple fairs also enhanced the commercial life of the whole community.

Temple associations are in evidence in some communities. Would this imply a kind of voluntary association which any member of the community was free to join or not? The activities of these associations and the actions of their leaders indicate that they were not.[44] They were organized to dispense public charity, to hold prayers in thanksgiving for the harvest, and to pray for the happiness of the ancestors.[45] These activities were seen as relevant to all members of the community, and all were "taxed" to pay for them.

The terminology used in these cases implies that the village community and temple community coincided. The temple processions and folk operas were not only religious rituals; they provided the glue of social integration in the village.[46] When Chinese Catholics attempted to separate themselves, to draw a distinction between themselves and the others in the community based solely on religion, the community reacted to defend its integrity. Traditional China did not distinguish clearly the sacred from the secular nor the political from the religious.[47] To have asked a nineteenth-century Zhili villager to submit to such a division was to ask him or her to do something which seemed both impossible and immoral.

Those who did so, the Catholics, were said to have embarked on a separate way of life (*shengmian*), and were termed sectarians (*jiaomin*) and no longer Chinese (*Hanmin*). This distinction rent the village community and called into question the symbols of social cohesion. In the next chapter, Roger R. Thompson also argues that this Christian challenge to the symbolic definition of local community had "traumatic implications." The Catholics' refusal to contribute to temple activities and their request for the division of communal lands made the social institutions in which these symbols were enshrined in effect voluntary associations. Although "legally" the unequal treaties had forced China to remove Christians from the category of religious heretics, most Zhili villagers continued to see the Catholic *jiaomin* as social and cultural deviants, betrayers of community solidarity.[48]

CHAPTER 4

Twilight of the Gods in the Chinese Countryside: Christians, Confucians, and the Modernizing State, 1861–1911

ROGER R. THOMPSON

On 13 July 1901, a year after several hundred Westerners and thousands of Chinese were killed in Shanxi Province during the Boxer Uprising, four Protestant missionaries and three Chinese officials met in Taiyuan, Shanxi, for an afternoon of negotiations.[1] They agreed that

> the greatest number of murders of Christians during last year's Boxer disturbance took place in Shanxi. In every local community (*xiangshe*) there had been a vibrant tradition of opera. The intense violence that broke out so suddenly was a result of grudges that had been building up for a long time because Christians had been refusing to pay opera subscriptions. For the time being opera performances are forbidden. Later, should Christians wish to attend opera performances they must contribute money like everyone else. As for useful public projects in rural areas (*xiangcun*) it is appropriate for everyone to donate money. This should put an end to the conflicts.[2]

Typically, Shanxi officials blamed banditry, famine, drought, and administrative incompetence for the rise of Boxer violence. Few people implicated the Allied invasion of China in the summer of 1900 nor was the Chinese official Lao Naixuan's thesis of sectarian origins, first proposed for Shandong, mentioned.[3]

Does the violence in Shanxi fit the recent profile drawn by Joseph W. Esherick for Shandong, where, he argues, the rampaging peasants comprising Boxer bands were a product of nonelite popular culture: a mélange of martial arts, sectarian religious beliefs, and models for action drawn from the repertory of local opera? These organizational resources and ideological motivations were tapped by peasants who struck at Westerners, Chinese Christians, and symbols of the "foreign" like railroads, telegraphs, and mission compounds. Esherick does not include the violence in Shanxi in this profile, attributing it to an "officially inspired Boxer 'militia'" organized after the March 1900 appointment of Yuxian as governor of Shanxi.[4]

Were the Shanxi officials meeting with Western missionaries in July 1901 trying to cover for the now-disgraced Yuxian, whose reported role in the massacre of 44 foreigners in Taiyuan on 9 July 1900 and apparent responsibility for other atrocities prompted enraged Westerners to call for his execution, which was carried out in 1901? If so, our search for the origins of the violence can end. But the evidence, while it does not exonerate Yuxian, certainly does not lend itself to scapegoating the governor. To understand the violence we must go back to the turn of the eighteenth century, when Catholic missionaries first proselytized in Shanxi. This heritage was preserved by generations of Chinese Christians. When Western Catholic missionaries returned to Shanxi after 1860, Christian communities still existed. This renewed Catholic presence, joined in the late 1870s by the arrival of Protestant missionaries, increased tensions between Chinese Christians and their nonbelieving neighbors.

The right of local communities to stage opera performances was at issue. The imperial government had begun issuing orders in 1861 that transformed the way local communities funded and organized the customary religious festivals that were usually highlighted by opera performances. That these orders, to be discussed below, were issued by the central government, underscores the significance of local opera in rural China.

The stage in 1861 was set by military and diplomatic battles waged by the French, British, and Chinese between 1858 and 1860. In the resulting treaties and conventions, provisions were made for the establishment of foreign legations in Beijing and the creation of a new metropolitan office — the Zongli yamen — for handling diplomatic affairs between the Chinese and Western governments. The issues in this new round of treaty making had not changed in the two decades since the first Opium War — treaty ports, extraterritorial rights, tariffs, and indemnities were specified and, for the first time, the Chinese were compelled to allow foreigners to travel and reside in China's interior. The Sino-French treaty, for example, not only guaranteed the right of French subjects to travel, as did the British treaty, but also noted the rights of missionaries to spread Christianity. These rights were also implicitly extended, by virtue of most-favored-nation status, to the two other countries — Russia and the United States — that signed treaties with China after deliberations in Tianjin in 1858. The treaty stipulations were reiterated in conventions in 1860 signed with France, Britain, and Russia. The Sino-French convention allowed the French not only to travel in the interior, but also to buy land.[5] This particular convention also affirmed the imperial edict of 1846 that called for the return to mission hands of land and buildings seized after 1724, when the Yongzheng emperor had branded Christianity an outlawed heterodox sect.[6]

These developments in Tianjin and Beijing were followed with particular interest by the Franciscan Gabriel Grioglio de Moretta (1813–91), the vicar apostolic of Shanxi since 1844. But it would be Moretta's successor, Luigi da Castellazzo Moccagatta (1809–91) who would be at the center of Roman Catholic affairs in Shanxi from 1861 until his death, in 1891, in Taiyuan, the provincial capital.[7] When the Sino-French Convention of Beijing (1860) opened up China's interior to Catholic missionaries traveling under the protection of the French government, the Franciscans who traveled to Shanxi reclaimed the mission their confreres of earlier generations had established before 1724. They were returning to a province that had weathered fairly well the phase of official intolerance from 1724 until an edict of toleration was issued in 1844. The number of Chinese Catholics in Shanxi at the end of that period has been estimated at 20,000.[8] Certainly the first figures for the post-1860 period suggest a continuity. In 1867, 13,832 converts were counted in Shanxi and the long-standing commitment of Rome to Catholicism in Shanxi ensured that at least four of the native priests had been trained in Rome. There were Catholic stations scattered throughout Shanxi.[9]

The Franciscans quickly claimed ownership of properties that had been seized in the early eighteenth century, but they also addressed another question: were Chinese Catholics responsible for customary subscriptions used to mount religious festivals? This was a familiar theological question — the Rites controversies of the seventeenth and eighteenth centuries ended with the definitive statement from Rome in 1769, which enjoined Chinese Catholics from contributing "to a community enterprise for restoring or building temples or for sacrificing to idols."[10] But this theological issue, largely moot during the period after 1724 when Christianity had gone underground, was joined with political and diplomatic issues after 1860. Catholic missionaries now instructed their converts not to pay, and insisted that Chinese authorities protect Christians from repercussions.

As we will see, this French triumph was pointed to repeatedly by Catholic missionaries from 1861 on. So too would the Protestants rely upon it. Protestant evangelization of Shanxi did not begin until 1876, after the signing of the Chefoo Convention, which elaborated upon the rights of foreigners, first expressed in the treaties of Tianjin, to travel in the interior. Representatives of the China Inland Mission (CIM), the first Protestant missionaries to travel in Shanxi, had explored the southern prefectures of Zezhou, Pingyuan, and Puzhou in the autumn of 1876 but they did not establish their first permanent station, in Pingyang, until 1879.[11] This delay had been caused in part by the devastating Great Famine of 1876–79. Timothy Richard, of the Baptist Missionary Society, had arrived in Taiyuan in November 1877.[12] Joined by three other missionaries, who reached Taiyuan on 2 April 1878,[13] the first Protestant efforts in Shanxi addressed the tremendous human suffering caused by the famine. Although the Protestants were recent arrivals, they outspent the Catholics. One scholar reports that 127,110 taels (ounces of silver) of relief were distributed by Protestants to 100,641 individuals in Taiyuan, Pingyang, and Zezhou prefectures. The Catholic effort, for which we have less information, was reportedly limited to 14,416 taels of relief to 2,800 families.[14]

After the famine crisis ended, the number of Protestant missionaries in Shanxi increased and their focus turned to preaching. The Pingyang station established in 1879 was joined by these additional CIM stations in the 1880s: Quwu (1885), Daning (1885), Xizhou (1885), Datong (1886), Huozhou (1886), Hongdong (1886), Xiaoyi (1887), Pingyao (1888), Yuncheng (1888), Lu'an (1889), and Lucheng (1889).[15] All of these stations, with the exception of Datong, just south of the Great Wall in the north, were in southern Shanxi. Other Protestant mission societies active in Shanxi in the nineteenth century included the American Board of Commissioners of Foreign Missions, which posted Oberlin College graduates to the central Shanxi cities of Fenzhou and Taigu in the 1880s.[16]

Although the Catholic and Protestant missionary efforts in Shanxi are part of two very different mission histories, the controversy surrounding the liability of Christians for subscribing to temple festivals is common to both. The French minister received specific guarantees from the Chinese on this issue in early 1862. Protestants received similar promises in 1881.[17] In his diary entry for 22 September 1881, medical missionary R. Harold A. Schofield reported that word had arrived in Taiyuan that "a proclamation has just been issued by the Chinese Government in Pekin [Beijing] extending to Protestant native Christians the same privileges which have long been accorded to the native adherents of the Romish priests, viz. complete exemption from all taxes levied for the support of idolatrous rites and ceremonies."[18]

By the mid-1880s Shanxi had witnessed, in a quarter of a century, the return of Catholic missionaries and the arrival of Protestant missionaries, and had been ordered by metropolitan authorities to exempt Chinese Christians from the customary fees used to fund local temple festivals.

The presence of several hundred Westerners and the conversion of only a few tens of thousands of Chinese to Christianity in a province of about twenty million people was given weight by the attention of Chinese and Western authorities, both ecclesiastic and diplomatic, to the question of liability for temple festival subscriptions in 1861–62. The policy discussions that began in 1861 would have far-reaching implications because the compromise reached in Shanxi would be applied to all of China in 1862. Moreover, we can see in these initial discussions the beginnings of a convergence of lines of analysis taken by Chinese metropolitan officials and Western diplomats and missionaries. The perspectives and demands of rural Chinese were scarcely perceived and, significantly, became tangential to the Beijing-based convergence.

By the fall of 1861 the Franciscans in Fengtai County, Zezhou Prefecture, had decided they needed a proclamation from the governor outlining the rights and freedoms of Chinese Christians. Accompanying their letter was a proposed set of regulations with five articles describing how the relationships between Christians and non-Christians in Fengtai should be ordered. These regulations, which would ultimately be sent on to Beijing and prompt high-level discussions between the French legation and the Zongli yamen, were: (1) those people outside the faith should not expect Christians (*jiaoren*) to contribute money for opera, sacrifices, or temple repairs because Christians, who believe in God (*tianzhu*), need to use this money to pay for their own chapels (*tianzhu tang*) and ceremonies (*libai*) so that they can show proper respect to their religion; (2) Christians are not responsible for giving financial support to activities that are harmful to their beliefs; (3) as for other monetary subscriptions, both public and private, that are not harmful, both Christians and non-Christians alike are liable for the same amount, neither more nor less; (4) should there be, in rural areas (*cunshe*), subscriptions for public matters (*gongshi*) that are actually used for heterodox (*yiduan*) affairs, then the Christians are only responsible for the monies used for nonheterodox matters; and (5) magistrates must punish any non-Christian who extorts from, harasses, harms the crops of, or acts violently toward or beats Christians who refuse to pay monies for activities injurious to their beliefs.

The French were well informed about certain aspects of village life and finances, for the picture in this document from 1861 is similar to one that can be found in a government compilation published almost half a century later. In the imperially mandated *Shanxi Financial Report* (*Shanxi quansheng caizheng shuomingshu*) an anonymous essayist explicates the convoluted structure of local finance. There were four main players on the local fiscal scene: the government, degree holders, merchants, and local communities (*xiangshe*). Elaborating on the *xiangshe*, this essayist divided the financial responsibilities of local leaders, who could be called *sheshou*, *huishou*, or *jiushou*, into the following areas:

1. Ritual. The *xiangshe* leader was responsible for organizing ritual operas and arranging for spring and autumn agricultural rituals.
2. Public Works and Welfare. The *xiangshe* leader managed the money disbursed for bridge-building, road work, and welfare.
3. Government Levies. The *xiangshe* leader collected the money needed by local leaders like himself to carry out his duties.[19]

But the Shanxi governor Yinggui, who had assumed his position in September 1858,[20] was less interested in local fiscal practice. Yinggui included the Franciscans' proposed regulations, which they wanted to be sent throughout the province, in his report of 14 October 1861 to the Zongli yamen. Yinggui was incredulous that missionaries leveled the serious charge of heterodoxy at non-Christians. As for the problem of temple festivals, Yinggui said he would look into it.[21]

The issue of funding temple festivals, however, would not go away; missionaries repeatedly asked the French minister to address this problem. For example, in a letter that arrived in Beijing on 2 December 1861 describing the situation in Yangqu County in Taiyuan Prefecture, a missionary complained that even though the Zongli yamen had sent a document on these matters to provincial authorities, nothing had changed. Furthermore, officials were actively opposing Christians. Throughout Shanxi, Chinese Christians were still required to pay for the opera performances that were at the center of temple festivals. If they refused to pay, then their liability for other levies was increased proportionately. Christians in Yangqu were also being beaten and imprisoned over this issue.[22]

On 21 December 1861 the acting French minister Michel-Alexandre Kleczkowski sent a cautious communication (*zhaohui*) to the Zongli yamen that was based in part on such missionary reports. Since he had little information on the Yangqu case, Kleczkowski simply repeated the propositions made by the Fengtai Franciscans in September 1861. He went on to complain that the Sino-French treaty had not been posted on official notice boards and where treaties had been posted, it was the recent Sino-British treaty. Kleczkowski closed with a proposed four-article regulation, similar to the September document, describing relations between Christians and non-Christians. Kleczkowski iterated that Chinese Christians could not be forced to subscribe to temple festivals. Moreover, they could not be required to pay any more than non-Christians for public projects like bridge and road repairs or irrigation works.[23] The total tax burden on Chinese Christians, then, would be less than on their non-Christian neighbors. Kleczkowski called for county magistrates to first determine the amounts of money being spent on religious festivals and public works, and then to make sure that Chinese Christians paid only the latter portion.

Kleczkowski's fourth proposal concerned the culpability, and responsibility for restitution, of village leaders who punished the intransigence of Christians by stealing from them or destroying their crops. Mindful perhaps of Yinggui's irritation at the claim of the Shanxi missionaries that any project that could not be supported by Christians was heterodox, he used a neutral "useless" (*wuyi*) to describe such projects.[24]

The Zongli yamen's response, issued two days later, did not mollify Kleczkowski. On 26 December 1861 he complained that recent dispatches by the Zongli yamen to Shanxi were being ignored. There were still problems in Shanxi, he claimed, soon to be expounded by a visitor to Beijing from that province. The French minister requested that his four-point plan be distributed throughout the province.[25]

The Zongli yamen replied on 5 January 1862. Prince Gong conceded that Christians could refuse, on the basis of conscience, to pay for opera and temple festivals organized by local communities (*xiangshe*). Nor could they be forced to pay. However, there was a whole range of local fees that Christians were still responsible for. These included public works, local security, crop-watching, and paying the converted corvée labor tax. Prince Gong reminded the French that "Christians can practice the religion of your country but they are still people of China (*Zhongguo zhi ren*); these other imposts should still, according to precedent, be collected."[26]

The French minister remained unsatisfied. Kleczkowski reiterated on 18 January 1862 his understanding of the nature of local fiscal responsibilities: there were "wasteful" expenses (*rongfei*), like temple festivals and opera performances that no Christian need pay, but everyone had to pay "useful" (*youyi*) ones like the corvée labor tax that were included under the general category of public expenses (*gongfei*). It was up to the magistrate to determine the proper breakdown between those two broad categories in order to determine the Christians' tax burden. Kleczkowski presented a hypothetical breakdown of 40 percent "useful" and 60 percent "wasteful." The French thought this document could serve as a model and the Zongli yamen agreed, sending copies to the governors-general of Guangdong and Guangxi and Zhili and then other provinces on 19 and 22 January 1862.[27]

Greater force was given to these arguments when the Zongli yamen, after consulting with the French, instructed provincial governors throughout China to turn Kleczkowski's 18 January 1862 statement into an "order" (*yudan*) to be reproduced in the hundreds for distribution to magistrates and missionaries. The Zongli yamen, in its 7 February 1862 cover letter, summarized Kleczkowski's argument and divided local imposts (*tanpai*) into the categories of "public" (*gongfei*) and "other," giving as an example for the latter the ones used to fund processions and operas.[28] But the new French minister, de Bourboulon, wanted imperial recognition of the issue and asked the Zongli yamen to memorialize these matters to the throne. The Zongli yamen submitted a memorial on 4 April 1862 based on the documents that had been sent out in February; an edict sanctioning this memorial was issued the same day.[29] All subsequent imperial edicts and Zongli yamen directives on the issue of temple festivals issued throughout the Tongzhi and Guangxu reigns (1862–1908) would echo the agreements of 1861–62. But the exhortations on paper were often ignored in practice, for conflicts between Christians and non-Christians over the issue of funding temple festivals would be unceasing.[30] The conflicts in Shanxi that came to the attention of the Zongli yamen in 1861 — prompting the flurry of documents just described — were not to be quelled by directives and edicts issued from Beijing.

Some incidents were documented; countless others were never recorded. There is a bias in this documentary record toward coverage of the Catholic missions, in part because there were more Catholics in Shanxi. By the time of the arrival of the first Protestant missionaries in the late 1870s, the Catholics already numbered (in 1879) 30 Western missionaries, 18 native priests, and 22,780 native converts.[31] This documentary bias is also a result of the predispositions of the missionaries involved. While Catholic missionaries and their diplomatic advocates aggressively claimed treaty rights, Protestant missionaries were less likely to resort to consular representation.

Protestant missionaries in Shanxi often prided themselves on their ability to withstand persecution, seeing it as a trial of faith. This brings us to another element that needs to be stressed in this search for the origins of the violence in Shanxi: the psychology of martyrdom that was fostered by Protestant missionaries. Inspired by their understanding of the early history of Christianity, some Protestant missionaries viewed violence and persecution as useful. For example, J. Hudson Taylor, the founder of the China Inland Mission, thought "[t]he opposition of pagan Rome, and of religious Jews, were essential elements of success; we lack these things, and our success can only be partial."[32] Many Protestant missionaries arriving in Shanxi in the 1880s and 1890s were affiliated with Taylor's mission society.

Speaking to CIM personnel in July 1886 on two separate occasions, Taylor argued that bearing persecution patiently allowed Christians to conquer by example. Weren't the victories won by enduring persecution "ten thousand times better than writing to the Consul, and getting him to appeal to the Viceroy?"[33] In fact, Taylor even wished that the political protection enjoyed by the missionaries would be withdrawn for then there would "be no hindrance to the spread of the Gospel."[34] If this happened, then the missionaries, having lost their privileged status, could "get shoulder to shoulder with our native converts, who are liable to be imprisoned, and robbed, and to have their tails and ears cut off."[35]

These ideas were conveyed by CIM missionaries to Chinese inquirers. On 5 September 1886, for example, at a special examination for candidates for baptism in a village in Xiaoyi County, "it was clearly pointed out that their profession would involve them in persecution, and even death might be the outcome."[36] These were prescient words: the first CIM members killed in Shanxi in 1900 were two women posted to this county. And their Chinese followers were tracked down after their names were noted on a silk banner that they had presented to the women and hung on the chapel wall.[37]

This acceptance of persecution was not unusual. Timothy Richard, the eminent British missionary responsible for opening up Shanxi to the Protestant missionary effort, wrote in 1884 that "missionaries make it a rule not to interfere on behalf of the native Christians at all, sometimes suffering greatly with their converts and giving them noble examples of patient endurance."[38] But Richard, who thought persecutions were neither inevitable nor desirable, blamed the Chinese government for not upholding treaty stipulations. Unless this was done "greater annoyances, severer tortures and more general massacres of foreigners as well as natives . . . may eventually get beyond the control of the government, ending, no one knows where."[39] Seventeen years later, after the Boxer Uprising, Chinese authorities asked Richard to mediate between Chinese and foreigners attempting to restore peace in Shanxi, where "general massacres" had taken place.

Much of this violence in these decades was undocumented. As mentioned above, Protestants often prided themselves on *not* bringing such incidents to the attention of consuls. Catholics were less reticent, so the archives of the Zongli yamen yield some data, but a local conflict could fester for months before it came to the attention of officials in Beijing.

In the section that follows I will describe three cases, from central, northern, and southern Shanxi, for which there is substantial documentary evidence: the first involved Catholics in Fenzhou Prefecture, Xiaoyi

County, in 1873–75; the second, from Datong Prefecture, occurred in 1881–82 and involved Catholics in Datong County; and the third involved Protestants in two incidents in the Hongdong area that cannot be precisely dated, but most likely took place sometime between 1896 and 1899. These cases will draw on three documentary bases: Catholic missionary reports to ecclesiastical authorities in Europe, the archives of the Zongli yamen, and a memoir published by a Protestant missionary in Shanxi.

This was a violent time in many of the villages of Shanxi. And it was a time of death, as the Great Famine of 1876–79 struck hard at the province. Drought and famine, as fearsome as they were, were at least familiar. What was new and unusual were the foreign missionaries. Although the missionaries were unseen by most peasants and townspeople, Shanxi villagers could infer the power held by these foreigners as they saw the extraordinary spectacle of village leaders unable to enforce the customary consensus on the nature of the local community — its customs, its projects, its identity. This impotence, wrought by distant powers in Beijing, both imperial and foreign, was beyond understanding.

Xiaoyi County, Fenzhou Prefecture, 1873–75

This well-documented case, reaching from Kusangyuan Village to the Zongli yamen, illustrates the nature of anti-Christian violence in the Shanxi countryside in the 1870s. Catholic proselytization, through the offices of the Chinese catechist Paul Wu (Wu Anchao), was at first not very successful. However, the refusal of Catholic Guo Qimao in 1873 to pay the customary subscription used to fund the local temple festival and to pay the village's crop-watchers contributed, in the end, to a breakthrough. It appears Guo avoided all tax liabilities, and when his crops were stolen in the fall of 1873 he sued a crop-watcher. The crop-watcher, also surnamed Guo, countersued. This case was still pending when a new magistrate came to Xiaoyi to take up his duties. One of the first items of business for the magistrate was the Guo case. In his decision of 6 January 1874 the magistrate wisely avoided the question of culpability, ordering the crop-watcher to make good Guo Qimao's loss and to await reimbursement when the thief was found. The magistrate allowed Qimao to withhold the money that was to be spent on village festivals but reminded him that he was responsible for paying the amount due to the crop-watcher. Nevertheless, Guo Qimao was kept in custody because he had neglected to pay a sales tax when he had purchased a draft animal.[40]

Tensions between Christians and non-Christians remained, even after the case appeared closed in February 1874. Indeed, the magistrate soon ordered that some of the new believers be beaten and thrown in prison on charges that "they had introduced a false religion, disturbed local order, and had disobeyed the law through their refusal to pay the temple impost."[41] Of course, under the new laws of the land it was the magistrate who was culpable. The vicar apostolic of Shanxi, Luigi Moccagatta, interceded with a letter to the governor of Shanxi, who ordered the Xiaoyi magistrate to release his Catholic prisoners. The "pagans" were "humiliated"; the Catholics were galvanized. One day in August 1874 a hundred people were baptized. By September Moccagatta could report that Catholic believers (neophytes) in Xiaoyi were scattered in fifteen towns or villages. His new concern was to build, in a central location, a chapel and some residences.[42]

Although the catechist Paul Wu thus had some success in converting the people of Xiaoyi County, the forces allied against Christianity in Xiaoyi that had been checked in 1874 were not defeated. Moccagatta's letter of 14 September 1875 describes the continuing struggle over demands for opera subscriptions and for money to rebuild the "Confucian" temple.[43] Once again the Catholics refused to pay; once again they were the objects of verbal and physical assault. And once again the catechist Paul Wu took the matter to the Xiaoyi magistrate. More cautious this time, the magistrate treated Wu with deference and courtesy, proposing that Wu's case be transferred to the yamen of the Fenzhou prefect. The decision granted by the prefect appeared to address the concerns of both parties: the "pagans" were instructed to return the objects they had stolen from the Christians and the right of the "pagans" to impose subscriptions on the Christians was upheld, but the prefect ordered the magistrate to bar non-Christians from entering Christian villages to collect local imposts.[44]

This partial victory frustrated the Xiaoyi magistrate. Although the Fenzhou prefect had supported the right of local authorities to levy imposts, enforcement would be compromised if authorities could not enter villages. And so the case, closed in the books of the prefect, was still grating on the magistrate, who boasted that he had ten counts of indictments against the Christians, sufficient to allow him to mete out corporal punishment. According to Moccagatta, this contributed to the next stage in this affair, for the "pagans," emboldened by the magistrate's statement, seized yet another believer, a catechumen, tied him up, and brought him to a temple. They accused the catechumen of stealing from a village chief "the instrument by means of which he convokes the people" and beating him. Once again Paul Wu came to the rescue. At first Wu was able to protect the catechumen, but the arrival of a new group of "pagans" turned the tide.

Paul Wu was brought before the Xiaoyi magistrate and charged with receiving stolen goods; the catechumen was arraigned for theft. The catechumen confessed his guilt and agreed to make restitution. The magistrate released him. But Paul Wu remained in prison and when news of this turn of events reached Moccagatta he asked the governor of Shanxi to take over this case. This meddling incensed the Xiaoyi magistrate and, on the pretext that Wu had tried to escape and that he was a threat to public order, he ordered a savage beating that left Wu "half-dead."

At this point the case began entangling more and more people. The governor transferred the case to the Fenzhou prefect and criticized the handling of the case by the Xiaoyi magistrates. The prefect said that Christians were to be recognized, as they were by authorities in Beijing, as "friends of order." The case was remanded back to Xiaoyi, apparently concluded.

But Paul Wu refused to sign an agreement in which he would have recognized his error, promised not to incite disorder, and accepted a punishment of 50 blows. Moccagatta was relentless. The Shanxi governor and then officials at the Zongli yamen, where he was granted an audience later in 1875, heard his complaint. Paul Wu's case continued to involve authorities at county, prefectural, and provincial levels. Wu's intransigence was finally worn down and he agreed, in the end, to sign a modified sentence, promising not to incite trouble. Obtaining his freedom at last, Paul Wu returned home where his recovery from the early beating was continuing as Moccagatta wrote in September 1875. But the struggle in Xiaoyi was not over, for "pagans" were still seizing believers, tying them up and suspending them from temple rafters to the point of death. Believers had better pay, they warned, the next time they came around asking for money to honor Confucius.[45]

Datong County, Datong Prefecture, 1881–82

The key elements of the Xiaoyi case can also be seen in the Datong County case of 1881–82 as reflected in documents from the archives of the Zongli yamen, especially the 31 May 1881 letter from the Franciscan coadjutor of the Shanxi vicariate apostolic from 1876 to 1890, Gregorio da Castellazzo Grassi (1833–1900),[46] to the Shanxi governor, and the 8 April 1881 report by the missionary in Datong on the incident.[47]

On 1 April 1881 three village leaders (*huishou*) in Yulin Village gathered together a group of people to go to the homes of the Christians Ji Yunchang and Guan Xiang to demand their share of the subscriptions for a local temple festival. Guan Xiang was not home at the time but his wife, three months pregnant, confronted the crowd and informed them that the Guan family did not pay these taxes and she resisted their efforts to take property. She was reportedly thrown to the ground and knocked unconscious, and subsequently suffered a miscarriage. Five days later in the same village a crowd of over twenty went to the home of Yang Tianzi, also to demand opera money. After this the Christians went to Datong City to tell the missionary what had happened in Yulin, leading to the missionary's 8 April 1881 petition to the Datong magistrate. The principals were called by the magistrate to a hearing on 11 May 1881.

The magistrate's exchange with Yang Tianzi is of particular interest. The magistrate asked: "You are a person of what country?" Yang answered: "I am a person of the Qing." The magistrate then began a blistering denunciation of Yang in particular and Chinese Christians in general:

If you are a person of the Qing dynasty then why are you following the foreign devils and their seditious religion? You didn't pay your opera money when requested by the village and you were beaten. But how can you dare to bring a suit? Don't you know why Zuo Zongtang went to Beijing? In order to kill — to exterminate — the foreign devils. You certainly ought to pay the opera subscription. If you don't you won't be allowed to live in the land of the Qing. You'll have to leave for a foreign county.[48]

This is a significant exchange, to which I will return. The Datong case was a subject of discussion throughout the rest of 1881 and into 1882. Yang Tianzi was again confronted, on 9 August 1881, to pay his opera subscription. After making serious threats, including death, the village leader (*sheshou*) left. Yang was again brought before the magistrate and asked: "What god (*shen*) do you honor? What is your religion (*daoli*)?"[49]

The case was not resolved, however, and finally the Franciscans were able to persuade the French legation to present the case to the Zongli yamen, which was done on 21 January 1882. A flurry of events then followed. The Zongli yamen told Shanxi authorities to look into the affair, a request passed along to Datong on 9 February 1882. The Datong report was completed less than two weeks later, allowing the Shanxi governor to inform the Zongli yamen that the problem was one of a lack of information: the simple country folk did not know about the treaties China had signed with other countries. He informed the Zongli yamen that he had ordered copies of the treaties to be distributed. The case finally came to a close in early May 1882, with the usual understandings exchanged between Chinese officials at the provincial and metropolitan level, foreign missionaries at the county and provincial level, and the foreign minister in Beijing: that China had guaranteed religious toleration in various treaties and conventions and that adherence was required and expected.[50]

Governor Zhang Zhidong, who became involved in this case after he arrived in Taiyuan on 10 February 1882,[51] launched a large number of reforms in his first posting as a governor: he punished corrupt officials, cancelled delinquent taxes, encouraged the local iron industry, and tried to limit the production and consumption of opium.[52] It was an ambitious program, far too much to accomplish before he was summoned to Beijing on 12 April 1884 and subsequently promoted to the position of governor-general of Guangdong and Guangxi on 22 May 1884.[53] But Zhang did leave Shanxi with one institutional innovation that grew out of his attempt to diminish the incidence of conflict between Chinese Christians and their non-Christian neighbors, conflict which he said was becoming more frequent.[54]

In a memorial submitted in early 1883, Zhang Zhidong asked for imperial approval for a new bureau — the Bureau for Missionary Cases (*Jiaoan ju*) — he had established in Taiyuan to take care of the conflict. He received this approval on 31 January 1883.[55] Zhang had established this bureau shortly after his arrival in the province and through the bureau's study and his own he had reached a conclusion that the Christians were in the wrong in these cases and the non-Christians in the right. Zhang argued that the people of Shanxi bore no animus against the missionaries and that most of the local difficulties had nothing to do with religion.[56]

The Hongdong Area, Late 1890s

Zhang Zhidong's reforms and analysis notwithstanding, there were still serious problems in Shanxi. By the mid-1880s Protestant missionaries were contributing their voices to the affray. And they too had their equivalent of Paul Wu, the protagonist in the Xiaoyi case described above. One of the first Protestant converts in Shanxi, the so-called Pastor Hsi of Pingyang County, bedeviled Chinese authorities in the first years after his conversion in 1879 and his association with the Hongdong station of the China Inland Mission. Hsi's proselytizing, and his effort to establish a network of opium refuges, brought him into numerous government offices. Hsi, according to one of his admirers, thought

that his zeal and energy must be employed to clear the way of the Lord, sweeping aside all obstacles and hindrances, with the means whereby he had hitherto successfully dominated those around him. Thus when troubles arose, and believers were persecuted contrary to treaty rights, he even went up to the capital and interviewed the Governor of the province, setting on foot legal proceedings that covered their enemies with confusion. For as followers of the Western faith, he and other Christians could claim the protection assured to foreigners.[57]

Hsi and the China Inland Mission missionary D. E. Hoste finally decided, however, that this policy was flawed because it attracted the wrong type of person to the Protestant fold. In 1891 their proposed resolution was passed by the churches in Hongdong stating that in the future those suffering persecution "should trust only in the Lord for protection, and not depend on their treaty rights."[58]

Yet the conflicts continued. Hoste's successor in the late 1890s, Marshall Broomhall,[59] said "constant persecution" was still a problem because village leaders refused to make a distinction between "public and idolatrous" expenses or "profitable and unprofitable" expenses. Writing about the village of An-loh, Broomhall says:

some years ago several men made profession of Christianity and applied to the village Council for exemption from the idolatrous portion of the taxes. This the council refused to allow, and as four villages were dependent upon the same water channel for irrigation, the several village Councils unitedly determined to oppose any attempt to break the ancient custom of their villages as to taxes. The Christians conscientiously refused to pay, whereupon the water supply was cut off. For three years they persisted in the decision, only obtaining poor crops where irrigation would have produced profitable returns. At length, weary with the contest, they yielded to the pressure and paid as before. Though they still profess faith in Christ, they have ceased to give any public acknowledgment and have fallen off from public worship.[60]

Broomhall goes on to note an occurrence in the village of Dicun, just north of the Zhaocheng County seat, also a part of the China Inland Mission Hongdong circuit: "a public notice was posted up by the village Council saying, that as the Christians refused to pay the temple taxes, the Council would refuse to accept even the lawful taxes from them, and thereby free themselves from all responsibility as to their property and persons."[61]

Almost 40 years had elapsed since the Zongli yamen had specified that Chinese Christians were exempt from some local subscriptions. The logic of the French minister — dividing local subscriptions into two categories, and exempting Christians from the portion going toward opera performances and temple festivals — was not making sense in rural Shanxi. The incident in Datong and the one in Dicun suggest that for both a county magistrate and a group of village leaders it was all or nothing. The villagers implied that anyone not paying the opera subscription was not welcome in the village; even a partial subscription was not enough. And the magistrate, perhaps in a fit of impotent rage, went even further: If you don't pay you might as well leave China. Clearly, more than a superstitious practice was at stake.

Broader Patterns

What connections are there between these conflicts and the violence of 1900? We know that each county—Xiaoyi, Datong, and Hongdong—was particularly hard hit.[62] But the violence was more widespread. In a telegram dated 3 May 1901 Shanxi governor Cen Chunxuan said violence had occurred in eleven departments (*zhou*), six subprefectures (*ting*), and 40-odd counties (*xian*).[63] Qiao Zhiqiang has argued that the Shanxi violence was directly related to Yuxian's presence in the months between his March 1900 arrival and mid-summer 1900, when he began to distance himself from the anti-Christian violence.[64] Qiao has also argued against any secret society or White Lotus links for the Shanxi participants. Furthermore, he has argued that, unlike Shandong, there was no martial-arts tradition in Shanxi that could help explain the rapid development of the movement.[65]

This argument—that the data from Shanxi support the thesis that the Boxer Uprising was a spontaneous anti-imperialist peasant uprising—is echoed in a recent standard treatment. Indeed, a distinction is made between the reactionary violence against missionaries ordered by Yuxian in Taiyuan on 9 July 1900 and the anti-imperialist struggle carried out by the Boxers in other localities. Thus, it is argued that the growth of the Boxer movement in Shanxi was aided by Yuxian, but its subsequent suppression was a cruel double cross that was his responsibility alone.[66]

But eyewitness accounts of Protestants, both Western and Chinese, in Shanxi describe a more complicated picture. For example, in Hongdong City it appears that Chinese had been drilling secretly during the spring of 1900 and on 14 May there was an open drill and a subsequent march to the house of the native Christian leader of the area. He was stabbed, almost fatally, and his house was plundered.[67] What is apparent in this and other accounts is the variety of responses and actions by magistrates, local elites, and others. Also, there is some evidence the elites supported the violence. For example, in Hejin County three military *shengyuan* were reported to be in league with the "Boxers."[68]

It was an extremely confusing situation—Yuxian could be encouraging violence while in nearby Shaanxi Governor Duanfang, like his colleagues in the south, tried to protect Westerners and Christians as much as possible.

Some magistrates could be virulently anti-Christian but others were protective, although sometimes they had to withdraw protection for fear they too would become objects of attack. Local leaders could also be found on both sides. And, significantly, there is evidence that local bandits sometimes took advantage of the crisis and portrayed themselves as Boxers.[69]

Although the picture of Shanxi in 1900 is confused, it becomes clearer in the retrospective of officials taken in 1901 and 1902. This evidence implicates local leadership structures and also hints at the long-standing tensions within communities. As mentioned at the outset, Shanxi officials, in 1901, thought the tension over opera subscriptions was a central cause of conflict. Moreover, these monies were soon eyed by acting governor Zhao Erxun, who issued a directive from the provincial yamen in Taiyuan in December 1902 requesting that the associations sponsoring opera performances reserve a portion of the money for the purpose of establishing new-style schools. Zhao noted that each of these occasions, which he recognized were too popular to suppress, could require expenditures ranging from 60 to 200 taels.

Although Zhao does not elaborate in this directive on the organizational characteristics of these associations, a reform directive issued the following month, in January 1903, makes clear that the leaders of the associations (*xiangshe*) responsible for organizing temple festivals could also comprise the secular leadership of local society. As Zhao pointed out, the structure and characteristics of subcounty administration varied widely. Jurisdictions under the rule of unofficial leaders could range from one village to a group of villages surrounding a market town. Furthermore, local leaders were selected in various ways, including rotational systems and community consensus.[70] Zhao's reform regulations ended with an article concerning Chinese Christians and their local leaders, noting that Christian *xiangshe* should select their own leaders and these leaders, in the case of intervillage disputes, would resolve issues with their counterparts from non-Christian communities.

In China's brief age of constitutionalism, the issues under discussion in this chapter were being transformed. In the past popular religious practices came under fire from urban Confucian elites because they were thought to be "useless." For example, the magistrate of Dingxiang County in Shanxi received a petition in 1780 asking him to reform local practices associated with opera and temple festivals. The petition began with a statement clearly in sympathy with imperial injunctions: "If we reduce the number of operas, stop evening singing performances, and abolish obscene plays, then we can save money and repress heterodox thought. . . . Although these events are referred to as paying respect to the gods, in reality the people are only planning for their own enjoyment. These are not rituals of respect for the gods." The petitioner goes on to ask the magistrate to order the leaders (*xiangguan*) of local communities (*cun*) to reduce the number of these occasions.[71] But there is little evidence that county magistrates actually suppressed these festivals and certainly no villager would be protected should he refuse to pay customary fees. But a century later foreign powers were expecting Chinese officials to uphold the right of Chinese Christians to refuse to pay.

Communities that shared symbolic resources manifested in rituals and discourse that were mutually intelligible had been challenged by Chinese Christians. Beginning in 1862 they could call on foreign missionaries to guarantee a tax holiday. The disputes became intractable. This was a stunning development for it introduced in local communities the rationale and outside support for dissident behavior. Local magistrates had learned it was impossible to compel Chinese Christians to conform to these customary practices, for disputes could lead all the way to Beijing and jeopardize careers. Local village leaders could wield their power more effectively, but this too had its limits. There are cases where the complaints of Chinese Christians finally led to a visit by the resident foreign missionary. In north Shanxi an outraged local leader tied up two such foreign missionaries in 1910 and marched them to the county seat. The terrified county magistrate freed the missionaries, questioned the local leader, and sent him back to the village in humiliation.[72]

What is particularly significant in the post-Boxer period, however, is the appearance of state authorities who began to affect the fiscal well-being of local communities with an extractive policy that, in the nature of its justification, resembled both the Confucian and Western critiques of popular religious practices.

It is fitting that Zhang Zhidong, the reforming Shanxi governor of 1882–84, should be the spokesman for this new synthesis of ideas. Writing in 1898 in the context of an argument for educational reform, Zhang combined traditional Confucian ambivalence toward local religious practices with his desire to find resources to fund the network of new-style schools he hoped to build throughout China. His answer: appropriate the money spent for "useless" activities like festivals and opera performances. Zhang Zhidong knew well this was exactly the rhetoric used in the toleration edicts issued in the past four decades.[73] If Westerners could gain control of a portion of local monies to build chapels, schools, and hospitals, certainly the Chinese government could too.

Rural communities had always had resources extracted by the state; this was not new. And there is evidence that a range of projects were funded by local communities. But the intent of Zhang's message was different. Combining Confucian distaste for popular practices with the Western effort to split rural society into secular and sacred spheres, Zhang Zhidong was laying claim to local resources with the voice of a secular, modernizing state. This message was just as unfathomable to rural Chinese as the missionaries' arguments that opera was frivolous and idolatrous.

In Shanxi we can see the eventual impact of this new policy from 1906 on, by which time Zhao Erxun's policy of simply trying to persuade local elites to spend money on new-style education was replaced by new efforts of county governments to appropriate that money for their own educational reforms. Furthermore, the language used to describe local fiscal practices reflects a Western influence. Local monies were described in terms that do not seem far removed from a familiar sacred-secular dichotomy.

It is unclear if this conceptualization was shared by non-Christian Chinese. It is well to remember that the fundamental division of sacred and secular in Western thought is rooted in the medieval struggle in which the Catholic church was able to establish a claim to ecclesiastical power that was distinct from the temporal power of feudal lords it was called upon to legitimate. The sacred-secular dichotomy, Mircea Eliade argues, is not characteristic of the non-Western societies he studied.[74] But by sanctioning the demand by Chinese Christians to avoid subscribing to temple festivals, the Chinese government had called into question an implicit communal understanding of proper behavior with respect to ritual observances. By defining the ritual observances of local communities as voluntary and non-inclusive, the stage was set for desacralizing temple resources. At the turn of the century the state was not only lamenting the resources wasted on local religious practices, a familiar Confucian complaint, but was also claiming the authority to redirect those resources for the purposes of fulfilling a centrally devised reform agenda.

In 1862 the government had translated the French critique of "pagan practices" into the Confucian category of "useless expenditures." In 1906 the government not only called these practices useless but also began to lay claim to the resources themselves. The money first taken from village communities beginning in 1862, on the basis of Sino-Western treaties, was now being taken from local communities in the name of combating superstition and building a strong nation-state. Not only was the state neglecting to support local communities in upholding local customs, the state was attempting to extract the very resources of the community.[75]

Final evidence of the desacralization of the world of Shanxi villages in the minds of county, provincial, and national elites can be seen in the policies adopted by the Shanxi Provincial Assembly in 1909 to resolve the still-present tensions between Christians and non-Christians in the province. After discussing past ways of dealing with these issues, the assembly looked to the imminent establishment of local elected councils. With respect to the problem of local fiscal resources and local expenditures, the assembly thought that the tensions that had split local communities would end with the practice of electoral politics. No longer would local community resources be defined as temple resources under community control; no longer would authorities try to maintain separate Christian and non-Christian communities. Instead, the assembly thought that by fiat these resources could be secularized, that the fiscal responsibilities of Christians and non-Christians would be equal, and that decisions on the disbursement of local revenues would be made by local councils to which Christians and non-Christians alike could be elected.[76]

As we have seen, this secularization had already begun by the time the assembly met. In 1906 imperial orders had been issued, in the context of educational reform, stating that any land belonging to temples not listed in a specific section in local gazetteers was open to expropriation by county-level authorities responsible for education.[77] This attempt to expropriate land whose revenue supported so-called useless activities would continue. In the midst of late-Qing constitutional reform the characteristic pattern of the twentieth century became apparent.[78] In the blithe belief that electoral politics would easily contain the passions of local politics and restore Christian and non-Christian amity within a secular political and administrative body, members of the Shanxi assembly suggested what has been typical of Chinese political elites throughout this century. This attitude, related in part to Confucian prejudices, consigned to insignificance popular religious practice, Christian and non-Christian alike. Employing the distinction used by French diplomats in 1861 between "useful" and "useless" expenditures of resources, national, provincial, and county-level elites began to expropriate the resources of local communities for state-mandated purposes.

CHAPTER 5

Christian Missionary as Confucian Intellectual: Gilbert Reid (1857–1927) and the Reform Movement in the Late Qing

TSOU MINGTEH

The last several decades of the nineteenth century marked an important period in Chinese history. The arrival of Westerners pushed Chinese society into a variety of changes. Some Chinese, such as Lin Zexu and Wei Yuan in the 1840s and later Zeng Guofan, Li Hongzhang, Zheng Guanyin, Kang Youwei, and Liang Qichao, had wanted to modify Chinese culture to suit the rapidly changing circumstances. But their efforts had been largely passive. It was Westerners who played an initiating role in the course of the transformation.

The influence foreigners were able to exert on China's transformation depended to a large extent on their knowledge of China and its history and culture. Only those who understood Chinese society well were able to transplant part of Western culture in China. Among missionaries who contributed to China during that period were Gilbert Reid (Chinese name Li Jiabai), Timothy Richard, and W. A. P. Martin. This chapter deals mainly with Reid's mission, the connections between his early experience in Shandong and his later activities, his attitudes toward Chinese traditional culture, and his contributions to the reform movement in the late Qing.

Youth and Education

Gilbert Reid was born in Laurel, Long Island, New York, on 29 November 1857.[1] His father, John Reid (1820–97), was a native of Scotland and a Presbyterian pastor all his later life in New York. Gilbert had three brothers. The younger two had died in their early years; the eldest went on to become a physician. Because Gilbert was more clever than his elder brother, his father trained him diligently to be not just a missionary but a missionary to the Chinese. Young Reid's preparation for his vocation began with the study of "Chinese and all Chinese classics." This reflected his father's conviction that a person who "did not study earnestly the classics of Confucianism could not recognize the profound truths of the doctrines of Chinese sages."[2] Whatever imbued John Reid with this unusual interest in China is not revealed in any of Gilbert Reid's own reminiscences or in the studies of his contemporaries. That early study, Gilbert Reid later said, not only helped him "regard China as really my second home" but, more important, contributed to the effectiveness of his mission in China.[3] For instance, because he was "strong in Chinese," with a knowledge of Confucianism, later he found it easy to write a paper on Mencius and to cultivate "a very large circle of acquaintances" among Chinese officials.[4]

Reid supplemented his initial education under his father at schools near his home. He attended Whitestown Seminary, then went on to Hamilton College. After obtaining his degree in 1879, he studied at Union Theological Seminary and graduated in 1882. During the period of his higher education, he was one of those "rare young men who knew what he wanted to do." He studied hard, refined his Chinese, and familiarized himself with Chinese customs, absorbing as much as possible its ancient traditions.[5]

Reid's determination to become a missionary to the Chinese and what he did in China, though partly attributable to his father's influence, were closely connected with the liberal education he received at Hamilton and at Union Theological Seminary. At the seminary, the class of 1882 was dubbed "the great missionary class" because most of its members signed a pledge to serve as home or foreign missionaries. Under these circumstances, Reid's career decision was natural. Nevertheless, just before his graduation from the seminary he changed his mind and decided to become a home missionary. But after a discussion with John L. Nevius, one of the teachers at the seminary on leave from the China mission, Reid changed his mind again and offered his services to the Presbyterian Board as a missionary to Shandong, Nevius's own field. He was licensed on 1 May 1882 and ordained by the New York Presbytery six days later.[6]

In the fall of 1882, Reid said goodbye to his parents and sailed for China.

Reid's First Mission in Shandong

In the late fall of 1882, Reid arrived in Chefoo (Yantai) via Shanghai and began his 45-year mission in China. At that time, like other missionaries, he stressed preaching the gospel and making converts. He was deeply impressed by the devoutness of native Christians in southwestern Shandong. Although living in the mountains, "barefooted and almost naked," and sometimes surviving on nothing more than grass roots, they lived a good life and found happiness in their faith. "It reminded me of the Christians in the Reformation, fleeing to the Alps to serve and praise God undisturbed," he said. Those scenes strengthened Reid's determination to preach among the impoverished and help them attain a happy life, both spiritually and materially. He believed that ministering to the poor was the best way to Christianize China, since the poor constituted the great majority of the Chinese.[7] He was pleased with the mission his church assigned him and sought to do his utmost to fulfill his duties.

In the nineteenth century, North China suffered from severe flooding of the Yellow River. In 1856, because the outlet to the sea changed, the people in southwestern Shandong had suffered untold misery.[8] While preaching in Ji'nan and Jining, Reid witnessed people crying out because of hunger and cold. He found that teaching the truth of God in churches was no longer sufficient; preaching the gospel alone could not rescue the poor from their suffering. The gospel was attractive and pleasant to listen to, but it did not answer their immediate needs. Reid felt that if he merely looked on and did nothing for these miserable people, not only would he lose his converts' trust and faith in the truth he preached, he would also contravene his own doctrine: "one who loves others will be respected by all." Helping the refugees, he believed, represented "the loyal idea of a lofty person."[9] He concluded that more practical ways were needed to help China. In November 1889 and December 1890, Reid wrote two papers on how to control the Yellow River. This was the first sign that Reid was no longer confining himself to narrow religious work, but had become interested in social issues and the reform of Chinese society. This was the start of the secularization of his mission.

Upon the suggestion of Xu Fu, then the deputy-minister of the Board of Ceremonies, the Qing court had decided to check the flooding of the Yellow River by constructing a giant dam. After the work had been going on for nearly eight months and nine million taels had been spent, the construction remained uncompleted. In the fall of 1889, the river overflowed again, and the area affected this time was "even greater."[10] Reid held that the plan had failed mainly because it did not control the river according to "its natural law." He criticized the Qing court for wasting so much time and money "with no result at all."

In November 1889, Reid made five suggestions for controlling the river for the Qing court to "consider and adopt."[11] Unfortunately, these suggestions were ignored by the court, and flooding recurred year after year. On rescuing refugees, Reid suggested that the court make refugees work instead of providing aid to them. Only the old, children, and women were to be supplied; the young would be paid for working. In order to carry out this plan smoothly, Reid proposed that the Qing court select "fair-minded and honest Chinese officials" and invite foreigners to join them, thus avoiding the severe exploitation of laborers typical of most official projects. Reid also indicated several times that he proposed this plan to help China and had no intention of interfering in "the internal affairs of the Chinese government." What he did was all for the benefit of the Chinese. But it came to naught. Later, in 1903, he lamented, "what a pity that those suggestions were not adopted."[12] Using the principles of Christian benevolence, he wanted Chinese officials to understand the missionaries' "goodwill to men" through their practice. However, no one showed interest in the plans he had so carefully elaborated. Indeed, his suggestions were known to few.

Another important impetus for the shift in the focus of Reid's mission was his experience in purchasing property in Ji'nan. The experience gave him a better understanding of the local elite and their role in Chinese society. In early 1881, American missionaries bought a parcel of land in downtown Ji'nan on which to build a church and a hospital. However, the sale was blocked by the local elite and prohibited by the local government.[13] In the winter of 1885, Reid was posted to Ji'nan. There he continued to search for property. Under his constant pressure, in the fall of 1887 local officials offered him a piece of land in a suburb. While negotiations were underway, the news leaked out. A riot protesting the foreign purchase broke out. The riot, according to Reid, was headed by "an ex-governor" and joined by "all" the local elite in the area. In the evening of 28 November, the rioters broke into Reid's room, threw him into the street twice and beat him. Because he, on behalf of the church, had maintained strong demands for the property purchase, the Chinese treated him as an enemy.

This was the first time that Reid had directly experienced an antiforeign riot. When other missionaries protested his mistreatment, the daotai replied that "we can suppress the people, but not the gentry. Not even the Governor is able to."[14] Reid was deeply irritated by all this because he had expected to reside in Ji'nan, which he had described as "an important place united with peace and good-will."[15] He claimed that the coming of missionaries as bearers of Western civilization would make a great contribution to Chinese spiritual life and to the development of Chinese society. Schools, hospitals and churches set up by missionaries all benefited the Chinese. But the elite resisted all this. They viewed all new things from the West as harmful. Reid's experience gave him a good understanding of the role of the local elite, and influenced his life and career as a missionary. As Donald MacGillivray said later, after the Ji'nan riot Reid devoted his whole life to "the work of cultivating friendly relations" with the local elite.[16]

Reid's Attitudes Toward the Local Elite

In spite of what happened in Ji'nan, Reid did not lose heart. However, he recognized that a mission among the lower classes could not easily succeed. The local elite held sway over all Chinese classes. Moreover, most Chinese officials came from the local elite. Reid came to believe that if missionaries acquired an understanding of, and help from, this class, then the mission could succeed and China could progress. It was necessary that Christianity absorb some doctrines of Confucianism, and missionaries adapt evangelization to Chinese culture, so that Christianity could be accepted by the Chinese. Reid came to the conclusion that encouraging the local elite to accept Christianity and Western culture must be the first step toward Christianizing China and the major duty of all missionaries. This was the turning point of Reid's missionary career.

In order to establish a good relationship with the local elite, Reid first identified sixteen impediments to amicable relations between the elite and missionaries. He criticized the local elite's prejudice against foreign religions, but also discussed the missionaries' capacities, their evangelistic methods, ideas, and aims, their poor experiences with the local elite, and the difficulties caused by foreign encroachment. He also suggested that his fellow missionaries abandon their prejudices and try to improve relations with the elite — to dispel Chinese prejudice through "hard fighting" with "the torch of truth" rather than with "the rapier of ridicule."[17]

The main features of Reid's new strategy were as follows. First, Reid was reacting to the change in Chinese attitudes toward missionaries and Christianity following the Western encroachment. The unequal treaties the Western powers imposed had destroyed the image of missionaries in Chinese eyes. As Reid argued, when the Western powers came to threaten China, "jealousy was added to contempt, and revenge and suspicion brooded in the breast." Though Reid saw Chinese prejudice against missionaries and foreigners as essentially a reaction to Western encroachment, ironically as a foreigner he was unable to disassociate himself from those treaties. Missionaries relied upon the treaties as their authority for entering the treaty ports and the interior. To the Chinese, missionaries were the incarnation of foreign encroachment. Reid wrote that the Chinese believed that the churches were supported "by force" and composed of bad elements.[18] If Christian missionaries wanted to work among the Chinese, Reid thought they first had to wipe out the local elite's prejudice by making that group the main target of their mission.

Second, Reid became sensitive to the clash between native cultural traditions and the preaching of the gospel. Most missionaries felt that Western culture was superior to Confucianism. The Chinese, on the other hand, viewed Christianity as a religion creating "troubles, causing riots resulting in lawsuits and revolutionary in its aims." Reid pointed out that this was the main reason friction and misunderstanding between missionaries and the Chinese had become rampant. It seemed to Reid that Confucianism, in spite of its ostensible comprehensiveness and profundity, contained not much substantial and useful knowledge. But unlike other missionaries, he recognized its role in Chinese society and respected Chinese culture. In this way, Reid made clear his aim of removing obstacles to Sino-foreign contacts, especially eliminating the local elite's hostility toward missionaries and their work. Thereby he could achieve his goal of influencing the Chinese with Christian culture and help China progress. He firmly maintained that what should be changed was the method, not the truth. In previous decades, some missionaries, such as Walter Henry Medhurst, held the same theory, but it was Reid, and later Timothy Richard and others, who put it into practice.[19]

Third, Reid believed that the Confucian elite would accept Western knowledge because of the "many similarities" between Confucianism and all other religions. Though there was a multitude of names and ceremonies in the various religions, "in reality" the nature of all religions was the same: all stressed "morality above anything else." Furthermore, he pointed out that there were "more similarities between Confucianism and Christianity than those" between Confucianism and other religions; thus Confucianism and Christianity could be united to work for China's prosperity.[20] If missionaries succeeded in influencing officials with Western knowledge, they could help the latter make better policies for the nation. That was Reid's hope, or his so-called indirect mission.

Finally, true to his original reason for working in China, Reid showed his concern for China's future. In a period when Western powers struggled to partition China, Reid said that though he could not fight on the battlefield "as a friend of China," he could contribute by enlightening the local elite and officials. These people, he believed, were in a position to save the nation. If China were equipped with "Western truths," Reid argued, it could be built "into a prosperous country modeled after the American and European powers." Clearly, he placed his hope on the elite and officials.

The Shift in Emphasis

Who constituted the upper classes? Reid's theories and his later practice make clear that he believed the upper classes included ministers of state in the capital, local officials, and the local elite.

The reason that the local elite were so powerful was that they represented Confucianism and were in some degree the leaders of the people. Since Confucianism was the pillar supporting their status among the people, any alien culture that did not accept Confucian teachings would destroy their influence and weaken their power. Because the local elite were the embodiment of native customs and Confucian teachings and "imbued with the idea of the precedence of the superior, filial piety and fraternal submission," he said, most people were ready to conform to their wishes. Even officials were afraid of them. In provincial capitals, they could "radiate influences throughout every district of the province," even "throughout the Empire." Based on these judgments, Reid believed that the future of China lay in the success of the new mission plan he had worked out. The local elite's cultural contact with the people provided the principal channel through which missionaries could influence China's development. Missionaries could in this way be the indirect promoters of China's progress. This is the path Reid chose and followed until his death.

If the local elite were friendly toward missionaries, they at least would "praise and adopt" the accomplishments of Christian culture, though Christian teachings were "largely rejected." Considering Chinese traditions and the Chinese political situation at that time, Reid thought that the positive role played by missionaries in modern China could be measured not by how many Chinese became Christians, but by how much of Western culture the Chinese accepted.

Reid's work among the upper classes also helped promote the Christian mission in China. On 9 November 1887, Reid discussed such a mission with his colleagues and called on them to turn their attention to the elite while working among the poor. He proposed that the new mission meet "the *felt need* of this class," satisfy "the highest aspirations of [their] heart[s] and conscience," and convince them to accept Christianity as a useful ideology.[21] Only then could they appreciate the gospel-preaching with its sincere aim to "persuade people to do good" and "not harm to China."[22] His new mission method was to seize "every opportunity" to demonstrate friendliness toward the local elite. As a result, Reid predicted, the image of foreigners in the eyes of the Chinese would be improved, peace would be established, and future troubles would be "largely prevented."

However, Reid's notion was seriously criticized by his fellow missionaries. They insisted that the Scriptures prescribed special attention to the poor—that "the poor have the Gospel preached to them," not the rich.[23] But Reid stuck by his plan. Two months later he made the same speech before the Beijing Missionary Association. He emphasized the need to enlighten the elite and officials, to make them understand the true light and to help them adopt Western knowledge as a lever to move China forward.

Moreover, he realized that he alone could not accomplish these aims. The General Conference of the Protestant Missionaries in China held in 1890 provided him an opportunity to appeal to all missionaries to join with him in working among the elite and officials, with the spirit of "relying upon treaties" and having "direct dealings with the authorities." Based on his own experience with officials in Shandong, he emphasized that maintaining friendship with and influencing local officials would reach only "a part of the Chinese government." The "mighty task" was to reach the princes, ministers and censors in the central government.[24] His appeal received a warm response from Richard, who proposed that the conference should immediately take measures to build trust between Christian missions and the Chinese government.[25] In early 1891, Reid further urged that this mission should begin "from the center" of the nation, Beijing. He warned that the mission would require persistent effort and "a number of years" to bear fruit.[26]

In 1892, Reid returned to the United States on furlough, bringing with him his agenda for a new mission and support from the Shandong Presbyterian Mission.[27] During his visit, he asked his church for permission to carry out his plan, saying that with the changing situation in China, "no ironclad policy of mission" could be possible. He requested an appropriation "for the purchase of apparatus for the lectures given to the officials and literary classes." An American newspaper, the *Utica Daily Press*, cheered his idea of turning aside from "the usual custom of preaching to the masses." If "he could interest Chinese leaders in Christianity, progress would be more rapid," it concluded.[28]

However, the leaders of the Presbyterian church declined to accept his plan because it was entirely new, and they did not think it could be successful. They directed Reid not to devote his "chief time" to the upper class. However, they suggested that he might try independently without their support. In spite of that frustration, his determination remained firm. The only choice for him was to resign from the church. On 18 June 1894, he did so, and went back to China. As MacGillivray commented on Reid's personality, "when he grasped what he regarded as the truth he went ahead perfectly regardless of consequence."[29]

Before he left the United States, Reid proclaimed the establishment of the Mission among the Higher Classes in China (MHCC) and issued the first report on it in San Francisco on 15 October 1894. The report declared that the new organization aimed to promote "a greater degree of friendliness and cordiality, of sympathetic cooperation and religious tolerance" among Chinese leaders. He also raised money for the MHCC to carry on his missionary enterprise. By the time he departed for China he had received funds from 92 persons in various American cities, including his mother — a total of $1,773.93. His mother promised to give him "one hundred a year so long as I live" because of her "sympathy for the special undertaking."[30] Because Reid had severed his connection with the Presbyterian church, the donations became his mission's only source of financial support in the following years.[31]

Once back in Beijing in the winter of 1894, Reid started his independent mission, in Housuipao near Xuanwumen.[32] He immediately put into practice his idea of working "with the Bible in one hand and the Four Books in the other."[33] In order to be accepted by the elite and officials, he wore "Chinese clothes including a queue of his own." Chinese officials seemed more open than before, so Reid thought the time was ripe to influence them.[34] He called on officials such as Prince Gong, Li Hongzhang, Weng Tonghe, Sun Jia'nai and Liu Kunyi frequently. Then no one knew who he was, so it was very difficult for him to gain interviews with them. For example, Reid called on Weng Tonghe three times and was rejected twice, because Weng felt that it was strange that Reid had requested an interview.[35] Once officials understood his intention, they were happy to have discussions with him. As a result of his efforts, Reid — "a poor foreign missionary," as he described himself — was granted the privilege of entering the Zongli yamen and presenting petitions, and even of "freely asking [for] interviews" with officials in a "friendly and informal" way.[36]

Until 14 March 1897, the MHCC was represented by Reid alone.[37] Because the new mission's methods and aims differed from those of other missionaries and organizations, Chinese officials were not alone in their suspicion that Reid harbored political ambitions. Some foreigners also doubted his real intentions. Questions, such as "What is Reid trying to do? What is his real purpose?" arose. Even his old friend Donald MacGillivray, whom Reid had met first in Ji'nan, questioned "the wisdom of his plans."[38]

Reid candidly explained his reasoning: defeat in the war with Japan had made Chinese officials eager to build friendly relations with Western countries and to seek possible advice and help from "true friends." Otherwise, they realized, China soon would "be dismembered and cease to be a nation in the world."[39] Reid was responding to this situation by building bridges between the Chinese and foreigners. Foreigners, he argued, had been provided "unexpected opportunities" to introduce into China Western education, missionary enterprise, and other elements of Christian culture, and to keep China's door wide open. He argued that his purpose was to influence "the wealthy and powerful Chinese, so that they will cooperate in measures to ameliorate the people and open up the commerce of the country." In reality, the MHCC was for the benefit of the poor.[40]

Reid's mission in Beijing proved beneficial to missionaries and all foreigners because of the good relations Reid developed with Chinese officials. When Timothy Richard came to Beijing, Reid introduced him to many of his friends in officialdom. Through his intercession Richard had discussions with Sun Jia'nai, one of the tutors of the Guangxu emperor.[41] At the request of Young J. Allen, Reid presented a copy of his book to the Zongli yamen, and three others to the emperor, Prince Gong, and the empress dowager Cixi.[42]

Reid's aim was not proselytism, which was controversial and had in fact impeded the elite's absorption of Western knowledge, but to "bring about harmony and union between the votaries of various faiths"[43] and to promote friendship and peace among the educated people, first "between the many schools of thought in this country as well as between Chinese and foreign sympathizers."[44] Thus, the MHCC was not a church, but an international and nonsectarian mission, open to all nationalities and religions. In the MHCC every religion had the right to advocate its doctrines, but none was allowed to force others to accept them. In this way, the mission could reduce obstacles "between the Chinese and foreigners, and between Christians and non-Christians," and "promote the spread of knowledge" in China.[45] The MHCC had the potential of making a great contribution to China's progress, since China needed "great moral stamina and a higher spiritual vision."

Reid chose Beijing as the location of his mission because he saw it as the center of the empire, in his words, "the hub of China." Because the mission's aim was to "break down" hostility toward the West and Christianity at the top level, its method should be to cultivate contacts with high officials, princes and ministers of the Zongli yamen and the six Boards, the tutors of the emperor, and censors. All were influential in making policy and shaping the nation's destiny. The imperial tutors, whom Reid fre-

quently visited in his efforts to persuade them to agree to his reform suggestions, would "mould the character of Kuang-hsu [Guangxu]."

Though censors were the "chief foes" of Western knowledge and Christian missions,[46] Reid emphasized the importance of maintaining firm
friendships with them, because they had the right to memorialize the emperor. If they should come to accept Reid's suggestions, they would support them in their memorials. As a result of his work, one of the censors
became very interested in Reid's paper "Minjiao xiang'an yi" (On harmony
between non-Christians and Christians) and presented it twice to the emperor. After that, more and more officials were willing to have direct contact
with Reid. What Reid hoped was not to convert them, but to make them
friends. His rationale was simple: "win the leaders of China, and China
itself is won." The main purpose, as Reid entitled one of his lectures, was
"Seeking the Best Results by Using the Best Agencies."[47]

Reid's one-man mission ended on 14 March 1897. On that day, Reid
called on W. A. P. Martin and they discussed the problems of the MHCC
and agreed to work together.[48] According to their agreement, a new name
was given to the mission — The International Institute of China — although
in the following years the old name was still in use, and both were translated
into Chinese as Shangxiantang. Thereafter, the mission grew into "an important endowed institution."[49]

As the result of Reid's efforts, the Qing court gave its official sanction to
the new institute. In the first document issued to encourage a missionary
enterprise started by a foreigner, the court expressed appreciation for Reid's
proposal to erect "an institute of learning" and highly praised his "benevolent motives." The court also promised in the coming years to "confer on
him additional tokens of approval" if the MHCC proved by its performance to be, as Reid had predicted, an organization "without any precedent,"[50] and "a new and wholly unique kind of Christian mission."[51] The
Chinese government's unprecedented action was especially impressive because it came at a time when antimissionary riots were erupting all over
China.

The MHCC had become well known in China by the end of the nineteenth century. However, its goals were "difficult" to attain. Reid clearly
understood what a hard job he had chosen and was fully aware of his "own
incapacity," but he was "ready to learn."[52]

Reid's Contributions to the Reform Movement

As Reid had perceived, the Sino-Japanese war of 1894–95 provided a
unique opportunity to promote his ideas. The retreat of the Qing troops

from Manchuria and the signing of the Shimonoseki treaty became a signal for a general carving up of China among the Western powers. After the war, the Chinese faced a crisis, and were looking eagerly for a way to rescue their country. Officials tried to explore ways to save the empire from collapsing and elites with new ideas petitioned the emperor for political, economic, and military reform. Several, including Kang Youwei, formed the Qiangxue hui (Strengthening Society), a reformist discussion society. All of them sought advice from Westerners who were sincere and ready to help China. They thought Reid was a real friend who could give the "blind" leaders "light and learning enjoyed in the West" and lead China out of "darkness."[53]

While preparing their reform ideas, Kang Youwei and Liang Qichao had several discussions with Reid in the summer of 1895. They hoped that he would take the lead in setting up an organization to spread Western learning and advocate reform because they believed that such an organization, if established by themselves, would be less influential and would be easily suppressed by the conservatives.[54] They frequently invited Reid, Richard, and W. N. Pethick, an advisor to Li Hongzhang, to dinners to win their confidence and help, and even offered Reid a room to live in, so that they could ask for his advice on reform whenever they felt it necessary.[55] However, Reid preferred to work through officials rather than literati, so he pinned his hope on the Qing court itself and waited to see what the officials would do.[56] From September 1895 to February 1896, when Richard stayed in Beijing to present the Qing court with a special statement on the mission, he participated in meetings arranged by Reid with Prince Gong, Li Hongzhang, Weng Tonghe, and other ministers. Richard discussed with them "the true aim of Christian Missions, and the requesting of religious liberty." Meanwhile he devoted himself to establishing a good relationship with Kang, Liang, and other reformers, and even invited Liang to become his secretary to assist him while he was in Beijing.[57] But his main aims were to present the statement on the mission and to build a friendship with Kang and other reformers.

Seeing Richard's willingness to give Kang and Liang his "wise counsel," Reid retreated and focused on officials in power. When, because of court suspicions, the Qiangxue hui was closed and most of its members had gone south, Richard left Beijing for England on furlough on 26 February 1896.[58] Reid now was surer than ever that only officials could push China forward, if they would accept new ideas.[59] Although Reid did not believe Kang and other reformers would succeed, he still gave his "moral support to the reform movement."[60]

Reid believed that the corruption of the Qing court and the elite's opposition to Western science were the most important causes of China's defeat in the war with Japan and the then current crisis.[61] In his interviews with Prince Gong, Weng Tonghe and Li Hongzhang, he repeated "the necessity of change" and urged them to adopt immediately "thorough reform measures." Otherwise, he averred, China would never prosper and become "consolidated."[62] Reid's advice not only attracted their attention, they applauded it. Sun Jia'nai returned his visit and had a talk with him, and Weng Tonghe "condescended his official position as Chinese prime minister to call upon Reid," just as he had called on Kang.[63]

Reid continued to carry out his enterprise with untiring vigor even when the Chinese reformers were absent from Beijing at the end of 1895. In trying to fulfill his ambition to "meet nearly all of the highest princes and officials," Reid donned Chinese dress and spoke in "excellent Chinese."[64] In order to attract their attention, he gave himself a "courtesy name," Qidong, meaning "to enlighten the Oriental." He became well acquainted personally with most "of the influential officials of the day." His increased activity from October 1895 to April 1896 is reflected in his own reports. He claims to have made the acquaintance of 150 officials of different levels and areas and contacted them 350 times. He was even busier in the ensuing six months. The number of his acquaintances rose to more than 250, and he met with them more than 468 times.[65] Through these tactics the MHCC became well known among officials. By the end of 1896 Reid was a prominent reform activist in Beijing and a prime source of advice: officials turned to him when drawing up reform plans.[66] The *North-China Daily News* commented that "this is the most telling testimony perhaps which has ever been offered to a missionary," and applauded Reid's mission as having "met with unexampled success."[67]

Reid also tried to influence the reform movement by preparing petitions and presenting them to the Chinese government. Before he left China for New York to attend his father's funeral on 19 August 1897, he published in the *Wanguo gongbao* several papers he had sent to the Zongli yamen, Prince Gong, and others urging the court to reform.

Six central points were emphasized in these papers. First, they maintained that China was going through a national crisis triggered by foreign encroachment, but originating in China itself. China had failed to keep step with the modern world, had adhered too rigidly to the established order, and had taken a stubborn stance against the introduction of Western knowledge.[68] However, there was still hope. Reid encouraged the Chinese government to follow the example of the Japanese who had developed their country along Western lines.

Second, the Sino-Japanese war provided a unique opportunity for re-form. Since the war had awakened the people, more and more local elites and officials were willing to put Western sciences into practice. The young were even more anxious to make progress. Reid also stressed the impor-tance of appointing scholars of good character as officials, regardless of their new or old approaches,[69] and of reorganizing the government by appoint-ing such scholars to carry out reform policies.

Third, the most critical task for China was not political reform but economic development. In Reid's opinion, it was not important whether China was monarchical or democratic.[70] He urged the Qing court to pay more attention to agriculture, encourage industrial development, and pro-mote trade. These policies, he said, would be the manifestation of the Chinese willingness to obey "the mandates of Heaven."

Fourth, Reid held that Chinese reformers needed to learn from the West. China had imported many Western machines and books on Western science, he said, but it was necessary to evaluate their advantages and disad-vantages. In addition, he stressed the importance of introducing qualified Western personnel into Chinese officialdom.[71]

Fifth, Reid, like the Chinese reformers, vigorously maintained that China should adopt the Western educational system and set up Western-style schools to train those who were badly needed in Chinese reform and development.[72]

Finally, Reid paid equal attention to the roles of Chinese and Western cultures. To him it seemed that both were important in reform. He felt that China should mix Chinese and Western cultures and add "new learning to old knowledge."[73]

Reid's suggestions appear to have been appreciated and encouraged by Li Hongzhang. Though Li was not confident that all of them would be adopted by the Qing court, he expressed his support for Reid's suggestions. The Zongli yamen also seems to have thought Reid's ideas worthy of high praise.[74]

Comparing Reid's reform doctrines with Kang's, the most important difference is that Reid focused on economic and educational development and Kang advocated a political transformation, an idea with which Reid did not agree. Reid thought that a parliamentary form of government could not be hurriedly set up and that the first necessity was to enlighten the peo-ple. Using the example of Western countries to buttress his argument, he pointed out that though political systems in the West might differ—some were monarchies, others were democracies or constitutional monarchies— their aims were identical: to benefit the people, rescue them from misery, encourage their morality, protect property and life, and train those who were talented.[75]

Reid's reform plan was filled with the core spirit of Confucianism, the doctrine of the mean. This was the result of his long-term mission in China. Reid insisted that foreigners could not totally ignore Chinese culture. What he as a foreigner had done was to inject Western learning into the Oriental cultural framework. Though Reid did not personally witness the launching of the Hundred Day Reform of 1898, his work influenced it.

Conclusion

As representatives of Western culture, missionaries came to China imbued with the strong spirit of Christianity. Some got involved in political activities, but on the whole, Protestant missionaries worked among the people at the bottom of society and preached the gospel to save their souls without becoming politically involved. Most showed little direct concern for China's secular development.

An early practitioner of a variety of the social gospel, Reid differed sharply from most of his colleagues in four essential respects. First, he was a pragmatic missionary who changed the methods of his mission according to the situation and was "free from preconceptions and ready to fight for truth and justice."[76] Like most other missionaries, Reid had first busied himself working among the poor after his arrival in China. After he realized the elite's hostility toward Christianity and their role in society, Reid changed his target to the upper classes. This change was closely related to his missionary experience and his understanding of Chinese traditions. It shows that if missionaries could think and act independently of their churches and do what they felt was suitable for the people, they could work in peace with them and attain their goals. N. E. B. Ezra, the editor of *Israel's Messenger*, later praised Reid's liberality, saying that Reid pointed "the way where peace and happiness may be found."[77]

Second, Reid encountered more obstacles than had Matteo Ricci and his colleagues when they worked among the upper classes; conditions in the late Ming and early Qing were very different from those in the late Qing. In the former period, Ricci and his colleagues made friends with Xu Guangqi, Li Zhizao and others on an equal footing. They not only introduced Western science, but paid due respect to the Chinese cultural heritage.[78] Neither treaty privileges nor gunboats supported them, so the elite and officials were willing, sometimes even eager, to maintain friendship with them.

After 1842 many missionaries, with their treaty rights, felt themselves as saviors of the nation. They attacked Chinese traditions at will. What is worse, they went to the interior, proselytized the natives and set up churches, and harmed the interests and wounded the pride of both the elite and the common people.[79] As a result, missionaries became devils in the eyes of the Chinese, and antimissionary riots broke out everywhere. Most of these riots were initiated and headed by the local elite. Although many of the riots were, in fact, antiforeign, foreign merchants and diplomats lived in the treaty ports and large cities, so it was easy for them to escape assault. Only the missionaries in the interior served as a target of attack. Reid clearly understood the situation and the difficulties he faced in carrying out his mission. To remove Chinese prejudice and overcome these obstacles, Reid declared that exterritoriality was a source of antiforeignism and that the dependence of missionaries on foreign political power was unwise. He proclaimed that the purpose of Christian churches was to save China "with all science and knowledge" without "giving any offence." Moreover, he declared himself a missionary rather than "a political agent."[80]

Reid also fought prejudice by paying frequent visits to Chinese officials, explaining to them the aims of his plans, and urging them "to get rid of established prejudice" and "enlighten the masses with new knowledge." With the establishment of the MHCC, he worked more for a society in which "natives and foreigners, Christians and non-Christians" might live together peacefully so that China could recuperate and grow strong. As a result of Reid's efforts, by the end of 1896 he had become someone whose advice was taken seriously by officials. They held the mission and Reid himself in great honor. The Zongli yamen issued a proclamation stating that his mission was "marked by sagacious insight" and his heart "animated by benevolent motives." Li Hongzhang admired his "bold and tireless energy" in furthering the "welfare of the people in various parts of China" and hoped that Reid would help lead the Chinese to "the bright future."[81]

Most missionaries were not aggressors but cultural intermediaries. One cannot deny that some of the Western knowledge they brought was beneficial to China. New knowledge was not a "dreadful monster." History has proved that much of what the missionaries transmitted played a positive role in Chinese society. Though not a pioneer in promoting cultural contact between Chinese and foreigners, Reid was among the first to promote contact in a way that respected Chinese culture and was congenial to the people of China.

Third, in important respects Reid differed from men like W. A. P. Martin and Timothy Richard. In the nineteenth century, some missionaries after a period of preaching in China came to realize that secular work was as important as soul saving. Reid, Martin, and Richard epitomized this belief. Their liberal theology, which, as aptly pointed out by Paul A. Cohen, was "uncommon" and "questioned" in the nineteenth century, led them to believe that flexibility would promote the development of the mission enterprise.[82] Reid and Richard proposed new mission methods to their respective churches almost simultaneously. Reid, as we have seen, suggested that the American Presbyterians in China shift their focus from the poor to the high, and Richard offered a novel educational scheme to the British Baptists.[83] When their attempts failed, both withdrew from their churches. Martin had already left the Presbyterian church in 1868. All of them held that preaching the gospel was not enough to convert the Chinese; Western science was needed as an auxiliary.

Though the three held similar opinions and were actively involved in secular activities, their choices after breaking with their churches were different. Martin devoted himself to education and translation. After 1864, most of his publications were scientific.[84] Richard, believing that "the written word could reach more people," became a prominent figure in Christian literary publication.[85] Reid's most distinctive characteristic, of course, was the great stress he placed on building friendly relations with the local elite and high officials and enlightening them with Western knowledge. The result, as Robert Hart pointed out, was that Reid "got hold of some Han Lin and interested them in foreign matters to the extent of desiring to learn and use — this will gradually create a 'public opinion' in the literate class which will be an ally, instead of an enemy, of the officials who desire to introduce reforms."[86] Although Martin and Richard, like Reid, sought to reach the upper class, Reid did so through personal contact and the other two worked mainly through literature.

Fourth, Reid loved China and was a friend of the Chinese. As discussed above, he set forth plans to help China at a time of crisis, and "time and again with good intentions" tried "to awaken benighted Qing officials" to the need for reform.[87] A skeptic might contend that Reid was disingenuous, or that he must have had an ulterior motive. But such an argument would be simplistic, based only on the fact that Reid was a foreigner. It is well to remember that at that time all of the powers wanted a piece of the Chinese territory. Thus, if Reid were supporting foreign interests he should have thrown himself into the struggle for partition. But he did not. Instead he asked the Qing court to "clear all age-old abuses" and "to adopt new policies" in order to save China.[88] Thus Lü Haihuan, then Chinese minister to Germany, praised Reid as a "self-restrained" and "gradually Confucianized" missionary, and Liang Qichao pointed out, "He loves our Chinese people deeply."[89]

Reid's Western education, coupled with his respect for China, led him to adopt new methods to carry out his mission. His judgment on Chinese culture and the road China should take differed from those of the Chinese local elite. He meant well in his severe criticism of Chinese laws and corruption among officialdom. Indeed much of what he asserted was true. When the reform movement broke out, he was excited and took an active part in it. Kang Youwei and Reid differed, of course, but the difference was mainly one of method. Kang presented his petitions to the emperor. Reid submitted his to the princes and state ministers. Both shared the same hope: they wished China to be independent, prosperous, and progressive.

CHAPTER 6

The Politics of Evangelism at the End of the Qing: Nanchang, 1906

ERNEST P. YOUNG

This is a tale of missionary and mandarin. It is an occasion to reflect on the way the missionary movement and Chinese society were reacting to each other at the beginning of the twentieth century.

Late in the afternoon of 22 February 1906, in the residence of the head of the Catholic mission in Nanchang, the magistrate of Nanchang County was found with his throat cut. His name was Jiang Zhaotang. He had come to the Catholic mission by invitation to dine and to discuss some outstanding issues between the Catholic mission and Chinese officials of Jiangxi Province, of which Nanchang was the capital city. He would die a week later.

Murder or Suicide at the Catholic Mission?

The question of whose hands cut Jiang Zhaotang's throat remains contended.[1] In this respect, the affair has the aspect of a detective story that still lacks its final chapter.

Magistrate Jiang, 56 years old in February 1906, was an experienced official, who, after an earlier career in the salt business, served seventeen years as county magistrate in several postings.[2] He had arrived at mission headquarters, inside the Nanchang city walls, at three in the afternoon. He was accompanied by two servants. His host was Jean-Marie Lacruche, a French Lazarist priest, age 35 and almost ten years in China, who had recently been appointed head of the Catholic mission in Nanchang by his bishop.

Unaccountably, Lacruche prevented Jiang's servants from following

Jiang into missionary quarters. They were therefore not direct witnesses to the subsequent crucial events. This incriminating detail, suggesting malice aforethought and always mentioned in Chinese accounts, was not denied in the mission's own rendition.[3]

After the meal, attention turned to current negotiations over two disputed legal cases involving Chinese Catholics: one dating from 1901 at Chigang and the other from 1904 at Tangpu. Chigang and Tangpu were market towns in rural Jiangxi. Heated arguments produced no agreements. Jiang then went to the room of Lacruche's Chinese secretary (Liu Zong-yao), ostensibly to draft some proposals for settlement but perhaps to escape from Lacruche's hectoring. After some minutes, in the mission's version of the event, he called in the Chinese secretary to hear an explanation of the proposals and to carry the draft to Lacruche. Then, at about 5:30 P.M., Jiang went outside to instruct one of his two servants to fetch the second county magistrate of the city (which was divided between two counties, Nanchang and Xinjian). The servant later testified that Jiang told him to summon this magistrate, with whom Jiang apparently had a subsequent engagement, because "I am prevented by Wang [Lacruche] from leaving."[4]

The see of Lacruche's bishop, Paul-Léon Ferrant, was in the Yangzi river port of Jiujiang, some 120 kilometers distant from Nanchang. In the bishop's reconstruction of the incident, based on what Lacruche conveyed by telegram and told his missionary colleagues in Nanchang, Jiang Zhao-tang, having refused tea, was alone in the Chinese secretary's room with the door shut, when moaning was heard by a servant of the mission. Through the glass window in the door, the servant saw Jiang lying on a chaise longue with blood streaming from his neck. Jiang was allegedly attempting to enlarge the wound. Informed, Lacruche took one look and set off to report the event to the provincial governor.[5]

The testimony of Jiang's attendants was that Lacruche's hurried departure from the mission only slightly preceded the arrival of the previously summoned Xinjian County magistrate. The Xinjian magistrate was allowed into the mission and found Jiang in the chair with his throat cut, but alive. The mission's secretary, Liu Zongyao, told the magistrate that Jiang had done the deed himself with scissors, but did not produce the weapon.[6] Before Lacruche returned from the governor's yamen, the Xinjian magistrate was joined at the mission by members of Jiang's family and by the salt daotai and Nanchang's prefect, officials intermediate in authority between county magistrate Jiang and the governor.

How were the Chinese officials to interpret this bizarre scene? The obvious answer was to ask Jiang Zhaotang himself, who was unable to speak but could write. That night and over the next days, Jiang wrote messages to several people, including these and other officials, his family, and the missionaries.

Instead of bringing immediate clarity to the situation, his many notes only served to deepen the mystery. Some were illegible, drenched in blood. The chief problem was that the remainder, when compared, were contradictory, frequently charging Lacruche with assaulting him and cutting his throat, but sometimes seeming to confess suicide. In yet other notes he combined the two possibilities, writing of an initial cut with a knife by himself, which was followed by an attempt by others to finish him off with scissors.[7] These are some of Jiang's notes: To his son:

Wang Anzhi [Lacruche] pressed me to release the criminals in the Chigang case, to pay 100,000 taels compensation in the Tangpu case, and to punish the three [accused members of the] Gong [family]. He pressed me to draw up an agreement and sign it. I would not consent. He threatened me many times. I was stabbed in the neck three times with a knife and a pair of scissors. When I die, please take this written statement and petition the high officials to redress my wrongs.[8]

To the missionaries:

I only entreat that the priest settle leniently and promptly. With my life I pay for the lives of several of the offenders. With the affair closed, religion could again be propagated. The Gong family are not savages. If I die, as [Lacruche] said before, the case will be considered settled. I won't be able to pursue [the Catholics prematurely released from prison in the Chigang case] nor to commit a slip of the tongue [probably a reference to his promise not to execute any of the Gongs of Tangpu]. I die without resentment. I cast no blame for pressing this old man to die. It is in order to save the people. In future evangelism, the important thing is that the people and the Christians are mutually peaceful. They must not be headstrong. The common people of Jiangxi are good. It is not a land of rabble. I look upon my death as a requiting, simply out of love for the people.[9]

To the prefect:

My throat has three wounds. First I was forced into a secret room. There was a sharp knife for smoking cigars. I noticed a knife of foreign pattern on the table, used in connection with smoking. Later, he pressed me immediately to release the criminal convert Deng Guihe [of the Chigang case]. We got into an argument, and it looked as if he intended to use force. I then went into Mr. Liu's room to discuss the matter. [Liu] is also crafty. I forthwith set to writing. I was under pressure to take up the knife on the table and cut my throat. Owing to the pain I did not dare make another cut. I saw someone take a pair of scissors and stab my throat twice, and there were also two people who held my hands.[10]

Jiang's conflicting notes were not the only confusing elements in the incident. Neither knife nor scissors were ever discovered, or if discovered, they were not presented to the investigating Chinese authorities. Lacruche refused to allow the mission's Chinese secretary or the servants to be questioned outside of the mission. Therefore, aside from remarks made by the mission staff in the immediate aftermath of Jiang's wounding, their testimony was not recorded until weeks later. Lacruche and Jiang were the only people testifying.[11] Both were soon dead.

Opinion about responsibility for Magistrate Jiang's mortal wounds varied. After some initial wavering among the British and the Americans, foreigners generally concluded that Jiang had done himself in. Despite allegations to the contrary both then and subsequently, examinations of the corpse by British, American, and French doctors tended to confirm the verdict of suicide.[12] The French legation became most anxious that Chinese authorities publicly endorse this view. Although attended by some ambiguity, the official Chinese coroner's report held that the death was not self-inflicted.[13] Much of the Chinese press reflected the widely held view that Jiang had simply been assaulted by the mission.

This was also the immediate popular reaction in Nanchang in the aftermath of the discovery of Jiang's wounds. We may take as the common understanding of the affair the version heard by Protestant missionaries from their Chinese parishioners. It went like this. During negotiations at the Catholic mission, the French priest insisted that Magistrate Jiang sign a dictated agreement about old cases. In a rage at the magistrate's refusal, the priest said that if Jiang were dead, the cases could be settled. As Jiang was trying to escape, the priest cut the magistrate's neck and then attacked him further with shears. The priest went off to the governor's yamen and attempted to portray the affair as a matter of attempted suicide. Meanwhile, lying in a pool of blood and using gesture and writing brush, in the presence of the prefect and members of Jiang's family, Jiang charged the priest with the crime.[14] This was an undoubted popular sensation. The subsequent official refrain that the people's feelings were uncontainable does not seem far-fetched.[15]

Common to all Chinese views was the judgment that Lacruche had been overbearing and high-handed in his negotiation with Jiang. (Bishop Ferrant himself wrote, approvingly, of Lacruche's "cold tenacity in upholding our rights."[16]) Therefore, whether or not Jiang had actually attempted suicide, the responsibility in any case was Lacruche's. If Lacruche had not tried to murder Jiang, then he had driven the magistrate to suicide.[17]

The Assault on the Missions

Nanchang seethed with the news of the dire wounding of the county magistrate. It was not inevitable, however, that the emotions would find forceful expression. The authorities wished to keep the lid on, and they were not without resources. This was, after all, the capital city of a rather prosperous province. The only resident foreigners were the missionaries. The Jiangxi governor, Hu Tinggan, set about protecting them.

Governor Hu had at hand in Nanchang 400 police, 1,500 New Army troops, and 1,000 old-style troops who had undergone retraining.[18] Contingents were stationed at the fourteen Catholic and Protestant mission establishments, and the streets were patrolled. The governor also had proclamations posted, urging the populace to stay calm while officials investigated the matter. By nineteenth-century standards, and in accordance with treaty requirements for guarding against antimissionary outbreaks, Jiangxi's officials were prudent and effective.

The occasion for a breach in public order was constructed, not by secret societies or xenophobic nativists, typical nineteenth-century perpetrators of antiforeign violence, but by the proponents of nationalism and the acolytes of modernization. By 1906 the educated classes of Jiangxi, as in most parts of the country, had begun to participate with patriotic enthusiasm in the Westernizing reform programs of the Qing dynasty's last years. The alleged assault on Jiang Zhaotang was not, in the view of the new nationalists, a moral violation of the sacred person of a "father-and-mother official" (*fumu guan*). It was rather a challenge to the Chinese nation, a derogation of sovereignty. On these grounds, students of the new schools sponsored a mass meeting.

On 24 February, two days after Jiang's wounding, Nanchang was blanketed with a leaflet calling for a meeting the next morning (Sunday) to "deliberate civilized means of resistance to redeem the country's authority," in response to the stabbing of the Nanchang County magistrate by a Frenchman of the Catholic church. The gathering place: the large memorial temple to Shen Baozhen in the ample Baihuazhou grounds near the center of the city, a favored social center for the town's elite. As governor of Jiangxi in the 1860s, Shen Baozhen had resisted the infliction of any retribution on leaders of an antimissionary action in Nanchang and came to despise the French policy of Catholic protection.[19] That he was also credited with saving Nanchang from the Taipings, Christian rebels, was powerful symbolism in the context of the moment. The invitation was addressed to people of all social classes, who were enjoined to avoid any "insurrection" as prejudicial to the overall situation. The call was issued in the name of "all students of Jiangxi," had been composed at one of Nanchang's new colleges, and had been printed up at the local newspaper, the *Jiangbao*.[20]

A reminiscence many years later claimed that the meeting was a project of the local branch of the Tongmenghui, the national revolutionary party organized the previous August in Tokyo.[21] Whether or not that was so, the announcement lacked revolutionary or inflammatory overtones, beyond the flat assertion of French responsibility for Jiang's wounds. Its posture was dignified resentment at foreign insult. It called for a nonviolent resolution. Its very modernity and reasonableness lent the proposed event some immunity from official repression.

The governor, Hu Tinggan, was uncertain how to respond. Rather than use force to prevent the meeting, he summoned leading gentry to his yamen in the late evening of February 24. They included two leaders in the provincial railway company, a project drawing on the patriotic and reformist mood of the time. The governor asked them to go to the place of the gathering and call on the people to disperse.[22] The gentry went, but their efforts turned out to be quite inadequate to the occasion.

Despite inclement weather, thousands showed up for the meeting.[23] The 700 students in attendance were vastly outnumbered and apparently intimidated by the common folk who joined in. Advocates of restraint addressed the throng, as the governor had arranged, but were shouted down by the call for revenge. The outcome was a large contingent setting out in a violent frame of mind. There was a rush to the kerosene shops and a march from the city center to the main Catholic establishment (Laogong-yuan), about a mile away to the southeast.[24]

The gathering of a critical mass of people bent on revenge, which the police and soldiers had hitherto successfully prevented, had formed under the umbrella of student nationalism. It was presumably shared nationalist feelings that had induced the officials and gentry of the city to permit the mass meeting.

Lacruche, like all other missionaries in Nanchang, was aware of the student-called meeting Sunday morning. He had decided that the Catholic missionaries should continue their routines and rely on the protection of the Chinese authorities. He had been assured by his bishop and through him by the French minister in Beijing that protection had been requested at the highest levels. In a message to the sisters at the hospital and orphanage in the suburbs to the south of the city, Lacruche instructed them not to go out until further orders, but that they should stay calm: "You will be protected. Monsignor cabled me yesterday that the French authorities are extremely busy on our behalf."[25] Although the Chinese faithful coming to Sunday offices advised that all missionaries should seek out safe refuge, Lacruche agreed only to advance mass one hour and dispense with the sermon.[26] An exaggerated notion of the power of France seems to have overcome his usual distrust of Chinese officialdom.

When it reached the mission, the huge crowd overwhelmed the military guard, discovered Lacruche, and tracked him through the streets of Nanchang as he fled a rain of blows. His efforts at finding refuge failed, and he succumbed after a long chase of an hour or two. The mission buildings at Laogongyuan were set ablaze. Nearby was the French College, a Catholic missionary project, where resided five Marist teaching brothers. They were warned by the sight of flames at the main mission compound and fled the city. The pursuing crowd cornered them in a pond beyond the city walls and stoned them until all five had died. A British family of Plymouth Brethren missionaries, the Kinghams, lived hard by the French College. Challenged by the marauders, Harry and Octavia Kingham strenuously denied any connection with the Catholic mission or the French, but to no avail. Both were beaten to death. Their elder daughter, seven years old, was so severely injured that she died that night. Nine foreigners had been killed or fatally injured within a few hours amidst the rain and sleet of 25 February in Nanchang. All Catholic mission buildings were burned, as was the Plymouth Brethren compound.

The other missionaries in town, some 35 including families, survived for various reasons. The largest Protestant mission in town was that of the American Methodist Episcopal Church. Its residences were mostly located in the northern part of the city and in the northern suburbs, far from Catholic headquarters, the crowd's primary target. Distance helped, and no large assembly challenged the official contingents protecting the Methodists. Proximity to military barracks also helped; when some of the pursuers of the Marist brothers south of the walled city began to show a hostile interest in the compound of the China Inland Mission, a fresh supply of soldiers was close at hand. Others, warned in time by news of the early attacks, found safety at various secure points in and around the city — military barracks, police stations, the mint, official yamen, jails, and the like. These refugees included five Catholic nuns from the hospital and orphanage, which were nonetheless burned down. Late the same night, the surviving foreigners were officially escorted to boats, and all, with the exception of one Methodist, took the governor's steamer to Jiujiang.

Measured by numbers of foreigners killed in one incident, the Nanchang affair of 1906 was one of the largest of the many outbreaks of violence against missionaries in the period after the establishment of the treaty system in the mid-nineteenth century. It also marked a transition. It bore many resemblances to *jiaoan* ("religious cases," incidents involving missionaries or Chinese Christians that became legal and diplomatic issues) of previous decades. Yet it also contained in it auguries of changes in the Chinese reception of Christian evangelism, and possibly stimulated change in foreign handling of local sectarian conflict in China.

I wish to use the incident to bring attention to the institutional setting of Catholic missionary enterprise and its consequences. I shall stress three themes. One is precisely the Catholic difference: how the institutional and policy setting of the Catholic missionary movement had special features and how these features affected, not just Catholic relations with Chinese society and authority, but general missionary relations. The second is the development of Chinese responses to the Christian foothold in China in the early twentieth century: how, amidst continuities, there had already emerged new themes, especially nationalism, which had begun to change the character of Chinese approaches to issues arising from missionary activity and Chinese conversion. The third is the way in which the treaty system and French policy within that system exacerbated tensions in Chinese society arising from Christian evangelism.

The Catholic Church in China and the Nanchang Mission

Contrary to most first assumptions, the Catholic church in late Qing China was seriously deficient in organizational coherence. It is true that the many missionary dioceses, or vicariates (about 40 at the turn of the century), were directly beholden to the Vatican. Yet Rome's authority was diluted, not only by distance, but more importantly by the interposition of the various religious orders and missionary societies that actually ran the vicariates. The supply of missionaries and, for practical purposes, the selection of the heads of the vicariates (the vicars apostolic, who bore episcopal dignity) rested with the order or society. The result was that a vicar apostolic, theoretically inferior to a full bishop in autonomy, was often able to ignore direction from his superiors, as he maneuvered between his religious order and the Sacred Congregation for the Propagation of the Faith in Rome.

Furthermore, there was no ecclesiastical authority in China empowered to coordinate policy among the vicariates. Despite the wishes of the late-nineteenth-century pope, Leo XIII, there was no papal representative in Beijing. Moreover, there was no hierarchy of prelates and no country-wide synod until the 1920s. The Catholic missionary effort in China around the turn of the century resembled more closely the anarchy of Protestant evangelism than one might imagine. Actually, all-China conferences of Protestants began almost half a century before their Catholic equivalent.

These structural features of Catholic organization in China greatly enhanced the role of the French government. From the middle of the nineteenth century, France claimed to protect all Catholics in China of whatever nationality, including Chinese. French authorities called this function their Religious Protectorate and based its legal authority on France's treaties and other agreements with the Qing government.[27] One of the effects, by no means unintended by the French government, was that its consular establishment provided the only organizational unity the Catholic church enjoyed in China.[28] From these circumstances, there arose a special closeness between Catholic missionary and French consul.

French diplomats strove to avoid becoming partisans in purely local disputes between Catholic and non-Catholic Chinese, but often unsuccessfully. Because missionaries regularly represented the interests of their flock to secular authority, French officials were vulnerable to being drawn in. They felt compelled to retain the missionaries' good regard. Ever sensitive to its inferior trading position in China, France saw the Religious Protectorate as its primary resource in keeping up with Britain, as well as with Germany and the United States. Hence, the logic of the situation inclined French diplomats to take up the Catholic side in any dispute, whatever the merits.

Moreover, the pretension to the protection of *all* Catholics in China, irrespective of nationality, ultimately depended on continually proving to concerned Catholics the value of French protection. The French based their claim on treaties and other agreements with the Qing government, not on any grant of powers from Catholic authority. Yet it was obvious that the perpetuation of the pan-national protectorate depended on the compliance of both missions and pope. The Paris government expended quite extraordinary diplomatic energy in keeping everyone in line. It was also crucial, however, that France appear to be serving each and every Catholic interest in China—better, say, than could Italy, Germany, or Belgium, not to mention Austria, Portugal, Spain, or the Vatican itself. The result could scarcely be anything but an orgy of intervention, heightening the tension surrounding the Christian fraction in China.

The French authorities in China permitted the Catholic clergy to negotiate local issues with Chinese officials. The practice had been reinforced by an imperial decree of 1899 that granted Catholic prelates official rank and endorsed direct dealings between ecclesiastical and imperial authorities. The results were subject to approval by the French legation, and in any case, difficult or stalemated disputes would soon reach formal diplomatic process. Commonly, French diplomats were called upon to lend their influence to the Catholic side in a negotiation still underway at the local level, such as happened in Nanchang in 1906.

The Catholic heritage in Jiangxi Province was venerable, if thin. Matteo Ricci, the renowned Jesuit missionary, founded the Catholic mission there during his residence in Nanchang at the end of the sixteenth century. But it was Lazarists (known as Vincentians in the U.S.), not Jesuits, who were in charge when the effort was made to revitalize Catholic missions in Jiangxi during the middle decades of the nineteenth century. After the new treaty system was in place, from 1860, Catholic work in Jiangxi began to grow significantly. Yet in Nanchang, the provincial capital but not a treaty port, there was successful resistance to early missionary attempts to set up shop. A Catholic missionary presence was reasserted in Nanchang only in 1898, amidst the "scramble for concessions." Property acquisitions favorable to the Jiangxi mission were secured only after escalating French pressure on Chinese authorities.[29] Although by this time missionary residence was common enough throughout most of the empire, the freshness of the missionary presence in Nanchang and the coincidence of the breakthrough with a barrage of foreign threats to China's "territorial integrity" are relevant history to events of the next decade in Jiangxi.

Under the leadership of Bishop Paul-Léon Ferrant, coadjutor and then vicar apostolic of the North Jiangxi vicariate, special effort was devoted from 1898 to building up the Nanchang mission. In addition to priestly residences, an orphanage, and schools for religious training, there were soon other institutions: a small hospital, a medical dispensary, a French college, and a vocational school. When the incident occurred in 1906, there were fourteen French men and women attached to these various mission works at Nanchang.

Turn-of-the-century Intensification of Sectarian Conflict

Near the turn of the century, conflict in several regions of China around the Christian presence intensified dramatically.[30] Conspicuous instances were the rash of attacks on Christians in Central China in 1891, the violent episodes in the late 1890s in and around Chengdu and Chongqing in Sichuan, and the Boxer affair of 1899 and 1900. Of the provinces supposedly removed from the effects of the Boxer affair by the "neutralization" agreements between provincial officials and foreign consuls, Jiangxi experienced the most widespread anti-Christian attacks during the summer of 1900. In retribution about 40 Jiangxi officials were later dismissed or demoted, and a large indemnity was exacted.[31] The experience left feelings raw in many Jiangxi communities.

I suggest we might attribute this intensification of conflict surrounding Christians in Jiangxi, as well as in China generally, to three developments around the end of the century: (1) the accelerated expansion of evangelical enterprise, especially marked from the 1890s, thereby introducing many previously untouched communities to the problems of adjustment; (2) the gradual spread of nationalist attitudes among Chinese, with the result that a principled political objection to foreign encroachments combined with older communitarian resentments at the local effects of missions; and (3) heightened rivalry among the imperialist powers, intersecting with antagonism between Catholics and Protestants at the local level. The denominational antagonism exacerbated and was reinforced by the national rivalries.

Let us elaborate these new factors, as they bear on the background to the Nanchang incident.

The growth of missionary enterprise in China in the late nineteenth and early twentieth century has often been described.[32] The Catholic effort in Jiangxi was no exception to this expansion. A foreign missionary complement of 6 in 1870 had become 42 by 1894; it was 102 in 1905, including priests, sisters, and teaching brothers. (Chinese clerics and sisters in the Jiangxi Catholic church proliferated less rapidly: 10 in 1870, 17 in 1894, and 37 in 1905.) Chinese Catholics in Jiangxi were counted by the mission as 9,000 in 1870, 20,000 in 1894, and 32,000 in 1905. The figures may not be accurate in detail, but in any case, the impact on Jiangxi society of this expansion is not so much in the numbers, which remained a very small, if increasing, proportion of the population. Rather, the effect was in the wide distribution. The number of churches, chapels, and oratories rose from 34 in 1870 to 329 in 1905. The mission claimed that evangelical or pastoral visits in 1904 and 1905 reached 724 different Jiangxi communities.[33] Insofar as a Christian or a missionary presence was a potential source of local conflict, the opportunity for mischief was spread broadly over the province.

A second feature tending to intensify, and perhaps redirect, conflict over Christian evangelism was Chinese nationalism. The increased currency of nationalism in the early years of the twentieth century is well established. The manner in which this new nationalism intersected with sectarian issues is illustrated by a revolutionary essay distributed at the beginning of 1904 in

Nanchang and other parts of the province.[34] It is entitled "A Lament for Jiangxi," and speaks emotionally of imminent appropriation of the province by Britain. Foreign occupation lies yet in the future, but the way is being prepared by steamer and railway, and by suborning Qing officialdom. An illustration of the latter is the *jiaoan*:

> Should we look to the local officials to devise plans for protecting Jiangxi? To the evils of other days the local officials add other and greater evils. These local officials . . . are accustomed to submit to the desire of foreigners to poison our brethren. If a missionary case occurs, the simple nonconvert suffers, even to the extent of gentry and elders being put to death. Even though a convert of the worst character does the vilest acts, and gets involved in a serious case, he need only forge a foreign letter, a foreigner's visiting card, and he is extricated from all trouble.

For this nationalist author, then, missionaries and Christian conversion had become an aspect of the foreign march of conquest. The British consul who collected and translated the text noted how different it was from the anti-Christian tracts accompanying the 1891 attacks, which were marked, in the consul's view, by obscenities and appeals to superstitious fanaticism.[35] Insofar as the Nanchang incident of 1906 partly partook of the new ideas of nationalism, it would also be different from the riots of 1891. Though its shape was the classic *jiaoan*, its content was more complicated.

The third of the hypothesized causes of increased sectarian conflict by the turn of the century was heightened imperialist rivalry and sectarian antagonism. The effects of the scramble for concessions and the jockeying for spheres of influence included the way they played out among the missions. Put simply — and it was often enough put just this way at the time — Catholics (whether foreign or Chinese) were surrogates for French power in China. Protestants were surrogates for British (or American) power. In the minds of rivalrous foreigners, Catholic success was thought to presage superior French influence in any particular part of China and to block British ambitions. Similarly, French prestige and power with the court in Beijing or with any provincial yamen would enhance the chances for a Catholic, rather than Protestant, evangelization of the Chinese. The fit was far from exact, and all named parties would have formally rejected the equation. Reflections of this imagined struggle, however, permeate the documents of the period.

Once the rivalry was in the open, it absorbed contentiousness from Chinese society and was thereby cranked another notch higher. Local frays among Chinese were transformed into a larger Christian sectarian game, or even into irritants in Franco-British relations. The tenor of Sino-foreign relations was further soured. These reifications, in turn, sharpened the local fray.

In other words, the business of protecting Christians in a period of imperialist rivalries produced a chain of reinforcing interactions from village China to Beijing and back again. The local disputes could have the most diverse origins, but might then be translated into sectarian terms, including those of Catholic versus Protestant, sometimes by the instant conversion of one or both sides in the dispute. By the agency of missionaries, a consul might be called upon to support one side in its appeal for Chinese government action or in its effort to nullify an adverse judgment by Chinese officials. If both sides were or became different varieties of Christian, then there was the possibility of the involvement of consuls of different nationalities and of their ministers in Beijing, who would compete to influence Chinese official action. Even when consular intervention was not competitive, it tended to heighten the degree of tension and conflict at the lower levels by raising the stakes: the prospect of indemnities, harsh punishments, public humiliations, and the dismissal of officials. In other words, as an issue traveled up and down the ladder of interactions, it tended to grow in weight and to accumulate ancillary aggravating features.

Protestant missionaries and their protectors commonly charged Catholic missionaries and their French protectors with an excess of secular assertiveness. Yet it was a style that the competitive climate invited in all the protected churches. The case of the American Methodist Episcopal mission in Jiangxi illustrates this point and, as we shall see, is relevant to the Nanchang incident in 1906.

Around the turn of the century, the Methodists in Jiangxi were in an expansive phase, especially in the area of Nanchang. By 1902, they were reporting a total of over 9,000 adherents in the province, albeit with different degrees of absorption into the church.[36] The bishop for the denomination in China was delighted and gave much of the credit to Rev. Don W. Nichols at Nanchang, who was, in the bishop's words in 1901, "the one supremely successful evangelistic worker in the Mission."[37]

Suspicions within the Methodist mission of questionable methods, however, led to two internal commissions of investigation, reporting in 1902 and 1903. The commissions found that pastors and other members of the church had raised money in various unseemly ways: by assisting Chinese who sought legal and other assistance before Chinese officials; by acting as mediators between disputants, whether or not they were church members; and by charging for enrolling members into the church according to ability to pay. The investigators judged the results to be that "the law resisting element of the country" had been recruited into the Methodist church in Jiangxi "by the thousand," and that a great deal of the property held by the church had been purchased with funds raised by these unworthy means.[38] After the internal shake-up ensuing from these investigations, Methodist adherents in Jiangxi were reported as dropping to 1,866, about a fifth of the previous year.[39]

The circumstance that had led to this scandal in the Methodist Episcopal mission in Jiangxi was the combination of virulent anti-Catholicism among Protestant missionaries and the usefulness to Chinese of a citadel against both Chinese officials and Catholic assertiveness. The letters and reports of the Methodist missionaries were punctuated by references to violent Catholic attacks on parishioners or Chinese pastors and to the avaricious and predatory manner of the Catholic missions. The second Methodist commission cited as first cause of the misuse of church membership, including its sale, "the conditions brought about by Roman Catholic oppression and persecution of the people, and wide spread official corruption. . . . [People] hoped to find in the Protestant Church a power that would counter-balance the power of the Catholic Church."[40]

Nichols's response to perceived Catholic aggressiveness had been to adopt, and permit his Chinese co-workers to adopt, the very methods that, in his view, condemned Catholic evangelism. While charging the Catholics with "constantly robbing the government and maltreating the people," he actually boasted of directly lobbying the provincial governor on behalf of his own Chinese charges.[41] French consular officials reported him to be "a man of action, very energetic, with few scruples," who tried to protect the "guilty" from their proper punishments.[42] Though an extreme case, Nichols was not unique among Protestants in his preoccupations.

Just as vehemently, Catholic missionaries denounced the wicked methods of Protestant evangelists. The bishop of East Jiangxi charged in 1901: "The ease with which [Protestant missionaries] admit without distinction all who present themselves, the zeal of some warmly to patronize their followers before the authorities of the country, even in unjust cases, maintains or creates constant agitation within the population. Decent families are unjustly levied. On occasion one comes to us, evincing the desire of embracing Catholicism to free themselves from the exactions of self-styled Protestants."[43]

From Taizhou in neighboring Zhejiang came this report in 1903: "The ruins that the Protestants and the pirates had heaped up in the Christian [that is, Catholic] communities have been cleared away. The pirates have since left us in peace; it is only the Protestants who do not lay down their arms."[44]

All this mattered because the missionaries on both sides had recourse to the treaty structure and consular backstopping. Behind the sensational events in Nanchang in 1906 were previous incidents that arose from these currents.

The Disputes at Issue in the Nanchang Affair

When Jiang Zhaotang, county magistrate for Nanchang, dined at the headquarters of the city's Catholic mission on 22 February 1906 — and was found with his throat cut — the ostensible purpose of the visit was further negotiations with Father Lacruche about two *jiaoan* whose disposition displeased the mission. One had occurred in 1901, at Chigang, a market town about 20 kilometers southeast of Nanchang City, but within the county. The other occurred in 1904, at the market town of Tangpu in Xinchang County, about 115 kilometers west of Nanchang.

Chigang had both Catholic and American Methodist outstations without resident clergy, as extensions of the respective Nanchang missions. In the summer of 1901, the area was agitated by lingering charges from Catholics regarding unpunished ringleaders of anti-Catholic violence the previous summer, some of whom were receiving Protestant protection. Indemnities had been paid, and resentment about their exaction and distribution also seems to have been part of the aura of bad feeling in the area.

Against this background and during severe flooding, violence broke out between groups largely but not exclusively defined by the two Christian camps in the town. One supposes that the groupings had deeper roots in the social history of the town, but the point is that the divisiveness acquired new implications when translated into sectarian struggle. The affair started on 2 July 1901, over Catholic non-payment for a short ride on a Protestant ferry, put temporarily in service when the local bridge was washed away by flood. In compensation, the ferryman grabbed some beancurd cakes from the freeloader, and one thing led to another. Coreligionists were recruited into the fray. Mediation by a local gentry failed. On 3 July a force of one hundred Methodists trashed some fifteen Catholic shops, though the county magistrate later reported that no severe damage was done them. The next day, over two hundred avengers, mostly Catholic, lured a band of battle-ready Protestants and their allies into an ambush. In the ensuing fighting, twelve died, some by drowning. None of the fatalities was Catholic and six were Methodists. To celebrate the victory, various non-Catholic shops (nine Protestant, two unaffiliated) were sacked and the Methodist chapel defaced.[45]

The subsequent adjudication of the incident proved contentious. In succession, a French and a British consul arrived in the area by gunboat. The Catholic mission in Nanchang provided temporary refuge for at least one of the leaders of the 4 July clash. Eventually a number of people were sentenced to terms varying from two years to life imprisonment. About three years later, however, the Nanchang County magistrate, who by this time was the ill-starred Jiang Zhaotang, was ordered to release all but the lifers. About a year after that, in December 1905 or January 1906, a new provincial judge, Yu Zhaokang, apprised of the irregular release, ordered Jiang to re-arrest two men (Catholics) whose sentences even then had not expired.[46]

These confusing events masked a choice piece of intrigue, in which Chinese bureaucratic politics and *jiaoan* were intertwined. It so happened that the Jiangxi provincial treasurer from 1903, Zhou Hao, was related by marriage to a former prefect who had been sacked over a quite different incident involving Catholics. According to a later Chinese investigation, Zhou or his agents made a deal with the French bishop of North Jiangxi whereby the bishop would support the former prefect's rehabilitation in return for release of some Chinese Catholics imprisoned in the Chigang affair.[47]

Jiang Zhaotang, as Nanchang County magistrate, was caught in the ricochets of this intrigue. He first had been ordered to breach the law to the private purpose of the provincial treasurer. Then, with the arrival of a new provincial judge, as we have noted, he was told to reverse himself and thereby cross the Catholics. In the latter task, he had to overcome Lacruche's refusal to countenance the renewed jailing of the released men.

Jean-Marie Lacruche had become head of the Nanchang mission only a few months before this effort to reincarcerate the Chigang perpetrators.[48] His path had crossed earlier, however, with that of Jiang Zhaotang. They were both deeply involved in the Tangpu incident of spring and summer 1904.

Tangpu, about 25 kilometers from the Xinchang County seat, in Ruizhou Prefecture, was a market town. It was in the district with which Lacruche was charged at the time. On 19 May 1904, two Chinese lay Catholics attempted to open a chapel there, in a town marked since 1900 by turbulence around the Catholic presence. They were beaten and drowned. Their bodies were never found. This act began more than two months of insurrection in Tangpu against all external authority. During this period, Catholics were attacked in various parts of Xinchang County as well as in several neighboring counties.

Whence the severity of the reaction to the attempted Catholic evangelism in Tangpu? The 1917 Xinchang County gazetteer attributes it to the resentment built up around the abuse of missionary protection by the ne'er-do-wells and bullies who responded to Catholic evangelism after 1900.[49] Basing themselves on memories collected a half-century later, some Chinese historians assert that one of the murdered catechists had raped or "insulted" a woman of the town.[50] The Catholic bishop, in his report at the time to French consular authorities, described the men as "worthy, peaceful," prudently brought in from another place for the purpose of reopening the chapel and replacing its signboard.[51] All accounts agree on the existence of festering antagonisms in Tangpu during the previous four years.

The catechists had made their move in Tangpu at market time. Young stalwarts of the locally prominent Gong family were out in force. They were led by Gong Dong, who was known as a fighter and was encouraged by the townsfolk. After the first murders, according to the account in the county gazetteer, the remaining Catholics fled during the night. Secret society elements (Hongjiang hui) were soon taking advantage of the opportunities offered by this contretemps.[52]

An interesting complexity is added by the report of a local British missionary who was neither Catholic nor Methodist. He reported to his consul that the leader of the outburst, Gong Dong, was a former deacon in the American Methodist Episcopal Church. He had been one of Rev. Don W. Nichols's men and had been responsible for 2,000 conversions. From these conversions, Gong Dong had raised $3,000. When his achievements were disavowed and he himself dismissed (in the wake of the Methodist inquiries previously discussed), he established a Chinese Protestant church of his own, which was the core of the Tangpu movement against Catholics in 1904.[53] We do not know whether Gong Dong's sojourn in Methodism was crucial or incidental to his anti-Catholic activism. In any case, it illustrates the intertwining of local conflict and sectarian rivalries.

In August 1904, over two months into the affair, talk was of an order for soldiers to move in and exterminate the whole Gong clan. At this point, Jiang Zhaotang, already county magistrate of Nanchang, was deputized by the governor to attempt a peaceful resolution. He had spent nine years as magistrate of the neighboring county of Shanggao and was favorably known to the gentry of Xinchang. He bypassed the missionaries and went directly to Tangpu. With the help of a military-degree holder of the Gong family, he negotiated the disarming of the town and the surrender of two leaders of the violence (the primary leader, Gong Dong, was arrested separately). As part of the arrangement, he promised that there would be no executions.[54] This was to be a fateful commitment, but the immediate crisis at Tangpu had passed by the beginning of September 1904.

The North Jiangxi Catholic mission was highly displeased with Magistrate Jiang's ban on capital punishment for the crimes of Tangpu and the Gong family, and insisted that the punishments reach beyond the three culprits under detention. It would appear that, before Jiang's arrival on the scene, Lacruche, the mission's representative in Ruizhou Prefecture, was calling for at least ten executions.[55] Although expressing a willingness to forego executions, his bishop, Paul-Léon Ferrant, assiduously pursued the matter of punishments over the next year and a half. He enlisted the services of both the French consul-general in Shanghai and the French minister in Beijing.[56] He was in Nanchang, consulting with his missionaries about the matter, a few days before the incident.[57] Actual negotiations were in the hands of Father Lacruche and County Magistrate Jiang Zhaotang, whom Bishop Ferrant wished reprimanded for his previous "double-dealing."[58]

Thus the stage was set for the suicide/murder of Magistrate Jiang in the chief residence of the Catholic mission of Nanchang. We may rehearse some of the meanings of the affair as we look at the aftermath and the lessons drawn at the time.

Consequences

Chinese commentary in the aftermath of the upheaval at Nanchang almost unanimously celebrated Magistrate Jiang and condemned Father Lacruche. Jiang was hailed as a national hero, whose resolute confrontation with foreign imperiousness was upheld as a model for all officials. A memorial service in his honor was sponsored by Beijing officials from Jiangxi and Anhui (Jiang's home province). In Tangpu, they erected a temple to him, complete with statue.[59]

A popular position was that expressed in a widely reproduced memorial by one Yun Yuding of the prestigious Hanlin Academy. Underlining the outrageousness of the assault by a foreign priest on an imperial official, he held that the popular outburst was an understandable response and expressed a kind of filial piety. He wrote that the British were innocent victims in this affair but should be indemnified, not by China, but by France.[60]

The outpouring of sentiment impeded the Chinese foreign ministry in its efforts at reaching a settlement. The demand hardest to swallow was the

French insistence that Lacruche should be publicly absolved of any responsibility in Jiang's death, which should be labeled a suicide. The quiet consensus among official Chinese seemed to be that Jiang had first cut his own throat but that the magistrate had subsequently been attacked at Lacruche's direction. This was the conclusion of the official investigators sent by the prominent governor-general of neighboring Hunan and Hubei, Zhang Zhidong.[61] It was what the Jiangxi provincial judge, Yu Zhaokang, told French representatives in Nanchang in mid-March: "A terrible altercation had to have arisen between them, and no one can know who dealt the second blow, if, as I believe, Jiang dealt himself the first one. Father Lacruche was violent. He often struck his fist on the table, and perhaps he was unhinged."[62]

Final agreement between the foreign ministry on one side and the French and British ministers on the other came in June 1906. Jiangxi governor Hu Tinggan and provincial treasurer Zhou Hao were both dismissed. The provincial judge, Yu Zhaokang, was demoted and left officialdom.[63] Thus, the two officials, Zhou Hao and Yu Zhaokang, who had been subjecting Jiang Zhaotang to contradictory pressures in his dealings with the Catholic mission, were both punished in the aftermath. Six military officials were either cashiered or demoted. Nine alleged offenders, named in the agreement, were executed in July for their direct contributions to the deaths of missionaries. Various jail sentences were allotted to thirty-three others. In addition, Gong Dong was also executed. Jiang Zhaotang's promise to the people of Tangpu was after all not sustained, even by his death. On the other side, the Catholic offenders of Chigang who had been prematurely released were sentenced to the completion of their terms — something that Lacruche had bitterly resisted.

The Chinese government did agree to a statement that Jiang had cut his own throat "in a fit of anger." This formula was weaker than desired by the French, who objected to the suggestion of Lacruche's moral responsibility for Jiang's rash act, but more than the Chinese had wished to say. As a balance to this concession to the French, the agreement contained an implied criticism of the Catholic mission in a paragraph warning against Chinese Christians making false accusations and, with untruths, soliciting "missionaries to intervene against the treaties." In the realm of publicly proclaimed moral judgments, then, there was something for both sides.

The financial terms of the settlement were as follows. For the British, about 33,000 taels: for a surviving Kingham child, two years old and now an orphan, and for rebuilding the Plymouth Brethren mission building.[64] The French exacted ten times as much. For property losses, including some dating back to the Tangpu affair in 1904, were allotted 200,000 taels. A monument to the murdered French was to be erected for 5,000 taels. Then the families of the five Marist brothers received a total of 40,000 taels, and the order was granted another 10,000 taels for the expense of bringing out new teachers. Nothing went to Lacruche's family, since French government policy distinguished the teaching function of the Marist brothers from the purely religious vocation of Lacruche, whose family lost any expectation of financial support from him when he took vows. Instead, in a pattern already established by the French in China, the agreement exacted a "moral indemnity" of 100,000 taels and free land along the river for the construction of a French hospital in Nanchang (quite apart from and in addition to the modest medical facilities that had been run by the nuns).[65] The total finally agreed upon here (355,000 taels plus some land) was 145,000 taels less than the original French request.

Actually, the Catholic missionary position in Jiangxi had been badly damaged. The losses, however, were by no means only in people and property. Shortly after the agreement was final, Bishop Ferrant wrote to his Lazarist superior general in Paris, "I have to fight off the idea that all is lost in North Jiangxi."[66] On the occasion of Ferrant's death in 1910, an old associate, the vicar apostolic of East Jiangxi, expressed the view that the Nanchang affair had set back the missionary effort all over the province with regard to its relations with people and officials. He blamed Ferrant and Lacruche for their aggressiveness.[67] In contrast to the experience in Zhili after the Boxers, this time there was no quick evangelistic rebound from tragedy.

There were signs, too, of disillusionment within the French diplomatic establishment. The French minister in Beijing who negotiated the final settlement of the Nanchang affair, cognizant of the origins of the trouble, inserted into his report the view that the Catholic missions tended to regard local Christians as removed from the jurisdiction of Chinese authority. "Under the influence of this tendency, the missionaries intervene too often with the local authorities on matters strictly Chinese, in which they have no right whatsoever to involve themselves." The result was sometimes serious conflict, he concluded.[68] Although not a brand-new observation, it came to occupy a more central position in French official consciousness after the Nanchang incident.

If the idea had not worked itself into focus spontaneously, it would have been forced into view by a remarkable démarche from the British foreign secretary, Edward Grey. In May 1906 he gave the French ambassador a memorandum deploring the Catholic practice in China of missionaries treating cases directly with the authorities on matters between Chinese Christians and other Chinese. "His Majesty's Government feel very strongly that this system is both inconvenient and dangerous" and was not authorized by the treaties. In the Nanchang case, he noted, this practice led to the massacre of three British subjects who were in no way parties to the precipitating dispute.[69]

The suspicious Whitehall watchers at the Quai d'Orsay were dumbfounded by this "unusual" communication, at a time when the two countries were drawing closer together. They focused first on divining Grey's hidden intentions. Only then did they get around to considering the note's explicit content.[70] Hence, it was not until October 1906 that a response was sent. The French legal defense was that the direct approach of Catholic clergy to Chinese officials was based, not on the treaties, but on a Qing imperial edict of March 1899 that authorized negotiations between Catholic missionaries and territorial officials in order to settle local disputes. The French response went on. Neither French officials nor Catholic missionaries were permitted to involve themselves in the mundane affairs of Chinese Christians. The Nanchang circumstances conformed to this principle and to the procedures stemming from the 1899 edict, which called for consular negotiation of religious cases only when they were of special gravity. In a concluding twist of the lion's tail, the French reply reported that the British chargé in Beijing had criticized the French minister for giving away too much when he agreed to a Jiangxi proclamation forbidding Chinese Christian solicitation of missionary intervention before Chinese authorities.[71] The French government scarcely concealed its anger at Grey's lecturing.

After Nanchang, however, the official French relationship to Catholicism in China was no longer viewed so confidently within the diplomatic establishment. The French Religious Protectorate was not formally abandoned until the French government negotiated away its old treaty rights in China in 1946. Nonetheless, in the years immediately following the Nanchang incident, French officials perceptibly drew back from the more extreme versions of the protectorate that had characterized the 1890s and the first years of the new century. Objections of a moral and legal character to the use of French power in internal Chinese quarrels were heard more and more frequently within the Quai d'Orsay and among French diplomats in China. The dampening effect that the Boxer affair has sometimes been described as having on foreign aggressiveness in China—by revealing an accumulation of hatred in the hearts of so many Chinese and dramatizing the unsavory consequences of letting that hatred fester—did not register at the time with those in charge of French policy. The Nanchang affair was a more prominent marker in the moderation of French interventionism in China, which was so intimately connected with religious issues.

We might observe, then, that the commonly noted lessening importance of *jiaoan* in Sino-foreign relations was not simply a result of changing Chinese attitudes. Nationalism did indeed call for more complex, long-term strategies in containing foreign interventions and reducing foreign pretensions within China. From the French case and the circumstances surrounding the Nanchang incident, however, we can trace a more interactive evolution of relations. The reduction in frequency and intensity of explosions over the presence of Christians in Chinese communities in the last years of the Qing had more than one cause. Surely one important factor was a reduction in the assertiveness of foreign governments in taking sides in local controversies where Christians were involved. Insofar as foreign interventions were a frequent cause of anti-Christian outbreaks, a first step in eliminating this cause would most effectively be a foreign one.

When we looked at the causes of intensified conflict over Christian evangelism around the turn of the century, I suggested that issues were exacerbated as they traveled up and down the treaty-constructed ladder of possible arenas: from local to missionary to consular to diplomatic and back down. The Nanchang incident captured all the worst possibilities of this dynamic. It had its roots in local quarrels about ferry crossings and establishing chapels in a couple of market towns in rural Jiangxi. The disputes were enmeshed in sectarian identifications. Missionaries took up the gauntlet. Consular officials quickly and rivalrously injected themselves into the quarrels. The French minister in Beijing was enlisted in the struggle. All this attention served to heat up the atmosphere in Jiangxi. The disputes spontaneously combusted as they were traveling downwards again, their shape much altered, of course, by these journeys. They were settled only to the accompaniment of much loss of life, foreign (by popular violence) and Chinese (by official execution), and of onerous new indemnities.

We should consider another way that the ladder might function. By conscious effort, one of these arenas could be used to lessen conflict, or at least taken out of the sequence, to reduce the tendency toward aggravation and reification of everyday contentiousness. The French, after 1906, seemed to have moved in that direction. Perhaps the new tone was in part a consequence of anticlericalism in France and the diplomatic rupture with the Vatican in 1904. Those developments alone, however, had not altered policy in China. A precipitant was required, and the shock of Nanchang in 1906 served the purpose. Any change in the politics of Catholic evangelism also had the potential for influencing the politics of Protestant evangelism, because of their competitive relationship, and thereby for having an impact on the Anglo-American posture toward these local disputes.

The Nanchang affair, in this light, contributed by negative example to an amelioration of relations between Christian and non-Christian in China. This was a result that Magistrate Jiang, in one of his final notes, had said he wanted.

PART II

Christianity and Ethnicity

Christianity and Ethnicity

DANIEL H. BAYS

Anthropologists and other scholars have observed that in many cultures ethnic minority groups may have a tendency to convert to Christianity, including via mass conversions. Chinese culture has many hegemonic features, and can exert strong and unwelcome pressures for assimilation and conformity on minority cultures within its reach. Thus it is not surprising that there have been many cases of minority group or ethnically related conversion in nineteenth- and twentieth-century China, and that ethnic communities of Christians are a feature of Chinese Christianity today, in Taiwan as well as in the PRC.

The 1989 symposium of the History of Christianity in China Project was fortunate to have four excellent papers by anthropologists dealing with these issues; those by John R. Shepherd, Norma Diamond, and Nicole Constable are in this volume, in revised form, and T'ien Ju-k'ang's work developed into a monograph published in 1993.[1] Two other chapters in Part IV relate to topics treated in Part II: Jessie and R. Ray Lutz's chapter on the Chinese Union tells us something about the background of later successful mission efforts to the Hakka, and Murray Rubinstein's chapter on Taiwan touches on Christianity among the mountain people today.

As Grant Wacker reminded the participants in the 1989 symposium, there are a variety of models that scholars of religious studies use to describe religious conversion, including conversion to Christianity. One of those is the "functionalist" model, which stresses how the conversion meets needs or deprivations that are generally not self-conscious, whether political, economic, social, or psychological. Shepherd's chapter on nineteenth-century Taiwan, positing the "marginality" of the several groups he studies and studying the results of conversion in terms of a cost-benefit analysis, is a clearly and cogently argued functionalist interpretation. The chapter here, with two case studies and brief reference to a third, has only a small portion of the extensive documentation of the symposium paper, which dealt with five different cases. Shepherd's paper sparked lively discussion at the 1989 symposium, partly because of its strongly functionalist interpretation. My own view is that it is an important perspective to keep in mind; conversion, especially of a group, is likely to have an agenda of some kind, obvious or not, rather different from that of missionaries.

Additional perspective on the complexities of Christian conversion, and the multiple factors involved, can be gained from use of the concept of "reference group" formation. Robert W. Hefner, in discussing this and related ideas, such as the process of "identity development," also sums up nicely the need to view religious change through believers' eyes as well as through sociological constructs: "The changing social environment in which conversion so often unfolds is not simply a product of material forces. Its effects register not only in actors' material well-being but also in their sense of self-worth and community and in their efforts to create institutions for the sustenance of both."[2] A variety of this approach can also be referred to as an "intentionalist" model of conversion or religious affiliation, one which stresses listening carefully to believers' own accounts of why their religious identification is important to them.[3]

Diamond, in her chapter on the creation and continued importance of the Miao script, describes the British missionary Samuel Pollard's rapid and eventually near-total identification with the Hua Miao after 1900, and how his linguistic creativity began a process of cultural and local political empowerment centered on the Stone Gateway community. Indeed, somehow Pollard and his successors developed their own religious, socioeconomic, and political vision of the Hua Miao, which meshed nicely with the agenda of the Miao themselves. The twentieth-century struggle of the Hua Miao to preserve their identity and better their position in relationship to Han society, much of that struggle centering on maintaining the integrity of the old Pollard script, has been eventful. The resourcefulness, and sometime success, of the Miao has been impressive; their ability in the early 1940s to go over the heads of the missionaries, who dragged their feet, and to approach the GMD government directly for more resources, is a good example. The permanence of their adoption of Christianity (here Christianity being tied up inextricably with their language and culture), despite the ravages visited upon them by state-sanctioned Han chauvinism in the 1950s and the condescendingly ignorant views of minority "experts" in the PRC even today, seems unquestionable. In this case of the Hua Miao, although

Shepherd's ideas certainly help to account for initial mass conversion early in the twentieth century, explanations of permanent Christian affiliation seem to require explanations along the lines of the "intentionalist" model discussed above. Another helpful perspective is to view the Hua Miao case in light of the thesis of Lamin Sanneh, that worldwide the process of Bible translation, and other use of the vernacular, guarantees the cross-cultural adaptation, or inculturation, of Christianity. Sanneh argues, "Missionary adoption of the vernacular, therefore, was tantamount to adopting indigenous cultural criteria for the message, a piece of radical indigenization far greater than the standard portrayal of mission as Western cultural imperialism."[4]

As Constable points out in situating her own work on the Hakka in relationship to the chapters by Shepherd and Diamond, the Hakka are not an ethnic minority, but are Han Chinese. Thus, while the ethnic minorities may not have been interested in being "Chinese," but in defining themselves in opposition to "Chineseness," the Hakka whom she studied present a case of consciously trying to balance Chinese and Christian identities, often in a self-conscious way. For the Christian Hakka of Shung Him Tong, Christianity has been both a magnet and a skeletal framework around which to construct a new community, one with a more enhanced and integrated identity than was the case before. The mediation between and melding of the two identities, Chinese and Christian, are shown by Constable in, among other things, the evolution of ancestor "commemoration" to be consonant with conservative Christian doctrines, and the blended Chinese and Christian norms represented visibly in the cemetery. However, as she points out, the dual identity is not an easy one to maintain; historically derived, as the Lutz chapter shows as well, it nevertheless has continuing tensions and ambiguities.[5]

As a final introductory comment to this set of chapters, I wish to draw attention to the applicability of one of the conclusions of a recent essay by Richard Madsen on Catholic communities in the PRC. That is, many Catholics in China today have as their main basis for continued affiliation with the church the simple fact that their parents and grandparents passed it on to them. Regardless of the motivation of the first believing generation, and their possible struggle with the idea that Christianity was not Chinese, for the present generations Christian faith "is now understood in a way that is entirely consistent with the reverence for familial obligations that constitutes the mainstream of China's historical heritage."[6] This concept may help to explain as well the continued Christian identity of other groups, including ethnic groups.

CHAPTER 7

From Barbarians to Sinners: Collective Conversion Among Plains Aborigines in Qing Taiwan, 1859–1895

JOHN R. SHEPHERD

A cursory review of the Chinese historical record of the final decades of the nineteenth century reveals numerous instances of conversions to Christianity taking place on a group basis. Latourette speaks of entire clans and villages that "professed conversion in the hope of obtaining support against an adversary."[1] Cohen reports that in 1863 whole villages in a rebel-infested prefecture of Guizhou sought to join the Catholic church as a means of enlisting the aid of the local bishop.[2] Esherick reports that in Shandong during the 1890s groups of sectarians fleeing persecution, bandits seeking protection from law enforcement, and tenants seeking leverage against oppressive landlords all sought on various occasions to enter the church.[3] Ethnic minorities also joined the church in large numbers: for example, boat people in Fuzhou in the late 1850s, Lolos in the 1870s, Miao in Guizhou beginning in 1895 and in Yunnan beginning in 1904.[4]

All of these groups were in one way or another "marginal" from the point of view of the power structure of Chinese society.[5] Chinese officials polled by their government in 1868 were of the general opinion that the only persons for whom the Christian religion had any appeal were the "impoverished, the ignorant, and the disreputable."[6] These marginal groups were known to convert en masse when it appeared that an alliance with the local mission station would bring some benefit vis-à-vis the local government, such as advantage over rival groups in litigation or protection from Chinese officials.

Foreign Christian missionaries were in a position to confer such advantages because of their extraordinary privileges under the Sino-French Treaty of Tianjin (ratified in 1860). This treaty won for the missionaries the right to propagate their religion anywhere in the empire under the protection of the Chinese authorities, and guaranteed Chinese subjects the right to practice Christianity without fear of punishment. The treaty gave the missionaries direct access to Chinese magistrates whom they might call on for protection, and the right to appeal to higher officials if such protection was not forthcoming.[7] In addition, missionaries could and did appeal to their own diplomatic representatives to apply pressure and, if necessary, military force, to enforce their rights. Because no official wished "to become embroiled with foreigners who through their consuls and ministers could make trouble for him with his superiors," missionaries could wield considerable power in local society.[8] Many missionaries (particularly Catholics under the protection of a French government anxious to assert its power) took advantage of their position to interfere with the local administration "either on behalf of their converts or in order to gain converts."[9]

Not all missionaries abused these privileges or took unscrupulous advantage of their position; but all missionaries (along with the religion they propagated) shared in the halo of power and the special prestige conferred by being associated with the foreign powers. As members of a uniquely privileged group, missionaries were inevitably identified by the populace with the imperialist powers that had defeated China in recent wars and caused the downfall of numerous officials. It was this special prestige that earned missionaries the enmity of great numbers of Chinese, commoners and officials alike, who as members of groups with an established position in the power structure of Chinese society could only feel threatened by the foreign challenge to the status quo in politics and religion. But this very same prestige offered a glimmer of hope to many groups marginal to the structure of power and in need of leverage against it. To these marginal groups the missionary and his religion represented a potential source of status and power waiting to be tapped.[10]

The structural position of the vast majority of Chinese was far from marginal in the late nineteenth century. The failure of the missionaries to win large numbers of Chinese converts in the nineteenth century is not the result of some peculiar strength or ability to resist change unique to Chinese culture, nor is it a function of the "cultural distance" between the two cultures and their religious practices.[11] Studies comparing the adaptation of overseas Chinese to a variety of societies show that when the avenue to upward mobility leads in that direction, Chinese immigrants readily acculturate, even adopting Christianity where appropriate.[12] "Cultural distances," no matter how great, could be bridged when interest beckoned. So long as the locus of greatest power and source of highest prestige in nineteenth-century China remained the imperial bureaucracy and the Confucian institutions and culture it fostered, Christianity offered little attraction to the vast majority. Only the traditional institutions of Chinese society could confer access to power, prestige, and wealth. Moreover, because Christian intolerance for so much of Chinese social practice (for example, ancestral rites) required converts to sever their connections to these institutions and forego the opportunities they provided, conversion to Christianity in the nineteenth century imposed a heavy social cost.[13] But for groups marginal to society, already denied access to wealth, prestige, and power on orthodox Confucian terms, conversion to the religion of the foreigners came at little cost and held out the promise of real advantages, psychic and material.

Taiwan's missionary experience in the nineteenth century provides five striking examples of this logic at work, all among marginal ethnic groups collectively known as "plains aborigines" (*pingpufan*; in Hokkien, *pepohoan*). In all the missions founded in nineteenth-century Taiwan, whether Spanish Dominican, English Presbyterian or Canadian Presbyterian, within a few years of their establishment plains aborigines accounted for more than half the membership. And most of this plains aborigine membership joined the churches in bursts of collective enthusiasm that swept entire villages. To understand the dynamics of these social movements in plains aborigine villages, I present in this chapter brief narratives of how the missionaries first came into contact with the plains aborigines and how the plains aborigines chose to receive them, in two of these five cases. But to explain the source of plains aborigine enthusiasm for the foreign religion we must first come to know who they are and how they came to occupy a marginal position in Taiwan's Chinese society.

Plains aborigines account for nine of the twenty-odd Austronesian ethnolinguistic groups that inhabited Taiwan before Chinese settlement.[14] During the seventeenth century nearly all of the groups that inhabited the western coastal plains of Taiwan came under Dutch and later Chinese control; it is the groups sharing this historical experience that are called the plains aborigines. In contrast, the groups that inhabited Taiwan's east coast and the high mountains remained beyond government control until subdued in the late nineteenth and early twentieth centuries.[15]

Let me sketch briefly the social history of the plains aborigines. In the seventeenth century Taiwan was the center of a flourishing export trade in deerskins, which were carried to Japan by Dutch and Chinese merchant ships. Plains aborigine hunters supplied huge quantities of deerskins to this commerce in exchange for trade goods and the cash they needed to pay the taxes levied by successive Dutch and Chinese regimes.

Early in the eighteenth century overhunting and the plowing up of grazing land by increasing numbers of Chinese settlers led to the depletion of the deer herds and the decline of the plains aborigine hunting economies.[16] Plains aborigine livelihoods became increasingly dependent upon plow agriculture and ground rents from tribal lands reclaimed by Han settlers. The Qing government recognized plains aborigine rights to large tracts of land in part because the plains aborigines rendered military service and paid taxes and because the Qing feared plains aborigine revolts which it saw as likely to be caused by the extortions of unruly Han settlers. The Qing viewed Chinese immigrants as intruders who would disrupt an already satisfactory status quo, and raise the costs of government control. Settlers therefore were required to enter into reclamation agreements that obligated them to pay to plains aborigines ground rents from newly reclaimed land (*fan dazu*).[17]

Despite these beneficial policies, plains aborigines found it difficult to compete economically with the Chinese. As their numbers shrank in proportion to the rapidly growing Han segment of the population, the government's interest in defending plains aborigine interests declined as well. Thus, in the course of the late eighteenth and nineteenth centuries plains aborigines became impoverished and began selling off their land and rental rights. Han settlers gradually displaced many of them from their original villages and groups of plains aborigines opened up hill colonies along the eastern edge of the coastal plain. Thus, contrary to popular textbook accounts, the plains aborigines were not exterminated, nor were they driven into the mountains to become the groups of mountain aborigines we know today. Instead, the plains aborigines have survived on the west coast of Taiwan where their modern history began in the seventeenth century.

It is within this political and economic framework that the plains aborigines have gradually but not entirely sinicized, first by adopting aspects of Chinese material culture and agricultural techniques and learning to speak a Chinese dialect, and more gradually by adopting Chinese ways of worship and the Chinese kinship system and ancestor cult. Frequent intermarriage, especially between plains aborigine women and Chinese bachelor immigrants, was an important channel for the introduction of Chinese ways. Today some plains aborigine descendants are ignorant of or deny their origin, some acknowledge it reluctantly, while others take pride in it and are fascinated by their history. In some instances, such as the Sirayan cult of the goddess Alizu, plains groups have continued to preserve and even to revitalize aspects of their traditional culture.[18] This pattern of uneven sinicization and incomplete Chinese identity betrays an ambivalence among the plains aborigine groups toward the culture of the dominant Chinese and their own sinicization. This ambivalence was more pronounced in the nineteenth century when European missionaries arrived on the scene in Taiwan.

With this background we can now review sketches of the cases of missionary success among plains aborigines.[19]

Wanjin and the Spanish Dominicans

The first missionary to arrive in nineteenth-century Taiwan was Fernando Sainz, a Spanish Dominican who landed in Dagou (Gaoxiong) in May 1859. It was not until March 1861 that Sainz and a catechist made their way to the Makatao plains aborigine village of Bankimcheng or Wanjin. The records available to me do not indicate how Sainz came to know of Wanjin, but it is likely he knew more than a little about the village before traveling there, as it was a long and somewhat dangerous journey from Dagou, through hostile Hakka ("Cantonese") territory. Fernandez comments that Sainz "surmised—and correctly, that the natives of Bankimcheng, not being Chinese, would prove more receptive and less hostile."[20]

Sainz's hopes were not disappointed in Wanjin. He and his catechist stayed more than ten days and Sainz was sufficiently encouraged by the results that he sent a catechist and another convert to stay an additional week later in the year. In January 1862, another catechist visited the village and Father Limarquez was assigned to the Wanjin church. The first two Wanjin converts were baptized early in 1862. In May 1863, Sainz bought a site and built a small church in Wanjin, and in August baptized 47 villagers. In December 1863, another 47 were baptized. The next year the mission spread to another plains aborigine village, Kao-a-khi or Gouzeqian.[21]

These early successes did not, however, go unchallenged. The neighboring Hakka, for long the hostile competitors of the Wanjin plains aborigines, soon began to spread rumors that the Catholics were using corpses to make medicines.[22] At Chinese New Year's in 1864, a group of Hakka attempted to burn down the Wanjin church. They complained that the converts were failing to contribute to the cost of local temple operas. These incidents inaugurated a series of conflicts that embroiled the Catholics in communal strife between Hakka and plains aborigines over the next few years. Under these conditions the priests took a leading role as advocates for Wanjin before the local authorities.

During 1867, a band of Hakkas kidnapped Father Sainz and held him for ransom. His fellow priests enlisted the help of the English consul and demanded that the Taiwan mandarins obtain Sainz's release. The Fengshan County magistrate, fearing an international incident, ordered the Hakka to release Sainz. Forewarned of the magistrate's action, the Hakka kidnappers tricked Sainz by promising immediate release if he would pay a smaller ransom.[23] The plains aborigines saw Sainz's capitulation as a serious blow to their hope of gaining advantage over the Hakka through a connection with the Catholics. Father Herce describes the plains aborigine reaction to this event in a letter of October 1867:

They felt that the missionaries were powerful, so powerful that they could even compel the mandarins to be on their side. If the missionaries were powerful, then they were the ones who could free them from the oppression of the Cantonese. It seemed only fair that they should help the missionaries, that they should all become Christians.

Such was their shock and disillusionment, therefore, when they were informed that the Father Vicar, instead of having the bandits punished, had in fact rewarded them for capturing him. . . .

Angrily, they remarked: "Is this what Christianity is? Must everything be patience and silence and suffering? When their house and church at Bankimcheng were burned, they were silent, no one was punished. When their head was kidnapped, they paid the bandits for kidnapping him."

From these remarks, it was easy to reach one conclusion. "How, then, can we afford to become Christians? If we become Christians, and we are kidnapped, we will be tortured and put to death because we do not have the money to pay the bandits. If this is Christianity, we don't want it. Let us, then, forget once and for all all thoughts of becoming Christians."[24]

The events of 1867 marked the low ebb for the Dominican mission in Wanjin.

More troubles came in 1868, but these troubles ultimately brought a reversal in the fortunes of the mission. A dispute between the foreign merchant community and the Taiwan intendant over the latter's attempt to monopolize the trade in camphor escalated into a general antiforeign disturbance.[25] In April 1868, mobs wrecked both the Spanish Dominican chapel in Kao-a-khi and the Presbyterian mission station in Fengshan. Attacks on and accusations against the missionaries were made again in July and September. This confrontation between the Chinese establishment and the foreign community was not resolved until a British gunboat landed troops at Anping (the port of Tainan) in November 1868. Faced with superior firepower, the Taiwan mandarins were forced to agree to pay indemnities for the destroyed property of both the merchants and the missions, and to issue proclamations denying slanders against the Christian missionaries and recognizing their right to work in the island.[26]

This application of foreign military power to humiliate the mandarins transformed the political climate in which the Dominicans worked. The Hakka, no longer able to assume the acquiescence of the mandarins and now having reason to fear the Dominicans, became less brazen in their harassment at Wanjin. Thus, when Father Herce was robbed on his way to Wanjin in the summer of 1869, the head of the town from which the bandits came took steps to ensure that the stolen articles were returned.[27]

Increased respect for the Dominicans from the Hakkas and the mandarins also brought with it increased respect and enthusiasm from within Wanjin. The humiliation of the mandarins had created an aura of power that now adhered to the Dominicans and their religion and endowed them with a newfound prestige. This we may attribute to the heightened status of the foreigner in the local balance of power.[28]

Because the villagers hoped to gain by seeking the protection of the Dominicans, the demonstration of superior power by the British in 1868 led to a surge in the villagers' enthusiasm for the religion of the foreigners. By September 1869, Father Colomer could report a flourishing mission and rapid growth in the number of catechumens.[29] It is the outcome of the events of 1868 that convinced many of the villagers of Wanjin that hope for the future lay in embracing the new religion. Many demonstrated their zeal by breaking with the old gods who had failed to provide the protection that now seemed to lie within the power of the Dominicans.

The mission in Wanjin grew steadily for the next few years and became a regular feature of the institutional pattern of life in the village. In 1870 the Wanjin congregation completed construction of a large church building. In 1872 the church was able to buy land to assist members whose land had been seized by the neighboring Hakka.[30] In the 1880s and 1890s the Dominicans found openings for their mission in other communities in central and northern Taiwan. Yet in 1894 when the church claimed a total of 1,290 converts in the island, the 582 plains aborigine members at Wanjin and vicinity still constituted nearly half the total.[31]

From this chapter in the history of the Dominican mission in Wanjin we can see that the fortunes of the foreign religion among the plains aborigines closely paralleled the general prestige of the foreign community and more particularly the ability of the Dominicans to aid the plains aborigines in their conflicts with their Hakka neighbors. Because of the marginal and powerless position of the villagers of Wanjin within local society, the modest ability of the Dominicans to extend protection to them was sufficient to make the new religion a source of hope in the face of continued oppression from the Hakka.

The Pazeh and the English Presbyterians

The English Presbyterian mission, which got its start in 1865 in Tainan and Dagou, experienced similar fluctuations in its ability to attract aborigine adherents. Local Chinese gave the English Presbyterians, as they had the Dominicans, a cold and at times hostile reception. But eventually the Presbyterians made connections with two groups of plains aborigines who proved receptive. The first, the Siraya in the hill stations of Tainan county, I have discussed elsewhere;[32] here I will focus on the Pazeh of Anli and Puli.

The second great expansion of the Presbyterian mission field came among the Pazeh of Anli Toa-sia (Dashe) and the Puli basin. The Pazeh were included in a broad category of plains aborigines referred to by the Chinese as *sekhoan* (*shufan*) or cooked aborigines, and it is by this label that the missionaries learned to refer to these central Taiwan groups.

The Pazeh, along with other plains aborigine groups in central Taiwan, were parties to an 1823 compact by which several *sekhoan* groups organized a plains aborigine colony in the Puli basin, within the mountains. In the Puli basin (known as Po-sia [Pushe] to the missionaries) the plains aborigines had sought to establish a refuge from competition with the Han Chinese settlers they saw daily encroaching on their lands in the plains of central Taiwan. A history of conflict with the Han had sharpened Pazeh ethnic consciousness.[33]

William Campbell, writing in November 1872, explained how the British trader William Pickering initiated the spread of Christianity among the Pazeh:

The agent of a mercantile house in Takow [Dagou] happened to be spending some days at Toa-sia about two years ago, and mentioned to some sick people that there was a foreign doctor in Taiwanfoo [Tainan] both able and willing to help them. Soon after, a party of far-travelled strangers presented themselves at the mission Hospital for relief. One of them was a native of Po-sia named Khai-san [Pan Kai-shan], who had relatives living at Toa-sia, and who came now to place himself under the skillful treatment of Dr. Maxwell. No difficulty was experienced in dealing with his bodily ailment, but the poor idolater was spoken to about another disease, which required to be dealt with in a very different manner. His interest was aroused, much prayer was offered on his behalf, and in less than three months the heavenly light and peace broke in upon his soul. On returning to the north, he lost no time in speaking to friends and neighbours about his new-found treasure. He produced God's Word, and although no scholar himself, others assisted him in deciphering the difficult Chinese characters, and in translating several little Gospel leaflets, which were read and reread and talked over by all sorts of people. Khai-san had also to explain about praising God, and tell what was meant by people meeting together for worship without any sacred object being placed before them. A new thing was seen in Po-sia. One here and another there gave up the practice of idolatry, some of our church hymns came to be familiar, and in one village an attempt was made to hold weekly Christian services. Thus the movement had fairly commenced.[34]

Thus Khai-san, having experienced both a healing and a conversion, began the movement among his fellow Pazeh entirely on his own initiative. This was done without the awareness, let alone the assistance or guidance, of the Presbyterian mission.[35] Nearly a year had elapsed when news of these developments reached Tainan in July 1871 and two native helpers were sent to investigate; Dr. J. L. Maxwell and Rev. Hugh Ritchie followed in September.[36]

Dr. Maxwell reported from this September 1871 visit that Toa-sia already had a regular worshipping congregation of 50 to 70 members and that Rev. Ritchie had baptized five men and five women, indicating that the missionaries were favorably impressed both with the earnestness of the candidates and the work of instruction conducted by the native preachers. Maxwell reports that at neighboring Lai-sia (Neishe) "the whole population have renounced idolatry for the worship of God; but excepting one or two visits from the Toa-sia helper, they have had no regular teaching."[37] Thus the missionaries witnessed with their own eyes the progress of a movement almost entirely initiated by the Pazeh alone.

Rev. Ritchie, along with Dr. Dickson and Rev. G. L. MacKay, visited Toa-sia again and Po-sia for the first time in March 1872. MacKay reports that "as we did not wear the queue they called us their kinsmen."[38] Thus the Pazeh saw in the foreigners "kinsmen" who would protect them against their Chinese rivals. Campbell's secondhand description of the same visit demonstrates his own awareness of the nonreligious sources of the enthusiasm for the missionaries: "The joy and hospitality with which they were received was overpowering. . . . Of course, no one would say that this interest proceeded altogether from genuine religious feeling. In such circumstances we never meet with a sudden and widespread desire to embrace the Gospel *for its own sake*. . . . Yet the opportunity was most precious."[39] Rev. Ritchie baptized 22 Po-sia candidates on that first visit and preparations were made to erect chapels in three Pazeh villages in Po-sia.[40] Notably, other plains aborigine but non-Pazeh villages in Po-sia did *not* participate.

The Pazeh, like the Siraya near Tainan, preserved memories of Taiwan's Dutch period (1624–61). Rev. Thomas Barclay reports that there was current among the Pazeh a legend predicting a return of the Dutch. When the missionaries and other powerful foreigners appeared on the scene, some Pazeh understood the legend to instruct them to adhere to the new religion.[41] Thus the decision to adhere to the foreign religion was understood by the Pazeh in terms of their own traditions and their own "worldly" and spiritual needs. It was this native understanding and not the teachings of the missionaries that accounted for the mass movement character of the collective conversion of the Pazeh. In 1872 Campbell lamented the quality of Pazeh participation in the church:

> Not that people fail in attending service, or show any lack of willingness to become members, but that little headway is made in getting them to understand the spiritual nature and function of the Church of Christ. It would almost seem as if the petty officials and older people of the place had taken the matter into consideration and decided in favour of Christianity *because no loss, at any rate, could arise in following the advice of foreign teachers who were quite as influential and far more sympathising than the Chinese around them.* This theory would account for the easy acquiescence of the younger people, and the irrepressible desire for baptism by many who do not possess the slightest knowledge of its meaning.[42]

Baptism was sought not as an act of spiritual rebirth but because it would make the Pazeh worthy of foreign protection. What Campbell presents as hypothesis was actively suspected by other observers. Consul T. L. Bullock reported from his 1873 visit that "in spite of the undoubted sincerity of many of the converts, I think that the movement towards Christianity commenced in *a vague hope of possible advantage to be obtained, probably of some protection against the encroachment of the Chinese.* The missionaries are careful not to foster any such feeling."[43] Campbell reported continued progress from his April 1873 visit to Toa-sia, Lai-sia, and Po-sia. At Po-sia, Campbell admitted fourteen candidates who were baptized at a large Sabbath gathering of all three village congregations, at which 450 attended. Campbell spent the balance of his time in Po-sia with the native preachers, visiting the non-Christian villages, distributing tracts, and handing out doses of quinine.[44] We learn from MacKay of one of the reasons requiring these visits. Writing in May 1873 MacKay reports that some opposition to the work of the missionaries had grown up among "jealous, discontented and covetous" *sekhoan* in Po-sia.[45] Thus the adoption of Christianity did instigate some opposition, not within the villages of the Pazeh converts, but between these Pazeh and villages of the other plains aborigine ethnic groups in Po-sia. MacKay mentions jealousy as a possible motive and perhaps these opponents feared that the Pazeh would gain an unfair advantage through their connection with the foreigners. In any case, this makes clear that not all *sekhoan* saw the foreign religion as a solution to their problems.

When Campbell revisited Po-sia in May 1874 he commented that the Po-sia churches "continue to show signs of spiritual life and progress. The outward boundary has not been much enlarged, our people for the most part being still confined to the three villages in which chapels have been erected."[46] Thus the movement in Po-sia remained confined to the original Pazeh villages. Despite some dampening of the early enthusiasm, the membership statistics indicate steady growth within the five initial Pazeh villages over the next years. By 1876, there were 176 baptized members and congregations totalling 540 in the five Pazeh stations.[47]

In the case of the Pazeh, village leaders spearheaded a social movement to accept the foreign religion. This contrasts somewhat with the movements among the Tainan Siraya and the village of Wanjin where there was the initial opposition by certain village leaders to the introduction of the new religion. This local leadership is linked to the most striking feature of the movement among the Pazeh: its initiation before the missionaries arrived in their villages. Indirect contact through a comrade who had been cured by the miraculous medicines of the missionaries, and with foreigners like Pickering who did not fear the mandarins, was enough to convince these villagers that they should befriend a force that appeared to them to be equal to that of their Chinese overlords. By embracing the foreign religion, the Pazeh hoped to win the protection of the Europeans, a hope that was nurtured in the desperation of a group fearing the dissolution of its culture and society under Chinese pressure.

Nevertheless, not all *sekhoan* agreed that adopting the foreign religion was the best means of securing cultural survival. Indeed, once one group among the multiethnic community of Po-sia made its alliance with the missionaries, the other groups seem to have kept their distance, despite Campbell's efforts at proselytization. We may speculate that these groups kept their distance out of jealous rivalry, because the Pazeh in fact sought subtly to exclude them, or because they perceived that what power and influence the missionaries had was too limited to benefit them all. Once one group had opted to adopt the foreign religion, other groups could distinguish themselves by preserving plains aborigine traditions or seek to impress the Chinese by sinicizing. The dynamics of group competition and ethnogenesis best explain why the movement to adopt Christianity in Po-sia halted at the borders of the Pazeh villages.

MacKay in North Taiwan

George Leslie MacKay of the Canada Presbyterian Church arrived in Dagou in late 1871.[48] After studying language and observing the methods of the English Presbyterians, MacKay took up mission work in the north of the island, settling in Danshui in March 1872. MacKay was also to find the bulk of his converts among plains aborigine groups, and his experience provides two additional cases that can only be mentioned here. His first plains aborigine congregation was founded in one of the three hamlets comprising the Taokas village of Xin'gang in Miaoli County in 1872. Growth of this congregation was stymied by interhamlet rivalries within Xin'gang, where the village head felt threatened by the missionary religion that had taken root first in a rival hamlet. Throughout the remainder of the 1870s, MacKay concentrated his efforts in primarily Chinese communities of northern Taiwan and achieved only slow growth. After furlough in 1880 and 1881, MacKay returned to Taiwan in 1882 and began to preach in Yilan, on Taiwan's east coast. Here he was enthusiastically received by villages of Kuvalan plains aborigines. By 1884 MacKay had baptized 630 Kuvalan, more than he had baptized in the previous decade of laboring among the Chinese of north Taiwan.

Conclusions

The case studies introduced above have emphasized the initial phases of the movements in the plains aborigine villages to adopt the foreign religion, so that we could come to an understanding of what attracted the plains aborigines to the religion of the missionaries, the nature of the social dynamics of the movements, and the social networks that brought the missionaries into these villages. The ability of the missions to maintain a hold in these villages after the initial wave of enthusiasm for the new religion remained problematic. But despite declining levels of enthusiasm, plains aborigines continued to account for a substantial majority of each denomination's converts.

By the end of Qing rule in Taiwan in 1895, each of the foreign missions had memberships that were both small and predominantly plains aborigine. After 36 years of effort the Spanish Dominicans claimed a membership of 1,290, of which half were plains aborigine.[49] After 30 years of effort the English Presbyterians claimed a membership of 1,256, of which approximately two-thirds were plains aborigine.[50] And by 1892, after 20 years of effort, the Canadian Presbyterian mission claimed a membership of 1,751, of which at least three-fourths were plains aborigine.[51] The dominant element of the population, the Han Chinese, had found very little attractive in the foreign religion, while certain villages of plains aborigines had at least at first reacted with enthusiasm.

The five cases discussed in the full-length version of this paper illustrate the dynamics of village-wide movements among the plains aborigines to adopt the religion of the missionaries. Each of the cases shows the importance of the perception that the missionaries would extend protection to these disadvantaged groups, a perception that was made by marginal groups of every description all over China. But in analyzing the specific character of the marginality of the plains aborigines, these cases also suggest that the plains aborigines sought more than short-term strategic advantage in local power struggles from adopting the religion of the missionaries.

The plains aborigines were also seeking a worldview and a reference group that would enable them to set a higher value on their cultural identity and that would restore their self-respect. Chinese society denigrated the plains aborigines as barbarians, while considering the Han to be the carriers of civilization.[52] Plains aborigines could not elevate their prestige in Han society by adopting the religion of the foreigners. Indeed, adopting a foreign religion that categorized plains aborigines as sinners rather than barbarians might seem to offer little advantage. But the plains aborigines surely derived psychic satisfaction from a religion that instead of looking up to the Han as the carriers of civilization, looked down on them as heathen idol-worshippers. While the conditions of plains aborigine life changed very little materially, the new religion radically lowered the ranking assigned to the rival Han on the hierarchy of civilizational prestige, and elevated the ranking of plains aborigine believers. That theirs was the religion of the powerful foreigner, and that respect came at least from that quarter, made the burden of adopting a religion that the Han despised more bearable. Adopting the foreign religion was an act of cultural rebellion that signaled the unwillingness of plains aborigines to continue to acknowledge to their Han neighbors the superiority of Han culture. No longer need deference be paid when Han censured "barbarian customs." In adopting the new religion, plains aborigines acquired a separate set of values and a prestigious reference group made up of powerful foreigners. This made Han attitudes of superiority irrelevant and immunized the plains aborigines from the humiliations directed at them by Han.

But it is fair to ask of this interpretation, if conversion to Christianity provided a set of values that restored plains aborigine self-pride, the opportunity of a connection to powerful foreigners, and leverage against oppressive Chinese, why did not *all* plains aborigine villages convert en masse, instead of only the villages prominent in the cases discussed? Surely these factors are too general, explain too much, when the actual pattern of conversion was historically contingent, and dependent on a number of limiting factors that had to be absent before conversion became attractive.

Let us list some of these limiting factors. There were of course only a few missionaries present in Taiwan who could effectively extend the network, although the Pazeh example shows that conversion could spread independently of missionary presence. We have alluded to the presence of interhamlet and interethnic rivalry that limited the spread of the new religion among the plains aborigines in the cases of Xin'gang and Puli. When the hoped-for protection and leverage failed to materialize, conversion brought persecution that went unavenged, and the missionaries were shown to lack the influence converts and potential converts hoped they would have (as in early Wanjin, and in the Siraya villages of Jiayi County), there was much backsliding and at least a temporary end to membership expansion. Some plains aborigine village leaders seem to have assessed the costs and benefits of adhering to the foreign religion and concluded that as the costs outweighed the gains they would remain firm on the course of sinicization.

The Siraya hill stations in Tainan seem to have experienced a minimum of persecution at the hands of Chinese. I think this was primarily because of the large preponderance of plains aborigine population and partial isolation from Chinese in the hill districts, whereas other villages or hamlets were exposed to direct scrutiny from nearby Chinese neighbors, or were already participating in Han Chinese networks and folk religious practices which involved them in relations they had no desire to rupture.[53] Thus the strength of the Tainan hill station churches can be explained in part by the low costs of conversion imposed on these villages. In the case of Wanjin, the desperation of the plains aborigines in the face of relentless Hakka persecution, which predated the introduction of Christianity, made the cost of conversion seem less, and the small victories of the Dominicans seem that much greater. In the case of the Kuvalan of Yilan, their desperation seems so great, and their lack of viable alternatives so few, that all their villages converted and none held back. Thus a wide range of intervening variables can be invoked (though the sparsity of data, especially on the villages that did not convert, prevent systematic testing of these hypotheses) to explain why group conversion proceeded in only specific locales and tipped the cost-benefit calculus against conversion in other locales.[54]

These variables are all of a sociological or political rather than religious or narrowly cultural character, and my argument locates collective conversion in strategies of ethnic competition and ethnic politics. The many differences in the distinct plains aborigine cultures represented in these five cases (Makatao, Siraya, Pazeh, Taokas, and Kuvalan) seem to me to have played little role in the reception given to the foreign religion, and the religious content of Christianity seems irrelevant to its power of attraction. The key to its attractiveness was that it was the religion of powerful foreigners, and that the foreigners could be engaged in a relationship by adhering to their religion. The Europeans might have been propagating *any* religion, and the dynamics of group conversion among the plains aborigines would have been little changed. The religious content of Christianity was important in three different and limited ways: first, for the way it motivated the *missionaries* (rather than the converts); second, for the way it alienated Chinese; and third, at a *later stage*, after group conversion had occurred, in the process of indigenization when affinities between religious practices helped the new religion become part of the institutional fabric of village life. It was the content of European Christianity that motivated missionary evangelization and that made common faith the basis of a social tie, and it was also the intolerant, exclusivist, monotheistic nature of Christianity that made it such an obstacle to Chinese living in a Chinese institutional context.

In conclusion, what made the religion of the foreigners attractive to Taiwan's plains aborigines and marginal groups (Chinese and non-Chinese) all over China was the relative powerlessness of the marginal groups and the apparent power of the foreigners; but whether conversion was a viable alternative in any case depended on the structural position of each group and how that affected the cost-benefit calculus of conversion. In the case of ethnic minorities, the additional element of cultural revaluation seems to be an important factor affecting the cost-benefit calculus. Because partial sinicization had not brought an end to their humiliation and oppression by Chinese or yet equipped them to compete effectively with Han, it was all the more reasonable for plains aborigines to give the foreign religion an opportunity to prove its worth.

Let us turn now to review some commonly held ways of explaining the movement among the plains aborigines, explanations that variously emphasize the comparative lack of obstacles among the plains aborigines to accepting the foreign religion, the character of the plains aborigines, and the decay of plains aborigine culture. Explanations offered by the missionaries for their success among the plains aborigines (in contrast to their very slow progress among the Han Chinese) commonly emphasized the nature of the obstacles they had to overcome. Rev. Ritchie, for example, in 1870 explained the receptivity of the plains aborigines by pointing to the lack of rival temples and priests, the weak hold of Chinese religion, resentment at Chinese domination, and the hope that foreigners would prove valuable allies.[55]

These explanations come from the point of view of the missionaries and emphasize the problems they encountered in overcoming Han Chinese opposition to Christianity, some of which they did not encounter among the plains aborigines, and ignore the fact that the plains aborigines were attached to their own religions. We must remember that only a small proportion of all the plains aborigines ever converted. By emphasizing the obstacles that had to be overcome, these explanations relegate the plains aborigines to a role of passive recipients of missionary teaching, and obscure the active role taken by the plains aborigines in adopting the foreign religion. The plains aborigines were not blank slates on which the missionaries could write; instead they had their own political and cultural agendas which they expected the missionaries to help fulfill. And those who were proselytized but did not convert judged for themselves the value of the new religion. The same absence of Han-style temples and priests, which the missionaries saw as opening the way to their work, we may see as indicating the marginal position of the plains aborigines in the cultural world of the Han Chinese. For from that marginal position, some plains aborigines could see in the missionaries a force that offered a new alternative, a glimmer of hope that the missionaries could help them escape from their degraded position in Han society. Ritchie acknowledges the plains aborigine resentment of Chinese domination and that they entertained the idea that "foreigners are their true friends." To prove themselves worthy of this friendship, and to revitalize their own culture and sense of worth, some plains aborigine villages converted en masse.

In the movements that swept the plains aborigine villages, it was plains aborigines who took the active role and the missionaries (who were sometimes not even present in the initial stages) who were relegated to a passive one. The missionaries commonly attributed this enthusiasm of the plains aborigines in contrast to the Chinese to a difference in personality; MacKay for instance writes that the "Pe-po-hoan character" was "more emotional, approachable, and responsive than the Chinese, although perhaps, less solid and stable."[56] In my view the sources of plains aborigine enthusiasm for the foreign religion lay not in a "simpler" character or more emotional personality, but in the marginal position of plains aborigines in Chinese society, which cut them off from orthodox sources of prestige and power;

the missionaries therefore had for plains aborigines a significance they could not have had for Han. The missionaries were aware of the operation of this cultural dynamic, but had to guard against it: for such "worldly" motives not only tainted their spiritual message and delegitimated missionary accomplishments, they were also most likely to lead to disappointed expectations. Indeed, in many instances the major challenge the missionaries faced was not to win converts but to maintain control over the movements and slow them down, such as by setting high standards for baptism and admission to the church.

Objections similar to those made above can be lodged against explanations that account for the success of the missionaries among the plains aborigines in terms of the "decay" of plains aborigine culture, in contrast to the strength of Chinese culture. Presumably a culture in decay would offer less resistance to the entrance of the new religion. We may immediately note that this approach too is flawed in positing an active role for the missionaries and a passive one for the plains aborigines; thus it cannot account for the actual roles played by either group in the movements we have documented. What is needed is an approach that looks at the problem from the point of view of the converts: an approach that asks why the plains aborigines found the foreign religion so attractive, rather than why plains aborigine culture offered so little resistance to the missionaries. But in asking what benefits the plains aborigines hoped to gain through adopting the new religion we must also reflect on why these benefits could not be obtained through their traditional culture.

It is in this context that the state of plains aborigine culture in the late nineteenth century has relevance for our problem. Dr. Patrick Manson found the plains aborigines abandoning aspects of traditional custom and adopting Chinese practices in their stead.[57] The most obvious example of this acculturation was the loss of the ancestral language of the Siraya. Senior generations had apparently decided that they would no longer transmit the ancestral tongue; instead their children's future would be better served by a mastery of the language of the Han-dominated society around them. Such a radical step made sense because theirs was a defeated culture, a culture of hunters and warriors, whose values could no longer be obtained in a social environment dominated by Han. Because many of their customs brought ridicule and contempt from the Han, the plains aborigines were often not reluctant to abandon them in favor of more prestigious Chinese practices. Some adopted Chinese customs, such as ancestor worship, because the practice of such customs was a mark of civilization in the Chinese cultural order, and would allow the practitioners to command respect from Han.

But their incomplete sinicization had not yet enabled the plains aborigines to compete effectively with the Han or to resist Han encroachment or oppression.

Some plains aborigines reacted to this situation by seeking to migrate away from the Han, to Puli or the east coast. Others sought to adapt by attempting not just to acculturate but to assimilate: to assume a Han identity and to reject all things aborigine. Many obstacles lay in the path of those who selected this option; a distinct physiognomy would elicit Han prejudice and ridicule, and feelings of guilt might plague those seen as having abandoned their own communities. Many adopted neither radical solution but created a syncretic culture that had for them its own consistency, and preserved aspects of their traditional culture which they continued to value, such as the cult of Alizu. But all things non-Han were denigrated in the larger society; the low status and inability of plains aborigines to resist Han encroachment made their failures obvious to all. This led to the desire for a new set of values that would accord both power and prestige; and to the plains aborigines the missionaries seemed to offer just that. It was not the "decay" of their culture, but its low status and their powerlessness that made the foreign religion an attractive alternative.

The contrast with Han Chinese is striking: theirs was the culture of the power holders of society; the foreign religion was seldom attractive to those not on the margins and in fact was repulsive because of its foreignness. So long as this culture remained entrenched in the institutions of society, the religion of the missionaries could hold little attraction. But that this strength inhered in the institutions, and not the culture per se, is demonstrated in the cases where Chinese emigrants left their institutions behind; where they found the path to advancement required acculturating to non-Han societies their culture was no obstacle.[58]

Christianity and the Hua Miao:
Writing and Power

NORMA DIAMOND

China's policy toward her minority peoples includes the right to use their own languages for schooling, publication, and public affairs. However, among China's 56 minorities (*shaoshuminzu*), the state recognizes only 11 as having a true writing system of their own, meaning one based on a system other than Chinese ideographs and which was in common use prior to 1949. These include Mongolian, Tibetan, Korean, Dai (Thai), and the Arabic-derived scripts used by the Islamic minorities. A few other ethnic groups were acknowledged to have indigenous writing systems, but these were judged unacceptable because they were understood only by a small elite group (as among Naxi or Yi) or because they were introduced and spread by the Christian churches in the twentieth century, as was the case among Miao, Lisu, Lahu, and Jingpo. After 1949, some of the preliterate peoples were encouraged by the state to adopt a Latin romanization (*pinyin*) and standardized spelling for what was determined to be the standard language of the group. Similarly affected were those whose writing systems had been developed and taught in Christian churches and schools. Members of at least 30 of the officially recognized minorities, or of dialect subgroups within those minorities, thus had no alternatives other than learning Chinese or the predominant dialect or sublanguage within their minority classification in order to gain literacy.[1]

Even today, relatively little is published in the minority languages other than primary school primers. Over half of the minorities do not have access to published materials in their own languages. Policy, in effect, demands that the minorities become bilingual, sooner or later. Higher levels of schooling require a knowledge of *putonghua* (standard Mandarin) and written Chinese. Some minority children begin learning Chinese in the first grade, either because there are no other textbooks for them, or because the nearest school serves an area with mixed ethnic population so that *putong-hua* becomes the classroom tongue by default. This sometimes occurs in the large "autonomous regions" of the country, and is even more likely to be the case for those living in areas designated as autonomous prefectures, autonomous counties, or "minority townships" (*minzu xiang*). By secondary school, a knowledge of Chinese is essential. In the state view of China's cultural history, the Han Chinese are presented as the most advanced of the nationalities: they are the most developed in the political, cultural, and economic spheres. Therefore a knowledge of Chinese language and literacy in Chinese is a necessity if members of all nationalities are to receive a full education and participate in the task of modernizing the country and building socialism.

This chapter is concerned with the Miao nationality, a population estimated at close to seven and a half million persons, and more specifically with a segment of that population known in earlier literature as the Hua Miao or Flowery Miao. For the Hua Miao, government policies regarding literacy have created problems. Government claims of having provided a written language for the Miao in the decades following the revolution gloss over the problem that there is no single Miao language. "Miao" is a minority classification that incorporates historically related but culturally and linguistically diverse populations scattered over several provinces in the southwest. Linguists in China and elsewhere disagree about the actual number of Miao languages, dialects, and subdialects that are in current usage. The consensus now seems to be that there are three major divisions.[2] The smallest division is that of the Xiangnan languages, spoken in west Hunan. It now has close to one million speakers overall, subdivided into two distinct dialects. Only one standardized romanization has been provided for them. A more complex problem exists for the Qiandong languages of eastern and central Guizhou. Again, only one standardized romanization is provided, though there are three major "dialects." At least one million people speak the officially recognized dialect; another half million or more are divided between the remaining two dialects. Most problematic is the third division, which is referred to as Chuan-Qian-Dian. As a category, it is a catchall for the various languages and dialects spoken by the Miao living in Sichuan, western Guizhou, and Yunnan. It is meant to imply a mutual intelligibility that in fact does not exist. Not only are these Miao languages distant from Xiangnan or Qiandong dialects, they are highly diverse within the category, dividing into seven main dialects that are almost distinctive enough to be termed "languages" in themselves. Until the early 1980s the standard romanization and school texts for all were based on one of the "dialects," namely the language spoken by one million Miao living primarily in Sichuan, with some scattered populations in Yunnan and Guizhou. In the scholarly literature they were formerly known as the Chuan Miao or River Miao.[3]

The Hua Miao, with which this chapter is concerned, is the second largest population within Chuan-Qian-Dian. Their language is called Dian Dongbei, and is sometimes referred to as Weining dialect or Shimenkan dialect. It has at least one quarter of a million speakers, living in scattered communities in the Yunnan-Guizhou border area between Weining, Yiliang, Zhaotung, and Xuanwei prefectures. There are also some settlements in Wuding and Lufeng counties, west of Kunming. The Hua Miao figured dramatically in the missionary writings of the early twentieth century because of their widespread and rapid conversion to Christianity.[4] One of the features that came to distinguish them from neighboring groups, including Han Chinese in some areas, was the high rate of literacy held by both men and women. The ability to read and write in their own language resulted from a village school network, encouraged by the church from 1905 until 1949, and facilitated by the adoption of a phonetic system sometimes referred to as the "Pollard script."

This script has continued in private use and church use up to the present, but it is not officially recognized by the government as a legitimate medium of communication. Despite its flexibility and its wide usage throughout the community by Christians and non-Christians, the government forbade its use at the same time that it closed many of the existing village schools. In 1983, a compromise of sorts was effected: the government allowed the publication of a set of school primers written in a *pinyin* (romanized) rendering of Dian Dongbei.[5] This was de facto admission that the language of the neighboring Chuan Miao was too dissimilar to be of practical classroom use. Moreover, to engage the cooperation of the adults or to ease their transition to the use of *pinyin*, the Pollard script appears throughout the initial primers as a guide to pronunciation. In effect, the children learn both *pinyin* and the older script. Around the same time, the Protestant Three-Self Church and the Bureau of Religious Affairs in Yunnan authorized the reprinting of the edition of the New Testament and hymnal in circulation before 1949. These, of course, were written in Dian Dongbei, using the Pollard script, which the Hua Miao call "old writing."

In official writings on the Miao, it is repeatedly stated that they were preliterate prior to 1949. Literacy, in the sense of ability to read the ideographic characters, has deep meaning in Chinese culture. It is one of the key markers that distinguishes the advanced Han Chinese from the backward minority peoples, and until recently distinguished the polished elites from the crude peasants. Those who were literate were fully cultured and qualified to rule. Defensively, Hua Miao mythic history tells of a past when they lived in a Golden Homeland. It mirrors the Chinese world: a land of rivers, lakes, lush fields of rice and cotton, towns and cities, and of course books and writing. This idealized world contrasts to the tiny mountain villages scattered over the less desirable lands of the Yunnan-Guizhou border area where most of the Hua Miao now live. For the past several hundred years, such villages have relied, not on irrigated fields, but on a combination of pastoralism and slash-and-burn farming. Their subsistence crops were "coarse grains" such as buckwheat, oats, corn, and potatoes, scorned by the Chinese. Their clothing was made from hemp and woolens rather than cotton and silk. Virtually all were tenants on lands held by Han, Hui, and Yi. The historic tales explain how the Golden Homeland and all the riches associated with it were lost as a result of successive waves of Chinese expansion, a series of battles, and eventual migration westward into the higher plateaux and mountains. It parallels Miao history of the late Ming and Qing periods.

Of course, the Miao were familiar with the concept of writing through their contacts with the Han and interactions with their Yi and Hui landlords in the area. They recognized that writing was linked to power as well as to special knowledge, and that it was almost inaccessible to the Miao. Learning to read in Chinese was prohibitively expensive: actually, most of the Han settlers and soldiers were also poor and illiterate. Only a tiny number of Hua Miao received even a few years of schooling prior to 1900. It was far from sufficient to open the road to the world of books and official positions through the imperial examination system. Study at Hui mosques required conversion and a total change of lifestyle. Yi writing was specialized, known only to a small group of religious practitioners.

Hua Miao tradition credits the missionaries with bringing literacy along with religion. I quote from a letter written in the Pollard script in 1988 to one of the former missionaries:

Thanks be that Pastor Chang-chong is well and happy. Thanks be to the Heavenly Father for his love and providence leading us at all times. Now he has come to help a people who are few in number, speaking to the teachers who were here before, making them again look to us Miao brothers and sisters, indeed Miao brothers and sisters, mothers and fathers. Years ago, teachers faced great adversity and hardship to help us Miao brothers and sisters. They made Miao books, built schools and hospitals and taught us to be clever and wise. They came and said to the Miao people "You have all the Heavenly Father's protection, peace and joy." When they had been told all this, their hearts were glad and rejoiced greatly. Thanks be to the Heavenly Father forever. Praise be that the Lord remains with you and also remains with us, protecting and embracing us and giving peace and joy in our hearts. This is only simple writing and some is written incorrectly. Teachers, pastors, please forgive us. Amen.[6]

A letter received a few months later expressed the hope that Teacher Pollard himself might return to build schools and hospitals and bring wisdom and leadership, though many Miao know that Pollard's grave is at Shimenkan.[7]

Samuel Pollard's mission to the Miao began in the summer of 1904 when four Miao men arrived unannounced at the CIM compound in Zhaotong City in northeastern Yunnan. They spoke some Chinese, and explained that they came seeking "instruction" from Mr. Pollard. They brought with them a food supply sufficient for a week's stay and their return journey, and a letter of introduction from another CIM missionary, James Adam, whose station was at Anshun in western Guizhou. He had sent them on to Pollard, whose station was much closer to their home villages.[8]

Pollard's diary entry for 12 July 1904 notes, "They were very much in earnest in learning to read." He was not sure whether it was that or the Christian message that had drawn them. However, he welcomed them, and housed them in an empty classroom, realizing that they would be unwelcome at Chinese inns even if they had the money to pay for lodgings. With the Zhaotong mission school on holiday, Pollard and his wife Emmy set to work teaching the four "scouts" (as he dubbed them) to read from the Chinese version of the Gospels. He preached to them in simple Chinese, taught them a few hymns, and they left at the end of a week when their food supply began to run low. To Pollard's surprise, five more "scouts" arrived in the following week, and after that a group of thirteen, all asking for "instruction." They told Pollard that thousands more were waiting in the hills "to see the missionary and hear Ie-su."[9]

By mid-August, the number of visiting Miao had risen to over 100. By September, there was growing concern in Zhaotong regarding the comings and goings of these hill people. Rumors swept the area: the Miao were planning uprisings and receiving secret poisons from the missionaries to use to kill the Chinese. Other rumors said that the missionaries had a "magic water" which gave the Miao instant literacy.[10] The first rumor drew on memories of the widespread nineteenth-century rebellions of the indigenous peoples, including the Hui rebellions in Yunnan. The second had to do with power and prestige. Pollard embarked on his first tour of the Hua Miao home areas, partly out of curiosity and partly to seek cooperation from local officials and strongmen to squash the rumors and end the escalating violence against the Miao. Throughout the region, individual Miao were being beaten, tortured, forced to pay over large sums of money, and threatened with exclusion from the market towns or the periodic markets.

Pollard's intervention, and his visits to a number of Miao settlements, had the effect of intensifying the pilgrimages to Zhaotong. The number of visitors rose to 40 or 50 a week. The Pollards were overwhelmed by the work of teaching and caring for the inquirers in addition to their regular duties at the mission. Mr. Pollard drew one of the mission's Chinese pastors, Stephan Li, into the work and together they produced a collection of Bible stories in very simple Chinese for Miao use. He also began learning Dian Dongbei and experimenting with a romanized transcription.

His involvement with the Miao work soon became total. The work in Zhaotong was a struggle to win a handful of Chinese converts. In contrast, the Miao sought him out as their teacher, and the number of potential converts was growing rapidly. He found the Miao to be receptive and quick learners. He saw many things in their traditional culture that he preferred to the Chinese way of life. He was particularly impressed by the spirit and confidence of the women, the absence of footbinding, and the courage and resourcefulness with which the Hua Miao seemed to face the difficulties of life. However, he did not totally romanticize them. He was appalled by their heavy use of alcohol, premarital sexual freedom, and continuing belief in what he termed "devils" and "witchdoctors." These failings were, in his view, the result of poverty and ignorance and his call was to help them overcome both.

The Chinese viewed the Miao as newly pacified barbarians, less able than the Hui or Yi. They were regarded as an inferior and rootless people. Pollard saw them as landless and poor, but kept that way by restrictions on purchase of land and by exorbitant rents in cash, in kind, and in labor service. Labor service included the forced growing of opium for their landlords; the Hua Miao did not use it themselves. Pollard's understanding of the Hua Miao differed considerably from the general view. Drawing on his Cornwall origins, he felt a kinship with the Miao; he compared them to the original Britons who were driven from their lands and oppressed by the Roman, Saxon, and Norman invaders. Drawing on his religious background, he saw them as a persecuted people who were already among God's chosen awaiting word of the renewal of the Covenant: "They are as slaves, like the Israelites in Egypt under Pharaoh; they are wanting liberty but are not getting it," he noted in his diary on 4 November 1904. In other interpretations, he saw them as the people to whom Christ himself would have preached or as the despised and rejected in whom Christ appears in this world. In a report written shortly before his death he wrote, "He is still the ally of the poor and downtrodden. He is still on the side of the lowly of the earth and does not object to be the Friend of the Miao, sharing their humble cottage and mud-floor fireside."[11]

As for the Miao themselves, they seem to have alternated between despair and resistance. Their historical myths told them that they had a glorious past, and that they had put up a good fight against the imperial troops. They saw themselves as a people who had been outnumbered militarily, dispossessed and scattered, and now exploited and cheated because they were poor, weak, and illiterate. In the local hierarchy of ethnic groups, they ranked near the bottom, below the Chinese, the Yi aristocracy (Black Yi) and free men (White Yi), and the Hui, closer to the Yi slave caste. Despite their position in the social hierarchy, they sometimes saw themselves as the original owners of vast tracts of land, as the pioneers who opened up new areas for cultivation and pasturage, as holders of a rich body of oral literature, and as the moral and cultural equals or superiors to many of their immediate neighbors. The Yi overlords, Chinese officials, and Hui merchants were intimidating because they had superior economic, military, and political power. But the Chinese settlers in the mountain areas were not impressive. Like the Miao, they were, for the most part, poor and illiterate. The demobilized soldiers and the wretched colonists brought from other areas of the empire did not inspire the urge to assimilate and "become Chinese." They were known sometimes to engage in violence: to burn down villages, loot, rape, kidnap, and even kill. They bound their women's feet and jeered at those who did not. Some smoked opium. The Yi were the lesser of two evils, and many Hua Miao fled to the protection of "native officials" (*tumu* or *tusi*) appointed from the ranks of the Yi nobility and enfiefed with large estates. There too they were forced to grow opium and render labor service, but life under Yi rule had one advantage, which was that the Yi did not pressure them to assimilate. One could only be a Black Yi or a White Yi by virtue of descent, and the Yi preferred to fill the slave ranks with kidnapped Chinese in hopes of ransom money.

The Chinese referred to the Miao (and many other ethnic groups) by various terms that meant "barbarians." Similar terms were used for foreigners, which may have been an advantage for Pollard and the other missionaries, making them seem closer and more accessible. The term "Miao" was only slightly more polite usage. It literally means "weeds." It is still in use today, but the Hua Miao's own name for themselves is *ad hmaob*, which might gloss as "the people."

As Pollard was aware, the Miao were at times optimistic about their ability to overcome stronger opponents. Some of their popular folktales are variations on the theme of the weak overcoming the strong by cleverness, bluff, or supernatural assistance. In one widespread tale, a small mother goat frightens off a fierce tiger. In another, a powerful Chinese king covets the wealth accumulated by a Miao man and also covets the man's wife. Thanks to the wife's supernatural powers, the king loses everything he owns, and the Miao emerges victorious. Such stories carried the message that the meek might indeed inherit the earth, which was one of the messages that Pollard stressed in his teaching.

By the end of 1904, Pollard was convinced that he had been specially called to work with the Miao and that the China Inland Mission in Zhaotong was not the appropriate place. Thus, he made further journeys into the surrounding hill areas, searching for a mission site. In March 1905 he persuaded an Yi landlord to cede him a small tract of land near a Miao hamlet at Shimenkan (Stone Gateway), some twenty miles east of Zhaotong in Guizhou. He took with him two dedicated Han Chinese ministers, the brothers James and Stephan Li, from the CIM Zhaotong mission. Save for a home furlough in 1908, he lived there continuously until his death in 1915. He became fluent in the Shimenkan dialect, often wore Miao dress, and lived as close to the local style as possible, which meant that he and his family lived in poverty.[12] This willingness to live among the Miao and to share their hardships is a core part of the contemporary tales told about him.

Within a short time, the Shimenkan mission had a chapel and a school building in addition to the rough housing for the missionaries themselves. Mrs. Pollard joined actively in the teaching and preaching, riding circuit when necessary. One of her important contributions was her skill as a trained nurse. The new mission maintained contact with the CIM hospital in Zhaotong: visits from missionary doctors were welcome. So were visits by other CIM missionaries who were interested in doing "tribal work" in neighboring regions. These included Arthur Nicholl, who was working in Wuding, and Harry Parsons at Dongchuan. Pollard was not eager to have more foreign missionaries in residence at Shimenkan. Eventually he welcomed Harry Parsons to take over the work during his furlough time, and in 1909 accepted an assistant, William Hudspeth, who had an unusually strong interest in linguistics and ethnology.[13] On principle he refused offers from the home mission board to send further personnel. Send us money instead, he argued, so that we can educate and train Miao clergy and teachers.

The request for funding rather than additional outside personnel flowed from Pollard's ideas about church organization and reflected his background in the Bible Christian church. It was the Bible Christians who had initially sponsored Samuel Pollard to go to China under CIM auspices. In 1907, the Bible Christians merged with the United Methodist Free Churches and Methodist New Connexion into the United Methodist Church. Pollard's work then came under the supervision and support of that larger body and its mission board.

The Bible Christians were a nineteenth-century Methodist dissenting sect, localized in Cornwall and Devon.[14] The membership was drawn from the lower middle class and working class: farmers, tradesmen, artisans, tin miners, and such. The disagreements with mainline Wesleyan Methodism were considerable. Bible Christians preferred chapel to church, and their meeting places were simple whitewashed cottages built by cooperative labor and community funding. They distrusted hierarchical structures. Lay leaders held a high degree of responsibility for the day-to-day operations of the chapels. Women were allowed to preach and teach. The chapels served as daytime schools for the children and as evening schools for adults of both sexes. Bible study was strongly encouraged and was at least as important as church ritual. Their ideal "church" was not a stone-and-stained-glass edifice used only on Sundays and high church holidays. Reaching back into Judeo-Christian tradition, they thought of the church as "synagogue," a place for daily study and worship.

This pattern appealed strongly to the Hua Miao. Within a few years after the establishment of the Stone Gateway station, most of the teaching and evangelizing was being done by the Hua Miao themselves. After training at the Stone Gateway school some returned to their home villages to establish schools and chapels. Some went out as teachers and evangelists to other Hua Miao communities and into areas settled by other ethnic groups. By 1914, Hua Miao students were attending colleges in Chengdu, Wuhan, and Kunming, many of them eventually returning as ordained ministers, doctors, teachers, and skilled technicians. Nineteen village schools were operating, aside from the expanding school complex at Stone Gateway.[15]

Stone Gateway grew as the center of the work with the Hua Miao and outreach to Chuan Miao and Yi. The church there attracted upwards of 5,000 people on church festival days. There was a secondary school as well as a primary school, a clinic, an orphanage, and a leprosarium on the outskirts. But the real success, for Pollard, was the growth of chapels and schools in the outlying villages stretching from Weining in southwest Guizhou to Yiliang in northeast Yunnan. Mountain villages of no more than 30 or 40 households voluntarily pooled funds and labor among themselves or with neighboring villages to build simple whitewashed adobe chapels that doubled as schools, to pay the salaries of the teacher-preacher, and to provide scholarships for their students to go on for further education. At its height, the number of village-based schools reached 75. The work stood out as the most dramatically successful of any single mission station in China. The Tribal Movement, as it came to be called, was seen as a great breakthrough in the spreading of the gospel in China. Certainly it answered the Hua Miao request for literacy.

For the Bible Christian model to work, the written word had to be accessible. Early in the Miao work it became increasingly obvious that Chinese Bibles, hymnals, and tracts were not the solution.[16] The experiments with romanization of Dian Dongbei were also unsatisfactory. Pollard then turned to the idea of an indigenous script such as had emerged among North American Indian groups or in the missionary work in Africa. In 1905, working closely with the new Hua Miao preachers that he had trained, he developed a series of symbols that would more effectively represent the phonetics and tone system of the language. One group of symbols represented initial consonants; another represented the vowels and were placed in different positions relative to the initial to indicate tone.[17]

A number of contemporary Chinese scholars deny that the script is "indigenous." Some describe it as a latinized romanization, though even a cursory glance at a text would show that only a few of the initial consonant signs derive from Latin letters, namely the *T*, *L*, *S*, *V*, and *Y*. Others insist it is borrowed from the writing of some "primitive African tribe" or combines Latin letters with African ones.[18] All such arguments are dismissive of the script.

The Hua Miao would not agree with these interpretations. Their own accounts, passed on by oral tradition or noted by researchers in discussion with contemporary Hua Miao intellectuals and ordinary villagers, credit the origins of the script to a group effort which drew on Hua Miao culture for its design. In an article written in the late 1940s, Wang Jianguang, himself a Hua Miao, stresses the input of the first generation of Miao teachers and evangelists into the early formation and later revisions of the script. He particularly singles out Yang Yake, Wang Shengmo, Yang Zhizhu, and Zhang Yohan (Yuehan), all of whom worked with Pollard on the translations of the New Testament and the creation of texts for school use and adult education.[19]

Zhang Yohan himself explained to generations of school children that the symbols were derived from Hua Miao batik and embroidery designs and the shapes of everyday implements. Possibly this explanation came after the fact, as a mnemonic device, but it led the Hua Miao to feel that the symbols came from their own cultural heritage and were not foreign borrowings. The *V*, which carries the same sound it represents in English, is said by the Miao to be the shape of the ox yoke and by extension the *v* initial in *vaif*, meaning "father." Similarly, the *L* is explained as the initial in *hlaot*, an L-shaped hoe. The symbol similar to a *Y* represents an initial *a* sound and is linked to the term for a Y-shaped wooden plow. Other symbols, such as a reversed *L*, an inverted *L*, or a triangle, are similar to batik and embroidery designs which represent rivers, mountains, rice fields, and so on. These traditional motifs are believed by many Miao to be evidence of their lost writing system. The women's batik skirts can be "read" as history.

The introduction of the script provided a new history. By the summer of 1906, Pollard and his Miao associates had begun the translation of the Gospel of Mark. It was completed at the end of the year, and arrangements made for it to be published in Chengdu by a woodblock printing method. The Gospel of John became available in the following year, and by the autumn of 1912 all four Gospels were printed in one volume by the British and Foreign Bible Society in Shanghai. Work on the remainder of the New Testament was completed late in 1914.

Pollard died in September of 1915, a victim of typhoid contracted while nursing the Stone Gateway students through an epidemic. His work was taken over by William Hudspeth and Harry Parsons. A revised edition of the complete New Testament was published in 1917, under Hudspeth's direction. This event had a great deal of meaning for the Hua Miao, involving not just the availability of the book itself but also the circumstances surrounding its publication. The book was printed in Japan rather than Shanghai. Yang Yake, by then a leading Miao preacher, traveled with Hudspeth to Japan to oversee the printing and make final corrections. He was hosted and treated as a person of importance in Japan and in church circles in the major cities of eastern China that they visited during the journey. It was the first time in memory that a Hua Miao had traveled so far, or under such dignified conditions.[20]

The use of the script extended well beyond the New Testament and the various hymnals and tracts that began to circulate in the Hua Miao areas of settlement. In the early grades of the school system the script was the medium for teaching basic science and general knowledge along with religious concepts. It was a guide to the pronunciation of standard Mandarin Chinese and the pronunciation and meaning of the Chinese ideographs learned in the higher grades. Miao teachers transcribed popular folktales and songs, some of which were incorporated into the school curriculum, while a larger collection circulated in inexpensive mimeographed booklets for a wider audience. Because it was easy to learn, it became the common medium for writing letters and keeping records. Starting in 1917, the Hua Miao had their own church newsletter, and during the 1930s and 1940s there was a small newspaper that carried local, national, and international news culled from Chinese and foreign publications and shortwave radio broadcasts. In the late 1930s, the Hua Miao college students published a fervent manifesto calling for a United Front against Japanese aggression. Thus, the script seemed to have unlimited uses, proving that the Hua Miao were indeed a literate people. Moreover, it demonstrated that they could be a part of the modern world without assimilating to Chinese culture.

The script had an appeal beyond the ethnic boundaries of Hua Miao society. Hua Miao evangelists, emulating Pollard, were willing to live among strangers and learn their language and customs in order to carry the Christian message. In the process, they became the bearers and teachers of literacy, offering a flexible system that was not patently "foreign" and that circumvented the problems of learning Chinese ideographs or another language. It required only minor revision for use with the White Miao (Chuan Miao) in Sichuan or with Lisu and Lahu in the Wuding-Saposhan area where CIM missionaries were working.

Another arena for interactions between the Hua Miao and their neighbors was the school network in the Miao villages and at Shimenkan. As late as the 1940s, the government school system was weak in the rural areas of Yunnan and Guizhou. Neighboring Han and Yi, eager for their children to participate in the new modern education, but without any facilities of their own, turned to the Hua Miao for help. The missionaries and Miao churches assisted in organizing schools for them, often staffing them with Hua Miao teachers. In some instances Han and Yi children came to the Miao villages for schooling, in a reversal of the earlier status ranking among the various ethnic groups. From their position at the bottom of the social ladder, mocked and despised for their ignorance and lack of "culture," the Miao became the carriers of modern education even to the Han Chinese. Hua Miao teachers and ministers found that they were addressed by title and honorifics even by upper-class Chinese, and government officials and Yi nobles attended the graduation ceremonies and the interschool sports meets at Stone Gateway.[21]

Still, prejudices die hard, and there were setbacks. Missionaries working at Stone Gateway in the late 1940s reported that there were still instances in which Han and Yi middle-school students bullied their Miao classmates. Miao parents were hesitant to send their children to the available government middle schools in Zhaotong and Kunming for fear that as a minority they would be harassed on the streets or even in the dormitories and classrooms.[22]

The Hua Miao schools were also a gateway for learning Chinese. The village schools provided an encouraging environment in which to learn Chinese as a second language, and the shift was gradual. Beyond the initial primary grades, the textbooks were in standard Mandarin, though Dian Dongbei continued as the language of the classroom, the dormitories, and the playgrounds. The classical (*wenyan*) texts used in the early years of the school system were dropped in response to the development of a modern school system nationwide and replaced by new textbooks for history, geography, literature, science, and mathematics. Various sports were encouraged and, at Pollard's insistence, the Stone Gateway complex soon included a swimming pool.

The school system was coeducational from the outset, though girls were clearly in the minority. Most parents seemed to feel that a few years' attendance at a village primary school was sufficient for girls. This remains an issue today. Most of the village schools were closed by the new government after 1950, with available schooling usually located in the larger Han Chinese settlements. Hua Miao parents are less willing to allow their daughters to make the long daily journeys back and forth. They cite as one reason their fear that the girls will be harassed or even attacked on the roads. Another reason is that by the age of eight or nine girls are needed to assist with the agricultural work and domestic tasks, and are also at an age when they must begin to learn weaving, batik work, and embroidery.

During the time that the Pollards were in residence, Emmy Pollard took charge of education for the older girls. She ran a split program of formal schooling and industrial arts, meaning cooking, nursing, public health, and handicrafts. The magistrate in Weining was so impressed by its success that he sent three young Chinese women there for several months to study alongside the Hua Miao.[23] However, during the 1920s this segment of the school system ceased to operate, and the only special classes for women were the Bible study groups. It was the Hua Miao who began pressuring for a resumption of women's education beyond the primary school level, while rejecting the idea that the older girls be sent to a church-run boarding school in Zhaotong. The girls' school at Stone Gateway reopened in 1932, and the United Methodist Church report for that year notes: "It was the boy students who morally compelled us to open it, by pointing out through their parents, that to give a sound education to the boys of a tribe and to neglect the girls was a fatal policy since, when the boys married, there was serious incompatibility."[24]

Throughout the 1930s and into the 1940s, the missionaries at Stone Gateway repeatedly made requests to the home mission for additional women teachers and deaconesses and for funding for expansion of primary and secondary schooling within the Hua Miao circuits. The earlier policies of self-help were no longer adequate to the demand for education. At best they supported three-year village primary schools. There was no funding from the national or provincial government. However, the directors of the Southwest District of the Methodist Missionary Society were mainly concerned with putting their major efforts and resources into the existent struggling Han Chinese churches, into work with the swelling flood of refugees from the Japanese-occupied areas, and into new outreach to the Yi, who were emerging as a strong political force in Yunnan under the governorship of Long Yun.

In 1943, the Hua Miao took matters into their own hands. Zhu Huanzhang, a teacher in the Zhaotong Middle School, led a delegation to call on Yang Zhizhong, an Yi notable on the Border Tribes Commission of the national government. Yang's sympathetic response led to government funding for an expanded middle-school complex at Stone Gateway. The Southwest District of MMS had no choice but to cooperate, turning over some of the buildings to the new enterprise. Governor Long Yun was appointed as chairman of the school board, the head of the Southwest District was appointed as vice-chairman, and Mr. Zhu became the headmaster, holding that post until his death in 1951 during the political turmoil following Liberation. To smooth the situation, it was agreed that all the school board members would be Christians.[25]

The Hua Miao confidence in going over the heads of the church bureaucracy was in part sparked by the greater control they had gained over the churches in the Miao circuit during the late 1930s and 1940s. By then, the circuit was supervised by Miao rather than by Chinese or foreign clergy. These were the students of the Pollard, Parsons, and Hudspeth early years, who had received theological training at seminaries in Chengdu, Wuhan, and elsewhere, and had been formally ordained. The various lay preachers and teachers came under their jurisdiction. Under their guidance, additional services were created and new hymns introduced. In 1941 they independently invited a Mr. Feng, a Chinese technician, to open a small industrial school at Stone Gateway. The Miao "subdistrict" leaders gathered once or twice a year in their own meetings, separate from the Yi and Han who made up the minority constituency of the Southwest District. Summer classes for the village teachers and preachers brought the participants together from the entire Hua Miao area of settlement to discuss problems specific to the Hua Miao as well as to engage in Bible study, and to discuss religious matters and practical teaching concerns.[26] In short, gatherings of the church network served as an informal political structure. It was in fact the only organization linking diverse villages. But its potential as a source of ethnic unity or as a representative voice for the concerns of all segments of the population was severely limited by exclusion of "pagan" leaders and representatives of non-Christian communities. Conversion of course requires giving up former religious beliefs and practices. The Methodist agenda further banned some aspects of traditional secular practice, particularly the complex of courtship customs (which often involved premarital sex), the use of alcohol, and playing of the lusheng pipes. These restrictions were threatening to the more conservative and unconverted segments of the Hua Miao population for whom such customs were an integral part of a Hua Miao (or non-Han) identity.

There were still many Hua Miao, certainly a majority, who were not formally affiliated with the church. Those numbers included some who were willing to send their children to church-run schools. It was not necessary for a family to be Christian in order for the children to attend, any more than it was necessary to be a Christian to attend school sports meets and religious celebrations at Stone Gateway. They sent their children to the nearest school, and were receptive to the new technological innovations that were being introduced through the churches and the mission station at Stone Gateway. These included improved seed for potatoes (a staple food), new vegetables suited to high altitudes, apple orchards, a more advanced weaving loom, and vaccinations against smallpox. The school graduations and the summer sports meets at Stone Gateway (introduced by the first missionaries as a substitute for the traditional "flower mountain festival") drew thousands of spectators.

The growing separatism of the Hua Miao churches was not entirely a matter of self-determination. It was initially encouraged by the fears of the Chinese representatives to the synod and foreign missionaries working outside of the Miao areas that they would be numerically swamped by the Miao at meetings of the Southwest District. The new rules for the synod, laid down by the home church in the early 1930s, based representation on the number of churches and the size of membership. The baptized and confirmed Hua Miao converts, plus adherents, numbered in the tens of thousands. The Chinese and Yi membership was counted in the hundreds. Thus the Miao could dominate the meetings and win important posts, a situation which some felt would adversely affect outreach to the Chinese. Funding was a serious issue here as well. The Miao village chapels and primary schools continued to be self-supporting, along the lines that Pollard had encouraged. The Yi congregations required a small amount of financial assistance, and the small Chinese churches were almost totally reliant financially on outside support. One district leader used the argument that the self-reliance of the Miao and Yi churches would be weakened if they were not kept separate from the Chinese: they would demand supplementary funding and their ministers would ask for the same salaries as were being given to ordained Chinese clergy and church workers.[27]

Miao teachers and ministers were already aware that their earnings were markedly less than those of the Han Chinese. In 1935, missionaries from the Seventh Day Adventist mission began to proselytize in the Hua Miao areas. They offered salaries for clergy and teachers that were double or triple their current wages, and also offered full scholarships to their middle school. In the summer of 1937, the Miao teachers at Stone Gateway went on strike, threatening a mass resignation if their salaries were not raised.[28]

Hua Miao suspicions that they were being shortchanged increased during the early 1940s. Due to the outbreak of war, funds from MMS had dried up. Local Chinese, Yi, and Miao assumed that the home church was withdrawing its support of the mission effort or, alternatively, that the leadership of the Southwest District was deliberately withholding monies in order to work with the flood of refugees from eastern China. The rumors were given further credence by the lessened visibility of foreign missionaries at Stone Gateway. They were in Kunming, or driving for the Friends Ambulance Corps and doing other war-related work (including, of course, work with the new refugees from Shanghai and Nanjing). For several years running, there was no full-time missionary at Stone Gateway, a situation which had occurred once before in the 1920s when political turmoil led to an order from the home church that all missionaries in the field be withdrawn for their own safety.

With the end of the war, the missionaries returned to Stone Gateway. The group included several young women who had volunteered to serve as teachers, nurses, and agricultural extension workers. They remained until late 1949.[29] However, enough Hua Miao had been educated and trained by then so that the foreign presence was less needed; there were some 30 university graduates, another large body of students enrolled in university, and a sizable number of middle school graduates. Some of that new intelligentsia "disappeared" for a time to join the Communist guerrillas and participate in the liberation of Guizhou and Yunnan, reappearing afterward as Party cadres. Others were less fortunate.

After the establishment of the People's Republic many of the more educated Hua Miao fared badly. The village schools and chapels were closed, and some of the Hua Miao teaching at middle schools were dismissed from their posts. Some of the teachers, ministers, and lay preachers were jailed, others were transferred to perform ordinary labor, and a few committed suicide under the pressure. Accusations against them included being "British spies" or active members and supporters of the disgraced Guomindang. Later, during the Cultural Revolution, even former attendance at the Stone Gateway Middle School became suspect because after 1935 the students were expected to join the Guomindang Youth Corps, as were middle school students everywhere in Nationalist-held territory.

The Pollard script was banned as an official medium for teaching or official matters after 1949. Nothing was offered in its place; one could only become literate by learning Chinese at the nearest government schools, often far from the Miao settlements, where all instruction was conducted in Yunnanese Mandarin. Still, the script remained alive within the villages. Church members met in private homes, using the increasingly worn Bibles and hymnals and making hand copies as needed. Letters to relatives and friends continued to be written in the script. Not until the post-Mao reforms of the early 1980s were Miao intellectuals able to gain permission to create a new romanized script to replace the earlier one, reopen some of the village schools, and reintroduce Dian Dongbei into the classrooms.[30] Until then the only reading materials in Dian Dongbei were the pre-1949 materials from the church and village schools, preserved even by non-Christians and treasured as proof that the Hua Miao were not illiterate and backward.

Chinese cadres in the region hold the opinion that Dian Dongbei is unsuited to modern times because it lacks vocabulary for the many new technical and political terms that have come into use in the wider society. This viewpoint is shared by some of the younger Hua Miao cadres. It is useless to argue that many of these terms are new coinages in *putonghua*, unknown to anyone until recently, while others of older vintage were known only to a small educated elite. There is blanket denial that equivalent terms can be constructed from the existent vocabulary of Dian Dongbei or any other of the minority languages. Publications in the minority tongues are studded with *pinyin* renderings of Chinese words: the Communist Party can only be called "gongchandang" and "socialism" is irrevocably "shehuizhuyi," though any student of first-year Chinese realizes that these compounds are composed of simple words that are likely to occur in many languages.

It is probably not politic for Hua Miao cadres to argue in response that Dian Dongbei and the Pollard script were adequate for translating the New Testament, many Methodist hymns, and the national and international news. The issue here is not linguistic flexibility but rather national unity and national policy. There is an official state language which must be recognized as the sole medium for higher education, socialist construction, and modernization, all led by the most advanced of China's nationalities. The viewpoint of China's scholars in the field of minority studies (*minzuxue*) is that the various nationalities are not just culturally different from the Han Chinese but are representative of earlier stages of human history that the Han long ago surpassed. In comparison to the Han, these peoples are portrayed as socially and culturally backward, lacking "culture" in the formal sense, and fixed at lower levels of social development such as the primitive communal society, the slave society, or various stages of feudalism. Within that reading of the Marxist evolutionary framework, the existence of an indigenous popular writing system based on the vernacular is a contradiction, and the ability of the minority languages to express new concepts and complex ideas generated by the more modernized sector is denied. Thus, the written materials for the minorities borrow heavily from standard Mandarin. From the start, they serve as a step toward learning *putonghua*, and subtextually carry the message that *putonghua* is the only legitimate language for participation in the modern sector and for political discourse.

Under these circumstances, Han cadres assigned to the minority areas have felt little or no pressure to learn any of the local languages. Pressure on the Hua Miao (and others) to learn standard Chinese has been heavy. Anyone aspiring to a lower-level cadre position in the village or commune (now township) needs some facility in speaking and reading Chinese. Of course, by 1950 some Hua Miao already spoke a more standard Mandarin than the local Yunnanese dialect of Mandarin, thanks to the church schools and the opportunities to study in various urban centers. Paradoxically, this worked to their disadvantage, barring them from Party membership and political office. As one informant explained, if you were truly illiterate you could not hold office. If you knew only the Pollard script you were still regarded as illiterate, and also politically suspect. If you had mastered Chinese before 1949, then even if you were avowedly non-Christian you might also be politically suspect. Thus, the best credentials were education in a Chinese school after 1950, followed by a period of service in the army.

Despite these difficulties, the Pollard script has survived the four decades since Liberation and continues to be regarded as an indigenous writing system by the Hua Miao, who refer to it as "the old writing." Similarly, a large segment of the population regard themselves as Christians and continue to hold worship services in private homes, or in the few churches and "meeting points" that have been allowed to resume activity since the early

1980s. Of all the missionaries who spent time in the area, Pollard's name is the best known. "Baikeli," as he is called, has become part of the local oral history, widely admired by Christians and non-Christians alike. Some of the tales credit him with superhuman powers or angelic protection. Others merge him with more recent political "model heroes" like Dr. Norman Bethune or Lei Feng as an exemplar of service to others and willing self-sacrifice.[31] The circulation of these stories causes bewilderment and concern among various levels of the state. Articles published in recent years denounce the missionary endeavor among the Hua Miao, linking it to imperialism and colonialist designs, and describing the Miao as a naive and backward people who were easily misled.[32] Still, the attacks stop short of direct accusations against Pollard himself. Even the local Party cadres say that he voluntarily gave up the comforts of home, lived in poverty, served the people and, like Bethune, died in that service. To them, he was the model of a good cadre; to the religious believers he was a saint as well as the restorer of the written word.

Some of the current articles from China also suggest that the Hua Miao converted because of the financial advantages of an association with foreigners. As indicated earlier in this chapter, the Hua Miao churches were largely self-supporting through tithing and labor contributions. Access to literacy and schooling, modern medical care, and technological assistance attracted followers, but these services were only in part provided by foreigners and conversion was not a requirement. It is hard to see the Hua Miao as "rice Christians," and that interpretation fails to explain the persistence of Christian belief and practice through underground churches after 1949 when the foreigners were withdrawn and all outside funding stopped. Nor does the "rice Christian" argument explain the growth of church groups during the years of the Cultural Revolution, a time when being a Christian or speaking well of the missionaries brought punishment in its wake.

What I hope to convey in this chapter is that an indigenized Christianity has been developing among the Hua Miao for some 80 years. It is closely linked to the introduction of literacy through a widely accepted writing system that has become part of the total ethnic identity of the group. The Hua Miao originally came to the mission stations requesting that they be taught to read, meaning literacy in Chinese that provided access to the canons of Chinese statecraft as well as to the powerful new texts rumored to be carried by the foreigners. What they received was unexpected: the sacred and powerful foreign texts appeared in their own language, along with new songs and school texts that conveyed knowledge both in the Miao vernacular and in Chinese. A significant segment of the young men (and a few women as well) became adequately prepared to move on to higher levels of education in Zhaotong, Kunming, Chengdu, Wuhan, and elsewhere with a head start on modern education during the first few decades of the century.

The importance of the coming of the written word, however, goes beyond creation of a small Hua Miao intellectual elite. For those larger numbers touched by the village schools and chapels and the complex at Stone Gateway, Dian Dongbei retained its status as the language of daily use, supplemented by a working knowledge of Chinese as a lingua franca that enabled them to communicate more effectively with neighboring Han, Yi, and Hui and within the larger Christian community. At the same time, Dian Dongbei was elevated as a literary language. The biblical texts linked them to ancient peoples of the Near East, to the Christian martyrs, the Protestant reformation, and the outside world. The songs in the hymnals became part of a widely known oral literature. As elsewhere, literacy strengthened self-identity and resistance against assimilation to some of the cultural and social practices advocated by the Han Chinese state, practices which were not only alien to the Miao but also seen as unchristian. The growing literacy tradition further served as a buffer against state definitions of the Hua Miao as a backward, undeveloped people and as a protest against political powerlessness.

With the liberalization of religious policies since 1980, the Hua Miao once again travel long distances to attend mass intervillage services on church festival days. Miao cadres express the hope that the schools at Stone Gateway will be restored as "key schools" for talented youth and as a cultural center for the Hua Miao people. The "old writing" has been incorporated into the new school primers. The Old Testament is being translated into the Miao vernacular, and a debate goes on about whether it should appear in Pollard script or in the new romanization.

Whether the Pollard script will eventually be replaced by the new romanization remains to be seen. Even for those Miao cadres who claim "atheism" and strongly identify with the Party and the state, the Pollard script is associated with their parents and grandparents who gained the respect of other ethnic groups because of their literacy and knowledge, and who learned modern skills which allowed them to play new roles within the larger society. For those who are now third or fourth generation Christians, the script is part of what they regard as "tradition," as intrinsically "Miao" as the costumes, foods, music, and dance that are the visible, state-approved markers of Hua Miao ethnicity.

CHAPTER 9

Christianity and Hakka Identity

NICOLE CONSTABLE

Less than a mile from the Fanling train station, in the northeastern region of the New Territories of Hong Kong, in an area that was once the heart of the Cantonese Tang (Mandarin: Deng) lineage's ancestral land, lies a very unusual community: the village of Shung Him Tong — the village of "humble worship" — a community of Hakka Protestants.[1] The area, also known as Lung Yeuk Tau, is located on Dragon Mountain, and as the local legends have it, the dragon holds a pearl in its mouth. On top of the pearl, at the opening of the dragon's mouth, a place which is reputed to have powerful geomantic features, Hakka Christians founded their village in 1903 despite local opposition.

In this chapter I examine the relationship between Christianity and the Hakka Chinese identity of the people of Shung Him Tong and suggest some of the broader connections between religious and ethnic identity. In the first part of the chapter I outline the historical connection between the Basel Evangelical Missionary Society and the Hakka of Hong Kong and Guangdong Province in the late nineteenth and early twentieth century. In the second part I turn to a case study of Shung Him Tong Village and assert that although the Christianity of the people of Shung Him Tong does not take a particularly "Chinese" form, their Christian identity has not served to undermine their sense of Han Chinese or Hakka identity. Rather, as I intend to show, Christianity has allowed Hakka Christians to reassert, reinterpret, and to some extent reinforce their Hakka identity.

Paul Cohen and other scholars have suggested that in China Christianity often attracted groups that were in some way "marginal" to the dominant Chinese power structure. For the plains aborigines in Taiwan described by John Shepherd in this volume, or the Miao described by

Norma Diamond, as well as the Hakka, such is the case. But the Hakka, although "disreputable," "impoverished," or marginal to the wider Chinese power structure during the nineteenth century,[2] are also—unlike the aborigines, Miao, or other minorities—Han Chinese. For the plains aborigines and the Miao, Christian conversion was an oppositional strategy, a way to avoid sinicization, and a means of empowering these groups in their resistance to imposed definitions, identities, and cultural categories of the Han. For the Hakka, Christianity was certainly a means of empowerment, and of resistance, but unlike for the aborigines and the Miao, Christianity was not constructed by Hakka Christians in opposition to Han identity or culture. For them Christianity could be used and renegotiated in their continued claims to legitimate Han identity.

The reconciliation of Christian and Chinese identity is not simple, straightforward, or unproblematic for Hakka Christians. It requires a reconstruction of Chinese values and beliefs within the acceptable framework of pious, conservative Reformed Basel mission traditions. Although Christian beliefs and values presented some beliefs that were fundamentally in opposition to certain Chinese ones, I hope to show that the Hakka church also provided an important context in which Hakka Christians could express and claim the distinctiveness of Hakka identity and in so doing, continue to assert their Han identity.

Who Are the Hakka?

As with most questions concerning identity, the answer depends on whom one asks, and those who claim the identity vary according to the situation and the context. In contemporary Hong Kong, many non-Hakka or Hakka who do not openly acknowledge their Hakka identity associate the name Hakka with a variety of negative connotations ranging from poor, uneducated, backward country bumpkins to "uncivilized," "tribal," or "non-Chinese barbarians." A positive description of the Hakka as patriotic, cooperative, "pure" Chinese also exists and can be consistently elicited from those who openly acknowledge their Hakka identity.

The definition of the Hakka that is most widely accepted by Hakka Christians of Shung Him Tong is that which has been popularized in the work of the famous Hakka historian Luo Xianglin, and is the same as that espoused by international Hakka associations the world over.[3] Luo's work has been referred to as a "veritable bible for the Hakka," an unambiguous statement of a number of Hakka beliefs.[4] As S. T. Leong summarizes, Luo believes that

(1) Hakkas were originally migrants from the Central Plain, true Han Chinese from the cradle of Chinese civilization, not hill aborigines as their neighbors repeatedly identified them, out of ignorance or malice; (2) Hakkas were historically identified with Han patriotism; they were patriotic loyalists of the Chin in the 4th century, Sung loyalists in the late 13th and 14th centuries against Mongol invaders, and anti Manchu patriots in modern times, as exemplified by Hung Hsiu-ch'uan and Sun Yat-sen; (3) the Hakka dialect is unmistakably rooted in prestigious northern, central Plain speech in Sui-T'ang phonology; (4) Hakkas justifiably take pride in their women, in academic achievement, and in the possession of all the orthodox Chinese virtues of diligence, frugality and culturedness in manners and customs.[5]

To Luo and most Hakka, the most important feature of the Hakka is that they are Han Chinese. Although this is officially acknowledged in the People's Republic of China today, Hakka have often felt, particularly during the latter half of the nineteenth century, that they must defend their claim.

According to most sources, Hakka migrated from north central China as early as the fourth century A.D. and arrived in Fujian and Guangdong in or around the fourteenth century.[6] It was after that time that most scholars believe the name Hakka (*kejia*), meaning literally "guests" or "strangers," became attached to this group of settlers in order to distinguish them in local registers from the Punti (*bendi*) or "native inhabitants."[7] The Hakka were despised by the Punti of Guangdong who considered the unfamiliar language and customs of the Hakka evidence that they were "tribal" people and not real Chinese. Dubbed permanent outsiders, settlers, or newcomers, as the name Hakka implied, the Hakka as later arrivals in Guangdong settled in the poorer, more remote mountainous regions of the province. As will become clearer in the course of this chapter, even such a basic and well-accepted definition of the Hakka can be said to be influenced to some extent by Hakka Christians such as Luo who became important spokespersons for the Hakka. Such images of the Hakka were also reinforced and perpetuated by European missionaries who became especially interested in the question of the origin and identity of the Hakka.

The Hakka and the Basel Mission

In the middle of the nineteenth century, a time of war, famine, and natural catastrophes in southern China, when violent conflicts between Hakka and Punti flared and prejudice against Hakka increased,[8] the first members of the Basel mission arrived in China.[9] In the wake of the disastrous Hakka-Punti wars and the defeat of the Taiping Rebellion, thousands of Hakka sought refuge and aid from the Basel mission. This further fueled

Punti hostility and the assertion that the Hakka would never have accepted the faith of the foreign devils had they been *real* Chinese. European missionaries, however, supported the claim that the Hakka originated in northern China.

The first two Basel missionaries in China, Theodor Hamberg and Rudolf Lechler, arrived in Hong Kong in 1847 at the request of Karl Friedrich August Gützlaff, who had founded the Chinese Union. Two Rhenish missionaries who arrived the same year were assigned to work with the Cantonese population, Lechler was sent to work among the Min speakers (Hokkien or Chaozhou) of eastern Guangdong, and Hamberg focused on the Hakka-speaking population of Guangdong in the Pearl River delta region and the area adjoining Hong Kong that later became the New Territories. After Lechler's repeated failures in attracting Hokkien converts, he joined Hamberg in his work among the Hakka. In 1854 Hamberg died; but under Lechler's leadership, the mission grew to include the Hakka regions of northeast Guangdong along the Mei and East rivers. Although in all probably less than 10 percent of all Hakka converted to Christianity, proportionally more Hakka appear to have converted to Christianity than other Chinese.[10]

From early on, the Basel mission came to be associated with the Hakka. As a man from Shung Him Tong explained, although there were other missions that also worked among the Hakka, the Basel mission became known by Hakka people as the "Hakka church." Hakka converts who became missionaries and church helpers worked with European Basel missionaries to translate the Bible, prayer books, and dictionaries into the Hakka language. The people of Shung Him Tong credit the Hakka and European missionaries for uniformly translating Hakka into a written language and devising new Chinese characters to represent colloquial expressions. Through the mission, a standard Hakka dialect was formulated. According to the people of Shung Him Tong, the church dialect allowed Hakka from Meixian, Baoan, and other regions of Guangdong to understand each other despite variation in their dialects. Although it is unlikely that the differences were so great that Hakka from different regions could not understand each other (people in Shung Him Tong who speak different Hakka dialects at home say they have little trouble understanding each other at church), the standard dialect did for the Hakka as a group what language unification has done in unifying many "nationalities" the world over: shared identity depended on a shared language.

Basel mission schools and churches provided important organizational structures for Hakka people. In 1876 there were 4 Basel mission stations, 16 outstations, 11 schools, and 953 communicants spread over the Hakka regions of Guangdong. By 1913, the mission had grown to include 18 mission stations, 108 outstations, and 80 schools (including a theological seminary, 2 normal schools, a middle school, 4 secondary schools, 13 boarding schools, and a total of 3,097 students). There were 2 hospitals, several dispensaries, 72 European staff, 271 Chinese staff, and 6,699 communicants.[11] By 1948 the Basel mission had close to 20,000 communicants.[12] Secondary school students who attended Basel mission schools were taught German and English, and many went on to university studies in medicine and engineering in Shanghai and Canton.[13] The instrumental role of Christianity in the upward mobility of Chinese Christians in Hong Kong has been well documented. Missions provided Western-style education and employment which enabled Chinese Christians to attain positions as middlemen in both business and government.[14] Similarly, the Basel mission allowed for the emergence of a Western-educated, Christian Hakka elite.

In the context of the mission, ties that went beyond surname and native place could be expressed, and Hakka social networks could be expanded. Marriages were arranged between Hakka Christian boys and girls who attended Basel mission schools, and friendships and business alliances were also formed. In the context of the Hakka churches, schools, and seminaries, Hakka people from various regions of Guangdong were brought together, but what linked them was not only their professed belief in a Christian God, but also ethnic ties which had, until then, few opportunities for articulation, with the noteworthy exception of the Taiping Rebellion.

The Taiping Rebellion is worth mentioning here in connection with Hakka identity for several reasons. First, similar to the Hakka churches, the Taiping Rebellion also served to unite Hakka from various regions, reaching beyond kinship or native-place ties. It has been well documented (though perhaps underemphasized) that an overwhelming number of the members of the God-worshipping Society, precursors of the Taipings, were Hakka.[15] We can also assume that some of the same factors that attracted the Hakka to the God-worshipping Society can account for their conversion to Christianity. According to Philip Kuhn, the "long-established congruence of ethnicity with settlement and kinship" in the Canton delta area "meant that no new symbolic structure was needed to express ethnic conflict."[16] But in contrast, "the fragmented kinship and settlement patterns in Kwangsi provided ethnicity no firm social base, and hence no established conceptual format. Amid the violent conflicts of the 1840s, ethnicity became, so to speak, a free-floating variable, one that demanded a new set of concepts for its expression (just as it demanded a new organizational framework — the God-worshipping Society)."[17] Similarly, Hakka churches throughout Hakka regions of Guangdong provided the organizational framework for Hakka ethnicity.

The Taiping Rebellion is also significant because to many Hakka it symbolizes patriotism, nationalism, and other positive Hakka qualities and characteristics. The central role of the Hakka in the Taiping Rebellion also attracted the notice of European missionaries. At first Hamberg and other missionaries were optimistic about the Christian aspects of the God-worshipping Society and the Taipings, though they were later disappointed. However, the Taiping Rebellion demonstrated to some European missionaries that the Hakka were "open to new convictions."[18] Participating in the Taiping Rebellion also displayed the Hakka's "political aptitude," their "military genius," and their "love of liberty."[19] Although the rebellion "turned out a sad failure" in the eyes of some European missionaries, they wondered if "it might have been attended with better results, had the movement been better directed."[20] Lechler and other missionaries also found the Hakka less xenophobic and "clannish" than the Punti and claimed that therefore "the gospel found easier access to them than the latter."[21]

In the wake of the Taiping Rebellion, as many relatives and supporters of the rebellion fled to the shelter of the European missions, the missionary interest in the Hakka grew. Numerous articles in missionary publications and gazetteers focused on the question of Hakka origins. Missionaries asked whether the Hakka were "a peculiar race or tribe, inhabiting the mountains near Canton and Swatow, who are of lower rank than the native Chinese . . . a mongrel race more civilized than the aboriginals, but hardly entitled to rank with the Chinese?"[22] Or were they a "very distinct and virile strain of the Chinese race," "Chinese *de pure sang*," "genuine Chinese," "not foreigners, but true Chinese" from the north of China?[23] There are numerous examples of the missionaries siding with the argument that Hakka were originally of high status and lending support that helped validate Hakka claims. As one missionary wrote:

The theory of the origin of a tribe from a mountainous corner in Fukien has frequently been met with suspicion, whereas among authors writing without accurate knowledge of the Hakka history, the assertion is often found that the Hakka belong to the aborigines of that province, and are not really Chinese at all — an idea which the Punti, who are disinclined towards the Hakka, have always been ready to endorse. Against this theory are the facts of language, character, and customs, and the impulse to migrate and spread out, which in the name "Hakka" finds striking expression. This impulse, moreover, is a characteristic of the real Chinese, but not of the aborigines. It is safe, therefore, to accept the tradition which relates that they migrated about A.D. 900 from the district of Kwangshan in South Honan, where even today the language and customs, especially in connection with marriage and funeral rites, are said closely to resemble those of the Hakka.[24]

According to Lechler, the most reliable sources for tracing the origin of the Hakka were the "family records which are religiously preserved by the heads of clans." He traced the "pedigree" of "catechist Li" back to the founder of the Tang dynasty in 620 A.D. and cites several other genealogies to demonstrate "that the Hakkas came from the North of China." This, he argues, explains "the similarity of their dialect with the mandarin, and their frequent moves bear out the meaning of their designation as strangers, or settlers."[25] For all Chinese, genealogies provide one type of "evidence" of Chinese, as opposed to barbarian, status.[26] Although many Chinese genealogies are not considered authentic or reliable, they play a central part in claims to Chinese identity and are an example of what Eric Hobsbawm and Terence Ranger refer to as "invented traditions"—those practices that attempt "to establish a continuity with a suitable historic past."[27]

Another theme that consistently resurfaces throughout the missionary literature dealing with the Hakka and that one often hears from the people of Shung Him Tong concerns Hakka women and hard work. That Hakka women did not have their feet bound and participated in "men's work" suggested to their Chinese neighbors that Hakka were more like "hill tribes" than Chinese. However, European missionaries found the "position of Hakka women . . . more natural and healthy" than among the Cantonese and Hokkien. As one missionary wrote, Hakka are more likely to have "a happy family life, because it is less hampered by such crying evils as polygamy and female slavery, which nip the growth of affection between man and wife almost in the bud and give little chance for the enjoyment of a quiet and happy home life."[28] Wilhelm Oehler observes that Hakka women are never sold as second wives or concubines, and that the Hakka would rather practice female infanticide than sell a girl into slavery, a custom which he believes "spring[s] out of the respect in which women are held."[29]

A famous passage written by a European missionary was later republished several times, including in translation in 1923 in Meixian and in 1951 by the Perak Public Association of the Hakkas.[30] In its original form it reads: "The Hakkas are certainly a very distinct and virile strain of the Chinese race. The circumstances of their origin and migrations go far to account for their pride of race and martial spirit. Probably they never had the custom of foot-binding. It is safe to predict that Hakkas will play an increasingly important part in the progress and elevation of the Chinese people."[31] Such positive images of the Hakka, as well as the missionaries' genealogical, linguistic, and cultural "evidence" of Hakka northern origins, were well received by the Hakka and probably contributed to the Hakka attraction to the Basel mission. These complimentary images of the Hakka are reflected in the works of Hakka historians and coincide with contemporary views about the Hakka espoused by the people of Shung Him Tong.[32]

The Establishment of Shung Him Tong

Following the defeat of the Taiping Rebellion, Taiping rebels and their relatives are said to have flocked to the European missionaries for shelter. According to the *Sabah Centennial Magazine*, Lechler arranged for hundreds of Hakka refugees to be resettled overseas. The refugees "were friends and relatives of the people involved in the Taiping Revolution and had been under the threat of massacre by Qing authorities since their defeat."[33] Hundreds of Hakka, aided in leaving Guangdong by the Basel missionaries, fled to, among other places, Sabah and British Guiana. Others settled in Hong Kong, and many joined one of a dozen Basel mission (now Tsung Tsin Mission) Hakka churches in the colony. The people of Shung Him Tong and other Tsung Tsin Mission churches still refer to the rebellion with pride and suggest that many of the early members of the community were either relatives or acquaintances of Taiping rebels.

Shung Him Tong Village was officially founded in 1903 by a retired Hakka Basel missionary named Ling Kai Lin.[34] Although other Hakka had previously attempted to establish themselves in the area of Lung Yeuk Tau, they stayed a few years at the most, and left because of the "hostility" of the local Punti. Ling Kai Lin was the first Hakka Christian to establish himself permanently in the area. His father, along with members of most of the other early Shung Him Tong families, had been converted to Christianity by Basel missionaries. Ling's father was baptized by Hamberg, and when the Basel missionaries were expelled from Buji, he took his family and moved with the Basel missionaries to Lilang where a chapel, boys' school, and seminary were established. Ling Kai Lin attended Basel mission schools and later served as a pastor for the Basel mission until 1903, when he retired and purchased land in what was to become Shung Him Tong.

Shung Him Tong Village is located in Lung Yeuk Tau, an area that was once considered the heart of ancestral lands belonging to a Punti lineage of the surname Tang.[35] The Lung Yeuk Tau Tang were a branch of the most powerful and wealthy New Territories Punti lineage, and in 1903 Lung Yeuk Tau had one of the smallest Hakka populations in the New Territories. Despite Punti opposition to Hakka Christians entering the area, and the feuds and conflicts that occasionally erupted between the two groups, Hakka Christians overcame the hardships to establish their community.

Hakka Christians often contrast their "moral strength" to the "moral decline" of the Punti and say that this is why they were able to establish themselves in Shung Him Tong Village. One is often told by Hakka Christians that it "was God's will" or "with God's help we overcame the hardships and managed to settle here," but the main explanation provided by the people of Shung Him Tong is that not only were the Hakka hardworking and honest, but the Tang were morally in decline. As one older man explained:

> The Tang lived in the area a long time and they didn't like newcomers. We were threatened and treated as aliens, outsiders. We had a hard time. . . . The Tang were very rich people, but we say that a family can never be rich for more than three generations. Perhaps this is because by the third generation the sons have forgotten how to make money and are lazy. . . . Well, the Tang were lazy. Perhaps they smoked too much opium, had concubines and played mahjong all the time and gambled and lost their money. . . . Pang and the Lings [two early residents in the village] got the land from the Tangs through their mortgage company. We Hakka have the reputation of going through China and usurping the land from the wealthy landlords because we are willing to work very hard.

Another explained that the Tang men were too lazy to work the fields or forgot how and the rest all moved to the city or overseas, which gave the Hakka opportunities to farm and buy up their land. The decline of powerful Punti lineages such as the Lung Yeuk Tau Tang is described by Hugh Baker in a similar way as tied to "failing manpower or misspent wealth."[36]

Fengshui, or geomantic features of a region, are often cited by villagers as reasons for the success or decline of lineages in the New Territories.[37] Even though the people of Shung Him Tong know of *fengshui*, they do not cite *fengshui* legends as though they believe them to be literal truth. They tell "history" — assumed by those telling it to be true and correct — and they tell "legends" about outsiders who believe in *fengshui* or about the power of Christianity over *fengshui*. According to one such legend:

> The village is set at the foot of Dragon Mountain and is bordered by Phoenix River. Before the Christians arrived, the Punti farmed some of this land, but no one dared to live here because the *fengshui* was very strong. So when the Christians asked to settle here they said "why not let them try?" Shung Him Tong people came and built their houses here and no harm came to them.

One informant ended the legend with the comment, "that tested the Christian's belief in the strength of Christianity"; another said, "the Punti then understood that the power of Christianity was stronger than that of *feng-shui*." With such a conclusion one might expect the Punti to flock to the church and convert to Christianity, but they did not. Instead they appear to have revised their view of the *fengshui*, as evidenced by the appearance of several large conspicuous Cantonese non-Christian family graves built on the hillsides surrounding the church.

A number of other factors may have contributed to enabling the Hakka Christians to establish their community. The decline of the power and property of some Punti lineages might have begun as long ago as the seventeenth century, during the period of the coastal evacuation and resettlement.[38] But the appropriation of the New Territories by the British also contributed to their decline.

Before the British, a complicated system of land tenure existed whereby dominant lineages claimed ownership rights to much of the land in the New Territories.[39] Members of the dominant lineages pocketed "taxes" from those who farmed the land which was not registered with the Chinese government. When the British began to register land, the "taxlords" claimed they had collected rent, not taxes. By 1905, the British government had registered all land that had proper ownership deeds. In cases where no deed could be produced "the cultivator was usually proclaimed owner."[40] The Tang of Ping Shan claim they owned more land in pre-British times, but at the time of the British land survey their tenants fraudulently claimed ownership.[41] According to Faure, with the arrival of the British the Lung Yeuk Tau Tang lost their control of bottom soil rights, which "changed the fundamental political situation of the New Territories."[42] The revised system of land ownership greatly benefited the Hakka at the cost of the Punti landlords, and also served to ally the Hakka with the British. Numerous examples of conflicts between the people of Shung Him Tong and their Punti neighbors reveal that Hakka Christians preferred to bring their problems directly to the British district administrators, enabling them to sidestep the authority of Lung Yeuk Tau village elders.

Although many volumes of land records were destroyed during the Japanese occupation of Hong Kong, enough exist to make some general statements regarding land ownership in the area of Shung Him Tong. Beginning at the turn of this century, little by little, land in and around Shung Him Tong that once had belonged to the Tang was sold to Hakka Christian immigrants, and the Tang receded to the northeasternmost regions of Lung Yeuk Tau. By 1905, Pastor Ling Kai Lin and his family owned roughly 20 percent of the land in and around Shung Him Tong (approximately 10.5 acres); Tang families owned approximately 30 percent (15 acres); and the rest was listed as crown land. Within the next twenty years the Tang sold almost all of their land in Shung Him Tong, and much of the remaining crown land was leased to Hakka Christians.

Between 1903 and 1934, families of eight surnames, mostly from Baoan District at first, but also from Wuhua, Meixian, Xingning, and other Basel mission stations, moved to Shung Him Tong. Unlike in most villages in the New Territories, what drew the immigrants to the community were not simply kinship and native-place ties, but also religious and ethnic ones. As recorded in family histories, the emigrants all left their native villages in Guangdong because of poverty, population pressure, increased Hakka-Punti conflicts, increased discrimination against Christians, and general dissatisfaction with their lives in their native villages, as well as the promise of a better life in the peaceful British-governed New Territories.[43] All of the first immigrants to Shung Him Tong were Hakka, and most were Christian or converted soon after moving there. Several were retired missionaries who had worked for the Basel mission in Guangdong or Hong Kong, and almost all claim to have suffered from persecution or to have been victims of violence in their native villages. A striking number of the household heads were missionaries who had attended Basel mission schools, and many chose to retire in Shung Him Tong rather than in their native villages. Religious networks seem to have been the main mechanism through which people learned of and came to settle in Shung Him Tong, but kinship and native-place ties were also factors.[44]

The first few people to arrive in Shung Him Tong after Pastor Ling purchased his land were some of his poorer relatives who came to work for him as tenant rice farmers. Between 1903 and 1905 Ling Kai Lin and his eldest son Ling Sin Yuen worked to spread the gospel among their tenants and to other Hakka in the area. By the winter of 1905 there were ten converts, so Pastor Ling requested that the Basel mission send a pastor to the village to set up a church. In 1905, they sent Pang Lok Sam, who was replaced in 1913 by Cheung Wo Ban. Pang, however, continued to play an important role in the New Territories, and in the establishment and growth of the village.

The people of Shung Him Tong shared the goal of establishing a model community. In the preface of the village history compiled by Pang, a visiting pastor from one of the other Basel churches in Hong Kong writes the following description of Shung Him Tong Village:

A model village should have the following: public roads for transportation and communication, a church for spiritual activities, a school for educating the young, a hospital for healing the sick, and a cemetery. In this model village everyone would be satisfied with their home and happy with their work. Everyone would live by the old lessons: love their neighbors, look after their friends, and help each other. . . . In the mid autumn of 192[?] . . . I found such a model village in Lung Yeuk Tau, New Territories, Hong Kong. . . . I often visited this village and was so impressed that I was reluctant to leave. . . . All villagers — there were over a hundred — were Christian. They loved their neighbors as much as they loved their families. . . . I awoke to find that this was the model village in my mind . . . and anyone who wants to build a model village should try to learn from this one.[45]

By the early 1930s, a church had been built and expanded. A road and bridge that connected the village to the main road had been constructed despite lengthy feuds and disagreements with members of the neighboring community. A local primary school was also founded. Although there was already a school in one of the neighboring villages, the Hakka Christians did not consider it an appropriate place for their children to study, in part because the classes were held in the Tang ancestral hall, but also because the Hakka Christians were not welcome there. The establishment of a cemetery was also of great significance to the people of Shung Him Tong because it demonstrated their concern for the ancestors and showed that their home was a permanent one. Some of the founders of Shung Him Tong transported the bones of their ancestors to the new Christian cemetery. They purchased land, built permanent homes, and came to regard members of the community as a "church family."

Every Sunday the Shung Him Tong church attracts about 150 people, and on special occasions such as Christmas and Chinese New Year's there have been as many as 400 or 500 people in attendance. Shung Him Tong is still labeled a Hakka Christian community by all who know of it, and those who belong to the church are labeled by insiders and outsiders as Hakka Christians. Yet in the broader context of Hong Kong, most people of Shung Him Tong pass as Cantonese without any problem. There are no visible markers which distinguish Hakka from Cantonese, and it is rare to find a Hakka person who does not speak Cantonese.[46] Most people speak Cantonese at work and at school, and Hakka increasingly speak Cantonese in their homes.

History and Hakka Identity

Christianity was "successful" among the Hakka of Hong Kong and China, writes a Hakka Christian missionary, because "becoming Christian" did not mean "leaving our beloved Hakka people."[47] As demonstrated in

Shung Him Tong, becoming Christian did not mean abandoning the ancestors and in effect abandoning Hakka identity. On the contrary, as members of the church, the people of Shung Him Tong were assumed to be Hakka, and in the context of the community there was little they could have done to escape their ascribed identity even if they so desired. To be a Shung Him Tong Christian was to also be Hakka in the eyes of Shung Him Tong people as well as from the viewpoint of people in the surrounding communities. One issue, then, was to replace the negative connotations associated with being Hakka with positive ones.

While Hakka Christians are aware that non-Hakka non-Christians may accuse them of not being Chinese at all on the basis of their different religious beliefs and practices — particularly the Christian disapproval of ancestral worship and care of the dead — Hakka define themselves as Hakka and therefore also as Chinese on the basis of their descent and shared history. A focus on shared descent allows Hakka Christians to escape a cultural definition of Chinese identity that depends on particular "Chinese" religious beliefs or practices.[48] While Hakka Christians are still concerned about ancestors, they focus on the genealogical position, the historical role, and the "commemoration," rather than the "worship," of ancestors. In the pious tradition of the early Basel missionaries, ancestral worship is still condemned and criticized by the people of Shung Him Tong. But alternatively they have transformed and redefined ancestral worship and care of the dead into "secular" concerns. As we shall see, however, these secular concerns are often still expressed on religious occasions and in religious settings.

Each year after the church service on Easter Sunday, at the time of year when non-Christians visit their family graves for the Qing Ming festival, Hakka Christians of Shung Him Tong walk in a slow procession to the Christian cemetery in back of the village and place flowers on their ancestors' graves. They pray at the grave sites, the pastor delivers a short sermon, and the choir sings a few hymns. As at non-Christian graves in Hong Kong, most graves have been repainted and "swept" for the occasion. Those that have been forgotten are conspicuously overgrown with weeds. There is no evidence of wine, fruit or other food, incense or paper offerings that are commonly seen at non-Christian graves in Hong Kong, and people in the Shung Him Tong cemetery do not bow or kowtow before the graves as do non-Christians.

In the course of my year of fieldwork, many people commented to me on the importance of the Shung Him Tong cemetery. Old people casually remarked that after they die, even if their descendants forget them, they will still be assured a visit each year by the pastor and the church choir. On most

of the grave markers are photographs of the deceased, genealogical information and the name of the place from which the person emigrated. People
explained that the cemetery is important as a place to show respect for the
ancestors, and to remember the family and the history of the village. Thus
the cemetery serves as a concrete, physical representation of church and
village history, and as a conscious mediation between Chinese and Christian values, representing a continued concern for the ancestors.

The ancestors are also commemorated in books of church, village, and
Hakka history. When I asked Shung Him Tong people questions about
Hakka identity, they repeatedly referred me to two main sources. One was
Luo Xianglin's history of the Hakka and the other was a village history
compiled by Pang Lok Sam. Although few people had actually read the
books, most knew of them and their content. On the many occasions when
church history is printed in the commemorative church and mission bulletins, the people of Shung Him Tong learn church history, in which is
embedded Pang's village history and Luo's more general Hakka history.

The history of the village compiled by Pang reflects his concern and
that of other Shung Him Tong church members with being both Chinese
and Christian. In it Pang raises the issue of Hakka Christians' loyalty to
their ancestors and their struggle to establish Shung Him Tong as a permanent home. The book provides a detailed genealogy of each family, and an
explanation of their reasons for emigrating. Pang envisioned it as both a
tribute to the ancestors and a lesson for the descendants.

Several of the authors of the eleven family histories stress the importance of keeping genealogies, and express their belief that it is one's duty to
know the family history. According to Pang, his manuscript was compiled
mainly for the purpose of preserving the history of the village for future
generations and encouraging them in their duty to their families and to the
community. In his introduction he writes of his concern for the community: "Whether or not a society can flourish depends not only on the pioneers who prepare the way, but also on the successors who carry forth and
develop the endeavor. If no one pioneers, even a good place will not be
discovered. If no one keeps it going, a flourishing community will decline."[49] In the Ling family history, Ling Sin Yuen begins by recounting the
belief that if a person does not know his ancestors, he will be worse than an
animal, and that one should trace one's family history as far back as possible.
He traces the Ling family back to Jiangxi Province, tracing their migration
to Meixian and Baoan, providing details about his grandfather, who "worshipped idols" until he was 40 and introduced to Christianity. He then "left
the idols, became devoted to the true God" and he and his family were

baptized. The Ling family history, like many others, describes how the hatred and persecution of Christians grew, and stresses their filial piety as well as their commitment to Christianity.

The famous Hakka historian Luo joined Shung Him Tong in the 1940s only after he had already written his first book on Hakka history.[50] He later became a church elder and his wife taught at the Shung Him Tong school. His best-known book on historical sources for the study of the Hakka draws in part from Pang's compiled volume of Shung Him Tong genealogies to provide evidence of the northern Chinese origins of the Hakka.[51] What Pang does with his book on Shung Him Tong history — recording the connection of local Hakka Christians with their ancestors — Luo broadens and generalizes to the level of all Hakka, establishing their genealogical ties to northern central China. In two of his books Luo introduces evidence that Sun Yat-sen was Hakka.[52] He also raises the topic of the heroic role of the Hakka in the Taiping Rebellion, and asserts what are now common claims about Hakka character and Hakka women.

Like Pang, Luo was concerned with how to be both Chinese and Christian. As his daughter explained, it was through his work on Hakka history that he was able to reconcile these two aspects of his identity. Luo, like Pang, was acutely aware of the importance of the ancestors in the definition of Chinese identity. As one villager explained, Luo spent much of his time collecting information from the grave markers at the cemetery, learning the connections between the past and the present. One of Luo's projects was to construct an ancestral hall in Pat Heung for the surname Luo which would be visited by both Christians and non-Christians and where both Christians and non-Christians could be commemorated. While non-Christians would go there to worship their ancestors, Christians would go to the side of the ancestral hall where they could pray under a cross and show respect for their ancestors.

Conclusion

Not all the people of Shung Him Tong today agree on the current importance or future significance of Hakka identity. Some consider Chinese ethnic distinctions divisive; others sadly regret that the youth do not show a "deep understanding" of what it means to be Hakka. All agree, however, that the Hakka share a history of migrations and a northern Chinese origin; and the hardships of their past have resulted in a common idea of Hakka character — namely that the Hakka are diligent, proud, hardworking, patriotic, and honest.

Hakka identity persists both because of and in spite of Christianity. Despite the official Christian disapproval of ancestral worship and other Chinese cultural practices, the people of Shung Him Tong have been able to adapt their expressions of commitment to the ancestors to a "secular" commemoration and display of respect. Despite the accusations of non-Christians that Hakka Christians are not Chinese because they have abandoned their ancestors, the people of Shung Him Tong maintain a definition of Chinese identity that hinges on the concepts of both descent and history. We can also say that the Hakka Chinese identity of the people of Shung Him Tong persists because of Christianity: positive images of the Hakka coincided with and were reinforced by the views of European missionaries; the church provided organizational structures for the Hakka that went beyond the traditional categories of surname or native place; and in the context of contemporary Hong Kong, the church provides one of the few settings in which Hakka identity is still relevant.

However, Hakka, Han, and Christian identities are not easily reconciled. There is a fundamental difficulty for the people of Shung Him Tong who have attempted to ally themselves at once with two prevailing hegemonic systems. The ultimate contradiction is that Christianity has legitimized their political and economic status and thus empowered their voices, but their claims to Christian superiority is at odds with Han identity. Ironically, Christianity is also important in maintaining their Hakka identity because they live and worship in a community that is labeled by others as intrinsically Hakka *and* Christian. Thus the people of Shung Him Tong may identify themselves as Chinese and Christian, but they continue to grapple with and attempt to rationalize the fundamental tensions between the two identities.

Protestant church in Qingdao, Shandong Province (formerly German Lutheran).

Protestant church in Jinan, Shandong Province, built in the 1920s (formerly an independent Protestant church).

Protestant church in Shanghai (formerly the All-Saints Anglican Church).

Protestant church in Zhengzhou, Henan Province (formerly Anglican).

Catholic
church in
Tianjin,
just before
reopening
in 1985.

The Jin Family Flower Garden mansion on Edinburgh Road (now Jiangsu Road), Shanghai, site of the McTyeire School after 1917. The building still houses the Number 3 Girls' School.

The McTyeire School class of 1921.

Catholic
church in
Fuzhou,
Jiangxi
Province
(formerly
Congregation
of the
Mission).

Beitang, or North Cathedral, Beijing, a traditional center of Catholic life in North China.

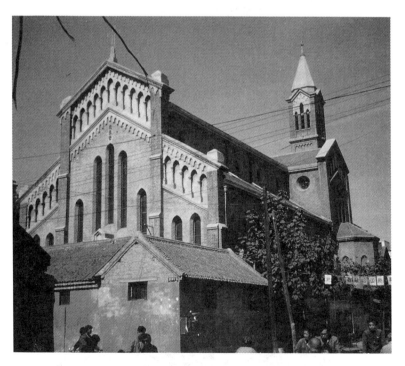

Catholic church in Kaifeng, Henan Province, an example of the "fortress style" of some churches built after the Boxer uprising.

Native assistants at the Basel Mission. Some are ancestors of the twentieth-century Shung Him Tong Christian Hakka community. Used with the permission of the Basel Mission Archives, Basel, Switzerland.

PART III

Christianity and Chinese Women

Christianity and Chinese Women

DANIEL H. BAYS

Jane Hunter's 1984 monograph on American women missionaries in China has become a benchmark for scholars dealing with various aspects of the mission movement, cultural change, or gender studies on the Western side. In the same fashion, Kwok Pui-lan's 1992 monograph on Chinese women and Protestant Christianity before 1930 will probably become a standard reference point for research and writing on Chinese women and Christianity from a "China-centered" approach. In Kwok's contribution to this volume, a few of the main points of that larger work are also made, in addition to a thoughtful discussion of the issues of sources and methodology. Her work begins to flesh out the detail, and to describe the richness and complexities, of Chinese women Christians. Much work remains to be done in this area (some of it pursued by the authors of the other chapters in this part), especially for the decades since the 1920s, where Kwok's work stops. But she has provided us with more sophisticated conceptual hardware than we had in the past with which to do it.

Besides stimulating concepts and approaches enriched by the insights of religious studies, which Kwok gives us, we need concrete historical case studies. Happily, we have four of them in the other chapters on Christianity and Chinese women. Robert E. Entenmann follows up his earlier chapter on eighteenth-century Sichuan Catholics and society with a chapter specifically on the interesting phenomenon of the Christian Virgins, a remarkably long-lived institution eventually surviving well into the twentieth century. A product of the period of indigenous development with minimal oversight by the European missionary priests, the Christian Virgins after a few decades were not eliminated, but marginalized, by those priests. Part of the lively documentation for the Virgins, as for other aspects of eighteenth-century Sichuan Catholicism, is the journal of the Chinese priest Li Ande, or Andreas Ly. Interesting to me is evidence of the broader presence of this Catholic women's institution, for example in Fujian, and the points of comparison with the role of women in the sectarian traditions of popular religion, especially the White Lotus, addressed by Entenmann.[1]

The last three chapters in this part fit together well, in that they all address in some fashion the issue of the social and value changes wrought by the women's educational institutions operated by the mission movement in the twentieth century. All are based on extensive interviews, but each also tries hard to set those interviews, in which events of 50 years or more ago are sometimes nostalgically recalled, into a context also informed by available printed and archival information. The stories of the McTyeire and St. Hilda's schools and their students, recounted by Heidi A. Ross and by Judith Liu and Donald P. Kelly, respectively, show us what Christianity may have meant in practical behavioral terms to Chinese schoolgirls in the first half of the twentieth century. The St. Hilda's alumnae today remember their Christian education as manifesting not religious doctrines, but order, courtesy, cooperation, a tangible sense of community, and a hope for a life that would reflect the ideals of the dignity of the individual and the importance of "service," to the nation and to society. This reveals something of the atmosphere and routine of the Christian boarding schools. However, it also points to a process of becoming self-reliant and eventually independent persons, because the urge to service, usually in careers as teachers, was almost always tied closely to the drive for self-sufficiency, in order to provide a solid economic and skills base for that service. Indeed, a remarkable number of these women never married, thus maintaining their independence, and apparently did have satisfying careers, in China and later often outside China. Deng Yuzhi (Cora Deng), discussed in Emily Honig's chapter, seems a classic example of the kind of women often produced by these Christian girls' schools.

A feature of women's Christian education, of course, was the relationship between foreign teachers and Chinese students, as well as the relationship between foreign and Chinese staff members. It seems clear that the single woman missionary teacher, who by the early part of the twentieth century was a professional reasonably well trained for and usually highly committed to her calling, had a crucial role in personifying for the Chinese students the ideals of self-improvement, equality, self-sufficiency, and service to which many of the girls responded positively. By the 1930s, Chinese staff members of these institutions, themselves graduates of the mission schools in earlier decades, could also play this role of model for the students. But, as Ross's essay indicates, the coexistence of foreign and Chinese staff could also bring with it tension and conflict, in the form of jealousy, resentment, and power struggles.[2] These are precisely the phenomena that are often downplayed in interviews, as they also tended to be suppressed or lightly passed over both in missionary documentation and in writings by Chinese participants as well. In Ross's chapter, there are several striking examples in her description of the very different content and tone of recollections of Xue Zheng, the longtime principal from 1936 to the 1950s, when compared to the memories of other interviewees. The girls' boarding schools run by the major missionary societies are obviously challenging subjects of historical analysis, but it is also clear that they were special places in many ways.

Honig's chapter on Deng Yuzhi, which concludes this part of the volume, takes an individual who could have come from the cohorts studied by Ross and by Liu and Kelly and creates a biographical study of depth and insight. Much of the depth, of course, comes from Deng herself, whom Honig encountered in the 1980s at a propitious time of self-revelation and self-reflection. But Honig provides much of the insight. Her hypothesis, that for Cora Deng Christianity functioned as an identity resource, useful in its own way much as feminism and communism or socialism were useful in their own ways, is well argued. One of the practical results of Deng's multiple identities was greater independence: she managed to preserve a certain degree of autonomy in defining precisely how she would live out her commitment to service to others, to society in general, and to the nation. Especially interesting in terms of the theme of this volume is how her Christian persona was considerably heightened, at her own initiative, after 1949. Perhaps, as Honig suggests, this was to enable her more effectively to demarcate her identity and her personal arena. Denominational or doctrinal specifics were not a part of this (for her) more visible Christian identity, nor as far as we can tell was personal piety. But the label "Christian" has obviously been very meaningful to her since the late 1940s. Deng's pattern of identification with Christianity, moral rather than doctrinal, and tied closely both to the ideal of service and to the desire for personal autonomy, may also explain much about the Christian beliefs and values of the alumnae of McTyeire and St. Hilda's.

CHAPTER 10

Christian Virgins in Eighteenth-Century Sichuan

ROBERT E. ENTENMANN

The Institute of Christian Virgins, an order of Chinese Catholic women, originated among Chinese women, living with their families, who chose to lead lives of celibacy and religious dedication in eighteenth-century Sichuan. Individual Christian Virgins were organized into an order under missionary supervision in 1744. Thereafter the institute evolved from a loose and informal group comparable to contemplatives into one called to a mission of active evangelism. Its aspirations, however, conflicted with the traditional role of women both in the church and in Chinese society, and in 1784 the church imposed new rules upon the order and brought it more fully under church control.

The history of Christian Virgins in China must be considered in the context of eighteenth-century Chinese Catholicism. It was a difficult time for Chinese Catholics: in 1724 the Yongzheng emperor proscribed their religion, European missionaries were expelled from China or forced into hiding, Chinese Catholic communities were driven underground, and the church was weakened by apostasy as well as persecution. Over the course of the eighteenth century the number of Christians in China fell by a third.

In Sichuan, however, Catholicism flourished, particularly in the second half of the eighteenth century. The number of Catholics in the province grew tenfold from 1750 to 1800, despite the church's insecure and illegal existence. The frontier environment of Sichuan, populated mostly by recent settlers from Central and South China, proved hospitable for illegal and "heterodox" religions such as Catholicism and the White Lotus sect, which provided their members with a sense of community and belonging. Moreover, the governmental apparatus was weak, and officials were more concerned with the potentially seditious White Lotus religion than with Catholicism.

The success of the church in Sichuan can also be attributed in large part to the active role of its indigenous leadership. European missionaries were visible and vulnerable to persecution and expulsion. Moreover, although Sichuan was under the jurisdiction of the Société des Missions Étrangères de Paris after 1753, there were too few French priests to serve a rapidly growing Catholic population. The society's aim, moreover, was to create a Chinese clergy and to build a native church. Thirty-three Chinese priests served in Sichuan during the course of the eighteenth century.[1] By 1804 there were eighteen Chinese priests but only four French missionaries in the province.[2]

By the end of the century Sichuan had 40,000 Catholics dispersed over a province the size of France. Most lived in tight-knit communities, known as *chrétientés* or "christendoms" in the writings of French missionaries. A *chrétienté* was the community of Christians within a locale, usually a small minority of the population, but sometimes including all the inhabitants of a hamlet. Priests traveled constantly to visit these communities, but many Catholics saw a priest no more than once a year. In the absence of clergy, leadership in these communities devolved to lay leaders. A *chrétienté* would elect a lay leader of the congregation (*huizhang*), who was vested with authority by a priest. He would take responsibility for religious instruction and assume leadership over the *chrétienté* in the priest's absence, conducting worship services, preparing the sick for death, and reporting to the priest when he visited. Lay evangelism was conducted primarily by catechists, from whom some of the Chinese clergy was recruited.[3]

Among those most responsible for the vitality and growth of the church, however, were the Christian Virgins. These women undertook the duty of teaching girls, training catechumens for baptism, and baptizing dying infants. They also engaged in famine relief and medical care. They actively sought converts as well. Their most lasting contribution was undoubtedly as teachers in schools for girls.

Origins of the Christian Virgins

There may have been Catholic women in Sichuan dedicated to a life of celibacy and religious contemplation as early as the 1640s.[4] Few of the late-Ming Catholic community in Sichuan, however, survived the devastation visited upon the province during the Ming-Qing transition. In the decades that followed, a Chinese Catholic presence in Sichuan was reestablished through immigration and evangelism.

There is evidence suggesting lay celibacy among Catholics in Sichuan as early as the first years of the eighteenth century. In 1705 the French missionary Jean Basset accepted as catechumens two young widows who were determined never to remarry, despite pressure from their relatives.[5] A few men, including some catechists, also chose to live as celibates.[6]

One of the earliest Christian Virgins was Agnes Yang, a woman of Mingshan District in western Sichuan. As is true of most Chinese Catholics of her time, her Chinese name has not been recorded. Basset had at first refused to baptize her because she was engaged to marry a non-Christian, and Basset feared that she would not be able to observe her faith after her marriage. She then took a vow of chastity. "God who inspired her aim delivered her from the great encumbrance," reported the later French missionary Joachim Enjobert de Martiliat, "for the fiancé died within the year." This occurred before Basset left Sichuan in 1707. Martiliat visited her in 1733, when she was over 50.[7]

By the 1740s there were, according to Martiliat, eighteen or twenty such women living in seven different *chrétientés*. They all lived with their families rather than in a community. They were, Martiliat reported, targets of slanderous rumors and attacks. "Most have been sorely tried by the infidels, who, full of envy seeing such rare virtues flourishing among the Christians, arouse a thousand evil incidents to make them abandon their sacred vow or at least obscure their fame," he wrote. "But the grace of God has rendered their efforts vain, and their virtue is now so well known that the gentiles themselves have developed much veneration for them."[8]

Voluntary celibacy was regarded with great suspicion in China. One scholar notes that women who chose celibacy "were suspected of being vampires or harbouring nefarious designs, and they were often persecuted, both by the authorities and by the population."[9] Marriage was nearly universal for women, although poverty prevented many men from marrying.[10] Sichuan was for much of the eighteenth century a frontier society where men outnumbered women and where there were strong pressures on women to marry. Occasionally men even resorted to the practice of *kang-qiang*, or abducting unmarried women or widows and marrying them by force.[11]

The choice of a vocation of celibacy violated Chinese norms and occasionally led to friction within families. In 1748, for example, the Chinese priest Andreas Ly (Li Ande) reported that the patriarch of the Zhao family refused to recognize his sisters and granddaughters who had taken vows of celibacy as members of his family. He treated them "as strangers and as Buddhist nuns."[12]

In 1754 Clara Sun, a "virgin devoted to God" (*virgo Deo devota*), was arrested in a local persecution of Christians. Andreas Ly records her interrogation by the local magistrate.[13]

> "What is your age?"
> "Thirty-eight years."
> "Why are you not married?"
> "My father had me betrothed twice, but both of my fiancés died. In any case, I never really wanted to get married. If anyone sought to compel me, I would sooner die here in front of you in this court. Such a death would be greater to me than any happiness. If you want me to marry despite my wishes, you would be undertaking an impossible task."
> "If you never get married, how will you live?"
> "I have adopted my cousin's son; he will support me to the end of my days. My father, too, has reserved part of his land to be left to me."
> "I order you to return to your home and marry."
> "There is no way I can obey this order of yours."

Clara Sun was thrown into prison. She was released after her father promised to arrange a marriage for her, but she never did marry.[14]

Her determination never to wed, although presumably for religious reasons, parallels that of women in late Qing and Republican Guangdong who formed sisterhoods, rejected marriage, and took vows before a deity never to marry.[15] Non-Christian Chinese women also could choose a religious vocation as Buddhist nuns. In some cases rejection of marriage, either of the institution or of a particular potential husband, may have reinforced religious celibacy.

Christians were often suspected of sexual license, a charge often made against the White Lotus sectarians. Christians sometimes met at night to escape detection, and their assemblies included both sexes. A magistrate of Xintu interrogating Christians revealed the suspicions of the Catholics' neighbors. "They say that every day, morning and night, you pray to God, and men and women gather together; that at night, you keep in good order as long as the prayer lasts, then as soon as it is over, you extinguish all lights and engage in shameful and abominable crimes. Is that true?"[16]

Such suspicions extended even to those bound by a vow of celibacy, both priests and Christian Virgins. Martiliat reports in his diary accusations against the latter, as well as against missionaries and Chinese Catholics, for committing "infamies avec les femmes."[17] In his diary Andreas Ly recounted rumors about sexual improprieties committed in confession and wrote a letter to his colleagues warning them to avoid occasion for such suspicions.[18] In 1769 a French missionary, Jean-François Gleyo, was questioned by officials about the manner in which he instructed women.[19] During a tenancy dispute in 1755 an apostate accused his Catholic landlord of hiding six nubile virgins in his home to be given in marriage to rebels.[20]

Both Agnes Yang and Clara Sun had fiancés who had died, evidently not an uncommon circumstance among Christian women who later chose to take vows of celibacy. Both could have perhaps justified their celibacy in Confucian terms as devotion to their late fiancés, although they did not follow the customary practice of living with their would-be parents-in-law. Legally they were regarded as widows, even though their marriages had never been consummated.[21] Martiliat's account of Agnes Yang indicates that she enjoyed that status: "to the title of virgin she has added that of chaste widow, which is much respected in China. She has reached the age of 50, which makes her eligible according to Chinese law for a monument to women of her status, for which her father is now working."[22] Neither Clara Sun nor her interrogator seems to have thought that she might claim the status of widow, however. In any case she would have had difficulty claiming to be a chaste widow, having been twice betrothed.

It appears that in 1746 Martiliat released one woman from her vow of chastity and gave her permission to marry, possibly because violations of her vow threatened a scandal. It was said that she had used drugs obtained from a non-Christian doctor to terminate three pregnancies. In February 1747 she was married to a young man who on his wedding night discovered to his consternation that his bride was not a virgin. He sent her back to her father; his mother prevented him from repudiating her on the grounds that it would bring shame upon both families.[23]

The Establishment of the Institute of Christian Virgins

The threat of such a scandal was one of the reasons that the European missionaries in Sichuan thought it necessary to regulate the lives of the Christian Virgins. The Dominican vicar apostolic of Sichuan, Luigi Maggi, began to formulate a set of regulations for them, based on rules established by Dominicans in Fujian for celibate women there.[24] Maggi died in 1744 before completing his task, and the project was continued by Martiliat, his successor as vicar apostolic in Sichuan. Martiliat dropped some rules that related specifically to Dominicans and added one regarding the frequency of sacraments.[25] He issued the regulations on All Saints' Day, 1744, and they continued in use into the twentieth century.[26]

Several of the regulations were designed to protect the Virgins' chastity and reputation. Christian Virgins were to live in their parents' houses, since there were no convents in Sichuan and unmarried women living together were suspected of being prostitutes. Moreover, Christian Virgins, unlike Buddhist nuns, did not shave their heads or wear distinctive clothing to indicate their religious vocation. They were not to go out without permission from their parents and the priest, and then only when accompanied by someone else. They were to avoid male relatives over the age of ten outside of their immediate families and maintain the strictest reserve with priests.

The Christian Virgins were to lead simple and austere lives. They were to wear simple clothing of black, white, or blue, and avoid ostentation in dress. They were to comport themselves with dignity; they were not to talk about "vain and useless things" but to confine themselves to pious matters. They were to worship separately from men, and were absolutely forbidden to take the role reserved to men in leading prayers. They were not to attend theatrical performances, eat dainty food, or drink alcohol except for medicinal reasons. Each day they were to recite the Apostle's Creed three times and the Lord's Prayer and Ave Maria each eighty-three times. Their time was regulated as well. Most of the day was to be spent in work "proper to women," such as weaving and preparing meals.

Martiliat declared that the Virgins were "entrusted to us," suggesting that they required the protection of male church authorities. This view accorded with Chinese attitudes, particularly the concept of the "three dependencies" (*sancong*) to which a woman was subordinated: to her father as a child, to her husband as a wife, and to her son as a widow.[27] Similarly the Christian Virgins were entrusted to both the priests (*shenfu* or "spiritual fathers") and their natural fathers, since they continued to live with their paternal families. They had no independent means of livelihood. Clara Sun, as we have seen, adopted a son to support her in her old age. In another case several decades later, a woman who had renounced an engagement to a non-Catholic and resolved to become a Christian Virgin was supported by her brother, who turned over to her and their mother land he had inherited from his father.[28]

The rules issued by Martiliat formally established the Institute of Christian Virgins. The institute was not a religious congregation but a loose organization of women united by common rule under the supervision of missionaries. The Christian Virgins took temporary vows of chastity and lived at home in lives of prayer and meditation. Twenty years later, in response to questions from the Sacred Congregation for the Propagation of the Faith, the vicar apostolic of Sichuan explained that "here there is no convent of nuns, but nevertheless, there are truly nuns here. They willingly stay with their parents, where they work with their hands for their livelihood. Nuns of this kind are bound only by a simple vow of chastity, and they make the vow in public before an altar."[29]

Martiliat's regulations were inspired in part by those for the women under Dominican supervision in Fujian, as well as similar orders outside of China. One model was the Daughters of Charity established in France in 1633 by St. Vincent de Paul, whose members take simple vows, renewed annually, and as their name indicates, do charitable work in society rather than remain in a cloister. Another was the Amantes de la Croix, founded in 1670 in Vietnam by Bishop Pierre Lambert de la Motte, a member of the Société des Missions Étrangères. Women of this order taught schools for girls; cared for sick women and children, both Christian and non-Christian; baptized infants in mortal danger; and were bound by strict regulations and vows of celibacy, poverty, and obedience. They lived in small communities, sometimes of only two women.[30]

In the years that followed, Martiliat brought the rules to celibate women he encountered in his pastoral visits to the scattered Christian communities of Sichuan.[31] "I gave them the regulations to sustain them and advance them on the path of perfection," he wrote. "The regulations must take the place of a director for them, for they are fortunate when they have the opportunity to see a missionary twice in one year. They all live with their families; it is not possible to cloister them in one house. Thus they are much exposed to temptation and dissipation, and it is for that reason that I wanted to bring them some remedy by means of the rules that I have prescribed for them."[32]

Moÿe's Reorganization of the Society

The transformation of the institute into an organization of women who went into the world to teach and evangelize occurred over three decades later. It was largely the initiative of Jean-Martin Moÿe, a French missionary who had founded the Sisters of Divine Providence of Portieux in Lorraine before coming to China in 1772.[33] Moÿe believed that women excelled men in piety, zeal, and prudence, as well as in their knowledge of religion. Unlike men, who according to Moÿe paid little attention to anything but commerce and the vanities of this world, women were the ideal servants of their faith.[34] Their lay evangelism became a main force in gaining new converts.

Moÿe recruited several women, married and single, to work for the church. Some were called to such service as an alternative to marriage or remarriage. One young woman of the prominent Christian Luo family of Chongqing, for example, had been betrothed to a non-Christian since childhood. Her father, in poor health, offered to secure her release from the engagement and dedicate her life to God. After making restitution to the fiancé, he regained his health and his daughter joined the Institute of Christian Virgins. Moÿe advised another woman, a young widow, not to remarry but to continue in her work in teaching prayers to other women.

In another case a girl of eleven or twelve joined the institute after recovering from illness. Moÿe had administered extreme unction; on the following day her mother carried the girl to mass in her arms so she could receive communion. The girl began to recover that evening. After learning to read and write she took vows as a Christian Virgin. Another missionary, Jean-François Gleyo, sent her to Suifu, where she instructed new converts and opened one of the two largest Catholic schools in Sichuan.[35]

The Christian Virgins of the late eighteenth century seem to have come from well-established Catholic families. Among them were two sisters of the Chinese priest Stephanus Tang Bairong and two aunts of another priest, Benedictus Sun.[36]

Married women as well served the church, although outside the institute. One of them, Monique Sen, was said to combine "a manly courage with the virtues proper to her sex." Her husband had been sent into exile during a local anti-Christian persecution in 1772. Monique and her sister Lucie traveled to proselytize until her husband returned from exile. Monique's aunt, Madeleine Ouen, was also active in spreading Catholicism.[37]

Moÿe was well aware of the reservations some had about this role for women. He justified it in part by pointing out that they were preaching only to other women. In a report to the Propaganda he wrote: "The Sacred Congregation may be astonished and take badly that in this country — I do not speak of others — women are charged with preaching the Gospel; but there are none but do it with prudence and according to the rules of strictest propriety, for the hearers are all women, and one easily comes across pious, wise, and fervent women in China."[38]

In 1777 a drought, bringing crop failure, famine, and disease, struck eastern Sichuan. Moÿe recruited both married and single women to baptize dying children — *l'oeuvre angélique*. He provided the recruits with a minimal livelihood and some were supported by their families. Subsisting on little but cakes of maize, the women sought out sick or abandoned children to baptize them. Moÿe later reported to the Propaganda that 30,000 children were baptized in his district in 1778 and 1779. Nearly all of them, however, had been *in articulo mortis*, and nearly all soon died. Moÿe reported that a third of the district's population had perished from famine or disease, and that the Catholics had suffered losses to the same degree.

Officials in Chongqing had established a camp for refugees outside the city and arranged for the distribution of rice. Many of the refugees died; some children survived their parents for but a short time before dying of neglect. Catholic women from Chongqing, led by the wife of a wealthy merchant, went to the camp to distribute medicine. At first soldiers barred them from the camp, thinking that they had come to pilfer the relief grain, but admitted them after learning of the women's purpose. Women carried out important relief works during the famine, and Moÿe recognized that they were a valuable resource for the church.[39]

Two years later, in 1779, according to Moÿe's letter to a fellow missionary, Moÿe heard a voice saying "Habe magnum zelam ad educandam prolem" (have great zeal for educating youth).[40] Moÿe resolved to recruit Christian Virgins for the task of teaching in schools for girls and to reorganize the order according to the model of the Sisters of Divine Providence, considering them a branch of that congregation. He tried to win the support of his colleague Jean-François Gleyo, but Gleyo at first felt that the obstacles to the project were insurmountable. Later, however, Gleyo wrote to Moÿe telling him that he had changed his mind after seeing a vision of the Virgin Mary, who told Gleyo that the project was her work. Gleyo enthusiastically endorsed Moÿe's efforts, and proposed calling the women Virgins of the Congregation of the Holy Mother (Shengmuhui de guniang).[41]

Moÿe charged Christian Virgins with the task of instructing new converts and daughters of Christian families. He sent one of the most able of them, Françoise Jen, to Gleyo's district in western Sichuan. She had learned to read and had studied Christian doctrine in order to teach others. At the age of eighteen she had taken a vow of celibacy. Gleyo sent her to a Christian family and she established a school for girls in their house. Later, after the mother of her host family died, she moved to the neighboring *chrétienté* and established a school there. Another school was established near Fu Zhou by Monique Sen, a married woman, who often traveled from *chrétienté* to *chrétienté*, stopping for a few days at each one to teach children the essentials of their faith.

Jean-Martin Moÿe reshaped the Institute of Christian Virgins into essentially a new order. He and Gleyo also established a normal school under Françoise Jen to train Christian Virgins to be schoolmistresses. At that school Moÿe introduced new rules, fixed hours for prayer and instruction, and established regular exercises of piety to strengthen the "four pillars" on which the institute was to be built: simplicity, trust in providence, poverty, and charity.

Moÿe also won the initial approval of his superior, François Pottier, bishop of Agathapolis and vicar apostolic of Sichuan. Pottier asked Moÿe to send one of the Christian Virgins to him to establish a school in western Sichuan with the help of another missionary, Jean-Didier de Saint Martin. Moÿe eventually sent Françoise Jen to Pottier for that purpose.

The schools did not always operate smoothly. Despite the austerity of the Christian Virgins' lives, it cost the equivalent of about sixty francs a month to operate a school for a dozen or fifteen girls. Some parents refused to send their daughters to school for a variety of reasons: they did not see the point of educating girls or they wanted their daughters to stay at home and work. Some feared that their daughters would follow their teacher's example and choose a life of celibacy, which would require their families to continue supporting them. Some *chrétientés* were composed entirely of people too poor to support a teacher. A few schools met regularly, particularly those in major cities such as Chongqing and Suifu, but schools in small towns generally met irregularly because of fear of attracting attention.[42]

Tensions Between the Church and the Institute

Despite his initial support, Pottier was soon expressing serious reservations about the new role of the Christian Virgins. In a report of September 1782, Pottier wrote that "although I have highly praised that institute, and although I have earnestly desired its success in the vicariate, I have discovered grave excesses in execution, which unless I deceive myself, will be avoided only with great difficulty."[43]

Pottier expressed his reservations in detail in a letter to Jean Steiner, director of the Société in Paris. Among the problems Pottier perceived was the young age at which some girls took vows of chastity, as young as eleven in one case. Pottier also feared that the Virgins were not adequately protected from threats to their virtue. The schools were established in private homes, but "the houses are not convents. The missionaries are not always there to watch what goes on, and relatives of both sexes come and go in the house." Moreover, despite their vow of chastity, the Virgins' dress did not distinguish them from other women, and there was always danger that someone might take advantage of them. In one case, Pottier reported, a Virgin was kidnapped by assailants but able to escape; in another case someone offered a house to a Virgin for use as a school with the intention of seducing her.

Another problem was that the Christian Virgins lacked assured sources of income and generally taught for free, relying on their neighbors' charity. "These Virgins have no dowry and cannot hope for one from their parents," Pottier complained, "for the goods go to the male children." Finally, Pottier objected that the Virgins read lessons and taught publicly, contrary to Chinese mores and the traditions of the church. "In many *chrétientés* they preside over communal prayer in assemblies including men; they read meditations in a loud voice and preach sometimes like a missionary. . . . I have discussed, criticized, and objected to a number of things in this establishment."

Pottier further reproached Moÿe for exceeding his powers in publicly receiving Virgins' vows of chastity, a power reserved to the bishop. Pottier also objected to anyone taking the vow before the age of 25, the standard age for such vows in Christian countries.[44] By that age, of course, nearly all Chinese women had been married for several years, so any woman taking a vow of chastity at 25 would have been long determined not to marry.[45]

Pottier's objections were supported by his coadjutor, Jean-Didier de Saint Martin. Nevertheless, Pottier was not willing to abolish the institute without advice from Rome. He wrote to the Propaganda for guidance. Gleyo, on the other hand, wrote to the Propaganda in defense of the institute and Moÿe's administration of it. He insisted that the Christian Virgins in fact lived in dwellings in which "they are as if in a convent," and notwithstanding the youth of the schoolmistresses, their discipline was maintained by teaching in pairs. Moÿe also wrote to the Propaganda, arguing that the Virgins, although young, were able and dedicated; they took simple, not solemn, vows, and they never taught before mixed assemblies as the bishop claimed they did.[46]

The Institute After 1784

Two years later, on 29 April 1784, the Propaganda issued new instructions for the regulation of Christian Virgins.[47] These instructions reaffirmed the 1744 rules established by Martiliat and added six new rules. The Propaganda advised abolition of the institute if it proved impossible to enforce these rules, indicating perhaps how marginal the institute was to the concerns of the church leadership. Nevertheless, the instructions also gave the Christian Virgins canonical recognition.

The regulations of 1784 prohibited the Christian Virgins from preaching or reading before assemblies including men, quoting the admonition in 1 Corinthians 14:34 that "women must be silent in the churches." The

Propaganda ruled that women not be permitted to take a vow of chastity before the age of 25 and that such vows be temporary, renewable every three years. Ideally, those chosen for the work of teaching girls should be "advanced in years," if possible over 30, coincidentally the age at which women were thought in China to have lost their sexual attractiveness.[48] No woman was to be admitted to the institute unless she could be supported by her family. Finally, pupils were to be taught with circumspection in order to avoid attracting the attention of "the gentiles."

The regulations issued by the Propaganda reflected the concern the church has always had for maintaining control over the vocation of chastity, fearing that without regulation it could easily fall into heresy or fanaticism. The catechism written by Jean-Didier de Saint Martin declared, for example, that the state of virginity is more perfect and grander than the state of marriage because it allows one to resemble angels and have a more intimate union with God. Yet it must be inspired by God and be "in accordance with the decisions of the Church."[49]

Ironically, these regulations were issued just as an outbreak of persecution brought the church in Sichuan into turmoil. Bishop Pottier escaped capture, but four other French missionaries and several Chinese priests and lay leaders were arrested.[50] Gleyo died in prison. Moÿe, disillusioned by his conflict with his superiors, had in 1782 returned to France, where he learned of the decision of the Propaganda.

A twenty-year period of peace returned to the Catholics of Sichuan after the persecution. Saint Martin, who had succeeded Pottier as vicar apostolic in 1793, had been an early critic of the Institute of Christian Virgins. At the time of his death in 1801, however, he asked his coadjutor and successor, Gabriel-Taurin Dufresse, to publish a retraction of his earlier views.[51]

Saint Martin nevertheless sought to circumscribe further the activities of the Christian Virgins by adding his own regulations to the order after his consecration as vicar apostolic. He reaffirmed the Propaganda's prohibition of vows before the age of 25 and the requirement that Christian Virgins be supported by their parents. Schoolmistresses were to be at least 25. Missionaries were not actively to recruit Christian Virgins in their districts, and the number of schools in each district was to be limited. Saint Martin ordered that missionaries avoid meeting the women unless accompanied by two aged women or other missionaries in order to avoid scandal. He also ordered that no Christian Virgin or other woman serve a priest at a table, enter his room, or offer him tea or tobacco. Saint Martin also ruled that it was not necessary for Christian Virgins to learn how to write.[52] Reading, presumably, was enough.

At the beginning of Saint Martin's vicariate in 1793, the mission in Sichuan had 32 schools: 11 for boys and 21 for girls. Six years later 10 more boys' schools had been established, as well as 5 more for girls. Chongqing had 2 Catholic schools, one for boys in which religious books and Chinese classics were taught by male teachers, and one for girls in which only religious books were taught. Christian merchants supported the education of daughters of poor families. The schools taught by Christian Virgins clearly gave girls an opportunity unusual in Chinese society, where girls' access to education was rare outside of the upper class.[53]

In 1803 Dufresse reported that schools were flourishing. There were now more schools for boys than for girls, 35 and 29 respectively. This was an increase of 13 boys' schools and 3 girls' schools over the previous year alone. Clearly, the church was attempting to put more resources than before into the education of boys. The Catholic boys' schools were so popular, Dufresse reported, that even non-Christian parents sought admission for their sons. The girls' schools, however, did not attract non-Christian pupils.[54] Non-Christian parents seem to have been unenthusiastic about educating their daughters; in any case the girls' curriculum was more religious than the boys'.

Renewed persecution broke out in 1805, eventually resulting in the martyrdom of Dufresse and several Chinese Catholics in the 1810s. Nevertheless, the Catholic church in Sichuan survived and grew. In the 1840s the French traveler Abbé Huc noted that Sichuan was the province in which Christianity was most flourishing, and estimated that there were 100,000 Christians there.[55]

The Institute of Christian Virgins flourished into the twentieth century. By 1892 there were 1,060 Christian Virgins in Sichuan, and 434 in other areas under the missionary jurisdiction of the Société des Missions Étrangères in Yunnan, Guizhou, Guangdong, Tibet, and northeast China. There were 2,945 pupils studying in 231 schools directed by Christian Virgins in Sichuan, as well as six orphanages under their direction in the province.[56] There were 2,450 members of the Institute of Christian Virgins in 1925.[57] The institute began to decline in the twentieth century because of the introduction of more regular religious communities of women. As one historian notes, however, these congregations failed to fill the role held by the Christian Virgins because their constitutions prevented their members from living in villages outside of convents, effectively limiting the role they could play in society.[58] Nevertheless, the institute, consisting of a dwindling number of elderly women, still existed on the eve of the arrival of the People's Liberation Army in Sichuan in 1950.

Conclusion

The Institute of Christian Virgins originated as a Chinese initiative. The first Christian Virgins were Chinese women who chose not to marry but to dedicate themselves to a religious life. Although they first apparently limited themselves to a contemplative life, they eagerly accepted a mission of evangelism and social service in the 1770s.

The importance of the Christian Virgins in promoting the Catholic faith parallels the role of women teachers in the White Lotus sect.[59] In both religions women were less vulnerable to persecution than men, whom the state punished more severely for heterodoxy. Moreover, both the Catholic church and the White Lotus offered women an outlet for their religious fervor not available within Chinese orthodoxy. In addition, a religious vocation was probably the only respectable alternative to marriage for Chinese women, both Catholic and Buddhist. This is not to suggest, of course, that the Christian Virgins were not primarily motivated by piety and a call to service.

The institute certainly conflicted with certain Chinese practices and mores. It demanded celibacy in a society in which marriage was a moral duty, but required women to wait past the usual marriage age to take their vows of chastity. It engaged in teaching girls in a society in which girls' education was not valued.

In 1744 the church brought the Christian Virgins under its authority through Martiliat's rules. These rules gave the order canonical recognition while at the same time ending the Christian Virgins' autonomy and bringing them directly under the control of European missionaries. Thirty years later many women responded enthusiastically to Jean-Martin Moÿe's vision of an expanded role for them. The Christian Virgins began a work of evangelism and social service. The regulations instituted by the Propaganda in 1784 again circumscribed their role while recognizing their vocation. After 1784 the church channeled the women's efforts into teaching children rather than seeking converts among adult non-Christians. At the same time the church put ever greater resources into establishing schools for boys, which were not run by Christian Virgins. It appears that the church regarded the work of these women as marginal. Nevertheless, the Christian Virgins remained central to the growth and maintenance of the Catholic community in Sichuan through the education of girls.

CHAPTER 11

Chinese Women and Protestant Christianity at the Turn of the Twentieth Century

KWOK PUI-LAN

In 1821, the wife, née Li, of Liang Fa, the first Chinese ordained Protestant, was baptized by her husband using water from a rice bowl.[1] When the Treaty of Nanjing (1842) was signed, missionaries reported that there were only six Protestant Christians; we do not know if any of them were women. The first missionary conference in 1877 estimated the number of female communicants to be 4,967.[2] About 100 years after the conversion of Mrs. Liang Fa, the number of female Christians had increased to 128,704, about 37 percent of the Protestant population.[3]

The relation between Chinese women and Protestant Christianity has seldom been the subject of serious and detailed scholarly study. In the past, the history of Christianity in China was primarily interpreted from the missionary perspective. Kenneth S. Latourette, in his monumental study, *A History of Christian Missions in China*, records comprehensively the work and contribution of the missionaries.[4] The numerous memoirs, diaries, reminiscences, and reports of both male and female missionaries fill out the details of their activities and private lives in China.

When scholars chose to study Chinese Christians, they tended to focus on the lives and thought of male Christians and their responses to social change at the time.[5] Even when female Christians were mentioned, they were invariably referred to as passive recipients of Christian benevolence, downtrodden objects to be emancipated, or feeble souls to be instructed and uplifted. Until fairly recently, Christian women were studied as missiological objects rather than historical subjects in the encounter between China and Christianity.

The oversight of women in the study of Christianity in China is hardly justifiable; it leaves out the experiences of a significant sector of the Christian community. More important, it might lead to an incomplete, if not one-sided, interpretation of the encounter between China and Christianity. Overcoming many barriers and obstacles, sometimes persecuted by family members and relatives, Chinese women began to join the church and participate in worship services in the nineteenth century. The Christian community had to make room for them and adapt to their needs, sending women missionaries, beginning "woman's work," and training Bible women. Since the gender construction of the Chinese was significantly different from that espoused by the missionaries, the Christian community had to walk a fine line of trying to appeal to women without rending the social fabric.

Chinese Christian women were not just onlookers in the unfolding drama of the missionary movement in China. They were integral members of the church, participating in worship and organizing their own Bible study groups and prayer meetings. Female leaders in the local congregations were often active community organizers, teachers, counselors, and arbitrators in their small communities. At the turn of the twentieth century, some of the Christian women responded to the needs of the time by organizing various social reform movements, such as the anti-footbinding movement, temperance unions, and health campaigns. Increased social participation and heightened political awareness provided a critical context for deeper religious reflection. Some of the more educated Christian women began writing religious confessions, testimonies, and short theological articles, giving us information about their journeys of faith and understanding of Christianity.

The study of Chinese women and Christianity will broaden our understanding of women in Chinese societies. For instance, the study of women's participation in local congregations will add to our knowledge of women's roles in religious communities. Through analyzing the changing relationship between the sexes in the church, new insights will be gained on how Chinese women and men responded to new gender roles, social expectations, and sexual morality introduced by another religion and culture. Furthermore, the study of Christian women's participation in the women's movement will help us understand how religious identity affected the development of feminist consciousness and what kind of institutional support women needed to step outside the bounds prescribed by the dominant culture.

From another perspective, research in this area will contribute significantly to our understanding of how Christianity adapts to and functions in a totally new environment. Historians studying Christian missions in China often affirmed that Christianity stimulated social change, including the emancipation of women.[6] But since the late 1960s, female religious scholars in the West have launched a far-reaching critique of the patriarchal nature of Christian symbolism and church hierarchy. They have argued that Christianity reinforces male domination by giving it sacred sanction.[7] The study of religious experiences of Chinese Christian women will offer us an example of how non-Western women interacted with Christianity, enriching our discourse on gospel and culture, feminism and Christian faith, and the role of religion in social change.

Sources and Methodological Issues

One of the major difficulties facing scholars doing research on Chinese women and Christianity is locating relevant sources and data. Christian women in China did not leave behind many books, articles, and religious writings; their voices were seldom recorded in conference reports and minutes of church gatherings. Their contributions were generally regarded as insignificant compared to those of their male counterparts. Secondary sources on Chinese Christian women are also very limited. With few exceptions, scholars who have worked on the history of Chinese women, including Ono Kazuko, Elisabeth Croll, Kay Ann Johnson, and Phyllis Andors, are not particularly interested in Christian women and their involvement in society. Some books and studies mention Christian women in passing, or recount the stories of a few notable Christian women, such as the Song sisters and Wu Yifang, without giving many details of the time and context in which they lived.

Since women's history became a respectable field several decades ago, scholars have paid more attention to oral history and have greatly expanded the sources of data to include not only published works but also autobiographies, letters, diaries, private papers, and other unpublished materials. Treating women as subjects, they have attached more importance to how women have experienced and interpreted their lives than to what has been written about them. What was formerly considered insignificant data or not data at all might become an invaluable piece of the mosaic when cast in a different light.

There are very few sources by Chinese women in the nineteenth century since the majority of women were illiterate or received little education. The first Protestant school for girls was opened by an English woman missionary in Ningbo in 1844, and Christian colleges for women were not established until the early twentieth century. There are some short articles by Christian women in *Jiaohui xinbao* (Church news) and *Wanguo gongbao*

(Globe magazine), published by Young J. Allen in the latter part of the nineteenth century, dealing with religious life in the church and the anti-footbinding movement.

In the early twentieth century, when Chinese women's journals and newspapers mushroomed in Shanghai and Beijing, Christian women also began to recognize the importance of women's literature in spreading new ideas and providing informal education for women.[8] Their writings appear in many journals, such as *Nüduobao* (The woman's messenger), *Nüqingnian* (The YWCA magazine), *Zhonghua Jidujiaohui nianjian* (Chinese Christian church yearbook), *Ginling College Magazine*, the *Chinese Recorder*, and *Woman's Work in the Far East*. Two Christian women's journals are worth special recognition. *Nüduobao* was first published in April 1912 by a woman missionary. As a monthly, it continued to be published into the 1940s and is the most important resource for Chinese Christian women's earlier writings. The YWCA began to publish its official organ in 1916, first as a quarterly entitled *Qingnian nübao* (Young women's quarterly). In 1922, its name was changed to *Nüqingnian bao* and subsequently shortened to *Nüqingnian*. In addition, several books and pamphlets were written by Christian women, such as Hu Binxia's study of the history of the Chinese YWCA, the autobiographies of Cai Sujuan and Zeng Baosun, and a study of the Chinese women's movement by Wang Liming.[9]

Besides these written materials, the papers of a few Christian women leaders, such as Shi Meiyu (Mary Stone) and Kang Cheng (Ida Kahn), are preserved by the General Commission on Archives and History of the United Methodist Church. The papers of the United Board for Christian Higher Education in Asia, located at the Divinity School, Yale University, contain invaluable resources on female Christian educators and graduates of the Christian colleges for women. Other valuable resources in placing the lives and activities of Christian women in context include the Chinese sermons of missionaries and Chinese preachers, church catechisms and religious tracts, church yearbooks, national church surveys, and even obituaries of women.

Because the early female converts were illiterate, it is unavoidable that we depend on the accounts of missionaries to a large extent. There are, generally speaking, two major kinds of missionary writings: published works and unpublished reports, correspondence, and private papers in mission archives. Published works were meant for consumption at the home base and often were written with the intention of soliciting support for Christian mission work. The titles of some of these books, such as *How England Saves China* and *The Uplift of China*, bespeak the feeling of cultural superiority and ethnocentrism of some of the missionaries. When using these accounts, special care must be taken to avoid the one-sided interpretation of some missionaries. Whenever possible, to gain a fuller picture published works should be checked against unpublished reports submitted to the mission boards.

The reports of women missionaries to the women's boards of foreign missions and their private correspondence are invaluable sources of raw data and interesting materials on the "native women" they worked with. The women of the American Board of Commissioners for Foreign Missions, for example, submitted annual reports giving details of the work of Bible women, the activities of Bible classes, and the responses of local women to catechism classes. Women missionaries of the Methodist Episcopal church were even more organized and they published annual reports of the women's conferences held at the various mission stations. In these reports, the details of the activities of missionaries, Bible women, local volunteers, and female converts were presented.

After the painful collection of data comes the equally demanding process of reconstructing the lives of Christian women from the pieces and sometimes fragments of materials gathered. First, we should emphasize that Chinese women were integral partners in the historical drama, and we have to place them at the center of our historical reconstruction. This often means that we have to ask a new set of questions and widen our scope of inquiry. Instead of simply commending the missionaries for opening mission schools for girls, we have to examine closely what these schools prepared the students for, and what were the options for graduates of these schools. It is also not enough to describe the work of medical missionaries without discussing how Chinese women responded to a foreign health care system with a different understanding of bodily functions and social hygiene.

Second, the relationship between Chinese women and Christianity must be interpreted in the context of the wider social and political transformation of modern China. The pattern of women joining the church, for example, was closely related to the changing response of the Chinese to Western culture and religion in the late Qing period. The roles of women in the Christian churches can be contrasted with the participation of women in the popular religious sects. Christian women's responses to social change need to be compared with those of the vast majority of women who did not share their faith. The impact of the women's movement on the self-identity and consciousness of female Christians has to be closely examined. Christian women's social analysis and strategy for social change should be contrasted with those of the socialist feminists and other secular feminists.

Third, since woman's work was carried out by women missionaries from both sides of the Atlantic, a cross-cultural understanding of the gender construction of the Western church and society is indispensable. Fortunately, there is a growing number of books on Western women's history in this period, including some interesting discussion of women's religious roles in local churches and mission societies.[10] Several books on women missionaries, including those by Jane Hunter and Patricia R. Hill, contribute to our knowledge of the motivation and private lives of missionaries.[11] Cross-cultural study will enable us to evaluate more carefully the impact of women missionaries on Chinese women and the strategy of woman's work in China.

Chinese Women and Protestant Christianity

In the following, I will discuss why Chinese women joined the church, women's religious activities and participation in the Christian community, Christian women and social change, and women's reflections on major themes in the Christian faith.

CHINESE WOMEN JOINING THE CHURCH

Chinese women joined the Protestant church at a very slow pace after the treaties of Tianjin (1858) and Beijing (1860) allowed missionaries to preach and build chapels anywhere in China. The early female converts were drawn from the relatives of male Chinese helpers and converts, as well as the domestic servants of missionary households. Women were reached through house visitations, small Bible classes, and mission schools for girls. Later, when Christian missions were more heavily involved in educational, medical, and welfare work, the church had additional channels to reach the female populace.

Chinese women had to overcome formidable barriers to approach the mission compounds, not to mention to become members of a foreign religion. First, many Chinese women were ardent followers of Chinese folk religions, which provided them with plausible explanations of evil and misfortune in daily life, reward and punishment, and the quest for immortality. The participation in Chinese shared rituals and festivals reinforced their sense of communal identity and belonging. Joining a foreign religion would sever these familiar ties and marginalize women from their own communities. Second, antimissionary riots and writings spread rumors that church members were involved in indecent sexual behavior and that male missionaries sexually craved Chinese women. Third, because the Chinese household was patriarchal, women did not enjoy the freedom of choosing their own religious affiliation. They were often harassed or persecuted by their husbands and other family members when they decided to join the church.

Because of limited information, it is difficult to generalize about the class and social background of female Christians. But missionary reports and obituaries of Christian women reveal that Christianity attracted particular groups of women.[12] In general, the majority of Christian women in the nineteenth century came from lower- and middle-class backgrounds and rural women responded more readily than women in the cities, since the non-elite rural population tended to be less bound by the dominant Confucian tradition and rural women were less secluded. Young girls and older women, especially widows, had more time to participate in church activities and more freedom to explore new identities, because they were situated somewhat at the margin of the family system.

Chinese women might join the church for many different reasons; we can only suggest a few possible ones because of the lack of documentation. Christianity offered women new symbolic resources with which to look at the world and themselves, helping them to affirm their sense of worth and dignity. In the process of adapting to the Chinese context and increasing the appeal of Christianity, there developed a process of "feminization of religious symbolism" in Christianity, especially in the nineteenth century.[13] The concept of a feminization of Christianity was introduced by historian Barbara Welter in her study of American religion in the first half of the nineteenth century. As women became more prominent in the church, Welter observed that sermons began to preach a Father-Mother God, and a loving and humble "feminized" Christ.[14] A similar process can be discerned in China as missionaries emphasized the compassion of God, used both male and female images of the divine, and stressed how Jesus loved and respected women, while downplaying the sinfulness of Eve. Although this feminized version of Christianity was not meant to be particularly revolutionary in America, it offered new possibilities for women to view their female identity in the Chinese context.

Similar to the Chinese popular religious sects, Christian congregations provided women the opportunity to participate in a range of activities and to experiment with new social roles. Besides attending worship services, women learned to read, sang hymns, listened to gospel stories, and made new acquaintances. Stepping outside their traditional family roles, Christian women could be students and teachers in Sunday school, counselors to younger converts, and volunteers in home visitations. The ability to read enabled some of these women to exert some forms of leadership in their village or local communities.

Some Chinese women might also have joined the new religion because of tangible material benefits and rewards. In order to attract adult women or to appease their husbands, some Christian missions gave these women a small sum of money as an incentive to attend church and Bible classes. Rural churches often provided a simple meal after church services for members who lived far away. In times of personal or family crises, Christian missions could provide security through famine relief and other forms of philanthropy and welfare. The privileged position of missionaries in the late Qing period offered Chinese church members additional protection. The Christian community and the mission schools provided institutional support to women when they wished to unbind their feet or escape an undesirable arranged marriage.

WOMEN'S RELIGIOUS ACTIVITIES AND PARTICIPATION

The kind of religious activities in which Christian women participated depended on where they lived. In the city mission stations, religious activities were centered on the mission compounds and spread throughout the week. In the rural outstations, most of the activities were concentrated on the weekends since church members were scattered throughout numerous villages. Religious meetings were also organized in the villages during itineration by missionaries and the Chinese helpers. Religious participation varied according to the seasons, since some rural women could only come when they were less busy in the fields.

On Sundays, city churches usually held one or two worship services. During the week, some missions opened a women's chapel or a guest room in the mission compound so that women could drop by to listen to gospel messages. In the evenings, "magic lantern shows" were occasionally held, using pictures to illustrate gospel stories to arouse the interest of the audience. During the week, prayer meetings were held in the church or in the homes of members. Christian women took turns as the hostess and were encouraged to invite neighbors and relatives. If there was a dispensary nearby, some women would accompany missionaries or Bible women in visiting and preaching the gospel to the sick. At the turn of the twentieth century, Christian Endeavor societies and branches of the temperance movement were set up in the city stations. Here church women had additional opportunities to discuss the relationship of religion and social life.

In the country parishes, women's prayer meetings were held on Saturday nights. On Sundays, besides the worship services, women attended the Sabbath school and women's gatherings or classes in the afternoon. On weekdays, gospel lessons would be taught and prayer meetings held during village visits. Although the range of religious activities might be limited in rural areas, village women participated eagerly in the life of the church and many offered voluntary services.

One of the favorite activities of Christian women was learning to sing hymns, although missionaries sometimes complained that many sang out of tune. Memorizing hymns was a good way to learn Chinese characters. In order to accommodate women's needs, missionaries wrote ballads, made up of simple and rhythmic popular expressions, to teach gospel messages.[15] Since the ability to read portions of the Bible was usually a prerequisite for baptism, the church was heavily involved in a literacy campaign. Christian women were taught the Bible, simple religious tracts, catechisms, the Christian version of the trimetrical classic (the *Sanzi jing*), and other works. More advanced students were taught books on the life of Christ or the Christian classic *Pilgrim's Progress*.

Because of the segregation of the sexes in Chinese society and the low educational level of women, women held their religious meetings, prayer groups, and station classes apart from men. In this way, women carved out a particular sphere in congregational life where they could develop their leadership and exert considerable influence. Especially in rural churches, where leadership depended more on lay people, women had the freedom to organize their own activities. Occasionally, some women even organized a house church in their homes, or formed prayer groups in their own villages.

Bible women, who were employed either full- or part-time, played a catalytic role in organizing women's religious activities. As missions grew, most women missionaries spent more time on educational and administrative tasks and less on evangelism, which required more patience and perseverance. The Bible women were typically older women, often widows, who had received some basic education, or who had been taught to read by the missionaries. Later, missions also opened Bible schools for training younger women to serve the church. The ministry of Bible women was very wide in scope, including house-to-house visiting, teaching Sunday schools or station classes, supervising younger volunteers, visiting the sick, and taking long country trips with or without missionaries.[16]

The leadership roles of women in Christian communities were in many ways similar to those of women in the popular religious sects. Women could be teachers of religious literature, founders of congregations, and leaders of local communities.[17] In fact, some of the female leaders of folk religious sects could exercise the same roles after their conversion to Christianity. Like the religious sects, Christian congregations provided an alternative structure for women to exert some influence. But precisely because of the similarities, the churches had to compete with these religious sects for followers, which sometimes created local conflicts.

Although women could exercise certain leadership roles in church, especially in their own groups, their influence in the overall Christian community was rather limited. Most denominations during this time followed a patriarchal church polity and barred women from preaching from the pulpit and from playing certain ritualistic roles. Even women missionaries were not given the same right as men to speak in church or missionary gatherings and they sometimes complained about the domination of the male missionaries. As employed workers, Bible women received far less recognition than their male counterparts, who could be ordained and take charge of a whole church. Given the hierarchical nature of most church structures, church women's participation in decision making was very limited.

The above discussion clearly indicates that the religious participation of women must be evaluated from two vantage points: that of women's own groups, and that of the church community as a whole. Women exercised more leadership in their own groups and less in mixed groups of women and men. In the early twentieth century, the changing circumstances of China and the emergence of the feminist movement prompted church women to struggle for greater equality in the church. Some of them demanded to be represented in church conferences, to be given the power to preach, and to be considered for the ordained ministry.[18]

CHRISTIAN WOMEN AND SOCIAL CHANGE

Sweeping changes around the turn of the century greatly affected Chinese women. Kang Youwei and Liang Qichao promoted the ideas of establishing schools for girls and abolishing the practice of binding girls' feet. Under mounting pressure, the Qing court instituted a national system of government-supported girls' schools in 1907. Some of the female students who went to study abroad, particularly in Japan, brought back new ideas and started women's newspapers and journals. Radical feminists, such as Qiu Jin, joined in the revolutionary struggle to overthrow the monarchy and some even formed women's battalions and military squads. Female students joined the demonstrations of the May Fourth Movement in 1919 and demanded equal rights in education, jobs, and politics.

The attitudes and responses of Christian women to these turbulent social and political changes depended on two factors: the social teaching of the Christian church during this time, and the understanding of womanhood by missionaries and the Christian community. The majority of the missionaries in China, especially those sent by the China Inland Mission, subscribed to an evangelical understanding of faith. They tended to emphasize salvation of the soul rather than critical involvement to change society. The more liberal missionaries, influenced by the social gospel, affirmed Christians' responsibility to society. They recommended Christian action through social services, reform movements, and cultural change. Very few would have condoned the more revolutionary tactics of throwing bombs or joining military corps.

The Victorian ideals of womanhood, stressing women's domesticity and female subordination, influenced the outlook of many women missionaries, and their evangelical upbringing reinforced the belief that women's God-ordained place is in the home. Their sense of cultural superiority led them to scorn footbinding, female illiteracy, and polygamy. But their understanding of womanhood as enlightened mothers and caring wives was not as revolutionary as it seemed. Their heroine was Frances Willard, a Methodist woman who tried to save the home through the temperance movement, rather than Susan B. Anthony or Elizabeth Cady Stanton, the leaders of the suffragist movement. These women missionaries supported the extension of women's housekeeping roles into the public realm. The traditional feminine virtues, such as self-sacrifice, caring for the young, and protection of the home, could be channeled to serve society in a new way. The attitudes of the missionaries influenced their teaching of Chinese girls and the range of social reforms they would support.

The first organized effort of Chinese Christian women to make some impact on society was the anti-footbinding movement. In 1874, nine working-class, illiterate women, encouraged by Rev. John Macgowan of the London Mission, formed an anti-footbinding society at his church in Xiamen.[19] Contrary to the common understanding, missionaries were not unanimous in their support of the anti-footbinding movement. Some feared the movement would further alienate the Christian mission from the richer class.[20] Women missionaries were more supportive of the movement;

they demanded that students of mission schools have natural feet. In the 1890s, the anti-footbinding movement spread to many cities, supported by girls in mission schools and women in local churches.[21] Bible women often played an important role in organizing women and setting an example by first unbinding their own feet. Although the Qing court had decreed against footbinding and Chinese intellectuals had espoused its abolition, the change of women's consciousness was fundamental in confronting this entrenched custom. Encouraged by the institutional support of the Christian missions, Christian women both promoted the idea of anti-footbinding and provided peer support for women to unbind their feet.

Christian women were also involved in the introduction of new conceptions of women's bodies, Western forms of health care, and social hygiene. The most notable Christian women of the nineteenth century, including Shi Meiyu, Kang Cheng, and Hu Jinying, were medical doctors who had received medical training in the United States.[22] In 1879, Chinese women gained access to medical training when Dr. John Kerr admitted the first group of women students to the Canton Hospital. These small groups of women doctors, together with the nurses trained in nursing schools, supported anti-footbinding, and promoted Western health care and child welfare. Later, the students of the women's colleges and the Chinese YWCA organized health campaigns and instructed the masses in social hygiene. These efforts introduced scientific knowledge about female biology and physiology, shattering the centuries-old myths and taboos surrounding menstruation, pregnancy, and childbirth.

Christian women participated in social reform activities when the Woman's Christian Temperance Union (WCTU) was introduced to China in 1886. The WCTU was formed in the 1870s in the United States when alcoholism threatened family life and caused many social evils. Members of the WCTU demonstrated in the streets, held prayer meetings in saloons, and picketed public places that served liquor. Modeled after the American unions, the WCTU set up small branches in China as a kind of "organized mother-love," committed to save the home from social peril. In China, the WCTU had to adopt less dramatic strategies and its aims were broadened to include movements against opium and cigarette smoking.[23] When Yuan Yuying and Wang Liming assumed leadership of the WCTU, the new generation of leaders became aware of the limitation of the ideology of "home betterment" as they began to introduce programs to deal with the more systemic problems women faced, such as poverty, illiteracy, and economic dependence.[24]

In general, Christian women adopted gradual approaches to social change, such as education, community organization, campaign movements, and moral persuasion. They were not encouraged to participate in more drastic revolutionary activities during the revolution of 1911, and some students in mission schools were dissuaded from joining the demonstrations of the May Fourth period. But this did not mean that Christian women were immune from the changing political circumstances and the development of a feminist movement in China. The YWCA played a crucial role in the promotion of women's social and political consciousness. In the 1920s, the YWCA drew the attention of the Christian community to the plight of women working in factories and sweatshops. YWCA literacy classes for workers in Shanghai cotton mills had the lasting effect of raising the consciousness of female workers and nurturing female leaders in the labor movement.[25] Influenced by the student movement, the Chinese leaders of the YWCA recognized the need to better serve poorer women, instead of simply providing services to middle-class, urban women and girls of mission schools.[26] They came increasingly to believe that the YWCA had to be integrated with the national aspiration for self-determination and political independence.

Some historians have attributed the rising consciousness of Christian women and their participation in society to the influence of women missionaries. It is true that women missionaries served as role models for their followers, introduced new ideas from the West, and provided the initial impetus for women to organize. But we should not overlook the changing internal dynamics of Chinese society, such as the rapid growth of women's newspapers and journals, the increased intermingling of the sexes, and the greater possibilities for women to explore their female identity. The influence of the secular feminist movement on Christian women should not be underestimated. Through their revolutionary activities and writings, the early feminists introduced a conception of womanhood much more radical than that offered by the missionaries. Later, socialist feminists also challenged Christians to integrate women's liberation with the wider economic and political issues of society.

WOMEN'S REFLECTIONS ON THE CHRISTIAN FAITH

Although Christian women did not write theological treatises as male Christians did, their autobiographies, religious testimonies, and short articles give us a glimpse of their theological thinking. Cai Sujuan, a well-known evangelist, described the overt oppression in her patriarchal family. Christianity revealed for her the moralism and hypocrisy of superficial Confucian teachings, and gave her new peace and power.[27] In spite of many job offers, she decided to devote her life to the propagation of the gospel.

Zeng Baosun, the great-granddaughter of Zeng Guofan, came into contact with Christianity while studying in mission schools. She was impressed by the power of Christianity to change people and motivate them to search for meaning in life. Encouraged by her missionary teachers, Zeng joined the Christian church. "The Christian spirit is so wonderful, it can make ordinary people extraordinary. . . . At that time I felt that China needed the spirit of Christian 'practice,' and I decided to become a Christian," Zeng wrote in her autobiography.[28] For Ding Shujing, the first Chinese general secretary of the YWCA, Christianity gave people wholeness of life, enabling them to develop their human potential and to search for higher spiritual ideals.[29]

Aware of the social problems and needs of China, Christian women affirmed the social involvement of Christians. Shi Meiyu commended the contributions of Christian women, citing the provision of social service, free education, community work, and publication of literature as examples.[30] Her colleague Kang Cheng further emphasized Christian women's effort in social change: "Already many of the recent reforms such as anti-footbinding and anti-opium smoking have been largely brought about by the Christian women of China, and their influence will become more patent as their circle enlarges."[31]

Christian women believed that Christianity enabled them to struggle against all forms of discrimination against women, since Christian doctrines stressed the equality of all human beings before the almighty God. God as the father of all was not understood to reinforce the domination of men over women in the family and society. Rather, divine fatherhood was interpreted to challenge and relativize all kinds of patriarchal control on earth.[32] Women, struggling for the rights of the female sex, often saw Christianity as their ally, not as their enemy. As Wang Huiwu wrote:

We know that Christians also espouse equality between men and women, and support the abolition of classes. They strongly oppose inhumane practices, such as concubinage, the keeping of domestic maids, and prostitution, and do not contradict the feminist movement. In terms of belief, the feminist movement differs from gospel preaching, but in terms of concrete work in society, the feminist movement and Christianity both elevate women's position.[33]

This emphasis of Christianity led Christian female leaders to challenge some of the patriarchal practices of the church. For Ding Shujing, the church, as a fellowship of believers, should recognize the equal participation of women and men in the Body of Christ. Discrimination against women hindered the witness and mission of the church and slowed down the pace of building an indigenous Christian community. She argued: "If the position of men and women is not equal in the church, the original mission of the church will not be fulfilled, and the development of church ministry will also be hampered."[34] Her idea was echoed by Cheng Guanyi, a prominent Christian educator, who dared to raise the issue of women's ordination at the National Christian Conference in 1922.[35]

In the wake of the May Fourth Movement, young students and radical intellectuals began to criticize Christianity during the Anti-Christian Movement (1922–27). Besides accusing Christianity of being unscientific and serving the interests of the Western powers, they also challenged the Bible and the churches for discriminating against women. This outside pressure prompted Christian women to reflect critically on their faith from their experience as women and to affirm the liberating aspects of the Christian tradition. Some Christian women emphasized the revolutionary attitude of Jesus toward women: He preached the gospel to the Samaritan woman at the well, challenged the patriarchal practices of the day, and befriended and respected women. Zeng Baosun came close to writing a feminist creed when she said: "Chinese women can only find full life in the message of Christ, who was born of a woman, revealed His messiahship to a woman, and showed His glorified body after His resurrection to a woman."[36]

The autobiographies and religious writings of Chinese women indicated that these women were able to analyze their faith and to draw out the social implications of Christianity. Although the majority of Chinese female Christians were little educated and believed in an individualistic evangelical faith, the more articulate leaders had begun to relate their faith to the needs of China at the time. Besides caring about their own spiritual needs, they also sought to follow the example set by Jesus to serve their own country and people. They emphasized the historical Jesus as the perfect human being, demonstrating the highest potential of humankind. As Ding Shujing said, "The life of Jesus is an exemplar, unique both in the past and in the present. He has perfect knowledge of God and is in complete harmony with God. He has genuine love for humankind. With steadfast and relentless power, He fulfills the task of saving human beings and the world."[37] During the trying time of the 1920s, the belief in a just and compassionate God and a humanistic understanding of Christology empowered these women to live out their multiple identities as Chinese, women, and Christians.

CHAPTER 12

"Cradle of Female Talent": The McTyeire Home and School for Girls, 1892–1937

HEIDI A. ROSS

(1)
Near the mighty Yangtze River
In the heart of old Shanghai
There's a school for China's daughters,
Bringing truth and freedom nigh.

(2)
May she live and grow forever,
Scatter knowledge far and near;
Till all China learns the lessons
That we learn at old McTyeire.

(3)
Blessings on thee, old McTyeire!
How we love thee, dear McTyeire!
May thy daughters live and love,
And grow forever, old McTyeire!

(4)
Here's our health to thee, McTyeire,
Here's our wealth for thee, McTyeire!
Though we live a thousand years,
We'll remember old McTyeire!

(5)
Near the mighty Yangtze River
In the heart of old Shanghai
Stood a school for China's daughters,
Bringing truth and freedom nigh.

(6)
And her spirit lives forever
In her daughters far and near,
Who are living, loving, growing,
As they did at old McTyeire.

(7)
God be blessed for thee, McTyeire!
Home of truth and love, McTyeire!
In thy dear name we'll live, love, grow,
Thy daughters, dear McTyeire.

(8)
Live, oh, live in us, McTyeire!
Speak again through us, McTyeire!
Though we live a thousand years,
We'll be true to thee, McTyeire.

—McTyeire School Song, *The McTyeirean*, 1933

Southern Methodist missionaries founded the McTyeire School for Girls (Zhongxi nüshu [Chinese-Western Girls' Academy]) in 1892 to provide a liberal education to young Chinese women of "the well-to-do classes." Sixty years later McTyeire was consolidated with St. Mary's School for Girls, and renamed the Shanghai Number Three Girls' School (hereafter referred to as Number 3).[1] In 1982 Number 3 was designated an advanced school (*jiaoyu keyan xianjin xuexiao*) for classroom-based research in female adolescent development and became China's only all-female municipal key secondary school.

This chapter examines McTyeire's history from its Wesleyan beginnings to 1937. The analysis represents a portion of a larger, ongoing study in which McTyeire provides the setting for exploring how North American and Chinese women in late-imperial, republican, and socialist China perceived the connections among schooling for women, indigenous and foreign oppression, and the transformation of Chinese society.

One of the assumptions underlying this examination of McTyeire is that schools, as primary agencies for transmitting cultural values, are exceptional locations for evaluating the power and meaning of a society's pivotal social and political contradictions. As a locus for dialogue about China's past, present, and future, McTyeire was a contested terrain, an arena for sometimes heated debate about the consequences of missionary school training for the educational, religious, professional, and political aspirations of young Chinese women. Scholars who have studied foreign-sponsored colleges in China have provided rich insights regarding the extent to which mission education supported Chinese nationalism and economic development or sponsored a depoliticized and "alienated academy" of foreign values.[2] Extending this question to the educational experiences of secondary school pupils broadens our understanding of how Chinese students developed the attitudes and values that shaped their political participation, social service, and cultural identity.

Readers are reminded that the conclusions drawn below are necessarily limited. Portraits of single institutions like McTyeire or St. Hilda's (elsewhere in this volume), far from depicting Chinese education writ small, represent all of the limitations of case study research that engages in "procedures for counting to one."[3] The use of personal narratives in this chapter highlights the partial nature of such analyses. The conflicting and nostalgic recollections of McTyeireans illustrate what historians have called the "not quite" status of personal narratives: not quite fiction, not quite factual evidence.[4] McTyeire's "true" legacy is to this day being reconstructed by alumnae, whose divergent claims indicate that McTyeire is very much an institution that has not one but multiple histories.

One theme does connect these competing histories, however. McTyeirean teachers and students consistently referred to their school as a garden of familial harmony, even as they argued about the extent to which McTyeire influenced their lives and acknowledged that pupils, wittingly or not, subverted McTyeire's explicitly communal goals. With fascinating regularity, McTyeire's family metaphor both concealed and encouraged student efforts to "put missionary offerings to their own uses," and seek "independence from missionary as well as Chinese social expectations."[5]

The Wesleyan Legacy: McTyeire's "Gospel of Gentility," 1892–1917

Young J. Allen, the "great Mandarin of the Methodists" in nineteenth-century China, was appointed the superintendent of the China Mission of the Methodist Episcopal Church South (hereafter referred to as MECS) in 1881 by Bishop Holland N. McTyeire (1824–89), founder of Vanderbilt University. In this capacity Allen coordinated the MECS Woman's Missionary Society in China, an organization he infused with a conviction that the elevation of Chinese women must be equated with the salvation of China. "The degrading systems of the East," Allen wrote, "are based mainly on the condition of woman; and experience has demonstrated that if we could make any permanent impress on society, she must receive more attention. To accomplish this female missionaries are necessary. They alone can reach the source of evil."[6]

In a manuscript entitled "Our China Mission," Allen declared that what the Chinese individual needed was "religion to bind him to God; morality to regulate his intercourse with his fellow man; and Science to teach him the properties and uses of things."[7] By fusing Victorian and Christian values, Allen sought to change Chinese social relationships through the work of female missionaries, who would, by educating Chinese women and their children, transform Chinese families, and ultimately the Chinese nation.

Allen was also convinced that the usual mission practice of running charity schools isolated missionaries from the very Chinese leaders who could assert influence within their communities. He advocated, instead, redirecting educational efforts toward the "best and most hopeful class" of students. The Women's Foreign Mission Society concurred with Allen's assessment, claiming that the time

had come when missionary work should cease to be a synonym for charity, and *vice versa*. We are pauperizing all our Churches and missionary work by the methods now in vogue, and yet we wonder and sigh for the time when the native Churches will become self-supporting. . . . We shut boys and girls in schools, pack them and cram them with hundreds and thousands of verses of Scripture, feed and clothe them at enormous expense, persuade them to make a profession of religion, hold out to them as an inducement to diligence and contentment a place ultimately as a preacher or teacher, etc; they accept it all, cleave to us, are orthodox converts, always looking to Mother Church to feed them! . . . I will not say they are all parasites, hypocrites, but it is certainly not the fault of the system that it is not so.[8]

With support from his home board, Allen proposed a sister school for the successful Anglo-Chinese School for Boys he had already established in Shanghai, and recruited Laura Askew Haygood (1845–1900) to be its principal.[9] Haygood graduated from Wesleyan Female College in Macon, Georgia, and became one of the founders of the MECS Home Mission Society.

Haygood agreed with Allen that a school for Chinese girls should enroll "girls of the better classes who *cannot* be brought into our day schools or charity schools — whose parents are able and willing to pay for having their daughters taught."[10] She assumed that most of these pupils would come from educated families, where a man "will care more or less that his sisters, his wife, his daughters, should be educated." Haygood explained to colleagues (usually when requesting financial contributions), "We long to open to some of these girls the doors, now closed to them, that lead to the beautiful world of light and truth."[11]

Like many women of the Wesleyan tradition in the second half of the nineteenth century, Haygood perceived her central responsibility as spiritual and educational leader in a primarily domestic sphere. Her conception of education for light and truth reflected the assumption that "the woman's sphere" of domesticity and care could be an enormous force in transforming society. Shifted from the home into the public arena of education, this transformative power seemed infinite. However, it also placed Haygood, as she tried to span the worlds of home and school, in the precarious position of reconciling her ideal of the role of women as reforming through "blessed influence" with the direct power, over finances and colleagues, she wielded as a school administrator.

Shortly before leaving for China Haygood revealed in a letter to a friend the frustrations she felt in battling the "costly superficiality" of women's education of her day.

Whether the accompanying course of study be geography and arithmetic, the philosophies and the higher mathematics, the arts and the sciences, or the making of a fair and beautiful home, she must know and feel that there are obligations resting upon *her*, because God has given her a soul and placed her among men and women, her brothers and sisters. . . . At whatever stage of her education she may be, or in whatever department of this great school of life, I care less for *what* she studies than *how* she studies. All the arts and sciences, the languages and the literatures of the world may be made tributary to this "higher education" for which we are pleading. No course of study can be too advanced, no learning too deep, no culture too broad, to help in the making of the *perfect woman*. . . . Why have we not told her that to grace her home, to make it bright and beautiful and good, is indeed womanly and wise, but for most of us need not, ought not, *must not* absorb all of love and time and mind? Why have we not made her feel that for her as truly as for her brother there is need of earnest, honest, thorough work, because the world has need of her?[12]

The tension and irony in Haygood's position is indicated by her expression of the ideals of self-liberation in the language of self-sacrifice.[13] Haygood asked, "Do we not too often in our schools shut our girls *out* from the real world with its real needs, and shut them *in* to the narrow ways of self and selfish aims?"[14] Once in China, her situation became further complicated as she was forced to redefine female education in a setting that demanded conformity not only to conceptions of North American femininity but also Confucian patterns of womanhood. Her letters home expressed grave doubts about her work, sufficiency of funding, and Chinese tradition, an "authority of the dead" which seemed to surround and consume her.

Not surprisingly, Haygood concluded that one of her mission's most urgent demands was the establishment of an institution that combined girls' school with comfortable way station and point of transition for female missionaries newly arrived in China. The Home, as it came to be called, would provide for unmarried foreign educators a touchstone of familiarity, a moral and physical preserve that could stave off the perceived threats of an alien environment.

The desire to make schools nurturing and privileged communities of educated women devoted to service had a profound influence on McTyeire. Haygood faced an inevitable tension as she pursued "partially feminist goals with anti-feminist means."[15] Some McTyeire alumnae from the 1930s and 1940s would look back at this contradiction and criticize McTyeire's "doctrine of 'ladies first'" as little more than a substitute for authentic equality. Nevertheless, during the late nineteenth century Haygood attempted to make McTyeire an environment in which tensions between private domesticity and public responsibility could be resolved.

After seven years of planning, the McTyeire Home and School opened in March 1892, five years before the establishment of Shanghai's first Chinese-managed girls' school. McTyeire initially occupied one building erected at the present site of Moore Memorial Church, and was named after the late Bishop McTyeire who supported the school's establishment and died just before it opened. The school's Chinese name, Zhongxi nüshu, selected to remind parents of Allen's successful Anglo-Chinese School for Boys, better embodies the school's purpose and tension. Its educational goal was to give girls *tong cai*, the capacity to understand and be of service to both Chinese and American cultural traditions.

The school's grand opening was a well-publicized affair attended by prominent Chinese officials, including Nie Qigui, Shanghai's daotai from 1890 to 1894, as well as the vice consul general of the U.S. and editors of local newspapers and magazines. In respect for Confucian protocol, two receptions were organized, the first for men, at which Haygood was represented by the U.S. vice consul, and the second for women, on 16 March, the first day of classes.

Although only seven girls "of aristocratic background" (including Nie Qigui's daughter) composed McTyeire's first class of students, Haygood and the two Chinese teachers with whom she taught described the turnout as "an excellent beginning, particularly for a school which charged tuition." By 1897 the school had 29 students. The students' fathers included three "mandarins," a manager of the imperial telegraph, an editor of a well-known Shanghai newspaper, and five Episcopalian and Methodist ministers.

Laura Haygood died in 1900, a pivotal year in McTyeire's early history. The school moved into a three-story structure known as the McGavock Memorial, which accommodated 75 boarders and 25 day pupils. McTyeire also graduated its first class of students, all three of whom became teachers. McTyeire accepted married women for the first time, and became fully self-supporting. This "encouraging progress" was recorded in annual reports of the Women's Foreign Mission Society with an accepted formula for measuring Christian modernity: of the school's 99 pupils in 1903, 6 were married, 30 were Christians, and only 5 had bound feet.

As noted above, American missionaries brought to China their own conversations about educating women. "Their mediations between public and private responsibilities, between expansive and defensive commitments, were dramatic versions of the central tensions within American female culture at the time."[16] McTyeire certainly embodied these conflicting conversations, but it was also an institution whose shape and purpose emerged in the process of American tensions being played out among different but equally complex tensions in Chinese society. By the early twentieth century, McTyeire's educational aims reflected both the accomplishments wealthy families desired in their daughters and the moral character and refined breeding that comprised the mission school's "gospel of gentility": to offer students a firm grounding in Chinese and English through a liberal arts education; to offer a series of elective classes in Western music; to build a wholesome educational environment which would cultivate young Chinese women of high moral character and mental habits; and to provide students with fundamental knowledge of Christianity.[17]

McTyeire's aims, fashioned from the meeting of two cultures of female gentility, reflected the tremendous changes taking place in China. Republican, utopian, and anarchist feminist writers (albeit in a fringe press) were linking the education of women to the strengthening of China, and even writing treatises on the relationship between class, gender, and the state. Even the empress dowager conceded that educational reforms once suppressed might now be advantageous for the protection of China's crumbling empire. In 1901 she issued an edict providing for the preparation of girls' textbooks to be used in home study. Two years after the imperial examination system which had existed since the seventh century was abolished by imperial decree in 1905, the first government-run girls' primary and normal schools were established.

American mission schools benefited from this ambition to achieve political and social ends through education, and the number of missionaries in China doubled between 1890 and 1905. Yet by 1908, although no more than 2 percent of pupils in government schools were girls, their numbers exceeded those of girls being trained in mission schools. This novel competition reinforced the missionary view that education was the path of least resistance to bring the hearts and minds of the Chinese people to God, just as Chinese reformers spoke out ever more forcefully that the education of Chinese women was crucial for building a strong, independent China.

This confluence of interest did not eliminate disagreements about the nature of appropriate education for Chinese women, particularly when rapid social change meant that Confucian and Christian models for womanhood existed alongside altered, "progressive" social relationships. Helen Richardson, Haygood's successor, expelled five pupils from McTyeire in 1906, one for insubordination, the rest for engaging in illicit correspondence with male admirers. Changing times brought confusion, and Chinese and Americans regarded each other as simultaneously radically outlandish and parochially conservative:

New temptations are coming to Chinese young women such as were never dreamed of by their grandmothers and their characters are being tested with every new opportunity. Fathers are proud of their educated daughters, and want them to participate in public functions. "Public functions" means being seen of men; and being seen of men means an attempt at a secret correspondence — sometimes a walk in the moonlight, a drive into the country, or to questionable entertainments, etc. The great difficulty comes through the inability of the unlearned, conservative mother to properly instruct and chaperon her progressive, educated daughter.[18]

Missionaries struggled to direct the consequences of a McTyeirean education by coupling appropriate behavior with religious study. The 1908 school catalog reminded parents and students that "the study of Christianity is not optional. All students must return on Sunday morning to Sunday school and church, after which they may return to their homes till

Monday morning."[19] The message that discipline and order were expected on the school's terms underlies the entire catalog, which spelled out precise requirements for everything from student fees (nine dollars a month room and board), bedding, clothing, examination and evaluation procedures, to the particular school entrances to be used by male and female visitors.

During the first two decades of McTyeire's development, educating young women became perceived as an important means to two very different ends: religious salvation on the one hand, and national salvation on the other. The developing tension between Christianity and nationalism in a single institution raises intriguing questions about the relationship between the activities of missionaries and the emergence of Chinese women as a social and political force. Some scholars suggest that female missionaries were more culturally imperialistic than were their male counterparts, because they became directly involved in the lives of Chinese families. McTyeire provides a paradoxical example of foreign penetration into the lives of Chinese girls because its role in training future wives and mothers to "be the center of Christian influence in the sphere of power with which Christ has gifted them [the family]" and its goal to train young women to use their study of English and the Bible, as well as history, science, mathematics, and Chinese, to become leaders in their communities, moved Chinese women into nontraditional roles. Any such movement was an implicit challenge to traditional cultural patterns of subservience, duty to mothers-in-law, and early betrothal. More importantly, the school's collective experience offered its students a forum for discussing their personal concerns, as well as untraditional role models in its unmarried, strong-willed, and highly educated teachers.

By 1913 McTyeire had become so overcrowded that a meeting of fourteen prominent Shanghai leaders, including Wu Tingfang, former minister to the U.S., was held to discuss a $60,000 fund-raising campaign for the purpose of buying new property for expansion. This plan was temporarily disrupted by political instability within China, and McTyeire's first student strike, what one alumna considered the most destructive conflict between Chinese students and American teachers at McTyeire prior to the school's registration with the Nationalist government in 1928.

Well over half of McTyeire's students were involved in the strike. In the autumn of 1915 several students talking during their afternoon study period were reprimanded by their principal, Helen Richardson. When they persisted, Richardson slapped the hand of one student. Shocked and offended at their ill-treatment by a condescending foreigner, two students criticized Richardson for her allegedly insulting and discriminatory response. The two students were expelled. When student representatives sent to Richardson to speak on their behalf were turned away, 82 students left the school, although 50 returned, sent back to school by their parents. Over 30 pupils withdrew permanently from the school. One of the students who left, with the help of a close friend who was also a McTyeire graduate, founded another girls' school, Qi Xiu, which enrolled the majority of the striking students. Students who returned to McTyeire were required to pay a five dollar reentrance fee, and a young teacher suspected of inciting the pupils had her teaching responsibilities revoked.

It is not clear how students made their decisions to stay at McTyeire or join the exodus. A graduate of the class of 1918 suggests that the daughters of Christian families remained at school, primarily because they defined themselves in opposition to classmates who were "stylish, wealthy, well-to-do, high-class Shanghai ladies." McTyeire administrators at the time, on the other hand, believed that such cliques within the student body were successfully discouraged by regulations that encouraged students to share their care packages from home, that prohibited extravagance in dress, and that limited knowledge of the identities of scholarship students to McTyeire's principal, treasurer, and head of the scholarship committee. Missionary teachers declared, "After a few years in McTyeire they all became McTyeire girls. Christianity leavens the whole lump and learning lifts it to the place where class distinctions give way and real worth becomes the determining factor of the student's place in the life of the school."[20]

Most alumnae who attended McTyeire at the time agree. "We have students from Christian families that served in the mission. So they weren't as well-off as the Christian families with independent businesses. Their income is a lot lower than most outsiders, and their children got scholarships to McTyeire. This was the inside story, though. Nobody knew. You can't tell the difference."

The strike of 1915 temporarily altered the size of McTyeire's senior high school student body. The graduating classes of 1915, 1916, and 1917 were each comprised of only two students, compared to fourteen in 1914. This figure was not surpassed until twenty-one students graduated in 1921. Nevertheless, rapidly increasing enrollments in McTyeire's earlier grades soon revitalized the once-tabled plan for school expansion. In 1917, the year Helen Richardson died, McTyeire's preparatory and high school departments moved to Edinburgh Road, currently Shanghai's Jiangsu Road in Changning District.

Nationalism and the Critique of "Ladies First": 1917–27

McTyeire's new campus, located on slightly more than thirteen acres, was the site known as the Jin Family Flower Garden. The four-story Jin family mansion, a fabulous Victorian creation that captured the sometimes inharmonious spirit of McTyeire's Anglo-Chinese enterprise, became the school's center of operation as well as residence for three teachers and fifty-five senior high school students.

McTyeire's 1917 catalog described the mansion as "a bright, happy Christian home" where the "Rules are few, the law of school is obedience."[21] Students paid an annual tuition of $60, and an equal sum if they wished to study music. The catalog stressed not only order but neatness, propriety, and frugality. Jewelry and extravagant clothing were forbidden, and money found in student rooms was confiscated and used for the "improvement of school premises." Students were forbidden to carry on correspondences with gentlemen and "questionable" letters were opened by the principal.

After 1919, it is clear that at least some of McTyeire's students and faculty became enmeshed in fervent debates about whether cultural or political activism should be the leading impetus for Chinese reform and about how Chinese women should serve China's reform efforts. Some members of the McTyeire student council were involved in May Fourth demonstrations. However, the majority of McTyeire students refrained from joining political movements, to the relief of both their parents and their foreign teachers. "We are just Christians, not political," say alumnae. "And the teachers all discouraged us from doing that. And especially our families. They don't like us to march in the street. We really had very little to do with political involvements. You grow up under that umbrella and you are all alike."

In-house histories written by Number 3 administrators since 1949 suggest that American teachers at first supported their students' political interests, "since the initial movement was ostensibly against Japanese imperialism." Xue Zheng, principal of McTyeire from 1936 to 1952 and current honorary principal of Number 3, contends that when missionaries realized anti-imperialist fervor might be directed toward their own efforts, they demanded that students attend at least two classes, English and mathematics, before they demonstrated. It is likely that American teachers did admonish students to balance activism with formal study, in the desire to preoccupy their charges and keep them off the streets. But what Xue Zheng saw as manipulation, foreign teachers saw as admirable calm in the face of struggle.

"Our students have gone on bravely with their work and we at McTyeire have not lost a single day of school. Three cheers for McTyeire students!"

Regardless of motive, political involvement by students outside McTyeire's walls was eventually discouraged. In the fall of 1919, the student council, which was directly affiliated with the Shanghai Student Union, was transformed into an independent council (*zizhihui*), perhaps to break the direct connection between McTyeire students and their peers in other institutions. The students' self-governing body was given added responsibilities for managing school activities, at the price of diverting student energies away from national politics. McTyeire's successful athletic competitions with other institutions were also discontinued.

Xue Zheng insists that McTyeire's response to student political participation marked a subtle shift in the school's management of the student body. Whenever trouble brewed in Shanghai's student communities, McTyeire authorities announced a "vacation" and sent students home. Parents who were concerned about their daughters' safety gave McTyeire administrators their approval. This is not to suggest that McTyeire students were not encouraged to take responsibility for much of their education. Political awareness, evidenced by sensitive essays written for *The McTyeirean*, the school yearbook, or the twenty-one graduates of the class of 1921 proclaiming themselves "the twenty-one demands," was not only acceptable but desirable, particularly if sweetened with precocious good humor. Independence and self-reliance was, after all, a McTyeire hallmark, but its expression was carefully contained.

Alumnae who attended McTyeire during the 1920s frequently make a clear distinction between their foreign teachers and foreign imperialism in China. A graduate of the class of 1929 recalls

the rickshaw that took me to school. And you know what I hated the most? I think all the students did. We had to pass that race course, and there was a sign that said Chinese and dogs not allowed. And that made me really boil. But, of course, I was so young so I held it inside. With the missionaries we never talked about that. Because missionaries were our teachers, right? And they are benevolent, they are thinking for your goodness. They also show their regret that all these bad things happen in China. We were almost on the same side.

Being "almost on the same side" captures the ambiguous complexity with which a student responded to missionary aims to offer the "knowledge, skill, and spirit to serve her home, her community, her nation and the world."[22] Some pupils interpreted McTyeire's devotion to service and community as developing a Christian identity. A graduate of the class of 1918, who entered McTyeire as a Christian, remembers that foreign teachers "really wanted you to become a Christian. But the missionaries came with a good purpose of spreading Christianity. I feel that way. So I'm proud I'm a missionary's daughter." A member of the class of 1929 who converted to Christianity during her years at the school recalls:

At school I heard an evangelist, a woman at an assembly. And everyone was crying, and I wanted to be a Christian so much. That's when suddenly I got up my courage, and I went to my grandmother, and I told her my school is really wonderful, a Christian school, and I wanted so much to become a Christian. You know what my grandmother said? She said, "Of course, your mother sent you to a Christian school, you will become a Christian." She said, "But, when you become a Christian, you'll be a good one. Buddha will bless you." And I never forgot that sentence. All my life I carried that with me. Then I immediately was baptized and I felt, "Oh! I'm one of them."

Other alumnae appreciated a camaraderie that allowed them to "feel loved," to resist families that took for granted the unhappiness of sisters, mothers, aunts. Their narratives vibrate with fury. China's first female lawyer, an extraordinary woman who graduated from McTyeire in 1920, struggled with her father to attend McTyeire in order to

fight the laws against women in China. I said I'm going to fight. My sister married, and her husband took her money to keep three women on the side. . . . My sister belonged to another dynasty. Whatever she thought was not what I wanted — she even wanted to bind my feet. She had bound feet, and she wanted me to look good. I said, "Ohhhh, no!" When I grow up I'm going to be a lawyer and fight for the rights of women. But the women of my time were so low, so below the men, the law school wouldn't take any women. So I taught mathematics at McTyeire, the hardest subject at my old alma mater. And I waited for nine long years until I heard that Suzhou Law School was open to women, and I said to myself, "I am going to show you boys that I have bigger brains than you have. I'm going to beat you all, because you think men are superior to women. I'm going to show you women are superior to you."

With such passions stirring, McTyeire's explicit educational program inevitably threatened its own mission enterprise. First embraced by pupils for the social and intellectual alternatives it offered them, the McTyeirean experience came to be defined as both barrier and pathway to personal and social transformation.

From Registration to War: 1927–37

As Chiang Kai-shek consolidated his political power, Chinese educational policies became increasingly tied to Nationalist Party (Guomindang) plans for the unification of China. In 1927 the Central Educational Administration Commission launched the Recovery of Educational Rights Movement which culminated in a series of regulations requiring the registration of all private schools in China.

After Helen Richardson's death in 1917, McTyeire's principalship had been held by four American women: Alice Waters, 1917–18; Martha Pyle, 1918–23; Lois Cooper, 1923–25; and Sallie Lou MacKinnon, 1925–29. There was no question that the first Chinese principalship would go to Mo Kyi Ying (Ma Jiying), a thirty-year member of the McTyeire family who had served in the capacity of school matron, teacher, treasurer, business manager, and vice-principal. But Mo died in February 1928, and in her place, McTyeire hired Grace Xizhen Yang, a daughter of a Methodist minister and graduate of Mt. Holyoke and Columbia Teachers College. Grace Yang was a woman of impeccable credentials, recipient of a Boxer Indemnity Scholarship, secretary of the student department of the National Committee of the YWCA, and later its executive secretary.

American teachers at the time expressed little concern about the impact of registration on McTyeire. "After all," said one,

we did not start out to build a world Methodism, we started out to build an indigenous church. McTyeire was able to remain strong, especially academically, through so many hardships. We built strong ideals and tradition was passed on from one group to another. By the time I got there we had daughters of McTyeire graduates in school. So, you see, you had among the faculty not only graduates of the best colleges in the U.S. and China, but they were born and bred McTyeire people.

Consequently, the McTyeire community was not prepared for the difficulties this transition brought about. It was Grace Yang who became the center of heated controversy. Although accounts in Number 3 archives suggest that Grace Yang left her post because she was disliked by foreign teachers, American teachers at McTyeire express confusion about why Yang failed to bring her considerable talents to a fruitful end at McTyeire. "I have a feeling that Grace Yang took McTyeire more as her school. Well, it was never anybody's her school. It was our school." Students who remember Grace Yang are divided about the effectiveness of her leadership. Some believe that she was able to gain the support of treaty port families of Shanghai with stylish aplomb, raising money and furthering McTyeire's already formidable reputation. Others feel her attention to fund-raising undermined academic standards. In fact, Grace Yang was discreetly dismissed from her position as principal because of her close relationship with a female American vocal teacher at the school. Alumnae mention her relationship with the American music teacher only in passing, and it may be that missionaries problematized a relationship that few students considered important. Nevertheless, Grace Yang was replaced by Xue Zheng, who began her formal schooling in the Confucian classics disguised as a boy and went on to study at Yanjing University and Columbia.

Whether McTyeire was significantly altered as a result of post-1927 registration is a matter of disagreement among former students and teachers. Frequently they identify the late 1920s as the beginning of a decline in the school's English language curriculum. In compliance with the requirements of registration, all junior secondary school classes, with the exception of English language study, were taught in Chinese. English was used to study world history, as well as mathematics and physics, in senior middle school. Religion was made an elective, although all students continued to study the New and Old Testaments.

Jean Craig, a missionary educator who arrived to teach at McTyeire while these changes were being implemented, insists that the order of McTyeire's Chinese name reflected a commitment to mutuality between foreign and Chinese colleagues. "It was *zhongxi* [Chinese-Western], not *xizhong* [Western-Chinese]. McTyeire was never a school run *by* foreigners for Chinese; it was always a cooperative venture in which Americans and Chinese worked together with mutual love and respect."[23] Craig maintains that it was this close community that allowed McTyeire to expand its enrollment and curriculum, despite outbreaks of violence and disruption. Refugees who found temporary shelter in McTyeire's relatively protected campus became such a fact of life it fazed no one. In a letter written in 1931, Craig describes "teaching my religion class, and it was working on the beatitudes. You could hear the gun go 'boooooom,' and you hear this 'whizzz' going over your head, and you knew it was going to explode. During periods of silence I taught. When the new explosion was going to come, I turned around and wrote the next beatitude. You see, we went right on."

Xue Zheng, however, remembers relationships between foreign interests and Chinese needs as filled with tension and suspicion. She recalls an argument with her American advisor over skits that students performed during their fifteen minute break before lunch. Missionary educators hoped to stop the students from depicting in their performances China's war of resistance, or oppressive landlords and impoverished workers, themes the missionaries felt too depressing for girls who should be engaging in light-hearted activities before the noon hour. Xue contends that the school's general orientation came "from the U.S. for the purpose of inculcating

Western culture. In all matters of management the foreign advisor had final say. We had a school committee of five to seven people which met each week. It sounds very democratic, but everything was in fact decided in advance. The Chinese principal's position was the office manager for the foreign advisor."

Personal narratives of alumnae, as well as letters written by teachers, annual missionary reports, and excerpts from *The McTyeirean*, support the claims of both Xue Zheng and Jean Craig. Students write fondly of their stage productions of *Little Women* and *Merchant of Venice*, their celebrations of Christmas and Halloween, their Campfire Girls' bonfires, their senior teas in shady school gardens. Many conclude that "the efforts of the missionaries were really to be commended, because they created something out of nothing. They were able to stay on and graduate class after class of women who became useful citizens. You know, at that age or looking at it from this point of view, I really didn't think they were imposing their culture."

The granddaughter of the founder of St. John's University, a graduate of McTyeire's class of 1937, believes that

when students went in to McTyeire maybe they were not Christians, but most McTyeire students left being Christians. Because we had a very strong Christian education. It's not forced upon us. You don't have to go to the prayer meetings. And for the religions we learned all of them, we studied comparative religion. And the teachers' examples, they were so well-liked by everybody. All of the teachers went to worship. Whenever we went, there they were. They never forced anything on you. That's the good part. They just lived Christian lives.

Even alumnae who became active communist supporters look back at McTyeire in appreciation of its relaxed and open approach to education: "What I liked about McTyeire was its liberal atmosphere. We didn't talk much about politics, but we also weren't controlled by the KMT [Guomindang] like a lot of public schools. We could read whatever we wanted. From Karl Marx to Byron, everything was on the shelf waiting. It was a joy. We were so young at the time. We were interested in everything from Hamlet to Hitler."

A smaller number of students, however, describe McTyeire as

a beautiful ivory tower, so very beautiful, forsythia, daffodils, peach blossoms, a lily pond, a little bridge, a little island, and the dragon wall and wisteria. And we took walks. We lay down on the lawn in warmer days, sang, played, talked. Later on when I became an adult, I looked back and thought what an isolated kind of life, when China was in a great turmoil. Warlords were fighting, Japanese were encroaching.

We knew nothing about those things. We were very isolated. For heavens sake! We didn't know anything about our own country. It is a very sad case that we, somehow, got the kind of perception or the kind of attitude of looking down on Chinese culture. They didn't intentionally do this, but they always talked about beautiful, bright America, and we imagined it must be so good. And at the same time China was herself in a very bad state.

Alumnae recount with chagrin their treatment of Chinese-language teachers. "We were awful to every teacher who taught Chinese — we bullied them. It was terrible in retrospect. Almost cruel, and the way we treated them, they had to leave. Thinking back, it was cruel. Because of the environment we just didn't pay attention to Chinese language. We were daughters of Westernized families."

On 4 November 1935 McTyeire held a formal dedication celebration for a newly constructed classroom building, Richardson Hall. A procession of students from every McTyeire class from 1900 to 1949 was headed by McTyeire's first three graduates of the class of 1900. The senior class that year would later convey in their class history a complex mixture of hope and the grave necessity of growing up quickly in times of crisis. "The clash between the Chinese and the Japanese in Chapei in 1932" made their "blood boil with patriotism as we saw injustice, conspiracy, and treachery right under our eyes. . . . The children of yesterday suddenly grew up overnight when they were brought face to face with human misery." Yet, illuminated by lanterns in the autumn twilight of their senior year, they stood with 50 years of McTyeire students in a circle of optimism and connection, as if in defiance of the war and political disruption that would soon follow.

The Japanese occupation of Shanghai after Pearl Harbor shattered McTyeire's ivory tower. American teachers were driven away from the school property in an emotional leave-taking, to be interned in concentration camps. McTyeire was eventually occupied by the Japanese Army Number Two Hospital, and the school was forced to move into an abandoned English girls' school on Haig (Hua Shan) Road, the current location of Shanghai's prestigious kindergarten. Although McTyeire's student body was reduced in size, and teaching operated in two half-day shifts, classes continued throughout the war. The absence of foreign teachers at McTyeire fostered a new sense of independence and control among Chinese teachers and students at McTyeire. Students of this newer generation came to look upon their prewar years at McTyeire "as Alice in Wonderland. After that, we had to grow up fast."

Conclusion: McTyeire's Legacy

Over 2,000 women returned to Shanghai in 1992 to celebrate the one hundredth anniversary of McTyeire's founding. The celebration has culminated in a controversial effort to pass on McTyeire's Chinese middle school name, Zhongxi nüzhong, to Number 3. Acceptance of this concrete connection between the two institutions, spearheaded by McTyeireans in both the U.S. and China, is by no means unanimous. Some alumnae eschew any possibility of historical continuity, advising me that "the McTyeire you know is not the one I know." Stalwartly anticommunist alumnae consider the special qualities of McTyeire lost, except in their own lives and cherished memories. This rupture of heritage much less frequently divides alumnae in the PRC. Number 3's newly articulated connection with the past, which began in the late 1970s through the formation of alumnae associations in China and abroad, confers concrete advantages as market socialism has made secondary school funding an institutional as well as state responsibility.

Current efforts to find McTyeire in the present have prompted women of McTyeire and Number 3 to reevaluate their disparate images of what the school was and has become. The school is still officially portrayed in Number 3 histories, and passed down in this form to current Number 3 students, with condemnation of McTyeire's re-creation of an upper-class American school on Chinese soil. In the most formulaic of these descriptions, McTyeire's influence is portrayed as monolithic. While breathtaking in its serene beauty, McTyeire forced religious training on its students and replicated the patterns of bourgeois American domesticity in home economics classes. Xue Zheng has written that McTyeire's decidedly upper-class school climate (*guizu xuexiao de xiaofeng*) "trained the wives and mothers of powerful men, rather than successful women."

Most alumnae (both those in China as well as those who live abroad) reject this characterization by pointing to the accomplishments of outstanding McTyeire graduates: Tsun Pei Wei Hsueh (1908), general secretary of the YWCA; Shun Zhen Yeh (1909), director of China's first women's bank; Cecilia Zung (1920), China's first female lawyer; Vivian W. Yen (1934), chairperson of the board of directors of Yue Loong Motor Company; Mae Yih (1946), the first female Chinese-American U.S. state senator.

Others respond indignantly, complaining, "It's not easy to get into McTyeire. McTyeire had a reputation of girls from wealthy families, luxurious in habits, but it's not true. It was not as if all we do is spend money, get clothes. It's not true. We had the highest academic standards in our school."

Although the personal narratives of McTyeireans belie the harshness of Xue Zheng's portrait of McTyeire's purposes, they do not contradict her critique of the powerful cultural claims McTyeire made on its students. McTyeire made foreignness attractive. The school's elaborate rituals and parties established strong emotional bonds between students and their alma mater. Their introduction to American culture and customs, coupled with unparalleled English fluency, set pupils apart, made them feel, especially upon leaving McTyeire, that they were different, entitled, cosmopolitan "McTyeire girls."

Many Christian and non Christian alumnae speak with fondness about "beginning to know the American way of life. This seemed very fascinating to me, and I loved English." They recall being impressed by how their missionary teachers carried "their Christian ideals in their attitudes." "I think what makes alumnae similar is that they had the same experiences, the American way of life. It's just more liberating, and we all caught their values, and this cannot be forgotten or repressed." They agree that prior to the late 1940s political engagement on the part of McTyeireans was extremely rare, but often seem impatient with the question, sighing, "At that age, well, how political could you get?!"

Yet, McTyeire was never just the "Peach Blossom Land" that so infuriated Chinese and foreign critics of privileged mission schools. McTyeire's emphasis on service was internalized by pupils who came to believe that the prestige of being a "McTyeire girl" carried with it heavy social responsibilities. Regardless of whether service was defined in religious or political terms, alumnae remember a McTyeire that "called out of themselves a better self." "The teachers all told us constantly, so we had no doubt that this was the best school certainly in Shanghai, and maybe in all of China. We were always told, pounded into our heads, that we represent not only ourselves as young women but we also represent the school, the nation."

The drive to be excellent, the kind of built-in standards. I think these were formed at McTyeire. You have a responsibility of returning part of it [the good life] to the society or to the community, in addition to passing it on to your children. I mean the training, education, a code of ethics. That's right. You should do that with your children. But I also feel you have to extend beyond the immediate family. If you want to become part of the community, you have to put some investment into that community.

In her fine book, *Composing a Life*, Mary Catherine Bateson characterizes successful living as an "improvisatory art."[24] Growing up as they did in the midst of disruptive social changes that left many caught up in violent political movements or displaced without financial resources abroad, McTyeireans have had to regard improvisation in their lives not as a last resort, but as an established way of creating new possibilities. Alumnae value McTyeire precisely because its precarious isolation extended to them a stable environment in which to develop the personal strength to live life in the face of great uncertainty:

> What McTyeire gave us was confidence — not just good academic training. It was that everyone was appreciated and cherished for whatever their individual skills and strengths. Everyone was made to feel they belonged, were valued. Like a big family. Perhaps we were protected, naïve, but we had the strength to survive suffering. Many left China with only a day to pack. Looking for jobs, working long hours, sacrificing. But somehow they not only survived, they were successful.

I have noted that "family" is the dominant metaphor McTyeireans use to evoke their nostalgic attachment to McTyeire. The powerful sentiment that surrounds the use of this metaphor calls to mind Carolyn Heilbrun's wise reminder that the tales women tell are rarely "truthful" in the conventional sense.[25] In fact, the McTyeire family metaphor has a remarkable power to smooth over a past that was far from conflict free. At the same time, it has allowed McTyeireans to maintain strong bonds across glaring political and religious differences. McTyeire women have defined their educational and social aspirations by reconciling in very different ways the competing claims of nationalist loyalties, socialist ideals, and Christian faith. Nevertheless, remarkable similarities exist in the intentions of American missionaries, who called their schools "nurseries for the engendering of pure principles, homes for the development of womanly virtues," and Chinese educators who continue to describe Number 3 as a "cradle of female talent."[26]

In this sense, one of McTyeire's most striking qualities is the effort by its teachers and students from different generations and cultures to accomplish the often mutually exclusive tasks of finding themselves and each other. In this sometimes rewarding and successful, sometimes painful and failed process, they have been forced, by their unusual historical circumstances, to balance Christian faith, nationalist loyalties, and revolutionary dreams, and to come to grips with what Carol Gilligan has called the potential in human relationships, including those that structure schools, for both care and oppression.[27]

CHAPTER 13

"An Oasis in a Heathen Land": St. Hilda's School for Girls, Wuchang, 1928–1936

JUDITH LIU AND DONALD P. KELLY

The history of Christian schools in China represents an interesting cross-cultural study of the impact of Western education in China, and it is particularly fascinating when the students being studied are females. China has been a rigid patriarchal society where the role of women has traditionally been circumscribed. As such, anything more than a rudimentary education for females was deemed unnecessary and even unwise. But for missionaries from the West, developing indigenous Christian missionaries—male and female—in order to spread the gospel throughout the vast expanse of China was paramount. Thus, in 1835, the Domestic and Foreign Society of the Protestant Episcopal Church in the United States established its first mission in China; however, partly because Westerners were legally segregated from the general populace, the mission failed.

This de jure segregation was soon to change. The signing of the Treaty of Nanjing in 1842 ended the Opium War and officially opened China to the West by permitting the establishment of five treaty ports along the coast from Guangzhou to Shanghai. As a result of the treaty, an American Episcopal mission was established in Shanghai in 1845.[1] By the terms of the Treaty of Tianjin of 1858, ten more treaty ports were opened, including Hankou, one of the three cities (Hankou, Wuchang, and Hanyang) comprising the conurbation of Wuhan. Located about five hundred miles west of Shanghai on the Yangzi River, Wuhan was the most inland treaty port, and hence the most likely place to begin proselytization in Central China. Consequently, an Episcopal mission was established at Wuchang in 1868.[2]

Because missionaries arrived concomitantly with the agents of Western imperialism, the two became inseparable. While missionaries preached that Christianity transcended Western culture, most nonetheless used and endorsed gunboat diplomacy as the principal means for achieving a foothold in China. The inseparability of Western missionaries from Western imperialism made the Christianization of China problematic: the two took on the appearance of a system of total cultural imperialism.[3] Furthermore, this inseparability challenged Chinese ethnocentrism by confronting Confucianism — the major moral code of the society, the educational basis of the bureaucracy, and the cultural justification for dynastic rule. Many Chinese responded to these cultural challenges by becoming more nationalistic in their rhetoric and more hostile in their actions. The brunt of this anti-Western animus tended to fall upon the missionaries. In fact, it was not until the abolition of the separate missionary school system in the late 1920s that missionaries and missionary schools ceased to be the major focus of nationalistic movements such as the anti-Western Boxer Rebellion of 1900 or the anti-Christian movement of 1922.[4]

"An Honored Name": The Jane Bohlen School

Within this historical context, the Jane Bohlen School for Girls at Wuchang was founded in 1875. The school was the result of a bequest to the American Episcopal Missionary Board by the son and daughter of Jane Bohlen of Philadelphia.[5]

Although the school would exist ostensibly to educate girls, its proposed function was to produce a Chinese women's Christian vanguard that would, in a militaristic analogy typical of the day, help "conquer" China for Christ. But because women could not be ordained into the ministry, they would be ancillary to their minister-husbands. Hence, they would represent the idealized vision of the good Christian wife, mother, and helper. In this way, they would offer a positive role model for China's women.

This was the dream, but the reality was very different. As mentioned, social and cultural conditions in China were not conducive to establishing a thriving girls' school; consequently, the school, with room for forty students, opened with just one. By the end of 1877, it had thirteen girls. And they were young; far too young to initiate a Christian vanguard in the foreseeable future. While enthusiasm for the school back in the United States was high, little thought was given to the actual recruitment of teachers. Thus, only the wife of an Episcopalian missionary stationed in Wuchang was available to teach these girls. With her uneducated Chinese helpers, she taught the girls rudimentary educational skills and gave them the "requisite" girls' knowledge in cooking, cleaning, and sewing. At this point, the school could not hope to create an environment suitable for the establishment of an enlightened Christian vanguard.

Conditions were further complicated when scandals in 1880 and 1882 involving pregnant students and an unmarried American teacher dying in childbirth rocked the school and the community.[6] Cries were raised by local Chinese that the school was being used as a house of prostitution.[7] When the Bohlen School's third American-born teacher in eight years married and resigned in 1883, and no replacement could be found until 1894, home economics courses represented the only education received by the girls during this eleven-year period. High hopes for the school arrived with a new missionary and his wife in 1894. When she died in 1897, the survival of the Jane Bohlen School was in serious doubt. If girls were to become enlightened and educated Christians, a more stable school environment had to be created. Although conversions to Christianity were proportionately low, there were enough Episcopalian converts in Central China to warrant establishing a boarding school for middle-school-aged girls. Consequently, the American Episcopal Missionary Board decided to act; it recruited teachers specifically for the school and decided to expand its size. The result was that in 1899, the Jane Bohlen School became the Jane Bohlen Building of the newly christened St. Hilda's School for Girls (Wuchang sheng xilida nüzhong).[8]

"A Fresh Start": St. Hilda's

Although the goal of the school remained unchanged—the creation of a Christian women's vanguard—the focus shifted. St. Hilda's, like Jane Bohlen, would be a boarding school; however, it would be solely a middle school. Its students would be the children of missionaries and/or the fiancées of the boys at the adjoining Boone School, Central China's training school for Episcopalian ministers.[9]

In both of its two phases, the school was anathema to prevailing Chinese culture. It existed to educate not only girls, but Christian girls. Furthermore, this education did not include the Confucian classics, the very basis of China's moral code. Thus, within the confines of traditional, dynastic China, St. Hilda's represented a foothold for disseminating Christian heterodoxy.

Although the charge of advocating heterodox views could be leveled at all missionary schools, St. Hilda's could be charged with cultural subversion as well. The perpetuation of traditional Chinese patriarchy depended upon the subservience of women, which in turn required that women remain ignorant. The very presence of St. Hilda's threatened the entire patriarchal system.

Because the girls who attended St. Hilda's during this period were the daughters of those who had already converted, the school had little chance of producing a large Christian vanguard as long as the Qing dynasty remained in power. The justifications for the perpetuation of gender roles within dynastic China, which defined a female's role as daughter, wife, or mother, were antithetical to the goals of St. Hilda's. By educating girls and by promoting the religious doctrine of evangelism and its attendant goal of personal salvation, St. Hilda's could only achieve limited success.

With the founding of the Republic in 1912 came changes, however slight, in the perception of women's roles in Chinese society. Reports at the time from St. Hilda's envisioned the imminent arrival of the long-awaited Christian vanguard. St. Hilda's was now seen as "an oasis in a heathen city."[10] Enrollment swelled, which led to the creation of a new St. Hilda's campus in 1914. This new campus, which included both a middle school and a high school, was located outside the city walls of Wuchang.[11]

From the perspective of the missionaries, all the years of working to create a Chinese Christian vanguard seemed to be on the verge of success; St. Hilda's was producing Christian high school graduates, and Boone was producing Christian college graduates. But this enthusiasm proved to be unfounded. As nationalistic pride grew in the years after the founding of the Republic, anti-Christian sentiment intensified. Consequently, the Republican Revolution did not have an immediate impact on the lives of St. Hilda's girls. In fact, it was not until the late 1920s that any tangible effects could be seen. The reasons why effects became apparent then had to do with changes in the composition of the student body at St. Hilda's, the political climate in Wuhan, and the religious orientation of the Western female faculty members of St. Hilda's.

The birth of the Republican era made it possible for significant numbers of girls to be educated. The gender-based animus that characterized education during the Qing dynasty was declining, and conversely, perceptions of the importance of education in the modernization of China were increasing. As a result, wealthy non-Christian families in the Wuhan area began to send their daughters to St. Hilda's. For these families that St. Hilda's was a boarding school was a major attraction. Traditionally in China, wealthy girls were sheltered from any contact with the world outside the family compound. Ironically, it was only missionary boarding schools that were able to continue this practice of isolation. In fact, the isolation was almost total: St. Hilda's permitted the girls to return home only for summer vacation and Chinese New Year's break. The sense of separation from Chinese society was made even more complete since classes were taught in English and religious study was mandatory. Thus, the daughters of a portion of Wuhan's economic elite were resocialized in an environment that facilitated their acceptance of a Western ethos and world-view.

It was not only this Western-centered education that distinguished St. Hilda's girls from the students in the public school system. As nationalistic fervor swept over China in the late 1910s and early 1920s, the school for-bade the girls to engage in the political demonstrations that were rife in the public schools; hence, confining the girls to the school grounds effectively made them apolitical. This political isolation continued until events altered the school's authority.[12]

These events were connected with the second set of circumstances that affected the lives of the girls at St. Hilda's: the changed political position of Wuhan. Wuhan was always at the forefront of nationalistic movements in Central China. These movements ranged from the 1911 revolt that led to the collapse of the Qing dynasty to the storming of the Japanese concession in 1925. That the people of Wuhan had the temerity to storm the Japanese concession shows the intensity of their nationalism. The next event that fundamentally altered Wuhan's political climate was the Northern Expedi-tion of 1926–28, the Guomindang's effort to consolidate its power.[13] While Hanyang and Hankou were liberated from warlord control quickly, Wu-chang held out for 40 days behind its great city walls. Following the libera-tion of the Wuhan cities in late 1926, Hankou became the capital of the Guomindang government. The political climate seemed conducive to na-tional unification under the banner of the Guomindang, and the foreign concessions of Wuhan were taken over by Guomindang forces. However, factional conflict soon erupted within the Guomindang, culminating in a major split in 1927 and the return of the concessions to foreign control. From late 1926 through early 1927, when the concessions were seized, mass nationalism was rampant and the situation became untenable for foreigners in Wuhan and other Yangzi valley cities. Most foreigners fled to Shanghai and other coastal cities. Only 500 out of 8,000 missionaries remained in the interior of China in 1927.[14] Thus, from the fall semester of 1926 through the fall semester of 1928, St. Hilda's held classes for only one semester.

"Outside the Little East Gate": Political Awakening

The closing of St. Hilda's from 1926 to 1928 had a direct impact on most of the girls. Released from their cloistered environment, they became politicized.

When school reopened in fall 1928, the girls were no longer politically naïve. The closure of the school had made it possible for them to become aware of and participate in political demonstrations. Thus, when Japan annexed Manchuria in 1931, the girls were no longer politically indifferent — they showed their heightened awareness by organizing a boycott of Japanese goods at the school. All girls' belongings were checked, and goods from Japan were dated with a chop. Henceforth, at each new semester, no unmarked Japanese goods were permitted into the school. Furthermore, girls cut their hair so that the clippings could be used as insulation for soldiers' jackets, tore clothing to make bandages, and donated money raised in school campaigns — principally by selling confiscated Japanese-made goods — to the Red Cross. Within the confines of the school itself, the students were also more politically active. When a student leader was threatened with dismissal for disseminating information she had obtained from reading government bulletins that had been discarded — unread — by the headmistress, the students organized a three-day silence strike to show their solidarity, and the girl was not expelled.[15]

This politicizing of the students occurred at a time when secularization of schools was at the forefront of government policies. Once the Guomindang achieved nominal control over China, missionary schools became the target of a program of school registration. Registration meant the end of the division of education into two separate and distinct systems — the regular Chinese public school system and the foreign-supported missionary school system. With registration, missionary schools would become, in theory, secularized Chinese institutions. From the study of the graduates of St. Hilda's during the period between 1928 and 1936, it is clear that registration had a significant impact on the school.

With registration, the focus of the school necessarily changed. Classes — most of which had been conducted in English — were now to be taught in Chinese, the principal of the school had to be Chinese, graduates would receive Chinese diplomas, and chapel attendance and religious instruction had to be voluntary.[16] Added to the curriculum were the Three Principles of Sun Yat-sen, which had to be taught by a member of the Guomindang, and a course in ethics, which had to be offered as an alternative to religious studies.

Registration sparked great debate within the missionary community.[17] From the perspective of many missionaries, education was secondary to evangelism, and thus to accept registration would mean placing evangelism in a subordinate role. Many schools chose to close their doors rather than to register, but St. Hilda's decided to remain open and registered in 1930.

Registration for St. Hilda's was not as traumatic as it was for many other schools. The reason for this involved the transformation that occurred in the religious orientation of the faculty at St. Hilda's. The American women who taught at St. Hilda's were all college graduates, they were single, and they came to China to do good work. Because Episcopalian women missionaries could not preach, they assumed the role of educators. But these women were unlike their predecessors; whereas many of their predecessors were the wives of ministers, which made teaching a mere adjunct to their lives, most of these women came specifically to be teachers and to teach the social gospel.

Basic to the concept of the social gospel is the belief that social service is a legitimate means of evangelism and that evangelism can be an effective instrument for social change as well as for salvation.[18] Whereas evangelism had once focused on the notion of personal salvation, the social gospel was directed toward the transformation of this world. The social gospel was predicated on the belief that a fellowship can exist between God and man and that this fellowship can be attained through the cultivation of correct attitudes and the development of the right skills.[19] Just exactly what these "correct attitudes" and "right skills" are is somewhat nebulous, but the proposed result — the creation of "purposeful activity . . . proceeding in a social environment" — is not.[20] It was hoped that service to the welfare of the whole community would result in a reconstruction of society. While the spiritualism of pure evangelism went unheeded, the fusing of spiritual with secular in the social gospel had an explosive impact on the girls of St. Hilda's.

The secular aspect of the social gospel legitimated the nascent nationalistic views held by these girls and, in a sense, broke the element of cultural subversion that hindered the spiritual side of the missionary movement. By secularizing the religious message, the social gospel transcended the sectarianism inherent in pure evangelism. It was able to separate the moral basis of Christianity from its old religious framework. As a consequence, between 1928 and 1936 St. Hilda's produced a significant number of Christians over and above the 78 percent who were nominally Christian in 1930.[21] By the same token, however, it produced very few Episcopalians. It was this inherent theological relativism in the social gospel that permitted the school to de-emphasize its sectarianism in order to register with the government.

Religious indoctrination for personal salvation gave way to the principle of "Christian love and concern for the true welfare of the people,"[22] in other words social service. Thus, the goal of St. Hilda's became the training of Christian educators, medical workers, and social workers who would work for the good of China. (Coincidentally or not, these were virtually the only occupations available to educated women in China.) In order for the girls to do the "good works" dictated by the social gospel, they had to develop the self-sufficiency that was also dictated by the social gospel. Yet women were still dependent and subservient in Chinese society. Thus, inculcating the values of self-sufficiency and independence was no easy matter. Everything at the school was designed to promote self-sufficiency and independence, a subject to which we now turn.

"A Nation Cannot Rise Above Its Women": St. Hilda's Girls

Students recall that the school grounds were beautifully landscaped — grass, trees, flowers — and groomed. The living quarters matched the physical beauty of the school. Dormitory rooms, located above the classrooms, housed a maximum of 40 girls in the large rooms and eight to ten in the smaller ones. Each student was assigned a bed and a small locker in which personal items and clothing were placed. Suitcases were kept in a larger storage room and students were permitted access during specific times; otherwise, the storage room was locked. The rooms were "spotless"; beds with white sheets were covered with white spreads and daily inspections insured that beds were neatly made and the rooms kept clean.

There was a regimen to daily life at St. Hilda's. Because the bathrooms could not accommodate all the girls at once, there were two shifts: half of the girls were awakened at 6:00 A.M. and the other half at 6:30 A.M. Upon arising, students were required to lay open their sheets and blankets to "air" their beds. After washing up, students were expected to make their beds and walk quietly to breakfast at 7:00 or 7:30 A.M. Students were assigned eight to a table and one person each day had the responsibility of equally dividing not only the breakfast of piping hot rice porridge and vegetables but the other meals as well. Voluntary morning vespers commenced at 8:00 A.M. and ended at 8:15. Classes were held from 8:30 until noon; lunch was served between noon and 1:00 P.M., when afternoon classes resumed. Classes ended at 3:30, at which time classrooms were locked and students were expected to spend time in the school yard exercising or relaxing in the fresh air. Voluntary evening vespers were at 4:30; dinner was served between 5:00 and 6:00 P.M. After dinner, students were expected to work on class assignments. Each weekday evening there was a tutoring session for students to obtain individual help in any subject. One teacher was present in the study hall. Lights out was at 10:00 P.M., and as early as 9:00 for those who were ill or on restricted activity.

To this day, women who attended St. Hilda's vividly recall the orderly lives they led at the school. They credit the social and physical environment as conducive to learning. Moreover, the orderliness had a tremendous impact on their lives. It provided a pattern to their daily lives that many have continued to follow. As one graduate recalls, initially she was not used to the strictness, but eventually she found it preferable to the chaos she faced when she returned home for her monthly overnight visits.[23]

If the social gospel was to have any effect on the girls at St. Hilda's, the faculty faced the task of fusing the social service mores of the social gospel to the value of self-sufficiency. The school employed the concepts of "courtesy and culture" as the means for instilling a moral code that emphasized the value of altruism in the service of others.[24] If this goal of selflessness was to have social consequences, then the girls had to be taught to take care of themselves — individually and collectively.

Because the student population was a combination of tuition-paying and tuition-free students, the wearing of simple uniforms leveled any visible class differences. During the spring and summer, students wore white cotton uniforms; late fall and winter, they wore padded blue uniforms. Students were not allowed to have extreme hairstyles, wear jewelry, or use makeup. The inherent differences between the baptized Christian girls, who paid no tuition, and the non-Christian girls, who did, posed the greatest obstacle to creating an egalitarian atmosphere. Religion was not the sole difference between the girls. Many of the non-Christian girls came from wealthy Wuhan families who wanted their daughters educated outside of the state schools, which they thought to be communist-controlled; the Christian girls came from poorer rural areas where their parents were stationed as pastors or church workers.[25] It is astounding that the school was able to overcome this difference. After registration, girls were permitted to leave the school one night a month, which realistically meant that only those girls who lived in the Wuhan area were able to go home; however, because they could have roommates and friends join them, it was possible for non-Wuhan girls to take part in these outings. Intermixing of the two groups through the various techniques used by the school was a conscious attempt at producing a communal spirit. Consequently, the primary focus of the social gospel at the school was the promotion of the morality expressed in the golden rule.

The school also worked to diffuse factionalism by designing a "sister class" system whereby a senior high class was responsible for a middle school class. Thus, seniors were assigned to the incoming ninth-grade class, juniors to the eighth graders, and sophomores to the seventh graders. "Big sisters" were expected to help their "little sisters" adjust to the boarding school arrangement and assist in any way possible. Although the school was never able to eradicate cliques altogether, it kept them to the minimum by rotating dining assignments every semester. Thus, girls from different social backgrounds and class standing were mixed together. Within each dormitory room, an older girl was usually assigned to be "dormitory leader." This post was normally reserved for a girl who not only had leadership qualities but was also a good student. Although the dormitory leader had primary responsibility, all older girls were expected to supervise and care for the younger ones. This fostered a closeness and cooperativeness among the girls at the school and discouraged segregation based upon class or status. These techniques — sharing equally at meals, older girls looking after younger girls, rotating table assignments each semester — were attempts to create as egalitarian an atmosphere as possible.

Students were placed on the honor system when taking examinations. Because classes were small, the girls knew each other well and would not compromise the integrity of another student by cheating. St. Hilda's reputation in the city for scholarship and strictness was further enhanced when students taking municipal examinations not only scored extremely high but also absolutely refused to cheat. Instead, students were encouraged to help one another in study groups. Of course there were always the good friends who were willing to let others copy homework, but overall there was little cheating or stealing at the school. Stealing was minimized by the faculty encouraging the students to share not only their snacks and treats, but their personal items as well. Girls from wealthy local families often had weekly shipments of special foods sent to the school. During the two scheduled breaks during the day, students were permitted to have these "treats." Poorer students were not fortunate enough to have such luxuries and many of them recall that their wealthier friends shared. This spirit of sharing came not from a sense of noblesse oblige but from genuine fondness and a spirit of generosity, or at least that was the way it was remembered. Alumnae recall the theft of a watch at the school. Not only were the students themselves shocked, but a search of the entire campus was made and when the culprit was found, she was expelled. Rather than feeling scorn for the girl, who incidentally came from a wealthy family, students who recalled the incident felt only pity and forgiveness.

Self-sufficiency and independence — the virtues most often named by the students as characteristic of the ethos of St. Hilda's — were promoted in a number of ways. Abilities of any sort were recognized and nurtured by the staff. Students with leadership ability were encouraged to run for student association offices, or were appointed dormitory leaders, class leaders, or the like. Those with athletic ability not only served on teams but were made the leaders of the required daily calisthenics. Those with scholastic ability were encouraged to tutor their classmates or teach in the community.

Students who needed a haircut, laundry washed, shoes repaired, or clothing mended could seek the services of the student association's self-help organizations. Any girl, but especially one needing financial assistance, could earn money by working at these various services. Surprisingly, this did not serve to drive a wedge between the wealthy, tuition-paying students and poorer, tuition-free students. Instead, not only did work in the self-help organizations teach students to cooperate, but it also provided an honorable means for students to earn income by exercising their individual abilities. Many of the wealthy students were excellent seamstresses (having learned sewing at home in preparing their trousseaux). Rather than keeping the money, many chose to donate their income to charitable causes such as the "Wounded Soldiers' Fund" or "emergency funds." During the war of resistance against Japan, students from all walks of life volunteered their services. These experiences not only gave the girls confidence in their own abilities but graphically illustrated to them that, regardless of their social standing, they could use whatever abilities they had to take care of themselves.

Each Sunday, a group of teachers and volunteer students visited the homes of local families. They taught parents about sanitation, nutrition, and hygiene; helped bathe the sick and elderly; administered minor medical care; groomed young children; and even helped with housecleaning. The school started a literacy program wherein both teachers and students served as tutors for neighborhood children. Although many of the girls who initially volunteered did so only to avoid boredom, many later chose professions that were being subtly promoted during these weekly excursions. Several women mentioned that their love for teaching or medicine was first stimulated by their community service activities. "It was during this time," one woman wrote, "that I discovered I loved to work with children. That is one of the major reasons why I became a teacher." Moreover, students learned never to consider themselves better than anyone else. "We learned the principles of equality — not to denigrate the poor or elevate the rich."[26]

Social service was also fostered in the school by its emphasis on "health and hygiene."[27] Prevention of tuberculosis, then rampant in China, was of great concern at St. Hilda's. Thus, the doctrine of the healing benefits of fresh air was rigorously followed. In fact, the rooms used for rehabilitation were surrounded by a porch and girls were assigned two to a room. Given the temperature extremes in Wuhan, these rooms were definitely conducive to a speedy recovery. As mentioned earlier, bedding was to be aired daily to promote sanitation. Even today, many of these women keep windows open year-round and still turn back their bedding first thing each morning. From this perspective, St. Hilda's had a lasting impact on the girls' lives, and one can see why it was so successful in preparing many of its girls for medical careers.

Good manners, such as pushing in chairs, holding doors open for the next person, speaking softly, walking with good posture and at a measured pace, being polite, eating with the mouth shut, being punctual, and being neat, were actively taught and, more important, practiced by the foreign teachers. Neatness and punctuality were learned through the daily regimen. Students recollect that teachers were kind, courteous, generous, and polite to one another and to the students. Thus teachers served as models.

The foreign teachers were all young (in their mid-twenties), single, self-supporting women who made the trek from the United States to Central China. They were independent and self-sufficient themselves. If these foreign-born teachers could do it, the consensus of the girls at St. Hilda's was that they could do it as well.

For all its good points, however, students also recounted stories of aspects they did not like about St. Hilda's. Chief among the complaints was the poor treatment of the Chinese male faculty. According to the students, not only were the teachers not treated with the respect that was their due, but their living quarters were far below the standards of the foreigners' housing. In addition, it was thought that some teachers as well as the headmistress curried favor with the parents of paying students and considered themselves "better than the Chinese."

Good and bad models alike, however, spurred the girls on to do their best. The ethnocentrism of some of the teachers was matched by a growing nationalism and an equal ethnocentrism among the students. Thus, some of the women interviewed stated that they became fierce in their determination to prove that Chinese were as good as Americans. They studied diligently and achieved high honors "to prove that the Chinese were as good as they [the foreigners]."[28] Later in their own lives, students emulated the qualities of the teachers they admired most while avoiding those of the teachers they disliked.

It was only years later that many of the women who attended St. Hilda's felt the effects of their Christian education. Looking back at their lives, a number of the women remarked that their faith sustained them through difficult times. During the Cultural Revolution, many alumnae and their husbands were arrested, interrogated countless times, sent down to the countryside, and even beaten. Throughout these ordeals, the women report that they "always knew the right thing to do." Although divulging a name or implicating another person might have ended their own ordeal, these women refused. Thus, allegedly they never lied, or gave false testimony, refused to denounce anyone, treated all their denouncers and attackers with respect and courtesy, and maintained hope. They say their religious faith provided them with "something to believe in." This transcendent idealism continued to give meaning to their lives. Hence, while countless others died during the Cultural Revolution because of physical abuse, suicide, or absolute despair, these women and their families were able to survive. The lifelong habits forged during their years at St. Hilda's served them well throughout their later tribulations.

The impact of self-sufficiency and independence on these girls was extraordinary. It is on this point that warnings of the cultural subversion inherent in missionary education have some merit. The major message received by the girls at St. Hilda's was that they alone were responsible for their well-being. Their future success was, therefore, independent of the cultural tradition that defined a woman's role solely as wife or mother. In fact, a disproportionate number of these girls chose not to marry or, if they did marry, they did so in later life.[29] While the reasons for this vary from fear of childbirth to having to support their families, the fact is that many of these girls were reacting to the tragedy of their mothers who, widowed early in life, followed the tradition of widow chastity and thus could not remarry. With no education and no sons to provide for them, it became incumbent upon their daughters to support them. For these girls to marry would have doomed their mothers. No matter what justification they had for not marrying, these girls had been taught that they could succeed on their own, and they learned that lesson well.

Inculcated with the social gospel, these girls acquired a social awareness and a drive to put that social awareness into practice. They filled the niches that were available to them as teachers, medical workers, and social workers. Thus, many of the goals of St. Hilda's were fulfilled.

The powerful ethos of St. Hilda's stimulated a sense of camaraderie, which lived on after graduation in an old-girls' network that continues to this day. Although this network is small, it is important. In the China of the 1930s, only one out of eight hundred high-school-aged children was able to attend school.[30] Thus the girls of St. Hilda's became part of the educational and intellectual elite of China — particularly since there was an even greater scarcity of college-educated females.[31] Moreover, their education was relatively uninterrupted since they attended school in the only period of comparative calm during the Nationalist era. Consequently, their education made them not merely an anomaly but a valuable resource for aiding in the modernization of China.

"Sources of Light and Centres of Power": St. Hilda's Legacy

St. Hilda's between 1928 and 1936 was a unique place. It offered a Western-style education to both Christians and non-Christians, it not only survived but thrived in the politically volatile climate of Wuhan, and it turned out women imbued with the sense of personal strength and social commitment that is the hallmark of the social gospel.

In earlier decades, St. Hilda's was to be an oasis in a heathen land, a place where a Christian vanguard would gather to "conquer" China for Christ. This personal evangelical approach had only limited success: it could not separate the moral basis of Christianity from its sectarian practices. Furthermore, the missionaries' desire to "conquer" China for Christ made it impossible to separate Christianity from Western imperialism. Therefore, Christianity was unable to transcend Western culture. Not being able to separate the moral tone of Christianity from its sectarian manifestations, the evangelical missionaries could not hope to offer to the non-Christians who attended St. Hilda's a plausible alternative to the traditional moral teachings of Confucianism, Daoism, and Buddhism. That is, prior to the introduction of the social gospel to St. Hilda's in the 1920s, Christianity, in its various sectarian manifestations, offered these students an alternative that was no better than China's existing moral systems.

However, Christianity, as mediated through the broad moral claims and promises of the social gospel, offered a new, more plausible alternative. By advocating social service rather than mere personal salvation, the social gospel was able to separate Christian morality from its sectarian practices. As such, it created a theological relativism that de-emphasized a specific sectarian orientation. The result was that St. Hilda's converted many non-believers into believers; however, those who converted became Christians, not Episcopalians. To this day, in fact, these women primarily attend non-denominational services.

A study of the girls who attended St. Hilda's between 1928 and 1936 offers some interesting insights into the impact of Christianity on their lives. Although the strength of the missionary movement in general began to wane after 1926, it reached its zenith at St. Hilda's in the years 1928–36. Clearly that St. Hilda's was a boarding school and that most of its students were already nominally Christian aided the school in shaping the lives of its girls, but how successful would the school have been if its faculty had not inculcated the principles of the social gospel? The one possible avenue to success open to Christianity in China during this period was to fuse itself to the nationalistic fervor of the time. And the principles of the social gospel made this fusion possible. Thus, by living their lives according to the social gospel, the girls at St. Hilda's came to believe that they could serve God and China simultaneously.

CHAPTER 14

Christianity, Feminism, and Communism: The Life and Times of Deng Yuzhi

EMILY HONIG

Unlike the twentieth-century Chinese women whose lives Western readers know the most about—the revolutionary martyr Qiu Jin, the writer Ding Ling, and Mao Zedong's controversial wife Jiang Qing—Deng Yuzhi (b. 1900; known to her Western friends as Cora Deng) considered herself neither a feminist nor a revolutionary. She described herself as first and foremost a Christian, yet as head of the Labor Bureau of the Young Women's Christian Association (YWCA), she played a major role in organizing women to participate in the Chinese Communist revolution from the 1920s to 1949. She exemplifies a group of urban, educated, Chinese women who equated Christianity with social activism and international sisterhood. Their quiet, understated contribution to the Chinese revolution has been largely ignored in studies that have focused instead on workers and peasants, the two groups the Chinese Communist Party (CCP) most explicitly tried to organize.

This chapter explores the relationship between Christianity, feminism, and communism in Deng Yuzhi's life. In spite of her own retrospective emphasis on her Christian identity, she devoted much of her life to instilling a working-class and feminist consciousness among women factory workers. Defining, juggling, and sometimes manipulating the Christian, communist, and feminist elements of her identity was a major theme in her career.

The integration of Christianity, feminism, and communism might at first seem paradoxical. Although liberation theologians in Latin America have insisted upon the compatibility of Christianity and communism, in the context of Republican-period China their synthesis seemed unlikely. The missionaries who went to China sought converts to Christianity, not Marxism. Instilling a revolutionary ideology was not their mission; nor did the church encourage people to get involved in the revolutionary move-ment. Deng Yuzhi was by no means the only Christian sympathetic to communism, for individuals such as Wu Yaozong (Y. T. Wu) devoted much of their career to establishing the potential connections. Deng, however, added a concern with women's issues to the amalgam.

Feminism and Christianity might seem as unlikely a combination in Republican-period China as Christianity and communism. A major as-pect of the missionary enterprise in China was the establishment of girls' schools, yet the missionaries' aims were limited. On the one hand, they attacked what they perceived as the most oppressive aspects of Chinese women's lives, such as footbinding and arranged marriages. Moreover, they provided young women an opportunity for education that in some cases made it possible for them to have professional careers. Yet the vision of gender roles that they advocated was one based on traditional Western values: a woman might have a career, but she should be a responsible housewife as well.[1] The generation of "Christian feminists" was not the goal. Although the YWCA night schools that Deng Yuzhi directed tech-nically belonged to the missionary effort in China, their message to women was far more radical, and feminist, than the more typical missionary schools Deng herself had attended.

Although feminism and communism might not at first seem incongru-ous, their union has been as troubled in China as in other countries experi-encing socialist revolution.[2] Particularly after the 1920s, most women who joined the CCP or who were sympathetic to the communist movement subordinated their feminist principles to the "larger" goals of the revolu-tion. The few who did not, such as Ding Ling, were silenced.

Deng Yuzhi, then, represents an unusual amalgam in the history of the Chinese revolution. Yet, as we shall see below, to describe Deng as a "Chris-tian feminist communist" is far too simplistic. In fact, what is most striking about her is that she never fully identified as any one of these: although sympathetic to the aims of the CCP, she never joined or called herself a communist; she devoted most of her career to women's work, yet never called herself a feminist; and although she calls herself Christian, her life has been a remarkably unreligious one. As we shall see, during different periods of her life Deng has drawn on — while never entirely subordinating herself to — each of these ideologies and structures to define a vision of politics that is her own.

What emerges is that although she was a Christian from childhood, attended missionary schools and college, and devoted her life to working for a Christian missionary organization, the YWCA, Christianity was not a prominent component of Deng's identity until the 1940s. A commitment to creating a feminist and working class consciousness was far more salient. In the 1940s, however, as her work and convictions drew her closer to those of the CCP, the articulation of a Christian identity became a way of protecting and maintaining her own agenda. Ironically, only after 1949 did Christianity become central to her identity.

In exploring the relationship between Christianity, feminism, and communism in Deng Yuzhi's life, this chapter draws on archival materials from the YWCA, Deng's own published writings, and interviews with her friends and colleagues. The primary source, however, is an extensive oral history that I conducted with her in 1985. I had first met Deng Yuzhi in 1979, when I was beginning research about the history of women cotton mill workers in Shanghai. For the two years I was in Shanghai, we met almost every week, to discuss my research, her past, and to share opinions about China's present. Her passion for recalling the past, as well as her extraordinary memory, made me determined to record her life history. By 1985, she, too, was unmistakably anxious to tell her life story to herself, and had set up a tape recorder of her own for that purpose.[3]

Like any historic inquiry, an oral history is inevitably shaped by the historical period during which it is recorded. Deng's life story, had she told it immediately after Liberation in 1949 or during the Cultural Revolution (1966–76), might have included the same events, but would have been colored by a different tone and interpretation from her account in 1985. The year 1985, nearly a decade after the end of the Cultural Revolution, was a relatively relaxed time. Relations between Chinese and foreigners were far freer of restrictions than they had been even five years earlier, when I first got to know Deng Yuzhi. The mid-1980s was also a period of political liberalization and openness to the West. Prior to the mid-1980s Deng might well have been reluctant to record her life history at all, fearful she might say things considered politically "incorrect." She certainly would not have told her story to a foreigner. The general admiration of the West that was popular in the mid-1980s most likely made her feel freer to speak about the time she spent abroad and her affiliation with a Western missionary organization. The YWCA, after all, was being revived in China in the 1980s, and Deng was playing a central role in that work.

Politics was not the only factor shaping the version of her life that Deng related in the mid-1980s. At the age of 85, she had resolved much of her past, and had a deep investment in presenting her life as nonconflictual. Thus, at points when one might expect emotional or political conflict, her account is conspicuously straightforward.

A Christian Education

Deng Yuzhi's Christian identity was not the result of individual deliberation and conversion, but rather the continuation of a family tradition begun by her grandmother. In this respect she was like many of her contemporaries. This "tradition," however, began only after her parents died. They had never been Christians and had raised Deng and her sisters in a manner considered progressive for its time. So long as her parents were alive, Deng's early experiences resembled those of a number of women who became well-known revolutionaries.

Deng Yuzhi was born in 1900 in the Hubei city of Shashi; her family moved to Changsha when she was eight, because her father had received an official appointment there. Changsha was the political, cultural, and educational center of Hunan, a province which since the 1890s was reputed for its radicalism.[4] When she arrived there, Deng joined the ranks of the relatively small number of Chinese women who had the opportunity of attending school. Not until 1906 had government-sponsored schools for girls been established in China, and even then, their mandate was to educate girls to become "good wives and mothers."[5] Although missionary schools had opened several decades earlier, they did not gain legitimacy among gentry families until the early twentieth century.[6] Unlike some girls, such as Xie Bingying, who had to threaten suicide or stage a hunger strike to overcome their parents' conviction that going to school violated codes of proper female conduct,[7] Deng, her sister, and sister-in-law were enthusiastically enrolled in the Zhounan Girls' Middle School by her parents. "My parents wanted to send us to a modern school because the atmosphere in Changsha was very progressive at that time," Deng recalled. "My father was a strict Confucian, but he was very progressive on social issues. He was one of those people who cut off their queues and he had joined the Anti-Footbinding Society."[8]

Of the schools in Changsha that admitted women, Zhounan was particularly known for its progressivism. Well before the May Fourth Movement of 1919 — when all aspects of women's traditional status were challenged — Zhounan students stood out for their public defiance of traditional female roles. At the time of the 1911 Revolution that replaced the dynastic system with a republican form of government, Zhounan students were conspicuous for their bobbed hair and practice of being in public unescorted, thereby appalling older women.[9] Had Deng stayed at Zhounan, her future might have been more like that of her schoolmates Xiang Jingyu, Cai

Chang, Ding Ling, and Yang Kaihui (Mao Zedong's first wife), all of whom became active in the CCP.

Deng unwittingly moved into a different, more religiously oriented social world when her parents died in the early 1910s. From then on she was raised by her grandmother, a devout Buddhist who had become a Christian through contact with missionaries at the Yale Hospital in Changsha where Deng's father was treated for tuberculosis. Deng attributes her grandmother's conversion to the help provided by missionaries:

There was a Bible woman from the hospital who came to our house every day, to try to help us, comfort us, and help with losing the breadwinner. I think one reason my grandmother was converted was that the church was a place where you could go for help with all of your problems. They were very friendly there and would do anything to help you. . . . Christianity was much better organized [than Buddhism]. After my grandmother was converted, she went to church every Sunday and took us along.

More influential than attending church services, however, was her grandmother's decision to send Deng to a missionary school once she graduated from Zhounan. This undoubtedly reflected her grandmother's Christian identity, even though Deng ascribes the switch to her own desire to learn English.

The move from Zhounan to the missionary-sponsored Fuxiang School for Girls marked a major turning point in Deng's life. Although it was not Deng's decision or desire to attend a missionary school, she immediately identified potential advantages (such as learning English and thereby gaining a familiarity with the West). Moreover, almost as soon as she moved to Fuxiang, she found a niche — the YWCA — where she could keep alive, within a missionary environment, the progressive political values she most likely acquired at Zhounan.

Upon entering Fuxiang, she became involved with the social service committee of the YWCA, which provided for her the link between Christianity and social activism that became central to her life's work. "I wanted to do something helpful for people — to serve, not just be served," she recalls. "I had caught that idea from my childhood, listening to all those sermons about how people should be good to others, like Good Samaritans. So religion did have some positive effect on me which lasted my whole life — not believing in God, but those ethical elements about how to live usefully to others. That's why I joined the social service committee of the YWCA." At this point in her life, Christianity was obviously not her most powerfully held conviction. She knew she wanted to "serve others," yet her ideas about whom to serve and how were vague, and she had not yet begun to focus on women or workers. The YWCA suited her needs well.

The YWCA was not typical of missionary organizations in China. Even in the United States and England, where the YWCA was first formed in the 1880s, spirituality and religion were subordinate to an emphasis on social work and the enhancement of women's opportunities. Although when the YWCA was established in China in the 1890s it devoted most of its initial energies to recruiting high school students (the number of female college students was still too small), its programs always aimed to educate school-girls about the problems of the urban poor.[10] Other missionary groups sometimes criticized the YWCA's emphasis on social work, charging that it was "not paying sufficient attention to religious pursuits and [was] in danger of losing 'its identity in church and community.'"[11] For Deng, however, this is what made the YWCA compelling — there was not a time in her life after Fuxiang (except during the Cultural Revolution of the 1960s) that she was *not* engaged in YWCA work.

The Challenge of May Fourth

As for many members of her generation, the May Fourth Movement in 1919 represented Deng's initiation into politics. When news reached Beijing of the Versailles peace conference proposal to cede parts of Shandong Province to Japan, students immediately mobilized massive demonstrations. They demanded that the Chinese delegation refuse to sign the treaty, called for the resignation of the pro-Japanese ministers in the government, and organized a boycott of Japanese goods. Almost immediately, these protests spread to campuses throughout China.

As president of the Student Self-Government Association at Fuxiang, Deng not only chaired meetings of the student body, but played a major role in organizing students to participate in the political demonstrations of 1919. That spring and summer, like students throughout China, she and her classmates took to the streets, making speeches and visiting shopkeepers in an attempt to persuade them to join the boycott of Japanese goods. It was the first time that she had to confront, and mediate, the potential conflict between religious and political convictions; it was also the first time she had to confront women's issues, albeit in the very personal context of her own marriage.

For students at a missionary school such as Fuxiang, the decision to take a political stand had to be considered in the context of religious beliefs.

Deng did not find it difficult to identify a Christian basis for participation in the May Fourth Movement, but her views were not shared by all her classmates. "Not all the students at Fuxiang joined the movement," she recalls.

> There was a small group who thought that we did not need to show our patriotism. There was a religious debate about it. There were these people who put all their hopes for change in God. But there were also people who thought that we not only had to have faith in God, but also to live in accordance with God's will. Since God does not want people to be exploited or suppressed by others, we thought that fighting for national survival was carrying out God's will. This internal debate went on for a month. We looked down on those who didn't join.

This belief in the relevance of Christian values to contemporary political struggles underlay almost all of Deng's future work.

The May Fourth experience not only affected Deng's ideas about the potential fusion of Christianity and social activism, but about women's roles as well. The May Fourth Movement made all previously prescribed social relationships subject to debate among the urban educated elite, as Confucianism and Confucian social organization were seen as the cause of China's inability to defend itself against Western imperialism. The traditional family system and women's roles in it became emblematic of everything corrupt about Confucianism; family revolution became "the center of revolutionary politics."[12] Some of the most famous writings of the time concerned the status of women. For example, one of Mao Zedong's earliest essays, "A Critique of Miss Zhao's Suicide," described how a young woman expressed her rejection of an arranged marriage by slitting her throat while riding in the sedan chair to the marriage ceremony. Henrik Ibsen's play *A Doll's House* was translated, widely published, and performed, the central figure Nora becoming a symbol to Chinese women of women's emancipation. In a speech to students at a Beijing women's college, entitled "What Happens After Nora Leaves Home?" China's preeminent writer Lu Xun dealt with the problem of women achieving individual liberation in an oppressive society.[13] New publications such as *New Youth* (*Xin qingnian*) and the *Ladies' Journal* (*Funü zazhi*), filled with accounts of women's tragic experiences as virtuous widows or child daughters-in law, were read and passionately discussed by Deng and her classmates.

The radical views of women's roles were more than abstract ideals for students at missionary schools, as many of their teachers were single women determined to establish their own careers and support themselves. Ironically, these women, who might have been caricatured as "old maids" or "spinsters" in their own countries, in many ways exemplified May Fourth ideals.[14] "I saw all those teachers at Fuxiang living independently," Deng recalled.

They earned their own salary and were free to use their money however they wanted. Some of them — both Chinese and American — were not married. No! No one thought it was odd that they were single. People respected them because they could earn their own living. That was the atmosphere in Changsha during those early days of the New Culture Movement. People wanted to be independent, and so did I.

In fact, refusing to marry was highly unusual in China at this time. According to one survey, less than one woman in a thousand in rural China never married, although the number was slightly higher in urban areas.[15] Nevertheless, inspired by the example of her teachers, Deng became determined to "support myself and not depend on a father, husband, or son." Like many of her classmates, she had no intention of marrying.[16]

The radical May Fourth values that Deng adopted during her high school years met their first major challenge when she graduated. Her hope of going on to college was suddenly dashed when her grandmother informed her that her marriage, long since arranged by her parents, was to take place immediately. Although arranged marriages were typical in China at that time, Deng belonged to the first generation of Chinese women who were committed to challenging the practice. Unlike some of her contemporaries, Deng was not resisting an arranged marriage for the sake of a mate she had freely chosen herself. Instead, she desperately wanted to remain independent, continue her education, and pursue a career — all of which she assumed marriage would preclude.

It was therefore only after extracting a promise that her husband's family would permit her to attend college that she acquiesced to the marriage. The marriage agreement also stipulated that the husband's family permit Deng to practice Christianity and not force her to engage in ancestor worship — a requirement issued by her grandmother. Although the ability to maintain a Christian identity was not crucial to Deng, it ultimately provided her a rationale to escape an undesirable marriage. When her husband's family forced her to worship their ancestors, forbade her from attending church (which had never been particularly important to Deng), and refused to allow her to continue her education, Deng seized her belongings and fled, seeking refuge at Fuxiang, where she had planned to study an additional year of English in order to pass the entrance exam for Jinling College.

Despite attempts by her husband's family to lure her back from Fuxiang, Deng finished the year of English, then moved to Nanjing to begin

Jinling in 1920. Jinling, at that time, was one of a handful of colleges open to women, and had been the first, in 1919, to have women graduates.[17] It was a small missionary college — there were scarcely more than one hundred students and five or six faculty members at the time Deng attended — and therefore very personal.[18] So, for example, when during her sophomore year Deng's husband, his relatives, and eventually a lawyer came to insist on her return, Jinling's president, Matilda Thurston, intervened in Deng's defense, arranging to send her to Shanghai.[19]

Learning About the Working Class

For the ten years following her flight to Shanghai in 1921, Deng Yuzhi's life was fragmented: she spent two years in Changsha working for the YWCA, two years back at Jinling finishing her undergraduate education, two more years working for the YWCA, and finally a year in England studying at the London School of Economics. Despite the many changes, however, a growing interest in understanding and analyzing the lives of workers was continuous.

Perhaps most influential in triggering Deng's interest in the Chinese working class was her friendship and working relationship with Maud Russell, a YWCA secretary from the United States who had been in China since the mid-1910s. Deng first met Maud when she returned to Changsha in 1922, to help her grandmother care for her brother's children while he was studying in England. Maud offered her a job in the Student Department of the YWCA. This represented not only Deng's first YWCA job, but also a turning point in the development of Deng's political thinking. Nearly 60 years later, Deng made a birthday tape to send to Maud, who lived in New York after her return from China in the late 1940s, single-handedly publishing the *Far Eastern Reporter* from her apartment on Riverside Drive. In it, Deng recalled how Maud had been the first to introduce her to revolutionary ideas.

Maud taught me to read something about revolution. She helped me study English and asked me to study with her a book called *Dialectical Materialism*. [laughs] I had very poor English then and there were so many big words in that book. I had to use a dictionary all the time in order to find out the real meaning. Whatever little knowledge I had about socialism at that time was started by my contact with Maud, and her helping me read those famous books about social revolution.

Perhaps unbeknownst to Deng was that when Maud first went to China in the mid-1910s to work for the YWCA she saw herself as a Christian missionary, not a communist; it was the experience of living in China, and working with people such as Deng, that radicalized her thinking and made her a Marxist, committed to socialist revolution in China.[20] Many considered Maud, along with Lily K. Haass and Talitha Gerlach, to represent the "radical" faction among the foreign YWCA secretaries. (Lily Haass was at one point criticized by the YWCA board for recruiting so many radicals or communists, to which she replied, "But they are the best students in China!")[21]

Maud introduced Deng not only to radical ideas that were becoming increasingly popular in China at that time, but to the workers' movement as well. Although an organized labor movement had existed in China since the early twentieth century, it had become particularly active and powerful during the early 1920s, as the CCP devoted most of its efforts to organizing urban workers to lead the revolutionary effort. Understanding the lives and struggles of workers was therefore a major concern of both Chinese and foreign radicals.

It was in this context that analyzing workers' lives became one of Deng's major interests, and when she returned to Jinling in 1924, she decided to major in sociology. She was encouraged by Mary Treudley, Jinling's sociology teacher, known for her philosophy of relating religious education to contemporary social problems. It is not coincidental that Deng chose Treudley as her advisor; she had identified the faculty member whose understanding of the relationship between religion and politics resembled hers at that time. Treudley's avowed purpose in going to China was "putting *all* I have into a constructive program for putting Christ into daily human life."[22] Yet she passionately believed in training her students to observe and analyze social problems surrounding them. "Every Sunday the girls visit in the homes of our neighbors," Treudley reported, "and out of these visits come some of the problems that give point to our discussion of poverty."[23]

Based on one of these expeditions, Deng wrote one of her first surveys of a group of urban poor — a report on a children's home in Nanjing that had been visited by her sociology class in 1925.[24] The next year, for her graduation thesis, she conducted a survey of the handicraft tapestry industry in Nanjing — the precursor, in some ways, to the more substantial study of women factory workers in Shanghai that formed the basis of her master's thesis at New York University in 1941.

Deng graduated from Jinling determined to become a teacher — an aspiration shared by many of her classmates and fueled by the severe shortage of qualified teachers to staff the growing number of girls' schools in

China. Before she could implement this plan, however, she was once again recruited by Maud Russell to work for the Student Department of the YWCA — this time, however, she would be based in Shanghai.

Deng's tenure as a student secretary represented the one time during the 1920s when she was not focused on workers, yet this interest was never far in the background, and her desire to pursue it caused her to change jobs. As student secretary she had to focus more on the religious aspects of the YWCA's program than at any other time in her career. At the Wuhan Student Conference in 1926, for example, Deng "led morning devotional hours," as well as a discussion on the "relation of government and mission school students."[25] Deng recalled that when, in 1926–27, she traveled to Fujian to meet with the YWCA Students Associations, "we would meet with the cabinet and they would report on what they had done during the semester. They would ask us to lead their prayers and help them to study the Bible and discuss some problems they found in their work. We thought of it as case work: each person could come and have a talk with us about how to *zuoren* [conduct oneself] — what we live for."

Ultimately, however, the emphasis on religion dissatisfied Deng, and she became increasingly restless with her job as secretary in the Student Department. Her frustration coincided with a concerted attempt by the Labor Bureau to lure her away from student work in order to direct its program of worker education. "It was a very big decision for me to switch to the Industrial Department," Deng recalled. "Just going on year after year doing the student work — reading Bibles, making speeches like sermons — was not really what I wanted. I was still interested in teaching, so I was going to leave the YWCA and find a teaching job." In other words, doing "social work" was far more important to Deng than a commitment to the YWCA or to Christian service. Just as she was about to leave the YWCA, another secretary told her about the possibility of doing direct work with factory girls, work that would involve teaching. "[She] knew that I was more interested in social problems than the religious aspect of the YWCA work."

In 1928 Deng began a year as a trainee in the Labor Bureau of the YWCA, headed at the time by Lily K. Haass. During this time she not only had the opportunity to acquaint herself with the programs for women workers run by the Labor Bureau, but also to develop her interest in economics. "In 1928 I started writing a book *Women and Money*," she recalled.

I had read books like Bernard Shaw's *The Intelligent Woman's Guide to Capitalism and Socialism*, or something like that, and we had discussed it in our discussion group. I thought that in Chinese society there was such a big gap between the poor and the rich. . . . Inside rich people's homes food was spoiling, while poor people were lying on the streets as corpses. We saw them every day—people dying of hunger and cold. As I went through the factories I saw the terrible living conditions and the long hours, the child labor, and all that. I was so impressed by the injustice. Then I tried to describe why women were not able to earn their own living, why they were subject to oppression in the home as well as the factory. . . .

I had the book all drafted out, but it was stopped before I finished it. I had shown it to the General Secretary Cai Kui, and she said, "Your writing is not good enough." I don't really think that was the reason, because you can always correct it. As I think back I believe she thought I was too radical.

Although her first writing project was aborted, she had the opportunity to pursue her interest in women's economic status when she was sent, in 1929, on a YWCA scholarship to study labor economics at the London School of Economics.

By the time Deng returned to China in 1930, she had an expertise in economics that was unusual for a Chinese woman at that time. She had also developed a commitment to working with women workers. On the surface, it seems that Deng's integration of Christian beliefs with a concern for women's issues and the working class was compatible with the YWCA, indeed that the YWCA provided an almost perfect niche for someone like Deng. A closer look, however, reveals that Deng already had views that differed from those of the YWCA, as exemplified by her recognition that her book *Women and Money* was "too radical." The differences, and the ways in which Deng developed her own vision, become particularly evident in the years during which she directed the Labor Bureau. The Labor Bureau, we shall see, provided a structure within which she could do the work she wanted.

The Labor Bureau

When Deng returned to China from England in 1930 she became head of the YWCA Labor Bureau. (Her appointment as head of the bureau represented a commitment of the YWCA to appoint Chinese, rather than foreigners, in leadership positions.)[26] For the next twenty years, she devoted herself to developing a program of education for women workers, the work for which she is best known.

Ever since the early 1900s, when the YWCA began a program in Shanghai—China's largest industrial center—it had been concerned with the plight of women workers, who represented nearly two-thirds of the city's work force.[27] Initially, the YWCA's industrial program had focused on attracting women mill workers to sing, crochet, learn to read, and engage in Bible study, with the hope of "developing workers who would carry on Christian work."[28] This goal of converting and training literate home-makers, as we shall see, was very different from Deng's aim of developing what can be described as a working-class feminist consciousness.

The program was sporadic until the early 1920s, when the association requested that someone with expertise in industrial problems be sent to China to assist in formulating a plan for industrial work. The appointment of Agatha Harrison, in 1921, represented the beginning of a shift away from a concern with Christian education. When interviewed for the job, Harrison was "very frank in saying that she is not a member of any church, although she has a very definite faith." She was asked "point blank whether she approved of the taking of Christianity to non-Christian countries and she replied that she was not sure, but that probably she would become sure on seeing the need for it on the spot. She would not be willing to take a Bible class."[29] After arriving in Shanghai, Harrison organized a campaign against child labor, which became the focus of the Labor Bureau's work for several years.

The Labor Bureau did not completely abandon its efforts to work with women themselves, and during the mid-1920s set up pilot programs for popular education in several working-class districts of Shanghai.[30] This was a period when the Chinese Communist Party, founded in 1921, was actively organizing workers to join unions and participate in strikes, causing at least some members of the Labor Bureau to advocate a greater emphasis on educating women workers. As Lily Haass explained to a YWCA Board that was less than enthusiastic about this shift, "The labour movement is the big factor in the future of our economic society and [it] makes all the difference in the world what that labour movement thinks. If we wish to help to create that thinking we will need to do it where the workers are. This does not mean that we care any less about public opinion or legislation."[31]

The shift to a program of worker education that emphasized politics more than religion culminated in Deng Yuzhi's directorship of the Labor Bureau. It would be misleading, however, to view Deng as simply continuing a preexisting trend, for she designed a program that represented a significant departure from that of the past, one that represented her growing sympathies with the goals of the Chinese Communist Party. The YWCA Labor Bureau, we shall see, provided her a structure through which she could contribute to the organizing of the communist revolution, without having to join the Party or subordinate her work to its dictates.

Under Deng's leadership, the Labor Bureau established night schools for women workers in China's major industrial centers. Ostensibly the purpose of the schools was to teach women literacy, but Deng designed a program that, couched in the rhetoric of Christian values, aimed to help them understand their position—as women and as workers—in China's social-economic system. To those who still expressed concern that the program represented too great a departure from the goals of missionary work, Deng replied:

> Some centres have Sunday Schools for the girls, others have Christmas services and parties, but the most important religious work done is through the secretary's personal contact with the girls. . . . The result of coming into touch with people who try to live a Christian life in all relations is a mighty factor in our religious work with workers, whose lives are in action more than in thought. Then day in and day out what the secretary does to help the girls in their one hundred and one personal and home problems; friendship with boys, friendship between girls, adjustment of marriages, the right kind of philosophy of life, enlarging their interest in life, are all religious work without fixed forms, and they represent the most important part of our work among industrial girls, for these give to us, as well as to the workers themselves, the permanent values of life.[32]

The notion of engaging in "religious work without fixed form" was extremely useful to Deng in justifying social and political work that might otherwise have been abhorrent to the YWCA.

In the curriculum Deng developed, students spent two years taking basic courses in writing, arithmetic, geography, history, and current events, followed by a third year taking elective courses about industrial problems, trade unionism, and labor legislation. Teachers supplemented the text required by China's ruling party, the Guomindang, with one Deng had helped them edit themselves. This text, according to one of the teachers, explained "what imperialism was, how to be patriotic, why workers were oppressed, and why workers' lives are so inferior to those of the capitalists."[33] Classroom activities often encouraged women to become activists. For example, allegedly teaching letter writing, one of the teachers familiarized students with the factory law of the Shanghai Municipal Council and then had them write letters to the Municipal Council reporting conditions in the factories where they worked that did not conform to the law.[34] The schools also taught women such practical skills as public speaking and singing that would enable them to participate more actively in the labor movement. The large number of night school students who became activists in the labor movement attests to the program's success.[35]

Although teaching women to understand (and ultimately to work to change) their position in the social and economic system was the major goal of the curriculum, Deng also saw the night schools as an arena where women workers could understand current political problems. By the 1930s, increasing Japanese aggression in China loomed as the major political issue. Teachers at the YWCA schools therefore organized discussions of Japanese imperialism, taught the students patriotic songs, and encouraged them to participate in the National Salvation Movement. Deng herself wrote a pamphlet for students, entitled *ZhongRi guanxi* (Relations between China and Japan). At the same time, people like Agnes Smedley, an American journalist who had close relations with leaders of the CCP, were invited to speak to the students about the attempts by the Communist Party to resist Japan and to organize a radically new type of society in Yan'an.

The 1930s were a time of severe political repression, when suspected communists were systematically arrested and executed by the Guomindang. Deng recognized that the YWCA provided an almost unique forum for political activity. The police were not likely to challenge meetings held by foreigners, she observed. "And of course we were Christians, so they shouldn't suspect us of doing things like being communists!" Deng was, in a certain sense, manipulating both the police and the YWCA, engaging in work that neither would have wholly sanctioned.

Christianity and Communism

The radical curriculum as well as the number of activists graduating from the YWCA schools attracted the attention of the Chinese Communist Party. It had been less than successful in its own attempts to organize women workers during the 1920s; following the coup of 1927, when the Guomindang attacked the CCP-organized labor movement in Shanghai, Communist efforts at labor organizing went completely underground. Thus, despite its earlier condemnation of the YWCA's religious orientation, the CCP, beginning in the 1930s, saw the YWCA Labor Bureau as an organization through which it could work to establish contact with women workers.

Deng's relationship with the CCP was complex. When, in the early 1980s, she was asked by a British friend why she had never joined the Party in the 1930s, she instantly replied, "But I was a Christian, so how could I have been a Communist?" Her answer implies a degree of religiosity that hardly characterized Deng's life at this time. One cannot help but wonder whether she drew on her Christian identity to separate herself from the CCP and as an excuse never to confront the decision to join. Why she preferred not to join the Party remains unclear. Perhaps she anticipated that her feminist concerns would be co-opted; at a minimum she knew that in joining the Party she would have to subordinate her own agenda.

Even if she never joined the CCP, she rarely disguised her sympathies for its beliefs and political aspirations. At the YWCA's student conference in summer 1933, for example, she assisted Maud Russell in teaching a course on "Christianity and Communism."

> We discussed what the October Revolution brought to Russia, how they were living, what their educational system is. We approached it from the Christian point of view—like we are all equal before God, should not have money as the incentive. Service should be the goal; serving people should be our aim. And that goes together with the communist idea of serving the general masses. Of course there was this idea of class struggle. I don't remember how Maud put it, but she did give us the sense that capitalism, the exploitation system, was bad. I shared her views at the time.

Throughout the 1930s, Deng continued to emphasize the benefits of socialist and communist revolution at workers' conferences sponsored by the YWCA. At a conference in the late 1930s, for example, the themes for discussion included "world unemployment," "capitalism, socialism, and communism."[36] Deng was never concerned with analyzing the relationship between Christianity and communism in a precise way. Instead, her work reflected, and sometimes foreshadowed, the endeavors of individuals such as Y. T. Wu to articulate the compatibility of Christianity and Marxism or communism.[37]

Perceiving the CCP as embracing the same "Christian" values in which she believed, Deng did not object to—but rather cooperated with—CCP attempts to influence women workers through the night schools. Moreover, she developed an argument that this was compatible with the goals of the YWCA, all the while knowing that not all YWCA staff members would agree. "The YMCA and YWCA are not churches," she explained. "They are social organizations with membership among the masses. So we got in touch with the more progressive groups, including the underground Communist group. They wouldn't tell you they were Communists, but they would appear as patriotic workers. That we would welcome." Thus, she helped the Party arrange to send its members (including Jiang Qing) to teach at the schools. She also enlisted the help of Party cultural workers, such as the playwright Tian Han, in helping the night school students produce skits that had an unmistakably revolutionary message. One such skit, "Where to Go?" depicted poverty-stricken peasants who left their rural homes in search of work. In the city they were abused by foremen and forewomen in the factories, their children had to work in silk filatures, and they were frequently unemployed.

So, where should they go? At the end of the play was the idea that they had to go and struggle to have a better society. But it was not stated so clearly. We might have raised suspicions from the local authorities there who were already suspecting that perhaps we had Communists among our students. So we tried not to make it so clear-cut that they must overthrow the capitalist system. The play didn't say it in those words, but it was in the conversations of the characters. We left it to the students and the audience to make their own conclusions about where to go.

Thus, although Deng never joined the Party, her work directing the night schools contributed in an indirect but crucial way to the growth of a Communist-influenced workers' movement in China.

The understated contribution of the night schools to the Chinese revolution, and the special role played by Deng Yuzhi, was acknowledged by the CCP in several ways. In the late 1930s, when the CCP had formed a united front with the Guomindang in order to fight Japan, both Zhou Enlai and his wife, Deng Yingchao, met with Deng to enlist her support in the Communist-organized resistance movement. In addition to her work in the night schools, Communist leaders undoubtedly saw Deng as a link to both women's and religious organizations. From Deng's perspective, the CCP represented values and engaged in struggles (such as resisting the Japanese) in which she believed. "What held us together," Deng recalled,

was that we wanted to be an independent country managed by our own people. That was in accordance with the Communist idea of a free China as well. So on those terms we worked together. As far as religious beliefs are concerned, they were atheists and we had our own beliefs. They didn't ask us to become atheists and we didn't ask them to become Christians. Zhou Enlai made it very clear to us, "You go on with your own religious activities and we are atheists. But we won't bother you. That's your freedom."

The Guomindang had observed Deng's importance as well, and Madame Chiang Kai-shek was dispatched to recruit Deng to work with the Guomindang-sponsored women's patriotic movement. Explicit refusal would have been dangerous; it was only because Lily Haass quickly arranged for Deng to go to the United States in 1939 — to publicize the Chinese war effort and to study for a master's degree at New York University — that she was able to evade Madame Chiang's overtures.[38]

Christianity and Liberation

Deng Yuzhi's importance to the Communist revolution was again recognized when the CCP prepared to assume power in 1949. Having been invited by Deng Yingchao to participate in meetings to establish the All-China Federation of Women, Deng traveled clandestinely to Beijing. Once there, she was also asked to join the newly formed Chinese People's Political Consultative Conference (CPPCC). And when the CCP declared its final victory on October 1, 1949, Deng was invited to join other government officials standing on the viewing platform at Tiananmen Square with Mao Zedong, celebrating the founding of the People's Republic.

Deng's affiliation with the CCP made her the subject of controversy within the YWCA. On the one hand, her political views and experience made her the most likely person to head the China YWCA after 1949. Cai Kui, who had been the general secretary of the China YWCA since the mid-1930s, resigned, recognizing the lack of support for her among the younger, more progressive secretaries.[39] In a confidential letter to the general secretary of the World YWCA, Cai Kui expressed her confidence that Deng "is the best person we have available to lead the association and to represent us to outside bodies."

She sees very clearly what the YWCA can do in these times and really understands the new China in general outline more clearly than many of us, so that she sees how to apply the YWCA to the situation. She also has conviction about the YWCA and speaks out in its support, sometimes managing to convince those among our younger staff who feel our whole future lies in complete identification with the Democratic Women's Federation. Few others can do this for they either do not see the issues clearly or else do not have the confidence of the younger group. Cora has the confidence of the staff and of many of the committee members, and in this she holds a unique position. I hope you will not let past prejudices come in the way of your staff in co-operating with her, nor let her different approach to things influence the place of the China YWCA within the world's family.[40]

Not everyone in the YWCA was convinced by Cai Kui, however. The "past prejudices" to which she alluded concerned Deng's radical reputation. "Deng is as erratic as ever," complained one YWCA secretary in China, "goes the 'whole hog' but insists that she is Christian, not Communist."[41] Another declared that she was "much distressed if it is true that Deng is to be GS [general secretary]—surely our National Committee folks aren't that stupid! It'll be wrangling, wrangling, wrangling!!!"[42] Yet a third worried that Cai Kui's replacement by Deng Yuzhi would undermine the efforts of the YWCA "to hold to its Christian ideals."[43] These concerns notwithstanding, however, Deng was appointed to the post.

Perhaps ironically, Deng's Christian identity became more pronounced in her tenure as general secretary throughout the decades following 1949. This may have been partly because the CCP treated her as a representative of Christian and religious people in China. It was as a Christian that she was appointed to certain government organizations, such as the religious federation; even her appointment to the state-sponsored All-China Federation of Women reflected the Party's desire to include representatives of Christian women. When she was invited to attend the Third World Peace Conference in Warsaw in 1953, she was to represent Chinese Christians.

Perhaps without forethought, Deng became a spokesperson for the interests and rights of Chinese Christians. For example, when she was invited to Beijing in 1949 to participate in the founding of the CPPCC, she joined other religious leaders in attempting to ensure that the newly established government would protect religious freedom. "At first," she recalled,

the Common Program stated that people are free to have faith. But faith meant faith in communism, not religious faith. Various religious groups carried on a discussion before the CPPCC met. In our Christian groups we had discussions, too. All of us came to the conclusion that there must be a separate clause in the Common Program protecting freedom of religious belief. We got it. That shows the Communists were very wise, and could really work with the people. We were quite moved.

While working to represent the interests of Chinese Christians to the CCP, Deng also represented the CCP to religious organizations, including the YWCA. Deng frequently found it necessary to defend the CCP to YWCA officials outside of China, who were deeply suspicious of the ability of the Chinese YWCA to adhere to the organization's principles. For example, at a meeting of the World YWCA in India in the fall of 1950, she encountered what she found to be a surprising degree of suspicion and hostility from other foreign representatives. Certain that Christianity and communism were contradictory and incompatible, they feared that the Chinese YWCA had become communist. She repeatedly explained that "we were a women's organization doing work from the Christian angle, according to Christian purpose, and according to our own program line."

At first glance it might seem that Deng's increased emphasis on the religious aspects of the YWCA was simply an expression of the new role she was placed in after the Communist Party assumed power. Yet scattered evidence suggests that her personal identification as a Christian also intensified in the years following Liberation. For example, in November 1950, when making what for her was an extremely difficult decision to violate the wishes of the World YWCA and attend the World Peace Conference in Warsaw, she wrote to an American YWCA colleague that "I thought hard and I prayed hard for wisdom from God to help me make a right decision. Yesterday I made the decision to go. There may be problems and difficulties, but most of the actions we take have problems and difficulties. However, I have faith in God and His hand will lead me through all the way. So, please pray for me."[44] The expression of faith in God is striking, for it is conspicuously absent from all her previous personal letters as well as her recollections. Nor is it coincidental that these sentiments were articulated shortly after Liberation.

The private and public expressions of her Christian identity suggest a change in the meaning of that identity wrought by Liberation. Before 1949, Deng defined and articulated a sense of purpose through a commitment to social change and revolution, particularly for women. Although she believed that this commitment embodied her Christian values, those values did not define the struggle in which she engaged, and she rarely spoke or behaved in ways that indicated they were central to her identity. As she had to affiliate more closely with the CCP in the years before 1949, however, she became more outspoken about her Christian identity, perhaps to establish a boundary between herself and the Party. Once the Communist Party won political power, it was her Christian identity that defined her individual agency and the arena for struggle in which she could engage. In this context, it is not surprising that she expressed religious convictions in ways that seemed discontinuous with her past.

The relationship of Deng's Christian, feminist, and communist identities from the early 1950s through the present is beyond the scope of this chapter. It is also more difficult to analyze, for besides her own recollections, few sources about her thinking and activities exist. As a member of a number of government bodies (the All-China Federation of Women, the CPPCC, and the national federation of religious organizations), as general secretary of the China YWCA (not director of its Labor Bureau, which was disbanded in 1952), and as the subject of criticism for her religious affiliation during a number of political campaigns, the context in which Deng defined, juggled, and continued to manipulate her Christian, feminist, and communist identities was radically different from the pre-1949 past.

PART IV

The Rise of an Indigenous Chinese Christianity

The Rise of an Indigenous
Chinese Christianity

DANIEL H. BAYS

The chapters in this, the concluding part of the volume, address what is in my opinion the single most important underlying issue of the past century of Christianity's presence in China: how soon (if ever) and in what ways would Christianity become Chinese, both in control of its institutions (indigenization) and in its cultural complexion (inculturation)?[1] The nineteenth century was the great age of building foreign-missions-dominated programs and institutions, not only in China but around the world. The twentieth century has seen a reversal, with national Christian movements succeeding to power and control over their own churches as foreign missions have been expelled, have withered, or have entered into partnerships with the "native" Christians over whom they formerly presided. In China, this has been a complex story, and these six chapters deal with only a few facets of the process. There is plenty of room, and need, for further biographical and institutional studies, especially of Chinese church leaders and all-Chinese Christian movements, as well as for investigations of the dynamics of cooperation, competition, and sometimes confrontation between the Chinese and foreign members of the Christian community.

In many ways it is revealing that these chapters begin in the 1840s with the early maverick missionary Karl Gützlaff, then leapfrog well into the twentieth century. There is a good reason for this. In the 1840s, there were still so few foreign missionaries that no one could contemplate personally directing all of the enterprise of evangelizing China. Probably about 200,000 Catholics were scattered around the country at this time, the legacy of seventeenth- and eighteenth-century Chinese Catholicism, most under the direction of Chinese lay leaders. It took a while for the arriving European Catholic missionaries to establish control over these communities, most of which had been getting along without foreign direction for decades.[2] For the Protestant missionaries, who had never been established outside Macao and Canton before 1842, and even after 1842 (until 1860) were limited in residence to five treaty port cities, there was no hope at all of directly reaching into the hinterland or the interior of China, and there was no earlier legacy of Christianity to reclaim, as there was for the Catholics. So for the Protestants, the choices were to labor in the five ports, with everything under their direct supervision, or to devise means of using Chinese nationals to reach into the interior. Karl Gützlaff, of course, came up with a flamboyant and at first apparently spectacularly successful strategy to do the latter. Jessie and Ray Lutz tell his story with sensitivity and insight.

Their chapter is a substantial improvement upon the usual references to Gützlaff, which approach caricature, and it sheds light on many important issues. For example, it provides a link to later evangelistic success among the Hakka, which in some ways perhaps vindicated Gützlaff.[3] It also shows the almost inevitable conflict of style and strategy that derived from the very different Protestant missionary communities even at this early time: the pietistic and evangelistic stress of Gützlaff on repentance and the personal transformative powers of faith, versus the confessional tradition and its stress on training, catechisms, and a hierarchy of control in the church (or mission). Gützlaff was of course also a threat to the full-time professional missionaries, with his language genius, simplistic strategy, and extravagant claims of success. So there were many hoping for his downfall, and fall he did. But I believe the verdict is still out on the nature and authenticity of the results of his efforts in the 1840s, despite the undoubted venality of some of his Chinese helpers. There were certainly cases of strange understandings of Christian doctrines by some who heard the message via Gützlaff's scheme, but perhaps no stranger than some of the understandings of Christianity rampant in the Chinese countryside today. In the end, Gützlaff seems prescient; his shadow reaches all the way into the twentieth century and its stress on indigenization of the church.

After Gützlaff's death and the collapse of the Chinese Union, the strategy of giving great responsibility for the work to Chinese nationals seemed to fade. I doubt that the former was more than incidentally responsible for the latter, although those who argued the need to go very slowly in turning over missionary responsibilities to Chinese Christians certainly found ammunition in the alleged disaster of the Chinese Union. Rather, the whole tenor of the age shifted. At mid-century, at least two major missionary leaders, Henry Venn of the Church Mission Society and Rufus Anderson of the American Board, still promoted a strategy similar to that of Gützlaff: to plant the seed of a native church, to pass on responsibility to it quickly, and then to liquidate the mission as soon as possible, thus keeping separate "Christ" and "culture."[4] But this was quickly forgotten in the late nineteenth century, as Christ and culture became conflated, and building the institutions of Western civilization came to be an integral part of the missionary effort.[5]

It was well into the twentieth century before prominent native Chinese Christian leaders and movements for greater Chinese participation and control appeared. The remaining five chapters deal with that phenomenon in the Protestant sector (revealing another of the lacunae of this volume, a corresponding movement in the Catholic church).[6] Of course, after the May Fourth Movement and the rapid growth both of mass nationalism and the organized political forces to tap into it in the 1920s (the GMD and CCP), the issue of who was in charge of the Christian movement in China was an explosive one, tied in directly with the emotionally charged causes of national unity and anti-imperialism. China missions, in the early twentieth century seemingly in the forefront of reform, educator of many of China's new leaders in mission schools, and enjoying unprecedented growth, suddenly found themselves on the defensive, under attack from non-Christian forces without and under more politely stated but unmistakable criticism from Chinese Christian leaders within. Peter Chen-main Wang's chapter deals head-on with this issue of control of the Christian movement, and is a provocative case study of the failure of the missionary movement to do what it said it wanted to do: to pass on real authority over the institutions of the "Sino-foreign Protestant establishment" to Chinese Christians. In reading the critiques of Christian literature that Wang presents, it is sometimes hard to remember they were written by Christians. In the end, a classic denouement ensued; the foreign funding agency withdrew its support, and the initiative died. It is no wonder that, as my own chapter indicates in a broad overview, a significant number of Chinese Christians left the missionary scene altogether during the Republican period (1912–49) and established wholly independent churches or Christian activities under their own leadership.

The chapter by Brook, which effectively uses new English-language and Chinese archival materials, argues for interpreting the period of the Sino-Japanese War as crucial in the decades-long movement of Chinese Christians toward independence, unity, and Chinese control. In documenting his hypothesis, he makes many useful observations, such as how the alacrity of the Chinese response to Japanese occupation authorities' pressures for consolidation of churches (in order to control them) indicates a long-standing desire among Chinese Christians to supersede Western denominationalism. The wartime experience also presaged in some ways what the churches would encounter in the 1950s under the new PRC regime. Practically the only Beijing holdout against the new unified federation of Protestant churches under the Japanese was the fundamentalist evangelist Wang Mingdao, who successfully defied pressures to take his Christian Tabernacle into the federation. There is evidence that this success led Wang to try the same defiance under the PRC, with the result that he lost the confrontation in the mid-1950s, and spent more than twenty years in prison.[7]

The volume concludes with two case studies of Protestant Christianity in recent decades, one in China and the other in Taiwan. Gao Wangzhi gives us an interpretive biographical study of Wu Yaozong (Y. T. Wu), one of the most controversial Christian figures of the past half century. Wu represented an important sector, the urban Christian intellectuals who insisted on a strong social and political relevance for Christianity and who were willing to participate in the state-supervised institutions devised to manage religious affairs. Although he was theologically different from evangelicals like Wang Mingdao, who was his nemesis, nevertheless simplistic terms like "liberal" or "modernist" probably do not do justice to the thought of Wu and his colleagues in the Protestant Three-Self Movement leadership. Chinese Christian scholars will undoubtedly grapple with historical judgments on Y. T. Wu for years to come, and this thoughtful assessment by Professor Gao will contribute much to their discussion.

Protestant Christianity in Taiwan is a varied and complicated phenomenon, retaining all the strands of the twentieth century historical legacy: some missionary efforts forced off the mainland after 1949 have continued to the present in Taiwan, permitting analysis of their changing strategies and results over several decades. Likewise, some of the independent churches begun on the mainland, such as the True Jesus Church and the Little Flock, have flourished on Taiwan. For the most part, this is not an unstudied phenomenon.[8] Yet in his chapter Murray Rubinstein does give us light on a most interesting and relatively unknown entity, the Pentecostal and charismatic movement in Taiwan Protestantism. Most readers will gain much new information from this chapter, and new insights into the complexities of the Protestant community. Pentecostal and charismatic Christianity is also one of the largest sectors of the Protestant movement in the PRC today, especially but not solely in rural areas. Rubinstein's discussion of "congruence" as a mechanism of inculturating these distinctive Christian beliefs and practices is useful, and reminds us as well of the deep wellsprings of popular religiosity in traditional Chinese culture, elements of which may be visible here.

CHAPTER 15

Karl Gützlaff's Approach to Indigenization: The Chinese Union

JESSIE G. LUTZ AND R. RAY LUTZ

The Chinese Union (Fu Han hui), founded by the German missionary Karl Gützlaff in 1844, was based on the principle that China's millions could never be converted to Christianity by foreign missionaries: Chinese Christians themselves must carry out the evangelization of the empire while Western missionaries would serve as instructors and supervisors. The union would send Chinese preachers and colporteurs into the interior to carry the gospel message to every province. Such an approach might seem to have considerable merit, for almost every missionary anticipated the eventual displacement of foreign evangelists by Chinese. Yet the Chinese Union lasted less than a decade, disintegrating soon after the death of its founder in August 1851. Why such short life? What was the union's legacy for the Chinese church and Christian missions? The history of the Chinese Union may be brief but it is complex.

Only five years after Gützlaff founded the Chinese Union, it had become the focus of a bitter dispute among China missionaries over techniques of evangelization and prerequisites for baptism. East-West relations and the volatile social and political environment of South China were part of the story, but differences between China missionaries and their supporting societies in the West also contributed to the controversy. In an era of slow communications, missions often reflected the personalities of the pioneer evangelists; consequently, personal animosities exacerbated problems.

Karl Gützlaff was an independent missionary. Though sent to Southeast Asia under the auspices of the Netherlands Missionary Society in 1826, he soon broke with the society over his desire to enter China, which at the time outlawed all Christian evangelization. From 1834 until his death, he found support as Chinese secretary to the British administration, first in

Macao and then in Hong Kong. Missionary activities were confined to weekends and off-hours.

Gützlaff's biographer, Herman Schlyter, distinguishes three types of Protestant missions: (1) the church mission wherein a specific denomination recruits missionaries and solicits funds primarily from among its own members; it ordinarily seeks to establish branch churches in the mission field; (2) the society mission, frequently characterized by ecumenism and public fund-raising campaigns; examples are the China Inland Mission (CIM) of Hudson Taylor and the YMCA; and (3) the free mission, of which Karl Gützlaff was the first modern Protestant model and Albert Schweitzer a renowned example.[1] Free, or independent, missionaries can choose their own field and methodology and guide their work from the field. Emancipated from human authority, they are responsible only to God. They must, however, find their own support, either by employment or by building a home base or both. Individual personality obviously is central to the nature of the free mission and because a strong personality is typical of independent missionaries, their careers are often marked by controversy.

For many reasons Gützlaff was convinced that Chinese, not foreigners, must effect the conversion of China. He had by the 1840s become isolated from the missionary community in Hong Kong and Canton and rarely joined in their activities. While holding a full-time job, he was driven by a sense of urgency to bring salvation to the heathen. The Chinese masses must be rescued from damnation and morally reformed by Christianity. Yet he, along with all other Protestant missionaries in China, had converted only a handful of Chinese. The minimal fruits of missionary efforts, furthermore, had been immensely costly; after years of language study in China to ready themselves, missionaries all too often had their careers terminated by illness, death, or resignation. Gützlaff craved success after a decade and a half of frustration and disappointment. "The evangelization of the world in this generation" would become a popular slogan during the late nineteenth century. "Evangelization of China in my lifetime" had been Gützlaff's driving ambition ever since he first rode sailing ships along the China coast making illegal forays into villages to distribute Scriptures and preach the gospel.[2]

Gützlaff's plan was to recruit missionaries to instruct and supervise a corps of national preachers who would do the actual evangelizing. He believed that the cultural gap between Westerner and Chinese and the difficulties of attaining true language facility were so great that few missionaries could ever communicate effectively with the masses. A Chinese Christian, even without great depth of theological knowledge, could always interact with the populace more effectively than a foreign missionary. As evidence, he could point to the fact that the majority of Christian converts thus far had actually been made by Chinese workers rather than by missionaries. Missionaries, for their part, should reduce the distance by going Chinese: dressing in Chinese style, including the queue, adopting Chinese cuisine, and living among the Chinese, preferably in the interior.

Theologically, Gützlaff advocated extensive, as opposed to intensive, evangelization. Jesus had commanded his followers to carry the gospel to all peoples. Deeply influenced by his Moravian, pietist heritage, Gützlaff was interested in promoting an awareness of sin and a conversionary experience of rebirth. Establishing denominational churches was not his goal. Training Christians in parochial schools was too slow. Christian communities would come into existence and continuing instruction occur after baptism, but Gützlaff defined a Christian as one who had seen the light and accepted Jesus' offer of grace. He did not require competence in the theology of Western Christianity before acceptance as a Christian, nor was he interested in the differences between Protestant denominations. With the conviction that the Holy Spirit was the ultimate source of all conversion and could accomplish all things came an unbounded faith in the power of the Word. Each of these stimuli to the founding of the Chinese Union, personal, methodological, and theological, left ample room for controversy. Furthermore, such a minimalist theology in combination with a considerable degree of autonomy enabled Chinese evangelists to adapt teachings and rituals to their clientele.

Brief History of the Chinese Union

As early as 1838, Gützlaff had sent two of his Chinese assistants to the borders of Jiangxi and Guangdong to preach; upon returning with glowing reports of converting relatives, they received funds to repeat the journey. The outbreak of the Opium War in 1839 interrupted Gützlaff's efforts, for in addition to heavy duties as translator and interpreter, he accompanied the British military north to the Yangzi and acted as civil magistrate on Zhoushan dao (Chusan Island). He returned to Macao in 1841 to find his little band largely dispersed, though a few of his converts welcomed him. Once again, he gathered Chinese believers for early morning and evening instruction leading toward baptism, and he had some of his converts accompany him on weekend itinerations in preparation for independent work as colporteurs and preachers. In 1844 Gützlaff gave his corps of assistants the title Christian Association for Propagating the Gospel (later changed to the Chinese Union). They reported a total of 262 baptisms, mostly in Hong Kong and its environs; a significant proportion came from the Hakka ethnic minority.[3]

Gützlaff, meanwhile, had cultivated support in England and Europe. Buoyed by the imperial edicts of 1844 and 1846 granting tolerance to Christians and Christian missionaries, Gützlaff waxed eloquent on the possibilities of penetrating every province of China, even Tibet, Korea, and Japan. Evangelists had only to follow the example of the Apostles and China's millions could receive the glad news of salvation. In a series of reports under the Chinese name Gaihan (*aihan*, lover of the Chinese), he repeated claims of Chinese converts forsaking their idols and the rise of numerous Chinese Christian communities.[4] He sent translations of letters attributed to Chinese Union members in which they expressed joy upon receiving the gospel of salvation and ventured to hope that all Chinese might be so privileged.[5] Needed were funds to support hundreds of Chinese evangelists and also Western mentors ready to sacrifice all in a heroic crusade.

Gützlaff's astute and ever sanguine publicity fell on fertile ground. The Second Great Awakening had generated a new awareness of the Christian obligation to missions and, moreover, churches had discovered that sponsoring overseas missions often vitalized home congregations. Appealing to a rising German nationalism, Gützlaff noted that Germans were far behind Americans and English in recognizing their moral duty to the heathen. Why not take advantage of the opportunity to rectify their neglect by supporting the Chinese Union? The Opium War had further aroused interest in China as it had raised hopes of an open door for Bibles and missionaries along with British cottons and other trade items. Some churchmen argued that the West owed China the gift of Christianity to offset the evils of opium brought by the West.[6]

One of Gützlaff's most enthusiastic supporters and publicists was Christian G. Barth. The lead article in the first issue of his *Calwer Missionsblatt* (1 Nov. 1844) carried the title "Morgenroth in China's Nacht" (Dawn in China's night).[7] It commended to its readers the needs of China and called attention to Gützlaff's project. News of the Chinese Union, letters and reports by Gützlaff and Chinese Union members, and statistical data on itinerations and converts became regular features of the *Calwer Missionsblatt*. Barth urged the Basel and Rhenish mission societies to answer Gützlaff's call and appoint evangelists to work with Gützlaff and the Chinese Union. Other magazines opened their pages to Gützlaff's exhortations and numerous church congregations expressed interest and support. The king of Prussia donated $400 to the great cause.

Chinese Union Membership and Converts

Year	Members	Preachers	Converts baptized
1844	20	—	262
1845	80	—	88
1846	179	36	601
1847	300	50	655
1848	1,000	100	487
Jan.–Sept. 1849		130	695

SOURCES: Selly Oak, Papers Relating to Gützlaff; *Jahresbericht*, 1846, p. 54; A. J. Broomhall, 1: 317; Schlyter, *Karl Gützlaff*, p. 297.

Reward came with the departure in November 1846 of four missionaries assigned to Gützlaff and the Chinese Union: Theodor Hamberg and Rudolf Lechler of the Basel Missionary Society and Ferdinand Genähr and Heinrich Koster of the Rhenish Missionary Society. In March 1847 Gützlaff welcomed them in Hong Kong and almost immediately sent them to Chinese quarters with their language teachers and assistants.[8] Each was assigned Chinese Union helpers with whom he was to go on a preaching tour the following Sunday, the assistants and not the Westerners obviously doing the evangelizing. Gützlaff set a goal of reading 300 characters a day plus practice in a spoken dialect. Each was to learn a different dialect of southeast China.

The Chinese Union expanded explosively. Though the figures are incomplete and differ according to source, the table approximates the claims. Generally, about 50 percent of the national evangelists were sent to the villages and towns in Guangdong with Jiangxi, Guangxi, and Fujian accounting for most of the rest. By 1848, however, Gützlaff reported one or more representatives in twelve provinces. Scriptures and tracts, mostly by Gützlaff, were also published under Chinese Union auspices and Gützlaff's translation of the Bible gained wide circulation in interior China. Expenses were running into thousands of dollars. Gützlaff began to envision his dream becoming a reality, his twenty years of labor for the Chinese justified. He would go to Europe to found support societies for thousands of Chinese evangelists and he would recruit dozens of men and women to instruct the national preachers. Departing Hong Kong in September 1849, Gützlaff turned direction of the Chinese Union over to Theodor Hamberg. The Hong Kong merchants presented Gützlaff with a farewell testimonial: "His official character has been as spotless as water; and not a cash has he received as bribe."[9]

Already, however, skepticism about Gützlaff's claims had been building, with J. F. Cleland and James Legge of the London Missionary Society expressing their concern and disbelief to their own society and to the British and Foreign Bible Society.[10] The latter had supplied Gützlaff with several grants for printing and circulating the Scriptures. Hamberg and Lechler had conveyed to Gützlaff their doubts about the reality of some reported journeys and the authenticity of diaries presented by itinerating preachers and colporteurs.[11] They offered evidence that some assistants had not ventured beyond the Hong Kong environs and had even spent their stipends on opium and gambling. Gützlaff brushed aside such information, relying on the word of his Chinese; he knew the Chinese better than these newcomers. By September 1847, Lechler and Hamberg had tried to dissociate themselves from the Chinese Union; they worked only with those assistants whom they deemed trustworthy and whom they employed directly.[12] Unbeknownst to Gützlaff, Hamberg's agenda as he took charge of the Chinese Union was radical reform and reconstruction.

Gützlaff's tour of England and Europe opened on a triumphal note. Preceded by an aura of romance and fame, Gützlaff was equal to expectations. He had a genius for inspiring confidence and enthusiasm upon initial contact and he made the most of it. He was, wrote one writer, like electricity.[13] Setting himself a killing schedule that called for travel by night after twelve-hour days of public lectures, meetings with executives of mission societies, sermons, and so forth, he conducted a blitz tour of England and Scotland. Crossing to the continent, he had an interview with the queen of Holland, received a commendation from the Literary Society of Leyden, met with Moravians about founding a mission station in Inner Asia, and established an English women's support society; all this in addition to meeting with various organizations and congregations interested in China missions. On to Germany, highlighted by an audience with the king and queen of Prussia and a hero's welcome in his home town of Pyritz, Pomerania. On to city after city in Germany, Belgium, Switzerland, Finland, Denmark, Sweden, and Austria-Hungary.[14]

Hundreds of support societies for the Chinese Union were founded and it was decided to allocate responsibility for specific provinces to specific societies so that all China could receive the Word. Several recruits for China volunteered. In England, Gützlaff enlisted Richard Ball, a businessman who had already published pamphlets on the Chinese Union. Ball became head of a support organization for the Chinese Union, the Chinese Association, later transformed into the Chinese Evangelization Society. This association, together with its journal, *The Chinese Missionary Gleaner*, edited by Ball, proved to be Gützlaff's most loyal advocate in England.[15] Gützlaff laid before the British Society for Circulation of the Scriptures in China an ambitious plan for printing thousands of inexpensive Bibles in China from wood blocks. There was even talk of sending to Beijing a missionary trained in mathematics and astronomy, à la the early Jesuit example.

Glowing reports accompanied Gützlaff's travels. The 1849 yearbook of the Cassel Missionary Society anticipated that one of the important events of the coming year would be seeing Gützlaff face to face and receiving an oral report on China's evangelization from one who for twenty years had shown himself "the chosen vessel of God."[16] Friedrich W. Krummacher, president of the Berlin Missionary Union for China, reported on Gützlaff's visit to his city.[17] In the midst of a dead and dying Christendom had stepped a worthy servant of God, he said. What Gützlaff offered Christendom was a chance to renew itself. Not simply China but European Christianity was at stake.

Nevertheless, undercurrents that portended trouble plagued Gützlaff and his advocates, while the sense of unease grew stronger as the tour progressed. Information leaked out from Cleland and Legge's reports expressing reservations about the existence of numerous Christian communities and doubts about the moral character and Christian knowledge of the Chinese preachers. Some of this information had reached Barth and he was deeply distressed, since he had led in publicizing Gützlaff's reports. One of the few places on Gützlaff's tour that did not form a support association was Württemberg, the principality in which Barth resided. Basel had similar data from Hamberg and Lechler so that here too Gützlaff found himself on the defensive.

During Gützlaff's absence, investigations were launched in Hong Kong. With Legge taking the initiative, Chinese Union preachers were summoned in late February for questioning by a committee of thirteen missionaries, mostly British.[18] The interrogation had the blessing of the London Missionary Society and the participation of Hamberg. The majority of the committee deemed the findings damaging, if not alarming. They expressed dissatisfaction with the Chinese preachers' understanding of Christian teachings. They were even more critical of the requirements for baptism set by Gützlaff and the preachers. Testimony indicated that a significant minority of the Chinese Union members were opium smokers, that some of the preachers had never left the Hong Kong area, and that some of the colporteurs had resold their tracts to book suppliers to be repurchased by Gützlaff. The committee resolved to have 100 copies of their proceedings, entitled the *Protocol*, printed for distribution.

By April 1850, copies of the *Protocol* had reached Europe. Gützlaff's protestations in response covered a wide range: the committee was biased;

the findings were more inconclusive than indicated in comments by Legge and Hamberg; most committee members had little or no previous contact with Chinese Union members and had never been in the field with them; the investigation was conducted after he left China, making it difficult for him and Chinese Union members to offer a defense; all missionaries had experienced instances of lapse by their converts, but publicizing such evidence did not help the cause of missions.[19]

Whatever the merits of Gützlaff's defense, the damage was great. Some societies, because of their commitment to the project, suspended judgment. Others expressed the hope that Gützlaff and new recruits from Europe could initiate reforms. Gützlaff's methods, they said, remained sound and offered the best hope for Christianization of China. If adequate instruction and controls were instituted, the goal of indigenous Chinese congregations could be realized. Barth recognized Gützlaff's contribution in generating interest in the China mission and he sanctioned the idea of evangelization by the Chinese themselves, but he recommended that control of the Chinese Union be taken from Gützlaff and placed in the hands of Hong Kong missionaries. Detrimental information mounted, however, while the controversy between Gützlaff and his critics grew ever more acrimonious. Maintaining faith in the rosy picture painted by Gützlaff before and during his tour became more and more difficult.

After taking leadership of the Chinese Union in September 1849, Hamberg had dismissed those preachers he considered untrustworthy, providing them with severance pay. Most of the remnant he retained in Hong Kong for instruction. Aided by two or three trusted assistants, Hamberg in May and June 1850 obtained reports from 42 Chinese Union members concerning their activities.[20] Some steadfastly insisted on the accuracy of their statements concerning place of origin and itinerations, but many acknowledged that their present home was in the Canton–Hong Kong environs instead of the distant provinces originally claimed. At least fourteen admitted that they had not visited the places they were paid to go.

Gützlaff left Europe in November 1850, determined to vindicate himself and the Chinese Union; he would reconstruct this great instrument for the conversion of China. Immediately upon arrival in Hong Kong, Gützlaff launched into a flurry of activities. He called together his preachers and secured counterconfessions; many stated that they had been coerced into signing false statements by threats of withdrawal of support.[21] He met with dozens of preachers for instruction and Bible reading in the morning and again in the evening; he preached to the people of Hong Kong, to the boat people, and to villagers on nearby islands in all kinds of weather. Letters of accusation and defense flowed back and forth between Gützlaff and Hamberg, Gützlaff and Barth, and Gützlaff and R. Ball, while both Gützlaff and Hamberg printed circulars justifying their actions.[22] Gützlaff tried to organize an executive committee of Chinese Union members, Hong Kong missionaries, and businessmen with the idea of formally dissociating himself from the Chinese Union. He failed to gain the support of the missionary community and, moreover, he could not really let go of what had become his alter ego. The will and desire of the man drove him on.

Gützlaff, however, was already a sick man. His European tour had been interrupted for several weeks by an attack of "rheumatic fever," and Gützlaff mentioned a little indisposition again in November 1850.[23] Genähr wrote shortly after Gützlaff arrived in Hong Kong in January 1851 that Gützlaff seemed disquieted and unsteady; he complained of aches and pains and spoke of dying.[24] For someone who had earlier delighted in physical challenges and hardships, such comments were most uncharacteristic. Gützlaff would die on 9 August 1851, seven months after returning to China.[25]

Despite the efforts of Gützlaff's widow, the Chinese Union could not survive Gützlaff's death. Gützlaff's major and most loyal supporter, R. Ball of the Chinese Association, had already held up funds pending clarification of charges leveled against the Chinese Union. The only missionary willing to assume administrative responsibility was a newcomer who retired because of ill health after a brief sojourn in China. In the face of damaging evidence after high hopes, many support societies disintegrated and interest in China missions declined. It appeared that the Chinese Union was so much the creature of the independent missionary and his personality that it ceased to have life when the umbilical cord was cut.

The Complexities of the Chinese Union Controversy

Many factors contributed to the rise and fall of the Chinese Union. Though the union included a number of dedicated Christians, a high proportion of the Chinese assistants were undoubtedly motivated by the desire for employment and a significant number failed to carry out their assignments. Many were minimally educated tutors or petty tradesmen hoping to improve their economic status. With the rapid expansion of membership and word spreading that enrollment meant easy income, increasing numbers apparently came from undesirable elements in the Hong Kong–Canton area. The aftermath of the Opium War brought a rise in piracy, robbery, warfare between ethnic groups such as the Hakka and the *bendi* (Punti), and clashes between villages and clans. As a disadvantaged minority that often suffered in the ethnic feuds, the Hakka seemed more receptive than most Han Chinese to heterodox teachings, including Christianity. According to Hamberg, a majority of native preachers in 1847 were Hakka.[26] The volatile social environment of Hong Kong–Canton defied Chinese and British attempts to police the Chinese populace. Opium compounded the problem. Some of the preachers had turned to Christianity hoping to cure their addiction, and there were a few success stories. More, perhaps, were simply desperate for money to supply their habit. Whatever the motive, a cure was not easy and lapse was common.

The "rice Christians" and charlatans in the Chinese Union were highly visible because of their numbers and because of the contrast between Gützlaff's sanguine reports and the later exposé. Such instances were, much to the sorrow of all missionaries, far from unique. Both Gützlaff's assistants and converts of other missionaries included the faithful as well as the opportunistic; it would be impossible to estimate the proportions in either camp. William Dean, an American Baptist missionary who had worked for several years to build a congregation in Hong Kong, reported on returning from home leave that he found many disappointments and the falling away of Chinese who had been left alone.[27] Chalmers and Legge regretfully dismissed a prime convert whom they were training as an assistant. He had proved "unworthy," and Chalmers concluded: "With this must end for the present at least the scheme of training up young men for ministry to [the] Chinese and supporting them while in training."[28] Examples such as this could be multiplied.

Those Chinese who associated with missionaries and their religion risked ostracism and identification with the "foreign devils." Moreover, reentry into Chinese society was not a simple matter, something that missionaries did not fully appreciate. Christian taboos against homage to the ancestors, concubinage, participation in religious festivities, gambling, smoking, and theatricals, plus the required observance of the Sabbath, made life difficult for the convert. Few support mechanisms were provided by Chinese society. Despite the toleration edicts, converts met hostility and discrimination. On 2 February 1855 the Basel missionary Philip Winnes reported on his visit to a Hakka village near Canton. The wife of a convert provided lodging and a place to hold evening religious service.[29] Her welcome, though friendly, was accompanied by unease, for her husband, as a Christian, had been forced to flee the village. Though ten villagers had been baptized, only three remained to attend the service. The rest had been driven out a year earlier.

Winnes traveled to a nearby village, where he encountered two more

Christians, one who had also been forced to flee his hometown and one who had worked for Gützlaff. Though Winnes reported that the latter's knowledge of Christian doctrines was deplorably deficient, he learned that the convert was so widely respected for his honesty and unselfishness that he was often called in as a mediator in local disputes. The convert housed Winnes and opened up his home to visitors desiring to converse with Winnes. The cost was high and yet there were those who chose to pay.

Accentuating the divide between converts and other Chinese was the concept of a permanent patron-client relationship and of the responsibility of each to the other. Some of the assistants apparently reasoned that once they had become identified with the Christian missionary, they should comply with the foreigner's wishes, but at the same time the foreigner had assumed responsibility for their welfare. A Chinese Christian, in relating the story of his conversion by Gützlaff and Chinese Union members, said that he had resisted baptism for many months. Though he found merit in Christian teachings, he was reluctant to abandon the gods and ancestors whom he had previously honored. The response of Gützlaff's assistant was: when one was in Hong Kong, one did as the foreigner did; when one returned home, one observed the traditional customs. This Chinese Christian expressed sorrow that Chinese Union assistants engaged in "squeeze" in relations with the foreign missionary without any apparent sense of guilt. He admired Gützlaff's affection for the Chinese people and commented that it was a shame that "dear Herr Gützlaff" was so easily deceived. Gützlaff, however, was not alone among the foreigners to be deceived, he said.[30]

Hamberg, Lechler, and other missionaries repeatedly accused Gützlaff of failure to monitor his preachers, especially those in the field. During the early years of the Chinese Union, Gützlaff had given considerable attention to instructing and training his preachers and on occasion members were deleted from the payroll until they repented and made amends. With rapid expansion, monitoring became more difficult and violations of trust became more flagrant. Preachers did bring converts to Gützlaff for baptism and many stayed for instruction preparatory to becoming preachers, but it was never possible to check reports of baptisms in distant provinces.

Gützlaff argued throughout that if one treated Chinese Christians as children, they would respond as children, taking no responsibility; if one treated them as adults and gave them responsibility, they would respond accordingly and accept the duty of evangelism as their own.[31] Like many of pietist persuasion, he looked for a conversionary experience as the mark of a Christian. A sense of sin, repentance, and rebirth was fundamental; outward practices, no matter how desirable, did not define a Christian. Future growth in Christian knowledge and moral reform would follow conversion as the Holy Spirit and the missionary did their work. He took sinners where they were; lapses were disturbing, though not necessarily cause for excommunication. Rather, one should love and trust the sinner and bring him to renewed repentance. True to his pen name, Gaihan, Gützlaff never abandoned his love for the Chinese people nor his goal of conversion of China in his lifetime. To do so would have been to acknowledge that his life had been a failure.

Reactions by Hamberg and many other missionaries to disillusioning and frustrating experiences contrasted with the hopefulness of Gützlaff. Hamberg became ever more critical of the Chinese. It was the hard heart of the Chinese that explained the difficulty of true conversion. Many missionaries agreed, concluding that the training of Chinese Christians by Western missionaries would be lengthy. The hope of Chinese leadership receded into the future.

Pietism (or evangelicalism) versus confessionalism was also a source of conflict among the missionaries. Gützlaff, William C. Burns of the English Presbyterians, Issachar Roberts, an independent Baptist, and Hudson Taylor of the CIM differed from church mission representatives over the definition of a Christian and the qualifications of an evangelist. During the interrogations in early 1850, examiners repeatedly questioned Chinese about the length of their training for evangelism and they contrasted their own experience with the average of three to six months' instruction for the Chinese. The Chinese preachers could repeat in some detail the stories of the Bible, but the committee members complained that the preachers recited as if by rote and provided stereotypical interpretations. One member, when asked whether those whom he baptized were already converted, replied that if the man believed and was sincere and upright, then he baptized and continued instruction. He expected only a partial change of heart before baptism; change would be completed after baptism. Such a procedure accorded with Gützlaff's methodology, but was hardly satisfactory to the mainstream missionaries. Hamberg stated to the committee: "I must confess . . . a strong doubt in my mind as to the members of the Chinese Union in general being truly converted Christians, and particularly so as respects their fitness for being employed as preachers and ministers of the Church of God."[32]

Gützlaff, to the contrary, did not find the information derived from the Chinese about their understanding of Christianity or their methods damaging.[33] The evangelists could repeat the Word of God and employ it to stress the need for repentance and the means to salvation through Christ and the Holy Spirit. He pointed out that when the report of a Chinese differed from that of a Westerner, the latter was assumed to be true. The Chinese had not had a chance to present a defense. He accused the committee members of putting a bad light on their findings. Burns, a committee member, did make several largely unsuccessful attempts to place the information in a different perspective. When one missionary asked, "Does any one in this meeting know of any member of the 'Christian Union' whom he considers to be a Christian?" Burns replied that he had worked with several members and found them honest. He could not attest to a "positive conviction of the spiritual regeneration" of these men but he found their knowledge of the Christian point of view considerable and their prayers suitable and apparently sincere. He was unwilling to criticize Gützlaff for not expecting a recently converted Chinese in a non-Christian environment to replicate Western evangelists.[34]

In view of the risks for China missions in general, why had Hamberg, Legge, and other missionaries insisted on an investigation and then given it such extensive and negative publicity? According to them, they saw it as their Christian duty to expose fraudulent claims and fraudulent Christianity.[35] From their standpoint, Gützlaff's flawed methodology was doing great harm to the cause of legitimate missions. But other motives, whether conscious or subconscious, entered, for some of the language was extreme and emotional. Burns had proposed that the findings of the committee be sent to London headquarters as requested, but without any interpretive opinions, since the investigation had been inconclusive. The London Missionary Society majority defeated the motion and secured agreement that 100 copies be printed and distributed to committee members; the missionaries could append their own comments to the copies they sent out.

Legge wrote to London: "My own impression is that the so-called Christian Union is more a sink of iniquity ten-fold than our report will make it appear and my opinion is that the opium traffic is not so injurious to the cause of Christianity in China as that so-called Christian Union."[36] Legge concluded that if Gützlaff would not alter his appeals to the European public, "it is because the man is so shameless that nothing but absolute force would put him down." Though Walter Medhurst had earlier collaborated with Gützlaff in translating the Bible, his letters regarding Gützlaff and the Chinese Union were laced with sarcasm. If, he wrote, one deducted for native duplicity and Gützlaff's credulity, little would be left. Why, if there had been such an effusion of the Holy Spirit throughout the provinces of China, were no other Protestant missionaries aware of it?[37]

Gützlaff had generated great enthusiasm and high expectations for the Christianization of China. He had reported hundreds of baptisms and dozens of evangelists in the far interior of China. He was preparing to print tens of thousands of inexpensive New Testaments. All this, while he was a full-time employee of the British administration. What were the full-time missionaries reporting? A few tens of converts, with counsels of patience and understanding. A few boys in parochial schools, but a high dropout rate. A new translation of the Bible, but irreconcilable disagreements over Chinese terminology for God, the Holy Ghost, and baptism. Some progress in mastering a fearfully difficult language. Medhurst remarked that Gützlaff almost made the full-time missionaries seem unnecessary. As early as 1848, the head of the British tract society had written Legge that strong appeals for the Chinese Union were being made in England and many were surprised at the society's apparent neglect of the openings noticed by Gützlaff.[38] The secretary of the London Missionary Society also wrote Legge that he was being asked what his society was doing to support the Chinese Union; perhaps some of the best members of the Chinese Union could be employed as colporteurs by the society's missionaries.[39] Church society missionaries felt that they were being unfavorably contrasted with Gützlaff and it was essential that they set the record straight.

Enmity between Legge and Gützlaff had a long and bitter history. In many respects, the two were polar opposites. A retiring scholar who took the pulpit regularly in the local church but rarely went on preaching tours, Legge concentrated on study of the written language, on supervision of a small school, and on translations. According to one report, he never mastered the local dialect sufficiently to be an effective preacher to the masses. He was typical of the church missionary in setting Western mainstream standards for baptism and ordination. Upon Gützlaff's departure for England and Europe in the fall of 1849, Legge had warned the London secretary not to be taken in by Gützlaff's eloquence. Gützlaff, he said, was a full-time government employee and he queried: Was it reasonable to believe that Gützlaff was able to find time to organize and carry on a great spiritual movement among a people so sunk in apathy, sensuality, covetousness, and deceit as the Chinese? Where was the necessary organization of infant communities, the oversight of them, and the discipline?[40]

The freewheeling and flamboyant Gützlaff was, in contrast, highly adept at picking up dialects and his goal was spreading the Good Word, not building denominational congregations. His relations with his Chinese helpers might have been that of patron to client, but they seem to have been cordial, and Gützlaff consistently defended the sincerity and dedication of his evangelists. One thing Gützlaff and Legge had in common: neither was easy to live with. Legge was frequently at odds with members of his own mission and the correspondence files of his mission contain more than one letter complaining of Legge's intolerance of those differing with him.[41] Likewise, however enamoring Gützlaff was on short acquaintance, his egotism, self-righteous obsession with his cause, and inability to accept criticism from colleagues alienated long-term associates.

By the late 1840s Gützlaff and Legge had ceased to be on speaking terms. Legge explained that one reason for the formal interrogation of Chinese Union members was that it was impossible for him to ask Gützlaff in person for information. Legge would, of course, go on to win fame as the incomparable translator of the Chinese classics. Gützlaff's empire went down in disgrace upon his death. How much this has affected the historiography of the Chinese Union would be difficult to say.

Hamberg, Gützlaff, and the Chinese Union

Hamberg was also defensive in relations with his home society and wished to prove the rectitude of his position. According to Gützlaff's plan, the Basel Society expected Hamberg and Lechler to go into the interior, to live with and as the Chinese, and to supervise the Chinese evangelists. On their first night in Hong Kong, Gützlaff took them to their Chinese home, which they were to share with their helpers and language teachers. They recoiled in shock before the dirt, darkness, and poverty of their cramped quarters.[42] Even Mrs. Gützlaff took pity on them, insisting that they stay in the Gützlaff home for a few days. When they did venture into Chinese villages, both Lechler and Hamberg had disheartening experiences: robberies, indifference and hostility among the populace, frustrations over their inability to communicate, squeeze by assistants, dissatisfaction with the preaching of the Chinese evangelists.

A rigid, perhaps even melancholic individual, Hamberg reacted negatively to the Chinese in a way that was self-defeating. On one of his early visits to the home of an assistant, he found pictures of gods and ancestors on the wall and immediately ripped them down.[43] The father of the Chinese preacher was enraged. The son might be a convert, he said, but the house belonged to the family, not to the son. If the family desired to pay homage to their ancestors and the deities, they had a right to do so. Less than four months after arrival, Hamberg was excusing his infrequent and restricted itinerations by detailing to the Basel Society the dangers and hardships, including the likelihood of illness.[44] Again in 1848, Hamberg explained that he was in Hong Kong because that was an excellent place to study the language, so necessary to effective preaching. He pleaded with Basel on more than one occasion to be patient in expecting results. In the summer of 1848, Hamberg moved to a market town on the mainland coast north of Hong Kong. He wrote that he was obeying the will of the Lord and the "dear committee," though he had a sense of isolation and unease in the midst of Chinese society.[45]

By the end of 1848 Hamberg had dismissed all of his Chinese Union preachers assigned to posts in the deeper interior, while retaining only three or four trusted helpers. These he worked with on a day-to-day basis. In May 1849 he returned unexpectedly to his station to find two of his assistants smoking opium; they were so stupefied, he remarked, that they just grinned and replied flippantly to his exclamations.[46] Such depression settled upon Hamberg that he went into seclusion and was unable to carry on any missionary activities for days. Hamberg decided on 15 June 1849 to abandon the station because of piracy and local feuding. He departed hurriedly in the middle of the night just ahead of the pirates. His assistants, temporarily left behind, absconded with his clock, his tub, and other items. Hamberg's reaction was that all goes well as long as you are giving the Chinese money, but if anything happens to stop the flow, they begin immediately to show their bad side.[47] As a result, Hamberg, who had once criticized most foreign missionaries for living in the "English manner," came to advocate their emphasis on intensive rather than extensive evangelization. By July 1849 Hamberg was expressing sorrow about a break in good relations with the Basel committee: "What the Committee asked of us, we could not deliver; what we wanted, the Committee was not inclined to endorse." Hamberg, unlike Gützlaff, was not an independent missionary and he had in the final analysis to account to his society and justify his actions. He remained associated with the Basel society, so that he had all the more reason to defend his stance vis-à-vis Gützlaff.

That Hamberg's relations with Chinese Union members would be uneasy comes as no surprise, and it is interesting to examine the tactics the Chinese assistants employed. When he sought to incorporate some Chinese assistants in administration, they declined, saying that the selection of headmen would be difficult and they feared that those elected would be inadequate. They requested Hamberg to continue in the Gützlaff manner, that is, take full responsibility. In a subtle defensive move, the Hong Kong assistants sent Hamberg a letter on 1 October 1849. They insisted that irregular conduct was impermissible and that those who remained in Hong Kong after being commissioned to a tour should be expelled. But they also requested that when slanderous reports came to the "teacher's" attention, he would hold a general open hearing, for "a biased ear will leave him in the dark." Above all, they desired that Hamberg continue Gützlaff's practices without change, sending out elder disciples to preach and instructing younger disciples. Hamberg acceded to the request of the Chinese that he retain sole responsibility.[48]

Dissatisfaction on both sides mounted. Like many Westerners, Hamberg failed to appreciate social mores designed to avoid direct confrontation and prevent loss of face. "Truth was truth," according to the Westerner, and Hamberg came to join those who viewed the Chinese as a nation of liars. In the confessions secured by Hamberg during May and June 1850, several members readily admitted that it was their father or grandfather who came from a distant province, not themselves. For Hamberg, this was evidence of deliberate falsification; for a Chinese who often identified himself with his ancestral home, the admission might have seemed less serious. Other confessions were more damaging: some admitted that they had not always gone to their stated destinations. Hamberg interpreted the evidence as a "general confession on the part of the members, as to their former deceitful conduct." His criticisms had been vindicated.

By late spring 1850, those studying in Hong Kong had been reduced to about forty out of the several hundred with whom Hamberg started, but the remnant membership was split into two factions: a small group of seven or eight who considered themselves clients of their patron Hamberg, and approximately thirty who looked to Gützlaff. Under these circumstances, discovering the reality behind accusations, confessions, and counterconfessions became next to impossible. Many of those who had in June signed a request to Hamberg to continue as administrator sent criticisms of Hamberg to Gützlaff in the fall. They contrasted Gützlaff's regular morning and evening instruction and his willingness to go out to preach in all kinds of weather with Hamberg's conduct. The latter, they wrote, remained quietly at home, looking out upon the sea but not venturing out upon it to preach. He had also ceased to send out Chinese preachers or to provide support. Though he was supposed to give lessons at nine o'clock, he often played the piano instead. He did not observe the separation of men and women, but talked intimately with his assistant's wife, "even caressing her." He and his assistants used economic threats to extract confessions and persuade members to defame one another. Other letters and journals sent to Gützlaff included protestations of faithful performance and a lamentation over the difficulty that a Chinese and a Westerner (i.e., Hamberg) had in understanding what was in the heart of the other.[49] Many of these criticisms would be repeated in the counterconfessions obtained by Gützlaff in January 1851.

Hamberg's group, meanwhile, complied with his suggestion that they make "a clear and brief report as to the real state of the union."[50] Though they confessed that there had been deceit after the rapid expansion of the union, the tone of the statement was equivocal. They insisted that the initial members had conscientiously fulfilled their duties and explained that later members were in such financial plight because of debts and the low pay that they were unable to complete their assignments. Gützlaff had, on the whole, exerted himself very much for a good object. A conflict of loyalties (patron, Chinese, economic?) pervaded the document and made it a vindication of neither Hamberg nor Gützlaff.

Relations between Hamberg and Gützlaff were going from bad to worse as personal egos and even careers and empires became involved. Gützlaff's reactions to criticisms undoubtedly contributed to the polarization. Gützlaff was so totally committed to his plan for conversion of China via national evangelists that he could acknowledge no alternatives. Like many radicals and revolutionaries, he yearned to see the accomplishment of his goals during his lifetime. Illness, age, obstacles, and criticisms only persuaded him to push ever faster and harder, ignoring mistakes and deterrents. Isolated from the Hong Kong missionary community, he had run the Chinese Union as his personal operation without checks by colleagues; as a loner, he had become less and less capable of assimilating negative information. Those who opposed his methods defied Jesus' commission to his Apostles and to all disciples to carry the gospel to every heathen. Those who questioned the efficacy of preaching the Word and distributing the Scriptures lacked faith in the Holy Spirit. They were answerable to God, not to him.[51] He never backed away from his insistence that conversion was the work of God, not man. "If God therefore has aroused men from the sleep of sin and drawn them to the Son of his eternal love, they may be safely received in baptism." In lands of darkness, relapses could be expected, for converts were subject to the allurements of their pagan countrymen and continued to be influenced by earlier training. The correct response of the missionary was forgiveness, kindness, and further instruction, not malice. Gützlaff berated Hamberg for harshness toward the Chinese, for not loving and trusting them, for alienating them instead of helping them return to the right path.[52]

As the son of an artisan, Gützlaff had found an avenue of social mobility in the ministry. As a venturesome romantic, he had found in the China mission an outlet for his ambition. Few other means of mobility existed in early-nineteenth-century Pomerania and few challenges were as great as the China mission. But Gützlaff, like many who had risen via this route, remained an outsider.[53] With his piety and total commitment to his cause, he could sweep people off their feet on initial contact, but he had difficulty in sustaining workable relationships with equals. In British-dominated Hong Kong, Gützlaff's sense of being outside was accentuated. He was looked upon as gauche, as an "enthusiast" lacking in moderation and decorum. One of Gützlaff's British defenders found Gützlaff's Pollyannaism unbecoming and tried to explain its source: either it was because he had adopted the Chinese manner or because in the British service he was constantly in contact with those who, he thought, were trying to thwart him.[54]

Gützlaff found more in common with other individualists such as William Burns and Issachar Roberts than with mainstream missionaries. He had not only itinerated with the two, but had provided housing and financial support to Roberts. His most cordial relations were with those who posed no social challenge, that is, those under his tutelage or in his employ. These he felt he could trust. Toward these poor souls, he could show compassion and understanding. They would return his favors in kind. The barrage of criticism from the missionary community, even those assigned to work under him, he found unacceptable and malevolent. By the time Gützlaff returned to China in early 1851, he was more isolated than ever, unable to enlist the cooperation of most missionaries and dependent on his Chinese assistants for contact and information. His defense had no audience.

The major reason for the decline in support on the home front was, of course, the contrast between Gützlaff's claims and what seemed to be reality. Christians in the West had even less of a context in which to place the failings of the Chinese converts than did missionaries. Their sense of letdown, of having been deceived, was unmitigated by experience in the field. With the founding of dozens of support organizations, existing mission and Bible societies had become uneasy about competition for funds and personnel. Legge and other missionaries believed that attention and monies were being shunted away from legitimate missions. Gützlaff had originally conceived of publicity and fund raising as the function of the support unions; the latter would feed into the regular societies, to whom the missionaries would be responsible. With significant support coming from outside church organizations and in the face of opposition from certain mission societies, Gützlaff began to expand his ambitions for the support unions. German mission societies, like the English ones, grew apprehensive. Gützlaff's death and the demise of most support societies occurred before transformation could be completed. Denominational organizations henceforth represented the mainstream of China missions.

Assessment and Legacies

Several support organizations survived and gradually became sending societies. Among these were the Berlin Missionary Society for China; the Berlin Women's Missionary Society for China; the Chinese Evangelization Society, precursor of the CIM; and the Pomeranian Mission Union for China.

Gützlaff was an early advocate of a change in the policy of sending only married women out. Single women, he thought, could accomplish more than missionary wives, for married women soon found much of their time devoted to rearing children and maintaining a household. The death rate among missionary wives, furthermore, was exceedingly high and they were not free to operate in the interior, as Gützlaff desired. Mission societies, including the Berlin Women's Missionary Society for China and the CIM, slowly began to commission single women. By the early twentieth century, single females constituted an important segment in the missionary community and they were making a contribution not only as evangelists, but also as educators and role models for Chinese girls. The foundling home for girls maintained by the Berlin women's society in Hong Kong provided a needed social service and, in addition, made Christian converts, furnished Christian wives, and trained missionary assistants. In 1905, for example, the society reported twenty-three baptisms and three former residents who had gone out as Christian workers or assistants.[55]

In some ways, progress toward indigenization of the Protestant church in China was retarded by the Chinese Union affair. Though all missionaries looked forward to eventual autonomy, they differed on the timing. Gützlaff would grant a high degree of autonomy to the Chinese from the very beginning, with foreign missionaries as tutors and guides. Most missionaries agreed with Hamberg that for years, perhaps for decades, the Chinese ought not to be left without Western control, ought not to be charged with heavier duties than they were ready to fulfill. Those who provided the funds for missions should be assured that their monies were employed responsibly. The fate of the Chinese Union, in the opinion of most missionaries, validated this viewpoint.

In other ways the work of the Chinese Union contributed to indigenization. During the late 1840s and early 1850s individual villagers had been converted and small Christian congregations and communities had slowly developed. These could provide a supportive environment and monitoring services helpful to converts and missionaries. As the Western evangelists ventured farther into the interior, they came upon individuals who had received copies of the Bible and Christian tracts.[56] They found villages with several Christian households, many in Hakka territory. A fragile infrastructure which the missionaries could expand and strengthen had evolved. The missionaries might question the depth of Christian understanding among the inquirers, but the Basel missionaries drew a significant portion of those baptized during the 1850s and 1860s from this group.

In contrast to Hamberg's disillusioning experience with robbers, unfaithful assistants, and local hostility, Philip Winnes met with considerable support on an itineration in Hakka territory during 1855. Twice, he was tipped off that robbers were lying in wait for him, so he changed his routing. He had little trouble finding housing because converts opened their doors despite the risks, and provided him with an entrée to other villages by contacting relatives there. On this tour Winnes met a Gützlaff convert holding the lowest-level examination degree; he and Lechler took the man in their employ as their Hakka-language teacher while giving him further instruction in Christian doctrine.[57] Expansion of Christian congregations in this territory enabled the Basel mission to raise one of the towns, Zhang-kengjing (Tschong hang kang), to a main station some 25 years later.[58] Many of the converts had originally been made by Chinese workers, even if baptism and acceptance into the church awaited the coming of the missionary.

The Basel mission continued to incorporate Chinese in its work and to rely heavily on them as evangelists. In the Hakka community, Basel missionaries had a field yielding a higher percent of converts than most other areas. Evangelists in the 1860s and 1870s came upon villagers who had learned of Christianity from the Taipings, from Chinese Union members, or from both, and they were able to build on these foundations.[59] Modifying Gützlaff's methodology, Lechler and Basel missionaries generally retained the right to baptize, at least until there were ordained Chinese ministers. They also worked in close association with a small number of assistants, many of the early ones having been recruited via the Chinese Union.[60]

Both major centers of the Basel Hakka church in Guangdong originated with former Chinese Union members. Jiang Jiaoren belonged to an influential Hakka lineage in Lilang, north of the New Territories. Despite Jiang's confession that he had not always made the trips on which he had reported, Hamberg retained him as an assistant. Jiang, after further instruction by Hamberg, became an ardent missionary and converted numerous

Hakka kinsmen and residents in the Lilang area. Building on the small congregations founded by Jiang, Hamberg and other Basel missionaries moved to the interior and in time the Lilang region became the locus of a boys' school, a girls' school, and a seminary as well as a dozen or so churches.

Zhang Fuxing, also a former Chinese Union member, founded the Basel mission to the Hakka in northeast Guangdong.[61] After further instruction and rebaptism by Hamberg plus experience with Jiang Jiaoren in Lilang, Zhang returned in 1852 to his home district of Wuhua, Meizhou. There he converted numerous relatives, some of whom joined him in proselytizing and distributing religious literature. Though Zhang and other evangelists made regular trips to the coast to report to the Basel missionaries and obtain funds and books, a Basel missionary first visited the area only in 1862. By this time there were about 170 believers located in some twenty hamlets.[62] With this foundation, Basel began in 1864 to station Westerners in Wuhua, while Chinese catechists continued to conduct much of the day-to-day personal work and at least one station came under the leadership of a Chinese preacher during the 1870s.[63] By the late nineteenth century, Meizhou, the Hakka heartland, had also become the heartland of the Hakka Christian church; even today some 90 congregations continue to function in this region. Whatever the original motives of Jiang and Zhang for joining the Chinese Union, nurturing by the Basel missionaries along with evangelistic work itself had led to internalization of the Christian faith. Not only did they become dedicated workers, but they founded Christian families which for generations provided the church with pastors, Bible women, and teachers.

Refinement of Gützlaff's approach enabled Basel to move more rapidly toward a self-governing and self-reliant church than did many other societies. Even the brief sojourns of Lechler and his Chinese Union assistants in the Shantou area had yielded results, as indicated in a letter of appreciation to Lechler by a Presbyterian missionary in Shantou in 1881.[64] Several of Lechler's converts had recently participated in organizing a presbytery and one congregation expressed a desire to call their own pastor, toward whose support they promised $150 annually. Basel often pointed with pride to the Wuhua mission as an early example of progress toward indigenization.

Despite disillusionment in Europe and a temporary decline in support for China missions consequent upon the plight of the Chinese Union, Gützlaff had raised the consciousness of Western congregations regarding world missions and China in particular. For a century missions would continue to be an important aspect of church activities. Dominating the work was the church mission, but society missions also participated, the most noted being the CIM and later the YMCA. Gützlaff, as an independent missionary, was an inspiration to Hudson Taylor, who collected funds for the Chinese Union and publicized the needs of its English support society. This society was in 1852 transformed into a sending society, the Chinese Evangelization Society, and it was under the latter's auspices that Hudson Taylor first went to China.[65] The Chinese Evangelization Society and its successor, the CIM, designated its field as interior China, where missionaries had not yet penetrated. Like the Chinese Union, the CIM espoused ecumenism and evangelicalism; by the turn of the century it had become one of the largest Protestant missions in China.

In contrast to the emphases of most church missions, these strains spoke to many Chinese Christians and became especially prominent in independent Chinese churches. Indigenization and ecumenism in missions have recently gained popularity among Christians of varying persuasions. With this has come a delineation of the foreign missionary's role more nearly in accord with that of Gützlaff than with the position of most nineteenth-century missionaries. Though Gützlaff's attempt to foster an indigenous Chinese Christianity via the Chinese Union met disaster at the time, in the twentieth century the goal has been revived. Direct historical linkages exist between the Chinese Union heritage and Protestant Christianity on the mainland and in Taiwan and Hong Kong today.

CHAPTER 16

Contextualizing Protestant Publishing in China: The Wenshe, 1924–1928

PETER CHEN-MAIN WANG

Wen yi zai dao (literature is for conveying the truth) has been a time-honored idea in the Chinese tradition. This phrase implies that if the writing is good, the truth will spread widely, and consequently there will be great harmony in the world. Conversely, if the expression of an idea is problematic, the truth cannot reach the people and great disorder will result. Therefore, in the Chinese mind truth and literature are closely related.

The mid-1920s were troubling times for Chinese Christians. The Christian community was constantly threatened by attacks from the scientific world, from nationalistic groups, and from various anti-Christian groups.[1] Chinese Christian intellectuals of the time therefore began to examine themselves and the situation of Christianity in China.[2] One of the most important conclusions they drew was that there must be something wrong with Chinese Christian literature, and that this deficiency constituted a hindrance to the dissemination of the truth.

The Zhonghua Jidujiao Wenshe (National Christian Literature Association of China, Wenshe for short hereafter) was the single most active and influential organization in the 1920s to advocate the indigenization of Christianity. This group was organized in 1924 by a few Christian leaders and foreign missionaries who felt that the lack of an effective indigenous Christian literature was hindering the spread of Christianity. Therefore, they decided to introduce Christian culture through a sinicized style of writing with the publishing of the *Wenshe Monthly* (*Wenshe yuekan*) and pamphlets and books. The association, however, was forced to cease operations in mid-1928 and to disband in early 1930 because of financial difficulties. During the four years of its existence, the Wenshe had a very strong impact on Christian circles and occupied a vital place in Chinese church history.[3]

This chapter examines the practical aspects of indigenization proposed by the Wenshe. It first provides a short introduction to the impact of nationalism and the anti-Christian movement on the church and the organization and history of the Wenshe. It then examines the Wenshe's attitudes and criticism of contemporary Christian literature in China. Finally, it considers the proposals and practices of the Wenshe as they related to the reform of Christian literature in China.

The Anti-Christian Movement and the Rise of the Wenshe

The anti-Christian movement of the 1920s had its origins in the New Culture and May Fourth movements of the late 1910s. These latter movements stimulated Chinese intellectuals to look upon questions of national affairs and social realities from the viewpoints of democracy and science. Under these influences, intellectuals began to criticize the warlords for obstructing the development of democracy and the foreign powers for imperialist transgressions in China and for providing assistance to the warlords. As a result, anti-imperialist and antiwarlord sentiment was widespread in Chinese society. At the same time, the spirit of scientism, accompanied by the growing popularity of pragmatism among intellectual circles, promoted the iconoclastic rejection of superstition and religious beliefs. Under these circumstances, Christianity, with all its Western cultural baggage, had not yet been criticized seriously, but it was soon to encounter organized anti-Christian sentiment.

The immediate source of the anti-Christian movement was a meeting of the World's Student Christian Federation at Qinghua University in Beijing in April 1922. Because of the propagation and wide discussion of the meeting in Christian periodicals, some Chinese students in Shanghai were stimulated to organize an Anti-Christian Student Federation. A public statement of their objectives was circulated, and this encouraged similar actions among students in other cities. Much of the criticism of Christianity was based on the perception of the wickedness of capitalism and the close relationship between Christianity and leading capitalist countries. Some critics also reflected Bolshevist influences in using such statements as "we are positive that Christianity is the transformation of capitalism and that churches and YMCAs are the capitalists' instruments in the exploitation of the proletarian class" and "Marx said that religion is the opium of the people."[4]

The second phase of the anti-Christian movement began in 1924 in association with the "educational rights recovery movement" and the general anti-imperialist sentiment of the time. Christian schools and churches enjoyed the protection of the unequal treaties and strongly emphasized religious instruction in curriculum and in school life generally. With the rise of the anti-Christian movement in 1922, Chinese educators and scholars began to criticize Christian education from the point of view of national rights and urged the government to rescind the special privileges accorded foreign missionaries and churches. In addition to the question of educational rights, criticism during the second phase of the anti-Christian movement focused on the close association of Christianity with the imperialist foreign powers. The authors of these criticisms pointed out that the imperialist countries took advantage of antimissionary riots to expand their claims to special protection from the law. They also alleged that many missionaries cooperated with the imperialists in order to expand the missionary enterprise.[5] The climax of the second phase of this movement was the outbreak of large demonstrations in many cities against Christian churches before and after the Christmas holidays in 1924.

The third phase of the anti-Christian movement began with the May Thirtieth Incident of 1925.[6] The nationalistic sentiment aroused by this incident led Chinese activists to denounce imperialism as well as Christian churches and their educational institutions, which in their eyes were closely related to imperialism. This anti-Christian sentiment was stimulated in part by measures taken by the Chinese Communist Party (CCP) to arouse peasants and workers into violent action against the church.[7] Some members of the Guomindang (GMD) were also antagonistic to Christianity; anti-Christian ideas were even incorporated into teaching materials at the Whampoa Military Academy.[8] Because of the spread of anti-Christian thinking among the GMD officer corps, and because of similar beliefs among the CCP membership as well as the left wing of the GMD, the Northern Expedition forces attacked and occupied Christian churches and church properties on their march north in late 1926. As a result, many churches, YMCAs, and church-sponsored schools and hospitals were forced to close. This phase was climaxed by the killing of several missionaries in Nanjing in March 1927. Following the protests of foreign diplomats as well as an anti-leftist party-purification campaign within the GMD, anti-Christian activities declined rapidly.[9]

The anti-Christian movement of the 1920s thus started in 1922 and came to an end in 1928. Although it lasted only six years, Christian churches in China suffered an unprecedented impact on their activities. Because of this situation brought on by nationalistic fervor, Bolshevist influence, and the Northern Expedition, many Chinese believers and Christian missionaries began to consider seriously the implications of the changing times.

The Wenshe was organized in the midst of the anti-Christian movement. The initial idea for the founding of this organization can be traced back to the establishment of the China Christian Literature Council, organized by the China Continuation Committee in 1918 at the request of the British and American Conferences of Missionary Societies to allocate the distribution of the missionary societies' literature grants and to promote cooperation among Christian literary institutions.[10] But even that organization was not instructed to develop the indigenous literary materials that some members of the council felt were sorely lacking.

The National Christian Council (Zhonghua Jidujiao xiejinhui, hereafter NCC) was established in 1922 and paid special attention to producing indigenous doctrinal literature. However, since the NCC was composed of representatives of many different denominations, it sought to avoid any literary project that might give rise to denominational contention.[11] Therefore, it authorized the China Christian Literature Council to consider the type of literature then needed and the ways and means of producing it. The latter then called in eleven Christian writers and several missionaries (including Frank Rawlinson, John Leighton Stuart, Henry T. Hodgkin, and R. Brooks) in September 1923 to discuss the issue. All of the participants concluded that Chinese Christian literature must be indigenized, or it would remain awkward, difficult to read, and lacking in vigor.[12]

At the end of 1923 a second meeting was held, at which it was decided to create an organization to be called Zhonghua Jidujiao wenzi shiye cujinshe (Society for the Advancement of Christian Literature in China), to be headed by Chinese with missionaries serving as their advisors. Two months later, the society was formally founded and it adopted a provisional organizational outline. Zhao Zichen (T. C. Chao) was elected president and Cheng Jingyi (C. Y. Cheng), Yu Rizhang (David Z. T. Yui), and others were named to the executive committee. Li Rongfang and others were designated to serve as members of the membership committee.

In May 1924, the society held its first formal meeting in Shanghai. Since too few members were in attendance, Zhao Zichen was authorized to appoint a general secretary to initiate the society's programs. Zhao selected Shen Sizhuang (J. Wesley Shen), who occupied the chair of Old Testament studies at Nanking Theological Seminary, as the associate executive secretary of the society and asked him to begin work at Soochow University. Since the society lacked any funds, it started with a loan of US $200 from

Dr. D. Willard Lyon of the YMCA and a donation of $1,200 from Rev. Edwin C. Lobenstine of the NCC. At this time, John R. Mott, longtime leader of the YMCA and head of the Institute of Social and Religious Research (hereafter ISRR), took an interest in this society that was to become the Wenshe and decided to offer financial assistance, which was a great help and source of encouragement to the members of the society.[13] From March 1925 on, a provisional office with two staff members was set up at Soochow University. A national conference was held on 18 February 1926, which adopted a formal constitution and changed the name of the organization to Zhonghua Jidujiao Wenshe. The conferees also decided to move its office from Soochow to Shanghai. The objective of the society was now "to promote the production of indigenous Christian literature to encourage the reading of such materials by the Chinese."

Most Wenshe members were church leaders of the time. Cheng Jingyi was the general secretary of both the NCC and the Church of Christ in China; Yu Rizhang served as the general secretary of the YMCA in China for twelve years and as the chairman of the NCC for ten; Liu Tingfang (Timothy Tingfang Lew) was the dean of the Religious College of Yenching University. Other distinguished church leaders included Frank Rawlinson, Henry T. Hodgkin, John Leighton Stuart, Zhao Zichen, Hu Yigu (Y. K. Woo), Wang Zhengting, Wang Zhixin, and Yan Yangchu (James Y. Yen).

The first issue of the official organ of the Wenshe—the *Wenshe Monthly*—appeared in October 1925, and the last (vol. 3, no. 8) in June 1928. Initially, the stated purpose of the *Monthly* was to promote indigenous Christian literature and indigenous Christianity. Later, the contents of the *Monthly* were enlarged to include articles on "Christian thought and practices," church history, church and society, church and state, and Chinese churches.[14] In 1926, Wang Zhixin, a professor of Chinese studies at the Nanking Theological Seminary, was invited to become the editor of the *Monthly*. According to one scholar, frequent contributors to the *Monthly* can be divided into three groups: professors at theological seminaries, church leaders, and those who worked for various literary institutions of the Protestant church.[15]

The *Wenshe Monthly* was the most outspoken religious publication of its time. During its life, the *Monthly* witnessed many important historical events, such as the anti-Christian movement, the Northern Expedition, and major reforms in Christian education initiated by the Nationalist government. The *Monthly* responded without hesitation to the questions of indigenization and the relationship between church and state, and it clearly expressed a political position toward the Nationalist government. The editors conceived of it as a forum for public debate and thus provided its readers with the opportunity to exchange views and opinions in a special section. These measures made the *Wenshe Monthly* both challenging and controversial in the eyes of various churchmen. Some conservative Christians and foreign missionaries were not happy about this situation and even sought to bring it to an end.

Although the opponents of the Wenshe occasionally voiced their criticism in print, the decisive attack on the Wenshe was launched clandestinely.[16] The opponents directly appealed to its financial sponsor — the ISRR in New York — charging the *Wenshe Monthly* with provoking unrest among the Christian population. Documentation of their discontent and the appeal can only be found in private letters between missionaries. For example, Donald MacGillivray, the general secretary of the missionary-run Christian Literature Society, wrote to John R. Mott, the chairman of the board of the ISRR, and stated that the Wenshe propagated "heresy."[17] As a result of these attacks and other factors, in a special meeting of the ISRR, called on 27 June 1928, the board abandoned its position of active support and decided to discontinue its patronage of the Wenshe.[18] This decision forced the Wenshe to suspend its activities with the publication of the June 1928 issue.[19] Thus, the main impetus of the indigenization movement during the Republican period died with this final issue of the magazine, a fact that underscores the unique position the Wenshe occupied in Chinese church history. The next section will illustrate the challenging themes that prompted the conservative reaction.

Wenshe's Criticism of Contemporary Christian Literature

The *Wenshe Monthly* paid great attention to Christian literature and repeatedly urged the creation of indigenous Christian literature. This position was maintained throughout its existence. The editors approached the issue in two ways: first, they called attention to the problems of contemporary Christian literature in China, and, second, they pointed out how to improve and create new indigenous Christian literature.

Although the authors of the *Wenshe Monthly* affirmed that the Christian literary enterprise had made a great contribution to spreading Christianity in China, they argued that it had failed to keep pace with the changing times and lacked contemporary relevance.[20] Operating from the standpoint that literature is intended to convey the truth, they held that pharisaical Christian literature would naturally cause difficulties in preaching the gospel.

Consequently, the contributors to *Wenshe Monthly* pointed out many problems in contemporary Christian literature.

The first objection was that foreign missionaries controlled the management, including the purse strings, and thus directed the Christian literary enterprise in China. Many missionaries followed publication plans as well as methods of supervision dictated by their mission boards. Most missionaries were handicapped in their service to China by the influence of their home churches, insufficient understanding of the Chinese situation, and a lack of true understanding of Chinese language and culture.[21] Naturally, these deficiencies caused Christian publications under their control to be out of tune with the needs of China. As one author insisted, "Those people [missionaries in literary enterprise] are at the same time like the masters of the church. If something lacks their permission, no matter how important the work is to the time, or how the work meets the urgent needs of the audience, [its publication] will be arbitrarily prohibited. There is no hope at all for its publication."[22]

The foreign missionaries' persistence in managing all church facilities made them behave arrogantly, and also made it difficult for Chinese Christians to cooperate with them. As a consequence, Chinese Christians had either to withdraw from literary service or compromise their positions. Those who conformed to missionary wishes could not bring their literary abilities into full play, since they were often prevented from touching upon certain issues because of the political or theological sensitivities of certain denominations.[23] Operating under the numerous restrictions imposed by the missionaries, Chinese Christians produced publications that were often regarded as vulgar and hence unable to win respect from inside or outside the church.[24] This tended to limit the impact of the Christian literary movement. Obviously, this critique had political as well as literary dimensions.

Still another problem of this period was that most Christian publications represented translations of English-language works; only a few were indigenous. According to a survey of the literary output of the period, prior to the founding of the Wenshe 90 percent of a total of 2,300 Christian publications were either translations or condensations of Western works.[25] This phenomenon was caused by two factors: first, as mentioned above, Chinese Christian intellectuals were not free to create their own theological literature, and second, foreign missionaries had a strong preference for Western materials, which they knew and could understand. Western religious tracts naturally reflected Western — not Chinese — cultural values, and thus were often ineffective in reaching a Chinese audience.

Large numbers of translations of Western-language religious works were completed by foreign missionaries and their Chinese assistants. Usually missionaries dictated translations in colloquial Chinese and their assistants polished the diction.[26] A few articles published in the *Wenshe Monthly* criticized those Chinese assistants for their poor literary skills. Some missionaries tried their own hand at writing Chinese, but this also often proved unsatisfactory. The consensus was that as literature works of this kind were shallow: they lacked any literary distinction and tended to be simplistic in thought and form.[27] One *Wenshe Monthly* writer explained that the reason missionaries with a good general knowledge of China could not compose good Chinese was that they lacked the stylistic skills needed to penetrate deeply into the Chinese mind and achieve any kind of popularity.[28] An opinion shared widely by *Wenshe Monthly* authors was that "the literature of the Chinese church must be composed by Chinese believers, not copied from the foreigners. It [should] not be replaced by English works, but also [should] not adopt English-style Chinese. Neither is suitable for Chinese society."[29] Thus this critique, like the earlier one, while on the surface literary in nature, was actually a hard-hitting indictment of foreign domination of the Chinese church.

This leads to the third problem pointed out by Chinese critics: Christian literature of the time was not able to relate to the contemporary needs of society. The Wenshe writers criticized the style of most Christian literature, which did not follow modern literary trends. Under the influence of the May Fourth Movement, *baihua* ("plain language" or vernacular Chinese) and the use of punctuation marks had become popular in China. However, some Christian authors resisted this trend and opposed the use of *baihua* as well as punctuation. Wang Zhixin, later the editor of the *Wenshe Monthly*, dealt with the problem in a straightforward fashion in his article "How to Make Christian Literature Enter the Center of Society": "In their institutions which spend great amounts of money annually, those who are in charge of writing are either old-fashioned pedagogues or diehards who have never seen books on the new culture. They want to fight and gain a victory in the battle of literature of the renaissance by holding an [old-style] breech-loading gun. Even the most foolish man will know that they have no chance at all."[30]

A critical problem was that most Chinese writers were unable to integrate Christian religious values with Chinese culture. This can be considered a mortal defect of Christian literary service. The authors of the Wenshe argued that the purpose of literary service was to cultivate the Way (*dao*) in the Chinese people. However, since Christian literature seldom touched upon Chinese beliefs, customs, or traditions, to say nothing of religious experience, it was difficult to move the Chinese.[31] This could be attributed to the missionary control of Christian literature at large.

In addition, the Wenshe criticized those who worked for literary enterprises. In the eyes of Wenshe adherents, the literary problem derived in part from a lack of true devotion to the work at hand. Generally speaking, there was an insufficient pool of Christian writers, which resulted in impoverished contents, ill-argued compositions, and deficient literary qualities. Only a few writers were recognized as having high literary skills, but because of the heavy demand for contributions, some writers responded in a perfunctory manner and failed to create anything significant, while others overworked themselves and were unable to carry on.

Furthermore, some contributors to the *Monthly* believed many contemporary Christian writers lacked sufficient understanding of Christianity and Chinese culture. Such writers, they felt, either drew absurd inferences from the literature or simply imitated Western Christian works. This phenomenon was described by a Wenshe writer with three Chinese characters: *tou* (to steal), *lou* (base), and *fan* (to engage in trade). He said:

This behavior, such as taking possession of the ideas of others and changing their outward look in order to avoid recognition by others, or copying the literature of other magazines without announcing the fact, is no different than robbing or stealing. What is it if it is not stealing?

They argue with shallow reasoning and compose vulgar and error-ridden works. They do not know the work *Shuo wen* and absurdly dissect Chinese characters [in order to suit their interpretations]. For example, they combine *si* (four) and *fei* (evil) as *zui* (sin), or *wu* (none) and *xin* (heart) as *e* (vice). They do not understand Confucian teachings and preposterously defame Confucius. . . . They even take communism to be the doctrine adopted by Jesus' disciples and regard war as not having been condemned by Jesus. They offer farfetched and dubious explanations [of doctrine] and thus are laughed at by those of profound knowledge. What is this if it is not base?

They respect lateral scripts [i.e., European languages] and believe in everything from abroad. There are many translations [of foreign Christian literature] and only a few original works of Chinese Christian literature. The so-called publishing institution is simply a foreign business firm to sell imported goods. The translation of foreign literature is not unimportant. But can we take it as the only purpose of the literary enterprise, without inquiring into the suitability of Western thought? That cannot avoid being ridiculed as cultural invasion. Furthermore, the purpose of Christian literature is to preach the truth, not business. Those writers [of Christian literature] work only for their monthly pay and do not question how a book can sell for such high prices. They treat their publications from the viewpoint of business. What is this if it is not engaging in trade?[32]

Chinese writers were also criticized for not being aggressive in their careers, in having no desire to achieve. They regarded their work only as a way of making a living, lacked any internal inspiration, had a propensity for materialism, and had no plan to cultivate the younger generation of writers.

At the same time, a lack of cooperation between various literary enterprises was also criticized.[33] Each enterprise only cared about its own publications and goals and rejected any cooperation on sales, circulation, or advertisements. Each enterprise placed strict restrictions on its employees, who were not allowed to write articles for other publications, even on their own time. Because of a lack of coordination, Christian enterprises seldom achieved individual distinction and often were repetitious and contentious. There were no joint publication offices, and literary enterprises had to rely on independent bookstores to sell their publications. Therefore, circulation was a major problem.

In sum, the *Wenshe Monthly* focused on three key problems facing the Christian literary enterprise: excessive control by foreign missionaries, ill-equipped and ill-prepared writers, and lack of coordination in publication efforts and logistics.

Reform Proposals and Practices of the Wenshe

Wenshe writers not only pointed out various problems that permeated church literary services, they also proposed many reforms and improvements. Their proposals were varied and addressed many different aspects of the problem, from the practical to the spiritual. Although they did not offer a complete program for the future, one cannot but be impressed by their sense of urgency as well as their persistent effort to move reform forward.

Let us consider their proposals for reform of church literary enterprises. The first is the right of autonomy. Since this matter involved the leadership of the church and church property, they did not wish to adopt radical methods, but suggested that Chinese Christians should make foreign missionaries aware of this matter by various means. They hoped that foreign missionaries would gradually transfer control to local people for the free expression of native opinion.[34] In order to promote and facilitate the devolution of church administration and property from foreign to Chinese hands, Shen Sizhuang drafted a "Recommendation for the Devolution of Church Administration and Property" and published it in both Chinese and English in the *Wenshe Monthly*.[35] His reason for providing an English version, the only such English-language writing published in the *Monthly*, would seem to have been for the benefit of foreign missionaries and readers. At the same time, some individuals suggested that Chinese Christians should organize and manage their own literary organizations. This was the only way, they argued, to assure the development of Chinese Christian literary enterprises according to Chinese visions and ideals.[36]

As for the lack of skilled writers, many articles suggested that the best way to settle this problem once and for all was simply to cultivate talent. Only with sufficient and able hands to help produce Christian literature could its effectiveness be increased.

The first set of solutions in effect constituted proposals for a wholesale revision of the curriculum and priorities of missionary-operated schools. Several writers suggested that every level in Christian schools should pay closer attention to Chinese history and literature, and at the same time improve the quality and treatment of their teachers of Chinese. At the time, Christian missionary schools claimed the protection of the unequal treaties; as a result, they were not subject to the supervision of the central government. Often a foreign missionary served as president of a school. The curriculum placed a strong emphasis on the Bible, Christian doctrine, Christian ethics, and English, instead of Chinese literature and history. As well, those who taught Chinese received a low salary. Under this kind of arrangement, students naturally lacked interest in Chinese language instruction and usually performed poorly in Chinese.[37]

Other articles suggested the establishment of an advanced institute or graduate school for the training of college graduates who were pious Christians and were interested in writing. These students would be trained in theology, Chinese, English, philosophy, ethics, and translation, as well as practical theology, such as mission work and evangelism. In order fully to develop their talents, those who completed this training would be well paid when they began their careers.[38] Other similar suggestions included adding related courses, such as composition, translation, and journalism, to the curriculum of Christian schools.[39]

In addition to advocating the cultivation of indigenous literary talent, the Wenshe introduced its own program to help young writers. It appropriated money for the education of talented students. Two students received financial assistance from the Wenshe; one of them, Zhu Weizhi, later achieved national prominence as a writer and was long active in Christian literary endeavors.[40]

The Wenshe also urged the integration of Christian faith and Chinese culture. Many writers cited the successful integration of Buddhist literature with Chinese culture as an example. Writers also argued that if Christianity was to become widely acceptable to the Chinese, it would have to follow the same path the early Buddhist monks had taken. There would have to be a vital core of Christian intellectuals with profound knowledge of Chinese culture, history, values, and the great literary works to introduce Christianity to the Chinese in terms they could appreciate.[41]

In order to improve the quality of Christian literature, some individuals suggested the formation of a literary examination board that would review all manuscripts before they were approved for publication and sale. In the past, many Christian publications had employed common language, poor reasoning, and absurd expressions, and this had aroused antipathy both within and outside the church. It was suggested on the one hand that comments from the examination board could help improve the quality of publications generally, and on the other that the board could assist in blocking the publication and distribution of much worthless and unattractive literature. Several authors urged the creation of a united church organization to preview all Christian literature. They believed that Christian publications, under the careful scrutiny of the proposed examination board, would become acceptable and even popular with the people, and therefore be influential.[42]

Wenshe writers suggested cooperation in many areas, including publication, responding to anti-Christian criticism, and dealing with the government. They recommended that a coordinating network among Christian literary agencies would not only be mutually helpful but also make it easier to create different features for different kinds of people. The *Monthly* called for the organizing of a new, strong, and powerful united front for the literary enterprise so as to deal with various problems, and for convening meetings for the cultivation of a spiritual life and personality.[43]

Another way to improve Christian literature, it was argued, would be to raise the spirit of criticism among Christian readers. As mentioned earlier, the editors of the *Wenshe Monthly* conceived of their publication as a forum for public debate and gave its readers an opportunity to exchange views and opinions in a special section. They believed that objective criticism based on truth, knowledge, and experience would promote the Christian literary enterprise.

The periodical paid great attention to the suggestions of its readers. At the beginning, the *Monthly* adopted a horizontal print format, but later, upon the request of its readers, changed to the traditional vertical columns of print. When a reader suggested in mid-1927 the readoption of the earlier format, the editor carried a note in the *Monthly* seeking others' opinions. Some readers' suggestions proved to be beneficial. For example, one reader,

Miao Qiusheng, suggested the publication of tracts. The *Monthly* accepted this idea. To everyone's surprise, in little more than a week's time the demand for these tracts became so great that a second and third edition had to be issued, each numbering 35,000 copies.[44]

Readers also suggested that Christian literature should respond to the changing times. The New Culture Movement, the vernacular language movement, and the May Fourth Movement had altered China's intellectual landscape. Responding to this new intellectual environment, readers suggested such things as using modern Chinese in translating the Bible, adopting modern biblical scholarly findings, and permitting Christian writers to observe Chinese living situations.[45] The *Wenshe Monthly* in turn responded to its readers. For example, it carried a notice (in vol. 2, no. 4) asking contributors to use modern punctuation. And in 1925 the Wenshe undertook a new translation of the Bible with modern punctuation. It asked Zhou Zuoren (T. R. Chow) of National Beijing University to undertake this task. Although Zhou did not complete the translation, Wenshe cherished this project throughout its existence.[46] Another important project, adopted in 1928 but left unfinished, was the founding of a Christian Book Club. The purposes of the club, according to the original plan, were to save Christianity from intellectual deterioration, to inspire Christian writers to produce better literature, and to create a market for the wider distribution of Christian literature in China.[47] However, the Wenshe did not have time to put this plan into practice, because it was forced to suspend operations in mid-1928.

Evaluation

The period from the late Qing to the 1920s constitutes a turning point in modern Chinese church history. Under the impact of various foreign and domestic changes, as well as the anti-Christian movement, Chinese Christians became more nationalistic and began to reexamine their religion and the issue of preaching the gospel in China. The case of the Wenshe shows how a Christian magazine dealt with the question of literary indigenization. The authors of the *Monthly* reviewed frankly all problems they encountered and offered many solutions.

The *Wenshe Monthly* attracted attention to its proposals from both inside and outside the church. Many major Chinese Christian publications, such as *Zhenli yu shengming, Jidutubao, Jidujiao chubanjie*, and *Zhonghua Jidujiaohui nianjian*, all made some response to the new magazine.[48] In academic circles, the historian Chen Yuan and men of letters such as Xia

Mianzun took public notice of the *Wenshe Monthly*.[49] Also, the leading missionary magazine in China, the *Chinese Recorder*, mentioned the *Monthly* and introduced its recommendations to its readers.[50]

The *Wenshe Monthly* articles on literary indigenization were visionary, incisive, and to the point. However, the Chinese conservatives and foreign missionaries who still controlled the church machinery were not pleased with the movement or its leaders. They regarded the Wenshe group as radicals and troublemakers.[51]

Moreover, despite their sharp analysis, articles in *Wenshe Monthly* often lacked agreement on specifics, and their suggestions were sometimes impractical. Proposals for change were usually set forth as general principles or a set of ideas, but failed to specify clear and concrete steps to carry them out. For example, on the question of an indigenized church or literature, the Wenshe's writers did not, or were unable to, define the term "indigenization," or to say to what extent Chinese Christianity should be indigenized. Therefore, while many writers adopted the term, they themselves were at odds over its meaning. On the integration of Christianity and Chinese culture, the Wenshe writers again were divided. Some argued that Christianity should be absorbed into Chinese culture, and some argued the reverse. The Wenshe's contributors simply could not reach agreement on many crucial issues.

Furthermore, the discussions in the pages of the *Wenshe Monthly* of the indigenization of literature were sometimes impractical. For example, the suggestion to establish an examination board to review all Christian writing for publication impinged on the matter of denominational differences, and individual as well as literary enterprises. When the various Protestant denominations could not agree on theology, homiletic methods, or attitudes toward worldly affairs, how could they establish an organization to set uniform standards for their publications?

Criticism of Christian institutions and their publications by the Wenshe authors inevitably offended foreign missionaries and caused discontent with church-sponsored publications. Even when the members of the Wenshe pointed out many undeniable problems in missionary work, two critical issues always surfaced in missionary minds. First, the missionary community did not believe that the Chinese Christians had matured to the point of self-propagation and the development of an indigenous Christian theology. Second, many missionaries still held paternalistic attitudes and believed Westerners were "more suited than the Chinese to bear the burden of responsibility for mission work." They did not wholeheartedly support the devolution of all mission administration to the Chinese.[52]

Another reason for the failure of the Wenshe was a conflict between "fundamentalist" and "modernist" groups in the Protestant church. Most Wenshe members were liberal in theology. They not only suggested that the Bible be examined scientifically, but suggested that all myths and "superstitions" be deleted from the Bible. Although the editors of the *Monthly* repeatedly claimed they were objective and open to any discussion, conservative Christians and missionaries remained unconvinced.

In the end, the mortal wound the Wenshe suffered in 1928 was financial. At that time, the Chinese churches and their followers did not have the funds to proceed with their reform plans. They were still basically dependent on foreign funds. Not yet having attained self-sufficiency, all proposals, such as building graduate schools and libraries, were of no avail. The result was that the *Wenshe Monthly* could not sustain itself after its American sponsor — the ISRR in New York — suspended its support. Although the *Monthly* ceased publication in mid-1928, its criticism of contemporary Christian literature, its ideas on literature indigenization, as well as its vigorous approach to reform and regeneration, were unique. Anyone studying the issue of indigenization in modern Chinese church history today cannot ignore the Wenshe and its journal. The root problems of Chinese Christian literature, addressed by the reform proposals of the Wenshe in the 1920s, still vex the Christian movement in China today. Even though today Chinese churches are financially much better off than in the Wenshe days, the essential needs of Christian literature as outlined by the Wenshe critics have yet to be fulfilled.

CHAPTER 17

The Growth of Independent Christianity in China, 1900–1937

DANIEL H. BAYS

This chapter discusses the new elements that appeared in Chinese Protestantism early in the twentieth century, with emphasis on those that were independent of foreign missions. Between 1900 and 1937, Protestant Christianity in China became considerably more diverse than it had been before 1900. In the nineteenth century, the Protestant mission movement was dominated by organized missionary societies, most of them (with the exception of the China Inland Mission) agencies of large denominational churches in North America and Europe. But from about 1890 on, considerably more variety came to characterize the Protestant scene in China.

The mission sector itself became much more diverse, as dozens of new mission groups established themselves. Some of these were unconnected with any denominational church, but established solely to send missionaries to China and other countries targeted for evangelization. Of these new missions, a few, like the Christian and Missionary Alliance or the Seventh-Day Adventists, became substantial and permanent; others were ephemeral, dissolving after a few years. After 1900 there was also a great increase in independent or "faith" missionaries. These were individuals who were not part of the old mission organizations, and were often not part of any organization at all, but came to China entirely on their own, leading a precarious existence and sometimes returning home after a short time. These were often from Western Christian sectarian currents such as the Holiness or Pentecostal movements, new on the Western as well as the Chinese scene. Indeed, in the early 1900s the theological menu for a potential Chinese Christian became much more varied than it had been in the late 1800s.

Another distinguishing feature of the decades after 1900 was the conspicuous growth in the sheer size of the Protestant church in China, especially in the 1900–1925 period. Naturally, part of this growth was in the old, well-established mission societies. These years were the culminating age of institution-building in China missions: schools, including universities; modern hospitals and clinics, staffed by increasing numbers of trained Western medical personnel; and sophisticated publication and communication systems, including traveling evangelists and Christian literature. All these created a much more complex and impressive presence than that of the 1890s. Moreover, the number of Protestant Christian church members grew rapidly, from 37,000 in 1889 to 178,000 in 1906.[1]

Yet, in retrospect, the most important feature of this period was the growth of the spirit of independence in Chinese Protestant churches. This had barely begun in the nineteenth century, but it was a prominent theme after 1900.

One category of "independence" that really did not amount to much autonomy for Chinese Christians, but did give them considerably more participation in what I would call the "Sino-foreign Protestant establishment" of these decades, was the so-called Three-Self Movement. This "movement," although it was not organized, aimed at making Chinese Christians responsible for "self-management, self-support, and self-propagation" in the churches. Many foreign missionaries, and Chinese Christian leaders working within the mission-related structures of the day, had spoken of this goal since the mid-nineteenth century. Karl Gützlaff, as shown in Jessie and Ray Lutz's chapter in this volume, had done more than most missionaries to promote this, but to little effect. From the early 1910s and the formation of the China Continuation Committee after the Edinburgh Missionary Conference of 1910, this goal was pursued more systematically, reaching a watershed in the National Christian Conference of 1922. Out of this conference came the ecumenical Church of Christ in China, a Sino-foreign body with a significant degree of Chinese leadership and responsibility, which eventually had a membership of about a quarter of the Protestant Christian community. The National Christian Council (NCC), a national Protestant coordinating and liaison body, was also a product of the conference and was operating by the mid-1920s.[2]

Not all denominations or mission groups joined the Church of Christ in China and/or the NCC. Some of them, like the Anglicans or Lutherans, pursued their own forms of Sino-foreign unity and nurturing of Chinese leadership. Others held back from the ecumenical push toward more Chinese leadership out of theological suspicions; the Church of Christ in China seemed too liberal in biblical interpretation for their taste. Some of these, like the China Inland Mission, continued in what was basically a foreign-dominated structure at the top levels, but tried to promote sensitivity to and encouragement of Chinese Christians' aspirations to responsibility and autonomy at the local level.

These developments were all important ones, and deserve more detailed and understanding treatment than they have so far received at the hands of scholars. However, my own view is that, all things considered, within the mission-related structures there was only slight movement toward an authentically autonomous or indigenous Chinese church before 1937. Even in the wartime years from 1937 to 1945, when as Timothy Brook shows elsewhere in this volume there was a forced shift toward independence in the Japanese-occupied areas, missions in the unoccupied parts of China remained much in the familiar pattern. From the 1920s to 1949, attitudes of paternalism persisted among many foreign missionaries, and the influence of foreign financial subsidy remained a potent, if usually an implicit, factor in most Christian institutions. Moreover, even capable Chinese Christian leaders sometimes failed to push as hard as they might have for full independence and control. This generalized conclusion may be a little unfair, for example to the YMCA/YWCA, but I think it is basically accurate.

An altogether different sector of Chinese Christianity, however, came into being during these decades, one which was independent of foreign missions, autonomous in operations, and indigenous in ideas and leadership. This category of Chinese Christians has been neglected by scholars of Chinese history and by scholars of the history of Christianity as well. It was quite diverse, made up of a combination of organized church groups (some nationwide with hundreds of congregations), individual congregations, and even individual Christian workers who made their mark in a more local setting. Some of these coexisted with and cooperated with the mission churches; others were quite separatist and had almost no contacts with other Christians, Chinese or foreign.

Having worked on the subject of twentieth-century Chinese Christianity for several years now, collecting considerable amounts of scattered data, I believe that this sector was far more interesting and significant than it might have been thought. An example of completely overlooking most of this sector was a 1936 handbook on Chinese Protestant Christianity produced by the NCC, which was in theory to serve the whole Chinese church. This volume included vast statistics on each of the mission societies and related Chinese church bodies, but it did not even mention the names of the True Jesus Church, the Assembly Hall, the Jesus Family, or the China Christian Independent Church federation, all of which were well established by that time and had at least several tens of thousands of adherents among them. In the preface of this handbook a paltry estimate of five thousand was made for communicants in the generic category of "independent churches."[3] Meanwhile, several mission denominations with only one or two thousand members were described in detail. The independent Christians were invisible to the Sino-foreign Protestant establishment.

I believe that this group of Christians was much larger than most have surmised. In the 1940s, the various independent Chinese Protestants may have accounted for 20–25 percent of all Protestants, 200,000 persons or more. Moreover, judging from what we know of the churches in China today, it is clear that a great many of the older Christians whose experience dates to before 1949 came out of these indigenous churches. Although denominational designations were abolished in the PRC in 1958, even today in some parts of China Christian groups still use the designations of the True Jesus Church, the Jesus Family, or the Assembly Hall to denote their local congregations and traditions, even though most of the believers are much too young to have known directly the old churches.[4]

Following is a brief introduction to the most important elements of this independent Protestant sector. In almost all cases, the relevant historical materials concerning these organizations and individuals are in Chinese. That is one reason why they have often been overlooked by historians of Christianity in China, who have tended to remain fixed on the foreign missionary presence and the English-language materials that document it.

The first category consists of church federations made up of independent congregations, most of which previously had been mission churches but had become self-supporting and self-governing. Independent Chinese Christian leaders, that is those who consciously broke away or distanced themselves from the foreign missionary structures, had been visible since the early 1900s. Early in the twentieth century the Shanghai Presbyterian pastor Yu Guozhen and several colleagues formed an all-Chinese organization called The Chinese Christian Union (Jidutuhui). In about 1906 they formed an independent, all-Chinese congregation, and in following years other churches in the region followed suit in becoming independent of missions. By 1910 Yu's group had a newspaper, *Zhongguo Jidutubao* (The Chinese Christian), which later became *Shengbao* (The sacred news). Out of these elements a federation of churches emerged called the China Christian Independent Church (Zhongguo Yesujiao zilihui). In 1920, this federation had over 100 member churches, an annual national meeting, and full bylaws, in addition to its own newspaper.[5] It continued to grow during the 1920s. Many of its member churches were formerly Presbyterian or Congregational, made up largely of urban middle-class Chinese. A comparable movement in North China beginning in 1912 produced a smaller but similar federation of independent churches centered in Shandong Province but also well represented in the cities of Beijing and Tianjin.[6] One of the Tianjin leaders of this federation was Zhang Boling (1876–1951), founder of Nankai University. Another was Cheng Jingyi (1881–1939), articulate pastor of an independent church in Beijing who came to hold every high office in the mainstream Sino-foreign Protestant establishment in the 1920s and 1930s.

Between 1917 and 1919 a very different Christian movement, the True Jesus Church, took shape. This was a dynamic movement drawing upon one of the "new" Protestant currents that came to China after 1900, Pentecostalism. Pentecostalism stresses the "Baptism of the Holy Spirit" and the use of supernatural spiritual gifts such as prophecy, healing, and speaking in unknown tongues, and is fired by a strong millennialism (expecting the return of Christ at any moment; this feature was also characteristic of many others of the newer mission groups, especially Holiness and Adventist ones). In addition to its Pentecostal beliefs and practices, the True Jesus Church was sometimes militantly antiforeign; its relations with foreign missions were usually contentious (unlike the fairly amicable relations with missions of the two independent federations mentioned above). In the 1920s this new church grew rapidly in central interior provinces, especially Henan and Hunan. It was highly exclusivist; that is, it insisted that Chinese Christians renounce their old churches and acknowledge the sole legitimacy of the True Jesus Church and its unique dogma (a mix of "unitarian" Pentecostalism, Seventh-day worship, and intense millenarianism). Its proselytizing efforts were widely felt, and thoroughly resented, by mission churches.[7] The True Jesus Church, which I interpret partly in terms of the heritage of Chinese sectarian folk religion, was almost certainly the largest of the independent Protestant churches from the 1920s to the early 1950s, when it was dissolved as counterrevolutionary and its leaders jailed. Its headquarters are today in Taiwan; it is very active there and in Chinese communities around the world.

The Assembly Hall (Juhuichu or Juhuisuo) or "Little Flock" (Xiaoqun), was organized in the mid-1920s and led before 1937 by Ni Tuosheng (Watchman Nee, 1903–72). Ni's name is familiar to many Christians around the world because several of his talks and a few of his writings have been translated and published abroad since the 1930s; many are still available, and widely read, today. From the mid-1920s onward Ni, strongly influenced by Brethren ideas (especially premillennialism) but also by a stress on the Holy Spirit derived from the Holiness tradition, was an inspiring and compelling teacher. His evangelistic meetings were not usually large and were often held in homes. But he had a gift of revealing the importance in the Christian life of a deeper spirituality; this, and his eloquence, drew many followers. Antagonism toward missions and foreign Christians often characterized his ministry. Seldom invited by or working within established congregations, his followers usually formed themselves into strongly proselytizing new groups, in effect forming a new nationwide denomination with headquarters in Shanghai. Like the True Jesus Church, the Assembly Hall was dispersed in the 1950s, and Ni was jailed as a counterrevolutionary; he died in prison in 1972. But the church migrated to Taiwan under the leadership of Li Changshou, one of Ni's lieutenants, under whom it became prominent and controversial; it is now a worldwide church, with joint headquarters in Taibei and Anaheim, California.[8]

The Jesus Family (Yesu jiating) was a unique Pentecostal communitarian church first established in rural Shandong Province (in a village called Mazhuang, in Taian County) about 1927. In later years, other Jesus Family churches were established in North and Central China, many of them in Shandong but others as far south as the regions of Wuhan and Nanjing. They were all in rural or semirural areas, and were formed into small communities of up to a few hundred, with the believers working and living together, and holding property in common, under the direction of the "family head" (jiazhang). Though it is hard to be exact, it seems that there were well over one hundred of these Jesus Family communities in 1949, with a total of several thousand members. All were run entirely by Chinese, under the overall leader Jing Dianying (1890–1953?). The Jesus Family was strongly millenarian, anticipating the imminent return of Christ, and it was very Pentecostal, basing its worship and behavior on the gifts of the Holy Spirit, including tongues, and also on the believers' receiving divine revelations through messages obtained while in a trance. All the Jesus Family communities were disbanded in 1953, but even today many former adherents are active members and leaders in the Chinese Christian community.[9] In the 1980s, some Jesus Family groups reappeared, but they are technically illegal and subject to persecution by the authorities. Unlike the True Jesus Church and the Assembly Hall, the Jesus Family did not move outside China.

The Spiritual Gifts Church (Ling'enhui) was the least organized of the independent churches mentioned thus far. It centered in Shandong Province in the early 1930s, and is perhaps best seen as a Pentecostal revival movement, not an ecclesiastically organized body. The movement encompassed Chinese churches and pastors who broke away from denominations or missions that refused to approve their controversial Pentecostal doctrines and practices. It was also linked to a famous revival among the missionary community called the "Shandong Revival," which spilled over into church splits, with denunciations of heresy on one side and jeremiads against indifference on the other.[10] The Chinese pastors and their followers who left their old churches, many of them from the U.S. Presbyterian mission, found a new home, at least temporarily, in this loosely structured movement. Unlike the organizations discussed in the previous sections, the Ling'enhui did not develop institutionally. I have found no publications or records indicating that it ever went beyond this informal stage of development, or survived past the 1930s.

The final category consists of several individual Chinese pastors, evangelists, writers, and teachers. These constituted a distinctive hallmark of the twentieth-century drive towards "selfhood" in Chinese Protestantism.

Before 1900, there was not a single Chinese Protestant figure with a nationwide reputation as an individual leader. After 1900, this changed rapidly. One of the first to develop national stature was Ding Limei (1871–1936), who attracted much attention as a YMCA evangelist in the 1910s.[11] Ding was a second generation Christian and an outstanding 1892 graduate of Calvin Mateer's Christian academy in Shandong Province.[12] He worked as a teacher, then as a pastor in his native province for many years. As a pastor in the years after 1900, he urged young men in Christian middle schools and colleges to choose Christian work as a career, and to make a spiritual recommitment to underpin that vocational choice. A turning point in his career came in 1909–10. Still a pastor, Ding visited his alma mater, now called Shandong Union College, in spring 1909. In a series of meetings, there occurred such a revival of Christian dedication in the student body that over 100 students committed themselves to enter the ministry.[13] Over the coming months Ding had a comparable impact on other Christian schools in North China. Then in 1910, at the annual meeting of the North China YMCA, there was organized a "Chinese Student Volunteer Movement for the Ministry," with Ding as its full-time traveling secretary. This was clearly modeled on the Student Volunteer Movement for Foreign Missions, which originated in the 1880s in the United States and was likewise affiliated with the YMCA.

For the next several years Ding traveled all over China, holding evangelistic revival meetings, especially in Christian mission schools. He had considerable impact on many students between approximately 1910 and 1918.[14] Although he had much stature of his own, Ding was a transitional figure, because he was part of the YMCA, a Sino-foreign institution still dominated by foreigners. Moreover, he cooperated with John Mott and Sherwood Eddy, YMCA evangelists from the U.S. who made several trips to China during the years 1907–18.[15]

After the May Fourth Movement, talented Chinese Christians who had few or no links with foreigners began to make their mark. Wang Zai (Leland Wang, 1898–1975) was an older colleague of Ni Tuosheng in Fuzhou in the early 1920s, then became a well-known traveling revival speaker with an effective Christian music ministry. Early in his career he made international contacts, and by the 1930s he had formed an evangelistic association that frequently took him outside the country as well as all over China. He often cooperated with foreign missionary churches, but his organization was independent.[16]

Wang Mingdao (1900–1991) was one of the best known Chinese Christian figures in the West because of his public resistance to the authorities in the 1950s and subsequent long imprisonment before his release in 1979. A stern and rather dogmatic man, often critical of missionaries and vociferously opposed to "liberal" theology, Wang was a powerful speaker and teacher. From the late 1920s he spent about half of every year on the road conducting revivals and evangelistic meetings in evangelical and fundamentalist churches, even after building his own church in Beijing. Wang did not create new churches nationwide but worked closely with others. He also edited and published a popular quarterly Christian magazine for over two decades, enhancing his national visibility. A fearless man, Wang defied the Japanese authorities during the early 1940s as well as the new Communist government in the 1950s. He was also proudly independent; foreigners could attend his church, but only a handful were ever invited to preach from his pulpit.[17]

There were several other prominent individual leaders in the years after 1920. Chen Chonggui (Marcus Cheng, 1884–1964) worked as a Bible teacher in the Swedish Covenant mission and seminary until he left the mission, possibly because of unequal treatment of Chinese and Western personnel, in the 1920s. Then he was chaplain to the warlord Feng Yuxiang for a time, and later the editor of an important Chinese Christian magazine (*Budao*; The evangelist) and a teacher in other seminaries. He ended up as a supporter of the new Communist government after 1949, but in turn angered it by his frank, critical remarks in the late 1950s and was subjected to a ferocious denunciation campaign, which hung over his head until his death.[18] Jia Yuming (1880–1964), like Chen Chonggui, began his teaching career in mission-run seminaries, but established a national reputation as a conservative systematic theologian with his publications, and had his own

Bible school for many years, entirely free from foreign support or direction. The last place he operated his school was in Shanghai, from the late 1940s to the early 1950s.[19]

Some of the most dramatic and flamboyant individuals on the Chinese Protestant scene in the 1927–37 period were associated with the "Bethel Bands" of the Bethel Mission in Shanghai. The Bethel Mission was an independent and self-supporting Holiness enterprise (hospital, church, Bible training institute) founded by Shi Meiyu (Mary Stone, 1873–1954), a Chinese woman M.D., and by Jennie Hughes, an American.[20] Both had been in the U.S. Methodist mission, but left the mission in the early 1920s because of its theological "modernism."

Although the Bethel Mission had some links to foreigners, it was an entirely China-based operation. It made its mark nationwide by sending out ardent Chinese young men and women from its training institute to conduct revival meetings at whatever churches would welcome them. Several of the young people who emerged in these "bands" showed appealing gifts of eloquence and of music. Five of the young men, including two who would later become stirring evangelists in their own right, Song Shangjie (John Sung) and Ji Zhiwen (Andrew Gih), set off in early 1931 as the unknown but ambitiously named Bethel Worldwide Evangelistic Band. By 1935, when the band dissolved, they had traveled over 50,000 miles, visited 133 cities, and held almost 3,400 revival meetings at churches of all denominations. Smaller, seasonal Bethel bands traveled on a regional basis.[21]

Ji Zhiwen went on to become a well-known revivalist in Hong Kong and overseas Chinese communities until his death in the 1980s. Song Shangjie, immediately after leaving the Bethel Band at the end of 1934, became the most controversial of Chinese evangelists during the next three years, until the invasion by Japan. Song (1901–44), the son of a Fujian pastor, studied in the United States from 1919 to 1927, receiving a Ph.D. in chemistry at Ohio State University in 1926. He then went to Union Theological Seminary in New York, where he had a religious and psychological crisis arising from the clash between his traditional Christian beliefs and the higher biblical criticism and liberal theology that surrounded him at Union. He ended up in a sanatorium for several months in 1927, after denouncing his teachers and local pastors, then returned to China freshly reconverted to the tenets of his childhood.[22]

Song developed a unique, abrasive style of forceful or "rude" evangelism which made him notorious. He was a creative Bible expositor and good song leader, but he was also ruthlessly direct and acerbic in his denunciations of those with whom he disagreed, especially "liberal" theologians and pastors. His meetings were often quite emotional, even spectacularly so. There also often seemed to be an antiforeign edge to his preaching, and he did not hesitate to denounce the pastors and leaders of denominational churches even as they sat before him in his meetings in their churches. In one place in 1935 he urged local Christians to boycott the upcoming meetings of the old American evangelist Sherwood Eddy on one of Eddy's last trips to China. This kind of behavior, both as a member of the Bethel Band from 1931 through 1934 and then as a lone revivalist until 1937, not surprisingly alienated many Christians, foreign and Chinese alike.[23] Yet Song must be reckoned as one of the most influential figures in Chinese Protestantism in the mid-1930s. Although eventually barred by some churches, he was highly esteemed by many others.

I have given only a superficial introduction to the fascinating array of churches and Christian leaders of the early twentieth century. But I think that the point is clear: there took place in these decades a remarkably strong and diverse flowering of independence in the Chinese Protestant movement.[24] Foreign missionaries had spoken for decades about the need for the Chinese church to move towards the "three-self" goals. But many foreigners were quite unaware of the extent and power of these new elements, especially the rural churches such as the True Jesus Church and the Jesus Family. Those who did have direct contact with the independent groups tended to distrust and dislike them, suspecting their theology and resenting their "sheep-stealing" from established mission congregations. From today's perspective, however, we can see clearly the importance of this independent sector of Chinese Protestantism in the first half of the twentieth century. It marked a crucial stage in the maturity of the Chinese church. Moreover, some parts of it have continued directly to the present, where they have contributed much to the dynamism of Christianity in China and among Chinese communities around the world.

CHAPTER 18

Toward Independence: Christianity in China Under the Japanese Occupation, 1937–1945

TIMOTHY BROOK

Being a European religion, Christianity has faced resistance from the non-European cultures to which it has been introduced over the past five centuries. The resistance has been natural: a culture protects the beliefs on which it constructs its view of the world, and those from outside are almost invariably unwelcome. That conceded, the non-European resistance to Christianity has not been a simple matter of self-preservation. If Christianity's foreign identity has been the hook snagging attempts to spread Christianity to the non-European world, its association with the power of imperialism has been the barb. Imperialism is what enabled Europeans to convey Christianity beyond its medieval boundaries; mission would have been impossible without it. But the success with which Europeans expanded their economic networks created for Christianity both opportunity and predicament. It brought missionaries into contact with non-Christian populations on a scale undreamt of; at the same time, it compromised the integrity of the mission project by introducing Christianity under the wing of military and economic coercion.

This predicament has plagued Christians in twentieth-century China. Their religion has been stigmatized as an arm of foreign domination. Reformers could take advantage of this foreign identity to ally Christianity to everything modern and metropolitan in the struggle against everything old and discredited; as well, they could cite the social gospel to show that the Christian purpose was to cross class and community barriers, not to serve imperialist interests. Such arguments in favor of Christianity's presence in China did not overcome the suspicion that belief in the Christian God was submission to foreign power. Whenever that power was under attack, as it was during the Boxer Rebellion (1900) or the Northern Expedition (1926–

27), Christianity went on trial. Chinese Protestants who rode out the anti-imperialist waves of the 1900s and 1920s developed a commitment to build a church that was independent of foreign missions. Given their personal ties to missionaries, their financial reliance on foreign funds, and their limited attainments in theology, they found it difficult to put this commitment into practice. Chinese Christians remained in the shadow of the West.

Japan's eight-year occupation of China substantially altered the political environment for Christianity. The invasion in 1937 was an act of military force, but what followed the initial conquest was more than just a military regime ruling a subject population by violence: Japan was obliged to create a state, and to devise social and economic policies to regulate the activities and associations of the people. Christianity was one form of association that fell under the scrutiny of the new state. Christianity along with other religions had already learned to live with incursions into its autonomy under the Guomindang state, but it would have to bend to greater pressures from the occupation state. Additionally, Christianity attracted particular Japanese concern for reason of its political identity. Not just a religion, it was part of the hegemonic ideology of Western nations whose power Japan aspired to exclude from the New Order in East Asia. This identity would further increase the pressures on Chinese Christians during the war years.

Despite these pressures, the occupation did not disrupt the history of Christianity in China. The period of 1937–45 was not an interlude in a composition scored to other themes. Rather, the occupation pushed Protestant Christianity further along the course it had already charted for itself: from a church that in 1937 was externally dependent, mission-oriented, and mission-dominated, to a church that in 1945 was moving in the direction of independence, union, and Chinese control. That the Chinese Protestant church gained independence from the West through the agency of a second imperialism was an irony not lost on foreign missionaries. Susie Kelsey, a Canadian mission nurse working in Henan Province, recognized that "self-support and self-government" had been the goals of both missionaries and Chinese leaders for a long time, but that these came about only when "suddenly forced upon the churches by the war."[1] So too a missionary in Shandong province observed that "duress" had brought church union and a strong self-identity to the Chinese church, and asked dryly, "Is it not a rebuke to Christian Missions and missionaries that such a union could be effected only after they had been eliminated or eclipsed? Can we profit by the lesson? It is not the Mission but the Christian Church that we must emphasize."[2]

This was a lesson that foreign missions would learn too late; the Chinese church learned it well, however. As I shall suggest at the end of this chapter, postwar Protestant Christianity is the direct heir of the accommodations that Chinese Christians had to make with Japanese imperialism. The Three-Self Movement can trace its intellectual origins back to the 1920s, but it grew directly out of the occupation. Before 1937, aspirations for independence, unity, and self-support seemed beyond reach. After 1937, the occupation brought these aspirations closer to reality. As well, the organizational means Japan used to dominate Chinese Christianity foreshadowed, and perhaps influenced, the Communist state's approach to subordinating Christianity to its own hegemonic goals.

A Case Study: The Church of Christ in China, Nanjing

On the eve of occupation, the Church of Christ in China (CCC) was the largest Protestant organization in Nanjing, and in China as a whole.[3] The church's history goes back to 1922, when several Protestant denominations in China decided to unite. At the first meeting of its General Assembly in 1927, the CCC could claim to represent close to a quarter of China's Protestants, making it the largest Protestant church in China, and the most powerful member of the National Christian Council (NCC). The Nanjing District Association (NDA) of the CCC was one of 53 constituent district associations.

Union and independence were the twin goals enshrined in the constitution of the CCC: "to unite Christian believers in China, to plan and promote with united strength the spirit of self-support, self-governance, and self-propagation, in order to extend Christ's Gospel, practise his Way of Life and spread His Kingdom throughout the world."[4] Church union had long been the goal of the CCC's founder and first moderator, Cheng Jingyi (1881–1939). Cheng had distinguished himself at the 1910 World Missionary Conference in Edinburgh by flatly declaring to the assembled Western missionaries: "Your denominationalism does not interest Chinese Christians." Cheng was a tireless champion of world church union and promoted cooperative links with Japanese Christians through the 1930s.[5] The other CCC goal was independence: from foreign funds ("self-support"), foreign mission direction ("self-governance"), and foreign preaching and theology ("self-propagation"). The CCC committed its member churches to replacing foreign missions as the dominant partner in the church-mission alliance.[6]

As the Guomindang capital, Nanjing was a natural target of the Japanese forces that landed in Shanghai in 1937. When the region came under attack in November, Chinese and foreign Christian leaders formed an International Commission to aid refugees fleeing before the Japanese army; it also took on the task of negotiating immunity from military occupation. When that negotiation failed, the commission demarcated an International Safety Zone in the center of the city. By early December some 290,000 refugees huddled there. When the city fell on 13 December, the Japanese soldiers exceeded everyone's worst fears. Through the next three bloody weeks, soldiers were permitted to run amok among the civilian population in what became the largest atrocity of the war, the Rape of Nanjing. The Japanese military police was annoyed at finding foreigners still in the city after they had been warned to leave.[7] Even though Japan negotiated with the commission regarding the safety of the refugees, Japanese soldiers violated the safety zone on several occasions. Of the estimated 300,000 killed from mid-December to early January, several thousand had sought sanctuary inside the zone but were taken out by the Japanese and executed in defiance of the zone's neutrality.[8]

Many Chinese, including CCC leaders, quit Nanjing before the Japanese arrived. Bao Zhong was among them. NDA vice-chair and pastor of the newly built Hanzhong Church on Mochou Road, Bao chose to flee west into Anhui Province. He got back to Nanjing in mid-April, working for a time at the smaller church of Banbianying, where a pastor who had returned two months earlier had already revived pastoral work. When yet another pastor returned to Nanjing in May, Bao was released from Banbianying for the task of reviving the Hanzhong Church. On Easter Sunday, Bao held a joint service there to celebrate the resurrection of the CCC in Nanjing. Aside from one church that lay inside an area designated as a military zone, the CCC's three other churches and three schools were also soon able to get back on their feet.

The Christian community of rural Nanjing fared less well. All CCC pastors and lay preachers working outside the city fled when the Japanese attacked. Four of the eight CCC churches were badly damaged in the attack, one was taken over by the Japanese army, and those in the south end of Nanjing District became inaccessible because of continued fighting. The attention of NDA leaders turned first to the Tongjing Church upriver, Nanjing's first rural church. Fighting had left nothing but a burned-out shell, but church leaders saw its revival as essential to demonstrate the viability of Christian institutions under the occupation. The man chosen for the task was Feng Rui, one of three lay preachers who had fled into the mountains of southern Anhui for the winter. Feng began work in Tongjing late in 1938 but had to abandon the project the next year when he fell mortally ill with consumption. No one else would be assigned to Tongjing. In fact, Feng would be the only lay preacher to serve in any of the rural churches even on a temporary basis for the duration of the war.

Despite these losses, attrition within the CCC community was not catastrophic. At the first wartime annual meeting of the Nanjing District Association the following October, NDA chair Wilson Mills estimated that of the 3,700 members of CCC congregations in the district, 2,700 remained.[9] Only sixteen had died, none of them clergy. The rest had fled, among them, unfortunately, the CCC's wealthiest members. Strapped for resources, the NDA could only review the many pressing needs without being able to afford solutions. The revival of the rural churches was foremost on the agenda as several were asking for pastors, but the annual meeting could only refer the problem to committee for further study. New evangelical undertakings seemed equally impossible. As the minutes record, "not only is the current situation difficult, but propagating Christian teachings is difficult in the extreme." The one new direction was a recognition of the need to pay more attention to women's work, women making up two-thirds of the NDA's membership. The meeting also urged that the CCC's work in education go ahead, although Mills pointed out that until new textbooks were available, teachers should take care to remove from existing texts and Bible readers passages that might offend the new regime. Accommodation to the powers that were, so as to restore something of what had been, was the order of the day.

The Japanese army was aware of Christianity in Nanjing, appointing a Japanese pastor to serve on the "pacification team" dispatched to restore order. Over the next year, Japanese religious personnel were posted as advisors to local Chinese Christian organizations. The YMCA was assigned two, one of whom had been a YMCA secretary in Japan. They told their Chinese colleagues that they were there to help their Chinese brethren through hard times and that they could put in a good word for them should problems with the new authorities arise.[10] The East Asia Mission (founded as the Manchuria Mission in 1933), Japan's Protestant mission society to Asian countries, also sent clergy to Nanjing that year. Mission representatives founded an organization called the Chinese Christian Church (employing the same name as the CCC) and set up a Japanese-language school.[11] In 1939, Japan went on to sponsor a Nanjing Christianity League, which engaged a Chinese pastor to hold a Christmas service attended by 35 people.[12] The league's goal was to encourage a union of Protestant churches in Nanjing. Initially, most Chinese would have nothing to do with the Japanese advisors and organizations, but as times got harder and Christians feared that their activities might be curtailed, they accepted their presence. The authorities made use of this acquiescence, calling on Christians to take part in the public demonstrations that were organized to create a facade of popular support for occupation policies.

Curiously, the forced Japanese presence in Christian circles is not reflected in the minutes of the NDA annual meetings, either in 1938 or in the next meeting in October 1940. The CCC annual meeting in 1940 was again preoccupied with the problems plaguing rural church work. Little had been achieved in the two years since the last annual meeting, and no new solutions emerged. It was agreed that a replacement for Feng Rui be sent to Tongjing, but none of the other requests for preachers or monthly visitors could be met. The one initiative was to seek to recover contracts for property belonging to the damaged Lishui Church should its pastor, Wang Junde, not return to Lishui to rebuild the congregation. The executive committee approached Wang, reassigned to work within the city, regarding his plans. Wang replied that the region was too unsafe for him to go back. The NCC Standing Committee, which Mills also chaired, urged him to return to Lishui by the end of December. Wang responded by quitting church work, although he asked to retain his status as a pastor. Despite the effort to accommodate to Japanese rule, pastors like Wang found themselves without the financial and personal security they needed to carry on their religious vocations. By the time Bao Zhong delivered his annual report in October 1941, little rural work had been accomplished. Bao had to conclude that, however bright the future might be construed, "we haven't been able to get back to the way things were before the 'Incident.'"

Records of the CCC in Nanjing fade out after the bombing of Pearl Harbor. The CCC's foreign executive secretary, A. J. Fisher, reported in 1943 following his repatriation to the United States that the Shanghai office had difficulty finding out what was happening in Nanjing after 1941. The news that got through was not encouraging. The three urban churches were said to be carrying on, while the rural churches "are at a low ebb. In many cases the work is carried on in the homes of Christians." The report closes with the faint conviction that "Christian work has not been eradicated" in Nanjing.[13] After the war, CCC general secretary H. H. Tsui (Cui Xianxiang), who had worked in Shanghai under Japanese supervision through the war, visited Nanjing. He found that "the strain of the war had told heavily on them. Each church had kept going, but this was due rather to the pastors supporting themselves than to the churches supporting the pastors. The Nanking Presbytery greatly needs fresh inspiration and vigorous planning for its future work." He also ventured that CCC churches "had not advanced much in the way of self-support."[14] The postwar chairman of the NCC in Nanjing, Yang Shoucheng, offered a more positive assessment the following October: "During the anti-Japanese war the NCC contributed to our member churches in two ways: (1) by promoting the unity of the Christian churches in Nanjing, and (2) by encouraging the Christian churches of Nanjing to learn self-governance and self-support."[15] Nanjing churches had survived the occupation, badly perhaps, but still they had survived without the benefit of foreign funds. Yang read this survival as triumph.

Yang's comments return us to the leading prewar concerns of the Church of Christ in China: union and independence. In the occupation years, the CCC made strong advances in the direction of both. The final withdrawal of foreigners in 1941 weakened the political clout the church previously enjoyed, yet the removal of foreign support and the church's vulnerability to more intrusive Japanese control precipitated important changes that were to alter the face of the Chinese church permanently. Union was imposed and independence of a kind achieved. Both would shape Christianity's postwar fate.

The story of the Church of Christ in China in wartime Nanjing is part of a larger history of accommodation and resistance throughout occupied China, to which we now turn. That history may be divided into three phases: the period of military assault, 1937–38, when most Christian work other than disaster relief had to be suspended until puppet administrations restored local order; the period of accommodation to Japanese rule, 1938–41, when Christian work resumed, largely continuing the organizational patterns of the prewar period; and the period of subordination to Japanese rule, 1942–45, when Japan strove to unify Chinese Christianity under its own umbrella organizations.

The Period of Military Assault, 1937–38

The opening months of the occupation were a time of emergencies, catastrophes, and windfalls for the Christian church. Despite substantial losses and great terror, the period of military assault initiated the church into a rite of passage toward indigenization more surely than any other event in the twentieth century.

The violence of the Japanese occupation of Nanjing was repeated, usually with less ferocity, wherever the invaders reached during their first year in China. The only places of sanctuary the Japanese army tended to respect were Christian churches and mission compounds. A missionary in northern

Henan, for instance, reported that not one Christian compound there was molested during the invasion in the fall of 1937.[16] Another noted in a letter at the end of 1937 that he found the local Japanese military authorities and their Chinese puppets easy to negotiate with, and was able to gain their respect and confidence to a degree. In a second letter a few months later he observed that "the Japanese caused the missionaries no trouble, but rather immediately offered protection and military mail facilities."[17] In some places, like Yangzhou, the Japanese military police posted signs on church doors declaring that this was foreign property and should not be touched.[18] Some Western missionaries reporting home to their mission boards were almost blithe about the new relationship they struck up with the invader.

By association, Chinese Christians sometimes received the benefits bestowed on the foreigners, and not only when missionaries personally intervened on their behalf. A missionary in Tianjin observed in a letter that "the Japanese often accept a Bible as a half-valid passport." He noted that Chinese Christians "get off with considerably less searching examination, and find it easier to get 'good citizen' certificates than some of the other folk. Some people are ready to take advantage of this, though, and we hear cases of where folk have got into trouble through falsely representing themselves as Christians. But on the whole we have had a privileged position."[19] As it became known that connections to missionaries could provide protection, Christians were moved to intensify their religious observances and non-Christians to develop links with the church. In some places there was a run on Bibles and crucifixes as tokens to secure safe passage. As a missionary in northern Henan commented in December 1937, "This is certainly a time when it has paid in a very material sense to belong to the church."[20]

Japanese indulgence toward Christians could cut two ways. Local people might be thankful to Christian leaders for the refuge and relief work they provided, but they could also regard Christian dealings with the Japanese with suspicion. When the Japanese army pushed into southeastern Henan Province in the fall of 1938, Ruth Elliott, an American working for the China Inland Mission, provided a refuge for over 200 elderly women and children in Huangchuan. The Japanese pulled out two months later. She reported that when Chinese guerrilla forces reoccupied the city, they charged the German Catholic mission in Huangchuan with having allowed its 800 refugees to help themselves to other people's property under the Japanese. The Polish father in charge of the mission was spared, but two Chinese Catholic leaders were tried and beheaded. Their heads were mounted on poles on either side of the bridge joining the northern and southern halves of the city as a warning to other collaborators.[21]

Like many missionaries, Elliott found that the Japanese threat induced ordinary people to respond positively to the Christian message. By furnishing safety and medical care, the church won the admiration of those who previously had treated it with indifference or contempt. The visible service that Chinese Christians rendered to their country did much to indigenize this foreign religion: the church was earning its right to a place in Chinese society. As a Canadian medical missionary reported, the work done by his mission hospital in Guide, Henan, meant that it was now being viewed as part of the local community. "I feel that the work of Christian missions and of the Hospital in particular have entered a new phase," he stated in a letter. "The Christian religion is now regarded more and more as a religion of the Chinese."[22]

Running parallel to this enthusiasm, however, were anxiety over opportunism and fear that the war was shaking some people's faith more strongly than it was planting that faith in others.[23] As a missionary in Henan testified, "Whole congregations, representing fifty years of patient toil and sacrifice, are on the point of being almost completely wiped out, either through starvation or the complete breakdown of morals."[24] The early opportunities for Christian service and evangelism that the war created with one hand were thus offset by the discouragement and loss of faith that it doled out with the other. Financial desperation only fed that discouragement. Carrying on with Christian work in the wake of bombardment and devastation often proved impossible. An American Lutheran missionary writing to his Board of Foreign Missions from Qingdao in January 1938, just after the Japanese navy had taken the city, was concerned that "perhaps the most tragic effect upon the Church is the disruption of the movement towards self-support, because of the disorganized economic life of the people." He noted gloomily in a letter two and a half weeks later: "A number of our congregations have been hard hit by the scattering of the people. Some will return, but perhaps there are many who will never get back to their former occupations and so we face grave problems as regards leadership and self-support."[25]

As its army moved across the eastern half of China, Japan sought ways of mobilizing Christian support for its occupation. At the invitation of the Army Ministry, a Japanese Catholic delegation spent three months in China in the winter of 1937–38. In the report he wrote at the end of the tour, Mgr. Paul Taguchi stressed that his mission was "without any political significance whatsoever." It was sent for two reasons: to see that the missionaries as foreign nationals were protected, and to attest to the Japanese government's awareness of the value of trying to win over world Catholic opinion to its cause in China.[26] Taguchi declared Japan's principal target to be communism, on which basis he hoped to build a bridge to Chinese Catholics. (The anticommunist appeal won a favorable response in some corners of world Catholicism: a Franciscan pamphlet published in Canada in 1938 went so far as to celebrate Japan's invasion as a double attack on Soviet-backed communism and what the authors call the "Free-Masonry" of the Guomindang.)[27] Taguchi also raised the sectarian appeal in his report that Catholics might "rejoice to see the existence of Catholicism so clearly recognized as a spiritual force and the distinction with Protestantism made much more exact."

The Catholic delegation was followed by a Protestant group three months later. That tour proved less successful. Protestants seemed to see less advantage in adapting to Japanese rule and internationally were less susceptible to anticommunist appeals. Indeed, some Protestant missionaries felt that international condemnation of Japan's aggression was too slow in coming.[28] One member of the delegation, who also attended the world missionary conference in Madras later that year, professed surprise when he found Chinese Christians suspicious that the delegation was trying to subvert the independence of Chinese Christianity in the service of Japan's war aims — which is, of course, precisely what it was intended to do.[29]

Although Japanese Christians sought to appeal to Chinese coreligionists by asking them to oppose communism, this formal ideological posture rested on a more fundamental goal: removing the Western presence from Asia. Chinese Christians were being called upon indirectly to repudiate those who shared their faith. This demand meant having to draw a line between what was Western and what was Christian, which is in any case never easy to do. Many missionaries were aware that Japan's ultimate goal was to sever their tie to the Chinese. An American missionary in Songjiang expressed this in a letter home early in 1938: "The Japanese do not want foreigners to go back to their work. I do not think they want us to mix with Chinese. They would like to disrupt all good relations between us and the Chinese, so that they may work their own plans."[30]

This recognition, while correct, led some missionaries to focus more on the threat to their mission work than on that to Christianity itself, assuming the suppression of the former to imply the destruction of the latter.[31] The real issue affecting Christianity in 1937–38 was not its right to exist. The Japanese army made that clear in its own internal documents, declaring in September 1938 that religious freedom should be respected in China to the extent that it did not interfere with Chinese solidarity with Japan and Manchuria.[32] What was at issue was the control of religion rather than its freedom. To this issue the occupation state now turned.

The Period of Accommodation, 1938–41

During the period in which Christians accommodated to Japanese rule, the occupation authorities continued to recognize the neutrality of missionaries and extend to them certain courtesies to encourage cooperation with the regime. But the authorities gradually came to view Christianity in relation to a broader concern with mobilizing educational and ideological means to legitimize the occupation. As this concern achieved greater focus, Christians found their activities coming under greater surveillance.

This process usually began with the arrival of Japanese clergy to work as advisors to Chinese churches. Inducted into national service, Japanese pastors and YMCA secretaries were dispatched to military administrations throughout the Japanese empire and assigned to local Christian organizations.[33] Some of these advisors were part of the East Asia Mission. The mission's goal was to establish mission stations all over China and for each of them to recruit a Chinese clergyman, assisted by a Japanese pastor. In the words of Shiraki Hachirō, a member of the executive committee, the mission was dedicated to nourishing "the wandering, helpless souls of Asia," and it was as culturally imperialistic as its Western counterparts. As Shiraki expressed it, "How can the Chinese become good citizens without Christianity? There is no question as to their need of Christ. We believe that the New Order of the Orient must be brought about through the spirit of our Lord Jesus Christ."[34]

Making the Chinese into "good citizens" was precisely what the Japanese army desired, and in 1939 it set about organizing Japanese missionaries of all religions for that purpose. The Japanese army's Asia Development Board (Kōain) set up the Central China Religious Unity League in Shanghai on 27 February 1939 to strengthen coordination among Japanese sects so that they could more effectively assist in Japan's cultural domination of China.[35] In addition, a series of joint associations were formed in the spring of 1939. For Christians, these included the Sino-Japanese Christian Association and the Japan-China Christian Federation. Non-Japanese observers at the time regarded these organizational initiatives as utterly inef-

fective at bringing about changes in the organizational life of Chinese religion,[36] but they did lay a foundation on which Japan would build after
1941.

As well as organizing religious work, the Japanese army sponsored
research on Christianity in China and on Chinese religion in general, beginning in 1939. Some of this work was done under the Asia Development
Board. The Office of the Army Chief of Staff and the South Manchurian
Railway Company (Mantetsu) also supported research on religion, as did
Japanese government ministries, special interest organizations, and Japanese religious bodics.[37] The reports that came out of these efforts — relying
on translations and published sources — are largely descriptive and statistical summaries rather than policy studies. They attest nonetheless to the
army's intense interest in developing a religious policy that would prevent
Chinese religions, especially Christianity, from serving as a base for anti-
Japanese sentiment.

Opinions on the effectiveness of Japan's religious work were divided. A
classified study on Japan's cultural policies in China produced in Tokyo in
1940 argued that religious work could contribute significantly to winning
the cooperation of the Chinese people.[38] (The army did in fact get this sort
of cooperation when it managed to establish a positive relationship with
local congregations.)[39] The report rejected the argument that cultural undertakings were simply a component of economic investment in China, yet
it insisted that cultural work had more than purely cultural significance. An
army Chief of Staff study, also from 1940, reminded policy makers that they
had no choice but to pursue religious work. The deep religiosity of the
Chinese masses could not be altered overnight: attempts rapidly to change
their religious organizations and customs would only backfire. Yet the
study also warned that Japan should be aware that Chinese Christians were
adept at taking advantage of the people's "spiritual wavering" to expand
their activities.[40]

This anxiety about an expansion of Christian influence in China fueled
a more agitated view. An Asia Development Board publication of December 1939 warned that Christianity in China was strong and that its privileges allowed it to serve as a cover for anti-Japanese activity. It advised that
any missionary found harboring such activity should be ordered out of the
country.[41] (The Japanese army suspected some missionaries of aiding the
resistance but was loathe to excite international complications by moving
against them.[42] With Chinese it was less circumspect, detaining them and
shutting down their churches and schools when it suspected them of anti-
Japanese activity.[43]) Some Japanese went further and argued that Japan's

policy of using religious personnel to monitor Chinese coreligionists had little value. Army special services officer Yamazaki Kaikō expressed this view in an account the army published in 1942 of his experiences as a pacification agent in rural Shanghai. Yamazaki had reason to be critical of Japan's accommodative policy: a guerrilla band once eluded his soldiers by fleeing to the sanctuary of a Catholic church. In his book he declared Western missionaries to be "the shock troops of foreign imperialism" and insisted that their presence had prevented Japanese missions from gaining a foothold in China. He allowed that joint Sino-Japanese religious organizations might help to foster international ties and provide educational and relief assistance, but concluded that "in terms of its significance for politics or state policy, the religious work our nation's religious organizations have done with respect to China cannot be regarded as having been particularly successful."[44]

"Success" for Yamazaki was winning Chinese allegiance to the New Order in East Asia. He felt that success was possible only by terminating the influence and extraterritorial rights of foreign missionaries. Among Japanese, the only disagreement here was over timing. Despite assurances Japanese diplomats were giving their foreign counterparts that missionaries would face a "minimum of interference with their normal lives," the ultimate goal was to force them out.[45] The question was how to do so without overly antagonizing foreign governments. The army Chief of Staff study already cited, which regarded most missionaries as unfriendly to Japan, recommended the slow course of restricting foreigners' privileges to the letter of existing treaties and seeing that their work be strictly limited to religious matters.[46] A Mantetsu study of the same year similarly noted that Japan's desire to end foreign privileges in China should begin with a passive policy of limiting the spread of foreign mission influence, combined with more active restrictions on the economic interests of missions.[47]

The Japanese army had already exceeded these recommendations in the summer of 1939 when it orchestrated an unofficial campaign against British subjects. This anti-British "popular movement" succeeded in removing British subjects and expropriating British mission property (particularly hospitals) in some areas of China. The Japanese at the same time put pressure on Chinese Christians for their alleged pro-British sympathies.[48] Most missionaries regarded this harassment as not solely anti-British or anti-foreign, but anti-Christian. A United Church of Canada missionary at the time feared that the pressures under which Chinese Christians were suffering while the missionaries were still in their midst would continue after his departure (as a Canadian he was also legally a British subject).

There was, he felt, "a deep anti-Christian feeling on the part of the Japanese military."[49] The threat to mission was causing some foreigners to read the situation subjectively. It was not Christianity that disturbed the Japanese authorities; it was its continuing susceptibility to foreign direction and control. Chinese Christianity had to be trained out of its habit of looking west. During the 1938–41 period, however, the Japanese army was obliged not to interfere too strongly with foreign missions; its goal of clearing China of foreign influence could not be achieved until war was declared.

Weakening the link between mission and church forced self-propagation and self-governance on Chinese congregations. The South China Mission of the United Church of Canada in its General Report for 1940 notes that "it is not desired by those in authority that we should have much to do with the Chinese. We have therefore deemed it wise to leave the work of the churches as much as possible in the hands of the Chinese workers. Most of these leaders have been able to call on us occasionally. The business part of the Presbytery was carried on by its executive composed of the evangelistic members of the Mission and a few of the Chinese leaders."[50] Canadian missionaries in the north similarly reported that year that the Chinese churches in Henan Province were carrying on well since their withdrawal. The number of Christians enrolled in the Northern Presbytery was growing, new famine relief projects under Chinese pastors were being undertaken, and a village bible school had been set up by one congregation, though the name appears to have been used to disguise a middle school under a religious label.[51]

Where the burden of forced independence was most onerous was in finances. With mission boards directing their funds to emergency relief and local congregations finding themselves without resources, many pastors could not afford to continue pastoral work. The weakness of self-support not only threatened self-propagation in the short term but contributed to tensions between Chinese and foreign clergy. A Lutheran report for Central China in 1940 mentions that a Chinese pastor "left his congregation and has gone into business" even though the church was "his first love." The report goes on proudly to claim that "otherwise our pastors have stuck faithfully to their posts, though war conditions and war prices make a pastor's position increasingly difficult."[52] The original typescript of the report preserved in a Lutheran archive says that he left "under a cloud," but the phrase has been penciled out, presumably because an editor feared it might convey the unwanted impression that some Chinese pastors were at odds with their missionary colleagues over financial matters.

In those areas of the country where missionaries were largely undisturbed during the years up to Pearl Harbor, churches not only continued to function but attracted more converts than at any other time in the present century. The Jesuit mission in Xuzhou (northern Jiangsu) experienced a remarkable increase in baptisms during the first years of the occupation, reaching a mission record of 5,666 adult baptisms and 3,133 child baptisms in 1939.[53] The official account of the Xuzhou mission observes that "the war brought the people to us. During these troubled years, the people searched for protection and the Catholic church effectively furnished it." The Catholic bishop of Qingdao in his annual report of 1939 was less confident about the rise in baptisms, for he doubted that wartime converts would keep their newfound faith once hostilities were over. He allowed, nonetheless, that the war presented the church in Qingdao with a "favorable situation."[54]

After 1941, the picture changes. Comparing the record of baptisms in Xuzhou before and after Pearl Harbor, it is hard to construe the pre-1941 confidence of missionaries as anything but wishful thinking. Adult baptisms in Xuzhou fell to 243 in 1943, the same year in which three Jesuit fathers were executed by the local Japanese commander. The missionaries feared that Christian life in Xuzhou was fading. In the words of the official mission history, Chinese Christians were becoming "refractory, indifferent, absent, ignorant."[55] Blaming this situation on local want of faith may be beside the point. It would be more appropriate to suggest that the windfalls the Xuzhou Jesuits achieved in 1938–41 derived entirely from the advantages their foreign status could wring out of the Japanese. When the moment came to rein in foreign influence, mission successes evaporated. In the beginning, war brought the people to the missionaries; for a time, accommodation allowed the missionaries to stay among the people; but in the end, it was once again war that drove them away. Thenceforth the fate of Christianity was in Chinese hands.

The Period of Subordination to Japanese Rule, 1942–45

The bombing of Pearl Harbor placed Japan at war with the nations from which most missionaries to China had come. Their movements were confined, though it was not until March 1943, after Japan's enemies interned people of Japanese ancestry, that Japan responded by gathering foreigners into concentration camps.[56] Several hundred were repatriated from Japanese-controlled territories in two exchanges for Japanese nationals in 1942 and 1943; the rest remained confined or interned until the end of the war.

Japan's entry into the world war left the occupation state free to "liquidate foreign influence" and require "allegiance to the Japanese regime," as a Lutheran missionary put it in the summer of 1942. The final symbolic gesture came in 1943 when the puppet regime formally cancelled extraterritoriality. Yet even though foreigners were removed from the affairs of Chinese Christianity, Christianity did not disappear from China. The Lutheran missionary was correct in estimating that among Chinese Christians "work may go on under Japanese scrutiny."[57] Indeed it did, so long as Chinese Christians could demonstrate that they were free of Western influence. When Japanese investigators visited the CCC General Assembly office in Shanghai right after Pearl Harbor, for instance, the Chinese staff was able to allay suspicions about the CCC's relationship with foreigners.[58] The CCC continued functioning through the war, hampered more by financial stress and insecure communications than by the Japanese. Unfortunately, mission property, which might reasonably have been expected to revert to Chinese hands, was often retained by the Japanese army for its own uses.[59]

Having severed Chinese Christianity's foreign ties, Japan was free to proceed toward the goal implicit in its religious work during the years prior to 1942: promoting union. Japan wanted to eliminate denominational divisions in the hope of thereby rendering a unified Protestantism amenable to the hegemony of the occupation state. Union would also symbolize a rejection of the Western face of Christianity. The Japanese state had already pressed union on Protestant churches in Japan during the two years preceding Pearl Harbor, culminating in the formation of the Church of Christ in Japan (CCJ) in November 1941. With the bombing of Pearl Harbor, Japan could turn to the task of building Protestant union in China.

This process was started in North China early in the spring of 1942, when a League for the Promotion of Church Union in North China was formed under the chief secretary of the Beijing YMCA. The first conference was not quite the happy event the Japanese advisors hoped for. A foreign missionary reported at secondhand that "there was a great deal of obstruction and wilful misunderstanding and heckling. When it was pointed out that the new church was now independent and received no funds from abroad, someone inquired innocently who was financing the present assembly — food, lodging and railway travel. The reply was that this was a special occasion, an organizational meeting!"[60] Bishop Abe Yoshimune, the CCJ's senior emissary to the Chinese church, was called up from Shanghai in June to shepherd the process along. The Japanese embassy participated by distributing to Chinese Christian leaders copies of the CCJ constitution as a model for their own organization of church union.

A second conference in October went more smoothly. A city newspaper reported that the goal was to create "a purely self-administered, self-supported missionary body for the propagation of the Christian faith by indigenous efforts, the realization and perpetuation of a long-cherished Christian ideal shared alike by enthusiastic native believers and the more far sighted foreign clergymen for at least a score of years." The conference was heralded precisely for its political significance, as ushering in

a bright new era in Christian missionary work in North China which will be independent of Anglo-American support and free of such domination and influence as have been responsible for all the evil stigmatizations in the past and which will engage in the preaching of the holy gospel in the spirit of Christianity's truthful self and incidentally to share with the Christian Church in Japan and Manchuria in the task for the reconstruction of Greater East Asia.[61]

The new North China Christian Union looked somewhat different than the CCC. Although the NCCU had greater governmental oversight built into its organization, it was, at least on paper, more ambitious. Its committee on evangelism mapped out an extraordinary range of activities, including discussion groups for church volunteers, women's meetings, itinerant libraries, prison outreach, factory evangelism, coeducational seminaries, even Chinese missions abroad. Still, the NCCU was not exactly what the Japanese wanted, for it allowed denominations to maintain separate identities and properties within the circle of unification. Church and mission properties, "for the sake of convenience and pending the formulation of definite plans of allotment and control by the new association, should independently be placed under the custodianship of the respective churches of the different denominations in the various areas." The effective control of churches thus remained in denominational hands at the local level, formally out of the reach of Japanese advisors. Additionally, the NCCU vowed to approach the authorities to ask that the Japanese army return all church properties it had occupied and was not presently using. The NCCU thus provided Christians of North China with a vehicle for challenging the army on property claims. Here was church union, but as much on Chinese as on Japanese terms.

The work of union that had begun in the north in the spring of 1942 was continued further south the following winter. A Central China Christian Federation was established in Hankou in December 1942, followed by a union for eastern China in Shanghai. According to a missionary, the Shanghai union was formally instituted in March 1943 "after much delay and repeated Japanese demands," the Chinese members yielding only on nonessential points.[62]

Some foreign observers were willing to concede that the forced union of Protestant churches was a positive development. Susie Kelsey, the Canadian nurse whose observations on self-support I have already quoted, felt that union, with its attendant promotion of independence from foreign missions, could help safeguard Christianity in China:

Closer fellowship and co-operation between the different branches of the Protestant Church, if not permanent union, will surely be the result of such bodies as the present United Church of North China [NCCU] formed under pressure from the Japanese army of occupation. Already one sees good results from this originally feared federation of churches as they are able to present a united front to the authorities in the face of demands which would compromise Christian consciences and assist each other in keeping and recovering Church buildings desired by the military.[63]

According to CCC executive secretary A. J. Fisher in 1943, many Chinese Christian leaders supported Japan's push for church union. They "throw themselves into it in the hope that something good may come out of it. They want union, of course, but not on the terms offered by Japan. On one hand they have to do it to save themselves and the church, on the other hand they hope to gain something out of it for a united church in China for the future. The Japanese have impressed the most prominent and ablest leaders."[64] Another missionary noted in 1943 that "the attitude of the leaders — preachers, Church workers, teachers, doctors, etc. — towards their duties has been one of devoted consecration in the midst of great danger. They have been forced in many cases to a degree of compromise and 'cooperation' as a means of preserving an inner liberty, and conserving the means for future recovery."[65]

"Preserving an inner liberty" was a weak defense in the eyes of Christians who had fled to western China, who tended to view the steps toward union and independence as collaboration with the enemy. Y. Y. Tsu (Zhu Youyu), Anglican bishop of Kunming, writing in 1944, anticipated this problem in the postwar dispensation:

What will happen to the enemy-sponsored federations after the war, only time will show. It is conceivable that those unfriendly to Christian churches may make it difficult for the churches and Christian institutions on the pretext of 'collaboration with the enemy.' There will possibly be also revulsion among the church members against certain church leaders who seemed to be too ready to seize authority under enemy auspices. On the other hand, it may be found that the Federation has given valuable experience in close cooperation. Certainly the cutting off of financial resources from abroad during this period has strengthened the movement for self-support.[66]

With much the same thought in the back of his mind, Fisher closed his assessment of union by wondering what relationship this "forced union," with its taint of collaboration after the war, might have to a "free-will union" after the war.

Independence Without Autonomy

Through the wartime experience of Christianity in occupied China run two strands, both of which are important to the fabric of postwar and postrevolution Chinese Christianity.

One strand reflects the negative impact of the occupation: the physical destruction of church property, the demoralization of clergy and congregation, and the absorption of Chinese Christian leaders into the schemes of the occupation state. Assessing occupation Christianity in these terms was common among commentators immediately after the war. A summary of conditions circulated by the CCC in early 1946 represents this strand when it declares: "From the surveys made thus far, we find discouraging features, ruin and devastation, many ardent church workers have given their all and are no more, others have lost their homes or their possessions. Yes, a few, it must be confessed, have succumbed to hardships and dangers and thereby lost their faith."[67] Although the authors of this summary round it off by declaring that "when all is added up, however, the encouraging features far outweigh the discouraging ones," the overall picture as they saw it was dim.

This analysis, mailed out to secretaries of the boards of foreign missions, was premised on the conviction that Western missionaries were once again needed in China. Chester Miao (Miao Qiusheng), a prominent Baptist educator who spent the war years in Shanghai, edited and published a little book in New York in 1948 that tends to reflect this view. Miao called for Americans to come to China "to strengthen the church in China with new missionary personnel, since the latter is still weak in its leadership, especially in view of the overwhelming new problems created by the war." He urged that they come "not as representatives of Western culture and society," however, but "as ambassadors of Christ." Miao also called on American industrialists "with Christian ideals and spirit" to invest in the Chinese economy.[68] In other words, nothing had changed: the China field still awaited missionizing.

The other strand regards the occupation in a different way. It judges the changes that Chinese Christianity underwent during the occupation as having contributed something positive to its development. By the chance of war, the Chinese church found itself thrust forward into a stage of independence it had not been able to attain on its own. The cutting off of Western mission funds forced the church to become self-supporting, the removal of Western missionaries forced it to become self-propagating, and the new responsibilities of leadership encouraged it to become self-governing. As Y. C. Tu (Tu Yuqing) of the YMCA observes with some pride in the second chapter of Miao's book,

> The churches and other Christian institutions in the occupied territory maintained themselves after help had been cut off upon the outbreak of the Pacific War. Suddenly they found themselves thrown upon their own physical and spiritual resources. The child was forcibly weaned from the mother. Some struggled against the pressure of occupation, and in many cases succeeded in keeping the properties intact and the work going. Others struggled to maintain their work and personnel intact, using whatever local support was available.[69]

Tu notes further that the end of extraterritoriality and the experience of self-help were assets for building "a genuine Chinese Christian movement." This brighter assessment understands that a genuine Chinese Christian movement is impossible so long as it is directed, organizationally or theologically, by missionaries tied to the privileges and capabilities of an external power. The occupation state promoted the independence of the Chinese church to serve its own purposes; that having been done, some Chinese Christian leaders felt there was no need for the missionary ranks of the prewar years to be refilled. It was time for the Chinese church to go it alone.

These two strands tangled in the immediate postwar context, generating both personal and historical contradictions. At the personal level, tensions between those Christians who went to West China during the war and those who stayed behind were palpable. Each suspected the other's motives; neither understood the trials and sacrifices the other had made to survive and keep Christianity alive in his own locale. Many who returned from West China assumed that the Christian world had to go back to the way it had been in 1937, whereas those who had not fled felt that the gains they had struggled for should be preserved.

At the historical level, the two strands also tangled over the relationship of Christianity to the state. It was not that one group supported state supervision and the other rejected it; but those who had accepted Japanese-sponsored union believed that they had manipulated the occupation state to their advantage, creating organizations that could better withstand improper state influence than loosely cooperating denominations. They had bowed to the necessity of working with the state without, they felt, sacrificing their Christian principles. Their critics, on the other hand, regarded anything created under the auspices of the occupation state as illegitimate because it had come from outside the church. They felt that the church had to follow its own path, autonomous from the state. "Free cooperation in the common interest" was superior to "police or bureaucratic ordering."[70]

The return of the Guomindang state in 1945 meant that the issue of Christianity's autonomy from the state, which the war had forced onto the agenda of occupied Christianity, receded from general concern. But the arrival of the Communist state four years later brought the issue once again to the fore, along with many of the organizational innovations of the occupation. With the triumph of the Communist Party, the leading principles of the occupation church — independence, self-support, and self-propagation — were invoked. Church union, itself a declaration of independence from Western denominationalism, was once again demanded.[71] With independence from the West now the hallmark of Chinese Christianity, Christians who had gone west during the war to avoid collaborating with Japanese imperialism found themselves vulnerable to the charge of having collaborated with Western imperialism. Autonomy from the Chinese state was henceforth impossible.

The grand irony in the history of occupation Christianity is that the Chinese church would not have become substantially independent or united were it not for the Japanese invasion. A further irony is that neither independence nor union would have been preserved were it not for the Communist revolution. The tragedy behind both ironies is that independence from the West is only half of what constitutes religious self-determination. The other half, autonomy from the state, has still to be attained.

CHAPTER 19

Y. T. Wu: A Christian Leader Under Communism

GAO WANGZHI

Wu Yaozong, also known as Y. T. Wu (1893–1979), founder of the Protestant Three-Self Movement and its leader for almost thirty years until his death, was a controversial figure and the subject of widely varying assessments by both Chinese and Western Christians. His successor, Bishop Ding Guangxun (K. H. Ting), wrote in 1983: "I think we may say that Y. T. in starting the Three-Self Movement was doing something comparable to the historical role that Paul played, in that they both caused the Christian religion to rid itself of certain deformities and narrowness and ushered it into a new stage of history." He emphasized that it was Y. T. Wu himself who enabled Chinese Christianity "to get a fresh image before the Chinese people." Ding also wrote about how he was inspired by his predecessor when he saw "how closely Y. T.'s love for Christ and his concern for the wellbeing of the people were harmonized and how his loyalty to Christ generated in him a great passion for truth, for life's ideals and for the people."[1] Most of the other leaders of the Three-Self Movement and certain Western Christians sympathetic to that movement cherish a similar respect for Y. T. Wu.

However, Wu was far from a positive figure in the eyes of quite a few Western critics. The editor of *Ching Feng*, a Hong Kong Christian periodical, wrote: "Wu has been branded by some as a heretic or an anti-Christ, while others would question his intentions and his integrity as a Christian and wonder if he has not betrayed his faith through the close alliance with the Communist government."[2] Although the majority of Western critics have made a negative assessment of Wu, there are also a few Westerners who take a middle position, critical but not denunciatory of him. For instance, Francis Price Jones wrote:

It seems clear that he was motivated by an honest conviction of the value of communism, a sincere love for the church, and a desire to save it from destruction. Approval cannot be given to all that he has done through the Three-Self Movement. He had allowed the church to be a "captive church," doing nothing but parrot the Communist line. But he undoubtedly felt that this was the only alternative to complete destruction. He was misled by a too optimistic expectation of tolerance of religion from the Communist government and by a failure to appreciate the depth of meaning in Tertullian's famous dictum that "the blood of martyrs is the seed of the church."[3]

There is a soundness in the view of Jones — who had long experience in China and a deep understanding of the Chinese Protestant church, and was able somewhat to rid himself of one-sidedness — not to regard Y. T. Wu as either an absolutely positive or an absolutely negative figure.

Now, more than fifteen years after Wu's death, we can look at his career more soberly. There is a Chinese saying, "A final judgment can be passed on a person only when the lid is laid on his coffin."

This chapter discusses some important aspects of Wu's career. Anyone who comments on this controversial figure inescapably will be involved in the controversy. But is it possible that we can attain in academic discussions or even debates some consensus on the evaluation of Wu? I think it is possible, provided that there is a common criterion, which might be formulated in one phrase: whether his career and actions were beneficial or detrimental to the survival and fortunes of Chinese Protestant Christians at large.

Before 1949

Y. T. Wu was born on 4 November 1893 in Guangdong into a non-Christian family, and did not convert to Christianity until he was an adult. His first enlightenment of faith came from a speech made by John R. Mott in Beijing in 1913 when Wu was twenty years old. Wu accepted the Christian faith five years later, in 1918, at a mass rally conducted by Sherwood Eddy, and was baptized soon afterward by Rev. Rowland Cross. By the end of 1920, he left his post at the Customs Office of Beijing and was appointed as a secretary of the Student Division of the Beijing YMCA, the starting point of his lifelong Christian career.

In the autumn of 1924 Wu arrived in the United States to receive theological and religious education. He studied both at the Union Theological Seminary and Columbia University, and in 1927 he received his M.A. in philosophy from Columbia with a dissertation entitled "William James' Doctrine of Religious Belief."

During the period of more than twenty years after he returned to China in 1927 through his inauguration of the Three-Self Movement, he worked for the National Committee of the Chinese YMCA, the headquarters of which was in Shanghai, except for the years of the Anti-Japanese War when it was in Chengdu. From 1927 to 1932 he was at the Student Division as its secretary and then executive secretary, and from 1932 onward he was in charge of publications, as editor-in-chief of the Association Press. Much of his time and efforts were dedicated to the editing and publication of the *Youth Library*, which was published in two series, consisting of 50 and 45 monographs respectively, including a number of books or translations done by himself. In 1946 he initiated the periodical *Tianfeng*, which has been the main magazine of the Protestant church of mainland China ever since.

During the three decades before 1949, Y. T. Wu's thought evolved through three stages, a subject to which we now turn.

1920–30. Y. T. Wu's thought during this earlier period of his life can be summed up in a single word: pacifism. Two historic events shook China on the eve of the 1920s: the Russian October Revolution in 1917 and the Chinese May Fourth Movement in 1919. The two ushered in the Communist movement in China and led to the establishment of the Chinese Communist Party on 1 July 1921. The Chinese Communists, though then still few in number, had considerable influence among students. As a student secretary of the Beijing YMCA, Wu consciously stood opposite the Communists. In April 1922 he participated in the Eleventh Enlarged Congress of the World Student Christian Federation. This congress took place at Qinghua University in Beijing, despite the vigorous objections of radical students who had tried to prevent the convening of the congress in China, and who had founded the Anti-Christian Federation about this time. During the congress Wu proposed to organize a Christian Student Movement in China, a proposal that was supported by other Christian delegates.[4] Wu later praised the congress for its achievement in bringing to Chinese Christian students a new spirit and motive force.

During this period Wu had no sympathy at all with Communist ideology. On the contrary, he cherished a strong belief in the power of "love." He understood "love" as a principle of action, by which he meant nonviolence; "love" was also the transcendent will of God. For Wu, the essence of Christianity remained the way of "love" as exemplified by Jesus Christ. In 1922 Wu founded in Beijing a China branch of the Fellowship of Reconciliation, an international Christian pacifist society. The Chinese name he gave to this branch was Weiaishe (literally "Society for Love Alone"). Wu began to publish a bimonthly journal bearing the same name.

Back in China in 1927 from the United States, now as the National Student Secretary of the Chinese YMCA, Wu continued his endeavor to organize a Chinese Christian Student Movement, and succeeded in establishing in the same year a preparatory committee for the movement. In Wu's words, the purpose of the movement was "to create fellowship among youth and to make our personality sound in the spirit of Jesus so as to strive for the liberation and development of the people's life."[5] His emphasis on fellowship and personality showed that he truly believed in the power of "love" and "reconciliation." In April 1927, the leadership of the Guomindang began to purge the Communists from the party, and in response the Communists rebelled against the GMD, claiming that the revolution had been sabotaged. At the time, Wu wrote nothing against the purge; on the contrary he gushed that "the great Chinese revolution of 1925–1927 inaugurated a new era, and all the Chinese people rejoiced over its victory." However, Wu's rejoicing over the victory of the GMD in 1927 did not last long. He continued, "The imagination of the students had been raised [in 1927] to the point of exhilaration only to be dashed by disillusion and disappointment." But his opposition to the Communists did not change: "The advocacy of class struggle, the use of brutal force, terrorism, the breaking down of all moral virtues, were their ideal methods and these were abhorred by the Chinese people, who held an entirely different philosophy of life."[6] In view of his conviction of "love" and "nonviolence," it was no wonder that he became an admirer of Mahatma Gandhi, whose autobiography he translated and eventually published in 1933.

1931–40. An enthusiasm for the social gospel characterized the next stage in Y. T. Wu's life. The social gospel — a reaction against unrestrained individualism and capitalism — was at that time a few decades old among American Protestants. The leaders of this movement, troubled by social injustice, advocated gradual social reform, which they believed would be predicated upon the goodness of human nature and the effectiveness of religious ethical persuasion. Wu's change of orientation began by the end of the 1920s, when he was deeply moved by the calamities of the great worldwide depression. He came to believe that the most urgent need of Chinese society was not just "love" but material reconstruction. The social gospel movement in the United States impressed him strongly. Early in the 1930s he wrote a number of articles advocating the theories of the social gospel, which were collected in a book published in 1934 under the title *The Social Gospel*. He also translated some works of Walter Rauschenbusch, an important American theorist of the social gospel, but he was never able to publish them.

The Japanese military occupation of Manchuria in September 1931, as Wu recalled later, was a turning point in his life. He resigned from the Fellowship of Reconciliation presidency and began to give up pacifism, which he no longer worshipped but regretfully labeled "a beautiful dream" of his earlier life. From then on, Wu became increasingly interested in the politics of China as well as in the anti-Japanese movement, which was developing all over the country; he even joined the patriotic National Salvation Society, a political organization in Shanghai.

All these testify to his firm belief in the social gospel, which was not absolutely new to him, because he had heard something about it during his study in New York from 1924 to 1927. When he went to the Union Theological Seminary for a second time from spring to fall of 1937, he was deeply influenced by the theories of Henry Frederick Ward (1873–1966), who was called the "leftist prophet of labor," and Reinhold Niebuhr (1892–1971), an outstanding popular liberal theologian. This helps to account for his radical inclination in the next decade.

1941–49. Y. T. Wu's thought during the last stage of his life before 1949 can be characterized as procommunist or Christian socialist. It is difficult to tell when and how Wu definitely came to favor communism; it might have been a gradual process starting from the mid-1930s. After 1934 he began to sympathize with socialist revolution. In 1943, he declared that he had no difficulties with communist theory. In his important theological treatise *No Man Has Seen God* (the title is a citation from John 1), he wrote:

Our conclusion is that belief in God is not contradictory to materialism, just as it is not contradictory to "evolution," because both "evolution" and materialism can be taken as the means by which God reveals Himself in nature. . . . A person who believes in God can also believe in materialism. . . . Even a materialist should be able to accept faith in God. . . . How do we know in the future the two seemingly contradictory systems of thought will not achieve a new synthesis?[7]

Wu had an in-depth talk with Zhou Enlai on 27 May 1943 in Chongqing; this may be regarded as symbolizing a finishing touch to his procommunist orientation.[8] Yet as late as 1947, he was not hostile to American Christian leaders and praised John Mott, whom he met in Europe that year, as the world's foremost Christian leader.

Not long after, in April 1948, he published a challenging article entitled "The Present-Day Tragedy of Christianity," which was actually his declaration of war against the foreign missions, particularly the American missions, in China. Jessie Lutz writes that the article criticized "the church for its negative attitude toward a developing world revolution" and declared that "the church and its institutions . . . needed drastic reform if they were to cease being reactionary forces molded by anachronistic capitalistic society." The "cries of outrage from Christian groups" in response to the article "forced the resignation of Wu as one of the editors of the magazine" *Tianfeng*.[9]

After 1949

After the Communist victory in 1949, Y. T. Wu emerged as the leader of the Chinese Protestants. He served as the president of the Three-Self Movement from its establishment in 1951 until his death on 17 September 1979. But his career actually did not last that long; it ended with the Cultural Revolution in mid-1966. Thus, his leadership lasted seventeen years, from the time when he was 56 until he was 73. In spite of his age and failing health, he did not spare himself in fulfilling his burdensome tasks. The Protestant church in mainland China was beaten almost to death by the Red Guards; however, it did not disappear. The survival of the church may be regarded as the principal achievement of Wu in his capacity as the leader of the Three-Self Movement. Indeed, saving the church was Wu's paramount goal in launching that movement. M. Searle Bates argued that "Wu's stand, as viewed closely in 1949–50, seemed to be—and indeed was, I believe—an earnest attempt to find a place for the Christian faith and people to live and to serve in a totalitarian revolution and reconstruction convinced of the early demise of religion."[10]

Of course, the survival of the Protestant church was not the achievement of Wu alone; it must also be attributed to the hard work and self-sacrifice of the Chinese Protestant Christians at large, clergy and laity alike. Besides, the CCP understands now that it is desirable to let the church survive. In short, the survival of the Chinese church has been the result of different causes, but one cannot deny the positive role played by Wu. Chinese Christians, no matter where they now live, on the mainland, in Taiwan, Hong Kong, the United States or wherever, and also their foreign friends, the former missionaries in particular, all prefer to see the Protestant church survive in mainland China, even though the church today may not seem quite satisfactory to them.

The Christian Manifesto. The famous Christian Manifesto—a short statement of less than one thousand Chinese characters—published in July 1950, is mainly a political rather than theological treatise. Its real title is *Direction of Endeavor for Chinese Christianity in the Construction of New China*, which sounds much different from a "Christian manifesto." Wu was its principal draftsman, and it fully represented ideas already expressed in his article of 1948, "The Present-Day Tragedy of Christianity," the appearance of which has been regarded by some scholars as the actual beginning of the Three-Self Movement. However, it would be inappropriate to say that the manifesto was merely Wu's personal writing. Rather, it was a product of a particular time—from 1948 to 1950—that witnessed the victory of the CCP and the establishment of the PRC. More specifically, it was an outgrowth of three interviews in May 1950 between Zhou Enlai and a group of Christian leaders headed by Y. T. Wu.[11]

The Christian Manifesto took as its principal theme anti-imperialism, and stressed "the fact that in the past imperialism has made use of Christianity," and the necessity to "purge imperialistic influences from within Christianity itself." Was it a manifesto of "betrayal," as Leslie T. Lyall asserted?[12] If one scrutinizes it word for word, one must conclude it was not. The manifesto confirmed the contributions made in the past by the Chinese church, and did not stigmatize the church directly as a tool of imperialism, but lamented that the church "unfortunately" had been tied to imperialism.

Nevertheless, if one reexamines the manifesto seriously, one will find that it was not favorable to Chinese Protestants at large. To many if not most Chinese Protestants it seemed too radical. Indeed, the Chinese Shenggonghui (Episcopal Church) refused to endorse the Christian Manifesto and issued a manifesto of its own. Soon afterwards, the Korean War broke out and the CCP intensified its anti-American propaganda. With these developments, the political atmosphere changed dramatically.

It was reported that within a span of two years the Christian Manifesto was endorsed by about 400,000 Christians, roughly half of the entire population of Chinese Protestants. The figure is meaningful from opposite perspectives: positively, it proved that Y. T. Wu and other procommunist Christian leaders had won a remarkable following; negatively, it demonstrated that half of the Chinese Protestants did not agree with severing all foreign links. It would be absurd to assume that half of the Protestant population were not patriotic. They were simply unwilling to endorse the manifesto or to be procommunist.

Apart from its overly radical tone, the manifesto had another important deficiency: it failed to give Chinese Christians any preparation for the forthcoming challenge from the Communist-ruled society in which they were destined to live. On the contrary, the manifesto conveyed a naïve and overoptimistic picture of the future. A paragraph under the subtitle "The Task in General" reads: "Christian churches and organizations give thoroughgoing support to the 'Common Political Platform,' and under the leadership of the government oppose imperialism, feudalism, and bureaucratic capitalism, and take part in the effort to build an independent, democratic, peaceable, unified, prosperous, and powerful New China." This paragraph implied that if Chinese Christians behaved well they would have a bright future. But actual historical developments were quite different. Christians responded to the call of the manifesto, but the church did not fare well and many Christians became victims of persecution. In this sense, the manifesto misled Chinese Protestants rather than providing them with a correct "direction."

In contrast, another contemporary Christian document, which was never published in China, contained some brilliant insights. This was the "Message from Chinese Christians to Mission Boards Abroad," written in December 1949 or about half a year before the Christian Manifesto was drafted. The authors of the Message wrote:

We are not unmindful of the challenges and difficulties lying ahead on a more fundamental way. Just how the Christian gospel can be witnessed in a clime that is by virtue of its ideology, fundamentally materialistic and atheistic presents a challenge stronger than ever before.

The banner of the Cross has never been easy to carry and it will not be easy in the new era of China.

The new philosophy [in the PRC] considers that all phases of life must necessarily come under the influence of politics in contradistinction to the traditional Protestant view of the separation between church and state. In a world where political influences play such an important part and affect our lives and work so extensively, it is a challenge how the church as an institution and how Christians as citizens in society can perform their Christian functions and discharge their duties to society at the same time.

In its assessment of missionaries, the document was fair-minded:

We do realize and so wish to assert that missionary work in China never had any direct relationship with government policies; mission funds have always been contributed by the rank and file of common ordinary Christians and church members; missionaries have been sent here for no other purpose than to preach the Christian gospel of love, and to serve the needs of the Chinese people. The central Christian motivation will not and can never be questioned, but these other social implications can very easily give rise to misunderstanding and accusation.

Finally, as a conclusion, this document correctly predicted that, for the Chinese church, "Its future road will not be a rose bed."[13]

According to Donald MacInnis, this document was written by an informal group of Protestant leaders who later became some of the founders of the Three-Self Movement. Y. T. Wu was probably not one of its drafts-men, because it did not represent his radical ideas at the time. Although he was apparently overoptimistic, one cannot say that he did not have any misgivings about the prospects of the Chinese church under the Commu-nists. But it seemed that he would rather not speak out, and was annoyed to be asked about any unfavorable possibilities in the future. Bishop Ding Guangxun met him at Prague in May 1949 and asked him whether, if the Communist government should try to extinguish religion, he would still support New China. Wu was unhappy with this question and criticized Ding for giving grounds too easily for talk in the Western press about the persecution of religion in China; and then he said, "Even in the eventuality that religion will be harassed, I will still love the motherland." He continued to say that he was sure that in New China problems or grievances of all sorts would be settled through a democratic process of consultation.[14] His words were sincerely spoken but unfortunately not justified by the course of events.

The Establishment and Activities of the Three-Self Movement. The Three-Self Movement of Chinese Protestants was formally inaugurated in 1951, and to no one's surprise, Y. T. Wu became its president. The terms "self-government," "self-support," and "self-propagation" were not the invention of Wu or his colleagues. Long before, Western missionaries had already talked about them with regard to Chinese Christianity. Shirley Garrett has written about the intention of Willard Lyon, who came to China at the end of the last century, to set up a Chinese YMCA: "The Association in America stipulated that the Chinese Association, like all others started by the In-ternational Committee outside the United States, should become self-propagating, self-governing, and self-supporting as quickly as possible. Lyon was pledged to start not a movement that would be an alien growth, but one that would become truly indigenous."[15] However, owing to a variety of hindrances and difficulties, this aim had not been fully realized before 1949. It was Y. T. Wu who made use of the political situation right after 1949 to accomplish the founding on a national scale of the Three-Self Movement.

Nominally speaking, this movement should have been an interdenomi-national patriotic association of Chinese Protestants rather than their high-est ecclesiastical authorities. Otherwise Wu in his capacity at that time as one of the leaders of the Chinese YMCA, instead of an ecclesiastical leader, would not have been eligible to be its president. Several prestigious eccle-siastical leaders were then still active, among them Bishop Chen Jianzhen (Robin Ch'en) of the Shenggonghui (Episcopal Church), Bishop Jiang

Changchuan (Z. K. Kaung) of the Methodist church, and others, but they were not as fully trusted by the new regime as was Y. T. Wu. According to M. Searle Bates, at the time Wu was the only Christian leader "who could give the word on the national scale."[16] Gradually the Three-Self took on the function of an ecclesiastical authority, especially after 1958, when Protestant denominations ceased to exist in China.

The unification of Chinese churches in 1958 was both a natural and unnatural event. The year 1958 in China was a time of the nationwide Great Leap Forward and the people's communes, and in that context it was natural that ecclesiastical unification would take place as a response of the Chinese churches to the call of making a "great leap forward." It sounded very desirable to Communist officials, who would have logically thought that since all the Chinese villages were being communized according to the principle of "large in size and collective in nature," why should not the churches follow suit? Eventually, various cities in China undertook ecclesiastical unification on their own, without thinking of the necessity to get the approval from corresponding denominational authorities. Nevertheless, such actions were quite unnatural because so abrupt a nationwide ecclesiastical unification was something unique in the universal history of the Protestant church.

Undoubtedly, abrupt unification meant the wholesale abandonment of ritual differences between the denominations and the curtailment of many activities. Unification on these terms was especially detrimental to the evangelical churches. In a sense, the government purposely took the opportunity of the unification to subjugate the evangelicals. An official document regarding the unification of churches in the city of Taiyuan instructed that:

(1) The Little Flock shall abolish its women's meetings, its weekly breaking of bread, its personal interview with members before the breaking of bread, and its rule against women speaking in the church.

(2) The Salvation Army shall give up all its military regulations.

(3) The Seventh-day Adventists shall abolish their daily morning prayers, and they shall work on the Sabbath. Their tithe system for the support of the clergy shall be abolished.[17]

After the unification of 1958, all the different Protestant churches in China became in fact Three-Self churches, although this has not been an official name for them. The government was pleased to see that the churches were now in the hands of those it trusted, but the aftermath of such a sudden change was traumatic to many Chinese Protestants. Francis Jones recorded that a female Chinese-British professor of chemistry visited

Chengdu in 1959 and discovered that "her several Quaker friends, after sitting together with the other denominations for several months, had decided that they did not feel at home in that kind of service and would go back to their own meeting for worship." She also found the other denominations were talking of doing the same.[18] In fact, much of the house church phenomenon, still strong in China today, dates back to the coerced unification of 1958.

Evaluating the work of the Three-Self Movement is a crucial problem in the assessment of Y. T. Wu's career. Essentially the movement served as a bridge between the Chinese government and Chinese Protestants, excluding those evangelicals who did not affiliate with it. The government undoubtedly has regarded the movement as an indispensable tool for ruling the Protestants. The Three-Self under the leadership of Y. T. Wu suffered serious failures, many of which resulted from its weakness in dealing with radical leftism in the policy of the government.

The contemporary Three-Self leadership has stressed three main achievements of their movement under Wu in the 1950s, namely: encouraging Chinese Protestants to become patriotic, helping the Chinese church to become self-governing, and urging Chinese Christianity to get rid of its foreign features.[19] I do not think such claims are convincing. First, the bulk of Chinese Christians had never been unpatriotic before 1949; second, the Chinese church is still not fully self-governing, because it has not been fully independent from the state in terms of supervision or financial support; and third, the indigenization of the church started long before the inauguration of the Three-Self Movement. In my opinion the main, if not the only, achievement of the Three-Self Movement and Y. T. Wu was their contribution to the survival of the Protestant church; everything else is negligible. Now let us turn to the topic of the denunciation campaigns, which are illustrative of Wu's failures resulting from his weakness in confronting leftism.

Denunciation Campaigns Among the Protestants. There were frequent denunciation campaigns in mainland China during the fifteen years between 1951 and 1966, especially in the circles of professors, scholars, writers, entrepreneurs, and religious leaders. Of course such campaigns did not happen spontaneously but were launched by the CCP. Today the Chinese people condemn those denunciation campaigns, and the leadership of the CCP has promised not to resume them, but still we have to learn lessons from them. The campaigns in the Protestant churches were extraordinarily intense, because many churches were closely linked with the American missions, and the United States was categorically the number one enemy at the time.

Many students in American missionary universities very naturally had grown attached to their missionary teachers, but this was abhorrent in the eyes of Communist officials. I myself remember a 1951 farewell party held at Yanjing University by students in honor of some American teachers, to whom was presented a red silk banner embroidered with a familiar eulogy in four Chinese characters, literally "[you are like] the spring breeze and rain [which have benefited our intellectual growth]." This event greatly irritated the officials, who immediately made use of it as "proof" of the necessity of their anti-American propaganda and denunciation campaigns.

If we were to draw up a list of the Protestant victims of the campaigns, we would easily see that the most influential theologians and the charismatic evangelical leaders were the most vulnerable to denunciation. To illustrate, there were campaigns against the prestigious Methodist leader Bishop Chen Wenyuan in 1951; against the renowned theologian and dean of the Yanjing School of Religion, Zhao Zichen (T. C. Chao) in 1952; against the founder of the Jesus Family, Rev. Jing Dianying (Ching Tienying) later in 1952; against the famous evangelical leaders Wang Mingdao and Ni Tuosheng (Watchman Nee) in 1955–56; against Rev. Chen Chonggui (Marcus Cheng), president of the Chongqing Theological Seminary and one of the vice-presidents of the Three-Self; and against Rev. Shao Jingsan (Luther Shao), leader of the Disciples' Church, during the Anti-Rightist Campaign in 1957.

The denunciations were generally unjustifiable; often the victims were selected not because they had done or spoken anything unpatriotic, but only because they were, in the eyes of the officials, too influential or too popular. For example, Rev. Chen Chonggui, an important conservative theologian, was denounced on the pretext that earlier in 1957 he made an "anti-Communist" speech, which was published in full in the *People's Daily* of 25 March 1957. This was actually a sincere and candid speech, in which Chen adopted a cooperative attitude toward the CCP and the government, while at the same time he persisted in his pious Christian faith. His criticism of Communist officials was severe but goodwilled. Chen said:

At the opening of a new bridge, an official of high rank gave an address, in which he emphasized that this bridge had been made by human effort, and was not the work of any so-called God. Then he said, "You Christians should throw your God into the dungheap." Such blasphemy of God, in the eyes of Christians, is worse than reviling one's mother. This is not criticism, but abuse of religion. . . . On the other hand, I must say that even when we are abused and our temples defiled, we can bear it and forgive. . . . We should bear it gladly, for Jesus said, "Great is your reward in Heaven."[20]

Obviously there was nothing improper in Chen's speech, let alone anything anti-Communist, but in a denunciation meeting his speech was condemned as "the greatest defamation ever made against the Communist Party, the People's Government, and the vast people of our nation."[21] Chen was then severely punished as a "rightist" and during the ensuing six years, until his death, he lived in unbearable humiliation.

We cannot let Y. T. Wu alone bear the responsibility of the absurd and cruel denunciation campaigns, but this does not mean that he should not bear a certain amount of blame. Many articles appearing at that time in *Tianfeng*, which was under his direct leadership, supported and even fostered these campaigns. For instance, in a 1951 article entitled "How to Hold a Successful Denunciation Meeting," Liu Liangmo, then national secretary of the Chinese YMCA, compared the denunciation campaigns to Jesus' rebuke of the scribes and Pharisees. He advised holding rehearsals first so as "to discover a few people who accuse with the greatest power and invite them to participate in the large accusation meeting; one can also correct certain weaknesses in their speaking." He also wrote, "the order of arrangement of the accusers is very important; they should be arranged as follows: first high tension, then moderate, then another high tension, etc.; only so can the accusation meeting be a success."[22] Everything was dramatized and performed under the instructions of the directors. People could never find the Christian principle of "love" in these campaigns; what was highlighted was hatred of one's own pastors and brothers and sisters in the faith.

Evangelical victims in the campaigns were especially numerous. In the 1950s there developed hostility between evangelical leaders on the one hand and the new regime and the Three-Self on the other. At first the contradiction was not serious, but later on it developed into a sharp conflict. The government adopted a policy of repressing evangelical leaders, and this has been one of the main reasons why the evangelicals have grown rapidly in China during recent years. Y. T. Wu was theologically a consistent modernist who was critical of fundamentalism and evangelicalism, and it seems that he did little to mitigate the conflict. An editorial in the February 1956 issue of *Tianfeng*, entitled "Drive Out the Sinister Wolves," condemned Watchman Nee and other leaders of the Little Flock. Surely the publication of this editorial was approved by Y. T. Wu. No matter what kind of justification there may have been for such an editorial, the effect could only have been to drive many Christians of the Little Flock into opposition to the government and the Three-Self. This alienation of the evangelicals was one of the most serious failures in Y. T. Wu's career.

"Socialist Religion": A Futile Suggestion. A few years before 1966, Y. T. Wu had a long talk with Li Weihan, an important leader of the CCP since the 1930s and at that time head of the United Front Work Department of the CCP Central Committee, the highest official in charge of religious affairs. Wu suggested to Li that the term "socialist religion" should be accepted by the CCP, and he made a detailed argument for his suggestion; however, he did not succeed in convincing Li.[23]

This anecdote, which is believable, is illustrative of Wu's thought as well as of the attitude of the CCP toward religion. As mentioned above, Wu had long asserted that belief in God was not contradictory to materialism, and that it was possible in the future the two would come together in a new synthesis. This was the theoretical basis of his suggestion, which he offered to the CCP for the purpose of attaining a legal status for religion in socialist China. Evidently it was his sincere expectation that if his suggestion was accepted, the Christian church would be able to get rid of discrimination and prejudice and enjoy a real freedom of faith.

However, this was a completely unrealistic expectation. The CCP consistently held to the theory that "religion is the opiate of the people," although recently it seldom states this openly. Mao Zedong himself was hostile to religious belief. In one of his important theses, *On Coalition Government*, published in 1940, he wrote that Communists may form an anti-imperialist and antifeudal united front for political action with certain idealists and even with religious followers, but "we can never approve of their idealism or religious doctrines." Today, several decades after Mao's statement, no fundamental change has occurred in the attitude of the CCP, although some Christian leaders still hope for a change.

Y. T. Wu's suggestion of "socialist religion" was not an exceptional Chinese idea; similar theories appeared in the former Soviet Union and East European countries. An article in the Soviet journal *Science and Religion* in the 1960s claimed that "Christianity is harmonious, fitting, and in step with the process of transforming social relations on socialist and communist principles," and that "Christianity has developed into 'Communist Christianity.'" Talking specifically about the situation in Russia, the article argued that "in the Russian Orthodox Church, the building of the kingdom of Christ on earth is more and more associated with communist transformation of the world."[24] This Soviet article was vehemently condemned in a critique in a 1969 issue of the CCP's official organ *Red Flag*. The critique declared that "scientific communism and religion are antagonistic. The struggle for the realization of the ideals of communism in the whole world and 'the building of the kingdom of Christ on earth' are just as incompatible as fire and water."[25] So far there is not any indication that this attitude will be changed in the future.

Y. T. Wu wrote in 1958, "I do not feel any anxiety about the future of Christianity. The Communist Party does not believe in religion, but it protects religion and respects religious faith."[26] By harboring such a naïve expectation, Wu failed to take measures necessary to safeguard the Protestant church. Bishop Ding wrote in 1983 that in the past

Y. T. and many other Chinese church leaders seemed to be only counting on the implementation of the policy of religious freedom by the government, without any strong realization yet that Chinese Christianity had no right to feel complacent by depending for its survival on that policy, and the Christians needed to work hard to make the Chinese church self-governing, self-supporting, and self-propagating, if we were to have a footing for carrying on conversation with our fellow-citizens, not to say bearing Christian witness to them.[27]

Y. T. Wu was not a heretic but a sincere Christian. Starting from the 1930s, he became more and more concerned with the sufferings of the Chinese people. Frank Price depicts Wu as "like an Old Testament prophet, his soul is seared by social sins and injustices that he sees around him, and his words, though quietly spoken and written, lash and cut."[28] The development of his thought and theology, which ultimately led to his advocacy of "socialist religion," was clearly evident.

It would be unfair to make Wu solely responsible for the serious difficulties of the Chinese Protestant church in the 1950s and 1960s; on the other hand, he was not blameless. The Protestant church of mainland China today is growing at a good pace, but it is still weak, loose, poor, and incoherent. Urban Christians cannot get rid of discrimination, and the large number of newly converted Christians in the countryside are in dire need of qualified pastors to give them biblical and ethical education. Many of the problems today may be traced to the failures of Y. T. Wu. Therefore to understand what lessons should be learned from his experience is still a task of great significance.

CHAPTER 20

Holy Spirit Taiwan: Pentecostal and Charismatic Christianity in the Republic of China

MURRAY A. RUBINSTEIN

This chapter is an introduction to an important but unexplored facet of modern Taiwan's religious life. Today Pentecostal and charismatic Protestantism is the most dynamic and expansive movement in Western Christianity.[1] It has also become a force in the Third World. Latin American and African nations are now the homes of large charismatic or "Spirit-filled" churches; these churches and sects are challenging the older, more established conciliar and evangelical churches.[2]

East Asia has also witnessed the birth of such charismatic and Pentecostal communities over the course of the twentieth century, communities that are growing in size and influence. Korean Pentecostalism has grown rapidly in the past four decades; the single largest church in South Korea is an indigenous Pentecostal church. Pentecostal and charismatic churches were important institutions within the larger Christian community of the pre-Communist Chinese mainland. A number of these communities have re-emerged in the wake of the opening up of religious life in the PRC that has taken place over the past decade.[3]

This powerful spiritual wave has also swept over Taiwan. Over the course of the past sixty years, this island, first held by the Japanese and now dominated by the Guomindang, has witnessed the coming of powerful and expanding Pentecostal and charismatic churches. Of those 300,000 citizens of Taiwan who are Protestant, almost a third define themselves as charismatics or Pentecostals.[4] Furthermore, members of more mainline conciliar and evangelical churches, such as the Presbyterians and the Southern Baptists, have participated in and have experienced the power of a nondenominational charismatic renewal movement. Each of these individuals — church members and participants in renewal — is a believer in a Holy

Spirit–centered, experiential form of Christianity that has continued to grow and to demonstrate dynamism even as mainstream churches have faltered.

The following section defines Pentecostal-charismatic Protestantism. I next suggest a spectrum, or continuum, that shows where individual churches in the Holy Spirit community exist in relation to each other. As I define the spectrum, I briefly profile a number of the churches that fall within it. Next I argue that congruence — the existence of parallel religious concepts and modes of behavior — is a basic reason for the gains such churches and parachurches have been able to make. But there is a downside as well, and the churches' theology and practices lay them open to threats from outside forces. These churches exist in a state of "double marginality." This issue is examined in the final section of the chapter, a section that explores the relationship of the charismatic Holy Spirit churches with the larger society of Taiwan and with the Protestant community at large.

Questions of Definition

The basic elements of Pentecostal-charismatic Christianity are these: the absolute authority of the Bible as the Word of God (inerrancy); orthodoxy–correct belief; personal salvation by grace; belief in and use of the "gifts of the Spirit," such as tongues, healing, and prophecy; dedication and commitment; a heavy stress on evangelism and missions.

These beliefs, ones that all Spirit-filled Christians hold dear, are mostly shared by evangelicals who belong to denominations such as the Southern Baptists and the Mennonites, and by those in the Methodist-derived Holiness tradition.[5] Pentecostal-charismatic Christianity, however, also strongly stresses the active role and gifts of the Holy Spirit, which the more mainstream evangelical churches often reject.

Belief in the direct and active work of the Holy Spirit, centered on the "gifts," has transformed the lives of the Pentecostal and charismatic believers and has shaped the history of these churches. Students of the movement contend it is because of this deep faith in the active presence of the Holy Spirit that these churches represent a return to the first-century Christian experience and to the Apostolic church itself. According to Paul Pomerville, an Assemblies of God missiologist, Pentecostalism and the more recent charismatic movement bring "a dimension of the Christian faith to light which has all but been eclipsed in Western Christianity — the experiential dimension." Pomerville takes this further. He argues that this principle of faith in the immediacy and power of the Holy Spirit — of experiential

Christianity—can be seen as the true dynamic nature of the Christian faith. This power of the Holy Spirit infuses those other facets of evangelical faith.[6]

This principle, the belief in the indwelling of the Holy Spirit, can be defined in experiential terms. Doing so allows the believer to accept new modes of behavior. Thus a Pentecostal-charismatic believer can experience, in an immediate and direct way, the power of the Holy Spirit and can be "baptized in the Spirit"; because of such a "baptism" one can "speak in tongues" (glossolalia) and can heal by the "laying on of hands."[7] What binds the Pentecostal-charismatic movement together is this belief that the Holy Spirit is at work transforming the lives of all those who accept it.

Those doctrines I have defined as Pentecostal or charismatic are shared by the Holy Spirit churches on Taiwan. At their core is the idea of the ongoing and ever-present work of the Holy Spirit. This is accepted as a fundamental reality in each of these Taiwanese religious institutions.

Though they share a common set of beliefs, these churches and parachurches do differ from each other in important ways. Such differences can be found in the way each institution developed, defines its theology, patterns its worship, and organizes both its central administrative organs and its local congregations. Such distinctions make each church unique. It is because of such differences that each church can appeal to a somewhat different constituency within the larger population of Taiwan.

The Pentecostal and Charismatic Community on Modern Taiwan

The Pentecostal-charismatic community on Taiwan is a small one, as is the Taiwanese Protestant community of which it is a part: at the same time, it is a community of some complexity. The churches within the community may be seen as making up a spectrum or continuum. At one end of this spectrum are churches that are very close to their Western roots and remain linked to the mission bodies that helped to establish them. In the middle of the spectrum are churches that owe their origins to Western theologians and missionaries and that maintain a careful relationship with these spiritual parent churches or missionary "fathers" but at the same time exist as aggressively independent entities. At the other end of the spectrum are churches that are both independent and indigenous. Such churches were founded by Chinese and have evolved theologies that demonstrate both their doctrinal independence and their leaders' ability to create a Chinese context for the Christian message. Specific churches lie in different places along this spectrum, and demonstrate the above-mentioned paradigms.

The Taiwan Assemblies of God is a Chinese Pentecostal church that lies at the mission-centered end of the spectrum. This church was founded by and continues to have strong ties to the Springfield, Missouri–based Assemblies of God, the largest of the American Pentecostal denominations.[8]

In 1952, the A/G mission board committed its men and women to the island in the hope of establishing Pentecostal churches in the militarily secure Republic of China.[9] They have been there ever since. On Taiwan these missionaries and their Chinese co-workers have been able to develop a small but dedicated body of believers who are part of the worldwide Assemblies of God network.[10] In Taibei, Taizhong, Tainan, and Gaoxiong and in villages in the reservation areas of the island's rugged interior are found A/G churches made up of mainlanders, Taiwanese, and mountain people.[11] There is a Bible school in Taizhong run by the mission and a large A/G run and financed correspondence school now operating in Taibei. Radio ministries such as that established by Jimmy Swaggart, a former A/G pastor, now operate as well and serve to attract Chinese to the church. The Assemblies mission on Taiwan is one that is rather traditional in its operating style.[12]

While some progress has been made, the A/G missionaries have not been able to expand among the Taiwanese majority or make much progress among the mountain people (or "original people," *yuanjumin*, as they have now become known).[13] The Assemblies missionaries knew of the work of the other churches when they began their own efforts but decided that there were unreached peoples in the mountain areas. They have been able to carve out a place for themselves but it has not been easy.[14]

Neither have the missionaries been able to plant a truly independent or indigenous Chinese A/G church. While there is a Taiwan Convention, many of the member churches are tied to A/G purse strings in Springfield, Missouri. This dependence has proven most disappointing to missionaries and to nationals but the reality is that the A/G community is just too small and too close to Western ways to be truly independent.[15] One senses that aside from certain older congregations it is a church that is relatively weak and is not growing.[16] Today, then, the Assemblies of God exists as a small church within the larger Protestant community. It holds fast to its Western roots and maintains close ties to its American founders. The Taiwan A/G can be seen as an example of middle American revivalist Pentecostal Christianity transplanted into an East Asian cultural and social environment.

In the middle of the Pentecostal and charismatic spectrum are those organizations that serve as a bridge between Western Protestantism and truly indigenized and sinicized churches. The best example of such a bridge is a parachurch known as the Prayer Mountain Revival Movement. The

Prayer Mountain Movement is not a church in any formal sense but is, instead, a nondenominational body that works with and for Protestant churches on the island. It creates a special religious environment for members of the various denominations — denominations that range from conciliar to evangelical to charismatic — and then leads these individuals through a complex process of spiritual renewal. While the movement's leaders and workers are open to the work of the Holy Spirit in the renewal process, and while these same individuals are clearly charismatic in style and in personal belief, they stress that they do not rigidly hold to any one form of Christian belief or practice. Daniel Dai, the Southern Baptist–trained minister who heads the organization, stresses that he provides the setting for Christian renewal and the emotional and religious atmosphere in which the renewal can take place, but does not present any one form of belief to his captive audience.

The renewal movement began in 1982. Since then, thousands of Taiwanese, mainlanders, and mountain people — members of the various churches that make up the island's Protestant community — have come to the mountain center and have participated in the prayer weekends.

For many the weekend renewal experience strengthened their faith. This did not mean that these people left their home churches, however. Rather, they returned more secure in their faith. They had experienced, at first hand, some of the power of God and of the man who leads the movement, Daniel Dai. Dai is a well-trained and highly intelligent man who is also a very powerful speaker with an attractive and magnetic personality; he can bring across his new vision with great force. Even in a formal interview, the power and the deep faith of the man come through.[17]

Not all who participated in a weekend retreat wished to return to the status quo. For these individuals, what they had undergone pointed the way to a new, more dynamic religiosity, a religiosity that involved an emotional and Holy Spirit–centered experience. Because of their new feelings and their sense that Christianity was more than what was preached in their home congregations, these returnees came home to threaten the stability of their congregations.[18]

Allen Swanson, a cofounder of the movement and later its major Western advisor, felt that much good was coming from the Prayer Mountain Movement. While he was fearful that the movement could slip into nonscriptural, that is, Christo-pagan patterns of belief, he felt that he could serve as guide and watchdog. Dai trusted him and used him as confidant and resident expert. Swanson, when interviewed at Prayer Mountain in December 1986, was convinced that this movement that he had helped nurture was of importance in breathing new life into the larger Protestant community. To an outside observer such as myself, the Prayer Mountain Movement is an important new organization on the Taiwanese Christian scene. It stands as a bridge between Western and Chinese churches and also serves to unite in spirit those separated by the formal walls of denomination.

On the indigenized wing of the spectrum lies the True Jesus Church. This church represents a truly indigenous Chinese Pentecostalism in its history, organizational structures, doctrines, and patterns of worship. The True Jesus Church has been able to take Western religious concepts and put them into forms with which Chinese and mountain people can be comfortable.[19] The church began on the Chinese mainland but was transplanted on the island of Taiwan in the 1920s.[20] It grew slowly under the Japanese, but has expanded rapidly since the Guomindang retreated to the island in 1949.

The True Jesus Church evangelists work with the two segments of the population they had evangelized in the decades preceding the Nationalist retreat, the Taiwanese and the mountain people. They use proven tactics, continuing to hold evangelical meetings, bear witness, plant new congregations, organize new churches, and as a result have been able to bring more Taiwanese and mountain people into their ranks.

Furthermore, church growth has been carefully systematized; each church member does his or her part in carrying it out. To be a True Jesus member means to be a missionary for the church. This is good evangelical practice. In practical terms, employing such a tactic means that the church has needed a smaller formal evangelical staff. Thus church leaders can devote less of their energy to the actual work of expansion and more to the relatively difficult task of creating an atmosphere to retain the new members.[21]

Central and local headquarters seem able to deal with the ever-expanding network of both rural and urban churches.[22] This can be seen in the way the church has set up and maintained control over its scattered congregations. Orders come out of Taizhong and reflect the decisions of the General Assembly. However, in each geographical area there is one main church that runs things on the local level. This church serves the needs of the community and is organized to take care of most aspects of congregational life.[23]

The church's publication effort has also helped the church to grow. Tracts have been written and produced in great numbers and these are made readily available to each church member. The press has become more sophisticated in its presentation of tracts and scriptural materials and is better able to meet the needs of the expanding church.[24]

The church has also been able to broaden its class base. The True Jesus

Church has been, since it began, a church of the lower and lower-middle classes. In recent years, however, the church seems to be attracting individuals in the new managerial and technocratic classes, as well.[25]

Finally, the church offers a safe haven in a troubled and uncertain political and social environment. The True Jesus Church is determinedly nonpolitical. It is removed from the type of activism that has led the Presbyterian church and the New Testament Church, another Holy Spirit–centered church, into direct conflicts with the Guomindang rulers of the Republic of China. It demonstrates to one and all that an alternative form of Christianity is available to Taiwanese, a form that is concerned with community but that will not challenge the existing political structure.

These, then, are the churches and parachurches that make up the Pentecostal and charismatic spectrum. What is the appeal of those churches and movements that have grown the most rapidly? One answer lies in congruence. I see in this concept one explanation for the success these churches have had in demonstrating that their doctrines and patterns of worship have much in common with traditional Chinese patterns. This concept will now be examined.

Congruence: Roots of Pentecostal and Charismatic Growth

Why have Pentecostal and charismatic churches been able to make homes for themselves on Taiwan? And why have they continued to grow while other churches have declined? One factor is congruence. It is a necessary precondition to the indigenization process. This concept goes far to explain the appeal of Holy Spirit–centered churches, especially to Taiwanese and mountain people.

Congruence may be defined as the existence of parallel structures. The term is one found in the field of geometry, but here it is used to describe structures and processes one finds in social and cultural environments. There are, in some societies, belief systems, patterns of intellectual analysis, and patterns of sociocultural interaction that can also be found in other, seemingly quite different, societies. The task of cultural transmitters—be they agents for the Agency for International Development, Christian missionaries, or indigenous evangelists—is to adapt the cultural and religious patterns of one society to the needs of another. They can achieve this end only if they can first find congruence—the existence of key parallel cultural patterns and structures. Once they have done this they can then show their clients—their target audience—that though the cultural and religious system they represent seems at first quite alien from what their hosts are familiar with, there exist numerous points of congruence—places where particular patterns on a given subtextual or deeper level are very similar. If they are successful in doing this then they have much of the battle won. Their host audience will now be ready to see why it is possible to accept the new belief system or religious pattern.

Does this theoretical framework explain the way Holy Spirit churches deal with the challenge of adapting Christianity to Chinese modes of religiosity? I will use True Jesus Church examples of congruence as models to argue that it does.

The first example of congruence at work is the use of the basic biblicism that is so much a part of the True Jesus belief system, as well as of the belief systems of the Prayer Mountain Movement and the Assemblies of God. The theologians of these churches believe in biblical inerrancy. They are careful to use scripture as the basis for all statements and arguments they make about the way the supernatural and the natural realms are constituted. They also use scripture as the moral basis for all acts and behaviors of individuals in society.[26] There is on the surface nothing here that is different from what most evangelicals do. The difference lies in the form such biblical argumentation takes—in the very way the True Jesus writers present their arguments.

There are two basic formats that can be found in True Jesus materials—tracts, paperback books, and hardcover volumes, as well as periodicals. In one format, scripture is quoted first and this is followed by comments showing why such scripture is relevant to a given situation or how it would provide guidance in dealing with one's problems. In the second format the procedure is reversed. The writers first discuss a given theological issue or a life-related problem. Then they go on to quote that passage in scripture that confirms the argument they are making.

Such forms of argument are congruent with traditional Chinese approaches to textual or scholarly argument. When one examines the classics—*Mencius* is one example, *Xunzi* is another—one finds similar patterns of argument. Usually a point is made or a specific point is presented and then reference is made to one or another of the pre-Confucian classics. In later works of scholarship and in the examinations for the civil service, *Mencius* or the *Lunyu* is used in much the same way.[27]

True Jesus evangelists make the existence of this pattern of congruence clear to those outside the Christian tradition in their many publications. By doing so they try to make this audience more willing to read True Jesus tracts. In the very way they present their material the True Jesus leaders demonstrate their Chinese roots and their familiarity with Chinese forms of philosophical and religious argument.

Congruence is also found in the fundamental theological concepts of the True Jesus Church. True Jesus writers and theologians, true to their biblicistic orientation, accept the idea that Satan, demons, and angels exist and play a role in the natural as well as the supernatural realms. John Yang, a True Jesus theologian, outlines the True Jesus perception of these beings and suggests the way they influence human life.[28] If one examines the Chinese popular religious tradition one finds a congruent structure: a formal supernatural bureaucracy with its higher gods, lesser gods, and demons, with each playing a specific role and each possessing the capability of directly affecting human existence. There can be found, in general terms, parallels between the biblical pantheon described in Yang's work and that defined in Chinese popular religious thought. There is an important caveat, however: within the Chinese tradition there does not seem to be the type of transcendent yet immanent being we find as the core figure in the Western (Judeo-Christian-Islamic) tradition. Neither is there the avatar — god becoming flesh — in any specific or formal sense; in China human beings become gods with some regularity and thus the thought of only one such being is looked upon as strangely limiting.

If the True Jesus writers can convince their Chinese audience that there is sufficient evidence of congruence then they take the next step: showing that they have adapted their faith to Chinese realities. For example, by arguing for the existence of a supernatural hierarchy and by setting forth, as they do, a theology of powers, they are able to make subtle linkages between their own Pentecostal theology and the mainstream Chinese folk theology. This emerges clearly in True Jesus literature; these discussions demonstrate the degree to which they are able to show how indigenized their own variety of Pentecostalism has become.

Congruence can also be seen in patterns of church practice as well as in doctrinal presentation and development. A key facet of True Jesus Christianity is the stress on the gift of the Holy Spirit. In True Jesus practice, believers pray for the gift of the Spirit and through such prayer open themselves up to possession by the Holy Spirit. This prayer takes place at a given point during the worship service. The atmosphere has been created through the singing of hymns as well as through the recitation of short prayers. At that moment when congregational prayer is called for, all individuals present — the men sitting on one side of the sanctuary and the women on the other — pull down their kneeling stools and, bowing down on their knees in supplication, begin to pray. They begin with simple words or verses. Then many begin to shake and sway. From their mouths come strange sounds; some of these resemble formalized chanting, while others are sharp glottal sounds. Such speaking in tongues, or glossolalia, continues for ten to fifteen minutes and, after a bell is rung, the sounds fade away. People then come out of their trance-like states and the service continues. A similar period of speaking in tongues takes place about twenty minutes to half an hour later, after the sermon.[29] Less formalized speaking in tongues is a common feature of American, Latin American, and African Pentecostalism.

There is congruence with the Chinese pattern of religious practice as well as the more obvious parallels with Western and Third World Pentecostalism. Within Chinese folk religious life there is the important personage of *tong khi* (*qitang*). These individuals serve as communicators with the gods. When a person is troubled he or she often turns to the *tong khi* who, when in a trance-like state, allows the god to speak to the client. The *tong khi* is a person of some importance in rural and urban Taiwan.

There is congruence between the baptism and gifts of the Spirit and the possession that the *tong khi* undergoes. True Jesus members, and other indigenous Pentecostals who undergo the baptism of the Spirit, appear to be possessed at those times during the service. At such times they become a collectivity of *tong khi*, and each shares the status and spiritual power that a *tong khi* possesses in his home village. When confronted by this apparent congruence, True Jesus theologians, as well as the theologians of the other churches, are quick to argue that *tong khi* are inhabited by evil spirits or by demonic spirits while those individuals within their church who are given the gift of the Spirit are possessed by the true spirit, by the Holy Spirit himself. What is important about this explanation is that there is no denial of the fact of possession. The focus instead is upon the nature of that spirit which takes over the believer. Thus, here too is congruence, an approach that church leaders use either implicitly or explicitly as a means of making their form of Christianity more attractive to the mass of Taiwanese who are of a traditional bent, as well as to the mountain people whose own religion is animistic.

By defining the Christian doctrines as they have and by demonstrating in various ways the congruence between their forms of Christianity and the basic forms of Chinese religion, the indigenous churches have also been able to carve out a place for themselves within the Pentecostal and charismatic community and within the larger Protestant community. But this does not mean that they are fully accepted. In spite of the strength of these churches, they and their members exist in a state of tension with the other Protestant churches on Taiwan and with the larger Taiwanese society.

Double Marginality

The members of the various Pentecostal and charismatic churches are seen as marginal in the eyes of two very different communities. In the eyes of the larger Taiwanese community, they belong to religious bodies that are marginal. At the same time, because of the Holy Spirit–centered Christianity they believe in, they are also seen as marginal by members of the larger Taiwanese Protestant community. Thus they bear the burden of "double marginality."

Simply being a member of the Chinese Christian community makes one marginal in the eyes of the mainlander and Taiwanese communities that control life on the island. Christians bore the burden of such marginality on the Chinese mainland: in the late Qing an unstable tension that often led to outbreaks of violence existed between the Chinese who accepted Christianity and the vast majority of the Chinese who rejected it. The years of the Nationalist revolution of the 1920s saw the anti-Christian feeling rise to new heights.[30] Since 1865, Taiwanese have also demonstrated an often deep-seated antagonism to the missionary presence and to the Christian community created by the missionaries. In Qing and in Japanese Taiwan there were attacks on the newly emerging Taiwanese Protestant communities.

The Nationalist government also demonstrated its own anti-Christian biases. It made use of the anti-Christian movement of the 1920s to gain control of the Christian-run schools in China.[31] On Taiwan, key members of the Taiwanese Presbyterian church were killed during the February 1947 Incident (the "2-28 uprising"). Presbyterian ministers and leaders have pointed this out in interviews and in articles in their church newspaper.

One does not witness overt anti-Christian sentiments in contemporary Taiwan, but one has the sense that the Chinese or mountain person who is Christian is still seen as unusual, at best, and at worst as somewhat suspect. Such feelings are not expressed directly, at least not to a foreigner, but do exist and are expressed in real, if oblique, ways. The following instances will suggest both the existence of anti-Christian sentiment and the real difficulty in pinning down this sentiment. In 1980 I expressed interest in studying the Presbyterians on Taiwan to members of the Academia Sinica institute in which I was working. The reaction of my Chinese colleagues was either "why bother" or "those people are dangerous." Similar comments were made in 1986 when I announced my intention to study the New Testament Church. Part of this was the natural caution of Chinese academics about dealing with politically sensitive issues, but I believe these comments also reflected a certain distaste for those Chinese who had become Christian. Furthermore, in my observation, academics who are known to be Christian are seen as belonging to a different world than the majority of their compatriots and are sometimes viewed with suspicion.

Anti-Christian sentiment was also reflected in comments made by a group of Chinese Christian seminary students who discussed their own conversions and the impact of these conversions on their non-Christian families. They felt that their decisions created great tensions between them and their parents. They suggested that their parents saw the act of conversion as one of desertion from traditional Chinese cultural values. These students do not make up a well-defined statistical sample; furthermore, their accounts are quite personal and subjective. But one can easily imagine that thousands of traditional Taiwanese and mainlander families felt hostility when their sons and daughters became believers of this "foreign religion," Christianity. Because of their exclusivist nature and because they demand a transformation of one's life, certain more evangelical forms of Protestant Christianity force one to a break from one's "heathen" roots. This creates tensions and ultimately resentment in the family that sees itself being abandoned by its children and thus cut off from its own future.[32]

Reinforcing the impression of marginality is the fact that the many seminaries and Bible colleges on Taiwan do not have the status of institutes of higher learning. They are supervised not by the Ministry of Education but by the Ministry of the Interior. Thus on a Taiwan where one's degree is everything, the graduates of these schools are seen as having no meaningful college degree. The graduates become ministers, Sunday school teachers, and church workers; thus they build their lives around an essentially alien institution. This further closes them off from the larger Taiwanese society. In the eyes of the Han majority, the Chinese Christian is one who has created his own world and is not involved in the larger world of Taiwanese life.

This burden of marginality that all Chinese Christians bear is but a part of the load that the Pentecostals and charismatics must shoulder. As believers in a radical experiential form of Christianity they are also seen as suspect by their fellow Christians, members of the more mainstream evangelical churches. In the West, Pentecostals and charismatics have long been suspect and kept at arm's length since the days of the first Pentecostal revivals in the early twentieth century. One reason is that these revivals were often attended by poor whites, blacks, and later by increasing numbers of Hispanics. The churches these people founded were tainted by the lower-class and pariah status of their members. That such meetings are the rallying point for the "disinherited" can still be seen by attending Pentecostal tent meetings in the countryside or prayer meetings held in meeting halls in the larger urban areas.[33] The mainline churches were wary of the people and were frightened of the phenomena they witnessed. Speaking in tongues was seen as unbiblical and healing was also seen as a distortion of scripture. Furthermore, the power and the raw emotion of such meetings was considered dangerous; good Christians simply did not behave in such a manner for they were sober and quiet folk who did not bring attention to themselves. The more established churches preferred to see Pentecostals as a fringe element and until recent years kept them at arm's length.

Mainstream religious leaders on Taiwan expressed similar viewpoints when dealing with the Pentecostals. Hollington Tong reflected this when he described the services of the Taiwan Assembly of God church. He described the work of A/G evangelists and noted that:

They hold crowded rallies in the T'ai Pei church. After preaching the Gospel, they have a healing service, inviting those who want to be healed to come to the altar. Throngs of people respond. Eye witnesses report that some of those who come to the altar appear to be healed. The danger to Christianity of such promises of healing is that they are apt to backfire. Those who believe themselves healed testify their belief in God, but those who are disappointed only too frequently go away to denounce the Christians.[34]

Misgivings similar to those that Tong voiced were expressed by missionaries in interviews I conducted in the years 1983 to 1987. Various groups such as the True Jesus Church, the Assembly Hall Church, the New Testament Church, and the Prayer Mountain Movement were also singled out for criticism. The fear was that such groups would give the other more mainstream Protestants a bad name. The missionaries and the Chinese nationals are wary of the charismatics for they do not know how to respond to their emotional forms of worship. They also may envy their successful church growth.

What all this means for the Holy Spirit–centered churches is that they live in a world that rejects them both as Christians and as charismatics. For many the response is to draw in the wagons and assume a defensive posture. This makes them more secure but it closes off chances for dialogue with the larger and more mainstream Protestant community. It makes them more convinced of the truth of their different vision of the Christian message and more secure in their sense that all other segments of Christianity are hetero-dox. Only the brave have begun to break out and try to deal with the larger Protestant community.

Conclusion

The churches of the Holy Spirit are paradoxes that reflect the basic dilemma of Protestantism on Taiwan. They are unique in the forms and varieties of Christian experience they convey and because of this they are often treated as pariahs. However, they have come the furthest toward creating a Christianity that is congruent with basic patterns of traditional Chinese religion. They are thus both the cutting edge of Christian progress and the outside fringe — the dwellers living on the edge. I see them as a symbol of the great problem Christianity faces on Taiwan. Will this religion sinicize itself and risk the danger of becoming more and more remote from acceptable Western and mainstream forms of this ostensibly universalistic faith, or will it remain an alien creed, forever outside the Chinese main-stream, with believers who are seen as suspect by the Chinese majority? The evolution of the Holy Spirit churches may provide a solution if the other churches are willing to accept such a solution as viable and valid.

Appendixes

Project Grants: History of Christianity in China Project, 1986–1990

Project director: Daniel H. Bays, History, University of Kansas
Advisory council:
  John K. Fairbank, History, Harvard University
  K. C. Liu, History, University of California, Davis
  Richard P. Madsen, Sociology, University of California, San Diego
  Lucian W. Pye, Political Science, Massachusetts Institute of Technology
  Grant Wacker, Religious Studies, University of North Carolina, Chapel Hill

Grant recipients:
  Suzanne Wilson Barnett, History, University of Puget Sound, "Chinese Reformers and the Early Protestant Missionary Press"
  Timothy Brook, History, University of Toronto, "Chinese Christians and the Japanese Occupation"
  Norma Diamond, Anthropology, University of Michigan, "Christianity and the Hua Miao"
  Robert E. Entenmann, History, St. Olaf College, "Indigenous Leadership of Catholic Communities in Eighteenth-Century Sichuan"
  Robert E. Entenmann, History, St. Olaf College, "Roman Catholic Communities in Eighteenth-Century Sichuan"
  Gao Wangzhi, Religious Studies, Chinese Academy of Social Sciences, "A Study of Y. T. Wu"
  Gu Changsheng, History, East China Normal University, "The Seventh-Day Adventists in China, 1902–1951" (travel grant to Andrews University)
  Emily Honig, History and Women's Studies, Yale University, "The Life and Times of Cora Deng (1900–)"
  Gail K. O. King, Library, Brigham Young University, "The Family Letters of Xu Guangqi: Public and Private Concerns of a Chinese Christian"
  Whalen Lai, Religious Studies, University of California, Davis, "The Buddhist-Christian Encounter in the Late Ch'ing and the Republican Era"
  Lin Jinshui, History, Fujian Teachers' University, "Giulio Aleni in Fujian Province"

Charles A. Litzinger, History, California State University, Bakersfield, "Temple Community and Christianity in Rural North China, 1860–1900"

Judith Liu, Sociology, University of San Diego, "An Oasis in a Heathen Land: A Study of a Cohort from St. Hilda's School for Girls, 1928–1938" (travel grant to China)

Kathleen L. Lodwick, History, Southwest Missouri State University, "A History of Protestantism in Hainan" (travel grant to China)

Jessie G. Lutz, History, Rutgers University, "Karl Gützlaff and the Chinese Christian Union, 1844–1851"

Sarah Mason, History, independent scholar, Minnesota (travel assistance grant to interview retired YMCA secretaries in Guangzhou)

Min Tu-ki, History, Seoul National University, "Xu Qian, A Christian Revolutionary in the Anti-Christian National Revolution (1924–1928)"

David E. Mungello, History, Coe College, "An Investigation of the Status and Accessibility of the Former Major Jesuit Libraries in China" (travel grant to China)

David E. Mungello, History, Coe College, "In Search of Zhang Xingyao" (travel grant to China)

Douglas R. Reynolds, History, Georgia State University, Atlanta, "Friction and Resistance in the Propagation of Japanese Buddhism in China, 1873–1915: A Comparison with Christianity"

Heidi A. Ross, Education, Colgate University, " 'Cradle of Female Talent': The Shanghai No. Three Girls' Middle School, 1892–1989"

Murray A. Rubinstein, History, Baruch College–CUNY, "Taiwan's Churches of the Holy Spirit" (travel grant to Taiwan)

Shen Dingping, Institute of History, Chinese Academy of Social Sciences, "Jesuits and Chinese Catholics at the Turn of the Ming and Qing Dynasties (1627–1662)" (travel grant to the U.S.)

John R. Shepherd, Anthropology, SSRC fellow, "Religion and Identity Among the Sinicized Siraya"

Paul Spickard, History, Capital University (travel assistance grant to interview Christians while in China on a Fulbright teaching appointment)

Alan R. Sweeten, History, independent scholar, "Christianity in Jiangxi: Community Conflict and Bureaucratic Control, 1860–1900"

Roger R. Thompson, History, University of Maryland, "Temple Festivals, Foreign Gods, and the Local Community: An Inquiry into the Origins of Violence Against Chinese Christians in Shanxi Province, 1900–1901"

Tsou Mingteh, History, Shanghai Jiaotong University, "The Missionary as Promoter of Chinese-Christian Cultural Contacts: A Study of Gilbert Reid, 1882–1927"

Carolyn Wakeman, Center for Chinese Studies, University of California, Berkeley, "From Christianity to Communism: Yanjing University, 1946–1952"

Arthur Waldron, History, Princeton University (travel grant to China to pursue possibilities of research in archives or materials of the former Christian colleges)

Joanna Waley-Cohen, History, Columbia University, and Mellon fellow, "Christianity and Militarism in Eighteenth-Century China: Jesuit Missionaries and the Military Campaigns of the Qianlong Emperor, 1736–1796"

Peter Chen-main Wang, History, Tamkang University, Taiwan, "The Rise and Fall of the *Wenshe*: A Vanguard of the Indigenization of Christianity, 1924–1928"

Philip L. Wickeri, History and theology, The Amity Foundation, Hong Kong and Nanjing, "The Christian Movement in Shanghai, 1946–1954"

Ernest P. Young, History, University of Michigan, "Christian Evangelism in Jiangxi and the Nanchang Massacre of 1906"

Project Symposia: History of Christianity in China Project, 1989–1990

Symposium I, June 18–23, 1989

Daniel H. Bays, History, University of Kansas, "Christian Revivalism in China, 1900–1937"

Chen Zenghui, History, Fujian Normal University, "New Light on the Gutian Incident of 1895" (in absentia)

Nicole Constable, Anthropology, Western Michigan University, "Christianity and Hakka Identity"

Norma Diamond, Anthropology, University of Michigan, "Christianity and the Hua Miao: Writing and Power"

Robert E. Entenmann, History, St. Olaf College, "Christian Virgins in Eighteenth-Century Sichuan"

Gao Wangzhi, Chinese Academy of Social Sciences, "Y. T. Wu: A Study of His Career"

Gu Changsheng, East China Normal University, "The Seventh-Day Adventist Mission in China, 1902–1950"

Charles A. Litzinger, History, California State University, Bakersfield, "Rural Religion and Village Organization in North China: The Catholic Challenge in the Late Nineteenth Century"

Douglas R. Reynolds, History, Georgia State University, Atlanta, "Japanese Buddhist Mission Work in China and the Challenge of Christianity, 1868–1915"

Murray A. Rubinstein, History, Baruch College–CUNY, "Holy Spirit Taiwan: Pentecostal and Charismatic Christianity in the Republic of China"

John R. Shepherd, Anthropology, SSRC fellow, "From Barbarians to Sinners: Collective Conversion Among Plains Aborigines in Ch'ing Taiwan, 1859–1895"

Alan R. Sweeten, History, independent scholar, "Christianity in Kiangsi Province: Community-level Conflict and Accommodation as Seen in 'Sectarian Cases' (chiao-an), 1860–1900"

Roger R. Thompson, History, University of Maryland, "Extraterritoriality and the Shanxi Countryside, 1861–1911: What is a Community? Who Belongs? Who Pays?"

T'ien Ju-k'ang, Sociology, Fudan University, "Cementation of Segregative Tribes: The Protestant Church Among Minority Nationalities in Yunnan"

Tsou Mingteh, Social Sciences, Shanghai Jiaotong University, "From Missionary to Reform Advocate: Gilbert Reid and the Reform Movement in the Late Qing"

Ernest P. Young, History, University of Michigan, "The Politics of Evangelism at the End of the Qing: Nanchang, 1906"

COMMENTATORS

Paul Cohen, Wellesley College, and the Fairbank Center
Terrill Lautz, The Henry Luce Foundation, Inc.
K. C. Liu, University of California, Davis
Richard Madsen, University of California, San Diego
R. G. Tiedemann, University of London
Grant Wacker, University of North Carolina

Symposium II, June 17–23, 1990

Suzanne Wilson Barnett, History, University of Puget Sound, "From Route Books to International Order: The Early Protestant Missionary Press and Chinese Geographical Writings"

Timothy Brook, History, University of Toronto, "Toward Independence: Christianity in China Under Japanese Occupation, 1937–1945"

Robert E. Entenmann, History, St. Olaf College, "Catholics and Non-Catholics in Jiangjin District, Sichuan, in the Eighteenth Century"

Emily Honig, History and Women's Studies, Yale University, "The Life and Times of Cora Deng"

Gail K. O. King, Brigham Young University, "The Family Letters of Xu Guangqi: Public and Private Concerns of a Chinese Christian"

Whalen Lai, Religious Studies, University of California, Davis, "Christian Love, Buddhist Compassion: A Comparative History of Religious Charities"

Lin Jinshui, History, Fujian Teachers' University, "Giulio Aleni in Fujian Province"

Judith Liu, Sociology, University of San Diego, and Donald P. Kelly, Sociology, University of California, San Diego, "An Oasis in a Heathen Land: A Study of a Cohort from St. Hilda's School for Girls, 1928–1936"

Kathleen L. Lodwick, History, Southwest Missouri State University, "A History of Protestantism in Hainan"

Jessie G. Lutz, History, Rutgers University, "Karl Gützlaff and the Chinese Christian Union, 1844–1851"

Min Tu-ki, History, Seoul National University, "Xu Qian: A Christian Revolutionary in the 1920s"

David E. Mungello, History, Coe College, "In Search of Zhang Xingyao"

Heidi A. Ross, Education, Colgate University, "'Cradle of Female Talent': The Shanghai No. 3 Girls' Middle School, 1892–1989"

Carolyn Wakeman, Center for Chinese Studies, University of California, Berkeley, "From Christianity to Communism: Yanjing University, 1946–1952"

Joanna Waley-Cohen, History, Columbia University, and Mellon fellow, "God and Guns in Eighteenth-Century China: Jesuit Missionaries and the Military Campaigns of the Qianlong Emperor, 1736–1796"

Arthur Waldron, History, Princeton University, Report on the Christian colleges records project

Peter Chen-main Wang, History, Tamkang University, Taiwan, "Contextualizing Protestant Literary Efforts in Modern China: The Case of the Wenshe, 1924–1928"

Philip L. Wickeri, History and theology, The Amity Foundation, Hong Kong and Nanjing, "The Christian Movement in Shanghai, 1946–1954"

COMMENTATORS

K. C. Liu, University of California, Davis

Shen Dingping, Chinese Academy of Social Sciences, Beijing

Erik Zürcher, University of Leiden

Reference Matter

Notes

Abbreviations used in this section are listed at the front of the book.

Preface

1. His 1968 American Historical Association presidential address promoted research using these materials and themes coming out of them. Fairbank, "Assignment for the '70s."

2. The phrase is that of Paul A. Cohen, in *Discovering History*; he himself did not use it to dismiss all missions-related history.

3. For a cogent historiographical discussion from the standpoint of missions studies, see Robert. One of her main conclusions is on this very point of how missions studies, if properly done, can provide an "entree into non-Western Christianity" (p. 158). This stress is also salient in the discussion by Andrew Walls, especially the last part of his stimulating article (pp. 21–25).

4. Hefner, p. 4.

5. Naquin, *Millenarian Rebellion*; Overmyer, *Folk Buddhist Religion*.

6. See Pas; a recent collection of documents is MacInnis, *Religion in China Today*; useful work by Chinese scholars from the Shanghai Academy of Social Sciences is in Luo Zhufeng.

7. All of the sources in note 6 have sections on Christianity. Among works specifically on Christianity in the PRC, the concluding section of Covell is still useful, and a thoughtful assessment of the resurgence of Christianity in Chinese social context through the mid-1980s is Whyte. The best overall work on recent and contemporary Protestantism is Hunter and Chan, which combines historical and sociological approaches, and also perceptively treats Catholicism in comparative analysis. A capable and well-documented evangelical Christian perspective is Lambert. Dependable ongoing documentation on Christianity and other religions, including government religious policy, is in *China Study Journal*, published three times yearly. Also see *ANS*, an Amity News Service publication of translations from the religious press in

China, published bimonthly by the Hong Kong office of the Amity Foundation, an agency of the Three-Self Protestant Church in China. Another bimonthly from Hong Kong, *Bridge*, often has independent firsthand reportage on Christian communities in China.

8. There has been considerable discussion among historians and social scientists in recent years about the applicability and usefulness of the concepts of the "public sphere" and "civil society" in studying China, past and present. For a set of several articles and responses by some of the major scholars involved in this discussion, see "Symposium: 'Public Sphere' / 'Civil Society' in China?"

9. Items already published as of this writing include books or monographs by Constable (*Christian Souls and Chinese Spirits*), Mungello, T'ien, and Peter Chenmain Wang, a major *American Historical Review* article by Waley-Cohen, and several other articles by scholars supported by the project, some presented at one of the symposia and some not. Interested readers are welcome to write to the editor at the History Department, University of Kansas, for a listing of these publications and continuing work in progress that may be published in the future.

Bays, *Dynamics of Qing Society*

1. Gernet. Another stimulating work, comparable in some ways to Gernet, is Rafael's study of the cultural and linguistic transmission process of early Tagalog conversion to Christianity under Spanish rule in the Philippines; his thesis is that many misconnections occurred.

2. Mungello; Zürcher, "The Jesuit Mission in Fujian."

3. Kwang-Ching Liu, p. 2 in his introductory essay, presents the concept of "religious pluralism and moral orthodoxy" in late imperial China.

4. A remarkable example of Christian ideas being used to reinforce Confucian orthodoxy in the late Ming is an official proclamation by a local prefect in Shanxi, discussed by Zürcher in "A Complement to Confucianism." Of course, the cases of Christian ideas being accepted as reinforcement of moral orthodoxy were probably relatively rare; Gernet, and Paul A. Cohen, *China and Christianity*, pp. 3–60, both show the considerable extent to which Christianity had become condemned as heterodox in the eyes of many of the elite by the mid-seventeenth century.

5. Zürcher provides us with a late-Ming example of supernatural emphases in popular Christianity in "The Lord of Heaven." The most recent work on the White Lotus, with some comparative ideas on Catholicism, is Ter Haar.

6. *China and Christianity*.

7. *ANS* 3.4/5 (Oct. 1994).

8. For example, Wang Shuhuai, and Kwong.

Entenmann, *Catholics in Eighteenth-Century Sichuan*

Research for this chapter was assisted by travel grants from the National Endowment for the Humanities and St. Olaf College. I am deeply grateful for the assistance and hospitality I received in Paris from Fr. Jean-Paul Lenfant, archivist of the Société des Missions Étrangères de Paris; Annie Salavert-Sablayrolles, librarian of the Bibliothèque Asiatique des Missions Étrangères; and Mgr. René Boisguerin, M.E.P. I am also very grateful to Anne Groton for her patient help with Latin sources; to David Mungello, Erik Zürcher, and other participants in the History of Christianity in China Project; and my colleagues in the St. Olaf College Department of History for comments on earlier drafts of this chapter. I alone, of course, am responsible for errors of fact, translation, or interpretation.

Sources from the Archives des Missions Étrangères, of the Société des Missions Étrangères de Paris, are indicated by the abbreviation AME, followed by volume number and page number.

1. Troeltsch, 1: 331–43.
2. Skinner, "Cities and the Hierarchy of Local Systems," map 1, p. 289.
3. Entenmann, "Migration and Settlement," p. 255. I have revised my estimates in light of those by Skinner, "Sichuan's Population," although I have not in all cases found Skinner's estimates persuasive. The poor quality of population and land registration data has led others to conclude that the demographic history of Sichuan is impossible to reconstruct. Cartier and Will, p. 221.
4. *Jiangjin xian zhi*, 3.13b–15b, 5.1.
5. Entenmann, "Migration and Settlement," p. 255. Skinner, in "Sichuan's Population," estimates the province's population in 1753 at 9 million and 12.8 million in 1773. I consider these figures too low; I think that the growth rate before 1750 was somewhat higher than Skinner estimates, and after 1750 considerably lower.
6. See "An Aridgment [*sic*] of the Life and Death of F. Gabriel Magaillans [Magalhães], of the Society of Jesus, Missionary into China. Written by F. Lewis [Luigi] Buglio, his inseparable companion for six and thirty years, and sent from Pekim [Beijing] in the Year 1677," appended to Gabriel Magaillans; also Martini, pp. 139–47. Mgr. René Boisguerin, former bishop of Yibin, has told me that there are still Catholics in Sichuan descended from the late-Ming converts of Buglio and Magalhães.
7. Dehergne, p. 258; Fang Hao, 3: 71–80.
8. Mullener to Artus de Lionne, Bishop of Rosalia, 13 Aug. 1713, AME 413: 467–70.
9. This account is taken from Gu Luodong (F. M. J. Gourdon, M.E.P.), *Sheng-jiao*, pp. 59–60b. Gourdon drew his information from the Luo genealogy, *Luoshi zupu*, possibly a manuscript, which I have not been able to locate.
10. Chinese Catholics had Christian names, often recorded in Latin or French forms, as well as Chinese names (*ming*), which are generally not recorded in church records. Sometimes the *ming* was a sinicized form of a Christian name, e.g., Ande for Andreas. Matthaeus and Anna Luo are mentioned in the diary, written in Latin, of a Chinese priest: Andreas Ly (Li Ande), p. 165 (15 Dec. 1750); p. 381 (7 Sept. 1756). For the Christian Virgins see my "Christian Virgins in Eighteenth-Century Sichuan" in this volume.
11. Joachim Enjobert de Martiliat, "Mémoire concernant la mission fondée dans une partie de la province de Seu tchuen par les missionnaires françois [*sic*] du séminaire des missions étrangères," 12 May 1740, AME 434: 1177–91. See Martiliat's biography in Launay, *Mémorial*, 2: 433–35.

12. Martiliat to François de Montocier, 10 July 1737, AME 433: 961–64. See biographical note on Gu (Joannes-Baptista Kou) in Gourdon, *Catalogus cleri*, pp. 3–4. Gourdon gives Gu's *ming* as Rohan, the Chinese transcription of Joannes, although Gu generally signed his name Gu Yaowen when writing in Chinese.

13. Martiliat to Mullener, n.d. (1741?), AME 434: 41–44.

14. Martiliat, Journal, Oct. 1740, AME 434: 634, and Jan. 1741, AME 434: 655.

15. Martiliat to the Superior and Directors of the Séminaire des Missions Étrangères, 14 Aug. 1746, AME 434: 920–39.

16. Gu to Martiliat, 5 Aug. 1746, AME 434: 870–88; Latin translation by Martiliat, AME 434: 997–1000. Gu was as far as I can determine the only Chinese priest in Sichuan to correspond with his European colleagues in Chinese rather than Latin.

17. Ly, "Relatio vexationum Christianitatis Kiang-tsin anno 1746 exortarum," in *Journal d'André Ly*, pp. 99–111.

18. Ibid., p. 100; Gu Luodong, *Shengjiao*, p. 60a–b.

19. Ly, "Relatio vexationum," p. 101. Lawsuits over land ownership were especially common in Sichuan because of new settlement, inadequacies of land registration, and the failure of an attempted land survey in the 1720s. Entenmann, "Migration and Settlement," pp. 132–33.

20. Accusation by Liu Mianshi and Zhou Qiyi, QL 11/5/3 (18 June 1746), copied by Gu Yaowen, AME 434: 886. Gu to Martiliat, QL 11/6/19 (5 Aug. 1746), AME 434: 870–88.

21. This record of the interrogations relies primarily on Gu's own account, AME 434: 870–88, supplemented by Andreas Ly's secondhand account, "Relatio vexationum."

22. Martiliat to Gu, 11 Aug. 1746, AME 434: 1000–1002.

23. Gu to Martiliat, QL 11/7/25 (11 Sept. 1746), AME 434: 870–72; Latin translation by Martiliat, AME 434: 1003. Abraham, incidentally, was in fact Sarah's half-brother. Gen. 12.13, 20.12.

24. Members of the Luo family and Paulus He Baolu, another Catholic in Shengchongping, also wrote to Martiliat in defense of Gu. Luo Andele [Andreas] et al. to Martiliat, QL 11/7/28 (14 Sept. 1746), AME 434: 999; He Baolu [Paulus] to Martiliat, QL 11/7/28 (14 Sept. 1746), AME 434: 999.

25. The wealthy Luo family of Chongqing was not related to the Luo family of Jiangjin. The two family names are written with different characters (see Character List).

26. Ly, "Relatio vexationum," pp. 105–10.

27. "Rescriptum Rectoris urbis Tchung-khing ad gubernatorum Kiang-tsin missum," QL 12/5/23 (30 June 1747), trans. in Ly, pp. 111–12. Ly translates several official documents in his diary, including transcriptions of interrogations, but does not indicate how he obtained them. Some Catholics were on the staff of provincial officials, however, and may have copied them for him. The originals of these documents have almost certainly been lost.

28. Launay, *Histoire de la Mission*, 1: 290.

29. Ly, p. 98 (3 Feb. 1749).

30. Ibid., pp. 95–96 (14 Jan. 1749). Because of the small number of priests,

lay congregational leaders and catechists were particularly important in the leadership and education of Catholics in Sichuan. See my "Chinese Catholic Clergy and Catechists."

31. Ibid., pp. 96–97 (19 Jan. and 29 Jan. 1749).

32. Ibid., p. 272 (2 Dec. 1753). Although "Dasheng" generally connotes Mahayana Buddhism, it here refers to a sect of that name related to the White Lotus.

33. This account is taken from Andreas Ly, "Relatio persequutionis Christianitatis Long-men-than et Ching-tsong-ping, oppidi Kiang-tsin suffraganei urbis Tchung-khing," in *Journal d'André Ly*, pp. 352–56.

34. Gourdon, *Catalogus cleri*, pp. 38, 47, 55–57, 59.

35. Gu Luodong, *Shengjiao*, p. 60b.

36. Huc, 1: 301–2.

37. Bays, "Christianity and the Chinese Sectarian Tradition"; see also Paul A. Cohen, *China and Christianity*, which puts the late Qing antimissionary movement into the perspective of the antisectarian tradition.

38. Ly, pp. 29–30, 42, 306, 388.

Sweeten, Catholic Converts in Jiangxi

This chapter represents part of a monographic study, still in progress, of Christianity in Jiangxi from 1860 to 1900. Through each stage of my work I have received encouragement and assistance from Professor K. C. Liu: to him I offer my thanks. Any shortcomings in my presentation of material or inadequacies in analysis are, of course, my responsibility.

JWJAD references are cited in this chapter as series number, volume number, document number, page number.

1. In this chapter, Christianity refers to both Catholicism and Protestantism: otherwise I try to be specific in my reference. In Jiangxi during the nineteenth century the majority of converts were Catholics. Therefore, my use of the unqualified term "convert(s)" should be understood to refer to Catholic converts. Whenever necessary and possible I distinguish between Catholic and Protestant converts, although some sources at times make this difficult.

2. Paul A. Cohen, "Christian Missions," pp. 556–60.

3. Latourette, pp. 94–95; D'Elia, pp. 36, 98.

4. One of the few books on this subject and period does include a short section on missionary work among the common people. See Gernet, pp. 82–104.

5. Latourette, p. 238. However, on p. 323 Latourette states that there were an estimated 6,000 Catholics in Jiangxi in 1832 and 13,000 in 1885. For an estimate of Catholic numbers in 1907, see Wolferstan, p. 450.

6. Latourette, p. 331.

7. Ibid., p. 332.

8. Ibid.

9. This progression for the convert was the ideal. In actuality, there was much variation and even some compromise by priests as to what were acceptable life styles and social practices. Priests were responsible for the baptism of catechumens. When

priests were absent, Catholic "headmen" (this term probably refers to catechists, *jiaotou* — which I discuss in the text) "administered baptism." The vicar apostolic was responsible for the final step, confirmation. His large jurisdiction, usually a province or a large part of one, meant that he had no choice except to let priests handle confirmation. Unanswered is the question of whether or not priests delegated confirmation to headmen. Latourette, pp. 331–36.

10. According to statistics for 1907, in Jiangxi's eastern and southern vicariates apostolic there were 170 and 53 catechists, respectively, and in the northern there were 101, but this last figure includes an unknown number of European and Chinese brothers and nuns. Wolferstan, pp. 436–37.

11. Latourette, pp. 191, 335, 339.

12. *JWJAD*, III/2/617, p. 794.

13. Specifically mentioned by three men, including Zou Yaya, was the establishment of a teacher-student relationship. Ibid., pp. 790, 792, 794.

14. Ibid., p. 785.
15. Ibid., II/2/721, pp. 925–26.
16. Ibid., II/2/712, pp. 904–5.
17. Ibid., p. 903.
18. Ibid., p. 904.
19. Ibid., II/2/704, p. 885.
20. Ibid., III/2/597, pp. 689–90.
21. Ibid., I/2/1082, pp. 974–75.
22. Ibid., III/2/597, p. 690.

23. Wiest, "Catholic Activities," p. 122.

24. *JWJAD*, VI/2/667, p. 1006.

25. Ibid., IV/1/379, p. 515. The six families included some 40 men, women, and children; all were Catholic converts. They only had a chapel for holding religious services. Ibid., IV/1/380, p. 525.

26. For a discussion of Guangdong lineages and how they split along socio-economic lines, see Wakeman, pp. 109–16.

27. For example, see *JWJAD*, II/2/715, pp. 906, 908; IV/1/367, p. 472.

28. There was one instance of a *juren* who masterminded the fraudulent sale of property to a Catholic priest. It is unclear from the material if the degree holder was a Catholic or not. *JWJAD*, V/2/1146, p. 1074.

29. Ibid., III/2/597, p. 689.

30. This conclusion contradicts Latourette, p. 334, and Paul A. Cohen, "Christian Missions," p. 557.

31. Fairbank, "Patterns," p. 493.

32. *JWJAD*, II/2/715, p. 908.

33. Ibid., III/2/614, p. 733.

34. Ibid., III/2/617, pp. 790, 792, 794.

35. Naquin, *Millenarian Rebellion*, pp. 39–46; Overmyer, *Folk Buddhist Religion*, pp. 39, 174–75.

36. General treatment, although dated, can be found in Morse, and in Cordier. More recent studies include Varg, *Missionaries*; Wehrle; and Chester C. Tan. These books, however, are all quite limited in scope.

37. For a model study on the Boxers in Shandong Province and border areas see Esherick, *The Origins*. Although similar research for other provinces will be difficult, Esherick's approach should be pursued as far as source materials permit.

38. *JWJAD*, III/2/568, pp. 641–42; III/2/571, pp. 645–47; III/2/573, p. 653.

39. Ibid., III/2/597, pp. 687, 690.   40. Ibid., pp. 687–88.

41. Ibid., p. 688.   42. Ibid., p. 689.

43. Ibid., p. 690.   44. Ibid., III/2/606, pp. 708–11.

45. Ibid., III/2/610, p. 721; III/2/619, pp. 803–28.

46. Ibid., III/2/619, p. 827.   47. Ibid., III/2/610, p. 721.

48. Ibid., III/2/619, p. 828.   49. Ibid., VI/2/710, p. 1062.

50. Ibid., VI/2/730, pp. 1078–83; VI/2/736, pp. 1089–93.

51. Ibid., VI/2/730, pp. 1079–80.

52. Ibid., pp. 1080–81.

53. At some point during the proceedings Yan tried unsuccessfully to involve the church at Hekou on his side. Ibid., pp. 1081–82.

54. Wang evidently tried without success to get the church to intervene on his behalf. Ibid., pp. 1082–83.

55. Ibid., VI/2/736, pp. 1091–92.

56. Ibid., pp. 1092–93. *Shoukui* has a range of meanings and can be taken to mean here a social setback (i.e., loss of face) or a financial loss, perhaps both.

57. Ibid., p. 1093.

58. The case discussed below is from ibid., VI/2/739, pp. 1095–97.

59. The *dibao*, the local subagent responsible for reporting matters such as this to the magistrate, had died of an illness. No one else acted in his place or acted independently to report the murder. Ibid., p. 1095. For details on the administrative importance of *dibao*, see Sweeten, "The *Ti-pao*'s Role."

60. Officials ordered Li Jingzheng returned to Fengcheng County for detention in jail there until such time as authorities apprehended Cai Mingliu and brought him to trial. It appears that officials never arrested Cai; how long officials held Li before executing his sentence is unknown. *JWJAD*, VI/2/739, pp. 1099–1100.

61. Ibid., VI/2/700, pp. 1041–42.

62. In 1849 there were ten Catholic priests in Jiangxi; in 1907 this number had increased to sixty. Latourette, p. 238; Wolferstan, pp. 436–37.

63. For example, see *JWJAD*, II/2/706, p. 893; V/2/1048, pp. 935–36; V/2/1100, pp. 1010, 1012–13; V/2/1112, p. 1048.

64. The involvement of the gentry and anti-Christian publications were both quite prominent in the Nanchang area during the 1860s. Paul A. Cohen, *China and Christianity*, pp. 88–94.

Litzinger, Rural Religion and Village Organization

1. This section of the Zongli yamen archives is published as *JWJAD*. Each citation to *JWJAD* in this chapter contains in order the numbers of the series, the volume, and the document, followed by the page numbers.

2. Topley, pp. 19, 40.   3. Hsiao, p. 275.

4. *JWJAD*, II/1/188, pp. 172–73.   5. Ibid.

6. Ibid., II/1/192, p. 180.   7. Ibid., I/1/563, p. 432.

8. Ibid., p. 436; I/1/593, pp. 523, 526.

9. Although originally a subdivision of the *baojia* system containing ten households, the *pai* under discussion here was a unit containing several villages. See Hsiao, p. 28.

10. *JWJAD*, I/1/183, p. 166; I/1/563, p. 451.

11. Ibid., I/1/563, pp. 429, 433, 442, 443.

12. Ibid., pp. 429, 430, 443, 451.

13. Dates have sometimes been left in their nineteenth-century Chinese form with the corresponding date of the Western calendar noted in parentheses to ensure the making of any significant connections between the date of events and the agricultural and ceremonial cycles of the communities under study here. The capital letter preceding a date indicates the Qing dynasty reign title: TZ for Tongzhi and GX for Guangxu.

14. *JWJAD*, II/1/189, p. 175.

15. Ibid., p. 176.

16. Ibid., I/1/491, p. 314.

17. Prasenjit Duara has written extensively on the importance of the cult of Guan Di in rural North China. See his *Culture, Power, and the State*, esp. pp. 139–48.

18. *JWJAD*, I/1/491, p. 317.

19. Ibid., I/1/504, pp. 353–54.

20. Ibid., p. 354.

21. Ibid., p. 356. On the ancient origin of the identity of people and place in Chinese culture, see Granet, p. 50. Granet holds that the "solidarity uniting the members of the local group was in essence territorial." Although millennia had passed from the time about which Granet was writing to the nineteenth century, this aspect of rural culture seems to have remained constant. Still it could be objected that all we are saying here is that the majority regarded its prayers as a duty for all. Perhaps from the point of view of a Western democratic culture in which religious pluralism is accepted as the norm, such an objection would seem well founded. However, we have attempted to describe the case from the point of view of the culture in which it occurred and in that culture the idea of religious pluralism seems out of place.

22. *JWJAD*, I/1/507, p. 373.

23. Ibid., I/1/503, p. 343.

24. Ibid., pp. 344–45.

25. Ibid., I/1/505, p. 364. For descriptions of such thanksgiving festivals in the twentieth century, see Gamble, *North China Villages*, p. 190, and Fei, pp. 103–4. Martin Yang (p. 197) reports that in Taitou, Shandong, the holding of a folk opera was seen as the essential method of expressing thanksgiving.

26. *JWJAD*, I/1/505, p. 364.

27. Ibid., I/1/497, p. 323; I/1/503, p. 342; I/1/507, pp. 372–73. The term *Momo* as a sect name could not be found in any standard dictionaries nor in works on secret societies or folk religion. The term *momodi* occurs in many dictionaries of Buddhist terms as the name of an office with the meaning "master of monastery."

28. Ibid., I/1/508, p. 376; I/1/510, p. 377.

29. Early in the present century an astute observer of village life in North China

analyzing the Christian withdrawal from participation in these kinds of village activities wrote that it was "obvious that the solidarity of the village system would be severely shaken if individuals were allowed to dissociate themselves at will from the actions of the village as a whole." See Reginald F. Johnston, p. 157. Gamble presents much interesting detail on the holding of temple fairs in the twentieth century in another part of Zhili Province in *Ting Hsien*, pp. 410–14.

30. *JWJAD*, III/1/299, p. 339; III/1/315, p. 351; other documents in the case refer to the sect as "Momo."

31. Ibid., III/1/311, pp. 346–47.   32. Ibid., III/1/315, p. 351.

33. Ibid., III/1/328, pp. 356–58.   34. Ibid., III/1/334, p. 371.

35. Hsiao, p. 564 n. 35. But see also p. 270, where Hsiao inclines somewhat to a view similar to the one presented in this chapter.

36. Note the situation in the Shuinian Village case above; and see also *JWJAD*, II/1/189, p. 175.

37. Ibid., II/1/183, p. 166; IV/1/211, p. 227.

38. Ibid., I/1/562, p. 426; IV/1/196, p. 190. The practice may have been modeled on that officially in force for Confucian temples. See ibid., II/1/283, p. 306. For evidence in the twentieth century that these activities were supported by assessments based on property, see Gamble, *North China Villages*, pp. 123, 283.

39. *JWJAD*, I/1/491, p. 317; III/1/328, p. 356; IV/1/181, p. 173; IV/1/184, p. 177; IV/1/196, p. 190.

40. Ibid., I/1/505, p. 361; II/1/189, p. 175.

41. Ibid., I/1/485, p. 310.

42. Ibid., I/1/562, p. 426; II/1/563, p. 440. On folk operas at temple festivals in the twentieth century, see Osgood, p. 334; Reginald F. Johnston, p. 130. Pasternak, working in Taiwan in the twentieth century, sees these festivals as expressions of community solidarity and as indications of the close connection between the village community and its temple (p. 95). Martin Yang reports that Christians in Taitou, Shandong, would not contribute money for the holding of folk operas, pleading that the performances were held in thanksgiving to the Dragon God and therefore contradictory to Christianity. They, however, attended and enjoyed the performances, causing much resentment among their non-Christian neighbors (p. 160).

43. See the Xiaoli Village and Neibu Village cases above, and also *JWJAD*, III/1/334, p. 372; III/1/563, p. 440.

44. Duara has identified four categories of rural religious organizations. Some, like those discussed in this chapter, he terms "ascriptive," others, "voluntary." *Culture, Power, and the State*, p. 119–32.

45. *JWJAD*, I/1/505, p. 364; IV/1/196, p. 188; IV/1/206, p. 218.

46. This view reflects the theory of Geertz, p. 168.

47. See Overmyer, *Folk Buddhist Religion*, p. 13. Gamble notes that purely secular projects such as crop-watching were undertaken by religious associations; *North China Villages*, p. 119. It also seems significant that when secular self-government institutions were set up in Chinese villages after 1911, they handled religious affairs in the village; ibid., p. 33.

48. *JWJAD*, I/1/563, p. 444; II/1/189, p. 176. If the situation in the villages of

North China was as I have described it here, then an intriguing question arises: How did some villagers, even if a minority, see their way clear to become Catholics? Unfortunately the documentation supporting the present chapter offers no answer.

Thompson, The Chinese Countryside and the Modernizing State

References to *JWJAD* in these notes are to series, volume, document, and page number.

1. Qiao, *Yihetuan zai Shanxi*, pp. 111–12. Dr. E. H. Edwards says in his account of these years that this statement was issued by Governor Cen Chunxuan as a proclamation. See Edwards, p. 53. The Chinese participants included the provincial treasurer, a circuit intendant, and the head of the *Jiaoan ju* (Bureau of Missionary Cases). See Qiao, *Yihetuan zai Shanxi*, p. 111.

2. Qiao, *Yihetuan zai Shanxi*, p. 112.   3. Chester C. Tan, pp. 36–45.

4. Esherick, *The Origins*, p. 1.   5. Li Chien-nung, pp. 84–88.

6. An imperial edict of 20 Feb. 1846 called for the restoration of mission property that had been seized since the reign of Kangxi. However, this did not apply to church buildings that had been converted into temples or houses. See Latourette, p. 230, and Morse, 1: 614–16, 692. Since foreigners were still prohibited from traveling beyond treaty ports, the real impact of this clause would not be felt until it was restated and elaborated upon in the Chinese text of the Sino-French Convention of 1860. This text not only called for the return of seized churches, schools, cemeteries, land, and buildings, but also permitted French missionaries "to rent and purchase land in all the provinces and to erect buildings thereon at pleasure." See Latourette, p. 276. This right, in conjunction with the freedom for foreigners to travel outside the treaty ports, guaranteed in the Tianjin treaties of 1858, was significant.

7. Streit, pp. 226, 243; Planchet, p. 27.

8. Latourette, p. 183.

9. Ibid., p. 320; Chardin, pp. 84–86.

10. Latourette, p. 151. For a survey of the Rites Controversy see ibid., pp. 131–55.

11. China Inland Mission, *Days of Blessing*, pp. 1–3.

12. Bohr, *Famine in China*, p. 103.

13. Ibid., p. 107.

14. Ibid., pp. 192–93.

15. China Inland Mission, *The Land of Sinim*, pp. 85–87.

16. Latourette, p. 366; MacGillivray, *A Century of Protestant Missions*, p. 289.

17. Latourette, p. 475, notes that the U.S. minister obtained an "exemption of Protestant Christians from contributions to festivals, processions, and theatrical performances in honor of non-Christian deities."

18. Schofield, p. 175.

19. "Shanxi quansheng," 3 (*difang caizheng*): 1–2.

20. Qian, p. 184.   21. *JWJAD*, I/2/741, pp. 687–88.

22. Qiao, *Yihetuan zai Shanxi*, p. 77.   23. Ibid., pp. 77–79.

24. Ibid., pp. 78–79.

25. Ibid., pp. 80–81.

26. Lü Shiqiang, p. 134.

27. *JWJAD*, I/1/9–15, pp. 4–5; Le Tobar, pp. 68–72.

28. Le Tobar, pp. 66–68; *JWJAD*, I/1/21, pp. 7–8; Lü Shiqiang, pp. 134–35.

29. Lü Shiqiang, p. 135; *JWJAD*, I/1/44, pp. 13–14.

30. Lü Shiqiang, p. 135. For examples of these conflicts, up to 1874, in Zhili, Shandong, and Guizhou, see ibid., pp. 135–37.

31. Cordier, 2: 473.

32. China Inland Mission, *Days of Blessing*, p. 42.

33. Ibid., p. 52.   34. Ibid., p. 41.

35. Ibid., p. 39.   36. Ibid., p. 158.

37. Marshall Broomhall, *Martyred Missionaries*, pp. 24–29, 110.

38. Timothy Richard, "Christian Persecutions in China," p. 245.

39. Ibid., p. 244.

40. *JWJAD*, III/1/405, p. 480.

41. *Les Missions Catholiques* 7 (1875): 99.

42. Ibid.

43. In Moccagatta's communication (*zhaohui*) to the Shanxi governor, written in Chinese, he only said the Christians refused to pay the temple tax (*miaofei*) and subsequently had their fall crops stolen. He made no specific reference to a "Confucian temple." See *JWJAD*, III/1/407, p. 481.

44. *Annales de la Propagation de la Foi*, 48 (1876): 375–76.

45. Ibid., 376–80.

46. Streit, p. 348; Planchet, p. 27.

47. *JWJAD*, IV/1/299, 305, pp. 312–13, 320.

48. Ibid., IV/1/305, p. 320.

49. Ibid., p. 321.

50. Ibid., IV/1/302, 310, pp. 316, 324–25.

51. Schofield, p. 189.

52. Hummel, p. 28.

53. Qian, p. 200.

54. Zhang's comment is corroborated by other sources. Latourette (p. 354) reports that a severe persecution, requiring the intervention of the French legation, broke out in southern Shanxi in 1882. See also Chardin, pp. 85–86.

55. Qiao, *Yihetuan zai Shanxi*, pp. 85–86.

56. *JWJAD*, IV/1/314, p. 327. Zhang's reform sharply diminished correspondence between Shanxi and Beijing. There are only ten documents in the Zongli yamen archives from the period of Zhang's tenure and only four of these came from the French minister. See *JWJAD*, IV/1, table of contents, p. 22.

57. Taylor, p. 363.

58. Ibid., p. 366.

59. Ibid., p. ix.

60. McIntosh, *The Chinese Crisis*, p. 37.

61. Ibid., pp. 37–38.

62. Marshall Broomhall, *Martyred Missionaries*, pp. 24–29, 126–43; Marshall Broomhall, *Last Letters*, pp. 51–61.

63. Qiao, "Shanxi diqu de Yihetuan yundong," p. 173.

64. Ibid., pp. 169–80.

65. Qiao, "Cong *Qian yuan suoji* kan Yihetuan," pp. 18–19.

66. Liao Yizhong et al., pp. 284–85.

67. Marshall Broomhall, *Martyred Missionaries*, p. 103.

68. Ibid., p. 265.

69. Marshall Broomhall, *Martyred Missionaries* and *Last Letters*; Qiao, "Shanxi diqu de Yihetuan yundong," pp. 169–76.

70. Roger Thompson, pp. 193–98. 71. *Dingxiang xian buzhi*, 12: 11.

72. Ricci, pp. 236–42. 73. Roger Thompson, p. 200.

74. Eliade. Max Weber wrote of the world becoming "disenchanted." "The locus of sacredness was removed from . . . everyday life." See Geertz, p. 174. Wayne Meeks discusses the significance of Christian conversion as "desacralizing the world." He writes: "Jewish-Christian monotheism has the potential to desacralize the world, a discovery [that permits the elite] to ignore the religious dimensions of civic life." Meeks, p. 136.

75. Roger Thompson, p. 201.

76. Qiao, *Yihetuan zai Shanxi*, pp. 100–102.

77. Roger Thompson, p. 201.

78. Duara, "Knowledge and Power."

Tsou, Gilbert Reid and the Reform Movement

1. "Gilbert Reid's Biographical Record."

2. Reid, "Meiguo jiaoshi," pp. 3–4.

3. Reid, *Renxu yanjianglu*, p. 8.

4. "Hart to Campbell," 3 June 1900, in Fairbank et al., *The I. G. in Peking*, 2: no. 1172; Reid, "*Mengzi* zhushi."

5. "Missionary in China for 45 Years."

6. Dwight, p. xxii.

7. Reid, *Glances at China*, pp. 68–71; Reid, "The Difficulties of Intercourse," p. 210.

8. Zhu, 4: 151.

9. Reid, "Chongshu," p. 3; Reid, "Zhihe jianzha shuo," p. 42a.

10. Zhu, 3: 1, 14, 61, 95; Guo Tingyi, 2: 821.

11. Reid, "Zhihe shuo," pp. 40–41; Reid, "Zhihe jianzha shuo," p. 41b.

12. Reid, "Yi gong dai zhen," pp. 42–43.

13. See West.

14. Reid, "An Experience of Missionary Trouble," pp. 276–80.

15. Reid, "Chinese Law," p. 445.

16. MacGillivray, "Donald MacGillivray to John Gilbert Reid."

17. Reid, "The Difficulties of Intercourse," p. 215; *Shanghai Mercury*, 10 Sept. 1927.

18. Reid, "The Difficulties of Intercourse," p. 209.

19. Latourette, pp. 389, 493; Bohr, *Famine in China*, pp. 171–81.

20. Reid, "Lecture," p. 32; Reid, "On the Duty of Every Religion," p. 30.

21. Reid, "The Duty of Christian Missions," pp. 363–64.

22. Reid, "Minjiao xiang'an yi," p. 33.

23. Reid, "The Duty of Christian Missions," pp. 359, 465, 469.

24. Reid, *Regulations of the Mission*, p. 2.

25. *Records of the General Conference, 1890*, p. 440. As a result of Reid's appeal, the conference set up several committees to work out measures for improving relations with the Qing government.

26. Reid, "The Importance of Christian Evangelization," p. 59.

27. Reid, *The Fifth Report of the MHCC*, p. 27. Reid reached New York in January 1893; see "Gilbert Reid's Biographical Record."

28. Reid, *The Second Report of the MHCC*, p. 2; "Missionary in China for 45 Years."

29. MacGillivray, "Donald MacGillivray to John Gilbert Reid."

30. Reid, *The First Report of the MHCC*, pp. 37–42.

31. See Reid's semiannual reports of the MHCC after 1894.

32. Song Bolu. Song was a supervisory censor in the Qing court at that time.

33. Reid, "Chongshu," p. 4.

34. Reid, *The International Institute*, p. 705; Reid, *The Third Report of the MHCC*, p. 2.

35. Zhao Zhongfu, pp. 1938–39.

36. Reid, *The Sixth Report of the MHCC*, p. 9.

37. Reid, *The Third Report of the MHCC*, p. 3.

38. MacGillivray, "Donald MacGillivray's Speech," p. 73.

39. Reid, *The Second Report of the MHCC*, p. 11.

40. Reid, *A Prospectus*, p. 3; *NCDN*, 2 June 1897.

41. Reid, *The Third Report of the MHCC*, p. 4; Reid, *The Fourth Report of the MHCC*, p. 15.

42. Reid, *The Fifth Report of the MHCC*, p. 37; "The Secretary-General of the Zongli Yamen to Reid," 8 Aug. 1895, in Allen, pt. 1, vol. 1: 11.

43. Ezra.

44. Reid, *Regulations of the Mission*, p. 4; *Shanghai Mercury*, 30 Sept. 1927.

45. Xu Run, p. 17.

46. Reid, *The Third Report of the MHCC*, pp. 4–5.

47. Reid, *The Second Report of the MHCC*, p. 3; Reid, *A Prospectus*, p. 14; *NCDN*, 24 Apr. 1897.

48. Reid, *The Fourth Report of the MHCC*, p. 15.

49. *Boston Evening Globe*, 30 Sept. 1927.

50. Reid, "Shangxiantang chuangban yuanyou," p. 4; Reid, *The Second Report of the MHCC*, p. 3.

51. Sunderland, p. 110.

52. Reid, *The Second Report of the MHCC*, p. 1; Reid, *The Seventh Report of the MHCC*, p. 13.

53. "Li Hongzhang to Reid," 12 Apr. 1897, in Reid, *A Prospectus*, p. 14.

54. Reid, *The Third Report of the MHCC*, p. 7.

55. Timothy Richard, *Forty-five Years in China*, p. 225.

56. Reid, *The Third Report of the MHCC*, p. 7.

57. Timothy Richard, *Forty-five Years in China*, pp. 242–52, 254–55.

58. Evans, p. 122.

59. Reid, *The Fourth Report of the MHCC*, pp. 16–17.

60. *North-China Standard*, 1 Oct. 1927.

61. Reid, "The Characteristics of China and Its People," p. 327.

62. Reid, *The Third Report of the MHCC*, pp. 2, 9; Reid, *The Sixth Report of the MHCC*, p. 11; Reid, *The Second Report of the MHCC*, pp. 2, 4.

63. Reid, *The Third Report of the MHCC*, p. 4; quotation from *Shiwubao*, 5 Nov. 1897.

64. "Missionary in China for 45 Years"; *Shiwubao*, 5 Nov. 1897.

65. Reid, *The Fifth Report of the MHCC*, p. 6; Zhao Zhongfu, pp. 1938–39.

66. "Mr. Gilbert Reid's Mission," *NCDN*, 5 Nov. 1896, p. 3; Zhao Zhongfu, pp. 1938–39.

67. *NCDN*, 24 Apr. 1897.

68. Reid, "Xinmin lun," pp. 8–11.

69. Reid, *The Third Report of the MHCC*, p. 5; Reid, *The Fifth Report of the MHCC*, p. 15.

70. Reid, "Shang Zhongchao zhengfu shu," pp. 5–8; Reid, "Xinmin lun," pp. 8–11.

71. Reid, "Xinmin lun," p. 9b.

72. Reid, "Chuangshe xuexiao yi," p. 4.

73. Reid, "Guang xinxue yifu," p. 45.

74. Reid, *The Sixth Report of the MHCC*, pp. 3–4; Reid, "Shangxiantang chuang-ban yuanyou," p. 4.

75. Reid, "Zhongguo neng huajiu weixin," p. 15; Reid, "Xinmin lun," p. 11.

76. McIntosh, "In Remembrance."

77. Ezra.

78. Xu Zongze, pp. 184–85; Spence, *The Memory Palace*, pp. 116–17; Li Zhigang, pp. 20–21.

79. Lü Shiqiang, pp. 6–7.

80. Reid, "The Duty of Christian Missions," pp. 364, 471; Reid, *The Second Report of the MHCC*, p. 3.

81. Reid, "Jingshi," p. 17; Reid, "Shangxiantang wenlu," p. 4; "Li Hongzhang to Reid," 12 Apr. 1897, pp. 13–14, in Reid, *A Prospectus*.

82. Paul A. Cohen, "Missionary Approaches," p. 36.

83. Ibid., pp. 36–37; Arthur J. Brown, p. 1108.

84. Duus; Arthur J. Brown, pp. 285, 1106.

85. Paul A. Cohen, "Missionary Approaches," pp. 49–50.

86. "Hart to Campbell," 27 Oct. 1895, in Fairbank et al., *The I. G. in Peking*, 2: no. 993; MacGillivray, "Donald MacGillivray's Speech," p. 73.

87. Review of *Xiangxuebao*, in Jian Bozan et al., 3: 318.

88. Reid, "Shang Zhongchao zhengfu shu," p. 5b.

89. Lü Haihuan, p. 24; Liang Qichao.

Young, The Politics of Evangelism

References to *JWJAD* in these notes are to series, volume, document and page number.

1. Most Chinese accounts have concluded — perhaps even assumed — that Jiang was murdered. Two recent examples: Li Ping, and Xu Wei. For a contrary Chinese view, see Zhang Qiuwen. I am grateful to Steven Averill, Daniel Bays, and Judy Wyman for help in discovering Chinese articles on the Nanchang incident.

2. Wu Erqi, pp. 21–23.

3. *JWJAD*, VII/2/616, p. 723; *JWJAD*, VII/2/626, p. 728; *ZZD*, 2: 1172.

4. Statement by Xu Rong, attendant of Jiang Zhaotang, enclosed in E. T. Werner, consul, to Ernest M. Satow, minister in Beijing, Jiujiang, 20 Mar. 1906, FO 228/2404.

5. *Annales CM* 71 (1906): 396–97.

6. Statements of Xu Rong and Wang Rong, enclosed in Werner to Satow, Jiujiang, 20 Mar. 1906, FO 228/2404.

7. These various possibilities were noted in the Chinese press at the time. Yan Fu.

8. A photograph of this note is deposited in ADNantes, Postes diplomatiques et consulaires, Pékin, carton 274. Substantially identical versions are printed in *ZZD*, 2: 1174, and *JSZ* 1 (1956): 99–100.

9. The original is deposited in ADNantes, Pékin, carton 274.

10. *JSZ* 1 (1956): 98. There were further writings on the same sheet, apparently, but not continuous with the section quoted here. For a different translation, see Werner to Satow, Jiujiang, 20 Mar. 1906, FO 228/2404.

11. The mission's secretary, Liu Zongyao, and two servants who were at the mission on 22 February 1906 did testify later in Nanchang before local officials and the representatives of the Chinese foreign ministry and the French legation. Their testimony confirmed the mission's version of the affair, although one of the servants spoke of Lacruche's bad temper and abusive behavior. For a Chinese transcription of the interrogation, see ADNantes, Pékin, carton 274. Xu Wei, pp. 107–9, provides a "script" for this climactic confrontation between Jiang and Lacruche, but the purported exchanges seem to be imaginative reconstruction inspired by selections from Jiang's notes.

12. C. H. Dawe, surgeon of the Royal Navy, to Werner, on H.M.S. *Snipe*, Nanchang, 3 Mar. 1906, enclosed in Werner to Satow, 20 Mar. 1906, FO 228/2404. Minister of the marine to minister of foreign affairs (Paris, 8 May 1906), enclosing report of Commander Grellier of gunboat *l'Olry* and naval doctor (2nd class) Edouard Fockenberghe, AMAE, n.s. 328. Bashford, notebook 13, p. 86. An example of the many Chinese accounts incorrectly characterizing the import of these foreign medical reports is *JSZ* 1 (1956): 104.

13. *ZZD*, 5: 3612.

14. Statement of Rev. A. P. Quirmbach (28 Feb. 1906), enclosed in Werner to Satow, 20 Mar. 1906, FO 228/2404. Bashford, notebook 13, pp. 86–88. A. E. Thor, China Inland Mission, to Hankou consul-general, Nanchang, 21 Mar. 1906, and

M. R. Charles to Hankou consul-general, Jiujiang, 16 Mar. 1906, Records of Hankou Consulate, Misc. Corres., 15 Dec. 1905 to 30 Oct. 1906, Record Group 84, National Archives. Thor and Charles also heard the other versions described above in the text. They had no contact with Catholic missionaries before the 25 February riots.

15. See Governor Hu Tinggan's report contained in Waiwu bu (Foreign Ministry) to French Minister Dubail, 25 Feb. 1906, no. 616, *JWJAD*, VII/2/616, p. 723.

16. Paul-Léon Ferrant to the French minister, Jiujiang, 24 Feb. 1906, in AD-Nantes, Pékin, carton 274.

17. *ZZD*, 2: 1173; *ZZD*, 5: 3609.

18. Dubail, French minister, to Prince Qing, Beijing, 27 Feb. 1906, enclosed in Dubail to the foreign minister, Beijing, 5 Mar. 1906, AMAE, n.s. 328.

19. Paul A. Cohen, *China and Christianity*, pp. 92–94, 96–100, 200.

20. *JSZ* 1 (1956): 102. "Express issued by students at Nan Ch'ang on Feb. 24, 1906," copy in Chinese, separately filed enclosure of Werner to Satow, Jiujiang, 20 Mar. 1906, FO 228/1602.

21. *Xinhai geming huiyilu*, 4: 345.

22. *ZZD*, 2: 1174. Consul Werner writes of a meeting on the morning of 25 February, which could refer to the extension of the 24 February nighttime meeting into the next morning, or might be a second meeting of similar character. Werner to Satow, Jiujiang, 20 Mar. 1906, FO 228/2404.

23. Xu Wei, p. 113, sets the crowd at thirty to forty thousand.

24. *JSZ* 1 (1956): 107, 109. *Annales CM* 72 (1907): 57; "Statement by Rev. A. P. Quirmbach," 28 Feb. 1906, in Werner to Satow, 20 Mar. 1906, FO 228/2404. A. E. Thor, China Inland Mission, to Wm. Martin, Hankou consul-general, Nanchang, 21 Mar. 1906, and M. R. Charles to Wm. Martin, Jiujiang, 16 Mar. 1906, Records of the Hankou Consulate, Miscellaneous Correspondence, Letters Rec'd, 15 Dec. 1905 to 30 Oct. 1906, Record Group 84, National Archives. The later Catholic reconstruction alleged that Jiang Zhaotang's son and brother were in the lead, but no such charge was made in the immediate aftermath of the incident. *Annales CM* 72 (1907): 203. Official Chinese accounts are uninformative about the Baihuazhou meeting.

25. Lacruche to Ma. Sr. Cayrel (copy), no date (apparently the morning of 25 Sept. 1906), Lazarist Archives.

26. *Annales CM* 72 (1907): 56.

27. I am currently pursuing a study of the French Religious Protectorate.

28. By 1901 two vicariates had seceded from the French Religious Protectorate, but the French government persisted with its policy of pan-national protection in the rest of the country.

29. Chargé Dubail to Zongli yamen, Beijing, 26 May 1898, and Bezaure, consul-general, to S. Pichon, minister in Beijing, Shanghai, 28 Oct. 1898, ADNantes, Pékin, carton 32.

30. For a discussion of the reasons for local conflicts over the Christian presence in the early decades of the treaties, and the patterns of those conflicts, see Paul A. Cohen, *China and Christianity*; Sweeten, "Community and Bureaucracy," chap. 6; and Litzinger.

31. Walter J. Clennel, consul, to Satow, Jiujiang, 14 Jan. 1901, FO 228/1405, reported that preliminary information was that Catholic churches had suffered damage during July and August 1900 in 23 of Jiangxi's 79 counties. Not all the indemnity was arranged through the negotiations in Beijing, and there are discrepancies regarding the total amount paid. French authorities counted approximately 500,000 taels for Catholics in Jiangxi. Chargé Beau to Delcassé, foreign minister, Beijing, 8 Feb. 1902, AMAE, n.s. 312. The British consul in Jiangxi referred to larger sums: 440,000 taels for just one of the three Catholic vicariates, and 1.5 million for all Christians in the province. Clennel to Satow, Jiujiang, 17 Apr. and 27 July 1901, FO 228/1405.

32. Latourette; Paul A. Cohen, "Christian Missions," pp. 553–59.

33. *Annales CM* 68 (1903): 412, and ibid., 72 (1907): 36–47. These sources do not distinguish clearly between foreign and Chinese in all categories of personnel. In my use of the Lazarist figures, I have assumed that secular priests and the Sisters of Saint Joseph were all Chinese. No reliable general population data are available from the early twentieth century. The census of 1953 reported the population of Jiangxi Province to be close to seventeen million.

34. Translation enclosed in Clennel to Satow, Jiujiang, 20 Feb. 1904, FO 228/1555. The original seems to have been passed on to Chinese authorities, who were well aware of the document. Although this text is not, as far as I know, included among his reprinted writings, I hypothesize that the author was Chen Tianhua, on grounds of style, themes, and occasion. Chen was assigned responsibility for Jiangxi as part of the aborted Huaxinghui plot of 1904. Young, p. 211.

35. Clennel to Satow, Jiujiang, 20 Feb. 1904, FO 228/1555.

36. *Eighty-fourth Annual Report*, p. 143. About 3,000 of the adherents were counted as full members and probationers, and 6,000 as inquirers.

37. Bishop David H. Moore to H. K. Carroll, corresponding secretary for the Board in New York, Shanghai, 22 June 1901, 74-11/1259-5-3:09, Methodists.

38. "Report of the Commission Appointed to Investigate and Report upon Property Conditions in KiangSi" (21 Dec. 1903), 74-11/1259-5-3:08, Methodists. This second report cites several of the conclusions of the first report, which I have not seen.

39. *Eighty-fifth Annual Report*.

40. "Report of the Commission Appointed to Investigate and Report upon Property Conditions in KiangSi" (21 Dec. 1903), 74-11/1259-5-3:08, Methodists.

41. Don W. Nichols to Carroll, Nanchang, 29 May 1901, 74-11/1259-6-2:20, Methodists.

42. Louis Ratard, consul-general, to Delcassé, Shanghai, 27 July 1901, AMAE, n.s. 327; L. Gayat, acting consul, "L'affaire de Sen-kan [Chigang]," ADNantes, Pékin, carton 274.

43. Casimir Vic, vicar apostolic of East Jiangxi, to the Propaganda, 6 Oct. 1901, Archivio della Sacra Congregazione per l'Evangelizzazione dei Popoli o "de Propaganda Fide," n.s. vol. 312, 1027r–1028r.

44. *Annales CM* 68 (1903): 186.

45. Clennel to Satow, Jiujiang, 27 July 1901, FO 228/1405. Clennel visited the

area himself in the immediate aftermath. He enclosed a report on the incident from the Jiangxi governor, Li Xingrui, from which most of the details recounted in the text are drawn. Clennel had hurried to the scene by gunboat to counter an anticipated French gunboat. The French consul-general did send a representative to Nanchang, instructed to seek peace between Catholic and Protestant, but at the same time to accept the view of the Catholic bishop in pressing for punishment "owed" from 1900. Ratard to Delcassé, Shanghai, 27 July 1901, AMAE, n.s. 327. For partisan Protestant accounts, see *North China Herald,* 17 July 1901, p. 109; and D. W. Nichols, Presiding Elder of the Nanchang District, reporting in *Minutes of the Twenty-eighth Annual Meeting,* p. 27. Nichols calculated Methodist losses from the incident, in addition to the six dead, to be not less than 20,000 gold dollars.

46. *ZZD,* 2: 1171–72.

47. Ibid.

48. Li Ping, p. 62, says that Lacruche was transferred to Nanchang in April 1905.

49. *Yancheng xian zhi,* pp. 609–10.

50. Wu Erqi, p. 27; Xu Wei, p. 104.

51. Ferrant, "Affaires de Sin-tchang-shien (Souei-tchéou-fou)" (18 July 1905), ADNantes, Pékin, carton 274.

52. *Yancheng xian zhi,* pp. 609–11.

53. Clennel to Satow, Jiujiang, 15 Aug. 1904 and 1 Sept. 1904, FO 228/1555.

54. *Yancheng xian zhi,* pp. 611–12; *ZZD,* 2: 1172; Clennel to Satow, Jiujiang, 16 Sept. 1904, FO 228/1555.

55. Clennel to Satow, Jiujiang, 15 Aug. 1904, FO 228/1555.

56. For example, Bishop Ferrant addressed the French legation in Beijing on the Tangpu affair in July 1905, in September 1905, in December 1905, and in February 1906 just before the fateful meeting of Jiang and Lacruche. Indeed, Ferrant's communication of early February 1906 stimulated the French minister to prod the Chinese foreign ministry on the matter. Most likely, this démarche precipitated a message to the Jiangxi provincial government, thereby intensifying the pressure on Jiang. "Note sur l'affaire de Sin Tch'ang" (no date), ADNantes, Pékin, carton 274.

57. *Annales CM* 71 (1906): 532.

58. Ferrant, "Affaires de Sin-tchang-shien," ADNantes, Pékin, carton 274.

59. Li Ping, p. 65; *Yancheng xian zhi,* p. 613.

60. *JWJAD,* VII/2/653, pp. 738–39.

61. *ZZD,* 5: 3612–13. Zhang Zhidong had initially heard this version from the Jiangxi governor himself. *ZZD,* 5:3609.

62. "Extrait du rapport de mission du Commandant de 'l'Olry'" (12 Mar. 1906), ADNantes, Pékin, carton 274.

63. Yu Zhaokang forthwith became a manager of the new provincial railway company in his native Hunan. Esherick, *Reform and Revolution,* p. 85.

64. "Confidential Prints," part 58, FO 405/168, pp. 154–55.

65. Edmond Bapst, minister, to foreign minister, Beijing, 22 June 1906, AMAE, n.s. 328.

66. Ferrant to Fiat (superior general), Jiujiang, 21 July 1906, Lazarist Archives.

67. Mgr. Vic to Lazarist superior general, 25 Nov. 1910, Lazarist Archives.
68. Bapst to foreign minister, Beijing, 11 June 1906, AMAE, n.s. 312.
69. "Memorandum communicated to M. Cambon, 22 May 1906," FO 228/2404.
70. "Affaire de Nantchang. Note du Foreign Office" (Paris, 14 June 1906), AMAE, n.s. 328.
71. Foreign minister to Paul Cambon, ambassador in London, Paris, 3 Oct. 1906, AMAE, n.s. 328. Memorandum from French minister to secretary of state for foreign affairs, FO 228/2404.

Bays, Christianity and Ethnicity

1. T'ien.
2. Hefner, p. 26.
3. Grant Wacker's informal presentation at the 1989 symposium.
4. Sanneh, p. 3.
5. On the earliest Hakka exposure to Christianity beyond Hong Kong, see Lutz and Lutz, "Zhang Fuxing."
6. Madsen, p. 116.

Shepherd, Plains Aborigines in Qing Taiwan

I would like to acknowledge the assistance of the staff of the United Church of Canada Archive at Victoria University, Toronto, particularly Rick Stapleton. Comments by Susan Naquin, Shih Lei, and Ch'u Hai-yuan have been of value in making revisions. I would also like to thank Pam Ling for typing the original manuscript. The chapter presented here is abstracted from a much longer and more detailed study ("Plains Aborigines and Missionaries in Ch'ing Taiwan, 1859–95") which will be published elsewhere. Selected Taiwanese names and place names are rendered in Hokkien romanization.

1. Latourette, p. 310.
2. Paul A. Cohen, *China and Christianity*, pp. 135–45.
3. Esherick, *The Origins*, pp. 86–90.
4. Latourette, pp. 238, 327; Clarke; Pollard.
5. Of course, not all converts to Christianity in the nineteenth century converted in groups. I shall be concerned in this chapter only with these group phenomena and not with the many instances of individual conversion.
6. Paul A. Cohen, *China and Christianity*, p. 162.
7. Ibid., pp. 68, 128.
8. Latourette, p. 310.
9. Paul A. Cohen, *China and Christianity*, p. 131.
10. I use the term "marginal" simply to mean "on the outs"; the particular cultural traits that adhere to this structural position depend entirely on situation and context.
11. My use of "Chinese" in the present context is not intended to apply only to majority Han Chinese. Other groups, for example, the Manchus, and the highly

sinicized Bai (Minjia) of Yunnan, also rejected missionary overtures because they identified with the Chinese order. See Fitzgerald, pp. 220–21.

12. See Wickberg; Loewen; Skinner, "Change and Persistence"; Patterson.

13. Latourette, pp. 41–43, 132. When, following the aborted reforms of 1898 and the Boxer Rebellion of 1900, the prestige of the Confucian order plummeted and that of Christianity rose, even the educated classes began to see value in the missionaries. Accordingly, the number of converts increased rapidly in the early twentieth century. See Kwok, p. 14.

14. The count varies according to how finely closely related languages are distinguished. A conventional list is Siraya (including Makatao and Tevorang), Hoanya, Favorlang, Pazeh, Papora, Taokas, Kulon, Ketagalan and Kuvalan. See Shepherd, *Statecraft*, pp. 31, 451.

15. The one exception to this broad division are the Kuvalan of the Yilan plain who came under intense pressure from Chinese settlers in the nineteenth century; for the purposes of this chapter I include them in the plains aborigine category. "Plains aborigine" is an historical category, not an ethnolinguistic or geographical designation.

16. After Qing forces triumphed over the descendants of Zheng Chenggong (Koxinga) in 1683, the new government repatriated large numbers of Chinese to the mainland and incorporated the plains aborigines into its system of administration (giving them a recognized status therein and continuing their taxpaying obligations). This respite from the pressure of Chinese agricultural settlement gave the plains aborigines the opportunity to make a gradual accommodation to Chinese influence before the second wave of Chinese immigration and settlement began in the eighteenth century. See Shepherd, *Statecraft*.

17. Ibid.

18. Shepherd, "Sinicized Siraya Worship."

19. Fuller accounts of the five cases, which have been condensed because of space considerations here, can be found in Shepherd, "Plains Aborigines and Missionaries."

20. Fernandez, pp. 8–10, 12.

21. Chen Jialu, pp. 33–35; Pan, pp. 1–3.

22. See Paul A. Cohen, *China and Christianity*, chap. 1, for a review of the tradition of popular Chinese anti-Christian propaganda, in which lurid accusations were frequently made to darken the name of the Christians.

23. Fernandez, pp. 89–92; Chen Jialu, p. 48.

24. Fernandez, pp. 92–93.

25. Pickering, p. 214.

26. Fernandez, pp. 105–8; Band, pp. 78–80; Davidson, pp. 192–98; James Johnston, p. 176.

27. Fernandez, pp. 111–12, 117.   28. Ibid., pp. 112–13.

29. Ibid., p. 111.   30. Pan, pp. 4–5.

31. *El Correo* 29 (1895): appendix.

32. Shepherd, "Plains Aborigines and Missionaries."

33. For an account of the migration to Puli, see Shepherd, *Statecraft*.

34. William Campbell, *An Account*, pp. 267–68.

35. See also *Messenger and Missionary Record* 7 (1874): 14; ibid. n.s. 1 (1876): 132.

36. Ibid. 4 (1871): 280; William Campbell, *An Account*, p. 269.

37. *Messenger and Missionary Record* 5 (1872): 13.

38. MacKay, pp. 36–37; William Campbell, *An Account*, p. 270.

39. William Campbell, *An Account*, pp. 270–71, emphasis added.

40. Ibid., p. 271.

41. Thomas Barclay.

42. William Campbell, *An Account*, pp. 257–58, emphasis added.

43. Bullock, emphasis added.

44. William Campbell, *An Account*, pp. 304–6, 308–9.

45. *The Home and Foreign Record of the Canada Presbyterian Church* 12.9 (1873): 243–44.

46. William Campbell, *An Account*, pp. 332–33.

47. *Messenger and Missionary Record* n.s. 1 (1876): 129–33.

48. MacKay, p. 31.

49. *El Correo* 29 (1895): appendix.

50. William Campbell, *Handbook*, p. xxxi.

51. Mrs. Richard. The fractions for each congregation are estimates based on the foregoing documentation; more precise figures are impossible in the absence of membership statistics broken down by congregation.

52. For negative stereotypes and contempt for aborigines common among Han, see Xie Shizhong.

53. Shih Lei found the degree and quality of contact with Han Chinese and their folk religion to be important in his comparative study of religious change in aborigine and mixed Han-aborigine villages in the postwar era. See Shih Lei.

54. Sparsity of data also makes difficult the important task of analyzing why certain Taiwan Han communities received the missionaries; were they also "marginal" to the power structure in their localities?

55. *Messenger and Missionary Record* 3 (1870): 288.

56. MacKay, p. 215.

57. Manson.

58. See Note 12.

Diamond, Christianity and the Hua Miao

I would like to express thanks to those who made the related research possible: in addition to the Luce Foundation, I am grateful to the Wang Foundation for field-work funding, to the Yunnan Academy of Social Sciences and the Central Minorities Institute (Beijing) for facilitating fieldwork and for access to their library resources, to the library of the School of Oriental and African Studies, London, which houses the archives of the United Methodist Church and Methodist Missionary Society, and to Yale Divinity School library. I particularly wish to thank the former missionaries to the Hua Miao for generous sharing of their time and assistance: Eleanor Cowles, Elliott Kendall, Keith Parsons, Kenneth Parsons, Charles Steele, and Ernest

Pollard for sharing his mother's memories. I regret that I saw the interesting study by Zhang Dan too late to make use of it for this essay. I intend to incorporate it into my future work.

1. For fuller discussion, see Ramsey.

2. Wang Fushi.

3. Also known as the White Miao. Despite their current location, they are closer linguistically to White Miao living in the southernmost parts of Yunnan and in northeast Thailand and Vietnam. See Graham.

4. See for example Grist, and Kendall, *Beyond the Clouds*.

5. The new primers for Dian Dongbei were published in October 1983 by the Zhaotong District Printing House. They had been compiled under the supervision of the local minority affairs commissions (*minzu shiwu weiyuanhui*) of the Zhaotong District (Yunnan) and Weining Autonomous County (Guizhou), locales which together contain most of the total Hua Miao population. The first two volumes to appear were a reader, *Ad Hmaob Ndeud*, and a picture dictionary, *Ad Hmaob At Got Ndeud*.

6. My thanks to Keith Parsons for sharing these letters with me and for his translation.

7. Samuel Pollard (1864–1915), the son of a Bible Christian preacher, was raised in the villages of Cornwall and the Isle of Wight. He attended Shebbear College in Cornwall and had a brief career in the civil service. He arrived in China in 1887 under the sponsorship of the China Inland Mission, after being appointed by the Bible Christian church as a missionary to China. After a short period of training in Shanghai, he was assigned to work in Zhaotong, Yunnan, as a minister and teacher. In 1891, he married Emma Hainge who was working as a missionary nurse in Kunming, also under CIM sponsorship. She joined him in his work at Zhaotong, and subsequently in his mission to the Hua Miao. After his death she returned to England, but continued to be in contact with the Miao work.

8. Kendall, *Eyes of the Earth*. The original and full texts of the diaries that Pollard kept throughout his years in China are housed now at the School of Oriental and African Studies, University of London, and are also available on microfilm at Yale Divinity School.

9. Pollard, pp. 25–26.

10. Pollard, diary entry, 4 Sept. 1904, MMS Papers.

11. Pollard, in *United Methodist Church Missions Report, 1915*.

12. Pollard, pp. 78–89.

13. Harry and Annie Bryant Parsons had been working in Dongchuan (Yunnan), and after Pollard's death spent several more years at Stone Gateway. William Hudspeth volunteered for Stone Gateway after hearing Pollard speak during his 1908 furlough. At the close of the First World War he returned to England and did a degree in anthropology and Oriental languages at Cambridge. He continued work among the Miao and Yi for a number of years and then took up a post with the Foreign Bible Society in Shanghai in the mid-1930s. During internment by the Japanese, his nearly completed manuscripts on Hua Miao ethnology and linguistics were confiscated and presumably destroyed.

14. See Thomas Shaw, and David M. Thompson.

15. Reports by W. Hudspeth and S. Pollard in *United Methodist Church Missions Report*, 1914 and 1915.

16. Pollard diary, 12 Oct. 1904, MMS Papers.

17. Pollard, pp. 142–43.

18. Wei Qiguang, "QianDianChuan"; Guo Jifeng; Chen Guoqun.

19. Wang Jianguang.

20. Yang Hanxian, unpublished memoir based on the notes and conversations of his father, Yang Yake. The version to which I have access is a 1977 mimeographed paper. It may have been formally published since that date.

21. MMS Papers, box 1318, includes a lengthy memoir written by H. B. Rattenbury, a leading officer of the society, about his on-site visit to Stone Gateway in May 1934. He was greatly impressed, since it happened to coincide with the Duan Wu festival, in its Christianized version of sports events, hymn singing, prayer meetings and feasting, attracting upwards of 7,000 participants and various regional notables. Hudspeth's account of the same event gives a more conservative estimate of the crowd at 4,000. The 1932 *United Methodist Church Missions Report* claims for the Miao circuit a membership of 4,468 confirmed persons, 8,017 on trial and 2,761 students at various levels of the system.

22. The question of the difficulties encountered by Hua Miao girls studying in church schools in the urban centers was raised by several of the missionaries I interviewed. One problem was that the girls were adamant about wearing their traditional dress and hairstyles. Another was their greater social maturity compared to Chinese girls of the same age. Also, the Zhaotong Middle School was heavily enrolled with Han Chinese drawn from wealthy urban and rural-elite families.

23. Reports by Emma Pollard on work with girls and women, in *United Methodist Church Missions Report*, 1913, 1914, 1915.

24. Report by Hudspeth, in *United Methodist Church Missions Report*, 1932, p. 59. Hudspeth gives a figure of 30 students for the first year enrollment, pointing out that this venture cost the mission no more than £5, the bulk of the cost being carried by the Hua Miao themselves.

25. MMS Papers, box 948, telegram of 20 May 1943 and letter of 7 Aug. 1943 from Kenneth May to Rattenbury.

26. Having Miao and Yi meeting separately in subdistrict meetings was actually approved and encouraged by the missionary leaders of the Southwest District during the 1930s and 1940s on the grounds that it would save time at full district meetings.

27. MMS Papers, box 946, contains several letters from W. Hudspeth to the home office that argue for keeping the Miao, Chinese, and Yi circuits separate and for organizing the Southwest District into four sections. Dated Mar. 1934; 5 Apr. 1934; and 18 May 1934. A long letter from Kenneth May of 19 Feb. 1935 supports the suggestion on financial grounds, letting Yi (Nosu) and Miao continue to receive lower salaries from the church and be self-reliant.

28. Ibid., letter of 7 Apr. 1935 from W. Hudspeth.

29. Eleanor Cowles, a teacher, had been at Stone Gateway since 1942. She was

eventually joined in 1944–45 by Nurse Edith Milner who had persistently requested transfer from Zhaotong to the Miao circuits, and by several more women in 1946–47 who were engaged in teaching, public health work, and agricultural extension work.

30. In areas where the primary schools are multiethnic, the new Miao school texts cannot be used, and smaller Miao villages are unlikely to have a village school of their own.

31. Among the tales of supernatural powers that circulate orally, one hears of how Pollard led a group of Miao through the wilderness and provided water for them by striking a rock, and how Pollard was saved by the intervention of an angel when threatened with a fatal beating by a gang of hired (Han) thugs. Pollard himself may have encouraged such tales by sometimes using his "powers" to exorcise devils. More in line with the contemporary model heroes of the PRC, one is reminded of how he tirelessly traveled on foot and horseback to visit the villages, how he healed the sick, how he stood up to the rapacious landlords and local *tumu*, and how he died nursing the sick students at Stone Gateway.

32. Wei Qiguang, "QianDianChuan," and "Shilun Jidujiao." See also Cen.

Constable, Christianity and Hakka Identity

I express my appreciation to the Joint Committee on Chinese Studies of the American Council of Learned Societies and the Social Science Research Council, and the Robert H. Lowie Fund of the Department of Anthropology, University of California, Berkeley, for their support of this research. I am also grateful for the help and suggestions of several participants in the first symposium of the History of Christianity in China Project, and to William A. Shack, Agnes Wen, and Joseph S. Alter. Some of the material in this chapter appears in Nicole Constable, *Christian Souls and Chinese Spirits: A Hakka Community in Hong Kong*, © 1994 by the Regents of the University of California. The author is grateful to the University of California Press for permission to use this material.

1. Hong Kong place names are romanized according to the Hong Kong government's *A Gazetteer of Place Names*, or *Hong Kong Streets and Places*. In most English-language publications, the Cantonese name *Tang* is written *Teng* following the Wade-Giles system of romanization. In *pinyin* it is *Deng*. A more detailed description of Shung Him Tong can be found in Constable, *Christian Souls and Chinese Spirits*.

2. Paul A. Cohen, *China and Christianity*, p. 162.

3. See Luo Xianglin, *Kejia yanjiu daolun*, "Kejia yuanliu kao," and *Kejia shiliao huipian*.

4. Leong, "The Hakka Chinese" and "The Hakka Chinese of Lingnan."

5. Leong, "The Hakka Chinese," pp. 5–6.

6. Hsieh; see also Luo Xianglin, *Kejia shiliao huipian*.

7. Leong, "The Hakka Chinese," p. 20; see also Hsieh, p. 217.

8. See Lo; also Myron L. Cohen, "The Hakka."

9. The Basel Evangelical Missionary Society was founded in Basel, Switzerland, in 1815 and supported by members in Switzerland, Germany, and the Austro-Hungarian empire. The society is international and interdenominational; its major constituents are Lutheran and Reformed churches. Partnerships exist today between the Basel mission and churches in Hong Kong, Singapore, Sabah, Indonesia, Taiwan, India, Cameroon, Nigeria, Kenya, Sudan, Zaire, Bolivia, Chile, Peru, Tahiti, and elsewhere. On the history of the Basel mission in China, see Voskamp; MacGillivray, *A Century of Protestant Missions*; Yu; Oehler; Schlatter; Hermann.

10. See Oehler, p. 352, and Voskamp, p. 374, on Lechler's work among the Min and Hakka. For a detailed discussion of the problems involved in estimating the number of Hakka Christians, see Constable, *Christian Souls and Chinese Spirits*, chap. 1.

11. Voskamp, p. 375. 12. Yu, p. 65.

13. Ibid. 14. Smith, *Chinese Christians*.

15. See, for example, Hamberg, *Visions of Hung Siu-Tshuen*; Laai, pp. 167–71; Shih, pp. 49–50, 305–6; Teng, pp. 54–55; Kuhn, pp. 350–51; Bohr, "The Hakka and the Heavenly Kingdom," p. 135; Constable, *Christian Souls and Chinese Spirits*, chap. 2.

16. Kuhn, pp. 364–65. 17. Ibid., p. 365.

18. Lechler, p. 359. 19. George Campbell; Oehler.

20. Lechler, p. 358. 21. Ibid.

22. George Campbell, p. 474.

23. Ibid., p. 480; Piton, p. 225; Oehler; Eitel, p. 65; Lechler.

24. Oehler, p. 351.

25. Lechler, pp. 353–54.

26. See Blake, "Negotiating Ethnolinguistic Symbols," pp. 80–81.

27. Hobsbawm, p. 1. 28. Eitel, p. 98.

29. Oehler, p. 352. 30. Nakagawa, p. 209.

31. George Campbell, p. 480.

32. For example, Luo Xianglin, *Kejia yanjiu daolun*; Hsieh.

33. Tsang, p. 5.

34. Personal names such as this one do not follow a standard system of romanization but reflect the most common rendition of the name as it is recorded in church, government and private records in Hong Kong.

35. For other studies of the New Territories Tang, see Rubie S. Watson, "Creation of a Chinese Lineage," and *Inequality Among Brothers*; Potter; Faure.

36. Hugh R. Baker, *Chinese Lineage Village*, p. 173.

37. Faure; Sung, "Legends and Stories," pts. 1–2.

38. Lo.

39. Rubie S. Watson, *Inequality Among Brothers*, pp. 55–59.

40. Ibid., p. 59. 41. Potter, p. 164.

42. Faure, p. 164. 43. Pang.

44. See Constable, *Christian Souls and Chinese Spirits*, chap. 3.

45. Pang, preface.

46. Although many people in Hong Kong say that the Hakka are shorter, stock-

ier, darker skinned and have larger feet than other Chinese, it is impossible to distinguish them on this basis. A few old women still wear a distinctive black cloth draped over their heads and tied over the top and behind the ears with an embroidered band. See Johnson; and Blake, "Negotiating Ethnolinguistic Symbols" and *Ethnic Groups and Social Change*. Other women who wear the flat, circular hat with the black "curtain" around the rim are usually assumed to be Hakka but often are not. The hats, as well as the notion of Hakka as being stockier and having darker skin than other Chinese, may well result from the stereotype of Hakka being involved in outdoor, heavy manual labor such as farming and construction work. See Constable, *Guest People*, chap. 1.

47. David C. E. Liao, p. 7.

48. Keyes argues that ethnicity entails both "instrumental" and "primordial" aspects, and that it "derives from a cultural interpretation of descent" (p. 5). While he views ethnicity as "a form of kinship reckoning," he stresses that "it is one in which connections with forbears or with those whom one believes one shares descent are not traced along strictly genealogical lines" (p. 6).

James L. Watson asserts that in late imperial China "to be Chinese is to understand and accept the view that there is a correct way to perform rites associated with the life cycle" (p. 1), and that "the proper performance of the [funerary] rites, in the accepted sequence, was of paramount importance in determining who was and who was not deemed to be fully Chinese" (p. 4). See Constable, *Christian Souls and Chinese Spirits*, for a detailed discussion of this point.

49. Pang, p. 1.

50. Luo Xianglin, *Kejia yanjiu daolun*.

51. Luo Xianglin, *Kejia shiliao huipian*.

52. Luo Xianglin, *Kejia yanjiu daolun*, chaps. 7, 8; and *Kejia shiliao huipian*, pp. 388–96. Other writers have questioned this claim. Cf. Tan Bian.

Bays, Christianity and Chinese Women

1. One point Entenmann could have made is that while women had scope for participation both in Christianity and in the White Lotus tradition, in the latter they could apparently only take a leadership or teaching role as spouse or widow of a male leader, whereas the Christian Virgins took on these roles directly.

2. Of course, this would be true of boys' schools as well.

Entenmann, Christian Virgins in Sichuan

Research for this chapter was supported by travel grants from the National Endowment for the Humanities and St. Olaf College. I am deeply grateful for the hospitality and assistance I received at the Société des Missions Étrangères de Paris, especially from Fr. Jean-Paul Lenfant, archivist; Annie Salavert-Sablayrolles, librarian; and Mgr. René Boisguerin. Jean-Paul Lenfant, Ann Waltner, and Jean-Paul Wiest commented on earlier drafts of this chapter, as did Gao Wangzhi, Charles Litzinger, and other members of the History of Christianity in China Project. I am also grateful to my colleagues in the St. Olaf History Department Colloquium for their valuable comments on an earlier draft of this work. Anne Groton kindly helped me with Latin sources. Only I am responsible, of course, for errors of fact, translation, or interpretation.

Sources from the Archives des Missions Étrangères, of the Société des Missions Étrangères de Paris, are indicated by the abbreviation AME, followed by volume number and page number.

1. Gourdon, *Catalogus cleri*, pp. 9–21.

2. Dufresse to MEP, 11 Oct. 1804, *Nouvelles lettres édifiantes*, 4: 94.

3. Entenmann, "Chinese Catholic Clergy and Catechists."

4. Launay, *Histoire de la Mission*, 1: 214. Launay indicates that the late-Ming Jesuit missionaries in Sichuan, Luigi Buglio and Gabriel de Magalhães, wrote of women who had "consecrated themselves to God." Launay does not cite a source, however, and I have not found any such references in the writings of these missionaries.

5. Basset to Artus de Lionne, 17 July 1705, AME 407: 559.

6. Basset to Artus de Lionne, 17 Sept. 1704, AME 407: 485–89; Martiliat, Journal, May 1738, AME 434: 569.

7. Martiliat, Journal, Mar. 1733, AME 434: 489.

8. Martiliat to MEP, 13 July 1745, AME 434: 347–48.

9. Van Gulik, p. 50. Van Gulik's observation applies to the pre-Han period, before Buddhism with its vocation of celibacy was introduced to China, but such attitudes have nonetheless persisted.

10. A field study conducted in rural China in 1929–31 indicated that fewer than one woman in a thousand never married. George W. Barclay et al., p. 610. Martiliat observed that marriage was nearly universal in China. Journal, Aug. 1734, AME 434: 519. Yet polygamy meant, of course, that some men had multiple wives and others none.

11. Famin, governor of Sichuan, memorial of Yongzheng 4/6/4 (3 July 1726), *Gongzhongdang Yongzheng chao zouzhe*, 6: 107–9.

12. Ly, 7 Sept. 1748, pp. 84–85. Ly's diary, written in Latin and sent by courier to Macao and thence to the Société des Missions Étrangères, is held in the Société's archives (AME 500).

13. Ly, "Relatio vexationum christianorum Mao-ping civitatis Fou-tcheou," *Journal d'André Ly*, pp. 306–7.

14. Ly, 9 Dec. 1755, p. 358.

15. Stockard, esp. chaps. 4 and 7.

16. Ly, "Relatio persequutionis christianorum Sin-Tou-Hien," *Journal d'André Ly*, p. 12.

17. Martiliat, Journal, Apr. 1733, AME 434: 492.

18. Ly, "Monita moralia ad presbyteros provinciae Sse-tchuen," 30 Nov. 1753; Journal, 15 Aug. 1757, *Journal d'André Ly*, pp. 258, 421.

19. Gleyo's account of his captivity, reprinted in Launay, *Histoire de la Mission*, 1: 406; see also "Extrait de la relation de la persécution qu'a essuié M. Gleyo, missionnaire apostolique de Séminaire des Missions Étrangères, dans la province de Su-tchuen en Chine 30 Mai 1769–27 Juin 1777," *Nouvelles lettres édifiantes*, 3: 44–88.

20. Ly, "Relatio persequutionis christianitatis Long-men-than et Ching-tsong-ping, oppidi Kiang-tsin suffraganei urbis Tchung-khing," *Journal d'André Ly*, p. 354. This persecution is examined in my other chapter in this volume, "Catholics and Society in Eighteenth-Century Sichuan."

21. For a discussion of widows in this period see Waltner, and Elvin.

22. Martiliat, Journal, Mar. 1733, AME 434: 489. After 1723, in fact, widows were eligible for honors if they had been widowed for as few as fifteen years. Elvin, p. 124.

23. Ly, "Infamia a Josephus Tchao sibi comparata," *Journal d'André Ly*, p. 9.

24. One of the Chinese priests in Sichuan, Antonius Dang Huairen, had served in Fujian in the 1720s, where his duties included supervising a group of "virgins dedicated to Christ." Martiliat to MEP, 13 July 1745, AME 434: 341.

25. Martiliat, Journal, Nov. 1744, AME 434: 733.

26. The Chinese text is *Tongzhen xiugui*; the Latin version is reprinted in Launay, *Histoire de la Mission*, 2: appendixes, 13–20. Later regulations for Christian Virgins are included in *Summa Decretorum*, pars prima, cap. 3, art. 5: De Virginibus.

27. *Yili*, 20.15b.

28. Gabriel Taurin Dufresse to his mother, 15 Aug. 1780, AME 1250: 116.

29. François Pottier, "Responsa ad questiones S. Congregationis de Propaganda Fide circa missionem Seu-tchuen," n.d., AME 436: 903. Internal evidence indicates that this report was written in 1765.

30. Launay, *Histoire générale*, 3: 141–46.

31. Martiliat, Journal, Jan.–Mar. 1745, AME 434: 740.

32. Martiliat to MEP, 13 July 1745, AME 434: 348.

33. Moÿe is the subject of several biographies. Father Jean Guennou kindly provided me with a photocopy of parts of his book. See also works by Marchal, Foucauld, Plus, Mary Generosa Callahan, and Tavard.

34. Marchal, p. 235.

35. Pottier to Steiner, 18 Oct. 1782, AME 438: 237–40.

36. Dufresse to Georges Alary, 4 Oct. 1782, AME 1250: 148; Dufresse to Alary, 30 Aug. 1789, AME 1250: 475. The aunts of Benedictus Sun are referred to as Lieu (Liu) Da guniang and Sun Da guniang. Da guniang (Great maiden) was evidently a title of respect for Christian Virgins.

37. Marchal, p. 230.

38. Moÿe, "Narratio rerum ad missionem in parte orientalis Su-tchuen et Kouei-tcheou attinentium pro anno 1778 finiente et sequenti," Archives of the Sacred Congregation for the Propagation of the Faith, East Indies and China, Scritture riferite nei Congressi, 1780, vol. 320, cited in Guennou, p. 221.

39. Moÿe to Propaganda, 27 July 1779 and 7 Apr. 1780, as cited in Mary Generosa Callahan, p. 142, and Marchal, pp. 359–61; Moÿe, "Narratio," cited in Guennou, p. 215.

40. Moÿe to Dufresse, 19 Aug. 1780, reprinted in Marchal, p. 441.

41. Ibid., p. 440.

42. Dufresse to Alary, 24 Sept. 1782, AME 1250: 148.

43. Pottier's report of Sept. 1782, quoted in Marchal, p. 462.

44. Pottier to Steiner, 18 Oct. 1782, AME 438: 237–40, esp. 238–39. See also

Guiot, pp. 335–36, for excerpts from a letter from Pottier to Jean-Joseph Descouvrièrs, procurer of the Société des Missions Étrangères in Macao, 16 Oct. 1782.

45. Martiliat had noted a half-century earlier that marriages were usually contracted when the woman was 17 to 20 years old. Martiliat, Journal, Jan. 1734, AME 434: 519. On one occasion he celebrated a wedding for a woman of 23, "an old age for these parts." Her father had turned down earlier marriage offers from non-Christians, waiting for a suitable Christian match. Martiliat, Journal, June 1743, AME 434: 720.

46. Marchal, p. 468. The original letters, which I have not seen, are located in the archives of the Propaganda.

47. Instruction of the Sacred Congregation for the Propagation of the Faith to the Vicar Apostolic of Sichuan, 29 Apr. 1784, *Collectanea*, 1: 351 (document 59).

48. Elvin, p. 124.

49. Saint Martin, *Shengjiao yaoli*, p. 50a–b. There are many editions of this work, which was used well into the twentieth century. See also the French translation: *Doctrine de la Sainte Religion*, pp. 109–10. I am grateful to Annie Salavert-Sablayrolles of the Bibliothèque Asiatique des Missions Étrangères for bringing this work to my attention.

50. On this persecution see Willeke.

51. Dufresse to MEP, 11 Oct. 1803, *Nouvelles lettres édifiantes*, 4: 64.

52. Saint Martin, pastoral letter, 1 Sept. 1793, summarized in *Summa Decretorum*, pp. 47–49.

53. Dufresse to Denis Chaumont, 26 Sept. 1798, *Nouvelles lettres édifiantes*, 3: 323. See Rawski's discussion of female literacy, pp. 6–8.

54. Dufresse to MEP, 28 Oct. 1803, AME 1250: 988.

55. Huc, 1: 301.

56. Launay, *Histoire générale*, 3: 557, 576, 588.

57. Foucauld, p. 49.

58. Wiest, *Maryknoll*, p. 87.

59. See Naquin's work on the White Lotus tradition, particularly her *Millenarian Rebellion*, pp. 47–48, and "Connections Between Rebellions"; Overmyer, "Alternatives"; and Rosner, pp. 239–46.

Kwok, Chinese Women and Protestant Christianity

1. McNeur, pp. 24–25.

2. *Records of the General Conference 1877*, p. 486.

3. Stauffer, p. 293.

4. Latourette.

5. Wu Liming, *Jidujiao yu Zhongguo*; Lam Wing-hung, *Chinese Theology in Construction*; Smith, *Chinese Christians*.

6. Latourette, p. 485; Paul A. Cohen, "Christian Missions," pp. 582–83.

7. See Daly, *The Church and the Second Sex*, and her *Beyond God the Father*; Ruether, *Sexism and God-talk*.

8. Chu, "Magazines for Chinese Women"; Yuan, p. 167.

9. Chu, *Zhongguo nüqingnianhui xiaoshi*; Cai; Zeng, *Zeng Baosun huiyilu*; Wang Liming, *Zhongguo funü yundong*.

10. For example, Ruether and Keller; Thomas and Keller.

11. Jane Hunter; Hill.

12. Some of these obituaries are found in *Zhonghua Jidujiaohui nianjian*, 3 (1916): sec. *wei*, 139–46; 4 (1917): 219–31; 5 (1918): 227–45; 6 (1921): 254–73; 7 (1924): 150–63; 8 (1925): 269–85; 9 (1927): 253–83.

13. See Kwok, pp. 29–64.

14. Welter, pp. 86–89.

15. Charles Hartwell, a missionary in Fuzhou, wrote many religious tracts, including one with ballads to be related after each lesson on the life of Jesus. See, e.g., Hartwell's *Zhengdao qimeng*, in Fuzhou colloquial.

16. Ella C. Shaw, p. 344.

17. On the roles of women in folk religious sects, see Overmyer, "Alternatives," pp. 165–67; and Naquin, *Millenarian Rebellion*, p. 41.

18. See Kwok, pp. 86–93.   19. Macgowan, pp. 53–66.

20. See, for example, Dudgeon; Kerr.   21. Little, pp. 305–70.

22. Burton.

23. Goodrich, "Woman's Christian Temperance Union"; Goodrich, "Woman's Christian Temperance Union of China."

24. Mrs. Herman C. E. Liu, "The Woman's Christian Temperance Union."

25. Honig, p. 217.   26. YWCA of China, p. 1.

27. Cai, pp. 98–105.   28. Zeng, *Zeng Baosun huiyilu*, p. 35.

29. Ding Shujing, "Fengmen de shengming."

30. Stone.   31. Kahn, pp. 660–61.

32. Li Guanfang, p. 6.   33. Wang Huiwu, p. 8.

34. Ding Shujing, "Funü zai jiaohui zhong de diwei," p. 23.

35. Ruth Cheng, p. 540.

36. Zeng, "Christianity and Women."

37. Ding Shujing, "Fengmen de shengming," p. 7.

Ross, *The McTyeire Home and School*

Many members of the McTyeire and Number 3 communities have welcomed and guided my interest in McTyeire with grace and good humor. Two individuals deserve special recognition. Chen Jinyu, Number 3's librarian, has offered me unfailing support and advice. Rosalyn Koo, graduate of the class of 1947, has assisted me in collecting the personal narratives for this study. In addition, I would like to thank Colgate University, the Spencer Foundation, and the National Endowment for the Humanities for their support of this research. Both Judith Liu and Emily Honig have provided thoughtful comments on my work, for which I am very grateful. Finally, I extend my gratitude to the fine staff at the United Methodist Church's Global Ministries Commission on Archives and History, Drew University, who have assisted me in my search for documentary materials on McTyeire's historical development.

Where uncited, quotations are from interviews with alumnae or other persons connected with McTyeire's history.

1. St. Mary's was an Episcopalian school informally affiliated with St. John's University. Its grounds were taken over in 1952 by the Shanghai Textile Engineering Institute.

2. See Yeh; Wasserstrom.   3. Punch, p. 5.
4. Personal Narratives Group.   5. Jane Hunter, p. 255.
6. Bennett, p. 56.   7. Ibid.
8. Women's Foreign Missionary Society, *Annual Report*, 1882–83, p. 24.

9. Haygood was celebrated in Southern Methodist literature in the first two decades of the twentieth century as "the Chinese girls' friend." Examples include Chappell, p. 63; also see Cook.

10. Oswald and Anna Brown, p. 166.   11. Ibid., p. 176.
12. Ibid., pp. 92–94.   13. Jane Hunter.
14. Oswald and Anna Brown, p. 94.   15. Jane Hunter, p. 45.
16. Ibid., p. xv.   17. "Shanghaishi."
18. Women's Foreign Missionary Society, *Annual Report*, 1907.

19. McTyeire High School Catalog, 1908, in Methodists, RG79, box 16, folder 1459-4-1:26, 6.

20. Cobb.

21. McTyeire High School leaflet, 1917, in Methodists, RG79, box 16, folder 1459-4-1:26.

22. Lewis, p. 89.   23. Craig, p. 5.
24. Bateson.   25. Heilbrun.
26. Jane Hunter; Chen Zilong.   27. Gilligan, p. 168.

Liu and Kelly, St. Hilda's School for Girls

This chapter, focused on a particular time in the history of St. Hilda's, an American Episcopal girls' boarding school in Wuchang, Hubei Province, derives partly from a personal link that enabled one of the authors, Judith Liu, to conduct 21 interviews of St. Hilda's alumnae in China and Taiwan in 1982. This original set of data was followed up by a 1987 questionnaire administered to the 1982 interviewees and by interviews in the United States of six more alumnae in 1984, 1987, and 1989. Interview findings were supplemented by important material in the Archives of the Episcopal Church, Austin, Texas. St. Hilda's itself lasted until 1952, when it was absorbed into the Wuchang municipal educational system. Yet many of its alumnae still strongly identify with the school, as do those of McTyeire in Shanghai, discussed elsewhere in this volume. Thus the St. Hilda's of the 1930s still has a vivid presence in the collective memory of a diminishing cohort of aging alumnae around the world.

1. Lin, p. 8.
2. Ibid.
3. See Schlesinger.

4. The anti-Christian movement arose over The World's Student Christian Federation conference held in Beijing in April 1922. The conference coincided with the publication of *The Christian Occupation of China*, which chronicled the growth of Christianity in China. The idea of "the occupation of China" inflamed students in government schools who distrusted the "de-nationalized" character of missionary school students. See Kiang, pp. 60–68.

5. Henrietta F. Boone, pp. 174–75.

6. William J. Boone, Shanghai, to Rev. J. Kimber, New York, 24 Aug. 1880, Report to the Home Office, file RG-64-5, The Archives of the Episcopal Church, William J. Boone file, 1880; William J. Boone, Shanghai, to the Reverend Secretary of the Foreign Committee, New York, 2 May 1882, "A," Report to the Home Office, file RG-64-6, ibid., 1882; William J. Boone, Shanghai, to Rev. J. Kimber, New York, 18 Aug. 1882, Report to the Home Office, file RG-64-6, ibid.

7. William J. Boone, Shanghai, to Rev. J. Kimber, New York, 24 Aug. 1880, Report to the Home Office, file RG-64-5, ibid., 1880. This attempt to impugn Christian schools was nothing new. Anti-Western pamphlets in the 1860s and 1870s contained graphic "accounts" of priests copulating with members of their congregations after the service and nuns sexually abusing, and even eating, the children in their orphanages. For a detailed study of this type of anti-Christian propaganda, see Paul A. Cohen, *China and Christianity*.

8. "St. Hilda's School," pp. 374–76.

9. For a discussion of the Boone School, see Coe.

10. "Impressions of St. Hilda's," p. 318.

11. Dorothy Mills, p. 227.

12. Descriptions of the isolation of and cloistering within St. Hilda's come from interviews.

13. The exact dates of the Nationalist revolution are open to debate. For differing analyses, see Isaacs; and Jordan.

14. Lutz, *China and the Christian Colleges*, p. 260.

15. Interviews, 1982, 1984, 1987, 1989.

16. Prior to registration, St. Hilda's graduates received diplomas issued in the United States.

17. For a discussion of registration, see Wood, pp. 653–55.

18. For a discussion of the social gospel as it pertains to the missionary movement, see Hill.

19. Clark, p. 380.

20. Ibid.

21. Ibid. In 1930, St. Hilda's had an enrollment of 181.

22. *Handbooks*.

23. The policy allowing monthly home visits was adopted following the registration of missionary schools.

24. The terms "courtesy and culture" were consistently used by the women who attended St. Hilda's to describe the educational focus of the school. Interviews, 1982.

25. The notion of communist control of state schools was a holdover from the 1927 split in the Guomindang that pitted the militaristic or "right" faction against

the political or "left" faction. The left, which was based in Wuhan, was defeated, but many of the more conservative, wealthy Wuhan families believed that its socialist philosophy was still being taught in the state schools.

26. Much of the information in this section comes from questionnaires that were distributed in the PRC and the U.S. in September 1987.

27. "Health and hygiene" were the terms used by those who attended St. Hilda's to describe the school's emphasis on sanitation. Interviews, 1982.

28. Interviews, 1987, 1989.

29. On women who attended missionary schools resisting marriage, see Jane Hunter, pp. 248–50.

30. Kiang, p. 2.

31. According to Jessie Lutz, female Christian colleges began around 1905, whereas the "government made no attempt to provide college education for women until after the May 4, 1919 movement." Lutz, *China and the Christian Colleges*, p. 132.

Honig, *The Life and Times of Deng Yuzhi*

The major part of this chapter has appeared in Cheryl Johnson-Odim and Margaret Strobel, eds., *Expanding the Boundaries of Women's History: Essays on Women in the Third World*, © 1992 by Indiana University Press, and is used here with permission.

Research for this project was also funded by the National Endowment for the Humanities. I am grateful to Robert Entenmann, Licia Fiol-Matta, Christina Gilmartin, Gail Hershatter, Carmalita Hinton, and Marilyn Young for comments on earlier versions of this chapter.

1. For a discussion of missionary education for women, see Jane Hunter.

2. For a discussion of the relationship of feminism to socialist revolution, see Kruks et al.

3. The oral history was conducted in English, by Cora's choice. (In conversation, we had always alternated between Chinese and English.) Possibly she simply enjoyed speaking English, or perhaps felt it afforded a kind of privacy from neighbors or whoever else might listen to the tapes, even though she was ordinarily remarkably unconcerned with the potential risks of talking to a foreigner with no "official" approval.

4. For a discussion of Changsha's radicalism in the early twentieth century, see Esherick, *Reform and Revolution*, p. 6; Spence, *The Gate of Heavenly Peace*, p. 125.

5. Jane Hunter, p. 25.

6. Croll, p. 51.

7. Feuerwerker, p. 156.

8. Unless otherwise cited, all quotations of Cora Deng are from the oral history I conducted in 1985.

9. Hume, p. 159.   10. Drucker.

11. Ibid., p. 430.   12. Stacey, p. 76.

13. For a discussion of these writings, see Spence, *The Search for Modern China*, pp. 304–5, 317–19.

14. For a discussion of single women missionaries in China, see Jane Hunter, pp. 52–89.

15. George W. Barclay et al., p. 610.

16. For a discussion of the tendency of women who attended missionary schools to resist marriage, see Jane Hunter, pp. 248–50.

17. Boyd, p. 66.

18. Thurston, 27 Sept. 1925.

19. Ibid., 17 Mar. 1922.

20. Interview with Maud Russell, New York, Sept. 1989.

21. Ibid.

22. Application to teach at Jinling College, 1921. China Records Project.

23. Treudley, p. 3.

24. Deng, "The Ping Erh Yuen."

25. Russell.

26. Drucker, p. 430.

27. Honig, pp. 24–25.

28. Bagwell, pp. 221–22.

29. Letter to Grace Coppock, 8 Dec. 1920, World YWCA Archives.

30. Bagwell, p. 225.

31. Lily Haass to Mary Dingman, 5 Jan. 1928, World YWCA Archives.

32. Deng, "Industrial Work."

33. Interview with Zhang Shuyi, Beijing, 16 May 1980.

34. Interview with Zhong Shaoqin (Helen Zhong), Beijing, 17 May 1980.

35. For a more detailed discussion of the curriculum at the YWCA night schools, see Honig, pp. 219–24.

36. Haass.

37. On Wu Yaozong, see Endicott, pp. 224–26.

38. Lily K. Haass to Sarah Lyon and Bessie Cotton, 4 Mar. 1938, YWCA National Board Archives.

39. Interview with Yao Xianhui, 16 Oct. 1989. According to Yao, who was a YWCA secretary herself in the mid-1930s, Cora Deng and Cai Kui were the two most likely candidates to replace Ding Shujing when she died. Although Cora played a more prominent role in the YWCA at that time, the board preferred Cai because she was not as overtly "progressive" as Cora. Yao believes that Cora's and Cai's views were fairly similar, but that once Cai was appointed general secretary, Cai became more moderate, placing greater emphasis on Christianity than on social action.

40. Tsai Kwei (Cai Kui) to Helen Roberts, 17 Dec. 1949, World YWCA Archives.

41. Letter from Florence Pierce to Leila Anderson, 3 Oct. 1949, YWCA National Board Archives.

42. Leila Anderson to Florence Pierce, 9 Dec. 1949, YWCA National Board Archives.

43. Letter from Quaker missionary in Shanghai, 26 June 1950, World YWCA Archives.

44. Cora Deng to Miss Barnes, 15 Nov. 1950, World YWCA Archives.

Bays, Indigenous Chinese Christianity

1. These are my own overly simple but functional working definitions of these two terms, both of which (along with "contextualization") are frequently used by

those discussing Christianity or religion in general in multinational and multi-cultural context. They are by no means synonymous. A stimulating discussion of the ambiguities involved is in Harper.

2. This is an important but understudied problem. See the summary by Hanson, pp. 17–19.

3. Constable's chapter in this volume, and Lutz and Lutz, "Zhang Fuxing."

4. There is a summary of this in Wickeri, pp. 36–38, including references.

5. A superb treatment of this great reversal is in Hutchison, chaps. 3–4.

6. Such a movement, to remove Catholic missions from the French Protectorate and with the encouragement of the Vatican to give greater authority to Chinese priests and to consecrate Chinese bishops, did occur, but needs systematic study; broad treatments such as Latourette and Hanson refer to it in passing.

7. Wang gives his own account of the 1940s in Wang Mingdao. Lyall, *Three of China's Mighty Men*, chap. 3, covers the 1950s, as does (from a very different interpretive stance) Wickeri, pp. 164–70.

8. See Rubinstein, *The Protestant Community*, and the three published works by Swanson.

Lutz and Lutz, Karl Gützlaff and the Chinese Union

1. Schlyter, *Der China-Missionar*, pp. 9–10. See also Schlyter, *Karl Gützlaff*; and Schlyter, "Karl Gützlaff und das deutsche Missionsleben."

2. Lutz, "The Grand Illusion."

3. Gützlaff, pp. 1–2, 50–53, 68; Schlyter, *Karl Gützlaff*, p. 98; A. J. Broomhall, 1: 311, 317.

4. Gützlaff, pp. 124, 186, 191, 203–4, 291. These reports were published by Christian G. Barth in *Calwer Missionsblatt* before being issued as a separate volume in 1850. See also frequent quotations from Gützlaff's letters in *Jahresbericht*, 1846, 1847.

5. Journals and letters of Chinese Union members, Archive of the Missions Library of Selly Oak College, photocopy of Gützlaff materials from Overseas Missionary Fellowship Archives (hereafter, Selly Oak, OMFA). There are both Chinese and English versions in many cases. Some of the letters and journals were published in Gützlaff; see, for example, pp. 149–50, 156–57, 163–79.

6. "China Mission," pp. 71–72; E. Dyer, Letter to the Editor, 9 Nov. 1839, *Evangelical Magazine and Missionary Chronicle* (Jan. 1840): 36; "Extracts from Communications by Dr. William Lockhart," *Evangelical Magazine and Missionary Chronicle* (Jan. 1840): 42–43. For further details on Protestant missions and the Opium War, see Lutz, "The Missionary-Diplomat Karl Gützlaff."

7. Barth had known Gützlaff personally before Gützlaff left for China and he had earlier publicized many of Gützlaff's writings, including Gützlaff's journals on his trips along the China coast.

8. Rudolf Lechler to Inspector [W. Hoffman], Victoria, 22 Mar. 1847, BMG, A-1.1, 1846–47, no. 4; Theodor Hamberg to Insp., Hong Kong, 27 Mar. 1847, BMG, A-1.1, 1846–47, no. 6.

9. Kesson, p. 231.

10. Extract of letter of James Legge to Tract Society, HK, 2 Feb. 1849, CWM, S. China, incoming corres., box 5; Legge to Arthur Tidman, HK, 23 June 1849, CWM, ibid.; Tidman to Legge, London, 24 Dec. 1849, CWM, E. China, outgoing corres., box 4. See also exchanges between Gützlaff and Cleland, in Cleland, HK, 30 Mar. 1848, CWM, S. China, incoming corres., box 5.

11. Hamberg to Insp., HK, 30 Mar. 1848, BMG, A-1.1, 1848, no. 3; Lechler to Insp., HK, 24 Apr. 1848, ibid., 1848, no. 4; Hamberg to Insp., HK, 23 Apr. 1849, ibid., 1849, no. 5; Lechler to Insp., Yamtsao, 12 Nov. 1849, ibid., 1849, no. 16.

12. Hamberg and Lechler to Insp., HK, 21 Sept. 1847, ibid., 1847, no. 14.

13. A. Tidman to J. Legge, London, 24 Jan. 1850, CWM, E. China, outgoing corres., box 4.

14. K. Gützlaff to Richard Ball, Islington, England, 22 Jan. 1850–3 Mar. 1850, Selly Oak, Chinese corres.; Gützlaff to Ball, Rotterdam, 1 Apr. 1850, ibid.; Gützlaff to Ball, Hague, 9 Apr. 1850, ibid. A copy of the Dutch commendation is in Selly Oak, Papers Relating to Gützlaff. For detailed coverage of Gützlaff's tour, see Schlyter, *Der China-Missionar*, pp. 102–33.

15. In addition to the letters of Gützlaff to Ball, cited above, see Gützlaff to Ball, Geneva, 24 Oct. 1850; Alexandria, Egypt, Nov. 1850; HK, 22 Apr. 1851; Hamberg to Ball, 25 Sept. 1850, and various publicity materials drawn up by Ball, including a human interest article entitled, "Charles Gützlaff, the Friend of China," all in Selly Oak, Chinese corres. See also the following issues of *The Gleaner*: Dec. 1850, June 1851, July 1851, Aug. 1851.

16. *Jahresbericht*, 1849, pp. 3–4.

17. Missionsverein für China zu Berlin, *Aufruf zur Betheiligung an dem Missionswerke in China* (Berlin, July 1850), BMG, A-1.1 (1B), no. 2 (pamphlet).

18. *Protocol of a Conference of Missionaries of Various Societies. Held at HongKong. Feb. 20–26, 1850*, BMG, A-1.1 (1B). Hereafter cited as *Protocol*.

19. Gützlaff to Gillespie, Rotterdam, 8 May 1850, Selly Oak, Chinese corres.; Gützlaff to Hamberg, Rotterdam, 15 May 1850, ibid.; Gützlaff, "Ein Schreiben Gützlaff's an das Comité des Pommerschen Hauptvereins für Evangelische Mission in China, Posen, 8 Oktober 1850," *Evangelische Kirchen-Zeitung, Beilage*, 26 Oct. 1850, cols. 867–68, in BMG, A-1.1 (1B), no. 4 (hereafter cited as "Ein Schreiben").

20. Hamberg, *Report*, pp. 6–11.

21. Carl Vogel, gegenwärtiger Sekretär des Vereins, ed., "Bemerkungen der Glieder des chinesischen Vereins hinsichtlich Hamberg's Betragen," HK, 21 Jan. 1851, BMG, A-1.1 (1B), no. 11. Genähr of the Rhenish Society and others questioned the authenticity of the confessions.

22. Gützlaff, untitled circular, HK, Jan. 1851, BMG, A-1.1 (1B), no. 12; Hamberg, *Report*.

23. Gützlaff to Hamberg, Rotterdam, 15 May 1850, Selly Oak, Chinese corres.; Gützlaff to Ball, Berlin, 4 June 1850, ibid.; Gützlaff to Ball, Alexandria, Egypt, 9 Nov. 1850, ibid. Rheumatic fever was a generic term in the nineteenth century.

24. Ferdinand Genähr to Barth, 28 Jan. 1851, BMG, A-1.1 (1B), no. 2 (Abschnitten von Briefen an Dr. Barth, 1851).

25. Most obituaries stressed Gützlaff's utter devotion to the cause of Christianiz-

ing China, his faith in the power of the Holy Spirit to accomplish this conversion, and his unceasing efforts to bring the Gospel to the Chinese. Rev. E. T. R. Moncrieff in his eulogy stated: *"The details of his system may admit of debate,* BUT THE GEN-ERAL PRINCIPLE CANNOT." *Overland Friend of China and Hongkong Gazette,* Aug. 1851, clipping in BMG, A-1.1 (1B), no. 16.

26. Hamberg to Insp., HK, 27 Mar. 1847, BMG, A-1.1, 1847, no. 6; Hamberg to Insp., HK, 26 Oct. 1849, ibid., 1849, no. 15.

27. William Dean to Samuel Peck, HK, 23 Jan. 1849, American Baptist Historical Society.

28. Chalmers to Tidman, HK, 26 Jan. 1854, CWM, S. China, incoming corres., box 5. See also "Journal of David Abeel," *Missionary Herald* 38 (1842): 469.

29. Winnes, "Report to the Basel Committee on 'a little mission trip,'" Feb. 1855, BMG, A-1.3, 1855, no. 33. Hereafter cited as Winnes, "Report to Basel."

30. "Report by Wong kong lau on Gützlaff and His People," trans. by Lechler and appended to Lechler to Insp., 22 Mar. 1853, BMG, A-1.2, 1853, no. 27.

31. *Jahresbericht,* 1846, pp. 53–56, quoting a letter by Gützlaff, 10 Apr. 1846; Hamberg to Insp., Tungfu, 9 July 1848, BMG, A-1.1, 1848, no. 7; "Ein Schreiben."

32. *Protocol,* pp. 1, 3.

33. Gützlaff to [Barth?], Sept. 1850, Selly Oak, Chinese corres.; Gützlaff to Ball, Rotterdam, 8 May 1850, ibid.

34. *Protocol,* pp. 3–4.

35. Legge to Tidman, HK, 27 Sept. 1849, CWM, S. China, incoming corres., box 5; Hamberg to Insp., HK, 15 Sept. 1849, BMG, A-1.1, 1849, no. 13.

36. Legge to Tidman, HK, 28 March 1850, CWM, S. China, incoming corres., box 5.

37. Walter Medhurst to Tidman, Shanghai, 17 Sept. 1849, CWM, C. China, incoming corres., box 1.

38. Extract of letters of Rev. Dr. Legge, 6 Dec. 1848, 24 Feb. 1849, CWM, S. China, incoming corres., box 5.

39. Tidman to Legge, London, 24 Dec. 1849; 23 Feb. 1850, CWM, E. China, outgoing corres., box 4.

40. Legge to Tidman, HK, 27 Sept. 1849, CWM, S. China, incoming corres., box 5.

41. See, for example, B. Kay to Tidman, HK, 25 May 1849, CWM, S. China, incoming corres., box 5. See also Tarrant to Gützlaff, Victoria, 25 Feb. 1850, Selly Oak, Chinese corres.

42. Lechler to Insp., 22 Mar. 1847; Hamberg to Insp., 27 Mar. 1847, BMG, A-1.1, 1846–47, nos. 4, 6.

43. Hamberg to Barth, HK, 28 Nov. 1847, BMG, Hamberg corres. file.

44. Hamberg to Insp., HK, 30 Mar. 1848, BMG, A-1.1, 1848, no. 3.

45. Hamberg to Insp., Tungfu, 9 July 1848, ibid., 1848, no. 7.

46. Hamberg to Insp., Tungfu, 21 May 1849, ibid., 1849, no. 7.

47. Hamberg to Insp., HK, 23 Sept. 1849, ibid., 1849, no. 13.

48. Hamberg, *Report,* p. 4.

49. Journals and Letters of Chinese Union Members, Selly Oak, OMFA.

50. Hamberg, *Report*, pp. 11–12.

51. C. G. Barth, "Der Chinesische Verein in Hong Kong," *Evangelische Kirchen-Zeitung*, 20 Nov. 1850, cols. 943–44; Gützlaff to Hamberg, Berlin, 30 Sept. 1850, Selly Oak, Chinese corres.; Gützlaff to Ball, HK, 26 Feb. 1851, ibid.; Gützlaff to Hamberg, n.d., n.p. (prob. Apr. 1851), ibid.

52. Gützlaff to Hamberg, Rotterdam, 15 May 1850 (printed formal reply), Selly Oak, Chinese corres.; Gützlaff to Hamberg, Gottenberg, 3 Aug. 1850, ibid.; Gützlaff to Directors of the Basel Missionary Society, Bern, 29 Oct. 1850, BMG, A-1.1 (1B), no. 6; Gützlaff to Insp., Rome, 9 Nov. 1850, ibid., no. 9.

53. See the thesis set forth by La Vopa, esp. pt. 1, pp. 19–133.

54. William Tarrant to Madame [Frederick?], Victoria, 29 Jan. 1850, Selly Oak, Chinese corres.

55. Latourette, p. 576.

56. Legge and Chalmers to Tidman, HK, 9 July 1854, CWM, S. China, incoming corres., box 5; Winnes, "Report to Basel"; Lechler to Insp., HK, 12 May 1866, BMG, A-1.5, 1866, no. 15; Lechler, "Dritter Quartalbericht to Insp.," 5 Oct. 1866, ibid., no. 21.

57. Winnes, "Report to Basel."

58. "Missionar Rudolf Lechler, 1847–1899, in China," *Evangelische Heidenbote* 5 (1908): 36–38, clipping in BMG, Schachtel A-10.

59. Lechler, "Schulbericht Nr. 12. Zugleich Jahresbericht," copy, HK, 30 Jan. 1868, BMG, A-1.6, 1868, no. 24; Lechler to Mrs. Rothlieb [in Stockholm], HK, 25 Oct. 1869, ibid., 1869, no. 25; C. P. Piton, "First Quarterly Report, The Station of Lilong to the Committee of the Evangelical Missionary Society in Basel," 31 Mar. 1880, BMG, A-1.14, 1880, no. 30. The connection of Gützlaff and the Chinese Union with the Taipings is a subject requiring further research. There are numerous linkages that have not yet been explored, but we are not at present able to add much information to that already available.

60. Winnes to Insp., Buge [Pukak], 3 Apr. 1855, BMG, A-1.3, 1855, no. 41; R. Lechler, "Zur Würdigung Gützlaffs, des ersten deutschen Chinesenmissionars," 1903, BMG, Lechler corres.

61. See Lutz and Lutz, "Zhang Fuxing."

62. Winnes to Insp., HK, 10 July 1862, BMG, A-1.4, 1862, no. 7, p. 3.

63. Otto Schultze, "Geschichte der Basler Missionsstation Tschongtschun," BMG, A-1.23, Tschongtschun, 1889, no. 120, p. 36.

64. Included in Lechler to Insp., HK, 12 July 1881, BMG, A-1.15, 1881, no. 17. See also, Piton, "Referat für die Chinesische General-Conferenz," May 1880, BMG, A-1.14. 1880, no. 2.

65. A. J. Broomhall, 1: 355, 359–61; ibid., 2: 23–46, 53–55, 89–94.

Wang, Protestant Publishing and the Wenshe

1. On the anti-Christian movement of the 1920s, see Lam, *Fengchao zhong*; Lutz, *Chinese Politics*; Yamamoto and Yamamoto; Yip.

2. On Chinese Christian and missionary responses to the anti-Christian move-

ment, see Chao, "The Chinese Indigenous Church Movement"; Ling; Varg, "The Missionary Response"; Yamamoto.

3. The significance of the Wenshe was recognized by contemporary Christians and later scholars. For example, in 1950 when three famed Christian writers (Tang Yin, Xie Songgao, and Ying Yuandao) were requested to write their reflections on the Chinese Christian publications of previous decades, all of them expressed high regard for the Wenshe. See Jinling shenxueyuan, pp. 76–88. The contemporary Chinese newspaper *Shenbao* even claimed that the Wenshe was one of the three authorities in religious circles. Shen, "Benshe yinian," pp. 2–3. Modern scholars also consider the Wenshe important. See Yamamoto, pp. 78–82; Chao, "The Chinese Indigenous Church Movement," pp. 209–10; Ho, "Zhonghua Jidujiao."

4. Zhang Yijing, pp. 67, 75.

5. Lutz, *Chinese Politics*, pp. 91–159.

6. On the May Thirtieth Incident see Rigby.

7. Yip, pp. 62–64; Chao, *Zhonggong*, pp. 39–60.

8. Chao, "The Chinese Indigenous Church Movement," pp. 88–89.

9. However, the CCP continued its anti-Christian policies in the areas it occupied. On its policies toward Christianity after 1927, see Chao, *Zhonggong*, chap. 4.

10. Shen, "National Christian Literature," pp. 383–90.

11. There were more than 130 Protestant societies operating in China by 1920. Both Chinese Christians and missionaries were resigned to the fact that so many Protestant societies worked independently. However, they preferred a central medium to coordinate missionary work. A National Christian Conference was called in May 1922, and created the NCC the following year. On the NCC, see Paul E. Callahan; Rankin.

12. Shen, "Benshe yinian," p. 1.

13. Chinese Christians appealed to the ISRR for financial support for such a society in 1923 and the matter was discussed by the ISRR in September 1923. Minutes of the 20th meeting of the Institute of Social and Religious Research, 28–30 Sept. 1923, Rockefeller Archive Center, IV 3 A 5 box 2, folder 10. The ISRR in 1924 decided to grant US$6,000 dollars for the first year and John D. Rockefeller, Jr., its sponsor, agreed that such an appropriation was within the scope of the purpose of the ISRR. Raymond G. Fosdick to Falen M. Fisher, 25 Feb. 1925, and John D. Rockefeller, Jr. to Falen M. Fisher, 27 Feb. 1925, Rockefeller Archive Center, IV 3 A 5 box 2, folder 14.

14. Ho, "Zhonghua Jidujiao," p. 9.

15. Ibid.

16. There was no overt hatred or opposition to the Wenshe from missionary circles. Even the Christian Literature Society, which was the first to be affected by the criticism of the Wenshe, only politely defended its position and activities. Ji Lifei; Morgan.

17. "D. MacGillivray to Dr. John R. Mott, 1 May 1929," quoted in Ho, "Zhonghua Jidujiao," p. 17.

18. Shen, "Wo fuwu Wenshe," p. 12.

19. At this time, the three members of the *Wenshe Monthly* board resigned. The

Wenshe then published a new magazine, *Yiwei*. However, the Wenshe ran a note in the second issue (February 1930) of *Yiwei* announcing that it had decided to end the "nominal existence" of the association. Yamamoto, p. 81.

20. Generally speaking, the *Wenshe Monthly* authors had a positive attitude concerning Catholic and Protestant contributions to the introduction of Western scientific knowledge to China in the late Ming and the late Qing, respectively. However, they also pointed out that nowadays Christian publications and institutes were not the "only" path to Western knowledge. See Stuart; Wang Zhaoxian; Wang Zhixin, "Ruhe shi Jidujiao"; Ying; Zhao Zichen.

21. Cheng Xiangfan, pp. 30–32.

22. Xie Songgao.

23. Li Fengqian, p. 53; Li Zeling, p. 32.

24. Li Fengqian, p. 53.

25. Wang Zhixin, "Zhongguo Jidujiao," p. 67.

26. This method of translation can be traced back at least to the early nineteenth century when Protestant missionaries first came to China. For examples, see Barnett and Fairbank. Missionaries still followed this practice in the early twentieth century. For example, Donald MacGillivray had once kept four Chinese writers busy in such activities. Margaret H. Brown, pp. 82–83.

27. Ying, p. 13.

28. Nie, p. 47.

29. Li Zeling, p. 33; Shen, "Weishenme," p. 39.

30. Wang Zhixin, "Ruhe shi Jidujiao," pp. 9–10.

31. Wang Zhaoxian, p. 34.

32. Wang Zhixin, "Ruhe shi Jidujiao," p. 11.

33. Western missionaries were not unaware of the need for and the advantages of a united national program for literary publication. There were various efforts to promote this idea, but none succeeded. Ho, *Protestant Missionary Publications*, pp. 132–49. The reasons for this failure are vividly summarized by Garnier, p. 398.

34. Nie.

35. Shen, "Jieshou jiaoquan banfa."

36. Jian Zhe, p. 10.

37. Cheng Xiangfan, pp. 35–37; Wang Zhixin, "Bense jiaohui," pp. 6–8; Stuart.

38. Zhao Zichen, pp. 26–27; Jian Zhe, p. 10; Wang Zhixin, "Bense jiaohui," pp. 8–9; Wang Zhixin, "Zhongguo Jidujiao," p. 68.

39. Xie Songgao, p. 41.

40. Shen, "National Christian Literature," p. 390.

41. Wang Zhixin, "Zhongguo Jidujiao," p. 67. For a broad view of the various models and proposals for the indigenization of Christianity in China in the 1920s, see Yamamoto, pp. 291–329; and Chao, "The Chinese Indigenous Church Movement," chaps. 3–4, 6–7.

42. Li Fengqian, p. 52; Jian Zhe, p. 10.

43. Jian Zhe, p. 10; Zheng, pp. 6–7.

44. Shen, "National Christian Literature," pp. 388–89.

45. Chen Xun, p. 68; Wang Zhixin, "Zhongguo Jidujiao," pp. 65–66, 69.

46. Shen, "National Christian Literature," p. 387.

47. Ibid., p. 391.

48. Wu Leichuan; *"Jidutubao."*

49. Chen Yuan mailed a letter to the *Wenshe Monthly* in which he pointed out some mistakes in an article. *WS* 2.7 (May 1927): 121–23. Xia Mianzun wrote an article in the magazine *Yiban* reviewing an article published in the *Wenshe Monthly.* Xia's review was later reprinted in vol. 2, no. 2 of the *Wenshe Monthly.*

50. Lyon.

51. Ho, "Zhonghua Jidujiao," p. 26.

52. Janet E. Heininger drew this conclusion from her examination of the activities of 151 Congregational missionaries of the American Board of Commissioners for Foreign Missions who were in China from 1911 to 1952. She found that although the political situation of the 1920s hastened the process of devolution, the missionaries still held reservations in this matter. Heininger, chaps. 4–6.

Bays, *The Growth of Independent Christianity*

Some of the material in this chapter previously appeared in Steven Kaplan, ed., *Indigenous Responses to Western Christianity,* © 1994 by New York University Press, and in Edith L. Blumhofer and Randall Balmer, eds., *Modern Christian Revivalism,* © 1993, University of Illinois Press.

1. MacGillivray, *A Century of Protestant Missions*, p. 669.

2. National Christian Conference; Merwin.

3. Boynton and Boynton, p. xi.

4. For intelligent discussion of Christianity in China in the recent past, see the items in note 7 of the Preface. Other useful sources are in my "Chinese Popular Religion and Christianity."

5. Sources on the Zilihui are: Zhao Tianen, "Zili"; Chabei Shanghai Church.

6. Zha, "Minguo Jidujiaohui," p. 135; Qu.

7. See Bays, "Indigenous Protestant Churches."

8. On Ni Tuosheng and his movement, Kinnear is basic; also see Lyall, *Three of China's Mighty Men.* A solid biography of Ni is in Zha, *Zhongguo Jidujiao*, pp. 305–40.

9. Wang Xipeng; "Zhongmin"; Zha, *Zhongguo Jidujiao*, pp. 217–26.

10. Bays, "Christian Revivalism in China," pp. 171–72.

11. A good biography is in Zha, *Zhongguo Jidujiao*, pp. 107–12. See also Scott; Wei Waiyang; an autobiographical article is Ding Limei.

12. On Mateer and his school, see Hyatt, chaps. 7–9.

13. See note 11; also "A Revival in the Shantung College."

14. Writings of later Christian leaders provide testimony to this impact. See, for example, Xie Fuya, p. 286.

15. A survey of these years is in Ma and Xin. Also Zha, "Minguo Jidujiaohui."

16. Zha, *Zhongguo Jidujiao*, pp. 267–78.

17. Wang's autobiography, first published in 1950, is *Wushinian lai.* A short biography is in Lyall, *Three of China's Mighty Men.*

18. Zha, *Zhongguo Jidujiao*, pp. 147–58.

19. Ibid., pp. 113–20.

20. A biography of Shi Meiyu is in ibid., pp. 91–96. For a stimulating work on aspects of Chinese women's role in Christianity, see Kwok. Very little has been written on Bethel; it still exists as a seminary in Hong Kong.

21. Ji Zhiwen later wrote several books, most in English: Andrew Gih, *Launch Out into the Deep, Twice Born — and Then?*, *Into God's Family*, *Fuxing de huoyan*.

22. See Song's own story in Song Shangjie. See also, Liu Yiling; Lyall, *Flame for God*.

23. In addition to the sources in note 22, see Zia; while unnamed, Song is clearly the target of Zia's criticisms of uncivil behavior.

24. I am working on a full-scale monograph on the independent churches of the first half of the twentieth century, in which many of the organizations, movements, and leaders mentioned in this chapter will be treated in considerable detail.

Brook, *Christianity Under the Japanese Occupation*

1. Susie Kelsey, "In Occupied China" (n.d.), MSCC, series 3-3, Leonard Dixon files, GS 75-103, box 78, file 1. Also Austin, pp. 276–78, 282.

2. George King, "Honan Notes" (Mar. 1944), UCA, FA 186, box 11, file 187.

3. This account of the CCC in Nanjing is based on two sets of documents: the minutes and annual reports of the Nanjing District Association between 1938 and 1941, preserved in ZLD2, FG 628, files 18 and 96; and the wartime correspondence and reports of the CCC General Assembly office in Shanghai to secretaries of foreign mission boards, copies of which are held in UCA.

4. "Constitution of the CCC," pt. 1, art. 2, UCA, FA 180, box 1, file 1.

5. A. R. Kepler to A. E. Armstrong, 4 Dec. 1939, UCA, FA 180, box 1, file 3.

6. General Council, "The Findings of the Church and Missions Relationship Conference" (1929), pp. 3, 7, UCA, FA 180, box 1, file 1.

7. George A. Fitch to A. E. Armstrong, 24 Dec. 1937, UCA, FA 186, box 8, file 129.

8. Gao, pp. 6–11, 38–42, 66.

9. Wilson Plumer Mills (1883–1959), a Presbyterian from South Carolina, was one of many foreign missionaries who stayed on in Nanjing. Mills served as the English secretary pro tem of the CCC General Assembly in Shanghai after the war.

10. Hiyane, p. 321. A handwritten constitution for the Nanjing District Association of the Chinese Christian Church, undated but probably from 1942, is misfiled in ZLD2, RG 628, file 95, which otherwise contains the minutes of the CCC Nanjing District Association meetings for 1930–35.

11. Interview with Situ Tong, Nanjing, 11 Apr. 1989.

12. Hiyane, p. 322. Other religions in Nanjing also came under Japanese organizational supervision: the Muslim Association was inaugurated in November 1938, and the Japan-China Buddhist League in April 1939.

13. "The Church of Christ in China in Occupied Areas," pp. 4–5, UCA, FA 180, box 1, file 6. The author is unidentified, but appears to be Rev. A. J. Fisher.

14. "Minutes of the Standing Committee of the CCC" (11 Feb. 1946), UCA, FA 180, box 1, file 7.

15. "Nanjing Jidujiao xiejinhui kangzhan shengli hou shouci nianyihui jilu" (Minutes of the first annual meeting of the Nanjing District Association of the National Christian Council after the victory of the anti-Japanese war) (14 Oct. 1946), ZLD2, RG 628, file 98.

16. Gillies Eadie, "Christian Work in the Changte, Honan Area" (n.d. [1938]), UCA, FA 186, box 9, file 136.

17. John C. Mathieson to A. E. Armstrong, 29 Dec. 1937, UCA, FA 186, box 8, file 129. See also Mathieson's comments in "Starving Chinese Victims of Floods and War Cry to The United Church of Canada for Relief" (n.d. [1938]), UCA, FA 37, box 11, file 220. A Canadian missionary in Hangzhou whose mission operated a refugee center similarly commented that "any early contacts between the missionaries and Japanese were quite happy." E. Bruce Copeland to A. E. Armstrong, 15 May 1938, UCA, FA 186, box 9, file 137.

18. Mantetsu, *Yōshū ni okeru*, p. 2.

19. William Mitchell to A. E. Armstrong, 9 May 1938, UCA, FA 186, box 9, file 137.

20. Don Faris to A. E. Armstrong, 15 Dec. 1937, UCA, FA 186, box 8, file 129.

21. Ruth Elliott to the Crossett family, 6 Dec. 1938, Billy Graham Center, CN 187, box 1, folder 1. The cloud of collaboration that hangs over Catholics is not entirely a Protestant slur. A secret Japanese military report from Hankou, *Hankōgun tokumubu geppō* 6 (May 1939): 175, records that Irish priests at the Catholic church in Anlu expressed extreme anti-British sentiments, prayed for the victory of the Japanese army, allowed the army to use their property, and reported on anti-Japanese activities in the parish; Bōei kenshūjo, Riku Shi bi dainikki S14-87, entry 9. Japanese authorities were also aware that many Chinese Catholics supported the resistance, e.g., Qin, pp. 60–64.

22. H. H. Gilbert, "Annual Report, Dec. 1, 1938–Nov. 30, 1939, Honan, China," p. 8, MSCC. This view is also expressed in 1939 in *The China Critic*, as quoted in Bates, *Missions*, p. 34.

23. See, for example, Ruth Elliott to Margaret Crossett, 27 Dec. 1938, and Ruth Elliott to the Crossett family, 8 Jan. 1939, Billy Graham Center, CN 187, box 1, folder 1.

24. Don Faris to "Friends," 8 Mar. 1938, UCA, FA 95, box 1, file 10.

25. Paul Anspach to George Drach, 12 Jan. 1938, 31 Jan. 1938, ELCA, RG 8, box 382, folder 7.

26. "Retour de Chine par le R. P. Paul Taguchi, Secrétaire de la Délégation." I am grateful to Alvyn Austin for sharing with me this and other materials he culled from the SMJ.

27. R. P. Urbain and M. Clouthier, "The Sino-Japanese Conflict" (n.d. [1938]), SMJ. The closing passage is quoted verbatim in Austin, p. 257.

28. "We are so bewildered by this undeclared war, that comment on it is very difficult. The cruel and tragic injustice of it all is overwhelming. We wonder if the entire world is going to stand by and watch China's ruin brought to pass."

Paul Anspach to Paul Kinports, Qingdao, 17 Sept. 1937, ELCA, RG 8, box 382, folder 8.

29. Iglehart, *Year Book 1939*, pp. 168–69.

30. William Burke to James Burke, Shanghai, 29 Jan. 1938, Robert W. Woodruff Library, coll. 187, box 1.

31. A missionary doctor who left his hospital to serve in the medical corps of the Chinese army observed: "A good many missionaries were coming to the conclusion that their chief business just now was to do all that they possibly could to defeat the Japanese for they realized that if the Japanese were to secure control in China, then missionary work would be impossible." Hugh Mackenzie to A. E. Armstrong, Kobe, 1 Nov. 1938, UCA, FA 186, box 9, file 137.

32. Hata, p. 160.

33. Richard Baker, pp. 14–15.

34. Iglehart, *Year Book 1940*, pp. 274–75. The Japanese also sponsored at least one Korean Christian mission to North China: see C. Y. Sun to Paul Anspach, 24 May 1942, ELCA, RG 8, box 382, folder 5.

35. Tōa kenkyūjo, pp. 17–18.

36. See, for example, Bates, *Missions*, p. 33.

37. For example, the Office of the Army Chief of Staff sponsored the five-volume work edited by Umino and Nishimura, vol. 3 dealing with indigenous religions, vol. 5 with Christianity. The South Manchurian Railway Company published a multi-volume series in Shanghai in 1940–41 focusing solely on missionary activities: Mantetsu, *Fukyō ken'eki shiryō*. The Mantetsu study of missions in Yangzhou (Mantetsu, *Yōshū ni okeru*) even includes the curricula vitae of missionaries.

The Ministry of Finance published *Tairiku ni okeru shūkyō kosaku jōkyō* (The situation regarding religious work on the mainland) in 1939.

The Kōa shūkyō kyōkai (Asia Development Religion Association) based in Beijing produced at least five such studies in 1941, of which three were on Christianity (*Daisankokukei kirisutokyō no jittai* [Actual situation regarding Christianity of third-country nationals], *Kita Shina ni okeru daisankokukei kirisutokyō dantai no genkyō* [Present circumstances of the Christian organizations of third-country nationals in North China], and *Kita Shina ni okeru tenshūkyō no gaikan* [A survey of Catholicism in North China]), one was on the Red Swastika Society (*Sekai kōmanjikai dōin no jittai* [The situation regarding the halls of the World Red Swastika Society]), and one was a handbook on religions in North China (*Kahoku shūkyō nenkan* [Yearbook of religions in North China]).

The Salvation Army in Japan published *Shina jihen to kyūseigun* (The China Incident and the Salvation Army) in 1939, though this was a report on the work of its Japanese members rather than on the Salvation Army in China.

38. Tōa kenkyūjo, preface.

39. See, for example, Bōeichō bōeikenshūjo senshishitsu, 1: 197, citing a 1939 report on pacification work in northern Shanxi.

40. Umino and Nishimura, 3: 209, 214.

41. Hashitsume, p. 27.

42. A case is cited in *Hankōgun tokumubu geppō* 6 (May 1939): 174.

43. See, for example, Qin, p. 60.

44. Yamazaki, p. 250; see also pp. 134, 248–50. Yamazaki is most critical of the efforts of Japanese Buddhists to support the New Order in East Asia, attributing the poor performance of Japanese monks to their inadequate understanding of Chinese monks.

45. Corbett, p. 18.

46. Umino and Nishimura, 5: 307–9.

47. Mantetsu, *Chūgoku ni okeru*, pp. 97–99.

48. "Report of the Anti-British Activities, July–September 1939," UCA, FA 186, box 9, file 156; Letter from Mr. Knight, Tianjin, 15 Jan. 1940, ibid., file 159.

49. H. A. Boyd to A. E. Armstrong, 14 Nov. 1939, UCA, FA 186, box 9, file 149.

50. "General Report: South China Mission for 1940," UCA, FA 80, box 4, file 69.

51. "North China (Honan)" (1940), UCA, FA 186, box 9, file 163.

52. "Report of the President of the Augustana Synod Mission for 1940," ELCA, RG 8, box 373.

53. Adult baptisms for 1937, 2,838; for 1938, 4,481; in 1940 the number fell to 2,146. "Süchow: Relations: Développements 1935–46," SMJ.

54. Bishop Weig's report is summarized in Qin, pp. 54–56.

55. Renaud, p. 302.

56. Corbett, pp. 177–78.

57. Anspach to Drach, 6 July 1942, ELCA, RG 8, box 382, folder 5.

58. "The Church of Christ in China in Occupied Areas," p. 3, UCA, FA 180, box 1, file 6.

59. See, for example, Rev. S. C. Hwang to Rev. A. A. Gilman, 8 Dec. 1942, regarding Japanese expropriation of mission properties in Changsha, as excerpted in the summary of letter intercepts from the China Intelligence Wing, National Archives, RG 165, M1513, roll 53.

60. George K. King, "Honan Notes" (Mar. 1944), UCA, FA 186, box 11, file 187. A Shanxi Christian Union was organized in April following the Beijing meeting: see Flora Heebner, *Our Mission Work in Taiku, Shansi, China* (Philadelphia: The Board of Home and Foreign Missions of the Schwenkfelder Church in the USA, 1942), p. 11, copy in School Sisters of St. Francis, Personal Papers — Sisters, P-1384, Sr. E. Bush, 1–18.

61. "Important Information about Church Union in North China," American Board of Commissioners for Foreign Missions, *China Bulletin* 60 (17 Apr. 1943), translating the *Peking Chronicle*, 13, 15, 17 Oct., UCA, FA 186, box 11, file 180. The conference was closed with a twenty-minute radio address by John Hayes of the American Presbyterian Mission congratulating the conference on the founding of the NCCU.

62. "Report Concerning Protestant Christian Missionary Work in China, June, 1942–September, 1943," UCA, FA 186, box 11, file 181. Bishop Yue was obliged to serve as chair against his will; executive committee members included H. H. Tsui, Chester Miao, and L. D. Cio. "The Church of Christ in China in Occupied Areas," p. 3, UCA, FA 180, box 1, file 6.

63. Kelsey, "In Occupied China," MSCC, series 3-3, Leonard Dixon files, GS 75-103, box 78, file 1.

64. "The Church of Christ in China in Occupied Areas," p. 5, UCA, FA 180, box 1, file 6.

65. "Report Concerning Protestant Christian Missionary Work in China, June, 1942–September, 1943," UCA, FA 186, box 11, file 181.

66. Tsu, p. 11.

67. H. H. Tsui and A. J. Fisher to Secretaries of the Cooperating Boards, 11 May 1946, UCA, FA 180.

68. Miao, pp. 3–4.

69. Y. C. Tu, "Profit and Loss in the War," in ibid., p. 9.

70. This opposition appears, in a slightly different context, in Bates, *Missions*, 39.

71. In an early 1950s retrospective on the United Church of Canada's mission to China, Margaret Brown expresses dismay at the lack of interdenominational cooperation among missions after 1945: "We have exported our own parochialisms and presented the world with a fragmented gospel and a divided Church." See "The Church and its Mission" (n.d.), p. 6, UCA, Margaret Brown Personal Papers, box 6, file 93.

Gao, Y. T. Wu: A Christian Leader Under Communism

1. Ding Guangxun, "Forerunner Y. T. Wu."

2. Editor's notes to Ng Lee-ming's "A Study of Y. T. Wu."

3. Jones, p. 62.

4. Wu Yaozong, "Zhongguo Jidujiao."

5. Ibid.

6. Y. T. Wu, "The Revolution and Student Thought."

7. Wu Yaozong, *Meiyou ren jianguo Shangdi*.

8. Wu Yaozong, "Lichang jianding."

9. Lutz, *China and the Christian Colleges*, p. 449.

10. Bates, "Christianity in the People's Republic."

11. Wickeri, pp. 127–33, has a detailed account of how the Christian Manifesto was drafted.

12. Lyall, *Come Wind, Come Weather*, pp. 22–26.

13. MacInnis, *Religious Policy*, pp. 151–52.

14. Ding Guangxun, "Xianjin de Wu xiansheng."

15. Garrett, p. 57.

16. Bates, "Christianity in the People's Republic."

17. Jones, pp. 156–57.

18. Ibid., p. 157.

19. Ding Guangxun, "Forerunner Y. T. Wu."

20. MacInnis, *Religious Policy*, pp. 201–7. This speech of Rev. Chen Chonggui was entitled "Protect Religious Belief, Respect Religious Belief."

21. *China Bulletin* 8.12 (1958).

22. MacInnis, *Religious Policy*, pp. 238–41.

23. This writer knew of this story that circulated in Beijing during the Cultural Revolution through a tabloid publication, which is no longer available. The story is believable because Y. T. Wu cherished the notion of "socialist religion" even as early as 1943, when he expressed a similar idea to Zhou Enlai. See his article written for the eighty-first anniversary of Zhou's birthday, "Lichang jianding."

24. *Hongqi* 8 (1969).

25. Ibid.

26. Y. T. Wu, "My Recognition of the Communist Party."

27. Frank W. Price, in *China Notes* 17.4 (1979), 18.1 (1980).

28. Ibid.

Rubinstein, Pentecostal and Charismatic Christianity

Some of the material in this chapter has appeared in *The American Asian Review*, © 1988 by the Institute of Asian Studies, St. John's University, Queens, New York, and is used with permission.

1. Pentecostalism is the earlier form of the Holy Spirit–centered movement and began early in the twentieth century. The term *charismatic* refers to the form of Holy Spirit Christianity that began in the years after World War II and that was more ecumenical than the earlier movement.

2. See Hollenweger for an overview of the Pentecostal and charismatic movement as it existed in the 1970s. Useful descriptions of the Latin American charismatic movement are found in Glazier.

3. The Korean experience and its impact upon the Pentecostal and charismatic movements on Taiwan were described to me by Allen Swanson, missionary and Professor of Church Growth in the China Evangelical Seminary; interview with Swanson, Miaoli, Taiwan, 16 Dec. 1986. On Pentecostalism in the Chinese mainland see McGee. See also Joshua C. Yang, pp. 1–30. Alan Hunter of the University of Leeds has studied the Pentecostal community in the PRC. See Hunter, "Continuities."

4. The most useful recent studies of that Protestant community are Swanson, *The Church in Taiwan*; and Swanson, *Mending the Nets*.

5. Ahlstrom, 2: 287–91.

6. Pomerville, p. 7. Pomerville's book is of great value in understanding the extent of the modern Pentecostal and charismatic movement.

7. There is a rich literature on glossolalia. Among these works are Goodman; Kelsey; Kildahl; and Watson E. Mills.

8. Joshua C. Yang, pp. 1–30.

9. The China-based missionaries of the Assemblies, a church well established on the mainland, decided that these efforts were being threatened by the civil war and in 1948 took a tentative step to develop another Chinese field that would prove to be both a safe haven for its missionaries and a new starting point for evangelism. Two families of missionaries from the Assemblies of God were sent from Shanghai to Taiwan in 1948.

10. Assemblies of God.

11. Ibid.

12. On the concept of the traditional mission paradigm see Rubinstein, *The Protestant Community*, pp. 59–94.

13. Here the A/G have faced major obstacles. There was intense competition for the minds and hearts of the mountain people. Catholic priests, Presbyterian ministers, and True Jesus evangelists have all worked with the mountain people and have established strong church communities among the various tribal peoples.

14. Much of this has been detailed in Assemblies of God, Clip File materials. The most useful of these documents is Fred and Peggy Martin, "Development of the National Church" (ms. no. 531, undated), pp. 20–23.

15. This can be demonstrated by briefly looking at one major A/G congregation. The Taibei Center Church, which was founded in 1953 and which moved to its present site in 1966, is typical of such Mandarin A/G churches. Services are held each Sunday morning and last about one and one-half hours. Services are preceded by Bible readings and Bible lessons and even as the adult service proceeds on the church's second floor, Sunday school classes are held in the classrooms on the ground floor. This was much the same pattern found when services in the Taiwan Baptist Convention churches in various parts of the island were observed. During the A/G service men and women sat apart from each other, as was true of both the Baptist church and the True Jesus church; this was the common practice on the mainland. The service began with a hymn, then went on to prayers, and then had a time in which church members greeted each other and all newcomers to the congregation. A sermon followed, based upon a text that all read responsively before the pastor began to speak. Hymns and a closing prayer ended the service. There was warmth and camaraderie but no overt displays of religious spirituality. No one spoke in tongues or went into any trance-like state in the services observed. The content of the sermon and the prayers were Pentecostal but the service was not an overtly emotional experience, such as the services conducted by the indigenous churches, nor did the level of emotion rise to that of the tent meetings run by Assemblies of God evangelists in the United States. Today, the Assemblies of God worship serves as a very establishment oriented, very middle class, and very proper form of Pentecostal experience for those who participate. The history of this church can be traced using materials in the Clip File. See Assemblies of God.

16. Ibid.

17. Interview with Daniel Dai, Miaoli, Taiwan, 15–16 Dec. 1986. Prayer Mountain is an interdenominational center in Miaoli where Christian retreats and revivals are conducted. I spent two days with Dai and Allen Swanson at Prayer Mountain and was able to meet some of Dai's staff and observe the routines of life in days between the actual revival meetings themselves.

18. As a result, the returnees were seen as a danger by the more mainstream ministers and missionaries. Some of the Western missionaries asked about this movement gave very deliberate and guarded answers. They admitted the value of the movement but were fearful of the charismatic aspects of it. One church, the Presbyterians, decided that certain ministers and missionaries had to serve as liaison between the home church and the movement. Others may well follow their lead.

Interview with Robert McCall, Taibei, 14 July 1987, 12 Dec. and 14 Dec. 1986, 31 July and 4 Aug. 1987.

19. Making use of the congruence of certain structures in each society, the leaders and theologians of the church have been able to demonstrate that one can be a Pentecostal who is at the same time comfortable with his or her indigenous Chinese or mountain people culture.

20. The roots of the True Jesus Church go back to the 1910s. The church's founders, from Hebei and Shandong, were Christians who were looking for a deeper spiritual experience. This they found in Pentecostalism. They took Pentecostal ideas and redefined them so that they fit better their emotional and cultural environments. Once the basic doctrines had been defined, these men and a handful of compatriots began to spread the new doctrines and plant the new church. The origins of the church have been explored in Bays, "Indigenous Protestant Churches"; see also True Jesus Church, *Description*; "History of the True Jesus Church," in True Jesus Church, *Thirtieth Anniversary Volume*, p. 6.

21. Swanson discusses this in his studies of churches on Taiwan. See Swanson, *Taiwan*, pp. 180–83, and Swanson, *The Church in Taiwan*, pp. 76–79.

22. An impressive central headquarters facility has been constructed in Taizhong. It houses the various administrative offices of the church, and contains a large and stately worship space. The structure also contains sufficient space for the convening of the annual meetings of the central legislative organ of the church, the General Assembly. This body was set up in 1926 and has met to decide church policy ever since. The detailed records of each meeting provide the outsider with a convenient means of charting the progress of True Jesus history. In style and in function the General Assembly seems much the same as the legislative organ of its great rival, the Taiwanese Presbyterian church. Yet, in theory, such an assembly and the basic ecclesiology of the church itself is based, according to church leaders, upon Apostolic precedent. On church ecclesiology, see True Jesus Church, *Description*, pp. 9–17; also True Jesus Church, *Jiaohui zuzhi yuanli*.

23. These activities included the holding of services, the providing for the communal meals, the education of the young, the creation of activities for both single adults and married members, and the administration of funds. This account is based upon information gathered during discussions and observation, Taibei True Jesus Church, 1979–80, summers 1983, 1984.

24. The authors and editors of the magazine are now able to target their audiences more clearly, writing different types of articles for different types of church audiences. A perusal of a typical issue of the monthly *Holy Spirit* demonstrates this point.

25. These comments are based upon interviews and upon observations at True Jesus churches on Taiwan in 1980, 1983, 1984, and 1986. In the summer of 1986 I obtained more hard data and was able to discuss the sensitive problem of the class base of the church with church leaders and officials themselves in the True Jesus headquarters in Taizhong.

26. The basic True Jesus work on this subject is John Yang.

27. It is my opinion that the most useful translations of the classics remain those of James Legge and Wang Tao. See Legge.

28. John Yang, pp. 54–64.

29. These comments are based upon observations made at True Jesus services over the course of the summers of 1983 and 1984.

30. On this movement see Rubinstein, "Religion."

31. Ibid., pp. 21–24.

32. On the Chinese family see Hugh R. Baker, *Chinese Family and Kinship*, pp. 27–48; also Myron L. Cohen, *House United, House Divided*, pp. 57–85.

33. On the history of the Pentecostal movement in the United States, see Anderson's powerful and sophisticated social history. I observed a tent meeting in the summer of 1983 in my place of residence, Peekskill, New York. It was a non-denominational meeting but was sponsored by the local Assemblies of God congregation. In that same year I witnessed a meeting similar in style and format. This second revival meeting was held at a hotel ballroom in downtown Chicago. In both cases, it was clear, from observation and from on-site interviews, that those attending were members of the socioeconomic underclass and that many were also members of the major minority ethnic populations such as African Americans and Latin Americans. Of course, at the same time, in recent years in the U.S. many suburban charismatic congregations have become distinctly up scale, even wealthy.

34. Tong, p. 98.

Works Cited

Abbreviations used in this section are listed at the front of the book.

Ahlstrom, Sidney E. *A Religious History of The American People*. 2 vols. Garden City, N.Y.: Doubleday, 1975.

Allen, Young J. [Lin Lezhi]. *Zhongdong zhanji benmo* (A history of the Sino-Japanese War). 13 vols. Shanghai: Christian Literature Society, 1896.

American Baptist Historical Society, Archives Center. Correspondence of William Dean, 1849–51. Valley Forge, Pa.

Anderson, Robert Mapes. *The Vision of the Disinherited*. New York: Oxford University Press, 1979.

Annales de la Congrégation de la Mission. Paris: Congrégation de la Mission, 1835–1963.

Annales de la Propagation de la Foi. Lyons.

Annals of the Propagation of the Faith. Baltimore and New York.

ANS. Amity News Service. Hong Kong.

Archives des Missions Étrangères. Société des Missions Étrangères. Paris.

Archives Diplomatiques de Nantes. Ministry of Foreign Affairs, France. Nantes.

Archives du Ministère des Affaires Étrangères. Ministry of Foreign Affairs, France. Quai d'Orsay, Paris.

Archives du Secrétariat des Missions Jésuites. Montreal.

Archives of the Episcopal Church. Austin, Tex.

Archives of the United Methodist Church (USA). The Archives and History Center of the United Methodist Church. Drew University, Madison, N.J.

Archivio della Sacra Congregazione per l'Evangelizzazione dei Popoli o "de Propaganda Fide." Rome.

Assemblies of God. Foreign Mission Division, Clip File, Taiwan. Assemblies of God Headquarters, Springfield, Mo.

Austin, Alvyn. *Saving China: Canadian Missionaries in the Middle Kingdom, 1888–1959*. Toronto: University of Toronto Press, 1986.

Bagwell, May. "An Account of the Industrial Work of the Shanghai YWCA, 1904–29." In *A Study of the YWCA of China, 1891–1930*, pp. 221–26. n.p. n.d. World YWCA Archives, Geneva.

Baker, Hugh R. *Chinese Family and Kinship*. New York: Columbia University Press, 1979.

——. *A Chinese Lineage Village: Sheung Shui*. London: Frank Cass, 1968.

Baker, Richard Terrill. *Darkness of the Sun: The Story of Christianity in the Japanese Empire*. New York: Abingdon-Cokesbury Press, 1947.

Band, Edward. *Working His Purpose Out: The History of the English Presbyterian Mission, 1847–1947*. London: Presbyterian Church of England, 1948.

Barclay, George W., Ansley J. Coale, Michael A. Stoto, and T. James Trussell. "A Reassessment of the Demography of Traditional Rural China." *Population Index* 42.4 (Oct. 1976): 606–35.

Barclay, Thomas. "The Aboriginal Tribes of Formosa." In *Records of the General Conference of the Protestant Missionaries of China Held at Shanghai, May 7–20, 1890*, pp. 668–75. Shanghai: American Presbyterian Mission Press, 1890.

Barnett, Suzanne Wilson, and John King Fairbank, eds. *Christianity in China: Early Protestant Missionary Writings*. Cambridge, Mass.: Committee on American–East Asian Relations of the Department of History, Harvard University, 1985.

Bashford, James W. "Journal." 50 manuscript notebooks. Burke Library, Union Theological Seminary, New York.

Basler Missionsgesellschaft, Archiv. Berichte und Korrespondenz, 1846–86; Schachtel A-10. Basel.

Bates, M. Searle. "Christianity in the People's Republic." *China Notes* 6.2 (1968).

——. *Missions in Far Eastern Cultural Relations*. American Council Paper, no. 6. Institute of Pacific Relations, 1943.

Bateson, Mary Catherine. *Composing a Life*. New York: Plume, 1989.

Bays, Daniel H. "Chinese Popular Religion and Christianity Before and After the 1949 Revolution: A Retrospective View." *Fides et Historia* 23.1 (Winter–Spring 1991): 69–77.

——. "Christian Revivalism in China, 1900–1937." In Edith L. Blumhofer and Randall Balmer, eds., *Modern Christian Revivals*, pp. 161–79. Urbana: University of Illinois Press, 1993.

——. "Christianity and the Chinese Sectarian Tradition." *Ch'ing-shih wen-t'i* 4.7 (June 1982): 33–55.

——. "Indigenous Protestant Churches in China, 1900–1937: A Pentecostal Case Study." In Steven Kaplan, ed., *Indigenous Responses to Western Christianity*, pp. 124–43. New York: New York University Press, 1995.

Bennett, Adrian. "Doing More than They Intended: Southern Methodist Women in China, 1878–1898." In Thomas and Keller, vol. 2, pp. 249–67.

Billy Graham Center Archives. Wheaton College, Wheaton, Ill.

Blake, C. Fred. *Ethnic Groups and Social Change in a Chinese Market Town*. Asian Studies at Hawaii, no. 27. Honolulu: University Press of Hawaii, 1981.

——. "Negotiating Ethnolinguistic Symbols in a Chinese Market Town." Ph.D. diss., University of Illinois at Urbana-Champaign, 1975.

Bōei kenshūjo senshi shiryō (Historical War Records, Self-Defense Institute Library). Tokyo.

Bōeichō bōeikenshūjo senshishitsu (War History Group, Self-Defense Research Institute, Department of Self-Defense), ed. *Kita Shi no chiansen* (The war of pacification in north China). 2 vols. Tokyo: Asagumo shinbunsha, 1968.

Bohr, Paul R. *Famine in China and the Missionary: Timothy Richard as Relief Administrator and Advocate of National Reform, 1876–1884.* Cambridge, Mass.: Council on East Asian Studies, Harvard University, 1972.

———. "The Hakka and the Heavenly Kingdom: Ethnicity and Religion in the Rise of the Taiping Rebellion." *China Notes* (Fall 1981): 133–36.

Boone, Henrietta F. "The Jane Bohlen Memorial School." *The Spirit of Missions: An Illustrated Monthly Review of Christian Missions* 44 (1879): 174–75.

Boston Evening Globe. Boston.

Boyd, Nancy. *Emissaries: The Overseas Work of the American YWCA, 1895–1970.* New York: Woman's Press, 1986.

Boynton, C. L., and C. D. Boynton, eds. *1936 Handbook of the Christian Movement in China under Protestant Auspices.* Shanghai: Kwang Hsueh, 1936.

Bridge. Christian Study Centre on Chinese Religion and Culture. Hong Kong.

Broomhall, A. J. *Hudson Taylor and China's Open Century.* Vols. 1–3. London: Hodder and Stoughton/Overseas Missionary Fellowship, 1981–82.

Broomhall, Marshall, ed. *Last Letters and Further Records of Martyred Missionaries of the China Inland Mission.* London: Morgan and Scott, 1901.

———, ed. *Martyred Missionaries of the China Inland Mission with a Record of the Perils and Sufferings of Some Who Escaped.* London: Morgan and Scott, 1901.

Brown, Arthur J. *One Hundred Years: A History of the Foreign Missionary Work of the Presbyterian Church in the U.S.A.* New York: Fleming H. Revell, 1936.

Brown, Margaret H. *MacGillivray of Shanghai: The Life of Donald MacGillivray.* Toronto: Ryerson Press, 1968.

Brown, Oswald E., and Anna Muse Brown. *Life and Letters of Laura Askew Haygood.* Nashville: Publishing House of the Methodist Episcopal Church, South, 1904.

Bullock, T. L. "Report of a Journey into the Interior of Formosa Made by Acting Assistant Bullock, in Company with the Rev. W. Campbell . . . and Mr. J. B. Steere." *Parliamentary Papers, House of Commons,* 1874, vol. 68, pp. 127–33. London.

Burton, Margaret. *Notable Women of China.* New York: Fleming H. Revell, 1912.

Cai Sujuan. *Anshi zhi hou* (Queen of the dark chamber). Hong Kong: Bellman House, 1982.

Callahan, Mary Generosa. *The Life of the Blessed John Martin Moye.* Milwaukee: Bruce Press, 1964.

Callahan, Paul E. "Christianity and Revolution as Seen in the National Christian Council of China." *Papers on China* (East Asian Research Center, Harvard University) 5 (1951): 75–106.

Calwer Missionsblatt. 1844–50. Württemberg.

Campbell, George. "Origin and Migration of the Hakkas." *CR* 43 (Aug. 1912): 473–80.

Campbell, William. *An Account of Missionary Success in the Island of Formosa*. London: Trubner, 1889.

———. *Handbook of the English Presbyterian Mission in South Formosa*. Hastings, Eng.: F. J. Parsons, 1910.

Cartier, Michel, and Pierre-Étienne Will. "Démographie et institutions en Chine: contribution à l'analyse des recensements de l'époque imperiale (2 ap. J.-C.– 1750)." *Annales de démographie historique* (1971): 161–245.

Cen Xiuwen. "Shilun Jidujiao dui Weining Miaozu de yingxiang" (Preliminary discussion of the influence of Christianity on the Weining Miao). *Guizhou minzu yanjiu* (Guizhou minority research) 1 (1983): 162–70.

Chabei Shanghai Church, ed. *Zhonghua Jidujiao Chabeitang liushi zhounian xintang luocheng jinian tekan* (Sixtieth anniversary volume of the new church building of the Chabei Christian church). Shanghai: Chabeitang, 1948.

Chao, Jonathan T'ien-en [Zhao Tianen]. "The Chinese Indigenous Church Movement, 1919–1927: A Protestant Response to the Anti-Christian Movement in Modern China." Ph.D. diss., University of Pennsylvania, 1986.

———. *Zhonggong dui Jidujiao de zhengce* (Chinese Communist policy toward Christianity). Hong Kong: Chinese Church Research Centre, 1983.

———. "Zili, ziyang yu jiaohui zengzhang" (Independence, self-support, and church growth). In Shijie Huaren fuyin shigong lianluozhongxin huiyibu (Chinese Coordinating Committee of World Evangelism Conference), ed., *Shijie Huaren jiaohui zengzhang yantaohui huibao* (Proceedings of the conference on world Chinese church growth), pp. 231–36. Hong Kong: Shijie Huaren fuyin shigong lianluozhongxin, 1981.

Chapman, H. Owen. *The Chinese Revolution: A Record of the Period Under Communist Control as Seen From the Nationalist Capital Hankow*. London: Constable, 1928.

Chappell, E. B., ed. *Heroes of Faith in China*. Nashville: Publishing House of the MECS, 1915. In Methodists, RG31, box 165, folder 1234.

Chardin, P. Pacifique-Marie. *Les Missions Franciscaines en Chine*. 3 vols. Paris: Auguste Picard, 1915.

Chen Guoqun. "Shimenkan de Miaoyu jiaoyu" (Education in Miao at Stone Gateway). In Zhang Yongguo et al., pp. 251–52. Originally published in *Guizhou Miaoyi shehui yanjiu* (Researches on the Guizhou Miao barbarians). Guiyang, 1942.

Chen Jialu. *Tianzhujiao lai Tai chuanjiao yibainian jian shi* (History of one hundred years of Catholicism in Taiwan). Gaoxiong: Tianzhujiao daominghui, 1960.

Chen Xun. "Shengjing wenxue yu Jidujiao wenzijie de zeren" (Biblical literature and the responsibility of Christian literary circles). *WS* 1.3 (Dec. 1925): 63–72.

Chen Zilong. "Nüzi rencai de yaolan" (A cradle of female talent). *Renmin ribao* (Peoples daily), 13 Aug. 1987.

Cheng, Ruth [Cheng Guanyi]. "Women and the Church." *CR* 53 (Aug. 1922): 538–41.

Cheng Xiangfan. "Wo duiyu Jidujiao wenzi shiye zhi yijian" (My opinion of Christian literature). *WS* 1.2 (Nov. 1925): 30–37.

China Bulletin. Far Eastern Office of the National Council of Churches, USA. 1947–62. New York.

China Christian Year Book. See China Mission Year Book.

[China Inland Mission]. *Days of Blessing in Inland China, being an account of meetings held in the province of Shan-si.* London: Morgan and Scott, 1887.

China Inland Mission. *The Land of Sinim: An Illustrated Report of the China Inland Mission, 1904.* London: China Inland Mission, n.d.

"China Mission: Report by the Rev. George Smith." *Proceedings of the Church Missionary Society,* 1844–45, pp. 71–72.

China Mission Year Book. Christian Literature Society for China. 1910–39. Shanghai. Beginning 1923, entitled *China Christian Year Book.*

China Notes. East Asia / Pacific Office, National Council of Churches of Christ of the USA. 1963–. New York.

China Records Project. Yale Divinity School, New Haven, Conn.

China Study Journal. Department for China Relations and Study of the Council of Churches for Britain and Ireland. London.

Chinese Recorder. 1867–1941. Shanghai.

Chu, Mrs. T. C. [Hu Binxia]. "Magazines for Chinese Women." *CMYB* 8 (1917): 454–58.

———. *Zhongguo nüqingnianhui xiaoshi* (A short history of the Chinese YWCA). n.p., 1923.

Clark, Julia A. "Voluntary Religious Education in China." *The Spirit of Missions: An Illustrated Monthly Review of Christian Missions* 95 (1930): 380–81, 402.

Clarke, Samuel R. *Among the Tribes in Southwest China.* London: China Inland Mission, 1911.

Cobb, Mrs. J. B. *The Story of the Years in China.* Nashville: Women's Foreign Missionary Society. n.d. In Methodists, RG31, box 165, folder 1235.

Coe, John L. *Huachung University.* New York: United Board for Christian Higher Education in Asia, 1962.

Cohen, Myron L. "The Hakka or 'Guest People': Dialect as a Sociocultural Variable in Southeastern China." *Ethnohistory* 15.3 (Summer 1968): 237–92.

———. *House United, House Divided: The Chinese Family in Taiwan.* New York: Columbia University Press, 1976.

Cohen, Paul A. *China and Christianity: The Missionary Movement and the Growth of Chinese Antiforeignism, 1860–1870.* Cambridge, Mass.: Harvard University Press, 1963.

———. "Christian Missions and Their Impact to 1900." In John K. Fairbank, ed., *The Cambridge History of China.* Vol. 10, *Late Ch'ing 1800–1911,* pp. 543–90. Cambridge, Eng.: Cambridge University Press, 1978.

———. *Discovering History in China: American Historical Writing on the Recent Chinese Past.* New York: Columbia University Press, 1984.

———. "Missionary Approaches: Hudson Taylor and Timothy Richard." *Papers on China* (East Asian Research Center, Harvard University) 11 (1957): 29–62.

Collectanea S. Congregationis de Propaganda Fide, seu Decreta, Instructiones, Rescripta pro Apostolicis Missionibus. 2 vols. Rome: Ex Typographia Polyglotta S. C. de Propaganda Fide, 1907.

Constable, Nicole. *Christian Souls and Chinese Spirits: A Hakka Community in Hong Kong.* Berkeley: University of California Press, 1994.

———, ed. *Guest People: Hakka Identity in China and Abroad*. Seattle: University of Washington Press, 1996.

Cook, Edmund. *Laura Askew Haygood*. Nashville: MECS Women's Board of Foreign Missions, 1910.

Corbett, P. Scott. *Quiet Passages: The Exchange of Civilians Between the United States and Japan During the Second World War*. Kent, Ohio: Kent State University Press, 1987.

Cordier, Henri. *Histoire des relations de la Chine avec les puissances occidentales, 1860–1900*. 3 vols. Paris: Ancienne Libraire Germer Bailliere, 1901–2.

El Correo Sino-Annamita o correspondencia de las misiones del Sagrado Orden de predicadores en Formosa, China y Tung-king. Manila: Imprenta del Colegio de Santo Tomas, 1866–.

Council for World Mission, Archives. London Missionary Society. East China, Outgoing Correspondence, 1849–51. South China, Outgoing Correspondence, 1849–51. South China, Incoming Correspondence, 1848–54. London: School of Oriental and African Studies, University of London.

Covell, Ralph. *Confucius, the Buddha and Christ: A History of the Gospel in Chinese*. Maryknoll, N.Y.: Orbis, 1986.

Craig, Jean. *A Brief History of McTyeire School for Girls (In Celebration of Her Ninetieth Birthday)*. San Francisco: Alumni Association, 1982.

Croll, Elisabeth. *Feminism and Socialism in China*. New York: Schocken Books, 1978.

Daly, Mary. *Beyond God the Father: Toward a Philosophy of Women's Liberation*. Boston: Beacon, 1973.

———. *The Church and the Second Sex*. Boston: Beacon, 1968.

Davidson, James. *The Island of Formosa, Past and Present*. New York: Macmillan, 1903.

Dehergne, Joseph. "La Chine du Sud-Ouest: Le Szechwan, le Kweichow, le Yunnan. Étude de géographie missionnaire." *Archivium Historicum Societatus Iesu* 42.84 (July–Dec. 1973): 246–87.

D'Elia, Paschal M. *The Catholic Missions in China*. Shanghai: Commercial Press, 1934.

Deng Yuzhi [Cora Deng]. "The Industrial Work of the YWCA in China." 29 Nov. 1934. World YWCA Archives, Geneva.

———. [Deng Yu-dji]. "The Ping Erh Yuen (A Report on the Children's Home Visited by Sociology 41, October, 1925)." *Ginling College Magazine* 2.1 (Dec. 1925): 31–37.

Ding Guangxun [K. H. Ting]. "Forerunner Y. T. Wu." *Ching Feng* 26.1 (Mar. 1983).

———. "Xianjin de Wu xiansheng" (The forerunner Mr. Wu). In *Huiyi Wu Yaozong xiansheng* (In memory of Mr. Wu Yaozong), pp. 87–102. Shanghai: Zhongguo Jidujiao sanzi aiguo weiyuanhui, 1982.

Ding Limei. (No title). *Chuandao jingyan tan* (Preaching experiences) 1 (1925): 25–29.

Ding Shujing. "Fengmen de shengming" (Fullness of life). *Nüqingnian* (The YWCA magazine) 7.4 (May 1928): 3–7.

———. "Funü zai jiaohui zhong de diwei" (The position of women in the church). *Nüqingnian* (The YWCA magazine) 7.2 (Mar. 1928): 21–25.

Dingxiang xian buzhi (Gazetteer of Dingxiang County, continued). 1880.

Drucker, Alice. "The Role of the YWCA in the Development of the Chinese Women's Movement, 1890–1927." *Social Service Review* 53.3 (Sept. 1979): 421–40.

Duara, Prasenjit. *Culture, Power, and the State: Rural North China, 1900–1942.* Stanford: Stanford University Press, 1988.

———. "Knowledge and Power in the Discourse of Modernity: The Campaigns Against Popular Religion in Early Twentieth-Century China." *Journal of Asian Studies* 50.1 (Feb. 1991): 67–83.

Dudgeon, J. "The Small Feet of Chinese Women." *CR* 2 (Sept. 1869): 93–96, 130–33.

Duus, Peter. "Science and Salvation in China: The Life and Work of W. A. P. Martin." *Papers on China* (East Asian Research Center, Harvard University) 10 (1956): 97–121.

Dwight, Francis E. *Class of '79, Post-Graduate History: Triennial Reunion.* n.d., n.p. In special collections, Hamilton College library, Clinton, N.Y.

Edwards, E. H. *Fire and Sword in Shansi: The Story of the Martyrdom of Foreigners and Chinese Christians.* New York: Revell, 1903.

Eighty-fifth Annual Report of the Missionary Society of the Methodist Episcopal Church for the Year 1903. New York: 1904.

Eighty-fourth Annual Report of the Missionary Society of the Methodist Episcopal Church for the Year 1902. New York: 1903.

Eitel, E. J. "Ethnographical Sketches of the Hakka Chinese." *Notes and Queries on China and Japan* 1.5–11 (May–Nov. 1867): 49, 65–67, 81–83, 97–99, 113–14, 128–30, 145–46. Rev. ed. *China Review* 2 (1873–74): 160–64; 20 (1891–92): 263–67.

Eliade, Mircea. *The Sacred and the Profane: The Nature of Religion.* New York: Harcourt, Brace and World, 1959.

Elvin, Mark. "Female Virtue and the State in China." *Past and Present* 104 (1984): 111–52.

Endicott, Stephen. *James G. Endicott: Rebel Out of China.* Toronto: University of Toronto Press, 1980.

Entenmann, Robert E. "Chinese Catholic Clergy and Catechists in Eighteenth-Century Szechwan." *Actes du VIe Colloque International de Sinologie de Chantilly,* pp. 389–410. Variétés Sinologiques, nouvelle série, no. 78. Paris: Institut Ricci, Centre d'Études Chinoises, 1995.

———. "Migration and Settlement in Sichuan, 1644–1796." Ph.D. diss., Harvard University, 1982.

Esherick, Joseph. *The Origins of the Boxer Uprising.* Berkeley: University of California Press, 1987.

———. *Reform and Revolution in China: The 1911 Revolution in Hunan and Hubei.* Berkeley: University of California Press, 1976.

Evangelical Lutheran Church in America, Archives. Chicago.

Evangelical Magazine and Missionary Chronicle. 1830–46. London.

Der Evangelische Heidenbote. Basel.

Evangelische Kirchen-Zeitung. 1850. Berlin.

Evans, E. W. Price. *Timothy Richard: A Narrative of Christian Enterprise and States-manship in China*. London: Carey Press, (1945?).

Ezra, N. E. B. "N. E. B. Ezra to John G. Reid." 2 Oct. 1927. In Reid's papers, in special collections, Hamilton College Library, Clinton, N.Y.

Fairbank, John K. "Assignment for the '70s." *American Historical Review* 74.3 (Dec. 1969): 861–79.

———. "Patterns Behind the Tientsin Massacre." *Harvard Journal of Asiatic Studies* 20 (Dec. 1957): 480–511.

———, ed. *The Missionary Enterprise in China and America*. Cambridge, Mass.: Harvard University Press, 1974.

Fairbank, John K., Katherine F. Bruner, and Elizabeth M. Matheson, eds. *The I. G. in Peking: Letters of Robert Hart, Chinese Maritime Customs, 1868–1907*. 2 vols. Cambridge, Mass.: Belknap Press of Harvard University Press, 1975.

Fang Hao. *Zhongguo Tianzhujiao shi renwu zhuan* (Biographies in the history of Chinese Catholicism). 3 vols. Hong Kong: Gongjiao zhenli xuexi, 1970. Reprint, Beijing: Zhonghua shuju, 1988.

Faure, David. *The Structure of Rural Chinese Society: Lineage and Village in the Eastern New Territories, Hong Kong*. New York: Oxford University Press, 1986.

Fei Hsiao-tung. *Peasant Life in China: A Field Study of Country Life in the Yangtze Valley*. New York: E. P. Dutton, 1939.

Fernandez, Pablo. *One Hundred Years of Dominican Apostolate in Formosa: Extracts from the Sino-Annamite Letters, Dominican Missions and Ultramar*. Trans. Felix Bautista. Quezon City, 1959.

Feuerwerker, Yi-tsi. "Women as Writers in the 1920's and 1930's." In Margery Wolf and Roxane Witke, eds., *Women in Chinese Society*, pp. 143–68. Stanford: Stanford University Press, 1975.

Fitzgerald, C. P. *The Tower of Five Glories*. London: Cresset Press, 1941.

Foreign Office, United Kingdom. London: Public Record Office.

Foucauld, A. G. *The Venerable Jean-Martin Moye: Apostolic Missionary, Founder of the Sisters of Divine Providence and the Christian Virgins of China*. Trans. Sisters of Divine Providence of Kentucky. Melbourne, Ky.: St. Anne Convent, 1932.

Gamble, Sidney D. *North China Villages: Social, Political, and Economic Activities Before 1933*. Berkeley: University of California Press, 1963.

———. *Ting Hsien: A North China Rural Community*. New York: Institute of Pacific Relations, 1954.

Gao Xingzu. *Rijun qin Hua baoxing: Nanjing datusha* (Japanese army atrocities during its occupation of China: The Nanjing massacre). Shanghai: Renmin chubanshe, 1985.

Garnier, A. J. "Urgent Needs in Christian Literature." *China Christian Year Book* 15 (1928): 392–401.

Garrett, Shirley S. *Social Reformers in Urban China: The Chinese YMCA, 1895–1926*. Cambridge, Mass.: Harvard University Press, 1970.

A Gazetteer of Place Names in Hong Kong, Kowloon and the New Territories. Hong Kong: Government Printer, 1960.

Geertz, Clifford. *The Interpretation of Cultures*. New York: Basic Books, 1973.
Gernet, Jacques. *China and the Christian Impact*. Trans. Janet Lloyd. Cambridge, Eng.: Cambridge University Press, 1985.
Gih, Andrew [Ji Zhiwen]. *Fuxing de huoyan* (Fire of revival). Hong Kong: Jidujiao Zhongguo budaohui chubanshe, 1957.
———. *Into God's Family*. Rev. ed. London: Marshall, Morgan, and Scott, 1955.
———. *Launch Out Into the Deep*. London: Marshall, Morgan, and Scott, 1938.
———. *Twice Born — and Then?* London: Marshall, Morgan, and Scott, 1954.
"Gilbert Reid's Biographical Record." Manuscript, Presbyterian Historical Society, Philadelphia.
Gilligan, Carol. *In a Different Voice*. Cambridge, Mass.: Harvard University Press, 1982.
Glazier, Stephen D. *Perspectives on Pentecostalism*. Lanham, Md.: University Press of America, 1980.
The Gleaner in the Missionary Field. 1850–55. London. Title varies; also entitled *The Chinese and Missionary Gleaner*.
Gongzhongdang Yongzheng chao zouzhe (Secret palace memorials of the Yongzheng period). 29 vols. Taibei: Guoli gugong bowuyuan, 1977–80.
Goodman, Felicitas D. *Speaking in Tongues*. Chicago: University of Chicago Press, 1972.
Goodrich, Sara. "Woman's Christian Temperance Union." *CMYB* 2 (1911): 452–55.
———. "Woman's Christian Temperance Union of China." *CMYB* 7 (1916): 488–92.
Gourdon, F. M. J. [Gu Luodong]. *Catalogus cleri indigenae in provincia Se-tchouan, 1702–1858*. Chungking: Typis Missionis Catholicae, 1919.
———. *Shengjiao ru Chuan ji* (An account of the entry of the holy religion into Sichuan). Chongqing: Zengjiayan shengjiao shuju, 1918.
Graham, David C. *Songs and Stories of the Ch'uan Miao*. Washington, D.C.: Smithsonian Institution, 1954.
Granet, Marcel. *The Religion of the Chinese People*. Oxford: Basil Blackwell, 1975.
Grist, William A. *Samuel Pollard: Pioneer Missionary in China*. London: Henry Hooks United Methodist Publishing House, and Cassell, n.d.
Gu Luodong. *See* Gourdon, F. M. J.
Guennou, Jean. *Une Spiritualité missionnaire: Le Bienheureux J.-Martin Moÿe*. Paris: Apostolat des Éditions, 1970.
Guiot, Léonide. *La Mission du Su-tchuen au XVIIIme siècle: Vie et apostolat de Mgr. Pottier*. Paris: Téqui, 1892.
Guo Jifeng. "DianQian bianjing Miaobao jiaoyu zhi yanjiu" (Research on Miao education in the Yunnan-Guizhou border area). In Zhang Yongguo et al., pp. 230–48. Originally published in *Bianzheng gonglun* (Border government public information) 4.9 (1945): 72–90.
Guo Tingyi. *Jindai Zhongguo shishi rizhi* (The daily records of the history of modern China). 2 vols. Beijing: Zhonghua shuju, 1987.
Gützlaff, Karl. *Gaihan's Chinesische Berichte von der Mitte des Jahres 1841 bis zum Schluss des Jahres 1846*. Cassel, 1850.

Haass, Lily K. "The Social and Industrial Programme of the YWCA in China." 9 May 1939. World YWCA Archives, Geneva.

Hamberg, Theodor. *Report Regarding the Chinese Union at Hong Kong*. Hong Kong: Hong Kong Register Office, 1851.

———. [Theodore Hamberg]. *The Visions of Hung Siu-Tshuen and the Origin of the Kwang-si Insurrection*. Hong Kong: China Mail Office, 1854.

Handbooks on the Missions of the Episcopal Church. Rev. ed. No. 1, China. New York: National Council of the Protestant Episcopal Church, 1932.

Hankōgun tokumubu geppō (Monthly report of the Special Service Department of the Hankou Army). Hankou, 1938–39.

Hanson, Eric O. *Catholic Politics in China and Korea*. Maryknoll, N.Y.: Orbis, 1980.

Harper, Susan Billington. "Ironies of Indigenization: Some Cultural Repercussions of Mission in South India." *International Bulletin of Missionary Research* 19.1 (Jan. 1995): 13–20.

[Hartwell, Charles]. *Zhengdao qimeng* (Enlightenment on truth). Fuzhou: Taiping jie fuyin tang, 1871.

Hashitsume Kokki. *Shina jihen to bunka kosaku* (The China Incident and cultural work). Tokyo: Shakai kyōikukai, 1939.

Hata Shunroku. *Rikugun: Hata Shunroku nikki* (Infantry: The diary of Hata Shunroku). Vol. 4 of *Zoku gendaishi shiryō* (Materials on modern history, second series). Tokyo: Misuzu shobō, 1983.

He Kaili. *See* Ho, Herbert Hoi-Lap.

Hefner, Robert W. "World Building and the Rationality of Conversion." In Robert W. Hefner, ed., *Conversion to Christianity: Historical and Anthropological Perspectives on a Great Transformation*, pp. 3–44. Berkeley: University of California Press, 1993.

Heilbrun, Carolyn G. *Writing a Woman's Life*. New York: Ballantine, 1988.

Heininger, Janet E. "The American Board in China: The Missionaries' Experiences and Attitudes, 1911–1952." Ph.D. diss., University of Wisconsin-Madison, 1981.

Hermann, H. "The Work of German Missions in China." *CMYB* 2 (1911): 257–69.

Hill, Patricia R. *The World Their Household: The American Woman's Foreign Mission Movement and Cultural Transformation, 1870–1920*. Ann Arbor: University of Michigan Press, 1985.

Hiyane Antei. *Shina kirisutokyō shi* (A history of Christianity in China). Tokyo: Seikatsusha, 1940.

Ho, Herbert Hoi-Lap [He Kaili]. *Protestant Missionary Publications in Modern China, 1912–1949: A Study of Their Programs, Operations and Trends*. Hong Kong: Chinese Church Research Centre, 1988.

———. "Zhonghua Jidujiao Wenshe yu bense shenxue zhuzuo" (The National Christian Literature Association and the indigenous Chinese literature movement). *Journal of China Graduate School of Theology* 5 (July 1988): 5–28.

Hobsbawm, Eric. "Introduction: The Invention of Traditions." In Eric Hobsbawm and Terence Ranger, eds., *The Invention of Traditions*, pp. 1–14. New York: Cambridge University Press, 1983.

Hollenweger, Walter J. *The Pentecostals*. Minneapolis: Augsburg, 1972.

The Home and Foreign Record of the Canada Presbyterian Church. Vols. 1–14, 1861–75. Toronto.

Hong Kong. Government Lands Office. *New Territories Crown Block Lease.* 1905.

Hong Kong Streets and Places. Hong Kong: Government Printer, 1985.

Hongqi (Red flag). Beijing.

Honig, Emily. *Sisters and Strangers: Women in the Shanghai Cotton Mills, 1919–1949.* Stanford: Stanford University Press, 1986.

Hsiao, Kung-chuan. *Rural China: Imperial Control in the Nineteenth Century.* Seattle: University of Washington Press, 1960.

Hsieh, Ting Yu. "Origins and Migrations of the Hakkas." *Chinese Social and Political Science Review* 13 (1929): 208–28.

Hu Binxia. *See* Chu, Mrs. T. C.

Huc, Évariste. *L'Empire Chinois, faisant suite à l'ouvrage intitulé Souvenirs d'un voyage dans la Tartarie et le Thibet.* 2 vols. Paris: À l'Imprimerie Impériale, 1854.

Hume, Edward H. *Doctors East, Doctors West: An American Physician's Life in China.* New York: W. W. Norton, 1946.

Hummel, Arthur, ed. *Eminent Chinese of the Ch'ing Period, 1644–1912.* 2 vols. Washington, D.C.: Government Printing Office, 1943.

Hunter, Alan. "Continuities in Chinese Protestantism, 1920–1990." *China Study Journal* 6.3 (Dec. 1991): 5–19.

Hunter, Alan, and Kim-Kwong Chan. *Protestantism in Contemporary China.* Cambridge, Eng.: Cambridge University Press, 1993.

Hunter, Jane. *The Gospel of Gentility: American Women Missionaries in Turn-of-the-Century China.* New Haven, Conn.: Yale University Press, 1984.

Hutchison, William. *Errand to the World: American Protestant Thought and Foreign Missions.* Chicago: University of Chicago Press, 1987.

Hyatt, Irwin T., Jr. *Our Ordered Lives Confess: Three Nineteenth-Century American Missionaries in East Shantung.* Cambridge, Mass.: Harvard University Press, 1976.

Iglehart, Charles, ed. *The Japan Christian Year Book 1939.* Tokyo: The Christian Literature Society, 1939.

———. *The Japan Christian Year Book 1940.* Tokyo: The Christian Literature Society, 1940.

"Impressions of St. Hilda's." *The Spirit of Missions: An Illustrated Monthly Review of Christian Missions* 76 (1911): 317–18.

Isaacs, Harold. *The Tragedy of the Chinese Revolution.* 2d rev. ed. Stanford: Stanford University Press, 1961.

Jahresbericht des Evangelischen Missions-Verein in Kurhessen. 1844–50. Cassel.

Ji Lifei. *See* MacGillivray, Donald.

Ji Zhiwen. *See* Gih, Andrew.

Jian Bozan et al., eds. *Wuxu bianfa* (The reforms of 1898). 4 vols. Shanghai: Shenzhou guoguang she, 1953.

Jian Zhe. "Zhongguo Jidujiao wenzi shiye fanlun" (A general discourse on Christian literature). *WS* 1.4 (Jan. 1926): 1–10.

Jiangjin xian zhi (Gazetteer of Jiangjin County). Comp. Nie Shuwen et al. 1924.

Jiaowu jiaoan dang (Zongli yamen archives on Christian affairs and on cases and disputes involving missionaries and converts). Series I, 1860–66, 3 vols.; Series II, 1867–70, 3 vols.; Series III, 1871–78, 3 vols.; Series IV, 1879–86, 3 vols.; Series V, 1887–95, 4 vols.; Series VI, 1896–99, 3 vols.; Series VII, 1900–1911, 2 vols. Taibei: Institute of Modern History, Academia Sinica, 1974–81.

"*Jidutubao* dui benshe de lundiao" (The view of *Jidutubao* on the Wenshe). *WS* 1.11–12 (Oct. 1926): 92.

Jindaishi ziliao (Materials on modern history). Beijing.

Jinling shenxueyuan (Nanking Theological Seminary). *Jinling shenxueyuan sishi zhounian jiniantekan* (Special issue commemorating the 40th anniversary of the Nanking Theological Seminary). Nanjing: Jinling shenxueyuan, 1950.

Johnson, Elizabeth L. "Patterned Bands in the New Territories of Hong Kong." *Journal of the Hong Kong Branch of the Royal Asiatic Society* 16 (1976): 81–91.

Johnston, James. *China and Formosa: The Story of the Mission of the Presbyterian Church of England*. London: Hazell, Watson and Viney, 1897.

Johnston, Reginald F. *Lion and Dragon in Northern China*. London: J. Murray, 1910.

Jones, Francis P. *The Church in Communist China: A Protestant Appraisal*. New York: Friendship Press, 1962.

Jordan, Donald A. *The Northern Expedition: China's National Revolution of 1926–1928*. Honolulu: University of Hawaii Press, 1976.

Kahn, Ida [Kang Cheng]. "The Place of Chinese Christian Women in the Development of China." *CR* 50 (Oct. 1919): 659–62.

Kang Cheng. *See* Kahn, Ida.

Kelsey, Morton. *Tongue Speaking*. New York: Crossroad, 1987.

Kendall, R. Elliott. *Beyond the Clouds*. London: Cargate Press, 1948.

——, ed. *Eyes of the Earth: The Diary of Samuel Pollard*. London: Cargate Press, 1954.

Kerr, J. G. "Small Feet." *CR* 2 (Nov. 1869): 169–70; 3 (June 1870): 22–23.

Kesson, John. *The Cross and the Dragon, or the Fortunes of Christianity in China*. London: Smith, Elder, 1854.

Keyes, Charles F. "The Dialectics of Ethnic Change." In Charles F. Keyes, ed., *Ethnic Change*, pp. 3–30. Seattle: University of Washington Press, 1981.

Kiang, Wen-han [Jiang Wenhan]. *The Ideological Background of the Chinese Student Movement*. New York: King's Crown Press, Columbia University, 1948.

Kildahl, John P. *The Psychology of Speaking in Tongues*. New York: Harper and Row, 1972.

Kinnear, Angus. *Against the Tide*. Wheaton, Ill.: Tyndale, 1978.

Kruks, Sonia, Rayna Rapp, and Marilyn B. Young, eds. *Promissory Notes: Women in the Transition to Socialism*. New York: Monthly Review Press, 1989.

Kuhn, Philip A. "Origins of the Taiping Vision: Cross-cultural Dimensions of a Chinese Rebellion." *Comparative Studies in Society and History* 19.3 (July 1977): 350–66.

Kwok Pui-lan. *Chinese Women and Christianity, 1860–1927*. Atlanta: Scholars Press, 1992.

Kwong, Luke S. K. *A Mosaic of the Hundred Days: Personalities, Politics, and Ideas of 1898*. Cambridge, Mass.: Council on East Asian Studies, Harvard University, 1984.

Laai, Yi-faai. "The Part Played by the Pirates of Kwangtung and Kwangsi Province in the Taiping Insurrection." Ph.D. diss., University of California, Berkeley, 1950.

Lam, Wing-hung [Lin Ronghong]. *Fengchao zhong fenqi de Zhongguo jiaohui* (Chinese theology in construction). Hong Kong: Tien Dao, 1980.

———. *Chinese Theology in Construction.* Pasadena, Calif.: William Carey Library, 1983.

Lambert, Tony. *The Resurrection of the Chinese Church.* Rev. ed. Wheaton, Ill.: Harold Shaw, 1994.

Latourette, Kenneth S. *A History of Christian Missions in China.* New York: Macmillan, 1929.

Launay, Adrien. *Histoire de la Mission de Chine: Mission du Se-Tchouan.* 2 vols. Paris: Téqui, 1920.

———. *Histoire générale de la Société des Missions-Étrangères.* 3 vols. Paris: Téqui, 1894.

———. *Mémorial de la Société des Missions Étrangères.* 2 vols. Paris: Séminaire des Missions Étrangères, 1912–16.

La Vopa, Anthony J. *Grace, Talent and Merit: Poor Students, Clerical Careers, and Professional Ideology in Eighteenth-Century Germany.* Cambridge, Eng.: Cambridge University Press, 1988.

Lazarist Archives (uncataloged). Congrégation de la Mission. Paris.

Lechler, Rudolf. "The Hakka Chinese." *CR* 9 (Sept.–Oct. 1878): 352–59.

Legge, James. *The Chinese Classics.* 5 vols. Hong Kong: Hong Kong University Press, 1960.

Leong, S. T. "The Hakka Chinese: Ethnicity and Migrations in Late Imperial China." Paper presented at the 32d Annual Meeting of the Association for Asian Studies, 21–23 Mar. 1980, Washington, D.C.

———. "The Hakka Chinese of Lingnan: Ethnicity and Social Change in Modern Times." In David Pong and Edmund S. K. Fung, eds., *Ideal and Reality: Social and Political Change in Modern China, 1860–1949,* pp. 1–27. New York: University Press of America, 1985.

Le Tobar, P. Jérôme. *Kiao-ou Ki-lio [Jiaowu jilüe]: Résumé des Affaires Religieuses.* Variétés Sinologiques, no. 47. Shanghai, 1917.

Lewis, Ida Belle. *The Education of Girls in China.* New York: Teachers College, Columbia University, 1919.

Li Ande. *See* Ly, André.

Li Chien-nung. *The Political History of China, 1840–1928.* Trans. and ed. Ssu-yu Teng and Jeremy Ingalls. Stanford: Stanford University Press, 1956.

Li Fengqian. "Jidujiao wenxue de jianshe" (Christian literary construction). *WS* 1.2 (Nov. 1925): 51–54.

Li Guanfang. "Zhongguo shehui ruhe keyi pingdeng" (How can equality be achieved in Chinese society?). *Nüduobao* (Women's messenger) 9.6 (Sept. 1920): 4–8.

Li Jiabai. *See* Reid, [John] Gilbert.

Li Ping. "1906-nian de Nanchang jiaoan" (The Nanchang religious case of 1906). *Jiangxi daxue xuebao* (Journal of Jiangxi University) 2 (1985): 51–66.

Li Zeling. "Jidujiao wenzi shiye zhi wojian" (My opinion on Christian literature). *WS* 1.3 (Dec. 1925): 32–37.

Li Zhigang. *Zaoqi Jidujiao zaihua chuanjiao shi* (History of early Protestant missions in China). Taibei: Commercial Press, 1985.

Liang Qichao. "Shangxiantang ji" (On the mission among the higher classes of China). In Liang Qichao, *Yinbingshi wenji* (Essays of the Yinbing chamber), 4:51. 1926. Beijing: Zhonghua shuju, 1989.

Liao, David C. E. *The Unresponsive: Resistant or Neglected? The Hakka Chinese in Taiwan Illustrate a Common Missions Problem.* Chicago: Moody Press, 1972.

Liao Yizhong, Li Dezheng, and Zhang Zuru. *Yihetuan yundong shi* (A history of the Boxer movement). Beijing: Renmin chubanshe, 1981.

Lin, Meimei. "The Early Educational Enterprise of the Protestant Episcopal Mission Among the Chinese, 1835–1900, Shanghai and Wuchang." Archives of the Episcopal Church, Austin, Tex. Photocopy, n.d.

Lin Lezhi. *See* Allen, Young J.

Lin Ronghong. *See* Lam, Wing-hung.

Ling, Samuel D. "The Other May Fourth Movement: The Chinese 'Christian Renaissance,' 1919–1937." Ph.D. diss., Temple University, 1980.

Little, Alicia. *In the Land of the Blue Gown.* London: T. Fisher Unwin, 1902.

Litzinger, Charles A. "Patterns of Missionary Cases Following the Tientsin Massacre, 1870–1875." *Papers on China* (East Asian Research Center, Harvard University) 23 (1970): 87–108.

Liu, Mrs. Herman C. E. [Wang Liming]. "The Woman's Christian Temperance Union." *CMYB* 11 (1923): 257–59.

———. *Zhongguo funü yundong* (The Chinese women's movement). Shanghai: Commercial Press, 1934.

Liu, Kwang-Ching, ed. *Orthodoxy in Late Imperial China.* Berkeley: University of California Press, 1990.

Liu Yiling. *Song Shangjie zhuan* (Life of John Sung). Hong Kong: Christian Communications, 1962.

Lo, Wan. "Communal Strife in Mid-Nineteenth Century Kwangtung: The Establishment of Ch'ih-Ch'i." *Papers on China* (East Asian Research Center, Harvard University) 19 (1965): 85–119.

Loewen, James W. *The Mississippi Chinese: Between Black and White.* Cambridge, Mass.: Harvard University Press, 1971.

Lü Haihuan. "Chushi Deguo dachen Lü Haihuan zhe" (Memorial to the emperor from Lü Haihuan, minister to Germany), 15 Apr. 1898. In Guojia dang'an ju Ming-Qing dang'an guan (National Ming-Qing Archives), ed., *Wuxu bianfa dang'an shiliao* (Archival materials on the reform of 1898), pp. 16–24. Beijing: Zhonghua shuju, 1958.

Lü Shiqiang. *Zhongguo guanshen fanjiao de yuanyin, 1860–1874* (The causes of the anti-Christian movement by Chinese officials and gentry, 1860–74). Taibei: Institute of Modern History, Academia Sinica, 1966.

Luo Xianglin. *Kejia shiliao huipian* (Historical sources for the study of the Hakka). Hong Kong: Institute of Chinese Culture, Lingnam Printing Company, 1965.

———. *Kejia yanjiu daolun* (An introduction to the study of the Hakkas in its ethnic, historical and cultural aspects). Xingning, Guangdong: Xishan Shucang, 1933.

———. "Kejia yuanliu kao" (An investigation of the origin and movements of the Hakka). In *Xianggang Chongzheng conghui sanshi zhounian jinian tekan* (Hong Kong Tsung Tsin Association thirtieth anniversary special publication), pp. 1–106. Hong Kong: Tsung Tsin Association, 1950.

Luo Zhufeng, ed. *Religion Under Socialism in China.* Trans. Donald E. MacInnis and Zheng Xi'an. Armonk, N.Y.: M. E. Sharpe, 1991.

Lutz, Jessie G. *China and the Christian Colleges, 1850–1950.* Ithaca, N.Y.: Cornell University Press, 1971.

———. *Chinese Politics and Christian Missions: The Anti-Christian Movements of 1920–1928.* Notre Dame, Ind.: Cross Cultural Publications, 1988.

———. "The Grand Illusion: Karl Gutzlaff and Popularization of China Missions in the United States during the 1830s." In Patricia Neils, ed., *United States Attitudes and Policies toward China: The Impact of American Missionaries*, pp. 46–77. Armonk, N.Y.: M. E. Sharpe, 1990.

———. "The Missionary-Diplomat Karl Gützlaff and the Opium War." In Li Chifang, ed., *Proceedings of the First International Symposium on Church and State in China*, pp. 215–38. Taibei: Danjiang (Tamkang) University, 1987.

Lutz, Jessie G., and R. R. Lutz. "Zhang Fuxing and the Origins of Hakka Christianity in Northeast Guangdong." Paper presented at the 1st International Conference on Hakkaology, 23–26 Sept. 1992, Hong Kong.

Ly, André [Li Ande or Andreas Ly]. *Journal d'André Ly, prêtre chinois, missionnaire et notaire apostolique, 1747–1763.* Ed. Adrien Launay. Paris: Alphonse Picard et fils, 1906.

Lyall, Leslie T. *Come Wind, Come Weather.* Chicago: Moody Press, 1960.

———. *Flame for God: John Sung and Revival in the Far East.* London: Overseas Missionary Fellowship, 1954.

———. *Three of China's Mighty Men.* London: Hodder and Stoughton, 1973.

Lyon, D. Willard. "Dr. C. Y. Cheng's Thoughts on the Indigenization of the Chinese Church." *CR* 56.12 (Dec. 1925): 814–20.

Ma Kezheng, and Xin Yifu. "Minchu banian zhi budao shigong yu fuxing yundong (1911–1919)" (Evangelism and revivalism in the first eight years of the Republic, 1911–19). *Zhongguo yu jiaohui* (China and the church) 35 (July–Aug. 1984): 15–20.

McGee, Gary B. *This Gospel Shall Be Preached.* Springfield, Mo.: Gospel Publishing House, 1986.

MacGillivray, Donald. *A Century of Protestant Missions in China (1807–1907).* Shanghai: American Presbyterian Mission Press, 1907.

———. "Donald MacGillivray to John Gilbert Reid on Behalf of the Christian Literature Society for China." 5 Oct. 1927. In Reid's papers, in special collections, Hamilton College library, Clinton, N.Y.

———. "Donald MacGillivray's Speech at the Memorial Service for Dr. Gilbert Reid." *Guoji gongbao* (International journal) 6.1 (Dec. 1927).

——— [Ji Lifei]. "Jidujiao wenzi shiye de leguan" (The optimistic view of the Christian literary enterprise). *WS* 1.2 (Nov. 1925): 20–22.

Macgowan, John. *How England Saved China.* London: T. Fisher Unwin, 1913.

MacInnis, Donald E. *Religion in China Today: Policy and Practice*. Maryknoll, N.Y.: Orbis, 1989.

——. *Religious Policy and Practice in Communist China*. New York: Macmillan, 1971.

McIntosh, Gilbert. *The Chinese Crisis and Christian Missionaries: A Vindication*. London: Morgan and Scott, n.d.

——. "In Remembrance of Gilbert Reid." Oct. 1927. In Reid's papers, in special collections, Hamilton College library, Clinton, N.Y.

MacKay, George L. *From Far Formosa*. New York: F. H. Revell, 1895.

McNeur, George H. [Mai Zhan'en]. *Liang Fa zhuan* (Life of Liang Fa). Hong Kong: Council on Christian Literature, 1959.

The McTyeirean. Shanghai: McTyeire, 1933.

Madsen, Richard. "The Catholic Church in China: Cultural Contradictions, Institutional Survival, and Religious Renewal." In Perry Link, Richard Madsen, and Paul G. Pickowicz, eds., *Unofficial China: Popular Culture and Thought in the People's Republic*, pp. 103–20. Boulder, Colo.: Westview Press, 1989.

Magaillans [Magalhães], Gabriel. *A New History of China, Containing a Description of the Most Considerable Part of that Vast Empire*. Trans., from the French trans., John Ogilby. London: Printed for Thomas Newborough, 1688.

Mai Zhan'en. *See* McNeur, George H.

Manson, Patrick. "A Gossip About Formosa by a Former Resident." *China Review* 2 (1873): 40–47.

Mantetsu chōsabu (Research Bureau of the South Manchurian Railway Company). *Chūgoku ni okeru kirisutokyō no fukyō ken'eki* (Rights of religious propagation of Christianity in China). Shanghai: Mantetsu, 1940.

——. *Fukyō ken'eki shiryō* (Materials on rights of religious propagation). Shanghai: Mantetsu, 1940.

——. *Yōshū ni okeru gaikoku kyōkai no genjō* (The present circumstances of foreign churches in Yangzhou). Shanghai: Mantetsu, 1940.

Marchal, J. *Vie de M. l'Abbé Moÿe de la Société des Missions-Étrangères. Fondateur de la Congrégation des Soeurs de la Providence en Lorraine et des Vierges Chrétiennes. Directrices des Écoles de Filles au Su-Tchuen, en Chine*. Paris: Bray et Retaux, 1872.

Martini, Martino. *De Bello Tartarico historia: in qua, quo pacto Tartari hac nostra aetate Sinicum Imperium inuaserint, ac fere totum occuparint, narratur; eorumque mores breuiter describuntur*. Antwerp, 1654.

Meeks, Wayne A. *The Moral World of the First Christians*. Philadelphia: Westminster Press, 1986.

Merwin, Wallace C. *Adventure in Unity: The Church of Christ in China*. Grand Rapids, Mich.: Eerdmans, 1974.

The Messenger and Missionary Record of the Presbyterian Church of England. Vols. 1–9, n.s. 1–3, 1868–78. London.

Methodist Missionary Society Papers. London: School of Oriental and African Studies, University of London.

Miao, Chester, ed. *Christian Voices in China*. New York: Friendship Press, 1948.

Mills, Dorothy. "St. Hilda's, Wuchang." *The Spirit of Missions: An Illustrated Monthly Review of Christian Missions* 81 (1916): 227–31.

Mills, Watson E. *A Theological Exegetical Approach to Glossolalia*. Lanham, Md.: University Press of America, 1987.

Minutes of the Twenty-eighth Annual Meeting of the Central China Mission, Methodist Episcopal Church. Shanghai: American Presbyterian Mission House, 1902.

The Missionary Herald. 1830–61. Boston.

"Missionary in China for 45 Years, a Graduate of Hamilton College, is Dead." *Utica Press*, 1 Oct. 1927.

Missionary Society of the Church of Canada Archives. Toronto.

Les Missions Catholiques. Lyons.

Morgan, Evan. "Christian Literature—The Lessons of Experience." *CR* 56 (May 1925): 314–18.

Morse, Hosea Ballou. *The International Relations of the Chinese Empire*. 3 vols. New York: Longmans, Green, 1910–18.

Mungello, David E. *The Forgotten Christians of Hangzhou*. Honolulu: University of Hawaii Press, 1994.

Nakagawa, Manabu. "Studies on the History of the Hakkas: Reconsidered." *The Developing Economies* 13.2 (June 1975): 208–23.

Naquin, Susan. "Connections Between Rebellions: Sect Family Networks in Qing China." *Modern China* 8.3 (July 1982): 337–60.

———. *Millenarian Rebellion in China: The Eight Trigrams Uprising of 1813*. New Haven, Conn.: Yale University Press, 1976.

National Archives. U.S. Department of State. Washington, D.C.

National Christian Conference. *The Chinese Church as Revealed in the National Christian Conference*. Shanghai: National Christian Conference, 1922.

Naundorf, Gert, Karl-Heinz Pohl, and Hans-Hermann Schmidt, eds. *Religion und Philosophie in Ostasien. Festschrift für Hans Steininger zum 65. Geburtstag*. Würzburg: Köningshausen und Neumann, 1985.

Ng, Lee-ming. *See* Wu Liming.

Nie Shaojing. "Wo duiyu Jidujiao wenzi shiye de yijian" (My opinion of Christian literature). *WS* 1.2 (Nov. 1925): 46–50.

North-China Daily News. Shanghai.

North-China Herald and Supreme Court and Consular Gazette. 1870–1941. Shanghai.

North-China Standard. Shanghai.

Nouvelles lettres édifiantes des missions de la Chine et des Indes Orientales. 8 vols. Paris: À le Clere, 1818–23.

Oehler, Wilhelm. "Christian Work Among the Hakka." In M. T. Stauffer, ed., *Christian Occupation of China*, pp. 351–53. Shanghai: China Continuation Committee, 1922.

Osgood, Cornelius. *Village Life in Old China: A Community Study of Kao Yao, Yunnan*. New York: Roland Press, 1963.

Overmyer, Daniel L. "Alternatives: Popular Religious Sects in Chinese Society." *Modern China* 7.2 (Apr. 1981): 153–90.

———. *Folk Buddhist Religion: Dissenting Sects in Late Traditional China*. Cambridge, Mass.: Harvard University Press, 1976.

Pan Juxian. *Wanjin zhuang bainian chuanjiao shisui* (One hundred years of propagation of the faith at Wanjin). Gaoxiong: Sheng dao ming tang, 1979.

Pang, Lok Sam [Peng Lesan]. *Xianggang Xinjie Longyuetou Chongqiantang cun zhi* (The history of Shung Him Tong Village, Lung Yeuk Tau, New Territories, Hong Kong). 1934. Hong Kong University Library. Mimeographed.

Pas, Julian F., ed. *The Turning of the Tide: Religion in China Today.* Hong Kong: Oxford University Press with the Hong Kong Branch, Royal Asiatic Society, 1989.

Pasternak, Burton. *Kinship and Community in Two Chinese Villages.* Stanford: Stanford University Press, 1972.

Patterson, Orlando. "Context and Choice in Ethnic Allegiance: A Theoretical Framework and Caribbean Case Study." In Nathan Glazer and Daniel P. Moynihan, eds., *Ethnicity: Theory and Experience*, pp. 309–49. Cambridge, Mass.: Harvard University Press, 1975.

Peng Lesan. *See* Pang, Lok Sam.

Personal Narratives Group. *Interpreting Women's Lives, Feminist Theory and Personal Narratives.* Bloomington: Indiana University Press, 1989.

Pickering, William A. *Pioneering in Formosa.* London: Hurst and Blackett, 1898.

Piton, Charles. "On the Origin and History of the Hakkas." *China Review* 2.4 (1873): 222–26.

Planchet, J.-M. *Les Missions de Chine et du Japon.* Beijing: Imprimerie des Lazaristes, 1929.

Plus, Raoul. *Shepherd of Untended Sheep: John Martin Moye, Priest of the Society of Foreign Missions of Paris, Founder of the Society of Divine Providence.* Trans. James Aloysius and Mary Generosa. Westminster, Md.: Newman Press, 1950.

Pollard, Sam[uel]. *The Story of the Miao.* London: Henry Hooks, 1919.

Pomerville, Paul. *The Third Force in Missions: A Pentecostal Contribution to Contemporary Mission Theology.* Peabody, Mass.: Hendrickson, 1985.

Potter, Jack M. *Capitalism and the Chinese Peasant.* Berkeley: University of California Press, 1968.

Punch, Maurice. *The Politics and Ethics of Fieldwork.* Beverly Hills, Calif.: Sage, 1986.

Qian Baofu. *Qingji zhongyao zhiguan nianbiao* (Tables on important officials in the late Qing). Beijing: Zhonghua shuju, 1959.

Qiao Zhiqiang. "Cong *Qian yuan suoji* kan Yihetuan" (Looking at the Boxers in the light of *A Trifling Record from Qian Garden*). *Shanxi daxue xuebao* (Journal of Shanxi University) 2 (1981): 17–23.

———. "Shanxi diqu de Yihetuan yundong" (The Boxer movement in Shanxi). In *Yihetuan yundong liushi zhounian jinian lunwenji* (Articles commemorating the sixtieth anniversary of the Boxer movement). Beijing: Zhonghua shuju, 1961.

———. *Yihetuan zai Shanxi diqu shiliao* (Historical documents on the Boxers in the Shanxi region). Taiyuan: Renmin chubanshe, 1980.

Qin Chuncheng. *Seitō ni okeru tenshūkyō* (Catholicism in Qingdao). Qingdao: Kōain, 1940.

Qu Zhengmin. "Meiguo zhanglaohui he Shandong zilihui shilüe" (The American Presbyterian mission and the Shandong independent church). *Shandong wenxian* (Shandong documents) 11.1 (1985): 19–37.

Rafael, Vicente Leuterio. *Contracting Colonialism: Translation and Christian Conversion in Tagalog Society under Early Spanish Rule*. Ithaca, N.Y.: Cornell University Press, 1988.

Ramsey, S. Robert. *The Languages of China*. Princeton, N.J.: Princeton University Press, 1987.

Rankin, Milledge Theron. "A Critical Examination of the National Christian Council of China." Ph.D. diss., Southern Baptist Theological Seminary, 1928.

Rawski, Evelyn. *Education and Popular Literacy in Ch'ing China*. Ann Arbor: University of Michigan Press, 1978.

Records of the General Conference of the Protestant Missionaries of China, Held at Shanghai, May 10–24, 1877. Shanghai: American Presbyterian Mission Press, 1878.

Records of the General Conference of the Protestant Missionaries of China, Held at Shanghai, May 7–20, 1890. Shanghai: American Presbyterian Mission Press, 1890.

Reid, [John] Gilbert [Li Jiabai]. "The Characteristics of China and Its People." In Student Volunteer Movement for Foreign Missions, ed., *The Student Missionary Appeal*, pp. 327–29. New York: Student Volunteer Movement for Foreign Missions, 1898.

——. "Chinese Law on the Ownership of Church Property in the Interior of China." *CR* 20.9 (Sept. 1889): 420–26; 20.10 (Oct. 1889): 454–60.

——. "Chongshu duiyu Zhongguo zhi youyi jihua" (The reiteration of Dr. Reid's project to promote friendship between China and other countries). *Guoji gongbao* (International journal) 6.1 (Dec. 1927).

——. *Chouhua chuyan* (The question of the time for the good of China). Shanghai: Commercial Press, 1904.

——. "Chuangshe xuexiao yi" (Educational reform is urgent). *Wanguo gongbao* (Globe magazine) 7.84 (Jan. 1896): 4a–5b.

——. "The Difficulties of Intercourse Between Christian Missionaries and Chinese Officials." *CR* 20.5 (May 1889): 209–16.

——. "The Duty of Christian Missions." *CR* 19.8 (Aug. 1888): 358–64; 19.9 (Sept. 1888): 398–402; 19.10 (Oct. 1888): 465–72.

——. "An Experience of Missionary Trouble in the Interior of China." *CR* 23.6 (June 1892): 276–84.

——. *Glances at China*. London: The Religious Tract Society, n.d. (1893?).

——. "Guang xinxue yifu jiuxue shuo" (Supplementing old learning with new learning). In Reid, *Chouhua chuyan*, pp. 43a–46a.

——. "The Importance of Christian Evangelization." *CR* 22.2 (Feb. 1891): 51–60.

——. *The International Institute of China*. n.p., 1929.

——. "Jingshi nichang shangxiantang xiaoji" (On the establishment in Beijing of the International Institute of China). *Wanguo gongbao* (Globe magazine) 9.101 (June 1897): 17b–18b.

——. "Lecture." *Shangxiantang jishi* (The institute record) 7.11 (Nov. 1916): 32a–34a.

——. "Meiguo jiaoshi xiankao yuehan xingzhuang" (In memoriam: Rev. John Reid, my respected father and American missionary). *Wanguo gongbao* (Globe magazine) 9.104 (Aug. 1897): 3a–4a.

———. *"Mengzi* zhushi" (Explanation of *Mencius* with notes). *Guoji gongbao* (International journal) 5.39–40 (Aug. 1927): 6–7; 5.41–42 (Sept. 1927): 9–10.

———. "Minjiao xiang'an yi" (On harmony between non-Christians and Christians). In Reid, *Chouhua chuyan*, pp. 32a–37a.

———. "On the Duty of Every Religion to China's Prosperity." In Reid, *Renxu yanjianglu*, pp. 29–37.

———. *A Prospectus of the International Institute of China*. New York: Caton and Mains, 1910.

———. *The Regulations of the Mission Among the Higher Classes of China*. Shanghai: American Presbyterian Press, 1897.

———. *Renxu yanjianglu* (The lectures of 1923). Shanghai: American Presbyterian Press, 1923.

———. *Report of the Mission Among the Higher Classes of China*. No. 1, San Francisco, 1894; no. 2, n.p. n.d.; no. 3, Beijing, 1895; no. 4, Beijing, 1896; no. 5, Beijing, 1896; no. 6, Beijing, 1897; no. 7, Beijing, 1897.

———. "Shang Zhongchao zhengfu shu" (Petition to the Chinese government). In Reid, *Chouhua chuyan*, pp. 5b–6a.

———. "Shangxiantang chuangban yuanyou" (The causes of the establishment of the Mission Among the Higher Classes of China). *Shangxiantang chenjilu* (Account of the beginnings of the Mission Among the Higher Classes of China) 1 (Feb. 1909): 2a–4b.

———. "Shangxiantang wenlu" (Documentation of the Mission Among the Higher Classes of China). *Wanguo gongbao* (Globe magazine) 9.102 (June 1897): 3a–4a.

———. "Xinmin lun" (The need for new citizens). In Reid, *Chouhua chuyan*, pp. 8a–11b.

———. "Yi gong dai zhen" (On working instead of relief). In Reid, *Chouhua chuyan*, pp. 42a–43a.

———. "Zhihe jianzha shuo" (Locks for the Yellow River). *Wanguo gongbao* (Globe magazine) 2.23 (1890): 41b–42a.

———. "Zhihe shuo" (On the management of the Yellow River). In Reid, *Chouhua chuyan*, pp. 40a–41b.

———. "Zhongguo neng huajiu weixin" (China should transform the old into the new). In Reid, *Chouhua chuyan*, pp. 11b–16a.

Renaud, Rosario. *Le Diocèse de Süchow (Chine): Champ apostolique des Jésuites Canadiens de 1918 à 1954*. Montreal: Bellarmin, 1982.

"A Revival in the Shantung College." *Missionary Review of the World* 33.4 (Apr. 1910): 244–45.

Ricci, [Giovanni]. "Catholics of North Chan-si, China." *Annals of the Propagation of the Faith* (Baltimore and New York) 74 (Dec. 1911): 235–48.

Richard, Mrs. "Canadian Presbyterian Mission: Formosa." In *The China Mission Hand-book*, pp. 286–88. Shanghai: American Presbyterian Mission Press, 1896.

Richard, T[imothy]. "Christian Persecutions in China—Their Nature, Causes, Remedies." *CR* 15 (July–Aug. 1884): 237–48.

Richard, Timothy. *Forty-Five Years in China: Reminiscences*. New York: Frederick A. Stokes, 1916.

Rigby, Richard. *The May Thirtieth Movement: Events and Themes*. Melbourne: Australian National University Press, 1980.

Robert, Dana. "From Missions to Mission to Beyond Missions: The Historiography of American Protestant Foreign Missions Since World War II." *International Bulletin of Missionary Research* 18.4 (Oct. 1994): 146–62.

Robert W. Woodruff Library. Emory University, Atlanta.

Rockefeller Archive Center. Tarrytown, N.Y.

Rosner, Erhard. "Frauen als Anführerinnen chinesischer Sekten." In Naundorf et al., pp. 239–46.

Rubinstein, Murray A. *The Protestant Community on Modern Taiwan: Mission, Seminary, and Church*. Armonk, N.Y.: M. E. Sharpe, 1991.

———. "Religion, Revolution, and Anti-Foreignism." *American Asian Review* 4.4 (Winter, 1986): 1–28.

Ruether, Rosemary Radford. *Sexism and God-talk: Toward a Feminist Theology*. Boston: Beacon, 1983.

Ruether, Rosemary Radford, and Rosemary Skinner Keller, eds. *Women and Religion in America*. Vol. 1, *The Nineteenth Century*. San Francisco: Harper and Row, 1981.

Russell, Maud. "Wuhan Student Conference." 5–8 Feb. 1926. World YWCA Archives, Geneva.

Saint Martin, Jean-Didier de. *Doctrine de la Sainte Religion à l'usage des missionnaires en Chine et leurs néophytes*. Trans. [Claude Philibert] Dabry [de Thiersant]. Paris: Typographie de Henri Plon, 1859.

———. *Shengjiao yaoli* (Essential doctrines of the holy religion). Chongqing: Zengjiayan shengjiao shuju, 1926.

Sanneh, Lamin. *Translating the Message: The Missionary Impact on Culture*. Maryknoll, N.Y.: Orbis, 1989.

Schlatter, Wilhelm. *Geschichte der Basler Mission, 1815–1915*. Basel: Verlag der Basler Missionsbuchhandlung, 1916.

Schlesinger, Arthur, Jr. "The Missionary Enterprise and Theories of Imperialism." In John K. Fairbank, ed., *The Missionary Enterprise in China and America*, pp. 336–73. Cambridge, Mass.: Harvard University Press, 1974.

Schlyter, Herman. *Der China-Missionar Karl Gützlaff und seine Heimatbasis*. Lund, Sweden: C. W. K. Gleerup, 1976.

———. *Karl Gützlaff als Missionar in China*. Lund, Sweden: C. W. K. Gleerup, 1946.

———. "Karl Gützlaff und das deutsche Missionsleben." *Evangelische Missionszeitschrift* 8 (1951): 141–47.

Schofield, A. T. *Memorials of R. Harold A. Schofield*. London: Hodder and Stoughton, 1898.

School Sisters of St. Francis Archives. Milwaukee.

Scott, C. E. "Ding, the Apostle of Shantung." *Missionary Review of the World* 34.2 (Feb. 1911): 125–27.

Selly Oak College, Archive of the Missions Library. Chinese Correspondence, 1849–51. Birmingham, Eng.

———. Overseas Missionary Fellowship Archives (journals and letters of Chinese Union members). Birmingham, Eng.

———. Papers Relating to Karl Gützlaff. Birmingham, Eng.

Shanghai Mercury. Shanghai.

"Shanghaishi disan nüzizhongxue yan'ge shi" (Historical development of the Shanghai Number Three Girls' School). Unpublished ms., Shanghai Number Three Girls' School, 1986.

"Shanxi quansheng ge fu ting zhou xian difang jingli gekuan shuomingshu" (Financial report on various locally controlled funds of prefectures, subprefectures, departments, and counties in Shanxi). In *Shanxi quansheng caizheng shuomingshu* (Shanxi financial report). Taiyuan: Shanxi qingli caizhengju, n.d.

Shaw, Ella C. "The Work of Bible Women in China." *CMYB* 6 (1915): 343–47.

Shaw, Thomas. *The Bible Christians: 1815–1907*. London: Epsworth Press, 1965.

Shen Sizhuang [J. Wesley Shen]. "Benshe yinian de huigu" (The first year of the Wenshe). *WS* 1.11–12 (Oct. 1926): 1–4.

———. "Jieshou jiaoquan banfa" (Measures for the devolution of church administration). *WS* 2.7 (July 1927): 100–108.

———. "National Christian Literature Association." *China Christian Year Book* 15 (1928): 383–91.

———. "Weishenme yaoyou Wenshe?" (Why is the Wenshe needed?). *WS* 1.1 (Oct. 1925): 35–40.

———. "Wo fuwu Wenshe de zuihou zongbaogao" (My last report on the Wenshe). *WS* 3.8 (June 1928): 1–15.

Shepherd, John R. "Plains Aborigines and Missionaries in Ch'ing Taiwan, 1859–1895." Unpublished ms., 1988.

———. "Sinicized Siraya Worship of A-li-tsu." *Bulletin of the Institute of Ethnology, Academia Sinica* 58 (Autumn 1986): 1–81.

———. *Statecraft and Political Economy on the Taiwan Frontier, 1600–1800*. Stanford: Stanford University Press, 1993.

Shi Meiyu. *See* Stone, Mary.

Shih, Lei. "Social Contact and Religious Change Among the Formosan Aborigines." *New Asia Academic Bulletin* 6 (1986): 219–28.

Shih, Vincent Y. C. *The Taiping Ideology: Its Sources, Interpretations and Influences*. Seattle: University of Washington Press, 1967.

Shiwubao (The Chinese progress). Shanghai.

Skinner, G. William. "Change and Persistence in Chinese Culture Overseas: A Comparison of Thailand and Java." In John T. McAlister, ed., *Southeast Asia: The Politics of National Integration*, pp. 399–415. New York: Random House, 1973.

———. "Cities and the Hierarchy of Local Systems." In G. William Skinner, ed., *The City in Late Imperial China*, pp. 275–351. Stanford: Stanford University Press, 1977.

———. "Sichuan's Population in the Nineteenth Century: Lessons from Disaggregated Data." *Late Imperial China* 8.1 (June 1987): 1–79.

Smith, Carl T. *Chinese Christians: Elites, Middlemen, and the Church in China*. Hong Kong: Oxford University Press, 1985.

———. "Notes on Friends and Relatives of Taiping Leaders." *Journal of the Hong Kong Branch of the Royal Asiatic Society* 16 (1976): 117–34.

Song Bolu. "Meiguo chuanjiaoshi Li Jiabai sheli xuetang bingzai dubanchu chengdi tiaochen qingchichapian" (The petition of verification of American missionary Gilbert Reid's plan to establish schools and his presentation to the Military Supervisory Office). 17 Sept. 1895. No. 1 Historical Archives, Beijing, from Kong Xiangji, *Wuxuweixin yundong xintan* (New light on the reform of 1898). Changsha: Hunan renmin chubanshe, 1988.

Song Shangjie. *Wode jianzheng* (My testimony). Hong Kong: Bellman, 1962 [1936].

Spence, Jonathan D. *The Gate of Heavenly Peace.* New York: Viking, 1981.

——. *The Memory Palace of Matteo Ricci.* New York: Viking Penguin, 1984.

——. *The Search for Modern China.* New York: W. W. Norton, 1990.

"St. Hilda's School, Wuchang, China." *The Spirit of Missions: An Illustrated Monthly Review of Christian Missions* 65 (1900): 493–94.

Stacey, Judith. *Patriarchy and Socialist Revolution in China.* Berkeley: University of California Press, 1983.

Stauffer, M. T., ed. *The Christian Occupation of China: General Survey of the Numerical Strength and Geographical Distribution of the Christian Forces in China, 1918–1921.* Shanghai: China Continuation Committee, 1922.

Stockard, Janice E. *Daughters of the Canton Delta: Marriage Patterns and Economic Strategies in South China, 1860–1930.* Stanford: Stanford University Press, 1989.

Stone, Mary [Shi Meiyu]. "What Chinese Have Done and Are Doing for China." *CMYB* 5 (1914): 239–45.

Streit, P. Robert. *Bibliotheca missionum.* Vol. 12, *Chinesische missionsliteratur, 1800–1884.* Freiburg: Verlag Herder, 1958.

Stuart, John Leighton. "The Production of Writers." *CR* 56.5 (May 1925): 289–93.

Summa Decretorum Synodalium Su-Tchuen et Hongkong. Hong Kong: Typis Societatis Missionem ad Exteros, 1910.

Sunderland, J. T. "Dr. Gilbert Reid and His Unique Mission to China." *Unity,* 24 Oct. 1924. Chicago.

Sung, Hok Pang. "Legends and Stories of the New Territories." 2 parts. *Journal of the Hong Kong Branch of the Royal Asiatic Society* 13 (1973): 110–32; 14 (1974): 160–85.

Swanson, Allen J. *The Church in Taiwan: A Profile, 1980.* Pasadena, Calif.: William Carey Library, 1981.

——. *Mending the Nets: Taiwan Church Growth and Loss in the 1980s.* Pasadena, Calif.: William Carey Library, 1986.

——. *Taiwan: Mainline Versus Independent Church Growth.* Pasadena, Calif.: William Carey Library, 1970.

Sweeten, Alan Richard. "Community and Bureaucracy in Rural China: Evidence from 'Sectarian Cases' (Chiao-an) in Kiangsi, 1860–1895." Ph.D. diss., University of California, Davis, 1980.

——. "The *Ti-pao*'s Role in Local Government as Seen in Fukien Christian 'Cases,' 1863–1869." *Ch'ing-shih wen-t'i* 3.6 (Dec. 1976): 1–27.

"Symposium: 'Public Sphere'/'Civil Society' in China? Paradigmatic Issues in Chinese Studies, III." *Modern China* 19.2 (Apr. 1993): 107–240 (entire issue).

Tan Bian. "Sun Zhongshan jiashi yuanliu jiqi shangdai jingji zhuangkuang xin-zheng" (New evidence on Sun Yat-sen's ancestry and his ancestors' economic situation). *Xueshu yanjiu* (Academic research) 3 (1963): 32–38.

Tan, Chester C. *The Boxer Catastrophe.* New York: Columbia University Press, 1955.

Tavard, Georges. *L'expérience de Jean-Martin Moÿe: Mystique et mission 1730–1793.* Bibliothèque de Spiritualité, no. 12. Paris: Éditions Beauchesne, 1978.

Taylor, Mrs. Howard. *Pastor Hsi (of North China): One of China's Christians.* 6th ed. London: Morgan and Scott, 1905.

Teng, S. Y. *The Taiping Rebellion and the Western Powers.* Oxford: Oxford University Press, 1971.

Ter Haar, B. J. *The White Lotus Teachings in Chinese Religious History.* Leiden: E. J. Brill, 1992.

Thomas, Hilah F., and Rosemary Skinner Keller, eds. *Women in New Worlds: Historical Perspectives on the Wesleyan Tradition.* 2 vols. Nashville: Abingdon, 1981.

Thompson, David M. *Nonconformity in the Nineteenth Century.* London: Routledge and Kegan Paul, 1972.

Thompson, Roger. "Statecraft and Self-Government: Competing Visions of Community and State in Late Imperial China." *Modern China* 14.2 (Apr. 1988): 188–221.

Thurston, Matilda. Edited letters. China Records Project, Yale Divinity School, New Haven, Conn.

T'ien, Ju-k'ang. *Peaks of Faith: Protestant Mission in Revolutionary China.* Leiden: E. J. Brill, 1993.

Ting, K. H. *See* Ding Guangxun.

Tōa kenkyūjo (East Asian Research Institute). *Nihon no zai Shi bunka jigyō* (Japanese cultural projects in China). N.p., July 1940.

Tong, Hollington. *Christianity in Taiwan.* Taibei: China Post, 1961.

Tongzhen xiugui (Regulations for virgins). Hong Kong: Imprimerie de Nazareth, 1905.

Topley, Marjorie Doreen. "Chinese Religion and Rural Cohesion in the Nineteenth Century." *Journal of the Hong Kong Branch of the Royal Asiatic Society* 8 (1968): 9–43.

Treudley, Mary. "At Work in a Social Laboratory." 1 Dec. 1927. China Records Project, Yale Divinity School, New Haven, Conn.

Troeltsch, Ernst. *The Social Teachings of the Christian Churches.* Trans. Olive Wyon. 2 vols. New York: Macmillan, 1931.

True Jesus Church. *Description of the True Jesus Church.* Taizhong: True Jesus Church Publishing Office, 1964.

———. *Jiaohui zuzhi yuanli* (Reasons for the organization of the church). Taizhong: True Jesus Church Publishing Office, 1980.

———. *Thirtieth Anniversary Volume.* Taizhong: True Jesus Church Publishing Office, 1956.

Tsang, Kwok Fu. *Centenary Magazine, 1882–1982.* (Basel Christian Church of Malaysia). Hong Kong: Tat To Printing Co., 1983.

Tseng, P. S. *See* Zeng Baosun.

Tsu, Y. Y. *The Chinese Church: Partner in a World Mission*. New York: Friendship Press, 1944.

Umino Ryōji, and Nishimura Shōji, eds. *Chū Shina ni okeru kyōiku, shisō, shūkyō, senden, gaikoku shiryoku ni kansuru hōkokusho* (Reports on education, thought, religion, propaganda, and foreign strength in central China). 5 vols. Tokyo, 1940.

United Church of Canada Archives. Toronto.

United Methodist Church Missions Report. United Methodist Church (Great Britain). School of Oriental and African Studies, University of London.

Van Gulik, R. H. *Sexual Life in Ancient China*. Leiden: E. J. Brill, 1961.

Varg, Paul A. *Missionaries, Chinese, and Diplomats: The American Protestant Missionary Movement in China, 1890–1952*. Princeton, N.J.: Princeton University Press, 1958.

———. "The Missionary Response to Nationalist Revolution." In John K. Fairbank, ed., *The Missionary Enterprise in China and America*, pp. 311–35. Cambridge, Mass.: Harvard University Press, 1974.

Voskamp, C. J. "The Work of German Missions in China." *CMYB* 5 (1914): 371–76.

Wakeman, Frederic, Jr. *Strangers at the Gate: Social Disorder in South China, 1839–1861*. Berkeley: University of California Press, 1966.

Waley-Cohen, Joanna. "China and Western Technology in the Late Eighteenth Century." *American Historical Review* 98.5 (Dec. 1993): 1524–44.

Walls, Andrew. "The American Dimension in the History of the Missionary Movement." In Joel A. Carpenter and Wilbert R. Shenk, eds., *Earthen Vessels: American Evangelicals and Foreign Missions, 1880–1980*, pp. 1–25. Grand Rapids, Mich.: Eerdmans, 1990.

Waltner, Ann. "Widows and Remarriage in Ming and Early Qing China." *Historical Reflections/Réflexions Historiques* 8.3 (Fall 1981): 129–46.

Wang Chengmian. *See* Wang, Peter Chen-main.

Wang Fushi, ed. *Miaoyu jianzhi* (Treatise on Miao languages). Beijing: Minzu chubanshe, 1985.

Wang Huiwu. "Nüquan yundong yu nü Jidutu" (The feminist movement and female Christians). *Nüqingnian bao* (Young women's quarterly) (Oct. 1922): 8–9.

Wang Jianguang. "Miaomin de wenzi" (Miao writing). In Zhang Yongguo et al., pp. 214–15. Originally published in *Biansheng yuekan* (Border voice monthly) 1.3 (n.d.).

Wang Liming. *See* Liu, Mrs. Herman C. E.

Wang Mingdao. *Wushinian lai* (These fifty years). Hong Kong: Bellman, 1982 [1950]. Partial translation, *A Stone Made Smooth*. Trans. Arthur Reynolds. Sholing, Eng.: Mayflower, 1981.

Wang, Peter Chen-main [Wang Chengmian]. *Wenshe de shengshuai — er ling niandai Jidujiao bensehua zhi ge'an yanjiu* (The rise and fall of the Wenshe — a case study of indigenization of Christianity in China in the 1920s). Taibei: Yuzhouguang, 1993.

Wang Shuhuai. *Wairen yu wuxu bianfa* (Foreigners and the 1898 reforms). Taibei: Institute of Modern History, Academia Sinica, 1965.

Wang Xipeng. *Ji Yesu jiating* (Remembering the Jesus family). Shanghai: National Christian Council, 1950.

Wang Zhaoxian. "Tianzhujiao de chuban shiye" (On Catholic publications). *WS* 2.5 (Mar. 1927): 16–36.

Wang Zhixin. "Bense jiaohui yu bense zhuzuo" (Indigenous churches and indigenous writings). *WS* 1.6 (Apr. 1926): 1–17.

———. "Ruhe shi Jidujiao wenzi dadao shehui zhongxin" (How to make Christian literature enter the center of society). *WS* 1.2 (Nov. 1925): 7–16.

———. "Zhongguo Jidujiao wenzi shiye zhi guoqu xianzai yu weilai" (Past, present and future of Chinese Christian publications). *WS* 1.8 (July 1926): 59–70.

Wasserstrom, Jeffrey N. *Student Protests in Twentieth-Century China*. Stanford: Stanford University Press, 1991.

Watson, James L. "The Structure of Chinese Funerary Rites: Elementary Forms, Ritual Sequence, and the Primacy of Performance." In James L. Watson and Evelyn S. Rawski, eds., *Death Ritual in Late Imperial and Modern China*, pp. 3–19. Berkeley: University of California Press, 1988.

Watson, Rubie S. "The Creation of a Chinese Lineage: The Teng of Ha Tsuen, 1669–1751." *Modern Asian Studies* 16.1 (Feb. 1982): 69–100.

———. *Inequality Among Brothers: Class and Kinship in South China*. Cambridge, Eng.: Cambridge University Press, 1985.

Wehrle, Edmund S. *Britain, China, and the Antimissionary Riots, 1891–1900*. Minneapolis: University of Minnesota Press, 1966.

Wei Qiguang. "QianDianChuan bianqu Miaozu xinyang Jidujiao shixi" (Preliminary examination of Christian belief among the Miao of the Guizhou-Yunnan-Sichuan border area). *Guizhou shehui kexue* (Guizhou social science) 4 (1981): 64–73.

———. "Shilun Jidujiao dui Weining Miaozu diqu de wenhua yingxiang" (Preliminary discussion of the cultural influences of Christianity in the Weining Miao region). *Guizhou minzu yanjiu* (Guizhou minority research) 2 (1985): 30–41.

Wei Waiyang. "Ding Limei Lijie xiongdi hezhuan" (A combined biography of the brothers Ding Limei and Ding Lijie). *Xiaoyuan* (Campus) 22.2 (Feb. 1980): 62–65.

Welter, Barbara. *Dimity Convictions: The American Woman in the Nineteenth Century*. Athens, Ohio: Ohio University Press, 1976.

Wenshe yuekan (Wenshe monthly). Oct. 1925–June 1928. Shanghai.

West, Philip. "The Tsinan Property Disputes (1887–1891): Gentry Loss and Missionary 'Victory.'" *Papers on China* (East Asian Research Center, Harvard University) 20 (1966): 119–43.

Whyte, Bob. *Unfinished Encounter: China and Christianity*. London: Collins, 1988.

Wickberg, Edgar. "The Chinese Mestizo in Philippine History." *Journal of Southeast Asian History* 5.1 (Mar. 1964): 62–100.

Wickeri, Philip L. *Seeking the Common Ground: Protestant Christianity, the Three-Self Movement, and China's United Front*. Maryknoll, N.Y.: Orbis, 1988.

Wiest, Jean-Paul. "Catholic Activities in Kwangtung Province and Chinese Responses 1848–1885." Ph.D. diss., University of Washington, 1977.

——. *Maryknoll in China: A History, 1918–1955.* Armonk, N.Y.: M. E. Sharpe, 1988.
Willeke, Bernward H. *Imperial Government and Catholic Missions in China During the Years 1784–1785.* Franciscan Institute Publications, Missiology Series, no. 1. St. Bonaventure, N.Y.: Franciscan Institute, 1948.
Wolferstan, Bertram. *The Catholic Church in China from 1860 to 1907.* London: Sands, 1909.
Women's Foreign Missionary Society, MECS. *Annual Report.* 1882–1939. Nashville.
Wood, John W. "The Pro and Con of Registration of Christian Schools in China." *The Spirit of Missions: An Illustrated Monthly Review of Christian Missions* 93 (1928): 653–55.
World YWCA Archives. Geneva.
Wu Erqi. "Jiang Zhaotang pingzhuan" (Critical biography of Jiang Zhaotang). *Nanchangxian wenshi ziliao* (Historical materials of Nanchang county) 2 (Dec. 1988): 21–36.
Wu Leichuan. "Wei Jidujiao Wenshe jin yiyan" (My advice to the Wenshe). *WS* 2.6 (Apr. 1927): 95–98.
Wu Liming [Ng, Lee-ming]. *Jidujiao yu Zhongguo shehui bianqian* (Christianity and social change in China). Hong Kong: Chinese Christian Literature Council, 1981.
——. "A Study of Y. T. Wu." *Ching Feng* 15.1 (Mar. 1972).
Wu, Y. T. *See* Wu Yaozong.
Wu Yaozong [Y. T. Wu]. "Lichang jianding qizhi xianming jianku pusu pingyi jinren" (Firm position, clear-cut stand, hard work, plain living, and amiability: Commemorating comrade Zhou Enlai on the occasion of the eighty-first anniversary of his birth). In *Renmin de hao zongli* (The people's good premier). 3rd ed., pp. 274–80. Shanghai: Shanghai renmin chubanshe, 1979.
——. *Meiyou ren jianguo Shangdi* (No man has seen God). Shanghai: YMCA Bookstore, 1945.
——. "My Recognition of the Communist Party." *China Bulletin* 9.3–4 (1959).
——. "The Revolution and Student Thought." *CMYB* 15 (1928): 223–24.
——. "Zhongguo Jidujiao xuesheng yundong de guoqu he jianglai" (The past and future of the Chinese Christian student movement). *Tianfeng* 109 (1948).
Xie Fuya. *Xie Fuya wannian wenlu* (The later writings of Xie Fuya). Taibei: Chuanji wenxue, 1977.
Xie Shizhong. *Rentong de wuming* (Stigmatized identity). Taibei: Zili wanbao she, 1987.
Xie Songgao. "Duiyu Jidujiao wenzi shiye zhi wojian" (My opinion on Christian literature). *WS* 1.2 (Nov. 1925): 40–41.
Xinhai geming huiyilu (Memoirs of the 1911 Revolution). Zhongguo renmin zhengzhi xieshang huiyi quanguo weiyuanhui wenshi ziliao yanjiu weiyuanhui (Committee on Research in Historical Materials of the National Committee of the Chinese People's Political Consultative Conference), comp. 5 vols. Beijing: 1961–63.
Xu Run. *Xuyuzhai zixu nianpu fu Shanghai zaji* (Xu Run's autobiography and Shanghai miscellanies). Xiangshan: Xushi yin, 1927.

Xu Wei. "1906-nian 'Nanchang jiaoan' de fandi douzheng" (Anti-imperialist struggle in the Nanchang religious case of 1906). *Nanchang wenshi ziliao xuanji* (Selections of historical materials of Nanchang) 4 (n.d.): 101–22.

Xu Zongze. *Zhongguo Tianzhujiao gailun* (An introduction to Chinese Catholicism). Shanghai: Shanghai shengjiao zazhishe, 1938.

Yamamoto Sumiko. *Chūgoku kirisutokyōshi kenkyū, Purotesutanto no "dochakuka" o chūshin to shite* (Studies on the history of Christianity in China with special reference to "indigenization" of the Protestant church in the first half of the twentieth century). Tokyo: Tokyo University Press, 1972.

Yamamoto, Tatsuro, and Sumiko Yamamoto. "The Anti-Christian Movement in China." *Far Eastern Quarterly* 12.2 (Feb. 1953): 133–47.

Yamazaki Kaikō. *Seikyō kosaku* (Rural pacification work). Tokyo: Aishi jigyosha, 1942.

Yan Fu. "Lun Nanchang jiaoan" (On the Nanchang religious case). *Guangyi congbao* (Comprehensive review) 106 (23 May 1906).

Yancheng xian zhi (Yancheng [Xinchang] county gazetteer [1917]). *Zhongguo fangzhi congshu* (Reprinted Chinese local gazetteers), vol. 281. Taibei: Chengwen chubanshe, 1975.

Yang Hanxian. Unpublished memoir (1977).

Yang, John. *The Essential Doctrines of the Holy Bible*. Taizhong: True Jesus Church Publishing Office, 1970.

Yang, Joshua C. "The Assemblies of God Missionary Effort in China: 1907–1952." Unpublished paper.

Yang, Martin. *A Chinese Village: Taitou, Shantung Province*. New York: Columbia University Press, 1945.

Yeh, Wen-hsin. *The Alienated Academy: Culture and Politics in Republican China, 1919–1937*. Cambridge, Mass.: Harvard University Press, 1990.

Yili (Book of ceremonies). *Shisanjing zhusu* (Commentaries on the thirteen classics). Comp. Ruan Yuan. Tokyo: Zhongwen chubanshe, 1972 [1815].

Ying Yuandao. "Bai yu nian lai zai Hua Xi jiaoshi duiyu Jidujiao wenzi shiye zhi gongxian" (Western missionary contributions to Christian literature in China in the last hundred some years). *WS* 1.4 (Jan. 1926): 11–36.

Yip, Ka-che. *Religion, Nationalism and Chinese Students: The Anti-Christian Movement of 1922–1927*. Bellingham: Western Washington University, 1980.

Young, Ernest P. "Problems of a Late Ch'ing Revolutionary: Ch'en T'ien-hua." In Hsüeh Chün-tu, ed., *Revolutionary Leaders of Modern China*, pp. 210–47. New York: Oxford University Press, 1971.

Yu, Wai Hong [Yu Weixiong]. "Chongzhenghui yibaisishinian laiwen gongzuo, yingxiang yu zhanwang" (Work, influence and prospects of the Tsung Tsin Mission in the past 140 years). In *Xianggang Chongzhenghui lihui yibaisishi zhounian jinian tekan, 1847–1987* (Hong Kong Tsung Tsin Mission one hundred and fortieth anniversary special publication, 1847–1987), pp. 55–70. Hong Kong: Tsung Tsin Mission, 1984.

Yu Weixiong. *See* Yu, Wai Hong.

Yuan Yuying. "Zhongguo nüjie baozhi zhi xianzhuang" (The present condition of

Chinese women's newspapers). *Zhonghua Jidujiaohui nianjian* (Chinese Christian church yearbook) 5 (1918): 167–69.

YWCA. *See* World YWCA Archives.

YWCA National Board Archives. New York.

YWCA of China. *Introduction to the Young Women's Christian Association of China, 1933–1947*. Shanghai: National Committee of the YWCA of China, n.d.

Zeng Baosun [P. S. Tseng]. "Christianity and Women as Seen at the Jerusalem Meeting." *CR* 59 (July 1928): 443.

———. *Zeng Baosun huiyilu* (The memoirs of Zeng Baosun). Hong Kong: Chinese Christian Literature Council, 1970.

Zha Shijie. "Minguo Jidujiaohui shi (1), 1911–1917" (History of Christianity in the Republican period, part 1: 1911–17). *Guoli Taiwan daxue lishi xuexi xuebao* (Journal of historical studies of National Taiwan University) 8 (Dec. 1981): 109–45.

———. *Zhongguo Jidujiao renwu xiaozhuan* (Concise biographies of Chinese Christians). Taibei: China Evangelical Seminary Press, 1983.

Zhang Dan. *"Zhaimen" qian de shimenkan—Jidujiao wenhua yu ChuanDianQian bian Miaozu shehui* (The stone threshold in front of the "narrow door"—Christian culture and the Miao people's society on the border regions of Sichuan, Yunnan and Guizhou provinces). Kunming: Yunnan jiaoyu chubanshe, 1992.

Zhang Qiuwen. "Guangxu 32-nian de Nanchang jiaoan" (The Nanchang religious case of 1906). *Zhongyang yanjiuyuan jindaishi yanjiusuo jikan* (Journal of the Institute of Modern History, Academia Sinica) 12 (June 1983): 61–80.

Zhang Yijing, ed. *Piping fei Jidujiao yanlun huikan quanbian* (A complete edition of the rebuttal to the critique of the anti-Christian movement). Shanghai: Meihua jinhui, 1927.

Zhang Yongguo et al., eds. *Minguo nianjian Miaozu lunwenji* (Essays on the Miao in the Republican era). Guiyang: Guizhou Provincial Minorities Research Institute, 1983.

Zhang Zhidong. *Zhang Wenxiang-gong quanji* (Complete works of Zhang Zhidong). Ed. Wang Shutong. 6 vols. Taibei: Wenhai chubanshe, 1963.

Zhao Tianen. *See* Chao, Jonathan T'ien-en.

Zhao Zhongfu, ed. *Weng Tonghe riji paiyinben* (A typeset edition of the diary of Weng Tonghe). 6 vols. Taibei: Chengwen chubanshe, 1970.

Zhao Zichen. "Wo duiyu Zhonghua Jidujiao wenzi wenti de ganxiang" (My impression of Chinese Christian literature). *WS* 1.1 (Oct. 1925): 21–28.

Zheng Zheng. "Xiang nuli Jidujiao wenzi shiye zhe jin yi zhonggao" (Advice to the people of Christian literature). *WS* 3.8 (June 1928): 3–8.

Zhongguo dier lishi dang'anguan (Number Two Historical Archives of China). Nanjing.

Zhonghua Jidujiaohui nianjian (Chinese Christian church yearbook). Vols. 1–13, 1914–36. Shanghai.

"Zhongmin." "Yesu jiating" (The Jesus family). *Xinyang yu shenghuo* (Faith and life) 36.1 (Jan.–Mar. 1985): 104–11.

Zhu Shoupeng, ed. *Guangxuchao donghua lu* (The records of the governing of the Guangxu reign). 5 vols. Beijing: Zhonghua shuju, 1958.

Zia, Z. S. "Indigenous Evangelism and Christian Unity." *CR* 67 (July 1936): 408–12.

Zürcher, Erik. "A Complement to Confucianism: Christianity and Orthodoxy in Late Ming China." In Huang Chun-chieh and Erik Zürcher, eds., *Norms and the State in China*, pp. 71–92. Leiden: E. J. Brill, 1993.

———. "The Jesuit Mission in Fujian in Late Ming Times: Levels of Response." In E. B. Vermeer, ed., *Development and Decline of Fukien Province in the Seventeenth and Eighteenth Centuries*, pp. 417–57. Leiden: E. J. Brill, 1990.

———. "The Lord of Heaven and the Demons: Strange Stories from a Late Ming Christian Manuscript." In Naundorf et al., pp. 359–76.

Character List

This list excludes most place-names found in Playfair's *The Cities and Towns of China*, personal names cited for purposes of illustration only, names of prominent individuals easily accessible through standard bibliographical dictionaries, and names of commonly recognized offices, jurisdictions, and other terms. The notation (E) indicates common English spellings used in Hong Kong.

aihan　愛漢
Anshun　安順

Baihuazhou　百花洲
Baikeli　柏恪理
Bao Zhong　鮑忠
Baoan　寶安
baojia　保甲
bendi (Punti)　本地
Budao　《布道》
Buji　布吉

Cai Chang　蔡暢
Cai Kui　蔡葵
Cai Sujuan　蔡蘇娟
chan dian　禪殿
Chen Chonggui　陳崇桂
Chen Jianzhen　陳見眞
Chen Tianhua　陳天華
Chen Wenyuan　陳文淵
Chen Yuan　陳垣
Cheng Guanyi　誠冠怡
Cheng Jingyi　誠靜怡

Chigang　茈港
Ching Feng (see *Jingfeng*)
Chuan Miao　川苗
Chuan-Qian-Dian　川黔滇
Cui Xianxiang　崔憲祥
cun　村
cunmiao　村廟
cunmin gongyong　村民公用
cunshe　村社
cunzhong　村眾
cunzhong gonggong dasi　村眾公共
　　大寺

daoli　道理
Deng　鄧
Deng Guihe　鄧貴和
Deng Yuzhi　鄧裕志
Dengjia (market town)　登家
Dian Dongbei　滇東北
dibao　地保
Ding Guangxun (K. H. Ting)　丁光訓
Ding Limei　丁立美
Ding Ling　丁玲

Ding Shujing 丁淑靜
dingkou 丁口
Dongchuan 東川

e 惡

fan 販
fan dazu 番大租
Feng Rui 馮銳
fengshui 風水
Fu Han hui 福漢會
fumu guan 父母官
Funü zazhi 《婦女雜志》

Gaihan (see aihan)
Gong 龔
Gong Dong 龔棟
gongfei 公費
gongshi 公事
gongxi 公戲
Gu Yaowen 谷耀文
guizu xuexiao de xiaofeng 貴族學校
  的校風
guojia chizi 國家赤子
Gützlaff 郭實臘 (郭施拉, 郭士立)

Han 漢
Hanmin 漢民
hecun gonggong zhi shi 合村公共
  之事
Hongjiang hui 洪江會
Hu Binxia 胡彬夏
Hu Jinying 胡金英
Hu Tinggan 胡廷干
Hu Yigu 胡貽谷
Hua Miao 花苗
Hua Shan Road 華山路
huishou 會首
huizhang 會長

Ji Zhiwen 計志文
Jia Yuming 賈玉銘
Jialan dian 伽藍殿
Jiang Changchuan 江長川
Jiang Jiaoren 江覺仁

Jiang Zhaotang 江召棠
Jiangbao 《江報》
jianmin 賤民
jiaoan 敎案
Jiaoan ju 敎案局
Jiaohui xinbao 《敎會新報》
Jiaokeng 焦坑
jiaomin 敎民
jiaoren 敎人
jiaotou 敎頭
jiaoyu keyan xianjin xuexiao 敎育科
  研先進學校
jiazhang 家長
Jidujiao chubanjie 《基督敎出版界》
Jidutubao 《基督徒報》
Jidutuhui 基督徒會
Jing Dianying 敬奠瀛
Jingfeng (*Ching Feng*) 《景風》
jingun 衿棍
jiushou 糾首
Juhuichu 聚會處
Juhuisuo 聚會所

Kang Cheng 康成
kangqiang 扛搶
kejia (E: Hakka) 客家
Kōain 興亞院
Kong Xiangxi 孔祥熙
Kusangyuan 枯桑園

Laogongyuan 老貢院
Li Ande 李安德
Li Changshou 李常受
Li Jiabai 李佳白
Li Rongfang 李榮芳
Li Weihan 李維漢
Liang Fa 梁發
Lilang 李朗
Ling Kai Lin (E) 凌啓蓮
Ling'enhui 靈恩會
Liu Bingzhang 劉秉璋
Liu Liangmo 劉良模
Liu Tingfang 劉廷芳
Liu Zongyao 劉宗堯
Longmentan 龍門灘

lou 陋
Lung Yeuk Tau (E) 龍躍頭
Luo (family in Chongqing) 羅
Luo (family in Jiangjin) 駱
Luo Xianglin 羅香林
Luoranggou 洛瀼溝

Ma Jiying 馬季英
Mazhuang 馬莊
Meixian 梅縣
Miao Qiusheng 繆秋笙
miaofei 廟費
minzu xiang 民族鄉
minzuxue 民族學
Momo sect 摩摩教 (默默教)

Ni Tuosheng 倪柝聲
nian jing 念經
Nie Qigui 聶緝槼
nongmin ziwei zhi shi 農民自爲之事
Nüduobao 《女鐸報》
Nüqingnian 《女青年》

pai 牌
Pang Lok Sam (E) 彭樂三
pingpufan (Hokkien, pepohoan) 平
埔番
Potou 陂頭

Qiandong 黔東
Qiangxue hui 強學會
Qidong 啓東
Qing Ming 清明
Qingnian nübao 《青年女報》
Qiu (family) 邱
Qiuxi 秋溪

rongfei 冗費

saihui yanxi 賽會演戲
sancong 三從
Sanzi jing 《三字經》
Shangxiantang 尙賢堂
Shao Jingsan 邵鏡三
shaoshuminzu 少數民族

shen 神
Shen Sizhuang 沈嗣莊
Shenbao 《申報》
shenfu 神父
Shengbao 《聖報》
Shengchongping 勝沖坪
Shenggonghui 聖公會
shengmian 生面
Shengmuhui de guniang 聖母會的
姑娘
shenshi 紳士
sheshou 社首
Shi Meiyu 石美玉
Shimen 石門
Shimenkan 石門坎
shoukui 受虧
shufan (Hokkien, sekhoan) 熟番
Shung Him Tong (E) 崇謙堂
Shuo wen 《說文》
Song Shangjie 宋尙節
Songshi 嵩市

Tang Dingxuan 湯鼎煊
Tang Yin 湯因
Tangpu 棠浦
tanpai 攤派
Tashui 塔水
Tianfeng 《天風》
Tianwang dian 天王殿
tianzhu 天主
tianzhu tang 天主堂
ting 廳
tong cai 通才
tong cunzhong 同村眾
tou 偷
Tsung Tsin Mission (E) 崇正會
Tu Yuqing 涂羽卿
tumu 土目
tusi 土司

Wanguo gongbao 《萬國公報》
Wang Anzhi 王安之
Wang Huiwu 王會悟
Wang Jianguang 王建光
Wang Junde 王峻德

Wang Liming　王立明
Wang Mingdao　王明道
Wang Shengmo　王勝莫
Wang Zai　王載
Wang Zhengting　王正廷
Wang Zhixin　王治心
Weiaishe　唯愛社
Wen Jukui　文聚奎
wen yi zai dao　文以載道
Wenshe　文社
Wenshe Monthly (*Wenshe yuekan*)　《文社月刊》
Wu Yaozong　吳耀宗
Wuding　武定
Wuhua　五華
Wusheng laomu　無生老母
wuyi　無益

xi ji'nian songgun shoubi　係積年訟棍手筆
Xia Mianzun　夏丏尊
xian　縣
xiang　項
Xiang Jingyu　向警予
xiangcun　鄉村
xiangdi　鄉地
xiangguan　鄉官
xianghuo di　香火地
xiangjian gongshi　鄉間公事
Xiangnan　湘南
xiangshe　鄉社
xiangzhang　鄉長
Xiaoqun　小群
Xie Songgao　謝頌羔
xieqiu hui　謝秋會
Xin qingnian　《新青年》
Xingning　興寧
xingtong qinshou　行同禽獸
xisu xiangyan　習俗相沿
Xu Zuanzeng　徐纘曾
Xue Zheng　薛正
Xuzhou　徐州

Yan Yangchu　晏陽初
Yang Hanxian　楊漢先

Yang Kaihui　楊開慧
Yang Xizhen　楊錫珍
Yang Yage (Yake)　楊雅各
Yang Zhizhu　楊芝諸
Yesu　耶穌
Yesu jiating　耶穌家庭
Yi　彝
Yiban　《一般》
yiduan　異端
Ying Yuandao　應元道
yitu　異途
Yiwei　《一葦》
Youxi　油溪
youyi　有益
Yu Guozhen　俞國楨
Yu Rizhang　余日章
Yu Zhaokang　余肇康
Yuan Yuying　袁玉英
yudan　諭單
Yulin　榆林
Yun Yuding　惲毓鼎

Zeng Baosun　曾寶蓀
zhai　齋
zhaifei　齋匪
Zhang Boling　張伯苓
Zhang Fuxing　張復興
Zhang Yuehan (Yohan)　張岳漢
Zhangkengjing　樟坑徑
Zhao Zichen　趙紫宸
zhaohui　照會
Zhaojiazhuang　趙家莊
Zhaotong　昭通
zhaoyi xiangyue　照依鄉約
Zhenli yu shengming　《真理與生命》
Zhongguo Jidutubao　《中國基督徒報》
Zhongguo Yesujiao zilihui　中國耶穌教自立會
Zhonghua Jidujiao Wenshe　中華基督教文社
Zhonghua Jidujiao wenzi shiye cujinshe　中華基督教文字事業促進社
Zhonghua Jidujiao xiejinhui　中華基督教協進會

Zhonghua Jidujiaohui nianjian 《中華
　基督教會年鑑》
Zhongxi nüshu　中西女塾
Zhou Hao　周浩
Zhou Zuoren　周作人
Zhounan Girls' Middle School　周南
　女校
Zhu Huanzhang　朱煥章

Zhu Weizhi　朱維之
Zhu Youyu　朱友漁
zhuma　主瑪
zhuri　主日
ziwei zhi shi　自爲之事
zizhihui　自治會
zui　罪

Index

In this index an "f" after a number indicates a separate reference on the next page, and an "ff" indicates separate references on the next two pages. A continuous discussion over two or more pages is indicated by a span of page numbers, e.g., "57–59." *Passim* is used for a cluster of references in close but not consecutive sequence.

Zhou Zuoren (T. R. Chow), 304
Zhounan Girls' Middle School, 246
Zhu Huanzhang, 151
Zhu Luoheng, 49f
Zhu Weizhi, 302
Zhu Youyu (Y. Y. Tsu), 334
Zongli yamen, 29, 41, 54, 81f, 85f, 88;
and legal cases, 5, 32, 43, 48ff, 57–67
passim
Zou Jiaxiang, 31
Zou Yaya, 27, 382n13
Zung, Cecilia, 225
Zuo Zongtang, 65
Zürcher, Erik, 3

Library of Congress Cataloging-in-Publication Data

Christianity in China: From the eighteenth century to the present /
edited by Daniel H. Bays.
    p. cm.
    Includes bibliographical references and index.
ISBN 0-8047-2609-4 (cl.) : ISBN 0-8047-3651-0 (pbk.)
  1. China — Church history — 18th century.   2. China — Church
history — 19th century.   3. China — Church history — 20th century.
I. Bays, Daniel H.
BR1287.C47   1996
275.1'08 — dc20
95-53046 CIP

Original printing 1996

Last figure below indicates year of this printing:

05 04 03 02 01 00 99